MW00474615

Oracle E-Business Suite Financials Handbook, Third Edition

Ben Prusinski
Gustavo Gonzalez

New York   Chicago   San Francisco
Lisbon   London   Madrid   Mexico City   Milan
New Delhi   San Juan   Seoul   Singapore   Sydney   Toronto

The McGraw·Hill Companies

Cataloging-in-Publication Data is on file with the Library of Congress

Oracle E-Business Suite Financials Handbook, Third Edition

1 2 3 4 5 6 7 8 9 0   DOC DOC   1 0 9 8 7 6 5 4 3 2

ISBN   978-0-07-177972-2
MHID   0-07-177972-8

Sponsoring Editor Paul Carlstroem	**Technical Editor** Molly McLouth	**Production Supervisor** George Anderson
Editorial Supervisor Jody McKenzie	**Copy Editor** Jeff Anderson	**Composition** Cenveo Publisher Services
Acquisitions Coordinator Ryan Willard	**Proofreader** Carol Shields	**Art Director, Cover** Jeff Weeks
Project Managers Harleen Chopra Cenveo Publisher Services	**Indexer** Jack Lewis	**Cover Designer** Pattie Lee

I dedicate this book to my mother and father, who encouraged me to write from an early age and to never give up on my dreams in life. Without their support, this book would never have been possible.

—Ben Prusinski

Like in every aspect of my life, teamwork is my driver for success. This book is the result of years of support from my family team: mom Silvia, sister Euge, and the memoirs of my dad Hector. It is also dedicated to the love of my life, Andrea—who has been my partner on this journey for many years—and our two beloved daughters Catalina and Amparo.

—Gustavo Gonzalez

About the Authors

Ben Prusinski is an Oracle ACE Director and Oracle Certified Professional (OCP) in the Oracle E-Business Suite. As an Oracle Subject Matter Expert (SME) working for VCE, the virtual-computing-environment company, Ben provides enterprise solutions to customers for virtualized ERP and database environments. With more than 15 years of real-world experience with ERP and database systems, Ben specializes in Oracle EBS and SAP solutions for a broad spectrum of vertical customers in various business sectors. He has performed migrations, implementations, and upgrades to Oracle R12 for dozens of large public-sector and *Fortune* 500 clients. In his free time, Ben enjoys scuba diving and travel to exotic locations around the world.

Gustavo Gonzalez is an Oracle ACE and chief technology officer at IT Convergence, leading decision making regarding technology strategy for technology platforms, partnerships, and external relationships. He specializes in E-Business Suite, Oracle Business Intelligence, and Fusion Applications, with more than a decade implementing and upgrading Oracle E-Business Suite for worldwide organizations; he has led early-adopter programs for Oracle E-Business Suite Release 12 and Oracle Fusion Applications. Based in Argentina, Gustavo enjoys travelling for business and leisure with his family around the world.

About the Technical Editor

Molly McLouth, MBA Sr. Software Engineer, Fusion App Framework Development, Oracle USA. Molly holds a master's of business administration. Since joining Oracle Corporation in 1999, she has served in different roles helping customers implement Oracle technology. She worked on the Flexfields Development team for Oracle E-Business Suite and currently works on Fusion Applications Technology Development. With 15 years' experience working with accounting and financials software packages, Molly leverages a unique blend of technical knowledge and business acumen, delivering best-fit creative entrepreneurial solutions. Molly is a published contributor to several Oracle manuals and white papers in the systems-administration area. She is active in a variety of local technical and community volunteer activities in Orlando, Florida, where she is based.

Contents at a Glance

PART III
Managing and Customizing an EBS Environment

Contents

PART II
The Financial Applications

PART III
Managing and Customizing an EBS Environment

Acknowledgments

As Lao Tzu once said, "A journey of a thousand miles begins with a single step." This best explains my voyage into the wide world of ERP systems and Oracle E-Business Suite. I am grateful to many folks who have patiently explained to me the ins and outs of Oracle's financial complexity over the past 15 years, including Steven Chan and Elke Phelps from the Oracle ATG product team as well as Daryle Karnes, with whom I had the pleasure to work in a past life at IT Convergence. I also want to thank Max Arderius and Molly McLouth for their technical review of our book and for adding feedback to ensure technical accuracy. Last but not least, I want to thank my coauthor Gustavo Gonzalez for stepping up to the plate under tight deadlines for contributions to the book. Without Gustavo this book would not have been possible, and I'm grateful for his valuable real-world insight into the functional aspects of the Oracle Financials. Furthermore, thank you to everyone at Oracle Press, especially Ryan, Paul, and Jody for providing support and helping to make sure that we stayed on track for the book. I also want to thank my wonderful colleagues at VCE and EMC who have provided timeless feedback and support on complex Oracle R12 EBS scenarios with cloud-virtualized environments. Thank you to Kevin Closson, Mike Guthrie, Mark Lin, Jason Han, and Brendan Hogan for your insights on many things!

Ben Prusinski
Mountain View, California, USA
August 2012

Writing a book is a great reward that would not be possible without the lessons learned from all the great people I have met during my professional career. E-Business Suite is such an enormous tool that no one can be an expert at the full extent of it, but over the years, different projects at different companies gave me the capacity and experience I was able to use in this book.

I'd like to mention some of those whom I worked with over the past years who contributed directly or indirectly in this book. At Danone, working with Mary Maya, Ricardo Rosendo, and Daniel Bourdieu on multiple aspects for the shared service center supporting and implementing Financials, Supply Chain, and Process Manufacturing was a challenging but rewarding endeavor.

Over the past years, I have had the pleasure to work for IT Convergence, one of the most inspiring and exciting companies that I've worked for, which has a passionate executive team who have allowed me to build multiple teams with expert Oracle professionals. The Business Systems team with whom we executed the internal Release 12 upgrade at an early stage of the product consisted of Silvia Colacioppo, Gustavo Canalis, Melisa Diaz, Dolores Espiño, Sebastian Iglesias, Flavio Rodriguez, Marcelo Chipana, Sergio Segura, Daniel Chan, Pablo Rodriguez, Dharmendra Bhatt, and Hernan Izaguirre. The Education team was also a huge help on multiple concepts and on the big picture of E-Business Suite: Melissa English, Margaret Wong, and Anne Ristau. Also the Marketing team was a key component for the next step in my career; Nancy Jaime, Keith Thomas, and Cecilia Aceti helped a lot in this transition. Each and every ITC department has supported and cooperated with many of these projects, such as the Near- and Offshore Development teams, professional services globally, and the global Enterprise Cloud and Managed Services teams.

Thanks to IT Convergence's executive team, who have consistently supported my initiatives. Thanks to Patrick Krause, Andrew Meinnert, Owen Welch, Jake Van der Vort, Jenette Garcia, Joe Long, Brian Koh, and Sameer Kanwar.

Finally, thanks to Molly McLouth for her technical review and to the Oracle Development Team—Steven Chan, Max Arderius, Elke Phelps, and Santiago Bastidas—whom I had the honor to work with over the last year on a beta program for the new E-Business Suite release. It has been a great learning process.

Gustavo Gonzalez
General Villegas, Argentina
August 2012

Introduction

Oracle E-Business Suite is one of the most widely used business software applications in the world. It handles solutions for small organizations to some of the largest multinational corporations. Some of them are in the process of implementation to adapt their business to best practices or support the growth of their business operations. Other companies are planning to upgrade to the latest release in search of opportunities to enhance supporting their business practices.

This book is directed to resources involved in implementation or upgrade who are eager to learn from the years of experience of the authors to avoid or overcome the complexities of this packaged software.

What's in This Book?

This book contains three parts, 29 chapters, and one appendix.

Part I: Getting Started

Chapter 1: An Overview of the E-Business Suite

In this chapter you'll learn the scope of Oracle E-Business Suite and its structure, with over 150 modules. A high-level overview of the integration is presented. The chapter also introduces some important aspects of the benefits of implementing or upgrading Oracle EBS at your organization.

Chapter 2: Implementing the E-Business Suite—Essential Concepts

You'll explore how to capture the most relevant financial information without having to tailor the system, reducing the total cost of ownership. The key concept of flexfields is introduced, as is how business flows are handled through Oracle Workflow.

Accounting has a starring role in Oracle EBS, and the different concepts for each application are introduced. Building the model on which the application will support the business process is another key area introduced in this chapter, taking into consideration legal requirements and security among the users.

Part II: The Financial Applications

Chapter 3: Oracle General Ledger

In this chapter, you'll gain a good understanding of the functional and technical concepts of General Ledger, a fundamental application within Oracle E-Business Suite that collects the information from all the transactional modules. Oracle General Ledger is capable of setting different accounting methods, including global configurations, which are discussed in this chapter. Also, some best practices in creating the chart of accounts and reporting are presented.

Chapter 4: Oracle Subledger Accounting

In this chapter, you'll learn about some of the benefits of the new Subledger Accounting feature introduced in Release 12. It is a major shift in how accounting is performed. The concepts and components are shared in the chapter, providing some examples and alternatives if you are in the process of upgrading your Oracle E-Business Suite.

Chapter 5: Oracle Payables

You'll learn how Oracle Payables is integrated with other applications within Oracle E-Business Suite, and you'll discover the new features and functionalities introduced in Release 12, such as the payment process, which will improve the efficiency of the payables department. In this chapter you'll learn how Subledger Accounting can be leveraged for the accounting methods within Oracle Payables for each of the transactions types. The chapter will also introduce some technical concepts of the tables that are part of the data model.

Chapter 6: Oracle Receivables

You'll learn how Oracle Receivables models interactions with your customers, invoicing, and collections. The integration with other applications will be introduced in order to explain the different Oracle E-Business Suite objects that are connected with this module. The concepts of accounting for each transaction type are presented, including some examples for clarity.

Chapter 7: Oracle Treasury

In this chapter, you'll learn how the out-of-the-box integration of Oracle Treasury with other modules brings a consistent view of operational exposures, profitability, and control of your treasury positions.

Chapter 8: Oracle Cash Management

In this chapter, you'll learn about the evolution of the Cash Management module and the importance of cash forecasting and bank reconciliation with a tight integration with General Ledger, Receivables, and Payroll, along with information from external systems.

Chapter 9: Oracle Assets

You'll learn how to manipulate and process depreciation-schedule records for property, plant, and equipment using Oracle Assets. The chapter will present some examples of depreciation and how the introduction of Subledger Accounting brings new capabilities of meeting multi-GAAP, corporate, and fiscal accounting requirements.

Chapter 10: Oracle Purchasing

In this chapter, you'll learn about how Oracle Purchasing can strengthen the supply-chain process by improving the sourcing, requisitioning, purchasing, and receiving functions. Many enhancements introduced in Release 12 are presented, including new Professional Buyer's Work Center.

Chapter 11: Oracle Inventory

You'll learn about how Oracle Inventory provides a definition and basis for managing items through Oracle E-Business Suite on Purchasing, Payables, Order Management, and Manufacturing. Multiple definitions of powerful tools to manage inventory stock, location, and cost are presented, as well as a strategy for migrating items from legacy systems.

Chapter 12: Oracle Order Management

In this chapter, you'll learn how Oracle Order Management integrates through Inventory to Purchasing and Manufacturing for a consistent best practice in order to satisfy customer demand. Each step in the process is elucidated to provide a deep view of this application, from the different options for order entry to credit checking to booking, to the integration of shipping and receivables.

Chapter 13: Oracle E-Business Tax

You'll learn how this new application, introduced in Release 12, provides a simplified view of tax requirements. The chapter presents the new data model, which allows global configurations, scalability, and a robust tax engine that enables third-party applications, or tax-service providers, to automate the tax setup and updates, minimizing mistakes.

Chapter 14: Oracle Projects

In this chapter, you'll learn how to manage Oracle Projects to set up and monitor costs against budget, margins, and account, and to show costs and revenues. Some options and examples are presented to show where many industries can take advantage of this powerful application.

Chapter 15: Oracle Credit Management

You'll learn about how Oracle Credit Management can help your organization, providing the monitoring tools to evaluate the creditworthiness of your customers and using a tight integration with other modules of Oracle E-Business Suite, such as Order Management, Lease Management, and Oracle Loans.

Chapter 16: Oracle Self-Service Web Applications

You'll see how Oracle E-Business Suite is moving toward a self-service strategy on multiple modules, providing an improved user interface. In this chapter, some self-service modules are examined in detail, such as Internet Procurement, Self-Service Time, Self-Service Expenses, and iReceivables.

Chapter 17: Oracle Workflow

In this chapter, you'll see how to implement workflow processes with Oracle R12 EBS to orchestrate business processes. In addition, you'll learn how to apply useful tips and tricks to manage and troubleshoot workflow issues within a complex Oracle EBS environment.

Chapter 18: New Applications in Oracle E-Business Suite Release 12

In this chapter, you'll see how to deploy new and existing applications within the Oracle R12 EBS environment.

Part III: Managing and Customizing an EBS Environment

Chapter 19: The Oracle Financials Environment

In this chapter, you'll see how to implement best practices for Oracle Release 12 Financials.

Chapter 20: Oracle E-Business Suite Technical Architecture

In this chapter, you'll see how to design a complete environment for Oracle EBS Release 12. You'll learn how to deploy the complex new infrastructure components of R12.

Chapter 21: Security

In this chapter, you'll see how to implement best practices for application security within the Oracle R12 EBS environment. In addition, you'll learn how to deploy new security tools such as the Oracle Identity Management Suite within an Oracle R12 EBS Financials landscape.

Chapter 22: Customization and Modification

In this chapter, you'll see how to manage and deploy customizations and modifications for applications running within Oracle R12 E-Business Suite.

Chapter 23: Project Organization and Management

In this chapter, you'll see how to prepare a project plan, team, budget, and methodology to implement Oracle E-Business Suite. The authors share experiences, tips, and techniques for a successful implementation or upgrade.

Chapter 24: Performance Tuning for Oracle R12 Financials

In this chapter, you'll see how to implement best practices for optimizing performance and scalability within the Oracle R12 EBS environment. In addition, tools and methods are provided to help you remedy performance bottlenecks in a proactive and reactive manner.

Chapter 25: Oracle SOA Suite and BPEL for Oracle EBS

In this chapter, you'll see how to implement Web-services architectures with the Oracle SOA Suite and BPEL business applications for the Oracle R12 E-Business Suite.

Chapter 26: Disaster Recovery and Business Continuity

In this chapter, you'll see how to implement best practices for disaster recovery to ensure maximum availability and business continuity for the Oracle R12 E-Business Suite. You'll learn guidelines for implementing Oracle RAC and Data Guard with Oracle R12 EBS.

Chapter 27: Business Intelligence with OBIEE and ODI

In this chapter, you'll see how to deploy business intelligence with OBIEE and Oracle Data Integrator to migrate third-party data to Oracle R12 EBS environments using best practices. You'll also learn how to apply these analytical tools within Oracle R12 EBS.

Chapter 28: Overview of CRM, HR, and Manufacturing

In this chapter, you'll see how by implementing some of the modules from the Customer Relationship Management, Human Resources, or Manufacturing families, your organization can decrease the total cost of ownership, taking advantage of the tight integration with other modules of Oracle E-Business Suite. An introduction of the modules that make up these families will help to identify if a legacy or custom system can be replaced without having to perform a new installation.

Chapter 29: Oracle Fusion Applications—A Preview

In this chapter, you'll see how the Oracle strategy with the introduction of Oracle Fusion Applications will affect the selection of Oracle E-Business Suite for your organization. A description of the product families provides an overview of the different available options to adopt a coexistence strategy and leverage the benefits of a new business software built on the latest Fusion Middleware technology with an improved user experience.

Intended Audience

This book's goal is to provide an extensive view of Oracle E-Business Suite to developers, database administrators, functional users, and executive management. The business aspect is the predominant portion, but it will contribute to the knowledge of technical staff to understand if the out-of-the-box suite can perform certain functions or if an extension or customization is needed.

The latest release of the E-Business Suite brought a global view to the integration of multiple modules. This feature is one of the most relevant aspects of Oracle EBS, providing organizations the advantages of a single source of truth.

This book is not intended to replace the reference manuals; it provides a different view of technical, functional, and project-management processes. We envisioned it for businesspeople with some accounting background and for technical resources experienced in information technology. In addition, technical staff members such as the development and database teams will learn a fundamental background on how the technical aspects of Oracle's flagship ERP software interacts with business processes.

Every implementation or upgrade project requires a mix of technical and functional skills, and some portions of this book will have a mix of both aspects covering different characteristics that will help the project team. Years of experience have been transferred to this book to help you avoid mistakes and take the best approach for a successful use of this world-class business software through the use of best practices.

Retrieving the Examples

All the SQL scripts, programs, and other files used in this book can be downloaded from the Oracle Press Web site at www.oraclepressbooks.com. The files are contained in a zip file. Once you've downloaded the zip file, you need to extract its contents. This will create a directory named `sql_book` that contains the following subdirectories:

- **`sample_files`**   Contains the sample files used in Chapter 15.
- **`SQL`**   Contains the SQL scripts used throughout the book, including scripts to create and populate the example database tables.
- **`xml_files`**   Contains the XML used in Chapter 17.

We sincerely hope that you enjoy this book and, even more important, take away important lessons that you can apply right away to your Oracle EBS environments.

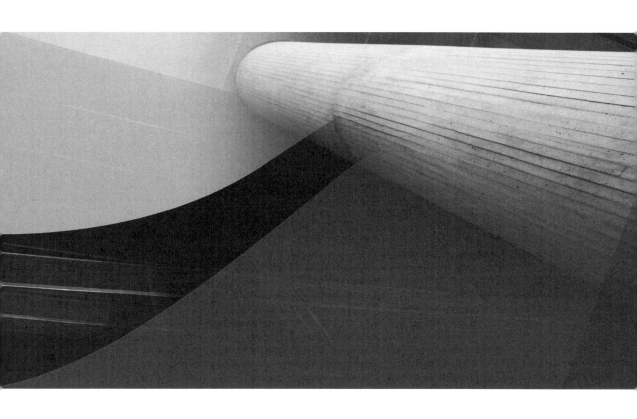

PART
I

Getting Started

CHAPTER
1

An Overview of the E-Business Suite

hoosing and implementing a new software package can be a monumental and expensive task for your organization. When considering the Oracle E-Business Suite, a number of questions arise: What is each application designed to do? What are the benefits? Is buying the suite a good business decision? What strengths of the Oracle Corporation might cause you to favor their software over their competition's? Once you've chosen Oracle, how can you succeed in installing the software, converting to it, and taking advantage of it to improve your business? Software is an intangible product, and the Oracle E-Business Suite of applications is a huge software suite, so answering these questions can be a detailed undertaking.

Although the Oracle E-Business Suite can satisfy almost all business needs while offering an excellent value and return on investment (ROI), it cannot be all things to all people. This is true with any of the commercial off-the-shelf (COTS) packaged enterprise resource planning (ERP) software currently available. However, Oracle's architecture, documentation, and tools are designed to make its code uniquely easy to modify to meet your specific needs.

The Structure and Scope of the E-Business Suite

The Oracle E-Business Suite (EBS) is a suite of more than 150 integrated software modules for financial management, supply-chain management, manufacturing, project systems, human resources, and sales-force automation. The modules vary in size and complexity from Oracle Inventory—the tables of which interface with a majority of the Oracle products and affect many different departments within your company—to Cash Management, which serves primarily as a supplement to existing modules.

Oracle EBS combines powerful features with state-of-the-art technology, which is configured to enable rapid implementation. Although Oracle EBS has grown over the last decade, its purpose has remained unchanged. It offers world-class business automation built on the preeminent Oracle database, using the full range of Oracle's own development tools. Oracle's corporate structure recognizes two major revenue streams: firstly, databases, development, and Web tools, which have been the core of the company; and secondly, the E-Business Suite, which is the likely growth business of the future. Recently, Oracle has acquired many software companies, including PeopleSoft and JD Edwards, thus covering a wide range of ERP modules and human resources; Hyperion, for enterprise performance management and business intelligence; and Siebel for customer relationship management (CRM).

The Oracle E-Business Suite serves a broad market, ranging from small organizations to *Fortune* 500 companies. Oracle EBS users and their data-processing support staff often find they have more in common than they originally thought. Both groups appreciate the benefits that Oracle's immense power and flexibility can bring, and they both almost always underestimate the amount of planning, preparation, and hard work required on their part to achieve those benefits.

This book focuses on the Oracle E-Business Suite application modules that are oriented toward financial management. Our aim throughout is to cover three basic areas: the business functions of these modules, the technical aspects of the software, and the management and organization of implementation projects. This book is divided into strategic sections to reflect these threads. Our focus, of course, is on the Oracle Financials modules; however, most of the technology chapters, as well as the project-management sections, apply equally to the Oracle Manufacturing and Oracle Human Resources product families.

The Oracle Financials components, which were the first modules released back in 1989, remain at the heart of the product line. Figure 1-1 shows the packages that have long been

FIGURE 1-1.   *Oracle Financials—the core modules*

considered to make up the Oracle Financials Suite. The ones in the inner circle handle money and generate General Ledger transactions. Components in the outer circle of the diagram—Purchasing, Inventory, and Order Management—usually are included under the title of Financials because they generate transactions with financial implications. These original modules (which we focus on in Part II of this book) remain the most widely used of the applications in EBS. They form the architectural anchor for the complete E-Business Suite, as illustrated in Figure 1-2.

NOTE
Figure 1-2 omits industry-specific applications. In addition, some of the applications might have undergone name changes since the printing of this book; their names are revised often.

The E-Business Suite is primarily designed to manage operations. Financial data are mere by-products. Financial measures are certainly the best reflection of how the business is doing, but they are only a reflection. True business activity is in the operations that generate financial transactions: warehouse receipts, services delivered, and orders entered. Oracle EBS provides the operational controls needed to optimize financial results and capture financial transactions at a level of detail that supports rigorous measurement of operations.

Figure 1-2 shows the products that Oracle now calls the Financial Applications in the inner circle. The other core applications are grouped by functional areas in the larger circle surrounding the Financials. Each package is a set of processes and tables designed to support a distinct business function. However, the key feature of all the EBS modules is data integration.

- **Master data are integrated**   All the applications share common files of customers, suppliers, employees, items, and other entities that are used by multiple applications.

- **Transaction data are integrated**   Oracle automatically bridges transactions from one system to another, as when Order Management must decrement inventory to reflect a shipment or send an order line to Receivables to be invoiced.

- **Financial data are integrated**   Financial data are carried in a common format, and the implications of any financial transaction in one application are accurately transmitted to other affected applications. For example, Oracle ripples the implications of a price change through the Inventory, Work in Process, and Purchasing systems.

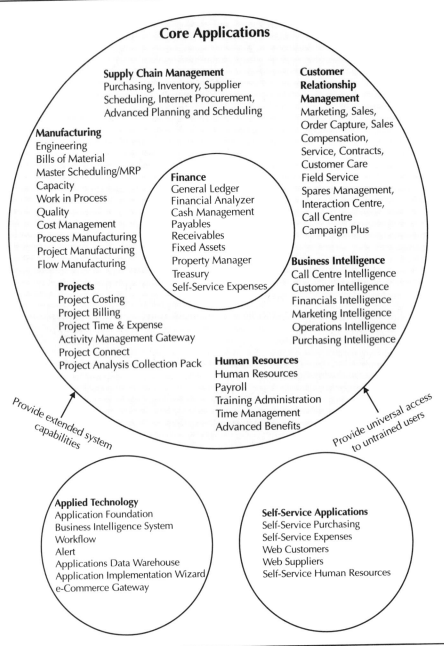

FIGURE 1-2.   *Logical organization of the Applications modules*

This level of cohesion brings major advantages over traditional "stovepipe" systems, which address the needs of individual functional areas. Although integrated systems have long been a major objective of systems design, large-scale integration has rarely been achieved in custom-written systems. Businesses evolve so quickly that few ever agree on an enterprise-wide design, much less develop and implement a comprehensive data-management system.

Oracle offers several additional E-Business Suite products that enhance the function of the Core Applications. The Applied Technology (ATG) products grouped at the lower left in Figure 1-2 give the Core Applications additional messaging and analysis capabilities. The Self-Service Web Applications function as front ends, enabling untrained end users—both inside and outside the organization—to query and submit transactions to the Core Applications under the control of Oracle Workflow.

Oracle incorporates best practices from the corporate, nonprofit, and government worlds in their software design. In buying Oracle E-Business Suite, you have purchased a very sophisticated integration model, broad enough to serve most businesses in most industries and flexible enough to be expanded to meet your individual needs.

Accounting Methods

Financial accounting satisfies the information needs of two major external audiences: investors and tax authorities. *Cost accounting*, also known as *management accounting*, is internal. It shows corporate management the financial workings of the enterprise in the formats best suited to support executive decisions. Although cost accounting works at a greater level of detail than financial accounting, both financial- and cost-accounting reports are derived from the same financial transactions. The Oracle E-Business Suite uses the same databases to satisfy both the internal and external kinds of financial reporting requirements.

In most cases the transactions that drive financial and management accounting are just by-products of corporate operations. Controlling those operations is the more significant function of the E-Business Suite. Consider a company that has bought office equipment from a supplier and is to receive the invoice later. The operational issues to consider are:

- Does the invoice represent a real obligation?
- When should the invoice be paid, to take best advantage of the supplier's terms?
- Is there enough money to cover the draft?

The financial transaction is comparatively simple: credit the payables account and debit the office-equipment expense account identified as the invoice was entered. In every package except the General Ledger itself, the financial reporting logic is subsidiary to operational control.

Cost and management accounts are generally intended for use by management; they are at a greater level of detail than statutory reports. They form the basis of informed management decisions and can answer a number of questions: Which groups of customers have large outstanding receivables? Should payment terms be changed? Which departments and product lines are most profitable? Which ones show the best improvement in gross margins? Should those managers be rewarded?

Operational Control

A company must control its operations to achieve optimal financial results. Control means satisfying customers: making commitments that satisfy customer needs and meeting those commitments. It means controlling assets, to get maximum use out of them. It means monitoring the performance of suppliers and people to keep their attention focused on supporting the company's mission.

Several requirements are common to control processes in various operations. These are the most frequent:

- **Defined routines, with defined exceptions** Business must be handled by routine. It is vastly less expensive to handle transactions by rote than to invent procedures for each new case. However, there are legitimate exceptions to almost every routine. Oracle modules are designed to minimize the effort involved in routine operations. They rely on a standard set of processes to bring exceptions to the attention of a human being as quickly as possible.

- **Workflow processing** Many transactions, such as approvals and inspections, require moving a transaction and the associated paperwork from person to person within an organization, the exact path depending on the nature of the transaction and the outcome of prior steps.

- **Defaulting** Oracle EBS makes processing decisions about individual records according to the value of field settings at that level. Payment terms are an example: should a given customer have to pay its bills in 30 or 45 days? Although it must be possible to set the terms customer by customer, they are much easier to administer if they are set for all customers, or at least by customer groups. Oracle makes broad use of defaulting hierarchies to allow you to control operations by setting field values for broad sets of records and override them for subsets or individual records.

- **Capturing and editing parameters for batch processes** Oracle EBS is fully generic to support a wide range of users. The trade-off is that most batch processes and reports require a series of parameters for exact control each time they are invoked.

Oracle uses more or less standard devices across all the EBS modules for these control functions. The system modules shown at the lower left in Figure 1-2 enhance the function of all the other packages. This standardization makes Oracle's products efficient for their customers to learn and efficient for them to support, and it means that enhancements are available across all of the packages.

The Package Families

The E-Business Suite has defied Oracle's best attempts at classification. Every year brings new packages and a new view of the organization of the older packages. It is not that Oracle is indecisive; rather, the packages are so well integrated that natural affinities exist between almost any two of them. Each time a new package enters the product line, it shifts the relative importance of the integrated relationships. The following are some useful classifications that can be imposed on the applications shown in Figure 1-2:

- Customer Relationship Management (CRM) covers the Marketing, Sales, and Service functions that face outward toward new business and servicing your existing customer base.

- Enterprise Resource Planning (ERP) covers the remainder of the product line. ERP activity is focused on Finance, Manufacturing, and Human Resources (HR).

- The Financials products in the inner circle are closest to the money and to General Ledger reporting.

- Supply Chain Management handles distribution—the business of getting materials from suppliers to customers.

- The Manufacturing modules shown in Figure 1-2 are limited to those that affect product design and manufacture. The Supply Chain Management modules are often included under Manufacturing.

- The Human Resources product family obviously deals with people. Information on organizations and hierarchies is maintained here to support other applications, such as Projects and Purchasing. HR deals with the administration of human capital, such as compensation and training for organization needs in terms of hiring, benefits, reviews, and termination of employees.

- The Projects applications apply a project dimension to Purchasing, Payables, Order Management, Receivables, and Inventory. Project Manufacturing links it with the rest of the Manufacturing suite. The project dimension serves both control and accounting ends. The project needs to stay on schedule. There is a financial need to see projects integrally—not period by period, but from inception to date—and, most important, to measure earned value and estimate profit and loss.

Although the classifications continue to evolve, each new module will only increase the level of integration and interdependence. Any business—your business—will benefit greatly by adapting this vast body of integrated features, then customizing it or integrating it with other packages to satisfy unique requirements. Many businesses will find that they can use most of the Oracle functions without changing them at all. In other cases, the effort made to install the packages will be minimal compared to the effort involved in developing those bits that must be unique. Other than customization and integration of Financial modules with Oracle EBS, you can also localize the functionality of the business data based on the requirements for each country—including tax, legal, and language requirements across geographic borders—providing for a global solution. Therein lies the value of proprietary software.

The Benefits of Implementing Oracle E-Business Suite

While implementing Oracle EBS, you will be making many far-reaching decisions. To make the right decisions for your organization you will need to fully understand the implications of the alternatives. You will also need to know why your organization is implementing packaged software. The "why" behind the project is often crucial to distinguishing among many otherwise similar alternatives.

These reasons should be clearly and objectively defined in business terms before the start of the project. Navigating a successful course through the project will ultimately depend on having clear business objectives to measure and assess any number of alternatives and dependencies. Every organization is different; your organization will have a variety and mix of different reasons for implementing Oracle EBS. It is always a good idea to identify the main reasons before you embark. These might include efforts to accomplish the following:

- Standardize on integrated, single-vendor solutions and move away from mix and match. *Business Objective ⇒ To reduce software license and support fees by 40 percent over five years.*

- Enable your organization to conduct business over the Internet using Oracle's Self-Service Web Applications and iStore. *Business Objective ⇒ To reduce the cost of acquiring new business to less than $35 per customer.*

■ Ensure that your systems are ready for international currencies and compliant with world currency systems such as the euro and Japanese yen.
Business Objective ⇒ To be fully euro compliant by December 31, 2011.

NOTE
Oracle EBS Release 12 and Fusion Applications are certified to be fully euro compliant.

■ Implement simplified processes, with no redundant dual keying of transactions.
Business Objective ⇒ To reduce head count in internal administration departments by 20 percent over two years.

■ Roll out shared service centers established on "single server" architecture.
Business Objective ⇒ To reduce the cost of processing POs to less than $50 per requisition.

■ Another business objective could be "to migrate into a single instance".
Many companies use different applications for different business flows. Migrating into a single instance can reduce costs by 50 percent.

■ Roll out shared service centers established on a "single server" architecture.
Business Objective ⇒ To reduce the cost of processing Purchase Orders to less than $50 per requisition

Identifying your particular business goals and then keeping them in focus will help your organization throughout the implementation process.

What Are Your Objectives? Setting Parameters and Expectations

Although taking full advantage of Oracle E-Business Suite can transform a business, most companies have more prosaic objectives. They need to be ready for the euro, to replace a few archaic systems that have become totally inadequate, to integrate their applications, or to implement a new chart-of-accounts structure.

Reengineer—Now or Later?

One of your first decisions as you implement Oracle E-Business Suite is whether to change your business procedures at the same time. Some companies opt for a two-phase approach. Phase 1 is to replace their legacy systems, function for function, with Oracle; and phase 2, usually in the indefinite future, is to use the features available in Oracle to reengineer the business. It turns out that just defining the current business processes involves more work than expected, but certainly much less than reengineering the business.

Reengineering the business as you install can make a lot of sense. You are spared the effort of defining your existing business processes in Oracle, your users are disrupted only one time, and you realize the full benefits of Oracle much sooner. On the other hand, reengineering is an even tougher job than software conversion. It takes lots more time and requires dedicated management to keep the staff inspired through the accompanying reorganizations, personnel actions, and retraining.

Oracle E-Business Suite truly is an enabling software product. Companies that fully exploit the features available in the Oracle modules put themselves at the forefront of modern business practice. The majority, those that merely convert to Oracle, realize significant tactical benefits in reliability, integration, and cost reduction. For the first time in the history of data processing, they also put themselves in a position where inadequate software is no longer a major impediment to progress. In most cases, Oracle is ready to support improved processes as quickly as the organization can absorb them.

Conclusion

Oracle Corporation, long the dominant vendor of database software, has increasingly emphasized applications software as the field in which they can offer the most value to their customers. Having developed their own database, programming tools, and Web support gives Oracle formidable advantages. Long known for their functional strength, Oracle's products have become the industry leaders in their use of technology.

Every business is different. The question for you is not whether the Oracle E-Business Suite works—that has been proven—but rather how your company can best achieve its objectives using the EBS. Each company has a unique answer to this question. A successful implementation will require knowledge of the individual modules and the ways in which they work together, knowledge of how to adapt them, and a management plan. Those are the primary themes of this book.

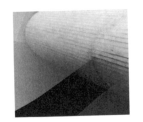

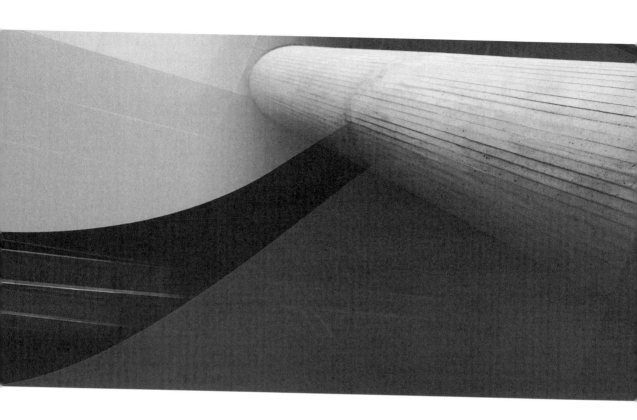

CHAPTER
2

Implementing
the E-Business Suite—
Essential Concepts

rganizations implementing the Oracle E-Business Suite must make important decisions about hardware configuration and application setup. EBS provides a vast array of features and business rules that can greatly improve your organization's productivity, enabling it to conduct business in ways not previously possible. During implementation, you take advantage of the E-Business Suite's built-in flexibility by tailoring the standard features of the package to meet your specific requirements. EBS is quick to implement and easy to adapt; however, the speed and ease of the process depend crucially on decisions made early in the implementation cycle and on the degree of customization you plan to make.

Do not allow shortsighted implementation decisions to hamper the long-term effectiveness of the software. You can avoid inappropriate decisions if everyone involved in the planning process has an early understanding of the concepts essential for implementing Oracle EBS Financials. This chapter introduces these concepts, highlighting decisions that will be difficult to change later on. Here you'll learn how to capture the level of financial information that you need, how to set up Financials within complex organizations, and how to meet the unique demands of the global business environment.

Capturing the Financial Information Relevant to Your Business

Oracle Financials can be configured to a remarkable extent without custom programming. All the forms and reports are designed to be flexible and accommodate many kinds of business rules for a wide variety of situations. Along with the innumerable predetermined fields that appear on each screen, most screens accommodate the entry of additional information through the use of flexfields. Flexfields are important building blocks in the Oracle E-Business Suite. They allow screens and reports to contain data that are uniquely relevant to your organization. Each flexfield can be configured to capture and display the specific information you want.

Flexfields

There are two types of flexfields: *Key* and *Descriptive*. Key Flexfields are used throughout EBS to uniquely identify information such as General Ledger (GL) accounts, inventory items, fixed assets, and other entities that every business needs to keep track of. Descriptive Flexfields (DFFs) enable you to capture additional pieces of information from transactions entered into the Oracle E-Business Suite. Information in key flexfields is composed of flexible ID data structures and a combination of many other IDs.

TIP
In the database, Descriptive Flexfields are stored in attribute columns, whereas Key Flexfields are held in segment columns. The Accounting Flexfield, a Key Flexfield, is stored in the GL_CODE_COMBINATIONS table in the columns named SEGMENT1, SEGMENT2, ... SEGMENT30. Descriptive Flexfields likewise are named ATTRIBUTE1, ... ATTRIBUTE15.

Descriptive and Key Flexfields share common features. They are multisegment fields; the number of segments and the length of each are totally under your control when you set up each application.

When you navigate to a flexfield in a form, a pop-up window appears; you enter appropriate values for each segment or choose values from a pull-down list. The application validates individual segments according to value-set rules and ensures that the combination of segments makes sense using cross-validation rules.

The Accounting Flexfield is Oracle's name for the account key used to record and report accounting information. The Accounting Flexfield is a Key Flexfield; it uniquely identifies General Ledger accounts and provides a flexible structure for any chart of accounts. You can set up the Accounting Flexfield to have any number of segments, up to a maximum of 30. Typically, an organization will need between five and 10 segments. You should aim to design your chart of accounts to have as few segments as possible for ease of use; the 30-segment limit should be seen as a theoretical, not practical, maximum. The more segments you have, the greater the range of segment reporting available to you. However, more segments can mean extra effort to code and categorize financial transactions. At the same time, you need to have a certain minimum number of segments for the flexfields for Oracle Financials modules. For instance, you can set up the Accounting Flexfield with at least two segments and up to a maximum of 30 for the chart-of-accounts flexfield. There is a delicate trade-off between capturing and validating data on each and every transaction and the potential insight the extra data will give into your business.

The following examples are intended to provide an idea of the Accounting Flexfield. Chapter 3 explains in more detail how to design a suitable Accounting Flexfield for your organization. Most companies will use at least three segments: Company, Department, and Account. A typical organization might set up the flexfield to have six segments called Company, Region, Cost Center,

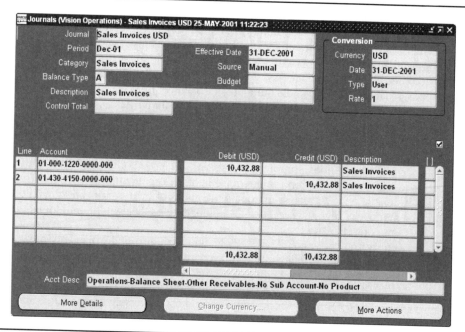

FIGURE 2-1.   *The Enter Journals form showing the Account Flexfield*

Account, Product, and Subaccount. During data entry, the flexfield appears on your form as a pop-up window containing a prompt for each of your established segments, as shown here.

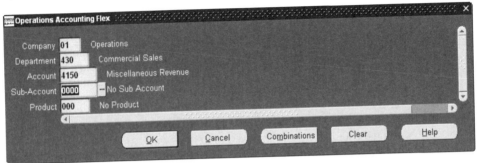

A combination of segment values, known as an *account-code combination*, uniquely identifies the Oracle General Ledger account. This is the finest granularity that Oracle General Ledger can record and report on. The management reports it produces present totals by code combination and accounting period. Transaction-level reports showing what went into a GL account balance must come from the systems that feed the General Ledger.

In Oracle Financials, monetary amounts are posted as debits and credits to account-code combinations. Each account-code combination has a balance at the end of each period. These balances form the basis of the balance sheet, profit-and-loss statement, and all other reporting in the Oracle General Ledger. These balances are readily available either from online inquires or on printed reports, and in some instances from the Web. The Accounting Flexfield segment structure determines the lowest level of detail for which account balances are held. The Accounting Flexfield is the lowest possible reporting detail attainable in General Ledger.

As mentioned, the Accounting Flexfield can contain as many as 30 segments, and you are required to define a minimum of two segments (one qualified as the balancing segment, the other qualified as the natural account segment). The balancing segment usually is the legal entity or company that Oracle E-Business Suite uses to balance journals for each value of the segment. The natural-account segment is classified with an account type of asset, liability, owner's equity, revenue, or expense.

If you intend to use other modules, such as Oracle Assets or Oracle Projects, you must assign an additional *cost-center segment*. Cost centers indicate functional areas of your organization, such as accounting, facilities, shipping, and so on. You also should consider creating additional segments to anticipate future reporting requirements or organizational changes. The Accounting Flexfield is flexible enough to accommodate the needs of your organization by allowing you to specify the number of segments you want, the length of each segment, and the name and order of the account-code structure.

Before you set up your Accounting Flexfield, you should carefully plan your organizational needs. It is easier to build flexibility into your account structure during setup than to try to change your account structure later. Consider future expansion and possible changes in your organization and reporting needs. Also consider the other applications you will be using now and in the future, because an incorrectly defined Accounting Flexfield can adversely affect your accounting data, chart-of-accounts structure, and other features. It is difficult to change your Accounting Flexfield after it has been frozen and has been used to capture data through transaction processing. Changing your structures after the fact may create data inconsistencies that could impact the behavior of your application or require a complex conversion program.

U.S. Operations

Detail Trial Balance
Year to date as of MAR-2002

Currency: USD
Company Range: 01 to 01
Company: 01 US- Global Computers

Acct	Description	Accounting Flexfield	Beginning Balance	Period Activity	Ending Balance
1531	Buildings- CIP Cost	01.000.000.1531.000.0000	4,851,183.78	0.00	4,851,183.78
1531	Buildings- CIP Cost	01.110.110.1531.000.0000	31,000.00	0.00	31,000.00
1531	Buildings- CIP Cost	01.110.410.1531.000.0000	10,000.00	0.00	10,000.00
1541	Buildings- CIP Clear	01.110.000.1541.000.0000	(8,467,359.47)	0.00	(8,467,359.47)
1541	Buildings- CIP Clear	01.110.000.1541.000.0000	3,200.00	0.00	3,200.00
1544	Machinery- CIP Clear	01.110.110.1544.000.0000	978,722.20	0.00	978,722.20
1550	Land- Acc. Depreciat	01.000.000.1550.000.0000	(700,000.00)	0.00	(700,000.00)
1551	Buildings- Acc. Depr	01.000.000.1551.000.0000	(506,805.58)	0.00	(506,805.58)
1552	Tenant Imp.- Acc. De	01.000.000.1552.000.0000	(4,409,599.52)	0.00	(4,409,599.52)
1553	Furniture- Acc. Depr	01.000.000.1553.000.0000	(2,099,245.69)	0.00	(2,099,245.69)
1554	Machinery- Acc. Depr	01.000.000.1554.000.0000	(3,038,271.76)	0.00	(3,038,271.76)
1555	Comp/Comm- Acc. Depr	01.000.000.1555.000.0000	(8,036,158.07)	0.00	(8,036,158.07)
1556	Vehicle- Acc. Deprec	01.000.000.1556.000.0000	(1,645,546.94)	0.00	(1,645,546.94)
1710	Intercompany Receiva	01.000.000.1710.000.0000	(693,143.87)	0.00	(693,143.87)
2110	Notes Payable to Ban	01.110.000.2110.000.0000	10,457.95	0.00	10,457.95
2210	Accounts Payable	01.000.000.2210.000.0000	(29,522.00)	4,200.00	(25,322.00)
2210	Accounts Payable	01.000.000.2210.000.0000	(156,794,819.96)	(10,875.00)	(156,805,694.96)
2210	Accounts Payable	01.110.410.2210.000.0000	1,950,000.00	0.00	1,950,000.00
2210	Accounts Payable	01.120.540.2210.000.0000	(125,000.00)	0.00	(125,000.00)
2210	Accounts Payable	01.130.000.2210.000.0000	31,461,094.53	0.00	31,461,094.53
2210	Accounts Payable	01.130.420.2210.000.0000	(5,678.00)	0.00	(5,678.00)
2210	Accounts Payable	01.310.000.2210.000.0000	(7,084,958.56)	0.00	(7,084,958.56)
2210	Accounts Payable	01.310.540.2210.000.0000	(40,961,256.42)	0.00	(40,961,256.42)
2210	Accounts Payable	01.320.000.2210.000.0000	68,834,743.00	0.00	68,834,743.00
2220	A/P Clearing	01.000.000.2220.000.0000	(50,340.00)	0.00	(50,340.00)
2330	Federal Income Tax P	01.000.000.2330.000.0000	(8,900.00)	0.00	(8,900.00)
2410	Accrued Payroll	01.110.110.2410.000.0000	(300.00)	0.00	(300.00)
2430	Accrued Commissions	01.110.000.2430.000.0000	(200,000.00)	0.00	(200,000.00)
2440	Accrued Bonuses	01.110.410.2440.000.0000	(2,000,000.00)	0.00	(2,000,000.00)
2520	State Sales and Use	01.130.440.2520.000.0000	(6,000,000.00)	0.00	(6,000,000.00)
2520	State Sales and Use	01.320.420.2520.000.0000	(58,602.83)	0.00	(58,602.83)
2542	Realized Foreign Exc	01.000.000.2542.000.0000	(7,197.29)	0.00	(7,197.29)
2543	Realized Foreign Exc	01.000.000.2543.000.0000	21,475.00	0.00	21,475.00
2550	Unearned Revenue	01.000.000.2550.000.0000	(50,125.98)	0.00	(50,125.98)
2550	Unearned Revenue	01.110.460.2550.000.0000	(152,460.11)	0.00	(152,460.11)
2550	Unearned Revenue	01.130.440.2550.000.0000	2,500.00	0.00	2,500.00
2550	Unearned Revenue	01.000.000.2550.000.0000	(30,000.00)	0.00	(30,000.00)
2550	Unearned Revenue	01.320.460.2550.000.0000	(22,000.00)	0.00	(22,000.00)

FIGURE 2-2. *A sample Detail Trial Balance report showing the Accounting Flexfield*

As soon as you are satisfied, freeze your Accounting Flexfield structure to prohibit unnecessary modifications. You must freeze and compile your flexfield definition before you use your flexfield. If you have more than one flexfield structure, you must freeze, save, and compile each structure separately. Do not modify a frozen flexfield definition if existing data could be invalidated. An alteration of the flexfield structure once you have any flexfield data can create serious data inconsistencies. Changing your existing structures also might adversely affect the behavior of any cross-validation rules or shorthand aliases you have for your structures, so be sure to manually disable or redefine these rules and aliases to reflect your changed structures.

NOTE
Changes made to flexfields are seen immediately after freezing or recompiling flexfields. However, other users will see these new changes only after changing responsibilities or exiting and signing back into Oracle EBS.

Key Flexfield Features

The combinations of a Key Flexfield, such as the Accounting Flexfield, uniquely identify a record in a database table. The philosophy of a relational database is that every table contains a group of columns known as the *primary key columns*, which uniquely identify records in that table. Other examples of Key Flexfields are the Asset Key Flexfield, used for identifying fixed assets, and the Items Flexfield, used for identifying inventory item numbers. There are 22 Key Flexfields in Oracle E-Business Suite; they are listed in Table 2-1.

All Key Flexfields share the same features; indeed, the flexfield concept is fully generic, or flexible, as its name implies. You can define shorthand aliases to speed up data-entry tasks, flexfield-value security to ensure that particular users can enter only particular segment values, and cross-validation rules to prevent users from creating new flexfield combinations that contain values that should not coexist in the same combination. You can allow, or intentionally prevent, dynamic insertion for any specific Key Flexfield.

Dynamic insertion is the creation of a new valid combination from a form other than the Combinations form. For example, a user could create a combination representing telephone expense for a new cost center without leaving the Journal Entry form. Sometimes it does not make sense for the application to allow a user to create a new combination "on the hoof." A user should not be able to create a new product item while taking an order for product items using the Enter Orders form.

The Accounting Flexfield incorporates all the generic features of Key Flexfields and some features that are not found in other flexfields.

- *Multiple rollup groups* are used to produce management summaries. You can define a hierarchy of parent and child values within each segment. When you report on a parent value, Oracle General Ledger automatically displays the total of the balances on all the children for that parent.

- *Summary accounts* provide online summary balances. Usually summary accounts are set up so that a total for each financial account is available irrespective of region, cost center, product, and so on. Summary accounts are useful for responding to questions like "What was our total revenue in the last period?"

Flexfield	Code	Owning Application
Account Aliases Flexfield	MDSP	Oracle Inventory
Accounting Flexfield	GL#	Oracle General Ledger
Asset Key Flexfield	KEY#	Oracle Assets
Bank Details Key Flexfield	BANK	Oracle Payroll
Category Flexfield	CAT#	Oracle Assets
Cost Allocation Flexfield	COST	Oracle Payroll
Grade Flexfield	GRD	Oracle Human Resources
Item Catalogs Flexfield	MICG	Oracle Inventory
Item Categories Flexfield	MCAT	Oracle Inventory
Job Flexfield	JOB	Oracle Human Resources
Location Flexfield	LOC#	Oracle Assets
Oracle Service Item Flexfield	SERV	Oracle Service
People Group Flexfield	GRP	Oracle Payroll
Personal Analysis Flexfield	PEA	Oracle Human Resources
Position Flexfield	POS	Oracle Human Resources
Sales Tax Location Flexfield	MKTS	Oracle Receivables
Sales Orders Flexfield	RLOC	Oracle Inventory
Soft Coded Key Flexfield	SCL	Oracle Human Resources
Stock Locators	MTLL	Oracle Inventory
System Items Flexfield	MSTK	Oracle Inventory
Territory Flexfield	CT#	Oracle Receivables
Training Resources Flexfield	RES	Oracle Training Administration

TABLE 2-1. *The Key Flexfields in the Oracle Release 12 E-Business Suite*

■ The *Financial Statement Generator* allows you to easily build custom reports without programming. You can define reports online with complete control over the rows, columns, and contents of your report.

You can readily consolidate balances up through the account hierarchy using tools such as summary accounts, parent accounts, and rollup groups. These tools are described in more detail in Chapter 3.

Accounting Flexfield Design

You should put considerable thought into the design and structure of your Accounting Flexfield before beginning your setup. Many companies put together a special project team to come up with a new chart-of-accounts structure before the implementation project. Companies use the implementation of the Oracle E-Business Suite as a catalyst for introducing a new chart of accounts or a common chart of accounts across their entire organization. You should question up front whether this is what your organization needs. Oracle E-Business Suite will support different Accounting Flexfield structures for each business unit in your organization that needs its own structure. You will still be able to use the native consolidation features in Oracle General Ledger to produce group consolidated accounts, even if different parts of your organization use different Accounting Flexfield structures.

CAUTION
The upheaval an organization experiences when introducing a new chart of accounts is similar in magnitude to what you would expect when introducing a new accounting system; introducing both at the same time can be particularly traumatic. Consider whether you can separate the two projects and minimize the risks.

The project team assigned the task of designing a new chart of accounts needs to consult widely within the organization to cover the reporting needs of all business areas. The team must be aware of the statutory accounting requirements and should be familiar with the mechanics of Accounting Flexfields within Oracle Financials. It is a mistake to think that the chart-of-accounts design is independent of the features of the Oracle E-Business Suite. You should design your Accounting Flexfield to make full use of standard application features. Such features as journal allocations, Account Generator, cross-validation rules, summary accounts, and rollup groups depend critically on the structure of your Accounting Flexfield. With a well-planned account structure, you will be better positioned to take full advantage of these built-in features.

For example, several standard Oracle General Ledger reports use a range of accounts as a selection parameter, and allocations can be defined to visit every cost center in a range in order to calculate an allocated cost for the cost center. A report such as the Oracle General Ledger Account Analysis, which takes a range of financial account codes as a parameter, will be considerably more useful if your account codes have been logically grouped into meaningful ranges.

For example, through grouping all current liabilities in an account range, say from 2000 to 2999, a report could easily be run on current liabilities. If there were no logic built in to the account codes and ranges, it would take considerably longer to obtain a list of all current liability accounts and would likely require custom report development at a later stage. The logical grouping of values in ranges is one example of good Accounting Flexfield design. A well-designed Accounting Flexfield is vital. Although the design process is not an exact science, there are a number of heuristic rules to help; they are described in detail in Chapter 3.

The finished design of the Accounting Flexfield is a milestone in the implementation of Oracle E-Business Suite. Before proceeding with subsequent phases of the implementation, ensure that the chosen design has the acceptance of people who will be working with it: the finance department, operational departments, and auditors. It is a good idea to ask Oracle Consulting Services or an experienced Oracle Financials consultant to validate the chosen design.

Workflow

Businesses thrive by acting on all sorts of information in a timely manner. Data must be delivered to people according to the type of data and the role of the individual. People act on the information and respond in a variety of ways. Purchase orders get authorized and routed to the supplier. Customers pass a credit check and goods are supplied. Stock levels fall below a reorder level and are replenished. Processes can be triggered by the arrival of goods from a supplier, a letter from a customer, a statement from your bank, and so on. Processes can result in financial transactions and journals being generated. Information can be routed to managers for authorization.

Business processes, seemingly always in flux, are many and varied. Oracle Workflow lets you automate and continuously improve business processes by routing any type of information to decision makers according to business rules. These key people can be internal or external to your organization. Oracle Workflow lets you model business processes using a drag-and-drop process designer. Perhaps company policy has changed so that purchase orders less than $100 no longer need manager authorization—you can redefine the purchase-order approval activity in Workflow to approve low-value purchases automatically. Workflow provides support for business processing as well as integration of the enterprise application environment.

Until now, finance systems have automated head-office processes but not reduced the burden of documentation sent by internal mail, faxes sent from one company site to another, and perfunctory telephone calls. Often, decision-making workers have e-mail and Web access but no access to finance systems. For example, the accounts-payable people must track down a project manager to get a project code before they can process invoices. The billing department has to contact the account manager before assigning sales commissions to a salesperson. The accounting department must talk with the corporate-tax department before deciding whether to capitalize an asset.

By delivering electronic notifications through e-mail or a Web page, Oracle Workflow extends the reach of office automation beyond the finance department. It generates notifications out of Workflow activities, and the responses are sent directly back into the Workflow process by e-mail or the Oracle E-Business Suite Notification Web Page. Finance and operational staff are relieved of the regular workload to concentrate their time and expertise on other issues.

The correlation of your business processes with the prebuilt flows within Oracle Workflow is a critical part of an E-Business Suite implementation. The features of Oracle Workflow and the purposes of the prebuilt processes are described further in Chapter 17.

Accounting for Transactions

Oracle Workflow is also used in the Account Generator—a feature that constructs account-code combinations automatically using user-defined criteria. The way Oracle Financials accounts for any particular event must be predefined during the setup of the system. First you must catalog all the events in your organization that give rise to accounting entries, such as raising a purchase order, issuing a sales invoice, depreciating an asset, and revaluing foreign-currency reserves at month's end. For each situation, you need to understand in detail how account codes should be assigned. Accounting policies vary from company to company, and sometimes even within a company.

To allow for all eventualities and provide a packaged solution that does not need reprogramming, Oracle Financials provides a variety of different methods to derive the account codes. The user can enter codes directly, select them from a hierarchy of defaults, look them up based on transaction type, or find them with AutoAccounting (used for assigning accounts to invoices in Oracle Receivables) or the Account Generator (a feature used elsewhere in the applications). The specific rules that Oracle Financials uses to assign accounting codes to transactions are described module by module in the chapters that follow.

At an early stage in the implementation, it is important to realize that there are a variety of methods for the assignments. Some are entirely under the user's control when the transaction is entered; others are entirely under the implementer's control and hidden from the user when the transaction is entered. Getting the structure of the predefined codes right during the implementation phase is a major objective of your preimplementation testing. Understanding the logic behind account assignments is part of mastering Oracle Financials.

Applications need to construct Key Flexfield combinations automatically for a number of reasons, primarily speed and accuracy. AutoAccounting and the Account Generator bring business logic and commercial rules of thumb to bear on account-code derivation. These mechanisms reduce errors, speed data entry, and provide coding consistency across the organization.

AutoAccounting

AutoAccounting is used in Oracle Receivables for generating default Accounting Flexfields for revenue, receivables, freight, tax, unearned revenue, unbilled receivables, finance charges, and *clearing* (suspense) accounts. AutoAccounting works on a relatively simple lookup-table concept; however, its simplicity does not preclude its effectiveness. Accounting Flexfields can either be defaulted as constants or be derived from one of several data sources related to the invoice. The data sources available to choose from are:

- **Sales reps** Account values associated with the salesperson.
- **Transaction types** Account values associated with the transaction type.
- **Standard lines** Account values associated with the standard memo line item or inventory item.
- **Taxes** Account values associated with the tax code.
- **Bill-to site** Account values taken from the customer's bill-to site (the address where the invoice is sent).

AutoAccounting enables you to default each segment for each account from a different data source if necessary. A revenue account can thereby be set up to default the natural account according to the type of sale (transaction type) and to default the cost-center and region segments according to the particular salesperson.

Account Generator

The Account Generator constructs account-code combinations automatically using predefined criteria and is a generalized, further-reaching successor to the Release 10 Flexbuilder tool. In Release 12, Oracle Assets, Oracle Order Management, Oracle Projects, Oracle Purchasing, and Oracle Receivables use Account Generator to create combinations. The Account Generator obtains data from sources such as Key Flexfield segments, application tables, value sets, and constants; applies the customized business rules; and produces an appropriate account-code combination.

Currently the Account Generator is used only for the situations described in Table 2-2. Used effectively, it is an extremely powerful tool, and it likely will be steadily introduced for situations within the E-Business Suite in which Accounting Flexfields are needed.

Application	Account Generator	Description	Initiation
Projects	Project Supplier Invoice Account Generator	Generates accounts for supplier invoices	From the Payables Invoices window
Projects	Project Web Employees Account Generator	Generates accounts for expense reports entered in Self-Service Expenses or the Invoices window in Payables	From the Self-Service Expenses, Enter Receipts window or the Payables Invoices window
Purchasing and Projects	Purchase Order Account Generator (POWFPOAG)	Generates the purchase-order charge account, budget account, variance account, and accrual account	
Purchasing and Projects	Requisition Account Generator (POWFRQAG)	Generates the requisition charge account, budget account, variance account, and accrual account	
Receivables	Substitute Balancing segment	Generates the balancing-segment values when you create finance charges or post exchange-rate gains and losses	Whenever you create finance charges for a transaction or post transactions to the General Ledger
Assets	Assets Account Generator	Derives the book-level account, the category-level account, and the asset-level account	From Depreciation run, Create Journal entries, Calculate gains and losses, and Mass Transfer
Inventory	Generate Cost of Goods Sold Account		
Order Management	Generate Cost of Goods Sold Account	Order Management and Oracle Shipping Execution insert a cost of goods sold (COGS) account for each inventory transaction line into Oracle Inventory through the Inventory Interface program. You can use the COGS account as a basis for COGS analysis in Oracle Inventory. The Account Generator dynamically creates a COGS account to transfer from Order Management and Oracle Shipping Execution to Oracle Inventory for each order and return line when it completes the Inventory interface cycle action.	The Account Generator process for Order Management builds the COGS account using the Cost of Sales account for the item and organization for each inventory transaction line and inserts the COGS account into Oracle Inventory through the inventory interface program.

TABLE 2-2. *Use of the Account Generator within Oracle R12 E-Business Suite*

Meeting the Varied Needs of Complex Organizations

Before you can embark on an Oracle E-Business Suite implementation, you must plan how your computing power and accounting data will be distributed among all the people who need access to financial systems. This is not a simple decision. The systems architecture has a subtle and pervasive impact on the features that can be readily delivered to users. For instance, a simple company will have only one ledger and will not make use of the Multi-Org functions (discussed in the following section). The following sections will help you determine how your company fits into the Oracle E-Business Suite organizational model.

The Organizational Model Within Oracle E-Business Suite

Oracle E-Business Suite is designed to be implemented in any organization, commercial or nonprofit, and at the same time support all possible organizational structures. Because the range of possible organizational structures is limitless, the design of Oracle E-Business Suite contains a general organizational model that can be customized to fit any actual organization. Part of the process of implementation involves planning how your organizational structure maps to the general organizational model within Oracle E-Business Suite.

An organizational model is needed to support fundamental business requirements. Multi-Org is a feature that supports multiple organizations within a single instance of the database. You can set up multiple ledgers within a single instance, with each ledger having its own subledgers or secondary ledgers. The biggest advantage is the capability to support different logical business entities. With Multi-Org, you can sell and ship products across different legal entities spread across different ledgers. In addition, even within the same legal entity, users can be assigned to different operating units so they cannot see or use data from other operating units, thus providing a high level of security. An enterprise must be able to perform the following functions:

- Record any number of organizations and the relationships between them, even if those organizations report separate sets of accounts.

- Support any number of legal entities, including jointly owned subsidiaries.

- Secure access to data so that users can access only the information that is relevant to them.

- Sell products from one legal entity and ship them from another legal entity, and automatically record the appropriate intercompany invoicing.

- Purchase products through one legal entity and receive them in another legal entity.

The multiple-organization architecture determines how transactions flow through different organizations in Oracle E-Business Suite and how those organizations interact with each other. Organizations in Oracle E-Business Suite can be *ledgers*, *legal entities*, *operating units*, or *inventory organizations*, which are explained in the following sections. Some terms have an everyday meaning as well as a very specific Oracle E-Business Suite meaning. In particular, the term *organization* serves a double purpose. Its everyday meaning refers to a company, corporation, government agency, or charity. It also has a specific meaning in the Oracle E-Business Suite model. Do not expect *organization*, as used in reference to the Oracle E-Business Suite, to correspond exactly to the everyday meaning.

Multi-Org is not required where subledger processing is centralized or where there is only one ledger. Similarly, Multi-Org is not required where one ledger has Accounts Payables (AP),

Purchase Orders (PO), Account Receivables (AR), and Order Management (OM) and another ledger has none of these, but only General Ledger (GL). Multi-Org requires only one installation of the software and only one database instance to support an unlimited number of ledgers; thus it provides viewing across multiple ledgers and easier administration of software upgrades. Multi-Org is defined by a hierarchy: a business group consists of ledgers, which are made up of legal entities, which are made up of operating units, which consist of inventory organizations.

NOTE
The multiple-organization architecture (Multi-Org) first became available with Release 10.6. Since Release 10.7, Multi-Org has become a standard part of the package. Operating units were first introduced with Multi-Org, and thus there are no references to them in any release prior to 10.6.

Subledger Accounting—A New Feature in Oracle R12 E-Business Suite

One of the key changes new with Release 12 of the Oracle E-Business Suite is the change to an accounting module for General Ledger. Previously, recall that sets of books were used to manage the setup and administration for chart of accounts, accounting calendars, and currencies. Now with Release 12, we have subledger accounting which provides all of these functions.

Subledger accounting contains the ledger with the chart of accounts, calendar, and functional currency. Legal entities that share the same chart of accounts, accounting calendar, and functional currency can be accounted for in the same ledger. Consider a US corporation that has a subsidiary in Germany. The German company must report statutory returns to the German authorities in the local currency (euros). Because the corporation in the United States accounts in dollars, the German subsidiary has to be created in Oracle Financials as a new setup within subledger accounting. Similarly, subsidiaries that use a different calendar or a different chart of accounts each need to be set up as separate subledgers.

The financial transactions and balances in Oracle General Ledger belong to one ledger. The user of one ledger sees only the journals that relate to that ledger. All other journals are hidden from the user on screens and reports. To access another ledger, the user would need the appropriate Responsibility privileges. The data within Oracle General Ledger are secured by ledgers. Within each ledger you can define one or more legal entities, described in the following sections.

Legal Entity

A legal entity is a company for which, by law, you must prepare fiscal or tax reports, including a balance sheet and a profit-and-loss report. In accounting terms, the legal entity is the smallest business unit for which you need to be able to produce a balanced set of accounts. For nonprofit organizations the legal entity is equivalent to a fund. Legal entities consist of one or more operating units.

Operating Unit

Operating units represent buying and selling units within your organization. The operating unit concept is most apparent in Oracle Order Management, Oracle Receivables, Oracle Purchasing, and Oracle Payables. The transaction data that these modules hold—purchase orders, invoices, payments, and receipts—are partitioned by operating unit. That is to say, one operating unit cannot see the purchase orders, invoices, payments, and receipts for another operating unit, even if the same vendor or customer is involved.

The customer and vendor lists are shared across operating units. The address sites are partitioned by operating unit. Purchasing and selling give rise to liabilities and receivables that are balance-sheet items. Consequently, all the transactions for an operating unit must appear on the balance sheet of only one legal entity. There is no reason to split the liabilities and receivables of one operating unit across two legal entities.

Inventory Organization

The inventory organization is a unit that has inventory transactions and balances, and possibly manufactures or distributes products. The inventory of an organization consists of the finished products that are ready for sale, all parts that are in stock waiting to be assembled into finished products, and all the assemblies of parts that are currently being assembled in the factory. A company's inventory changes continually as products are sold, new parts are purchased, and work progresses on assembly lines. Some organizations, such as banks, hospitals, and consultancies, do not have tangible inventories; they sell their services, expertise, and time.

The Oracle Manufacturing modules, including Oracle Inventory, are partitioned by inventory organization. From an accounting perspective, inventory is a balance-sheet item and therefore belongs to one legal entity. You do not need to split an inventory organization across two or more legal entities.

The organizational model is a strict hierarchy. The minimum configuration is a server supporting one Financials database instance, with one ledger, one legal entity, and a single operating unit related to one inventory organization, as shown in Figure 2-3. More complex organizations can be modeled by introducing multiplicity at any level.

Logical Financials Database

Although not explicitly part of the Oracle E-Business Suite multiple-organization architecture, the number of logical Financials databases has a bearing on the intercompany capabilities you will be able to deliver readily to the end users. Information held in the applications is protected from unauthorized access. Access is restricted to authorized users, who are able to log in and work through an application's screens with their passwords. Each logical Financials database has a single list of authorized users. The repository for the user list, the Applications Object Library, is installed in the database once—as the first application module created when you install Oracle EBS—and it controls user access to all organizations within the database.

Although it is possible to distribute the processing across nodes in a network system, Oracle Financials does not support databases distributed across machines. The distribution of the processing load provides fault tolerance in case one or more nodes fail. Oracle Financials databases therefore are essentially stand-alone database systems; they form islands of data. A global organization might implement one database instance for operations in North America, a second database instance for Europe and Africa, and a third for Asia. The accounting setup, user names, accounting calendar, and currencies will not be shared by those three database instances.

If you do decide to run multiple database instances, you can easily consolidate General Ledger transactions using the Release 11 feature Global Consolidation System (GCS). GCS caters to data collected from any source and any number of subsidiary accounting systems. These accounting systems do not need to be Oracle General Ledger systems. GCS can upload financial data from a spreadsheet as well as through a dedicated open interface. GCS makes it unnecessary to organize a consolidation mechanism outside Oracle Financials. Even so, before choosing multiple financial databases or servers, consider the overhead of maintaining reference data, such as currency-conversion rates, in separate databases.

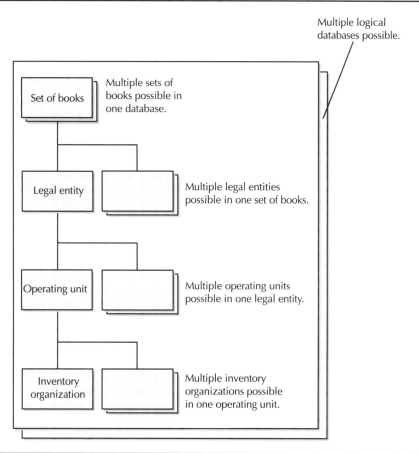

FIGURE 2-3.   *The organizational model*

Financials in the Global Businesses Environment

Hardware and network configurations can be complex. A large multinational organization with several operating units has finance users in many countries around the world. The corporation has a choice: run one centralized server and link all users by high-speed data connections (called a *wide area network*, or WAN) or install smaller machines in each operating unit and connect the users by a *local area network* (LAN). Each option should be costed, because there is a trade-off between network communication cost (which is higher for a centralized server) and machine cost (which is lower for a centralized server). The hardware strategy has a subtle and pervasive impact on the software features that can be delivered readily to each user.

Centralized servers are excellent for allowing regular and fast consolidation of financial data to produce group-wide accounts. In addition, a centralized server allows simplified creation of a common chart of accounts and common categories and classifications for all users. By contrast, local servers allow independent operating units a great deal of autonomy to run their businesses the way that suits them. Businesses have to adapt the hardware strategy to their corporate culture. However, local independence might be seen as a bad business practice because it can degrade the data being uploaded to corporate reporting systems. New technologies such as Oracle Exadata servers provide massive computational power with minimal server sprawl, reduced operating costs, and a smaller data-center footprint for enterprise Oracle E-Business Suite environments.

The hardware configuration and the implementation of organizational structure are subtly related. The strategy for each should be chosen together, after you have fully researched the structure and needs of your business.

Cloud Computing and Oracle Applications

Virtualization and cloud computing are the wave of the future for data-center environments that host the resources required to power the Oracle E-Business Suite infrastructure. So what exactly is cloud computing? To simplify this concept we can think of virtualization first. Virtualization provides you with the ability to operate multiple servers with individual operating systems on the same server through the use of hypervisor technologies such as VMware and Oracle Virtual Machine (Oracle VM). Cloud computing takes virtualization to the next level by implementing joint solutions with computer, storage, and network resources in a single environment coupled with virtualization technologies. For example, the Vblock platform from VCE (//www.vce.com) provides a true cloud-integrated solution to power data centers running the Oracle E-Business Suite. Fortunately, Oracle has validated support with VMware and Oracle VM technologies, so you can be assured that stability is provided with the cloud-computing paradigm and Oracle E-Business Suite.

Creating a Model of Your Business

Before you implement Oracle Financials, model your entire business and determine your actual organizational structures. How many legal entities do you own? Where are your warehouses and manufacturing plants located? Are the finance, marketing, and personnel departments run at the group level or by each business unit individually? Determine your reporting needs and the levels of autonomy in your business. Keep in mind that reporting hierarchies might not match physical locations; for example, the marketing manager for Asia and the Pacific might operate out of group headquarters in New York. The global effort can be broken down into smaller manageable chunks. A large multinational company might choose to implement Oracle E-Business Suite in one business unit as a prototype and later roll out the system to its other units.

Prototyping

The prototype might be a full implementation in a single business unit or it might be a pilot implementation of a subset of the functionality across the whole organization. Pilots can be implemented rapidly and used to validate new business processes and procedures. They allow managers, accountants, and implementers to build up confidence and understand how Oracle E-Business Suite works. From the start, the analysis of the business should consider all business units. Prototyping is a very powerful way to get up to speed fast and show some immediate return for the prototyping effort. The prototype must be seen in perspective. Decisions about hardware distribution, staff organization, the structure of a chart of accounts, and other setup issues have to be made with the needs of the entire organization in mind, not just those of the pilot business unit.

The final decisions about the hardware configuration and about organizational structure cannot be made independently of each other; both areas have to be considered. The configuration is not determined by the size of your organization but rather by the complexity of your organization, its geographical spread, the level of autonomy in different parts of your organization, and the similarity between their lines of business.

Modeling Process

The modeling process can be likened to a process of mapping your actual organizational structure onto the implied organizational model of logical databases, each database catering to multiple organizations and each organization consisting of multiple legal entities. If you are converting to Oracle E-Business Suite from an existing or legacy system, do not make the mistake of simply reimplementing your existing model; instead, start the modeling process at the database level. Determine how many databases are needed to support your business. You then can model upward to decide how many servers are needed and which database instances will reside on each server. For each database instance, you can model downward to determine the organizational structure implemented within each database.

Financial Reporting

The Accounting Flexfield segments support statutory and management reporting from the General Ledger. There has to be a corporate-wide plan for financial reporting. Reporting needs that are not covered by a segment in the Accounting Flexfield have to be satisfied by a report from one of the other modules, or from a feeder system if the data are imported directly into Oracle General Ledger.

Each module provides several reports, each one detailing a specific type of financial-transaction data. These standard reports can be requested by an authorized user at any time. Standard reports have a fixed format and layout; however, their content can be focused each time the report is submitted by specifying selection parameters. The standard reports in Oracle General Ledger include Trial Balance reports, several Account Analysis reports, and Consolidation and Budgeting reports.

In addition to the standard reports, other tools are associated with Oracle General Ledger for reporting financial data in a way that exceeds the intention of the standard reports. One such tool is the Financial Statement Generator (FSG), which can be used for producing any financial report such as a balance sheet or income statement. The FSG reports on account balance, either actual or budget, per Accounting Flexfield combination. It does not report on transaction detail. Refer to Chapter 3 for more information on defining FSG report formats.

Oracle Financial Analyzer is a separate module with an OLAP (online analytical processing) multidimensional database at its core, which is used to produce complex analysis reports. Transaction data are exported out of Oracle General Ledger and imported into Oracle Financial Analyzer. It provides a complete set of tools for budgeting, forecasting, analyzing, and reporting corporate financial data.

The Application Desktop Integrator (ADI) started life as a quick and simple way to import budgets and actual journals in Oracle General Ledger. It now includes the Request Center, a centralized report-management tool from which you can submit, monitor, and publish any type of report to a variety of different formats—Web, spreadsheet, and text—all from a single user interface. The Request Center not only supports publish-and-subscribe Web publishing; it also allows you to download a spreadsheet version of the report on demand for analytical analysis. In Oracle E-Business Suite Release 12, ADI has been replaced by Web ADI, which is browser based rather than being a stand-alone desktop client application.

Many customers are using Oracle Discoverer to deliver custom and ad hoc reports, driven directly off the underlying table structures or using an end-user layer, such as the Business Intelligence System. Discoverer is a standard Oracle database tool, which was renamed as BI Discoverer in the latest release. Through a spreadsheet-like window, users can browse data in the database and construct their own query reports to pull out the data elements that interest them.

Global Financial Applications

Oracle's globalization strategy is simple: provide one global product that meets local, regional, and global requirements. Business requirements for national and multinational users have been built into the applications for 44 countries worldwide. Oracle's ultimate aim with globalization is to put all features into the core product.

Oracle's earlier approach was to deliver the package in American English, with accounting features that closely corresponded to the generally accepted accounting principles (GAAP) of the United States, together with extensions—additional-language versions of screens and reports, extra software features, local statutory reports—that could be applied on top of the base package. Oracle called these extensions *localizations*. The same features are now developed, packaged, and released centrally in one global product for Oracle EBS. Oracle R12 EBS provides two types of localizations: regional and country based. Regional localizations provide general practices as well as statutory and legal practices for a given locality for multiple countries. In contrast, country-specific localizations focus on more specific legal requirements unique to a country versus an entire region.

National Language Support

National Language Support (NLS) permits you to run Oracle E-Business Suite in languages other than American English. There are two distinct categories of NLS: the language *character set* that users are able to use when they key data into forms and web pages, and the language *translation* of the fixed text on forms and reports. The character set available for user data need not correspond to the language of the fixed text on forms and reports. For example, the American English translation of the forms and reports can be used simultaneously with a data-entry character set such as US7ASCII that allows local-language characters to be entered. In contrast, you would use a character set such as UTF-8 for Unicode applications to avoid conflicts with data conversions, since the UTF-8 character set is backward compatible with the ASCII character set and avoids conflicts with endian data types.

Translations The Oracle E-Business Suite forms and reports are available in more than 29 languages in addition to American English. When you install Oracle E-Business Suite in a language other than American English, all the forms, menus, help text, messages, and reports appear in the selected language. If you need to view this information in more than one language (not including American English) within a single database instance, you can install Multilanguage Support (MLS). This feature enables users on the same system to view fixed text, appearing on screens and in reports, in different languages according to their user-setup designations.

Foreign Character Sets Choose a character set that includes all the printable characters you are likely to need. Character sets are grouped according to the number of bits and bytes needed to uniquely identify each character. Regular ASCII is a 7-bit character set. If you want to work in German you need an 8-bit character set to store extra characters such as ä, ü, and ß. The Japanese character set requires 16 bits (2 bytes).

You can always store data in American English with any of the available character sets. However, you may use only one character set in any given database instance, a limitation that could be a determining factor in the number of database instances you end up installing at your site. Before Release 12 of Oracle EBS, you were not able to store both Japanese and German in the same database, because they used different character sets. With Release 12, E-Business Suite supports Unicode character sets including UTF-8. This allows you to store text in multiple languages that use a subset of UTF-8, such as Spanish, German, and French. Your database administrator will need to know which character set you intend to use before the database is created. The default character set in Oracle R12 EBS is now US7ASCII for American English after a default installation is performed.

Address Styles

Oracle E-Business Suite enables you to enter customer, supplier, bank, check, and remit-to addresses in country-specific formats. For example, if you have customers in Germany and the United Kingdom, you can enter German addresses in the format required by the Bundespost (the German mail service) and enter addresses for customers in the United Kingdom in the format recommended by the Royal Mail. The data will still be stored in the same database columns, but the input-screen format and syntax will be specific to each country instead of always reflecting the US Postal Service requirements.

Localizations

Localizations are designed to meet the specific needs of certain territories or countries. Most localizations are necessary because the local laws or accounting practices differ from those that are common in the United States. For example, most countries have their own special formats for checks and electronic correspondence with banks. The electronic-payment formats for each country also are included in the localizations. Unlike translations, in which one language must be chosen as the base language, it is possible to install the localizations for several territories. This would be necessary for a Dutch company that intends to use electronic payments with both French and German banks.

Each territory that has localization modules belongs to one of three regions: Asia Pacific; Europe, the Middle East, and Africa (EMEA); or the Americas (Canada plus Latin America). An additional region, called Global, is for localizations that apply to territories throughout the world. For example, localizations used in both Europe and Latin America are classified in the Global region. Localizations are classified according to four groups:

- Asia Pacific (JA), for regions in the Asian Pacific Rim such as Japan and China
- European Localizations (JE), for regions in Europe including France and Spain
- Regional Localizations (JG), for regions clustered together
- Latin America Localizations (JL), for Central and South America

The effects of localizations vary widely; some could have only a minor effect on one module, whereas others might have wider-reaching effects. As a general rule, if a process is a generally accepted practice or is government required, it probably will be included in the localization for your country or territory.

NOTE
Translations and localizations are separate from and independent of each other. For instance, suppose you were to install the French localization software, but not the French translations. You then would be able to issue commands in French, but all your screens and reports would remain in English. Or suppose you wanted all screens and reports in Italian, but none of the Italian localizations. Both of these configurations are possible and common, especially within multinational companies.

Conclusion

Implementing the E-Business Suite is a major undertaking for most organizations. Business managers have to appreciate concepts such as flexfields, the organizational model, and regional features early on in order to be able to close out important implementation decisions that have to be parameterized in the initial setup of the application. Most of these decisions have to be made once for the entire company, and once made are difficult to change later. Pilots and prototypes are effective devices to enable your organization to quickly get up to speed with the structure and behavior of the E-Business Suite; they allows key users to design an optimal configuration of critical setup, like business organizations and charts of account—decisions which will pervade the fully implemented system forever.

This chapter has provided an overview of these concepts. Each is described and expanded on in the chapters that follow.

PART

II

The Financial Applications

CHAPTER
3

Oracle General Ledger

racle General Ledger (GL) is the collection point for all financial transactions. It is a tool for integrating subledger activity, consolidating group-wide accounts, and producing statutory financial reports. It provides a comprehensive financial-management solution that enforces financial controls and enables data collection and financial reporting throughout an enterprise. For businesses operating in a global environment, Oracle General Ledger handles the common setup components that are shared across Oracle Financial Applications, including legal entities, ledgers (primary and secondary), and currency-conversion rates; provides support for the euro; and tracks and reports balances in multiple currencies. For companies operating in a strict spending regime, Oracle General Ledger enforces absolute budgetary control.

Reporting drives everything you do in the General Ledger. Provided with an abundance of native reporting tools—BI Publisher, Financial Statement Generator, Web ADI, Business Intelligence System, and BI Discoverer—the implementer's task is to match the appropriate tool to the circumstance and, by judicious planning of the Accounting Flexfield, ensure that a company's reporting needs are met simply and efficiently.

The Heart of Your Accounting System

General Ledger is at the heart of any accounting system. It is the central repository of all subledger activity, maintaining the highest summary level of financial information from the transaction details supplied by its subledgers. All events that have a financial or monetary impact are ultimately reflected in General Ledger.

Anything that has a financial impact on the company has to be accounted for. Normally, transactions are entered into Oracle subledgers. For example, a customer invoice is entered into Oracle Receivables after Oracle Shipping has notified Receivables that a product has been shipped to the customer. To purchase office equipment, a purchase order is recorded in Oracle Purchasing. When the equipment arrives and the invoice is received, the purchase order is closed and a liability is recorded in Oracle Payables. Finally, Oracle Payables sends information to Oracle Assets to capitalize the equipment and initiate depreciation. The data in all of these subledgers are then transferred to Oracle General Ledger through a standard transfer program. Oracle E-Business Suite (EBS) is built on the principle that such events, or financial transactions, are entered only once, whether in General Ledger or its subledgers.

Transactions that are not entered into any other subledger can be entered directly into Oracle General Ledger using the Enter Journals form (see Figure 3-1 for sample journal entries). Companies must ensure that all financial transactions are represented only once in the ledger. A control mechanism outside the accounting system should be in place and maintained to ensure that accounting entries are entered and not duplicated. Not all companies implement all the Financials modules; for example, a company with a small number of assets can choose not to implement Oracle Assets and will instead have to enter asset additions, disposals, and depreciation information directly into Oracle General Ledger. A company using Oracle Assets would key the asset information into Oracle Assets; Oracle Assets would prepare a journal entry that would then be transferred into Oracle General Ledger.

On the other hand, a company using Oracle Assets and Oracle Payables would have asset information already available in Oracle Assets if an invoice were created in Oracle Payables. The Mass Additions feature in Oracle Assets allows you to transfer asset information from any feeder

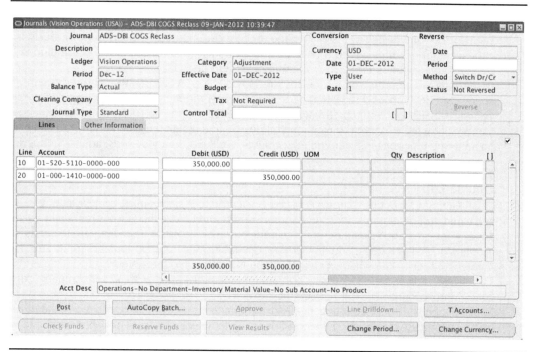

FIGURE 3-1.   *Sample journals shown in the Enter Journals form*

system, such as Oracle Payables and Oracle Projects, into Oracle Assets. Then, from Oracle Assets, you can send asset journal entries to Oracle General Ledger. Either way, the financial transaction finds its way into Oracle General Ledger.

Overview of General Ledger

Most people are familiar with their own bank statements, which show an opening balance, transactions that occurred throughout the period, and a closing balance. That statement is a snapshot of your account at a particular point in time. A company keeps an account, like the records the bank keeps of your bank account, for every organization or customer the company does business with. The balance sheet summarizes accounts and financial activities in three broad categories: assets, which represent everything the company owns; liabilities, which show how much money the company owes to others; and capital and retained earnings, which show the total cash invested in the business by the owners or shareholders. In addition, accounts are kept for all the revenues and expenses of the company. These accounts are summarized in an income statement, also called a *profit-and-loss* (P&L) statement, which represents the performance of a company over time.

The first step in capturing your transactions is to set up your chart of accounts. Your chart of accounts determines how your accounting information is collected, categorized, and stored for reporting purposes. Across the entire E-Business Suite, all accounts are identified by a unique

Accounting Flexfield (AFF) combination, which encapsulates your chart-of-accounts structure. You assign each account the qualifier of *asset*, *liability*, *owner's equity*, *revenue*, or *expense*. The structure and design of the AFF is one of the most important aspects of any E-Business Suite implementation. Guidance on how to go about the design and what to avoid is included later in this chapter in the section on Accounting Flexfield design.

Periods are identified by names such as FEB-2012 or WEEK12-2012 and represent nonoverlapping consecutive date ranges. FEB-2012 would include the date ranges 01-FEB-2012 to 28-FEB-2012 and would be followed by MAR-2012 starting on 01-MAR-2012. You choose the names, following whatever convention you devise, and assign the date ranges. You can also set up adjustment periods for year-end adjustments. Unlike ordinary periods, adjustment periods can overlap.

Double-Entry Accounting

Double-entry accounting requires constant symmetry; total debits must equal total credits. Every accounting transaction results in one or more debits and credits that always remain in balance. For example, a $5,000 purchase of office equipment would result in an increase to the asset account, posted as a debit, and an increase to a liability account, posted as a credit. AFF is used throughout Oracle EBS whenever a transaction is entered into the system.

The Accounting Flexfield consists of multiple segments, such as those for company, cost center, and account. One full Accounting Flexfield is called a *combination*. Each journal-entry line is tagged with an Accounting Flexfield combination. For expense transactions, the AFF usually identifies who incurred the cost (for example, which company or department) and what the cost was for (for example, travel expense). If you want more detailed information, such as which region, cost center, and product incurred the cost, you can design your AFF structure to include that information as well. Because total debits must always equal total credits in every transaction, Oracle General Ledger requires that all journals balance. If you try to enter an unbalanced journal, Oracle General Ledger will either reject the transaction or force the transaction to balance by posting the difference to a suspense account. This later behavior is controlled by a parameter that is configured when General Ledger is first set up (on the Ledger Definition screen under the Accounting Setup).

Legal Entities

In today's global economy, many large organizations perform transactions which are entered into by a legal entity. Oracle Legal Entity Configurator is a new addition to Oracle E-Business Suite that enhances the ability to manage a legal corporate structure and track data from the legal perspective. The solution provides the foundation for features such as securing the specific tax calculations corresponding to the local legal requirements and reporting at legal entity, and establishment legal entity with state and other authorities in addition to its central registration. It also keeps track of the intercompany documentation as well as providing basic process control to facilitate the IT governance.

Oracle EBS delivers through the Oracle Legal Entity Configurator a centralized data model supporting legal information for internal legal entities, legal authorities, and jurisdictions.

Multiple Charts of Accounts

Companies that operate globally might require the use of multiple charts of accounts. For example, a company with subsidiaries in different geographical regions might have to adapt to different account structures based upon various laws by region or base currency requirements. Oracle General Ledger allows you to define as many charts of accounts as desired, all within a single installation of the product.

Accounts and Periods

You can enter transactions only in an open period. Many times, two or three periods are open at once to allow for prior-period transactions and future-period transactions. Once you know that you no longer need to keep a period open to enter transactions, you should close the period to prevent accidental entries into it.

A transaction is dated in the accounting system according to when it actually occurred, not according to when it was entered into the system or processed. This is in contrast to the way online transaction processing (OLTP) systems tend to work. Transactions in an OLTP system are dated with the day and time when they were created. In an accounting system, the actual date and time a transaction was entered is not an important factor in controlling functions or report-selection criterion. In fact, it is stored in Oracle E-Business Suite as part of the *who/when* audit trail associated with every data record (see the following tip). The accounting period in which a financial transaction falls is likewise determined by the date when the transaction actually occurred, not when it was entered into the accounting system.

TIP
Most every transaction table has who/when columns, which record the user who created each record, the user who last updated the record, and the date and time these events happened. These columns are CREATED_BY, CREATION_DATE, LAST_UPDATED_BY, and LAST_UPDATE_DATE. They are referenced by the menu option Help | Record History, which displays the audit trail for the currently selected record on your screen.

Finance and accounting departments often have targets for the prompt closure of accounting periods. An important role delegated to the system administrator or a key person in the finance department is opening and closing the accounting periods. A one- or two-week time scale is a reasonable closing schedule for companies that operate on calendar-month periods. However, the number and timing of the periods can be chosen to suit your company's local accounting practice.

Various common accounting calendars are shown in Table 3-1. The accounting periods in Oracle Financials can start and finish on any day of the year, and the start and end days can differ from year to year; but the number of periods each year must remain constant. This limitation is required in order to produce year-to-year comparisons. The financial year can also end on any chosen day. Common year ends are December 31, because it fits in with the calendar year; March 31, because it fits with the United Kingdom's fiscal year (which runs from April 6 to April 5); September 30, for the US government's fiscal year; and June 30, which is favored by auditors who otherwise have a resource problem dealing with all the companies with December 31 year ends.

Posting is simply the process of updating the account balances of your detail and summary accounts. Posting can be done at the time of journal entry, at a later time to post a group of journal batches, or automatically using AutoPost. AutoPost uses criteria sets that are a combination of journal sources, journal categories, balance types, and periods. When you run this program it

Calendar	Number of Periods	Duration of Each Period	Usage
Quarter	4	13 weeks	Rarely used except by low-transaction, dormant companies
Month	12	Calendar month	Standard business calendar; the financial year ends on December 31 or any other chosen day
4-4-5	12	Each quarter is three periods of four, four, and five weeks	Alternative to calendar month; provides equal-length quarters, giving better quarter-to-quarter comparisons; users normally put odd days into the first and last weeks of the year, so fiscal years are directly comparable
Week	52	52 periods of one week each	Favored by retail companies that require rapid feedback on sales figures—a month is too long to wait for critical figures; odd days at year end are usually swept into the dead time around the holidays
Day	260 ± 25	Each trading day is a separate period	Favored by banks, which have to show day-end balances for regulatory compliance

TABLE 3-1. *Common Accounting Calendars*

selects the journals that meet the criteria and posts them automatically at specific times and submission intervals defined by you. Each time you post journals, the system keeps a record of the total debits and the total credits posted to each account in the period; it uses these totals to keep a running total of the account balance for each period. The following formulas shows how the account balances are calculated:

Account Closing Balance = Opening Balance + Total Debits – Total Credits.
Account Opening Balance for One Period = Closing Balance for the Previous Period.

These two rules determine how the balance of each account develops over a period of time. An example of this is shown in Figure 3-2. Box 1 shows the account balances, Box 2 shows the posted journal, and Box 3 shows the updated account balances. The journal in this case is simply a salary payment to employees from a bank account with some other administration cost.

There is a variation on the second rule for revenue and expense accounts at year end. Revenue and expense accounts are part of the profit and loss for the company. The definition of *profit* (or *loss* if the profit is negative) is

Profit = Total Revenues – Total Expenses.

At the end of the financial year, the profit or loss for the year is calculated and transferred to the balance sheet as retained earnings. The revenue and expense accounts start the new financial year with a balance of zero.

1. Opening Balances

Natural Account	Debit	Credit
Cash and receivables	137,000	
Other current assets	140,000	
Plant and equipment	120,000	
Land	40,000	
Investments	76,000	
Liabilities		60,000
Common stock		250,000
Other contributed capital		47,000
Sales		1,290,000
Investment income		3,000
Other revenue		2,000
Salary and wages	65,000	
Cost of goods sold	900,000	
Exchange rate losses	5,000	
Depreciation and amortization	47,000	
Administration	3,000	
Provision for bad debt	119,000	
Grand Totals	**1,652,000**	**1,652,000**

2. Salary Journal

Natural Account	Debit	Credit
Cash and receivables		37,000
Salary and wages	35,000	
Administration	2,000	
Grand Totals	**37,000**	**37,000**

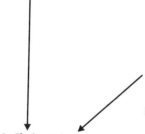

3. Closing Balances

Natural Account	Debit	Credit
Cash and receivables	100,000	
Other current assets	140,000	
Plant and equipment	120,000	
Land	40,000	
Investments	76,000	
Liabilities		60,000
Common stock		250,000
Other contributed capital		47,000
Sales		1,290,000
Investment income		3,000
Other revenue		2,000
Salary and wages	100,000	
Cost of goods sold	900,000	
Exchange rate losses	5,000	
Depreciation and amortization	47,000	
Administration	5,000	
Provision for bad debt	119,000	

FIGURE 3-2. *Account balances develop over time as journals are posted*

NOTE
Oracle General Ledger calculates the profit figure and transfers it to the account designated as the retained-earnings account for that set of books. The calculation takes effect when you open the first period of the new accounting year, and it is based on the account type defined for each Accounting Flexfield combination. For this reason, it is important to set up the account types in Oracle correctly when the segment values for each account are defined. Mixing up profit and loss accounts (revenue and expense) and balance-sheet accounts (asset, liability, and owner's equity) will inevitably result in an incorrect profit figure carried forward into the next financial year.

The two rules, plus the variation of the second rule at year end, completely describe the processing logic encoded into General Ledger. The mechanics of the system have their origins in paper-based lists of accounting records, known as *ledgers*. The processing logic needed to run a computerized ledger system is not complex. Small companies and sole traders can run a perfectly adequate general-ledger system on a spreadsheet. Oracle General Ledger has significant advantages for larger organizations, which need several users to access the system at the same time. Large organizations must be able to perform the following tasks:

- Process high volumes of data
- Provide transaction processing through journal approvals and secured access to journal posting and reversal
- Create custom and standard reports using Oracle General Ledger's reporting tool, the Financial Statement Generator (FSG)
- Account for multiple currencies
- Account for multiple accounting methods
- Create and maintain budgets
- Consolidate groups of companies or subsidiaries
- Provide a spreadsheet interface for entering journals, creating budgets, and creating and analyzing reports using the Applications Integrator (Web ADI)
- Provide OLAP capabilities using Oracle Business Intelligence Suite to further analyze information and expand reporting capabilities in a multidimensional environment

Primary Ledgers, Secondary Ledgers, and Ledger Sets
Oracle General Ledger linked all the previous definitions in the Accounting Setup Manager, the workbench for all the accounting setups. In previous releases, what is now called Ledgers was known as Set of Books; besides the change in the name, the definition also has changed, introducing new definitions.

The new definition of the ledgers is determined by the currency, chart of accounts, accounting calendar, ledger processing options, and subledger accounting method—if used—for a legal entity, group of legal entities, or some other business purpose that does not involve legal entities.

There are two types of ledgers. A primary ledger, which is required for each accounting setup, is the main record-keeping ledger. The secondary ledger, which is optional, is associated with the primary ledger and can be used to represent the primary ledger's accounting data in another accounting representation that differs from the primary in the chart of accounts, accounting calendar, currency, subledger accounting method or ledger processing options. The most common representation of this secondary ledger is when a legal entity is a subsidiary of a parent company and must produce its financial results according to the parent company's reporting requirements in addition to its own local reporting requirements; a secondary ledger may be used to satisfy the additional reporting requirement.

The introduction of secondary ledgers and the different data-conversion levels improved the ability to store and report information from the primary ledger in multiple ways:

- **Subledger**   This data-conversion level uses both Oracle Subledger Accounting and General Ledger posting to create the necessary journals in both your primary and secondary ledgers simultaneously.

- **Journal**   The journal-level secondary ledger maintains your primary-ledger journal entries and balances in an additional accounting representation.

- **Balance**   The balance-level secondary ledger maintains your primary-ledger account balances in another accounting representation.

- **Adjustments Only**   The adjustments-only secondary ledger is an incomplete accounting representation that only holds adjustments. To obtain a complete secondary accounting representation that includes both the transactional data and the adjustments, you must then combine the adjustments-only secondary ledger with the primary ledger when running reports.

Oracle E-Business Suite introduced another new feature related to the ledgers, which is the concept of the *ledger set*. A ledger set is a group of ledgers that share the same chart of accounts and combination of calendar and period type. Ledger sets allow you to run processes and reports for multiple ledgers simultaneously. The main objective of this new feature is to speed up processes that incurred multiple clicks, such as opening periods for multiple ledgers or summarizing balances across ledgers using FSG.

For example, you can open or close periods for multiple ledgers at once, run recurring journals that update balances for multiple ledgers, or run consolidated financial reports that summarize balances across multiple ledgers in a ledger set. You can group all types of ledgers in a ledger set, such as primary ledger, secondary ledgers, and reporting currencies (journal and subledger levels), as long as they share the same chart of accounts and combination of calendar and period type.

Auditing and Security

Oracle General Ledger maintains an audit trail for every financial transaction, to allow you to go back to the original entry for purposes of reconciliation and auditing. This audit trail helps accountants validate their reports and ensures data security. Tampering with accounts and figures is much more difficult with proper controls in place.

An important feature and a strong business requirement in many countries in Europe, Asia Pacific, and Latin America is the sequential numbering of accounting entries. The system allows the assignment of sequence numbers to journals during the posting process to ensure that finalized journal entries are properly sequenced.

The introduction of a new Management segment for reporting and entry of management adjustments is a huge advantage for security and reporting. This new segment can be any of the chart of account segments except the balancing segment, natural account segment, or intercompany segment. It will provide the ability to secure the information utilizing out-of-the-box Oracle General Ledger's security model avoiding customizations or extensions.

The setup of the control accounts will help the organization to secure the data entry to an account by ensuring that the account contains data only from a specified journal source, and to prevent users from entering data for the account either in other journal sources or manually within General Ledger. This is required when using accounts that are specific to a particular source system, such as Oracle Payables, and prevents other subsystems from entering data into a particular designated account for this subsystem.

Journal Entries

Journals can be entered into Oracle General Ledger using various methods: manual entry, subledger entry using the Journal Import interface, and spreadsheet entry using the Web Applications Desktop Integrator. A typical journal entry is shown in Figure 3-1.

New features were introduced in Release 12 to improve processing efficiency by reducing steps on the user interface. Among them are

- simultaneous data access to multiple legal entities and ledgers within a single responsibility;

- cross-ledger allocation, mostly used when allocating corporate or regional expenses to local subsidiaries' ledgers;

- automatic copying of an existing journal batch to create a new journal batch with the same journals and journal lines;

- automatic posting of journals across multiple ledgers simultaneously; and

- replacement of disabled accounts—a very useful functionality that can prevent transactions that include the account from returning an error during journal import by defining a replacement account for the disabled account.

Automatic Journal Reversal

General Ledger will reverse journals for specified journal categories. You choose the reversal method (either switching the debits and credits or changing the sign of each entry) for each category, and select the rules for General Ledger to use to determine the effective date or period of the reversal. You can use automatic journal reversal efficiently to reverse the effect of accrual journals in the following accounting period, or to wind out the effect of depreciation journals after the management accounts have been produced.

Integration with Other Financials Modules

Unless you opt for a manual solution using only General Ledger, you will inevitably need to import data from your subledgers. The Journal Import interface is the common tool for importing transactions into Oracle General Ledger. When you transfer data from Oracle subledgers, the system automatically populates the database table called GL_INTERFACE, from which the journal-import process captures its data.

The Journal Import Interface

Journal transactions can originate in subledgers or in an external feeder system. Each Oracle subledger that transfers transactions prepares the journal-entry records, inserts them into the GL_INTERFACE table, and starts the journal import process. Figure 3-3 shows the main accounting transactions that flow from the Oracle subledgers and a few symbolic external feeder systems.

The Journal Import interface uses the GL_INTERFACE table as a bridge between external systems and the Oracle General Ledger base tables where journals are stored. For each journal line that needs to be imported, a single record is inserted into the GL_INTERFACE table. The journal-import process is started and an execution report shows what has processed. If journals are not imported successfully, the errors are listed in the execution report. Each of these errors needs to be corrected using the Correct Journal Import Data window; then the journal-import process must be restarted. Alternatively, if the journal data set is beyond repair, all records can be deleted using the Delete Journal Import Data window and the data prepared again from the feeder system. Figure 3-4 diagrams the process.

For transfers initiated from Oracle subledgers, the system automatically populates the GL_INTERFACE table, then starts the journal-import process. The journal data transferred from Oracle subledgers seldom shows data errors. Although errors are rare, they do happen, so it is advisable to check each and every process to ensure that it has completed successfully. The most common and easily rectified error is attempting to import into a closed period. To correct, open the period and rerun the import.

Alerts, managed from Oracle Workflow, are a good device for performing checks such as these, precisely because they advise users when exceptions occur. You can write an alert to send a simple e-mail to the accounting manager (or whoever is in charge) when a process such as this—which is expected never to fail—actually fails.

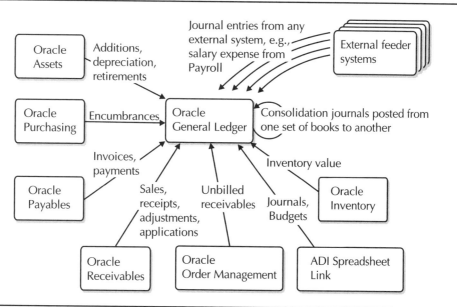

FIGURE 3-3. *Integration of Oracle General Ledger using the Journal Import interface*

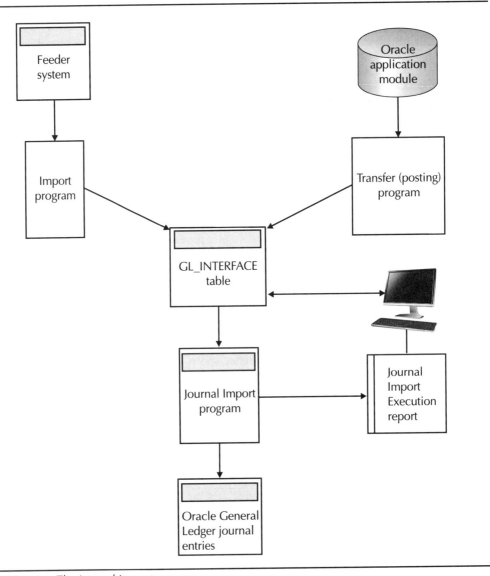

FIGURE 3-4. *The journal-import process*

Journal-Import Validation The Journal Import interface performs validation on all journals. This is intended to ensure that all journals entered into Oracle General Ledger are right and proper. Journal Import validates batches, journal entries, and journal lines. The data attributes of the journals are checked in detail, ensuring that all the accounts are valid and that attributes like the journal category are appropriate. You can import into any period that is open or future enterable. Journals in future-enterable periods can be imported but not posted.

Additionally, a journal needs to balance. Error codes are printed in the Journal Import Execution report next to the GL_INTERFACE data that are in error. A list of all the error codes and their meanings can be found at the end of the Journal Import Execution report. The validation ensures that all accounts, sources, categories, and dates are valid. Oracle uses the journal source to identify the subledger (such as Oracle Payables); the category represents the type of transaction, such as adjustments. The Journal Import program allows you to select what you want to import by source. If there are errors in your import process, you can review the error codes in the Journal Import Execution report.

Importing from External Systems   Importing financial transactions from external systems is very simple. Data records are inserted into the GL_INTERFACE table, then the journal-import process is started. You can use SQL*Loader, an Oracle utility, to insert data read from files directly into a database table, or you can use more complex import programs written using any programming language that supports embedded SQL. Whatever the mechanism for inserting the records, the GL_INTERFACE columns shown in Table 3-2 must be populated.

The interface program that populates the GL_INTERFACE table can also submit a concurrent request to run the journal-import process. Doing this is particularly useful for regular or overnight imports from feeder systems. Programmers can initiate concurrent programs by calling the submission routines from the operating system, PL/SQL, or Oracle Forms. Each time the routine is called, the appropriate parameters (such as the name of the concurrent program) and the parameter values should be passed. Refer to the Oracle Applications Object Library reference manual for more details.

Column	Purpose
SEGMENT1 through SEGMENT30	Identifies the Accounting Flexfield segment values of the journal
CODE_COMBINATION_ID	Is used as an alternative to the SEGMENT values
ACTUAL_FLAG	*A* for actual amounts
REFERENCE1	Used to create a journal batch name of the format REFERENCE1 Request ID Actual Flag Group ID
REFERENCE4	Used to format the journal-entry name
ACCOUNTED_DR	A debit amount
ACCOUNTED_CR	A credit amount
ACCOUNTING_DATE	Determines in which accounting period the journal appears
STATUS	The value *NEW*
LEDGER_ID	Determines in which ledger the journal appears
USER_JE_SOURCE_NAME	Determines which source the journal has
USER_JE_CATEGORY_NAME	Determines which category the journal has
CURRENCY_CODE	Determines which currency the journal has

TABLE 3-2.   *GL_INTERFACE Required Columns*

Transferring from Other Modules   The journals from each module are clearly identifiable according to their batch name and journal name. Each subledger transfer is tagged with a unique identifying number, as shown in Table 3-3.

When you run the Journal Import program or any of the transfer programs from the subledgers, you must specify whether the import should operate in summary mode or detail mode. Summary mode produces one journal-entry line per distinct Accounting Flexfield combination (for example, company, department, and natural account). Conversely, detail mode imports the journal with as many journal-entry lines as there are transaction lines in the GL_INTERFACE table. Summary mode reduces the size of journals, the amount of disk space required, and the time it takes to retrieve the data.

Summary mode is good for performance, but the direct one-to-one correspondence between General Ledger and the subledger is lost. To retain the audit trail back to the subledger, details taken from the imported journal lines can be retained in the GL_IMPORT_REFERENCES table. By default this feature is deactivated, but it can be activated from the Define Sources window. Provided this feature is activated, several drill-down inquiry screens are available to trace transactions back to the subledgers. Activating this feature increases the clarity and visibility of the audit trail and is strongly recommended.

Other Uses for Journal Import   Journal Import is used internally by the standard consolidation process to transfer account balances or detail transactions from one set of books to another. The consolidation process can take account of mapping account codes and period names between the source and destination set of books.

If you have chosen to implement multiple instances of Oracle EBS, use Journal Import to consolidate account balances from the remote databases into one central database that holds a consolidated set of books. Many of the routine tasks involved in multi-instance consolidation have been annexed within the Global Intercompany System (GIS). GIS takes care of intercompany transactions that are distributed across multiple application-database instances. The company that initiates the intercompany transaction enters and submits an intercompany transaction to a receiver company for review. Once the receiver approves the transaction, both entities may post

Batch Name	Journal Name	Transactions Included
user-ref Payables	Payments *CUR*	Payments transferred from Oracle Payables (*CUR* is the currency of the payments and *user-ref* is the reference given to the transfer by the user who started it)
user-ref Payables	Purchase Invoices *CUR*	Purchase invoices transferred from Oracle Payables
AR *control-id* Receivables	Sales Invoices *CUR*	Sales invoices transferred from Oracle Receivables (*control-id* is a sequential number assigned to each transfer by the system)
AR *control-id* Receivables	Trade Receipts *CUR*	Trade receipts transferred from Oracle Receivables

TABLE 3-3.   *Journal Identification*

the intercompany journal. Journal Import can load or convert opening balances from a legacy system when you first go live with Oracle General Ledger.

Journal Import can be used to import budgets or encumbrances. To do this, enter the value *B* or *E* in the ACTUAL_FLAG column and the appropriate budget-version ID in the BUDGET_VERSION_ID column or the appropriate encumbrance-type ID in the ENCUMBRANCE_TYPE_ID column of the GL_INTERFACE table.

The import process is often useful for statistical journals. For example, the manufacturing system might control the units-of-production figures that GL needs for allocations. Common practice would be to write a simple script to generate a statistical journal to post to the ledger. The same would apply to head counts from Human Resources and billable hours from Projects, and of course, statistical journals can be imported from non-Oracle subledger systems as well.

Posting

After importing your journals, you can post them in Oracle General Ledger to update the account balances. When you post to an earlier open period, actual balances roll forward through the latest open period, budget balances roll forward through the end of the latest open budget year, and encumbrance balances roll forward through the end of the latest open encumbrance year. If you post a journal entry into a prior year, General Ledger adjusts your retained-earnings balance for the effect on your revenue and expense accounts. You can automate the posting process by scheduling the Automatic Posting program to periodically select and post batches.

You can also set the criteria for the Automatic Posting program to post transactions based on combinations of journal source (such as Payables), journal category (such as manual year-end adjustments), and effective date at different intervals for different transaction groups. With the Journal Approval System, you can require that journal entries from any source be approved before posting. Oracle General Ledger offers security to control which users can post and reverse journals.

The Closing Schedule

At the end of an accounting period, all companies go through a closing process to close the period and produce final financial reports. These reports are considered final because once the period is closed, the figures for that period can no longer be changed.

Some companies allow for closed periods to be reopened so staff can add any missed journal entries. However, this practice should not be taken lightly. If your company's policies and procedures allow for the reopening of closed periods, you can do so in Oracle General Ledger using the Open and Close Periods form. You should restrict access to this form to a few select individuals, to protect your accounting data. New transactions posted to a reopened period will invalidate subledgers and cause you to re-create financial statements and consolidation reports. Most companies have strict closing procedures that prohibit the possibility of reopening closed periods. Instead, they use current-period journals to make prior-period corrections.

The following list outlines the events required to process transactions and close a period. The tasks do not have to be performed in the exact order described.

1. Set the status of the first accounting period in the new fiscal year to open.
2. (Optional) If your business rules require you to create reversing entries at the beginning of every period, generate and post accruals from the prior period now.
3. Transfer data from all of your subledgers and feeder systems to the GL_INTERFACE table.
4. Run the Journal Import process to populate the GL_JE_BATCHES, GL_JE_HEADERS, and the GL_JE_LINES tables. This can be done automatically from the subledger systems, or manually from Oracle General Ledger.

NOTE
*If you allow suspense posting in your set of books, you can choose a
Journal Import run option that will post any journal-import errors to a
suspense account. If you do not choose this run option, Journal Import
will reject any combination of source and group ID that contains
account errors.*

NOTE
*Posting from the subledger systems transfers data to the General
Ledger interface and journal-entry tables, but does not update GL
balances. You must run the posting process from General Ledger to
update the GL_BALANCES table.*

5. Review the Journal Import Execution Report to check the status of all imported journal entries.

6. Journals imported from external systems can be corrected at the source and reimported or corrected in Oracle General Ledger. The corrections can be made in the GL_INTERFACE table using the Correct Journal Import Data window. If you encounter a large number of errors, delete the journal-import data from the GL_INTERFACE table, correct the information in the feeder or subledger system, and run Journal Import again.

7. Journals imported from another Oracle application are a special case; they rarely error. When they do, you ought to proceed with caution and log a Service Request (SR) with Oracle Support. On no account delete the journal data, except in concert with Oracle Support, who will have considered whether to fix the data in GL_INTERFACE or in the subledger and will arrange for the batch to be retransferred. Transactions will have been flagged as posted in the subledger to prevent double transfers, and these flags have to be reset by script.

8. Close the period for each subledger. This prevents future subledger transactions from being posted to General Ledger in the same period.

9. Review and post the imported journal entries. You can review them online or in reports. The following reports will be useful at this stage: Journal Batch Summary Report, General Journal Report, Journal Entry Report, Journal Line Report, Journal Source Report, Journals Document Number Report (when document sequencing is used), and Unposted Journals Report.

10. Perform reconciliations of subsidiary ledgers by reviewing and correcting balances. The following reports are useful to help you reconcile: Account Analysis with Payables Detail, Account Analysis with Subledger Detail, General Ledger Report, Posted Journals Report, Journals Report with Subledger Detail, and Accrual Reconciliation Report.

11. Generate all recurring journals and step-down allocations.

12. (Optional) If you did not generate and post your prior-period reversals at the beginning of this period, be sure to generate reversals now.

NOTE
*Although it is customary to post reversing entries at the beginning of
a new period, many companies will leave this step as a period-end
procedure.*

13. Revalue balances to update foreign-currency journals to your functional-currency equivalents.

14. Post all journal entries, including: manual, recurring, step-down allocations, and reversals. Be sure to generate and post the step-down allocations in the correct order.

15. Review your posting results. Posting Execution Report and Error Journals Report are helpful.

16. Update any unpostable journal entries and then post them again. Common reasons for unpostable batches include violating control totals, posting to unopened periods, and having unbalanced journal entries.

17. All errors in the journal-entry batches must be corrected and resubmitted for posting.

18. Run General Ledger reports, such as the Trial Balance reports, Account Analysis reports, and Journal reports. It is convenient to group period-end reports in a report set to maintain a consistent audit trail.

19. Translate balances to any defined currency if you need to report in foreign currencies.

20. Consolidate your subsidiary sets of books if you have multiple companies.

21. If you are performing a year-end close and your accounting calendar includes an adjusting period that represents the last day of the fiscal year, close the current period and open the adjusting period.

22. Create and post adjusting entries and accruals in the adjusting period.

23. Run Trial Balance reports and other General Ledger reports in the adjusting period after adjustments are made.

24. Close the last period of the fiscal year using the Open and Close Periods window.

25. Open the first period of the new fiscal year to launch a concurrent process to update account balances. Opening the first period of a new year automatically closes your income statement and posts the difference to your retained-earnings account.

The period-end reports include a balance sheet, income statement, and statement of cash flow. In addition, companies produce a suite of management reports showing actual sales against budgeted sales and any other key indicators that managers need. These reports, whose layout and content are specific to your organization, are not available as standard reports in Oracle General Ledger; they must be defined as FSG reports or BI Discoverer workbooks, or possibly defined in Oracle Business Intelligence Suite, if you are using this tool.

It is important to manage and rationalize the number and volume of reports produced at period end. If managers had their wishes, you probably would have to produce three or four distinct reports per manager. The sheer volume of report output for a large organization would be overwhelming. Some big organizations, including Oracle, are migrating rapidly from a *push* organization, in which FSG reports are distributed to managers, to a *pull* organization, in which managers look in a data warehouse to retrieve the figures they need. The Web Application Desktop Integrator and the Business Intelligence Suite both allow for report output to be broadcast directly to an intranet Web site.

Financial Reports

The trial balance ensures that total debits equal total credits. This is the basis of the double-entry bookkeeping system. It tells you whether or not your accounts balance. A simplified trial balance is shown in Table 3-4. The Grand Totals line at the bottom shows that the debits do indeed equal

Natural Account	Debit	Credit
Cash and Receivables	100,000	
Other Current Assets	140,000	
Plant and Equipment	120,000	
Land	40,000	
Investments	76,000	
Liabilities		60,000
Common Stock		250,000
Other Contributed Capital		47,000
Sales		1,290,000
Investment Income		3,000
Other Revenue		2,000
Salary and Wages	100,000	
Cost of Goods Sold	900,000	
Exchange-Rate Losses	5,000	
Depreciation and Amortization	47,000	
Administration	5,000	
Provision for Bad Debt	119,000	
Grand Totals	**1,652,000**	**1,652,000**

TABLE 3-4. *Simplified Trial Balance*

the credits. The figure itself—$1,652,000 in the example—does not have any useful significance for the company or its managers.

The balance sheet is a snapshot of the financial position of a company. It is one of the key reports included in regulatory reporting. Like most financial reports, it is used for external purposes by investors, customers, and creditors. The balance sheet demonstrates the following accounting principle:

Assets = Capital + Liability.

Whereas the content is similar, the format and layout of the balance sheet vary from company to company. The essence, though, is to show all assets of the company with a total, and to show all capital and liabilities of the company with a total. The simplified trial balance shown in Table 3-4 has been recast as a balance sheet in Table 3-5. The totals on a balance sheet, in contrast to those shown on a trial balance, have major significance to the business and its managers.

The Retained Earnings line, shown in Table 3-5, is usually included as a current-period net income. As described earlier, the retained earnings are calculated at the end of the financial year

	Debit	**Credit**
Assets		
Cash and Receivables	100,000	
Other Current Assets	140,000	
Plant and Equipment	120,000	
Land	40,000	
Investments	76,000	
Total Assets	**476,000**	
Liabilities		60,000
Common Stock		250,000
Other Contributed Capital		47,000
Retained Earnings		119,000
Total Capital and Liabilities		**476,000**

TABLE 3-5.   *Balance Sheet*

by calculating the profit (or loss) for the year. The income statement, or profit-and-loss report, is the worksheet used by accountants to perform the following computation:

Profit = Total Revenue – Total Expense.

A very basic income statement is shown in Table 3-6.

	Debit	**Credit**
Revenue		
Sales		1,290,000
Investment Income		3,000
Other Revenue		2,000
Total Revenue		**1,295,000**
Expenses		
Salary and Wages	100,000	
Cost of Goods Sold	900,000	
Exchange-Rate Losses	5,000	
Depreciation and Amortization	47,000	
Administration	5,000	
Provision for Bad Debt	119,000	
Total Expense	**1,176,000**	
Profit		**119,000**

TABLE 3-6.   *Income Statement*

Accounting Methods

There are two main accounting methods. The *accrual method* records revenues and expenses when they are incurred, not when payment is received. For example, a sale on account would be recorded as revenue even though the customer has not paid the bill. The *cash-basis method* records transactions when payment occurs, regardless of when the transaction takes place. For example, when the company receives the customer's check, revenue is recorded even though the goods were shipped two months earlier.

Generally accepted accounting principles (GAAP) require companies to use the accrual method for financial-reporting purposes; it is considered a more accurate depiction of a company's income and expenses. However, different companies may account for transactions using different accounting methods based on their own countries' laws and regulations. Oracle Financials has been developed to meet GAAP requirements as well as the special needs of different countries, such as the International Financial Reporting Standards (IFRS). For example, in Oracle Payables you can choose whether to record journal entries for invoices and payments on an accrual basis, a cash basis, or a combined basis. With combined-basis recording, journal entries are posted to one set of books and cash-basis journal entries are sent to a second set of books.

Average-Balance Processing

General Ledger can automatically maintain average balances on an account-by-account basis for all balance-sheet accounts. Averages are calculated from actuals and are needed by some financial institutions for regulatory reporting. Average-balance processing can be enabled for each set of books, and the average and standard balances can be stored in the same set. General Ledger stores period average-to-date, quarter average-to-date, year average-to-date, and end-of-day balances for every day. Average balances are updated each time journal entries are posted.

You can translate average balances to any reporting currency and consolidate average balances between accounting entities. Average balances can be reviewed online or in standard reports, and the General Ledger FSG can be used to create custom financial reports that comply with the Federal Reserve's statutory reporting requirements. You can also reference average balances in formula journals, such as recurring journals and Mass Allocations, and archive and purge average balances for any range of accounting periods.

General Ledger Setup

With Oracle General Ledger and the entire E-Business Suite, you do not need custom programming to tailor your applications to reflect your enterprise's operations and policies or to keep pace with your changing business needs. The mantra is "Don't modify the software; simplify and standardize business-process flows instead." Plenty of tailoring and customization can be accomplished through standard setup of the application. For example, you can create an unlimited number of charts of accounts to reflect the way you do business; use General Ledger's Account Hierarchy Editor to reorganize account structures with drag-and-drop ease; take advantage of user-definable flexfields to add new types of information to your database; and make your windows reflect the way you do business, using folder technology under Oracle Forms or Personalizations on Oracle Application Framework—all without programming. In addition, any changes you make are preserved through subsequent software upgrades automatically.

The Oracle Implementation Manual is an essential source of information to help you implement Oracle Financials. It explains all the mandatory and optional steps, including those with dependencies on other setup steps. Also, every company ought to have an accounting-procedures manual that spells out how to create manual journals, accruals, and allocations.

It should also explain the period-closing process and year-end activities. Needless to say, the manual must be intimately tied to the Oracle processes. You should continually modify a draft of the manual throughout the setup process; it is especially important in testing. As part of cutover, the transition phase from legacy accounting to Oracle E-Business Suite, make sure there are test data to check every procedure in the manual.

Open and Close Accounting Periods

Once you have defined the calendar with accounting periods, you are invited to open an accounting period. Be aware that once you have opened the very first period, you can never open a prior period. A common mistake is to open the current period during the setup and then attempt to convert historic balances into prior periods. Unfortunately, by that stage it is too late to open any prior periods.

To avoid this pitfall, get agreement on the earliest period that is ever likely to be used. Open that period, then open all subsequent periods up to and including the current one. Then close all the prior periods to prevent accidental entry into a prior period. When the conversion of history is ready to take place, the pertinent prior periods can be reopened and journals can be imported or keyed in. When the GL period remains future enterable, a department such as manufacturing has no problem transacting against it. If accounting accidentally opens and then closes the period, manufacturing can no longer transact. This is an extremely important point; you should take great care to ensure that accounting be very careful not to open or close a period prematurely.

Setting Up Parents, Rollup Groups, and Summary Accounts

Value sets can be more than one-dimensional validation tools, especially in General Ledger. The user can define hierarchies of values through parent–child relationships. The Financial Statement Generator (FSG) and the Global Intercompany System (GIS) use the concept of rollup groups to simplify reporting. Unlike parent–child relationships, rollups go across all segments of the Accounting Flexfield.

Management reporting is the ultimate objective of General Ledger. It must be succinct—top management needs only the aggregate numbers. Oracle General Ledger uses several different devices to adapt its relational database—essentially flat in structure—to companies' hierarchical reporting needs. Figure 3-5 depicts the relationships graphically.

The sequence needed to define rollup groups is as follows:

1. Define the flexfield segment format.

2. Define value sets for the flexfield values.

3. Define parent–child relationships over the individual segments within the Accounting Flexfield, to as many levels as appropriate.

4. Set up your ledger.

5. Determine what summaries will be required for reporting and online-inquiry purposes. This is essential. The Oracle structures will support almost any reporting requirements that have been defined, but Oracle cannot be structured to anticipate requirements that have not been defined.

6. Ideally, assuming the reporting requirements are known in advance, define rollup groups before defining key segment values. See the discussion of parent–child relationships and rollup groups in the Flexfields Reference Manual.

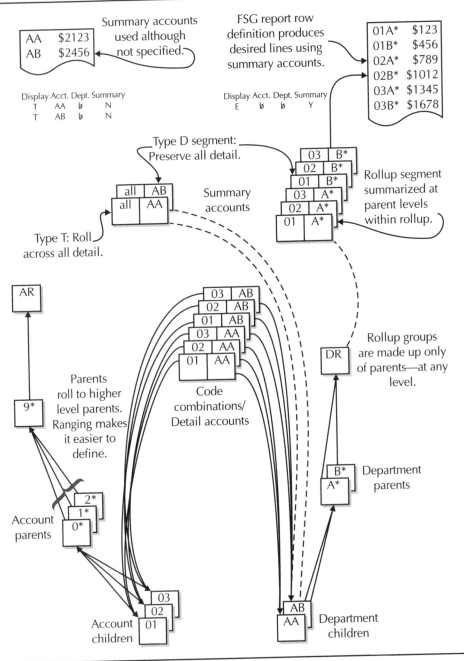

FIGURE 3-5. *Rollup group mechanics*

7. Define summary accounts as required for the rollup groups. They are needed to support online inquiry and for performance purposes.

8. Define FSG reports. All report definitions use Accounting Flexfields, not rollup groups. The Accounting Flexfield may include parent segments, which fit the Accounting Flexfield structure. However, they take advantage of the summary accounts that have been defined through rollup groups and wildcards.

It is a user's responsibility to define parent–child relationships and rollups, because they are wedded to the account- and department-number data, which users own.

Several independent hierarchies can be laid over the department structure. Three are shown in Figure 3-6. Each hierarchy serves a different purpose:

■   Divisions are used for sales analysis. Many departments belong to the default division, 00, which indicates No Division.

■   Locations equate to plant locations. Every staffed department belongs to a location. The location hierarchy is used to consolidate and compare plant operations.

■   Companies represent the formal structure of the corporation. Each department belongs to only one company; thus companies can be used for balance-sheet as well as profit-and-loss reporting.

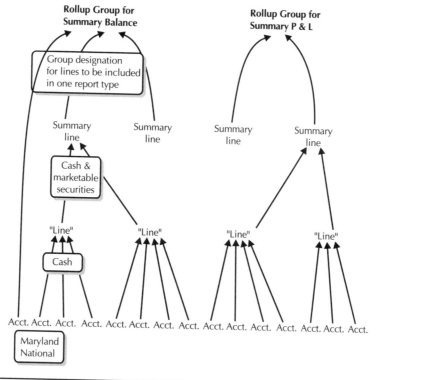

FIGURE 3-6. *Account parent–child rollup*

- Legal entities are one matrix rollup of companies. This rollup is useful for tax purposes.

- Management is a second rollup of companies, representing the management structure at higher levels. Reports produced within this hierarchy are used for management purposes.

Figure 3-7 shows the parent–child and rollup groups defined on the account segment. These first-level parents roll into second-level parents used for more summary reports. First- and second-level parents can be combined in any combination into rollup groups, which can be used in specifying summary accounts. FSG reports can be set up to print only summary accounts within the account range specified for reporting. Doing this reduces the effort involved in specifying certain reports.

Currency

For businesses operating in a global environment, Oracle General Ledger handles currency-conversion rates, supports the euro, and tracks and reports balances in multiple currencies. You can enter daily conversion rates between any two currencies, regardless of your functional currency. At the setup of the primary ledger, you are required to define a ledger currency as the primary record-keeping currency to record the business transactions and accounting data within General Ledger. A reporting currency is an additional currency representation of the primary or secondary ledger. In Figure 3-8, the primary currency is the US dollar (USD) and the reporting currency is the euro (EUR).

This is a great feature for organizations willing to maintain their ledger transactions in multiple currencies, using them for supplementary reporting purposes (such as management reporting or consolidation), or operating in countries with highly inflationary economies. When a journal is entered in General Ledger, on any of the different method of entry, it is converted into the ledger currency and each of the reporting currencies.

Enter Journals (Vision Operations)

Batch Status	Batch Name	Journal Name	Period	Journal Debit	Journal Credit
Posted	ADI: 14-DEC-97 18:01	ADI: 14-DEC-97 18:01	Dec-98	1,161,566.00	1,161,566.00
Posted	AP Invoice Payables	Payments USD	Apr-97	20.00	20.00
Posted	AP Invoice Payables	Purchase Invoices U:	Apr-97	20.00	20.00
Posted	AR 1000 Receivables	Sales Invoices USD	Jan-96	17,637,547.00	17,637,547.00
Posted	AR 1000 Receivables	Sales Invoices FRF	Jan-96	1,516,500.00	1,516,500.00
Posted	AR 1000 Receivables	Sales Invoices CAD	Jan-96	1,522,000.00	1,522,000.00
Posted	AR 1020 Receivables	Sales Invoices GBP	Jan-96	1,985,500.00	1,985,500.00
Posted	AR 1020 Receivables	Sales Invoices USD	Jan-96	6,946,010.00	6,946,010.00
Posted	AR 1020 Receivables	Sales Invoices DEM	Jan-96	2,772,000.00	2,772,000.00
Posted	AR 1020 Receivables	Sales Invoices JPY	Jan-96	21,600,000	21,600,000
Posted	AR 1060 Receivables	Sales Invoices USD	Jan-96	22,140,200.00	22,140,200.00
Posted	AR 1060 Receivables	Sales Invoices CAD	Jan-96	165,000.00	165,000.00

New Journal	Review Journal	Requery
New Batch	Review Batch	More Actions

FIGURE 3-7. *Department segment, parent–child, and rollup groups*

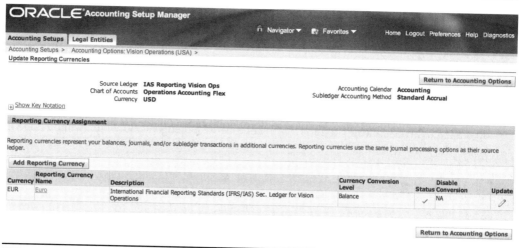

FIGURE 3-8. *Ledger with a primary currency of the US dollar and a reporting currency of the euro*

Accounting Flexfield Design—Best Practice

The accounts tracked by General Ledger are collectively referred to as the *chart of accounts*. The chart of accounts defines how your accounting information is categorized, collected, and reported. The first step in implementing Oracle General Ledger is setting up your chart of accounts. The design and use of your chart of accounts is crucial. It should fit the needs of your organization and allow for meaningful analysis. For example, if your company is small, a simple account structure with only two segments—one for account and one for department—might suffice. However, if yours is a large corporation with multiple products and sales organizations, you need a more robust structure that includes additional segments for company, product, and region. When defining your chart of accounts, consider the following suggestions:

- Define an account structure that is flexible enough to accommodate your current organization and anticipate the way you will run your organization in the future.

- Define an account structure large enough to reflect the important aspects of your organization, but small enough to be manageable and meaningful.

- Define an account structure that accommodates and properly classifies information from your other financial information sources.

- Define an account structure that provides a logical ordering of values by grouping related accounts in the same range of values. Additionally, it should allow for expansion and development of new categories.

What to Consider

To arrive at an optimal design for your organization, there are many aspects to consider. Some of these aspects are discussed in the following sections. The discussion is intended as a road map so that you can assess which areas are of relevance to your situation and focus further research on these topics. The Oracle Applications Flexfield Manual is a good source for detailed instructions. If you have not worked with Oracle EBS before, you are strongly advised to seek help in the initial design and implementation of your Key Flexfield. This task should be taken on by an experienced Oracle Financials functional consultant.

Reporting Needs

The setup of flexfield segments should support your reporting requirements and be part of a corporate-wide plan for financial reporting. Remember this major principle: do not include segments that do not get fed from most subledgers. Also consider the corollary to this principle: determine in advance which reporting will be done in subledgers and which will be done in Oracle General Ledger.

TIP
If you intend to use Oracle Projects, do not put a project segment in the Accounting Flexfield. Project reporting should be driven from Oracle Projects. Similarly, if you will be using Oracle Assets, do not track asset categories within the General Ledger.

Organizational Structure

The chart of accounts belongs to the ledger level in the organizational structure. Each ledger has only one Accounting Flexfield structure, which means when you set about designing an Accounting Flexfield, you will already have in mind the legal entities, operational units, and inventory organizations that the Accounting Flexfield is going to support. So whether you are considering the entire enterprise or a subset of it, the important point is that you know in concrete terms which parts of the enterprise you are analyzing. Unless you know this, you are likely to vacillate between the planned use of the organizational features in Financials and the proposed Accounting Flexfield. You will bounce back and forth without any objective way of choosing between alternatives. It is far better to get agreement on the planned use of the organizational features and the number of servers and databases, and then venture forward from this solid foundation to design the Accounting Flexfield for each ledger.

Security

Often you will want to restrict which accounting transactions users can see and what range of accounts they can post to. The primary level of data security within Oracle Financials is the Responsibility. Once a user chooses a Responsibility, he or she will only see the accounting transactions for the operating unit connected to that Responsibility. This takes care of which accounting transactions a user can see, in a way that does not depend on the design of the Accounting Flexfield. The segment-level security feature is intended to restrict the range of accounts that users can post to. Security rules define ranges of account-code combinations that are excluded, and then the rules are assigned to a Responsibility. All users of that Responsibility are restricted from entering or viewing that range of accounts.

A common use is restricting the salary and wages accounts to the personnel department. Doing so ensures that confidential payroll data are not freely available to all users. Another use is for companies that have one chart of accounts but many sets of books or legal entities. These companies want to ensure that users do not inadvertently make a cross-company posting by using the wrong company code. A security rule can be set up for each Responsibility, restricting the range of company codes that can be entered to the companies that belong in that set of books.

As mentioned earlier, you can require that journal entries from any source be approved before posting with the Journal Approval System, and you can also control which users can post and reverse journals in Oracle General Ledger.

Code-Combination Validation

Not every AFF combination makes sense. For example, it might not make sense to put a department number on an asset account, because assets are owned by companies, not departments. It might not make sense for an overhead department such as plant security to post to a revenue account. You set up cross-validation rules in Oracle to prevent creation of AFF combinations that do not make sense. The rules block out permissible and impermissible ranges of numbers. For asset accounts, the typical range of allowed departments is 000 to 000 (none). It makes a simple rule.

A new feature introduced in Release 12 is replacement for disabled accounts. It is very common in large organizations to disable accounts, but that is not necessarily reflected in the setups of the other modules or legacy systems feeding into the Oracle General Ledger. This new column next to the definition of the account defines the replacement account that will be replaced during the journal-import process. This highly improves efficiencies by preventing the journal-import process from erroring and by enabling the successful creation of the journal entry with minimal user intervention.

Complex cross-validation rules can be an early warning sign that your proposed flexfield design is not optimal. Suppose you have two segments: one for sales region and another for Canadian province department. You would need complex rules to indicate that the combination of British Columbia and Eastern Region is invalid. Moreover, the rules could change. Your Central region could split into the Quebec and Ontario regions. In a good flexfield design, each segment (other than dependent segments) is reasonably independent of the others.

Values That Change over Time

The Accounting Flexfield is the basis for year-to-year comparisons. If you change it, the comparisons become invalid. Plan your natural-account segment so that it changes little over time. Accommodate change in this area through reporting devices and consolidations, not in the ledger itself. However, for all your planning, some reorganization is inevitable. Plan your departments in such a way that the rollups can be used for year-to-year comparisons even as the organizations within them are redefined.

Some segments have a limited life span, such as those for project, program, and funding. There are two ways to take an existing account-code combination out of use. When you disable a segment value, Oracle will no longer create code combinations using that value, although you can still post to combinations that have already been created using it. For instance, when a project ends, you might assume it would be an error to create new code combinations using that project (although it could be proper to post adjustments for a while). You disable posting on a combination-by-combination basis. If you want no activity against a project, set the Disabled flag for every combination using that project value.

Plan how you will take segments and code combinations out of use. There are many places in the system where you specify default segment values to be used by Automatic Account Generation. It creates significant difficulties for your users if you disable one of these default values.

Summarization

Summarization can be accomplished with the Accounting Flexfield using several different mechanisms; assuming your analysis of reporting needs has revealed some need for summarization, you must decide which mechanism to use. Top management needs only the aggregate numbers to make their decisions. Because management reporting needs to be succinct, summarization plays a very important role in Oracle General Ledger. The following five mechanisms are available for summarization:

- dependent segments,
- parent-segment values,
- summary accounts,
- rollup groups, and
- explicit calculations in FSG reports.

Only the first of these, dependent segments, needs to be decided when the Accounting Flexfield is set up. However paradoxical it might seem, you should not restrict your attention to dependent segments; rather, plan how the other techniques are going to be used while you design your Accounting Flexfield. The reason for this is that parent-segment values can often provide a more straightforward way of achieving the same result as dependent segments. To understand this, some explanation of the five mechanisms is needed.

A *dependent segment* is a segment whose meaning depends on a previous segment. A common example of dependent segments comes from airplane seat numbers. Airlines number the seat rows and allocate letters to designate window, center, or aisle seat. That way, seat 14A is unique on the aircraft—row 14, window seat. In Oracle terminology, 14A is two segments; the seat segment depends on the row. A designation of seat alone is not sufficient to mark out a single seat on the aircraft.

Airlines could give a unique number to every seat on the plane, but then passengers would have no easy way of verifying if they have a window, center, or aisle seat until they board the plane. Seat 14B (coach) is a center seat, whereas 1B (first class) is on an aisle. Dependent segments are useful in this respect because they convey more meaning than an arbitrary numbering scheme. Use dependent account segments when you want a context-sensitive segment whose values have different meanings when you combine them with different values of the primary segment. A common use for a dependent segment is account and subaccount. Table 3-7 shows a basic chart of accounts using a subaccount-dependent segment.

Account Code	Description	Subaccount Code	Description
2800	Cash at Bank	29	Standard Chartered Bank
2800	Cash at Bank	30	Royal Bank of Scotland
2800	Cash at Bank	31	ING Bank
2800	Cash at Bank	32	Citibank
3060	Fixed Assets	10	Machinery
3060	Fixed Assets	20	Buildings
3060	Fixed Assets	30	Office Furniture
3060	Fixed Assets	40	Vehicle Fleet

TABLE 3-7. *Basic Chart of Accounts Using a Dependent Segment*

Subaccount 30 is both the Royal Bank of Scotland and Office Furniture; of these two meanings, the relevant one in any particular circumstance is determined by the account code. The total for Cash at Bank is the balance on the account 2800; the total for Fixed Assets is the balance on the account 3060. The summarization is implicit in the scheme.

Dependent segments are the only form of summarization that reaches into the subledgers. Dependent segments are an integral part of the Accounting Flexfield, and if you use a dependent segment you must enter it at any point that you enter an account-code combination. If you need reporting summarization within a segment value from a subledger, having a dependent segment is an elegant way of achieving it.

Often the dependent-segment approach works well for some segment values but not for all. Some accounts fall neatly into the hierarchy of account and subaccount; other accounts do not. It becomes laborious to enter the dependent-segment value when in fact no value is appropriate. Reporting segments such as regions made up of many districts, or projects composed of subprojects, are more likely to be successful candidates for implementation as dependent segments. Unless the hierarchy of segment and subsegment can be applied rigorously to all segment values, you should not use dependent segments. The same effect can almost always be achieved using a single segment and parent accounts.

NOTE

A dependent segment can always be redesigned to avoid using the dependent-segment feature of the Accounting Flexfield. You can increase the length of the primary segment and incorporate the dependent segment into the primary segment.

The account-and-subaccount schema shown in Table 3-7 has been recast as amalgamated account codes in Table 3-8. Structured keys with hidden meanings such as these are frowned upon by relational-design purists. From a practical point of view, users prefer structured codes; and from an application-implementation perspective, there is no overriding reason to avoid building structure into a list of segment values. The codes are easier to learn and they convey a meaning—before too long, accountants and users no longer need to see the description to recognize the account. Common sense tells us that only pairs of segments with a similar meaning

Amalgamated Account Code	Description
280029	Cash at Standard Chartered Bank
280030	Cash at Royal Bank of Scotland
280031	Cash at ING Bank
280032	Cash at Citibank
306010	Fixed Assets—Machinery
306020	Fixed Assets—Buildings
306030	Fixed Assets—Office Furniture
306040	Fixed Assets—Vehicle Fleet

TABLE 3-8. *New Representation of Account Codes*

are amalgamated. Account and subaccount segments are good candidates for amalgamation, whereas cost center and project are not.

The problem with dependent segments is their all-or-nothing hierarchy. You cannot switch it on for some values and switch it off for others. However, this capability is exactly the forte of parent segment values.

Parent segment values and their children form a hierarchy within a segment. Parent segment values are like any other segment value, except they have other values defined as their children. There are two applications that allow you to graphically create and modify account hierarchies and related information stored in General Ledger. The Account Hierarchy Manager is accessed through the General Ledger Navigator.

Table 3-9 shows how parent accounts might be introduced into the account-code segment. Parents can be defined with any child value or range of child values. The child values do not need to be consecutive and they do not need to be ranges. If the segment values have been assigned according to some logic, they will already contain an implicit structure; and the child ranges, as in this case, will fall neatly into consecutive ranges.

The balance on a parent account is equal to the sum of the balances on all its children. Be aware that a child value can belong to several parents, and that a parent itself can have a parent. The hierarchy can be as deep as you like. Oracle General Ledger does not store the balance of a parent account; the balance is calculated each time it is needed. For this reason, the account balances of parent segment values are not available for online inquiry. This shortcoming of parent segment values is overcome by summary accounts.

Summary accounts are account-code combinations. You cannot post to summary accounts; the account balances associated with them are calculated by the system during posting to be the sum of other account-code combinations. Exactly which accounts are summarized is determined by the summary-account template; the template specifies whether to summarize all segment values into one value (which appears as *T* for total) or whether to retain the detail for each segment of the Accounting Flexfield.

A company with the Accounting Flexfield defined as *Company-Account-Department* could set up a summary-account template *Total-Detail-Total*. The system would then maintain one summary

Account Code (with Parents)	Description	Child Range
280000	**Cash at Bank (Parent)**	**280001–280099**
280029	Cash at Standard Chartered Bank	
280030	Cash at Royal Bank of Scotland	
280031	Cash at ING Bank	
280032	Cash at Citibank	
306000	**Fixed Assets (Parent)**	**306001–306099**
306010	Fixed Assets—Machinery	
306020	Fixed Assets—Buildings	
306030	Fixed Assets—Office Furniture	
306040	Fixed Assets—Vehicle Fleet	

TABLE 3-9.   *Parent Accounts Introduced to the Segment Account*

account for each separate value of the Account segment. That way it would be possible to inquire about the balance of the summary account T-2800-T online, which would be the total for Cash at Bank for all companies and departments, or the summary account T-3600-T, which would show the total for Fixed Assets for the entire enterprise.

Summary-account templates can be created or removed at any time, and there is no limit to the number that you can maintain at any one time. In contrast to parent segment values, summary accounts do have stored balances in the system. Whereas parent segment values encode a hierarchy within a segment, summary accounts create a hierarchy of flexfield combinations. Because summary accounts have stored balances, processes such as generating FSG reports and generating consolidation batches can be faster if summary accounts have been used.

A *rollup group* is a collection of parent or child segment values. Rollup groups are a shorthand entry for a particular group of accounts.

Table 3-10 shows a comparison of features provided by the different methods of summarization.

Application Features

The Accounting Flexfield pervades Oracle EBS. Many application features add value to a particular Accounting Flexfield design. Your ability to use these features easily is closely related to your Accounting Flexfield design.

	Dependent Segments	Parent Segment Values	Rollup Groups	Summary Accounts	Explicit Calculations in Reports
Is the feature only visible in GL?	No	Yes	Yes	Yes	No
Is reorganization of the hierarchy possible?	No	Yes, easily	Yes, easily	No	Not without reprogramming
Are summarized numbers stored in GL?	Yes	No	No	Yes	No
Is posting possible at all levels of the hierarchy?	Yes	Yes	No	No	No
Are account balances available by online inquiry?	No	No	No	Yes	No
Are account balances available using FSG?	Yes	Yes	Yes	Yes	Yes
Are account balances available in Allocation formulas?	No	Yes	No	Yes	No

TABLE 3-10. *Comparison of Features of Different Methods of Summarization*

Four qualifiers single out three segments for special treatment by EBS. As mentioned in Chapter 2, two different segments have to be qualified as the balancing segment and natural-account segment. There is also a cost-center qualifier, and a segment can be designated as the intercompany balancing segment. The balancing segment is reserved for the segment that holds your company code, legal entity, or fund. General Ledger ensures that all journal entries balance for each value of the balancing segment that is referenced. Many reports, such as the General Ledger Trial Balance reports, either break on the balancing segment or have the balancing segment as a parameter. The year-end process that calculates retained earnings does so once for each value of the balancing segment.

The natural-account qualifier determines which segment is categorized as asset, liability, owner's equity, revenue, or expense. Here again, many reports make hidden use of the natural-account qualifier—the Trial Balance reports use it to determine which segment to report on, and dozens of reports have an account-segment range in their list of parameters.

The intercompany balancing segment shares the same value set as the balancing segment and is used in the account combination that General Ledger creates to balance intercompany journals. By including an intercompany segment in the Accounting Flexfield, you can track the trading companies involved in an intercompany transaction. Every time an intercompany transaction is generated, the intercompany segment is automatically populated with the balancing segment of the trading partner.

It is not only the segment qualifiers that have a distinctive effect on application features; there are many mechanisms for generating default values for Accounting Flexfield segments. The effectiveness of these mechanisms often hinges on the design of the flexfield. AutoAccounting is used in Oracle Receivables to automatically assign Accounting Flexfield codes for transaction accounts, such as receivables, freight, or revenue. The Account Generator tool can be used in an increasing number of circumstances to intelligently generate Accounting Flexfield values. Anyone planning to use these features should be aware of the implications while designing their Accounting Flexfield.

Segment-Value Maintenance

To simplify maintenance of the chart of accounts, changes to segment-value attributes are automatically replicated to the accounts that contain that segment value. For example, if you disable a particular cost center in your chart of accounts, you can choose that all accounts that contain that cost center be automatically disabled. You can also prevent selected accounts from being affected by segment-value attribute changes.

Legacy-System Analysis

You should consider which data were collected by the old system. Were they adequate or were there gaps that prevented certain sales analysis? What gaps were there? Gaps in the old system should be filled by reporting segments in the new system.

An Externally Imposed Chart of Accounts

Some countries, such as France, impose a chart of accounts—or at least an account-numbering scheme—for reporting purposes. Whereas a French company might want to use the nationally imposed chart of accounts throughout its organization, a multinational company with its own chart of accounts frequently needs to meet the reporting requirements of the host nations where it conducts business. Most reporting requirements can be satisfied by Oracle General Ledger through creating a national chart of accounts that can be deployed in a National or Alternate segment of your corporate chart of accounts and mapped to the corporate accounts. Oracle Applications provides French charts that can be deployed in this way; you can set up a ledger using your corporate chart of accounts and make it your primary entry book, with a national chart of accounts in a secondary ledger. Or you can do it in the opposite way, setting up a ledger to accommodate the national chart of accounts and making it your primary entry book, with a corporate chart of accounts in a secondary ledger. Oracle Subledger Accounting will populate both ledgers appropriately and simultaneously. See Chapter 4 for more details.

You can create a corporate book using your corporate chart and use Oracle Financial Consolidation Hub to link and map national bookkeeping to it. Or you can consider creating a consolidated book using the national chart, and use Oracle Financial Consolidation Hub to link and map your corporate bookkeeping to it.

After period end, the balances are transferred to the secondary, statutory ledger using Oracle General Ledger's Global Consolidation System (GCS). The statutory reports are then produced from the secondary ledger, based on the statutory chart of accounts. You can use GCS to consolidate between any chart-of-accounts structures. However, if some reports can be satisfied only from the subledgers, those subledgers must have a sense of the French accounting structure. Because it gets its AFF structure from the ledger, you must support it with a French-structure General Ledger chart of accounts. You would post to the French ledger, produce tax reports from the French books, and then consolidate to another set for management reporting.

After completing your consolidations, you can review consolidated balances online and drill down to the subsidiary balances that you consolidated. The Consolidation Hierarchy Viewer displays multilevel consolidation structures in an expandable hierarchical format, enabling you to immediately visualize and analyze the entire consolidation structure, no matter how many intermediate parents it contains.

Good Design Principles

It is easier to build flexibility into your account structure during setup than to try to change your account structure in the future. After considering the preceding topics, you are in a good position to start designing your Accounting Flexfield. The design will be complete when you have finalized the number of segments, their order and length, the valid values for each, and the separator symbol that will appear between them.

Number of Segments

Commercial businesses all face similar accounting and management challenges, so it is reasonable to expect that the same sort of business dimensions will apply to different companies. You might find that the classifications are different from company to company, but the underlying dimensions are the same. Nonbusiness organizations operate in similar if not identical circumstances. They need to track the same sorts of things, but often name them differently. Table 3-11 lists common business dimensions for both business and nonbusiness organizations. Each of these dimensions will become a separate segment in the Accounting Flexfield.

Order of Segments

The order you assign the segments of the Account Flexfield will determine their order of appearance on reports and screens. Segments that are frequently defaulted should appear toward the end of the flexfield. This will increase data entry speed.

Some claims have been made that the order of the segments has an effect on performance. This might be true, but only in a badly tuned application database. In a well-tuned application,

Dimension	Business	Nonbusiness
Legal entity	Company	Fund
Natural account	Account	Account
Responsibility	Cost center or department	Program
Sales analysis	Product-distribution channel	
Geography	Region or district	
Intercompany	Intercompany	
Project	Project	Funding vehicle
Fiscal reporting	Tax code	Appropriation year

TABLE 3-11. *Common Business Dimensions for Both Business and Nonbusiness Organizations*

the order of the segments should make no difference to the application's performance. Application tuning is a large topic that falls outside the scope of this handbook. Note, however, that the following tuning parameters should be set within the application before a DBA tunes the database by creating new indexes and such:

■ In Oracle General Ledger, you should run the Optimizer after you create a large number of segment values or add or delete summary templates. The Optimizer stores statistics, creates indexes, and improves the performance of long-running programs such as FSG, Posting, and MassAllocations.

■ You can tune Journal Import control parameters in the Define Concurrent Program Controls window.

Length of Each Segment
Consider the structure of values you plan to maintain within the segment. For example, you might use a three-character segment to capture project information and classify your projects so that all administrative projects are in the 100–199 range, all facilities projects are in the 200–299 range, and so on. If you develop more than 10 classifications of projects, you will run out of values within this segment. You might want to add an extra character to the size of each segment to anticipate future needs.

If you anticipate frequent restructurings, which require you to disable values and enable new ones, you should allow for enough digits to avoid having to recycle values. For example, if you disable old cost centers and enable new ones frequently, you will use up cost-center values quickly; therefore, you should use a larger maximum size for your cost-center value set, so that you can have more available values. For example, three digits would allow you to create 1,000 different cost centers (numbered 000–999).

Defining Valid Segment Values
Is a value required for a segment? Even if a particular dimension cannot be assigned a value, it is usual to implement the segment with the validation Value Required = Yes, and to create a segment value of zeros, 00000, meaning None or Not Specified. It is unwise to allow a Not Specified value for either the segment you specify as the natural account or the company (balancing) segment.

Such values allow users to post to a ghost account in a ghost company, which sooner, if not later, would have to be explained.

For each segment, you must define a value set, which restricts the valid values that can be entered. The value set can be either numeric or alphanumeric. You should set up alphanumeric value sets, because (as mentioned before) summary accounts use the value *T* to represent Total. However, the segment values you actually use should be numeric, if at all possible, for the detail accounts that are used day to day. Numeric segment values can be keyed far faster than alphanumeric values. It is also much easier to specify ranges with numbers than with letters, and ranges are extremely useful in rollup groups, parent–child relationships, and FSG reports. Parent accounts, on the other hand, can be set as alphabetical characters. Indeed, setting details as numeric and parents as alphabetical is a handy way to distinguish each type.

To reduce maintenance and maintain consistency between ledgers, you can reuse value sets when defining multiple charts of accounts. Using the same value sets allows two different ledgers to reference the same segment values and descriptions for a specified segment. For example, the values in your natural account segment, such as 1000 for Cash and 2100 for Accounts Payable, might be equally applicable to each of your sets of books. Ideally, when you set up a new ledger you should consider how you will map your new Accounting Flexfield segments for consolidation. When a common natural-account segment is used between ledgers, it is easier to map account balances from your subsidiary ledgers to a consolidating entity.

Cross-Validation Rules

Not every Accounting Flexfield combination makes sense. For example, if your organization manufactures both computer equipment and trucks, you might want to prevent the creation of hybrid part numbers for objects such as truck keyboards or CPU headlights. To prevent users from entering invalid combinations of segments, Oracle General Ledger allows you to set up cross-validation rules. Cross-validation rules define whether a given value of a particular segment can be combined with specific values of other segments.

The Separator

The choice of a suitable symbol to separate the segment values is not trivial. For quick data entry, choose numeric segment values followed by a period ([.]; "full stop" in British English). That way the entire Accounting Flexfield can be entered from the numeric keypad on the keyboard. For example, the numeric account-code combination

01.320.420.4110.000.0000

is significantly faster to enter than the alphanumeric combination

USA/NYC/420/4110/NON/NONE.

Maintenance

Your account structure and Accounting Flexfield must be maintained as your business grows and changes. Oracle General Ledger reduces the effort of maintenance through the Mass Maintenance Workbench, which allows you to move balances from one account to another or merge balances from multiple accounts into a single account and maintain financial integrity between Oracle General Ledger and its subledgers. You can also automatically create new account combinations based on existing combinations. In addition, Oracle General Ledger allows you to create new mass allocations and mass budgets by copying existing definitions and then making incremental modifications.

"For Future Use" Segments

Spare segments that might one day be activated are considered good design by some and unnecessary by others. If you incorporate a spare segment for fear of having missed something critical in your business analysis, it is a bad idea; go complete the analysis more thoroughly. You might expect that spare segments would become useful if the company develops a new line of business or acquires a rival. In the authors' experience, that is rarely the case. Businesses do change, but when change comes it is rapid and far-reaching. Seldom would an extra segment be sufficient to administer new with old. If you must create a spare segment, define it as character and hide it from ordinary users.

What to Avoid

Good design is like elegance and beauty—it is hard to define, but everyone recognizes it when they see it. It is easier to be specific about what contributes to a bad design. The following pitfalls should be avoided.

Accounting Flexfields That Are Too Long

The maximum length of the Accounting Flexfield is 240 characters, in up to 30 segments. A practical limit is much smaller, as a long Accounting Flexfield becomes unwieldy and tiresome to enter. Some reports in Oracle General Ledger report only the first 30 characters of the Accounting Flexfield. If the length of your flexfield (all the segments plus the separator between the segments) is longer than 30 characters, these reports will be less useful to your organization; therefore, it makes sense to define your Accounting Flexfield to be fewer than 30 characters.

Two Segments Used for the Same Thing

Group similar business dimensions into one segment. For example, you need only one segment to record and report on both districts and regions. Because regions are simply groups of districts, you can easily create regions within a district segment by defining a parent for each region, with the relevant districts as children. Use these parents when defining summary accounts to maintain account balances and when reporting hierarchies to perform regional reporting. This method accommodates reorganizations. If you want to move Dallas into the East US region, redefine your parents so that Dallas rolls up into the East US region. This method also avoids excessive cross-validation rules.

Poorly Defined Segment Usage

Ensure that the use and meaning of a segment are well understood. Ensure that people are referring to the same thing when they say "Southern region" or "headquarters cost center." This concern might seem trivial, but confusion can lead to a rapid decline in the usefulness of stored data. Consider geographic location. What exactly is being recorded? Is it the location of the salesperson who made the sale or the location of the customer? The two might not be the same.

For example, a salesperson for Gas Turbine Limited (GTL) based in the United Kingdom makes a sale to a customer in the Middle East. The UK regional sales manager will want to see total sales for all salespeople, irrespective of customer location. There has been a recent Middle East marketing campaign, so marketing manager will want to see the effectiveness of the campaign by monitoring sales by customer location. The marketing manager will not see the expected increase in Middle East sales if that sale is accounted for as UK revenue.

Suppose the company that bought the gas turbine calls the local representative office of GTL in the Middle East for engineering support. The cost of providing the support is allocated to the Middle

East region. The revenue is accounted for against the United Kingdom and the maintenance costs charged to the Middle East. It would be very difficult to determine whether conducting business in the Middle East is a profitable venture for GTL. Insight into the business is lost from the lack of clarity in the segment definition.

In the GTL example, staff had not realized that they were dealing with two geographic splits—salesperson location and customer location. Look for early warnings that a segment definition is unclear or ambiguous. Does the choice of segment value seem arbitrary, or are there two equally good options and no objective way to choose between them?

Two segments that genuinely represent the same dimension should be combined into one segment; however, two distinct business dimensions should never be combined, even if they appear superficially to be the same. The design and use of the Accounting Flexfield is crucial. Failure to optimize the structure of the Accounting Flexfield is a primary reason that implementations do not deliver the benefits that were originally envisioned.

General Ledger Reporting

Oracle General Ledger increases your decision-making capabilities by ensuring that the right business information reaches the right people at the right time. Oracle provides sophisticated operational- and financial-reporting tools that include proven high-volume reporting capabilities, interchangeable report components, desktop extensibility for customizing standard reports, powerful server-based processing, and the latest BI Publisher (formerly known as XML Publisher).

The introduction of Oracle BI Publisher enriched even more the complete set of reporting within Oracle General Ledger. It is a template-based publishing solution delivered with the Oracle E-Business Suite. It provides a new approach to report design and publishing by integrating familiar desktop word-processing tools with existing E-Business Suite data reporting. The flexibility of BI Publisher is a result of the separation of the presentation of the report from its data structure. The collection of the data is still handled by the E-Business Suite, but now you can design and control how the report outputs will be presented in separate template files. At run time, Oracle BI Publisher merges your designed template files with the report data to create a variety of outputs to meet a variety of business needs, including spreadsheet, PDF, HTML, and flat files.

A rich range of reporting techniques can be brought into action in concert with Oracle General Ledger. In addition to a suite of standard reports and BI Publisher, Oracle General Ledger has its own integrated report generator: the Financial Statement Generator. There are many standard reports and BI Publisher, including Trial Balance reports, General Ledger reports, Journal reports, Budget reports, and Consolidation reports. There are no predefined balance-sheet or income-statement reports, but these can be created easily with FSG within General Ledger. If your organization demands "what if" reporting or forecasts, the native reporting features of Oracle General Ledger will probably not be powerful enough. You can consider using the Business Intelligence Suite, which provides through the Fusion Analytics product a good number of prebuilt dashboards, key performance indicators, and analytic reports.

Financial Statement Generator

The example balance sheet in Figure 3-9 is typical of the style of report that FSG can produce. This is an end-user report generator. Businesspeople should be able to define and run their own finance reports without intervention from the Information Systems' (IS) department. At the same time, FSG security prevents users from viewing data for accounts to which they have no access.

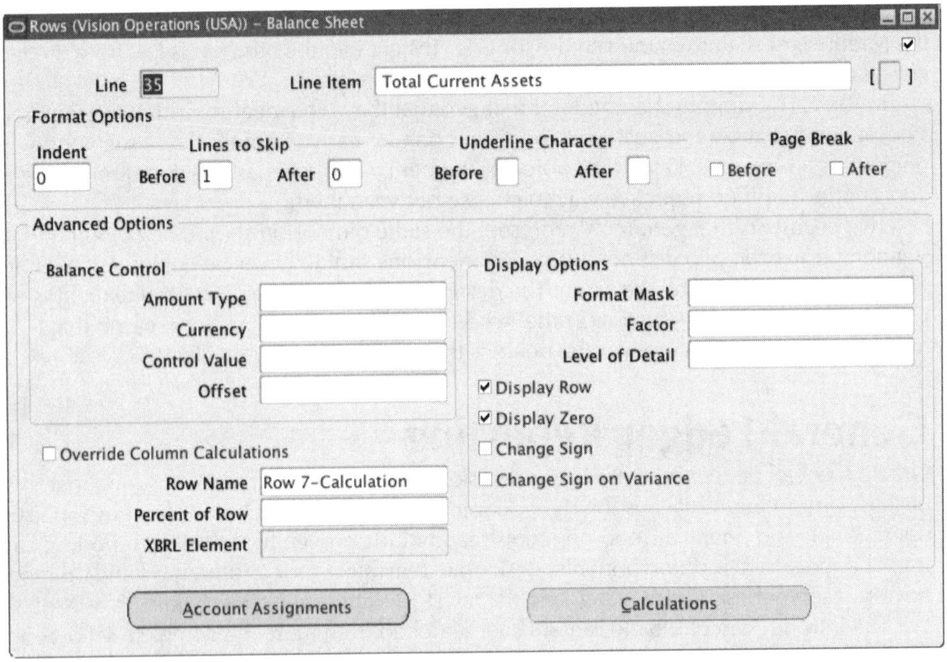

FIGURE 3-9. *Example of a Financial Statement Generator report*

The FSG is built on two premises: it reports only on data in General Ledger, and it provides granularity only down to the account balance per Accounting Flexfield combination. Within the bounds of these two premises, you can define almost any report data and layout you want. That said, report generation with FSG is not as simple as using PC desktop tools, and the final result is improved by the combination of FSG and BI Publisher by generating presentation-quality financial reports so that you can have more control with report-formatting options, including changing font characteristics, inserting graphical images or logos, and adding color.

Why Use FSG?

Oracle realized that it would be impossible to design one version of the financial reports that would meet the needs of all its customers. Some accountants include in the cost of a fixed asset not only its net invoice price but also its acquisition and installation expenses; others do not. These fine distinctions could not be covered by one or two standard balance sheets. Instead, Oracle has provided the FSG, a complex and powerful report generator that can produce tabular reports on any account balance. You will not find a balance sheet or income statement in the list of standard reports within Oracle General Ledger, but such reports can be produced with FSG.

FSG report output is not always the most attractive, and sometimes it is important for reports to look good. The alternatives to using the FSG are to set the output to BI Publisher by selecting a spreadsheet as export type; to program custom reports in Oracle*Reports to use as a data source and a BI Publisher template; or to use Web ADI to apply format themes to your reports and publish them to a Web site or spreadsheet. Oracle*Reports programs have to be written from a zero start point, and all the business logic, accounts to summarize, and accounts to show in detail are often stored in the program rather than as data. That means that modification can be a programmer task and not an end-user task. On the other hand, Web ADI integrates directly with FSG so that report output can be published directly to spreadsheet format. Also, any calculated result can be analyzed to reveal the account-balance entries from which it was derived.

FSG Components

The components of an FSG report are similar to spreadsheet rows, columns, and formulas. Report generation proceeds in a two-step process: define the report components, then run the report. The next time you need the same report layout, you do not need to define the report components again; you can simply run the stored report definition for a new accounting period. The capability to recycle and reuse report components is a great advantage that FSG has over custom programming. A report includes the following independent components:

- row set,
- column set,
- content set,
- row order, and
- display set.

The simplest reports are defined by a row set and a standard column set. Optionally, you can define your own custom column set. Also, you can add a content set, row order, or display set to enhance the report or refine the information in it.

Reporting with the FSG is a mix-and-modify, recycle-and-reuse activity. A new report can be defined simply by mixing an existing row set with an existing column set. If what you need is similar to what you had previously, but you now want comparison-to-the-budget figures as well as actuals, simply copy the column set and modify it to include a column for budget and a column for variance. The new report layout reuses the old row set without any extra effort from you.

The FSG Concept

The Financial Statement Generator is a tool for reporting on account balances by period. It cannot report on individual journal entries in General Ledger. Accounting data can be visualized as an array of cells. The array is like a large stack of dice, each one holding an account balance according to its position in the structure. The three dimensions that make up the array are the Accounting Flexfield, accounting periods, and type of balance.

In FSG terminology, the Accounting Flexfield dimension becomes a row set, whereas the type of balance is encoded into the column set. The reporting period is supplied by the user at run time.

Reports generated with the FSG can cut, slice, sort, and summarize the dice in all ways imaginable. However, the FSG cannot show more detail than allowed by the three dimensions of Accounting Flexfield, accounting period, and type of balance. None of the dice can be broken down into smaller units, such as individual journal transactions within a period. Account balances are balances, and no transaction detail is available. Periods cannot be split into weeks or days, and the chart of accounts cannot be split by attributes that are not contained as segments.

Defining Reports

Many users commit the error of approaching FSG the same way they approach custom report development with a regular programming tool. After an extensive effort to analyze all user requirements across the company, a finite number of reports are designed with a fixed layout and purpose. Intended to meet as many user requirements as possible, the reports are created as FSG reports and made available for the users.

Inevitably, such reports will not satisfy all the users, because compromises had to be made during the design, and as the business develops and grows, the reports either are never used or fall slowly into disuse. A better approach, for which the FSG is ideally suited, is to provide adequate training to end users and delegate the responsibility for defining reports to the people who actually work with the report output. To prevent users from going off on their own and duplicating each other's work, some central coordination can be provided for allocations and standard row sets.

A report is defined by specifying the report objects FSG should use to build the report. Once you define and save a report, you can use it anytime—to run the report, define a report set, or copy and save it as a new report.

Running FSG Reports

To run an individual report, follow these steps:

1. Navigate to the Run Financial Reports form, shown in Figure 3-10.
2. Choose Individual Reports, Single Report Set, or Multiple Report Set from the pull-down list.
3. Enter the name of a predefined FSG report.
4. Specify the report parameters, such as Period, Currency, Segment Override, and Rounding Option.
5. Click the Submit button.

The report is submitted as a job on the Concurrent Manager request list. If you press the Define Ad Hoc Report button, as shown in Figure 3-11, you can specify a row set and column set to be used to generate a report without first having to link these two as a predefined FSG report.

TIP
Define ad hoc financial reports as necessary to meet one-time reporting needs.

More on FSG Techniques

Building a basic FSG report is straightforward. The tools used can be extended to produce delimited output that can be transferred directly to a spreadsheet. If you build new FSG reports regularly, you will want to reuse report components such as row sets, and to avoid needless duplication of calculation, you will want to build the business logic into parent values and not FSG formulas. These advanced techniques are explained next.

Producing Spreadsheet-Compliant Output
You can download FSG report output into a spreadsheet on your personal computer. When you define or run the report, choose Spreadsheet as the output option. FSG produces the report in a tab-delimited format, so that report columns

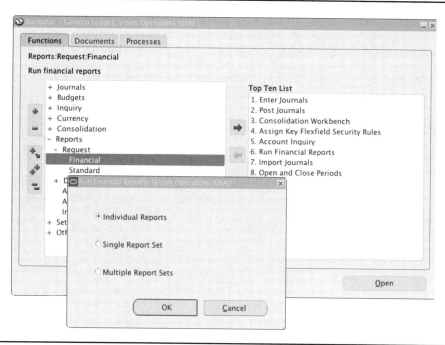

FIGURE 3-10.   *Run Financial Reports form*

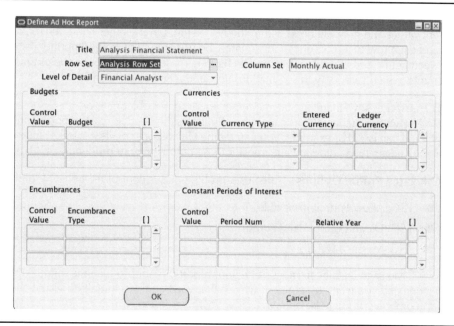

FIGURE 3-11.   *Define Ad Hoc Financial Report form*

get interpreted as spreadsheet columns when you load the report file into a spreadsheet. Once imported into a spreadsheet, the numbers can be made visually distinctive using the text-formatting tricks and graphics that are available in a spreadsheet but not in the FSG. The Web ADI request center has further simplified the process of publishing report output to the Web or a spreadsheet.

Reusing Row Sets   Row sets contain knowledge and logic about your company in a way that other components such as column sets and content sets do not. This attribute derives from the fact that the row set specifies which accounts appear and in which sequence, as well as which detail accounts are summarized into headings. If you have many row sets, each containing the same logic, you increase the maintenance workload that kicks in when your business logic changes. This creates an unwanted opportunity for your reports logic to miss segment values in calculated aggregate results, even though the underlying numbers are correct.

For this reason, it makes sense to reuse each row set in as many report definitions as is feasible. Define a row set for each distinct report family: balance sheet, income statement, cash flow, contribution analysis, source and application of funds, and so on. However, avoid the temptation to have several balance-sheet row sets that are all similar but not identical. You can still generate several different balance-sheet reports by combining the single row set with different column sets, or specifying that parent values should be expanded at run time, or overlaying a content set to produce a balance sheet for each cost center.

This might seem to contradict earlier advice to delegate the report-definition task to the end users, inviting them to do whatever they like. However, normally a single financial accountant will be in charge of the balance-sheet row set; a treasury manager will be responsible for the cash-flow report row set; and a cost accountant will be taking care of contribution reporting. They all are masters of their own sphere of interest.

Where to Store Business Logic   Maintainability is key. If business logic changes, it needs to be changed in only one place. The logic available in parent values is available for all reports without having to be repeated in each row-set definition. Therefore, business logic should be built into parent values and not contained within the FSG setup. On the other hand, the math capability behind each row of a row set can legitimately be used for calculating report totals, variances between actual and budget, or percentage figures. These formulas cannot be put into parent accounts, which cater only to summation, not subtraction or division.

FSG Transfer   Any Financial Statement Generator report object, report, or report set can be copied between databases. This capability eliminates the need to rekey report definitions in multiple databases. For example, you can define FSG reports in a test system while implementing General Ledger, then automatically transfer those reports to your production system.

FSG-Related Profile Options   Three user-profile options control the behavior of the FSG:

- FSG: Allow Portrait print style,
- FSG: Expand Parent Values, and
- FSG: Message Detail.

FSG: Message Detail can be useful if your report did not produce the output you were expecting and you want to figure out why so that you can fix it. Initially, a visual check of the report components might be enough to identify the problem, which could be an incorrectly specified range of accounts or a wrong calculation. If you have examined the report components and still cannot find the problem, you can access the FSG: Message Detail profile option. This profile option controls the degree of detail that appears in the message-log file while your report runs. The default value for this profile is Minimal, which prints only the error messages in the log file. If you change the profile option to Full, you get detail memory figures, detail timings, and SQL statements, which are useful for report debugging.

Report Listings on FSG Components   A range of report listings on FSG components helps you debug and fine-tune report definitions. For example, the Where Used report shows where specific segment values are used in row sets, column sets, and content sets. If you are considering changing the use of an account code or redefining a parent value in the account segment, you can use this report to quickly tell you which predefined FSG reports will be impacted, then use this information as the basis for modifying these reports, if necessary.

Web Applications Desktop Integrator (Web ADI)

The Web ADI gives users an alternative spreadsheet-based front end to perform full-cycle accounting. Most functions can be performed in a disconnected mode. You can create budgets and use a flexfield pop-up window to enter and validate new budget accounts. Segment-value security is enforced for accounts included in your budget worksheet. You can record journal transactions and define and publish reports to a Web site, a spreadsheet, or a standard text document. Web ADI includes theme formats you can apply to your reports as well as custom formatting you can apply to individual cells in both spreadsheet and Web report output. After reports are completed, you can perform data pivoting and account drill-down to analyze your financial results in a multidimensional user interface.

Some of the key features of Web ADI are

- ■ It works via the Internet, so no installation is required on client machines. It requires only a Web browser and a spreadsheet program.

- ■ It validates data against Oracle EBS rules before they are uploaded.

- ■ It enables customizations to determine which fields will appear in the spreadsheet and to save those definitions for the future.

- ■ It automatically imports data into the Web ADI spreadsheets, modified, validated, and uploaded into Oracle EBS. This is very useful when migrating data from legacy systems to Oracle E-Business Suite.

Oracle General Ledger Data Model

This section contains a brief description of the transaction tables in the Oracle General Ledger module. If you need to write custom extract scripts or GL reports, you should have an understanding of the GL database layout and how the accounting data are stored.

Table 3-12 lists some transaction tables in Oracle General Ledger and their contents. Journals are stored in the three tables GL_JE_BATCHES, GL_JE_HEADERS, and GL_JE_LINES. A journal batch is a group of related journals that are posted together. The period in which the journals belong is stored at the batch level. Each journal in a batch gives rise to a separate record in the GL_JE_HEADERS table.

Table Name	Contents
GL_JE_BATCHES	Journal batches
GL_JE_HEADERS	Journals
GL_JE_LINES	Journal lines
GL_BALANCES	Balances for every code combination, currency, and period

TABLE 3-12. *Some Transaction Tables in Oracle General Ledger*

TIP
*Whereas records in GL_JE_BATCHES are called journal batches on
the Oracle General Ledger forms, and records in GL_JE_LINES are
referred to as journal lines, the records stored in GL_JE_HEADERS are
simply referred to as journals on the application forms.*

A *journal* is a group of journal lines that balance. The sum of the debits is equal to the sum of the credits. The currency code is stored at journal level. The GL_JE_LINES table holds a record for each journal line. The lines record the accounted amounts—either debit or credit—and the account-code combination that the amount will be posted to.

In Figure 3-12 you can see the intricate relationship between a ledger and the GL_BALANCES table. A record in the GL_BALANCES table is the balance for a specific account-code combination for a specific period and currency; therefore, balances belong to a ledger.

FSG reporting and much of your own custom reporting is driven by balance rather than transaction data. Here again, the table structure is simple. Table 3-13 lists the major tables you need.

The first four tables help you select what you need out of GL_BALANCES, the repository where the actual balance numbers are held.

The Posting Process

The posting process takes a journal batch and updates the account balances in GL_BALANCES according to all the individual debits and credits that are contained in the GL_JE_LINES table belonging to that journal batch. Once the journal batch has been posted, the attribute GL_BATCHES. POSTED is set to Yes, so that the batch cannot be posted a second time. Each of the balances stored

Table Name	Contents
GL_LEDGERS	Ledger
GL_PERIODS	Calendar period
GL_CODE_COMBINATIONS	Account Flexfield segment values
FND_CURRENCIES	Currency
GL_BALANCES	Balances for every combination of account code, currency, and period

TABLE 3-13. *Major Tables in General Ledger Needed for Custom Reporting*

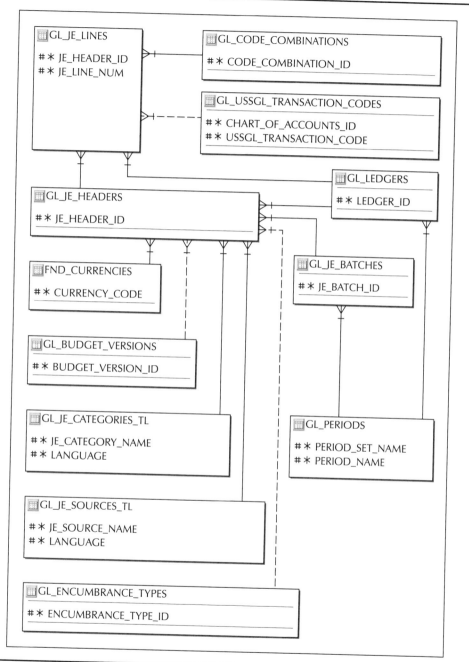

FIGURE 3-12. *Entity-relationship diagram of General Ledger module*

in GL_BALANCES has been calculated from summing the relevant records in GL_JE_LINES. The GL_BALANCES table is used to improve performance.

Many processes, such as standard reporting and all FSG reporting, require the use of account balances that are contained in the GL_BALANCES table. Without a balances table, the system would have to recalculate the balance each time it was needed by summing the journal lines. Calculating the balance once and then storing the value makes much better use of CPU processing power.

Conversion from Legacy Systems

The strength of Oracle's General Ledger and the Oracle E-Business Suite lies in their superior technology and software architecture. Oracle products are built according to open industry standards that provide flexibility, high performance, and extensibility. You can easily migrate from your legacy system to Oracle EBS, or you can integrate Oracle EBS with your existing third-party products through numerous open interfaces.

Unless you are using Oracle General Ledger from day one of operations, you will have some form of conversion to perform—for example, transferring account balances or transaction history from a legacy system. Your conversion plan needs to recognize the requirement to retain an audit trail of prior years' data. Therefore, before you perform your conversion, make sure you have that audit trail of prior years' data, such as hard-copy journal reports and archived copies of the legacy-system files. It might be useful to put them into spreadsheet or desktop database systems to help accountants access them more easily.

Although the budgets of prior years can be converted as easily as balances, it is uncommon to bring them forward through automated conversion scripts. Most users are content to import what they need into Oracle from the spreadsheets in which the budgets are developed.

Converting Historical Data

There are three basic options for how much balance history to convert: none, back to the start of the financial year, and back through prior years; be guided by your reporting needs. However, bear in mind that once you have a program in place to convert any historical period, you can pretty much convert as many periods as you want.

A conversion program uses legacy data to generate one journal per accounting period. Complexities arise if there are multiple sources of legacy systems (both a legacy financial system and a legacy cost-accounting system, for example). Conversion will need to merge both systems. The base datum in all cases is an account trial balance from the legacy systems. You might need to map accounts between legacy and new systems. If you are really lucky, the accounts will map one to one or many to one—in either case, it is simply a matter of sorting and summing to produce the new account balances. If the mapping is one to many (as is the case if the new chart of accounts carries more detail and finer graduations than the old), you must inject some logic into the conversion to split the balances. It is not always possible to split them precisely in half; most end users will be pragmatic about this. The following techniques are for mimicking a one-to-many mapping:

- Post legacy balances to parent accounts when parent accounts in Oracle are a closer one-to-one match to the legacy accounts.

- Inject the splitting rules into the conversion by allowing users to explicitly enter a splitting factor in transit between the legacy and new system.

- Code the logic into the conversion programs using whatever extra data or algorithms are necessary.

The maximum extent of transaction conversion is usually this: the user will want to translate and repost current-year journals in Oracle. It is useful to have a whole year's journals available under a single system.

Balances Versus Transaction Detail

Most users convert little or no transaction history. It is really useful only when the Oracle system will post in detail, when there are subledgers to exploit drill-down, and when transactions can be converted for the subledgers as well. This combination will almost never happen. Exceptions exist, of course; for example, clearing accounts will need their detail transaction history in order to be useful after conversion. For the vast majority of situations, though, transferring balances is sufficient and users do not need the transaction history.

Opening Balances and Movements

Whether you are transferring balances or transaction history, the same method is used: You import journals through the Journal Import interface. To that extent, even if you are loading balances, nothing is loaded directly into the GL_BALANCES table (there is no interface for that); the balance amounts are cast into the form of a journal and loaded and posted in the normal way. The balances journal is constructed to have a line for each distinct Accounting Flexfield that you intend to load. The amount for a line within the journal is the current-period balance less the prior-period balance (called the *movement*), so the year-to-date numbers are always right.

The exception is the first period you choose to convert. Into this period you must post an open balance as well as a movement. Open balance plus movement is equal to closing balance, so you can also choose to post only a closing balance into the first period and a movement in all subsequent periods. Either way, the ledgers will balance because the legacy ledger was balanced.

TIP

Clean up the data in the legacy system as much as possible before a conversion. At least make sure that the legacy ledger balances and reconciles internally. Turn off suspense accounting temporarily and continue attempting to import your conversion journals until you are confident that all segment values are defined and the cross-validation rules permit creation of the needed combinations.

Bridging—An Extension of Conversion

Until now, we have considered conversion a one-off process at the point of cutover from legacy to Oracle systems. A phased cutover, in which Oracle General Ledger goes live first and subledger modules are cut over some time later, introduces the need to have *bridging programs*—conversion programs that run on an ongoing basis translating account postings from legacy subledger systems into Oracle General Ledger. Whether you consider these programs as bridging conversion programs or full-blown interfaces depends on how long you plan to use them. The function they perform is identical; however, an interface should be elegant and robust, as it will probably need to be maintained at some stage in its life. A conversion program is a one-off, throwaway piece of code—it needs to work and no more. It makes no sense to build it to the same quality standards as an interface.

Either way, bridging programs and interfaces need a more permanent lookup table to hold the account mappings. Implementing the mapping in a table makes it easy to maintain the mapping, make corrections, or add new mappings if new codes are created in the legacy system.

Other Methods for Loading Legacy Data

Another method to transfer balances and transactions from legacy systems involves using Oracle General Ledger's Global Consolidation System. Even though GCS was created to perform consolidations, you can use this feature to load transactions or balances contained in a legacy set of books to a new set of books in Oracle General Ledger. GCS provides exceptional flexibility in allowing you to transfer data across any chart-of-accounts structure, any source, any calendar, any currency, and any level of detail. Because GCS offers an open interface, including a spreadsheet interface, it can be accessed by non-Oracle systems through programs that load data from legacy systems. GCS does this by providing sophisticated features for mapping data between accounting entities. For example, you can automatically map source accounts from the legacy system to destination accounts in the new system.

You can also use the Mass Maintenance Workbench to automatically create new account combinations based on existing combinations.

Coordination with Subledger Conversion

General Ledger conversion has to be carefully coordinated with other subledger conversions. Open items imported into Payables and Receivables are treated by Oracle Financials as fresh transactions; these will post to General Ledger. Left unchecked, the fresh transactions could give rise to journals that duplicate legacy journals or account balances imported directly into Oracle General Ledger. There are three common strategies for avoiding duplication:

- After performing the subledger conversion, transfer subledger balances to General Ledger and then reverse the resulting journal batch in General Ledger. You must take care to ensure that this batch contains only conversion items.

- Segregate the chart of accounts into GL accounts and subledger accounts; ensure that the GL conversion references only GL accounts and the subledger conversions reference only their accounts. A complete and watertight segregation is not as easy as it might sound.

- Fudge the open-item conversion in the subledgers so that, when posted to General Ledger, they create a net movement of zero. This can be achieved by coding Payables invoices with the same account-code combination for the liability account as for the expense-distribution account. Likewise, for Accounts Receivable invoices the Receivables account-code combination is used for both the receivables account and the revenue account.

Be especially careful that the same account mapping is used for General Ledger and subledger translations. In particular, receivable-account balances converted to General Ledger will, in the fullness of time, be reduced to zero by postings from Oracle Receivables. A mismatch between the translation mappings could cause problems for many months to come.

Loading and Copying Segment Values

There may be thousands of natural accounts and thousands of organization codes for General Ledger. The accounting staff almost always pulls them together in a spreadsheet. As most organizations use the Oracle installation as an occasion to change their chart-of-accounts structure, the spreadsheet also might include a column for the old account value. It usually includes parent–child relationships as well, showing the reporting hierarchy or hierarchies.

Transcribing all this data from the spreadsheet to Oracle even one time is a major job—but once is never enough. While the data-processing staff is working to bring up the Financials environment, the accounting staff is invariably engaged in the never-ending task of perfecting their account structure. The same can be said for other flexfields: item numbers, fixed assets, locations, and jobs. For the sake of accuracy, all these values need to be loaded fresh at conversion time. That, in turn, means they need to be loaded for each dry run of the conversion process.

Generations of users facing this requirement developed scripts to insert values directly into Oracle Applications. Because of the flexibility they offer, such scripts might still be valuable in an R12 environment.

A Novel Way to Create New Account-Code Combinations
The GL interface will create code combinations dynamically if they are needed. To enable this feature, check the Allow Dynamic Insertion box in the Key Flexfield Segments window. That done, you can prepare a journal import that has all the new code combinations that you need to create and zero amounts everywhere. Once this has been loaded, the code combinations will have been created. The dummy journal can be deleted later. The same principle can be applied with the Web ADI.

Conclusion
Oracle General Ledger is the heart of your accounting systems and allows your business to respond proactively to changes in today's business climate. Oracle EBS provides quick and easy implementation; painless migration from existing financial systems; accurate and timely processing of all your transactions; improved decision support through better reporting and analysis; and quick, automated closing procedures. It can greatly increase the operational efficiency of your business—an advantage crucial to success in today's fast-moving corporate arena.

CHAPTER
4

Oracle Subledger Accounting

he subledger, or subsidiary ledger, is a subset of the general ledger used in accounting. The subledger shows detail for the accounting records such as customer invoices, adjustments, and payments. The subledger detail includes such items as the actual date something was sold, whom it was sold to, and when the invoice was due. The total of the subledger would match a line item amount in the general ledger.

For many years, the General Ledger module of Oracle E-Business Suite covered most of the accounting complexity, particularly that that involved some manual processes, customizations, or third-party systems to fulfill the needs of today's corporate requirements. Organizations nowadays are highly controlled and the Enterprise Resource Planning (ERP) software needs to provide the highest standards of transparency and controls.

Oracle E-Business Suite Release 12 introduced a new centralized function, called Subledger Accounting (SLA), that works together with Oracle General Ledger (GL). SLA is a service, not an application or module; it addresses the needs of different accounting behaviors and controls, proposing an unmatched visibility to the accounting information in a single source of truth.

Legal requirements in multiple countries requires companies to document and enforce an accounting policy, which creates a challenging task for information-technology (IT) and accounting departments to keep it up to date and make sure their users follow it. It requires creating some procedures, extensions, and possibly some customizations. Oracle Subledger Accounting provides a centralized repository where every accounting policy can be documented as a user-defined accounting rule. The biggest advantage to this is that enforcement of the rules is automatically accomplished when SLA creates the accounting entries for every subledger transaction using these rules.

If your company is running Oracle E-Business Suite 11i, the upgrade to Release 12 will install SLA, but it is complementary to the account-generation tools you have configured. Every application within E-Business Suite has its own account-generation tool, which remains the same—with some new features, as explained in later chapters of this book—but does not modify the current Workflow Account Generator or AutoAccounting for account generation.

A common mistake is to look for new standard responsibilities for Subledger Accounting; but there are no responsibilities, nor a log-in for SLA. Every new form and program is embedded within the standard menus of each module that has SLA as a new way to generate accounting.

There are at least three functionalities that are worth exploring in SLA, which will be described in detail in further sections of this chapter.

- Accounting rules can be configured based on virtually any attribute of a transaction. The setup of the accounting rules is a common headache whose workarounds are manual entry, reclassification, or even customization.

- The limitless possibilities for adding any piece of transaction information, including journal and journal line descriptions, improves understanding of the originating transaction without your having to navigate to the subledger transaction for details.

- SLA rules are defined and stored within the system and can be queried and reviewed at any time by interested parties. These rules are even date effective, so changes to them over time can be recorded as historical backup. This is a huge step forward for providing proof of accounting to internal or external auditors.

The Subledger Accounting Concept

The new Oracle Subledger Accounting is an open and flexible accounting service included as part of Oracle E-Business Suite. It defines and generates accounting for transactions captured by the transaction-processing systems in the Oracle E-Business Suite. SLA includes a posting engine that sums the contents of the subledger tables and posts them to General Ledger to provide a clear audit trail.

There are many organizations that are using non-Oracle systems; Oracle Financial Services Accounting Hub can take advantage of SLA to support transactions being processed in those systems. It is a separately licensed product designed to account for non-Oracle input, and the advantage is that these non-Oracle systems can feed the Financial Services Accounting Hub with their transactions and let the application apply the rules defined by SLA, so any changes on the accounting can be transparent for the systems feeding the general accounting.

Subledger Accounting (shown in Figure 4-1) is a central transactional data repository with its own data model, reports, and inquiry window. This chapter will provide details of how each component of SLA is integrated.

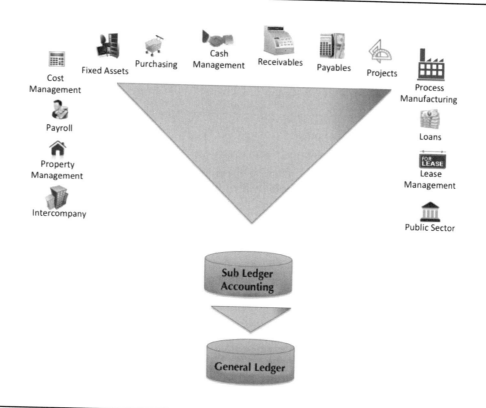

FIGURE 4-1. *Application subledgers using the SLA engine when accounting entries are created*

Set of Books	Ledger
Chart of accounts	Chart of accounts
Currency	Currency
Calendar	Calendar
	Accounting convention (or accounting method)

TABLE 4-1. *Introduction to the Ledger Setup of the Accounting Convention*

The new concept of ledgers in Release 12 that replaced the set of books, as explained in Chapter 3, introduces the concept of the accounting method (or accounting convention) to what was called the four Cs in Oracle E-Business Suite versions prior to Release 12. It is now known as the four Cs.

Table 4-1 compares the previous definition of a set of books and the new definition of a ledger, including the introduction of the accounting convention.

This introduction of the accounting convention is a key concept to understanding the implications of Subledger Accounting, due to the multiple accounting representations of a single transaction that can be performed within General Ledger. An example that might look trivial, but can show the capabilities of this new feature is the ability to have a primary ledger using a standard accrual accounting convention while a secondary ledger is configured with a cash accounting convention. In this case, when the accounts-payable (AP) clerk creates an invoice of $100 in Oracle Accounts Payable, the accounting will be created as shown in Table 4-2.

Since the accounting convention is cash, then there will not be any accounting impact on the secondary ledger.

For some end users, such as the AP clerk, the new functionality of Subledger Accounting will not have a major impact on their work—they will use perhaps a few screens for querying the accounting online. Some new procedures and reporting, though, will need to be added to the closing process as part of the implementation of Subledger Accounting.

Figure 4-2 shows the different elements used in the Subledger Accounting architecture that will be described in this chapter.

The first definition for the primary ledger is the accounting method. The accounting method is made up of multiple application accounting definitions (AADs). These AADs are unique to each subledger.

Natural Account	Debit	Credit
Expense	$100	
AP Control		$100

TABLE 4-2. *Accounting on a Primary Ledger with the Standard Accrual Accounting Method*

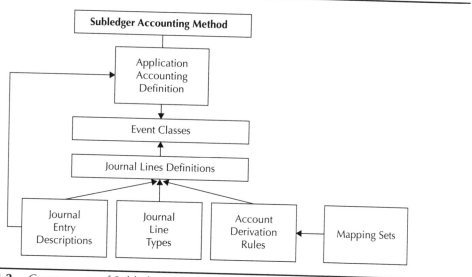

FIGURE 4-2. *Components of Subledger Accounting*

Oracle E-Business Suite comes with prebuilt events. There are three levels to an events: the event entity, allowing Subledger Accounting to handle the business events; the event class, which is the category for a particular transaction type or document; and the event type, which is the business operation and the most granular level with an accounting impact.

Each event comprises different components that can be defined using rules or through the setup screens provided by SLA for each application. For example, Oracle Payables provides classes like AP invoices and payments and a subsequent level for each type or business operation that can be performed for an event class.

Chapter 5 provides a detailed explanation of how accounting is performed for Oracle Payables, but we will cover how the feature of online accounting, introduced in Release 12, has its impact on Subledger Accounting.

In Oracle Payables, as shown in Figure 4-3, users can enter invoices and post the accounting immediately in General Ledger. After the validation of the invoice, the action button gives the possibility to create accounting using the options of Draft, Final, or Final Post.

The Draft accounting option allows the user to correct the accounting by changing the transaction and then create the draft accounting again.

The Final option acts the same as Draft, but only accounting in Subledger Accounting, with no possibility to rerun the accounting. This is a very important change in Release 12. Once a user performs this option, the next step is a new concurrent program in Payables called Transfer Journal Entries to General Ledger. This process picks up all SLA entries that have not yet been transferred to GL.

The Final Post option creates accounting, transfers the journals to General Ledger, and posts the journal batch.

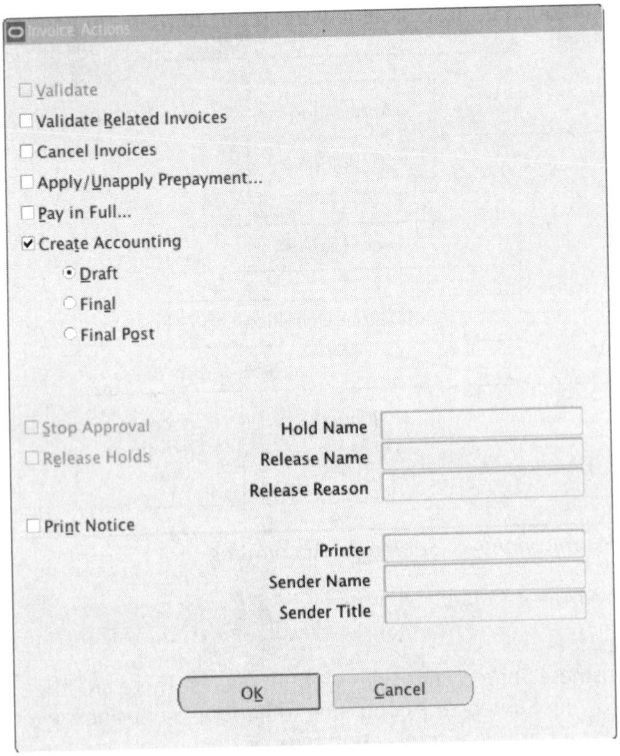

FIGURE 4-3. *Oracle Payables's action button for online accounting*

Components of Subledger Accounting

This section will cover the different components that are part of Subledger Accounting setup.

A review of the Accounting Setup Manager will be presented and then an introduction of the Accounting Method Builder (AMB). AMB is the functionality that enables users to define customized accounting rules.

Accounting Setup Manager Considerations for Subledger Accounting

The Accounting Setup Manager is a new screen using the Oracle Application Framework (OAF) technology enhancing the user experience of performing financial setups. Using this screen, located under the General Ledger Responsibility, users can define the accounting context for one or more legal entities, or a business need if legal entities are not involved.

Figure 4-4 shows the introduction of the accounting method as part of the ledger setup within the Accounting Setup Manager. As explained previously, starting with Release 12 the definition is based on the four Cs: chart of accounts, currency, calendar, and accounting convention.

Oracle provides the following seeded accounting methods: Standard Accrual, Standard Cash, Accrual with Encumbrance Accounting, Cash with Encumbrance Accounting, China Standard

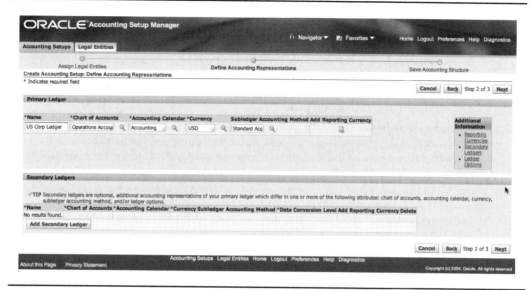

FIGURE 4-4. *Oracle General Ledger Accounting Setup Manager with the introduction of accounting method*

Accrual, and United States Federal Accounting. These methods can be changed by creating new methods using the latest functionality of Accounting Method Builder (AMB), introduced in Release 12.

An example of how you can leverage the accounting-method functionality is shown in Table 4-3. Consider a United States–based global company with three legal entities: one in the United States, one in the United Kingdom, and one in France. Table 4-3 describes the ledger attributes required for each legal entity.

Ledger Attributes	US Operations	UK Operations	France Operations
Chart of accounts	Corporate	Corporate	French statutory
Accounting calendar/ period type	Monthly/month	Monthly/month	Fiscal/Fiscal
Currency	USD	GBP	EUR
Subledger accounting method	Standard accrual	Standard accrual	French GAAP
Ledger options	Average Balances and Journal Approval enabled	Neither Average Balances nor Journal Approval enabled	Neither Average Balances nor Journal Approval enabled

TABLE 4-3. *Ledger Attributes Required for Legal Entities in Global Operations*

An important capability within the Subledger Application setup in the Accounting Setup Manager determines whether subledger journal entries are summarized when they are transferred to General Ledger. The options are

■ **Summarize by GL Period** This is the default option; it indicates that all subledger entry lines with the same GL period, GL journal category, account, entered currency, side, and balance type are summarized into a single GL entry; the GL effective date defaults to the last date of the accounting period.

■ **Summarize by GL Date** This indicates that all subledger entry lines with the same GL date, GL journal category, account, entered currency, side, and balance type are summarized into a GL entry; the GL effective date is equal to the subledger GL date.

■ **No Summarization** This indicates that the subledger journal entries in SLA and GL will have the same level of detail. The GL effective date is equal to the subledger GL date.

The impact of the different summarization options is shown in Table 4-4, which illustrates the different alternatives to meet business requirements.

Accounting Method Builder

The AMB is a key component of the Subledger Accounting service and determines the Accounting Flexfield for the primary and secondary ledgers. It defines the accounting entries the system will create based on the definition provided through the different setup screens within the AMB and will allow the organization to meet specific fiscal, regulatory, and analytical requirements. These definitions are grouped into subledger accounting methods and later assigned to a ledger. In the previous section, we mentioned some of the accounting methods that are seeded in E-Business Suite in Release 12. Some of the definitions or changes to the seeded methods that a user can perform using AMB are

■ determining some characteristics of the journal entry based on the accounting options;

■ adding descriptions that will appear at the journal header or lines providing additional information about the journal entry for reporting or reconciliation purposes;

Option	Journal Line Type Summary	Journal Line Type Detail
Summarize by GL Period	One journal entry per period; journal entry lines summarized	One journal entry per period; journal entry lines not summarized
Summarize by GL Date	One journal entry per day, based upon the GL date; journal entry lines summarized	One journal entry per day, based upon the GL date; journal entry lines not summarized
No Summarization	No Summarization Level of detail in General Ledger is the same as the level of detail in Sub ledger Accounting.	The level of detail in General Ledger is the same as the level of detail in Subledger Accounting

TABLE 4-4. *Impact of Summarization Options in Accounting Setup Manager*

- a powerful engine for account derivation rules to construct the accounts for a subledger journal-entry line; and

- tailoring conditions to determine a journal-entry creation.

Accounting Method Builder Components

The components of the AMB are based on the event model and its three levels. The highest level is the event entity, which there is usually one of per subledger application. The second level is the event class, classifying the transaction type for the accounting rule. Finally, the third level is the event type, defining the possible actions with accounting meaning.

Table 4-5 shows some example event classes and types used by the AMB for Oracle Payables, Receivables, Fixed Assets, and Purchasing.

The last layer of the Accounting Method Builder components, shown in Figure 4-2, is composed of three elements: Journal Line Types, Journal-Entry Descriptions, and Account Derivation Rules.

- Journal Line Types control journal entry line options such as balance type, side, and summarization.

- Journal-Entry Descriptions control the description for the journal entry headers and lines and provide additional information about the journal entry.

- Account Derivation Rules control the derivation of Accounting Flexfield combinations for the journal-entry lines to construct the accounts.

Application	Event Class	Event Type
Payables	Invoice	Validated
		Adjusted
		Cancelled
Receivables	Receipt	Created
		Applied
		Unapplied
		Updated
		Reversed
Fixed Assets	Depreciation	Depreciation
		Rollback
Purchasing	Purchase Order	Created
		Distributed
		Cancelled
		Rejected
		Finally completed

TABLE 4-5. *A Few Examples of the Event Model of the Accounting Method Builder*

The journal-entry setup components are associated with journal-line definitions that are attached to application accounting definitions. You can group detailed subledger accounting definitions for different kinds of transactions into consistent sets, each of which addresses different needs. While one application accounting definition can generate subledger journal entries to meet a particular set of requirements, another definition can be defined to satisfy completely different requirements. To use application accounting definitions, they must be included in a subledger accounting method and then assigned to a ledger. Users can group accounting definitions from multiple products, such as Oracle Payables, Oracle Receivables, and Oracle Assets into a single accounting method. A subledger accounting method can be assigned to multiple ledgers.

The Subledger Accounting service needs the definition of the following steps to create subledger journal entries.

TIP
Before creating or modifying any components or definitions, check whether the seeded application accounting definitions meet your requirements. In the event that more detail is required than is provided by the default definitions, modify them or create new ones.

1. **Define Journal-Line Type.** Journal line types are defined for a particular event class. They must then be assigned to a journal-line definition along with supporting references, account derivation rules, and journal-entry descriptions. These are data seeded by Oracle; users can modify these definitions or create new ones.

   This setup defines whether the component is a debit or a credit, what the accounting class is, where the amount should come from, which conditions needs to be accomplished for a line creation, and even more granular information, such as amount, currency, and conversion rate.

   An example is shown in Figure 4-5, where the definition of the journal line type for the exchange rate of Payables Invoices has a condition composed by an Invoice Distribution Type equal to Exchange Rate Variance and using the conditional Accrue on Receipt option set to Yes.

2. **Define Journal-Entry Descriptions.** When a transaction is transferred as a journal, every journal has a credit or debit description. The journal entry also has a description at the header and line level. The Journal-Entry Descriptions window lets users define the elements of a description that appear on the subledger journal header and line. The definition determines both the content and sequence of the elements of the description. It provides great flexibility for using any of the available sources for the application; it is possible to use literal strings or a combination of both sources and literals. Some of the sources can only be used for descriptions applied at the line level. For example, an individual segment of an Accounting Flexfield can be included in the description, but a source associated with invoice line number can only be applied to a line description. Figure 4-6 shows the journal-entry description for a Payables invoice; when the Invoice Voucher Number is not null, then apply some extra information to the journal-entry description.

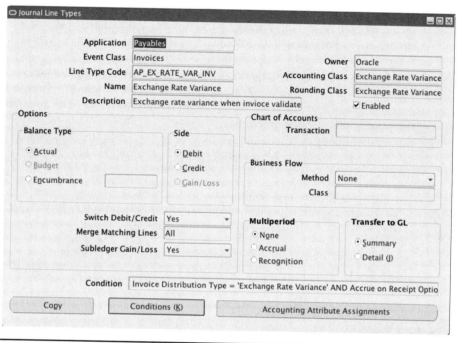

FIGURE 4-5. *Journal line type definition for Payables Invoices*

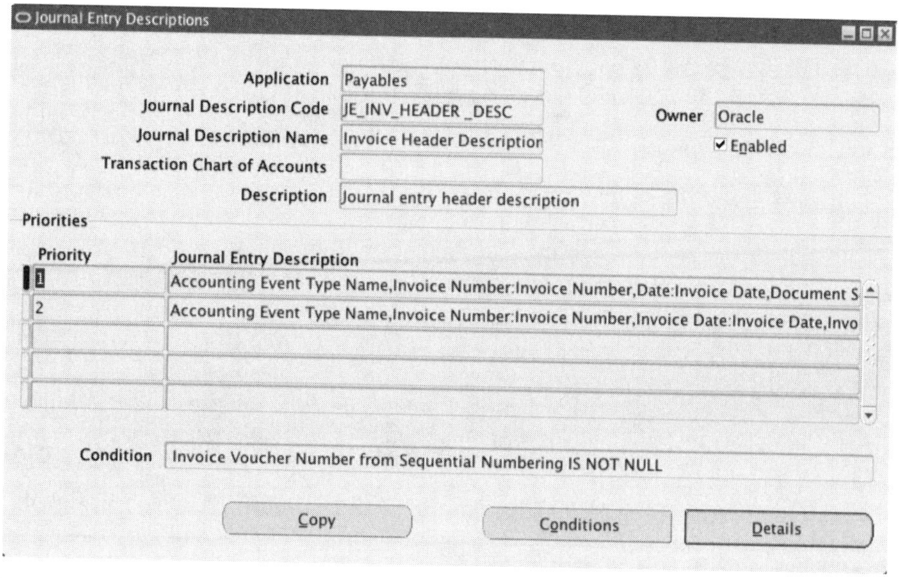

FIGURE 4-6. *Journal-entry description using a logical condition*

3. **Define Mapping Sets.** The optional feature of mapping sets provides multiple capabilities to associate a specific output value for an Accounting Flexfield or Accounting Flexfield segment based on the input value. It can be assigned to a single segment or to the entire Accounting Flexfield. Leveraging mapping sets in account derivation rules to build the Accounting Flexfield is an excellent complement.

   The definition of a mapping set is done through specified pairs of values, as shown in Figure 4-7. For each input value, a user specifies a corresponding account segment or Accounting Flexfield output value. Value sets or lookup types can be used for validating the input values of the mapping set.

4. **Define Account Derivation Rules.** Account derivation rules determine the Accounting Flexfields for subledger journal entries. You can also define conditions that determine when a particular rule is used.

   This functionality lets users define a rule by Accounting Flexfield, segment, or value set. If the rule is by Accounting Flexfield, it determines the entire Accounting Flexfield combination. As an example, you can set an account derivation rule for Accounting Flexfield to determine the complete supplier liability Accounting Flexfield in Payables; or a definition for a particular segment, like company, can be determined from the Distribution Accounting Flexfield.

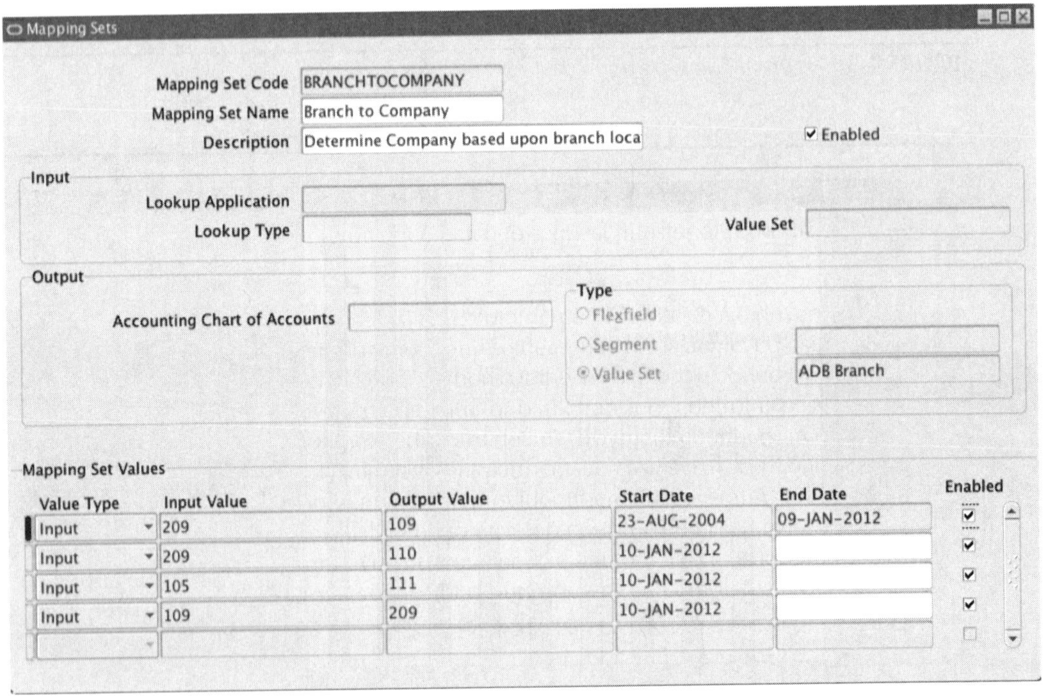

FIGURE 4-7. *Definition of mapping set*

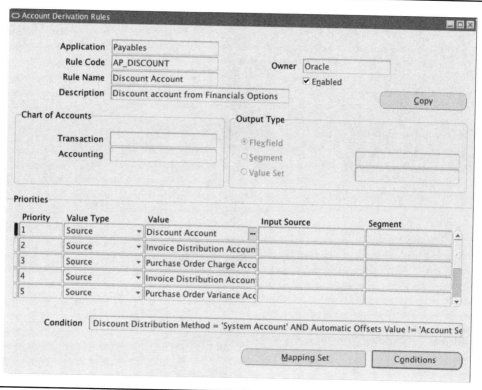

FIGURE 4-8. *Account derivation rule definition*

From a setup perspective, you have to plan in advance and document well, because this wide flexibility requires more setup and increases the maintenance.

Figures 4-8 shows the Account Derivation Rule for the Payables Module. The rule is defined for the payables' discount accounts, which has a condition shown in Figure 4-9 that checks the system different sources in order to produce an output account.

5. **Define Supporting References.** All the additional information fields that were required for reporting purposes in Release 11i were transferred to the General Ledger interface table in the Descriptive Flexfields. An important new functionality was built for Release 12 in OAF, allowing users to create customized sources as supporting references and transfer the values of these sources from the different application subledgers. These supporting references are linked at the event-class level and stored in a new table under the XLA schema. See section "Technical Overview of SLA" in this chapter for more details.

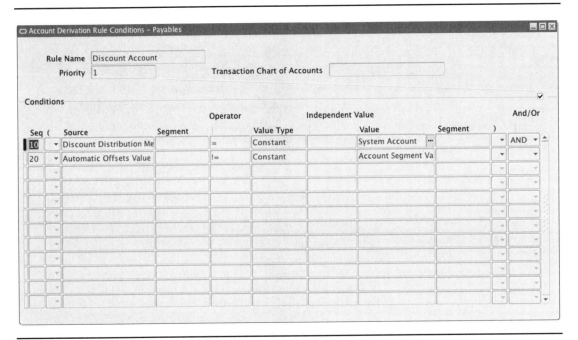

FIGURE 4-9. *Account derivation rule conditions*

Supporting references may be used as follows:

■ providing additional business information about a subledger journal entry at the header or line level;

■ establishing a subledger balance for a particular source value or combination of source values for a particular account; and

■ assisting with reconciliation of account balances.

Even though the use of supporting references is optional, we recommend exploring this, since it can provide valuable information for reporting and analysis to the accounting team. Some supporting references are seeded in Release 12, and you can navigate and copy the seeded version to create your own or start from scratch. An example of some supporting references for the Inventory application are shown in Figure 4-10.

6. **Define Journal-Line Definitions.** The setup of journal-line definitions is required. Oracle provides seeded values, which are used as part of the upgrade process if you migrate from 11i to Release 12.

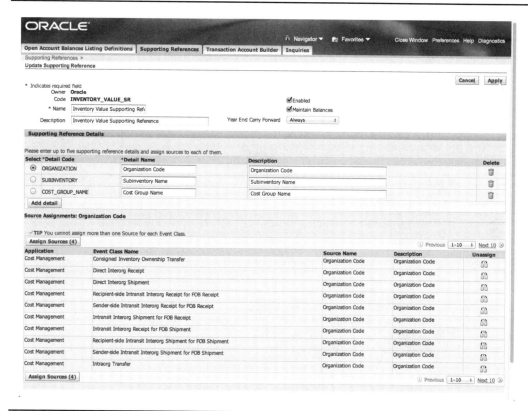

FIGURE 4-10. *New supporting references*

The journal-line definitions are used to group and assign journal-line types, account derivation rules, and journal-entry descriptions into a complete set of journal entries within an event class or event type. These groups or sets can be shared across application accounting definitions.

Figure 4-11 shows the Oracle Journal-Line Definitions screen with all the different sections that are required for the setup. At the bottom right side of the form is a copy function, which is used to copy and create your own definitions. It is important to mention that it is not possible to copy the journal-line definitions across charts of accounts, as the line assignments are dependent on the transaction and accounting chart of accounts.

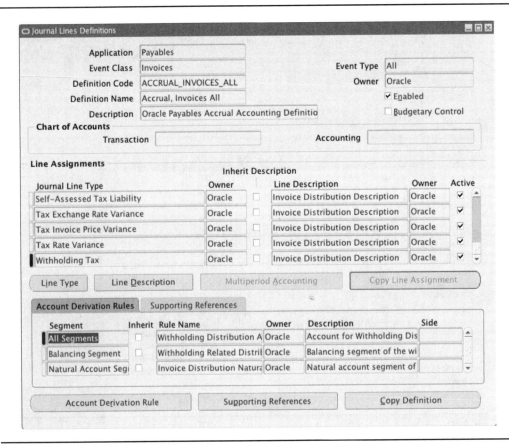

FIGURE 4-11. *Oracle Journal Line Definitions screen*

7. **Define Application Accounting Definitions.** The application accounting definitions (AADs) are used to group journal-line definitions and header assignments for event classes and event types. The AAD form (shown in Figure 4-12) allows adding one or more supporting references and specifying whether to create accounting for a particular event class or event type. You can use virtually all data captured by the Oracle E-Business Suite as points of reference when drafting a rule. Subledger Accounting rules are date effective, which allows better audit controls and identification for troubleshooting.

Oracle Release 12 provides seeded data for all Oracle subledgers; if there are specific requirements that are not met by the seeded accounting definitions, a user can modify them or create new ones. The owners of the AADs can be Oracle-seeded data, or User meaning a tailored AAD.

Accounting events represent transactions that have a financial accounting impact and require accounting information to support the transaction. Examples of accounting events include issuing an invoice and disposing of an asset. These accounting events are not

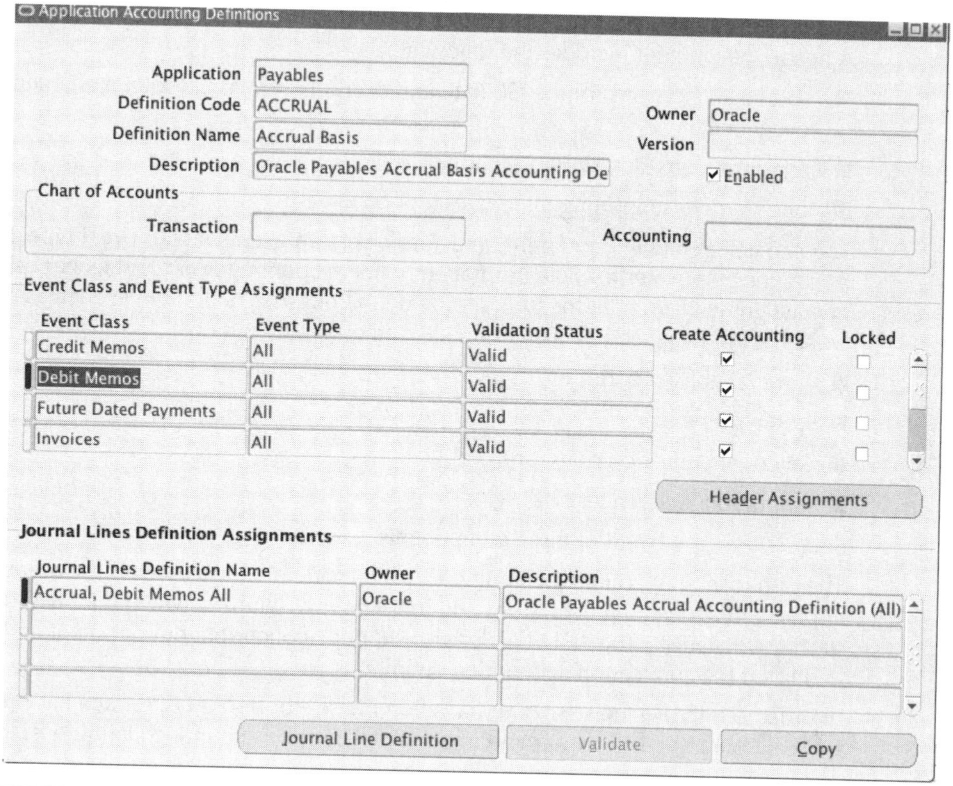

FIGURE 4-12. *Application accounting definitions*

comparable to system events and programs that update transaction tables; accounting events are events in the real business sphere. Accounting events are captured when transactions are saved in the subledgers of each application.

Application accounting definitions enable your organization to meet the subledger accounting requirements of multiple accounting representations. While one application accounting definition can generate subledger journal entries that are compliant with one particular set of accounting requirements, another definition can be defined to meet a completely different set of accounting requirements. For example, a complete set of US GAAP accounting definitions can be used for Payables as an application accounting definition for the ledger US operations. A complete set of French GAAP accounting definitions can be used for Payables for the ledger French operations. These two sets of definitions have differences based on the setup of the various components that make up their application accounting definitions.

In the Application Accounting Definition, entering the accounting definitions validation status at the levels of event class and event type enables you to generate subledger journal entries for certain event classes or event types even if the accounting definitions for other event classes or event types are invalid. Each event-class and event-type assignment consists of a header assignment and one or more journal-line definition assignments. A header assignment includes the following:

■ source assignments for the GL date and accrual reversal GL date, if enabled for the event class;

■ a journal-entry description (optional); and

■ one or more supporting references (optional).

You can assign multiple journal-line definitions to an event class or event type. Subledger Accounting generates a single journal entry per accounting event and ledger using the line assignments from all the journal-line definitions assigned to the event class or event type. The following can be assigned to a journal-line definition:

■ journal-entry description,

■ journal-line type,

■ account derivation rules, and

■ supporting references.

Sources are used by all of these components.

The Application Accounting Definition (AAD) Loader enables users to import and export application accounting definitions and journal-entry setups between the file system and database instances. The AAD Loader also supports concurrent development and version control of the application accounting definitions.

In order to improve the setup and transition phases for the AADs, Oracle has provided tools allowing users to export and import Application Accounting Definitions.

The Export Application Accounting Definitions program exports all application accounting definitions of an application from a database to the file system and produces a report of the results. All application accounting definitions and journal-entry setups for an application are exported to the same data file.

The Import Application Accounting Definition concurrent program enables importation of the definitions from a data file (previously exported) to the AMB context specified in the SLA: Accounting Method Builder Context profile option and produces a report of the results. In the concurrent program, some definitions will have to be made, such as running the merge analysis, merge, or overwrite processes.

8. **Define Subledger Accounting Methods.** The subledger accounting method (SLAM) groups application accounting definitions that comply with a common set of accounting requirements into a subledger accounting method. Each subledger accounting method can be assigned to one or more ledgers.

As mentioned before, the Application Accounting Definition is defined for each E-Business Suite application. Oracle EBS is, however, a suite composed of many modules, so it is necessary to perform accounting across various different applications. Consequently, the SLAM engine will generate the accounting journal lines for each Oracle application. Among the many advantages of this functionality are the reduction of setup time and the consistent method of accounting for all subledgers feeding into a particular ledger.

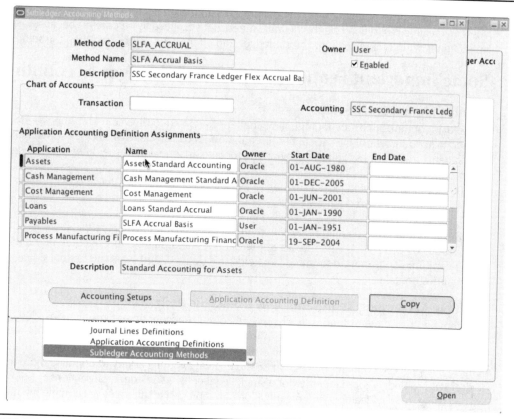

FIGURE 4-13. *Subledger accounting method for France*

For example, a subledger accounting method entitled "French GAAP" can be defined to group application accounting definitions that are accounted for using French GAAP criteria (a screenshot is shown in Figure 4-13). As another example, a Cash Basis Accounting Method can be defined to group application accounting definitions that are used to account for transactions on a cash basis. By assigning different subledger accounting methods to ledgers, the AMB enables users to create multiple accounting representations of transactions.

Accounting Method Builder Warning

During setup of each Oracle module within E-Business Suite, the users determine the default accounting. Once your organization starts operating the application, during the transaction processing each Oracle subledger utilizes the default accounting via AutoAccounting, Account Generator, or free format entry. An explanation of these accounting options is contained in the chapters for each Oracle E-Business Suite application.

In each of the applications, the Create Accounting function will call the AMB; the input to the AMB is the default accounting from the default accounting of the application. Through the setups, you can create rules to override the default values, but you have to be careful, because the applications will not go back into the subledger and change the values based on the setups.

Some Important Features of Oracle Subledger Accounting

Flexible Journal-Entry Setup

These days, organizations are facing many challenges related to diverse requirements—from corporate accounting policies, local fiscal regulation, and cash-basis or business-driven analysis—which demand E-Business Suite to provide the tools to adapt, such as the different subledger accounting methods.

The addition of Subledger Accounting to E-Business Suite also creates another point of control. Oracle has covered that with a flexible journal-entry setup, which controls every aspect of the subledger journal entries.

There are customer-defined rules which are based on data drawn from the subledger transactions by controlling which types of journal lines are created, how account numbers (code-combination IDs or Accounting Flexfields) are derived, and what the journal-entry descriptions contain.

Multiple Accounting Representations from a Single Transaction

It is common to see organizations that have very complex accounting representations, due to how they perform business. A major feature—in which Oracle invested a lot—is the ability to create multiple accounting representations from a single transaction performed on any of the applications. Oracle Subledger Accounting makes that possible, giving you the ability to populate more than one ledger with subledger journal entries for a single legal entity's subledger transactions.

By using this new feature, your organization can represent an alternate accounting interpretation of the original subledger transaction and even more, because each accounting representation can use different charts of accounts, calendars, currencies, and subledger accounting methods.

This is a requested feature from many multinational corporations for designing and implementing—through setup rather than customizations or extensions—global accounting policies independent of considerations that apply to subsidiaries operating in particular countries or in highly regulated vertical markets.

A corporate global template can be designed and implemented following single accounting policies without prior knowledge of the wide range of local fiscal regulation encountered in countries where the corporation runs businesses.

Default Transaction Distributions

Another feature of Subledger Accounting is the ability to modify the default distributions that are populated by the source application within E-Business Suite. Each application—such as Receivables, Projects, Fixed Assets, or Procurement—creates transaction distributions by referencing the defaults that indicate how the transaction will accomplish the accounting needs of your business. If you direct Subledger Accounting to amend the accounting impact of the product-supplied defaults, then SLA will modify the defaults. For example, a sales invoice might be distributed over several revenue accounts. You can edit the distribution defaults at the product level.

Create Accounting and Transfer Journal Entries to GL

The creation of accounting and the later transfer to GL are carried out by several programs that initially create the subledger journal entries by selecting the accounting events and applying the definitions created in the AMB.

The first program, called Create Accounting, initially validates and creates the subledger journal entries. Once all the entries are created, they are transferred into General Ledger and the General Ledger posting process automatically begins. After the completion of the posting, the program will trigger the Subledger Accounting Program Report, which will document the results of the Create Accounting program for use in verification and support. It lists the following:

- successful events and the subledger journal entries created for those events, and
- errors for failed events.

As mentioned in this chapter, you can create in Oracle E-Business Suite some journal entries into Subledger Accounting. Then the Transfer Journal Entries to GL program enables the transfer of any eligible journal entries to General Ledger, including those from previous batch runs that have not yet been transferred to General Ledger.

TIP

If you have already created accounting in Final mode but have not transferred the entries over to GL, and you run the Create Accounting program with the Transfer to GL option, the application does not pick up the events that have already been created in Final mode. You must run the Transfer Journal Entries to General Ledger program to do that.

Conversion of Historical Data for Reporting Currencies and Secondary Ledgers

It is very important to plan a strategy when defining a new subledger reporting currency or secondary ledger for an active primary ledger. A new subledger-level secondary or reporting ledger should not be added to an existing primary ledger that already has final accounted subledger journal entries.

There is a concurrent program called SLA Secondary/ALC Ledger Historic Upgrade which takes care of the initialization of the reporting ledger or secondary ledger. It creates journals in Oracle Subledger Accounting. These journals are created with a posting status of "Posted," but are never actually posted to Oracle General Ledger. To maintain historic balances in Oracle General Ledger, you must initialize balances for the new reporting-currency ledger or secondary ledger. If you are initializing a reporting-currency ledger, you can run the program Reporting Currency: Create Opening Balance Journals in Reporting Currency. If you are reinitializing a secondary ledger, you can use the Consolidation Workbench to copy initial balances.

You can determine the period from which to create ledger balances by selecting the first period for conversion. The journals are created from the selected period onwards. The first period of historic conversion should be the earliest period for which you have open transactions.

When a subledger-level secondary or reporting ledger is added to an existing primary ledger, the accounting in the secondary or reporting ledger fails in the following scenarios:

■ **When a final accounted transaction is reversed**   A Payables invoice is created and final accounted in the primary ledger. Then a new subledger-level secondary or reporting ledger is added to this primary ledger. The same invoice is cancelled. When the Create Accounting program is run, accounting for the invoice cancellation fails for the secondary or reporting ledger, as the accounting program does not find the corresponding Invoice accounting entry to generate the transaction-reversal entry (Invoice Cancellation accounting) for the secondary or reporting ledger.

■ **When a Payment accounting entry needs to be created using business flows**   A Payables invoice is created and final accounted in the primary ledger. Then a new subledger-level secondary or reporting ledger is added to this primary ledger. A payment is generated against the same invoice. When the Create Accounting program is run, accounting for this payment fails for the secondary or reporting ledger, as the accounting program cannot find the corresponding upstream entry (Invoice accounting) to generate the downstream entry (Payment accounting) for the secondary or reporting ledger.

Subledger Accounting Inquiry and Reporting

Oracle Subledger Accounting provides detailed subledger accounting reports and inquiries. The vast list will mostly satisfy the needs of your business and fiscal requirements. It also adds a detailed reconciliation between subledger transactions and accounting.

Since it is a new functionality, Subledger Accounting uses Oracle BI Publisher extensively. Extracts are made from the Subledger Accounting tables (see the technical overview later in this chapter) and formatted with XML Protocol templates. One advantage for users is that a template delivered with the product can be easily changed (without the users having to be technical developers) and formatted for legal requirements by extracting a seeded report and merging with the new template. For more information on BI Publisher, please refer to Chapter 20.

Using the Oracle Application Framework, Oracle Subledger Accounting introduces a Subledger Accounting Inquiries Overview window. As you can see in Figure 4-14, the Accounting Events inquiry window allows the entry of multiple search parameters and drill-down and inquiries related to accounting events.

This form allows inquiries into accounting events, journal entries, and journal entry lines based on multiple selection criteria, including transaction date, primary ledger, transaction number, and the SLA components event class, type, status, and date. It lets you compare subledger journal-entry information for any two journal entries, which is important for audit and reconciliation purposes. Some other view capabilities are

■ viewing information about an accounting event or journal-entry error;

■ viewing detailed information about the subledger journal-entry headers for a given accounting event;

■ viewing subledger journal-entry lines for a number of different documents or transactions;

■ viewing subledger journal entries in T-account format;

■ viewing transactions underlying the accounting event or journal entry; and

■ viewing supporting references associated with the subledger journal line.

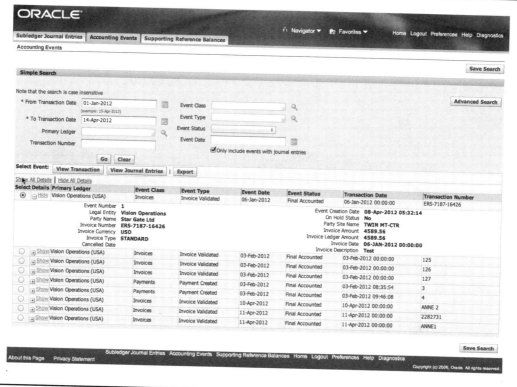

FIGURE 4-14. *Accounting Events inquiry window*

Another option in the Subledger Accounting Inquiries Overview window is to navigate to the Supporting Reference Balances page to inquire on account balances for a particular supporting reference, then drill down to the journal lines that contribute to the balances.

The Open Account Balances Listing report displays balances created by subledger transactions and detail transactions supporting the balance. An output of the report, defaulted by the BI Publisher template to Rich Text Format, is shown in Figure 4-15. A variety of seeded BI Publisher templates are included to provide multiple representations and summary levels of the data.

Subledger Accounting provides the following reports:

- Journal Entries Report,
- Account Analysis Report,
- Third Party Balances Report,
- Multiperiod Accounting Reports,
- Period Close Exceptions Report, and
- Subledger Accounting Rules Detail Listing Report.

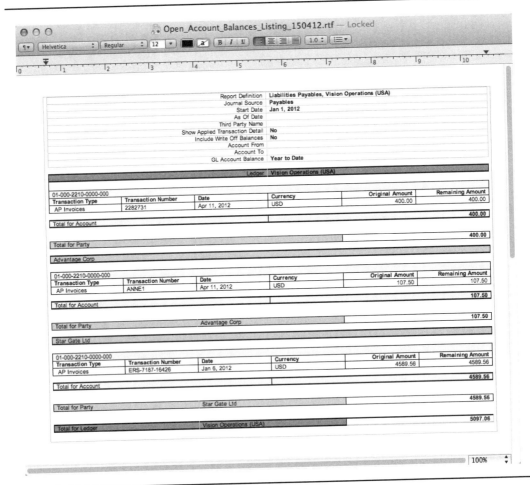

FIGURE 4-15. *SLA Open Account Balances Listing report*

Subledger Accounting's Impact on End Users

We stated early in this chapter that one of the main confusions for super users with Subledger Accounting is the misconception that it is a new module, so that the users look for a new Responsibility instead of using the existing Responsibilities for the transactional modules that are interfacing into General Ledger.

On the other hand, the end users (accounts-receivable or accounts-payable clerks) have heard about SLA but will never notice the change or impact in the modules, because it is transparent from a transactional perspective. This new functionality does, however, have an impact on processes, such as the month-end procedures.

From a reporting and inquiry side, there are changes to the standard reports which are most frequently used; the Account Analysis with Payables Details in 11i, for example—which was converted to the new Account Analysis with Subledger Details in Release 12—might have an impact on month-end procedures. It is very important to test and review the impact on every procedure, even more so in cases where organizations are heavily audited.

Even though the new Oracle Application Framework interfaces are more user friendly and intuitive than the forms, it is possible that some existing 11i users who are being exposed to OAF pages for the first time will have a marked learning curve. It is very important to train them in order to speed up the curve on topics such as adding new fields to the query page, exporting the information into a spreadsheet, and others. Training on the drill-down capabilities need be thoughtful, because it is likely that some users after the second drill-down will not understand how they got there and what exactly that screen is showing.

As explained previously in this chapter, within Subledger Accounting it is possible to enter manual subledger journals. The Create Journal Entry button is shown in Figure 4-16.

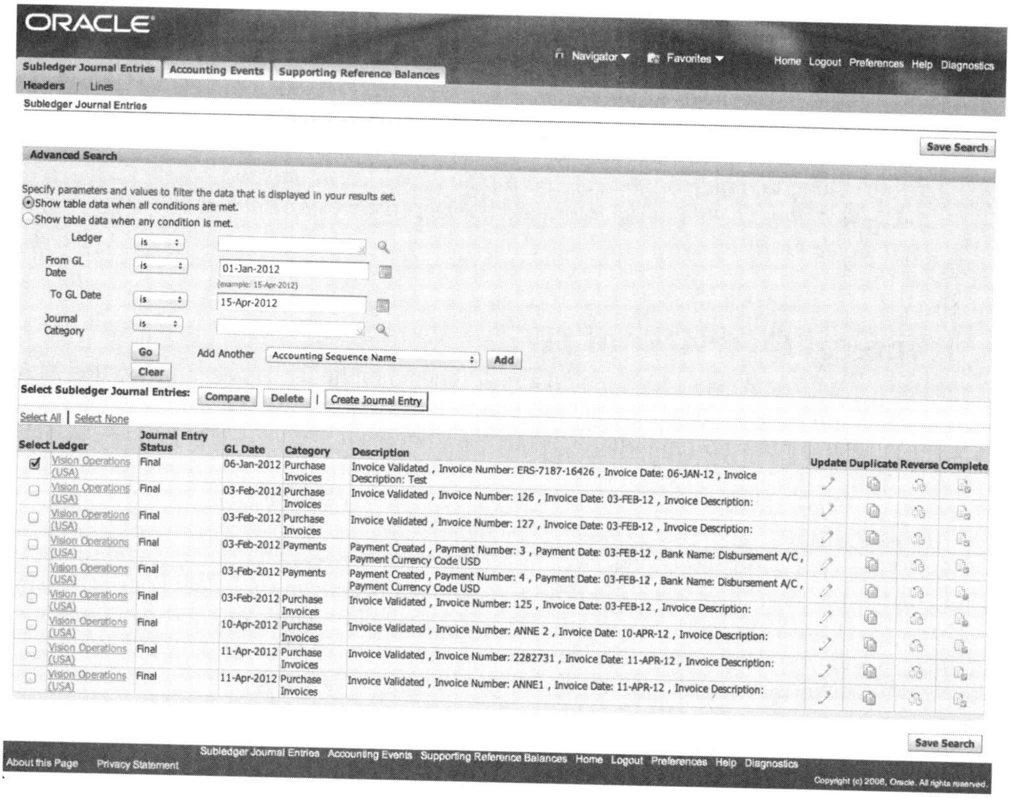

FIGURE 4-16. *Subledger Journal Entries with the Create Journal Entry button*

This functionality was requested by many organizations, but it has generated some concerns because this create function comes out of the box in a inquiry screen, and an incorrect use can create multiple reconciliation difficulties. The administrator of E-Business Suite can remove this function from all the users and implement an analysis of roles and responsibilities to determine who will have access to this feature and be trained accordingly.

Oracle presents SLA as a robust, centralized accounting engine and repository that enables true global accounting, facilitating a smoother period close and easier reconciliation (My Oracle Support Notes 986783.1 and 961285.1 provide a good point of view on the business benefits and how to assess the period-end procedures in R12). Even this could be on papers a facilitation it is strongly recommended to perform multiple tests for closing processes for period, quarter, and year end in your user acceptance tests to make sure that any impact of the "unknown" is mitigated.

The choice of using user-configured SLA rules or standard rules is a key component of the training, since the team that performs reconciliations and account analysis will have to be trained in order to understand how these rules are deriving accounting values. The mitigation for this is training and performing multiple test scenarios with the team responsible for these activities in your organization.

Understanding the SLA rules for diagnosing problems is also been part of the new product. Oracle provides a profile option SLA Enable Diagnostics, which you can set to "Yes" and then run Create Accounting. The process will store the information on the diagnostic tables within the XLA schema and report the results in the Transaction Objects Diagnostics report.

TIP
Make sure the profile option SLA Enable Diagnostics is only set to "Yes" when it is required, since the performance will be impacted because of the creation of the transaction-objects diagnostics (stored in the diagnostic tables).

Technical Overview of SLA

Subledger Accounting has incorporated a new schema in the E-Business Suite, called XLA. It has 143 tables, 165 views, 41 concurrent programs, and 94 lookup types.

A diagram of the most important XLA tables is shown in Figure 4-17. The XLA_HEADERS table stores subledger journal entries. There is a one-to-many relationship between accounting events and journal-entry headers. The XLA_LINES table stores subledger journal-entry lines. There is a one-to-many relationship between subledger journal-entry headers and subledger journal-entry lines. XLA_DISTRIBUTION_LINKS stores the link between transactions and subledger journal-entry lines. There is a one-to-many relationship between subledger lines and distribution links. XLA_DISTRIBUTION_LINKS also determines whether duplicate subledger journal lines are merged and whether the accounted amounts are calculated by SLA or passed through.

We mentioned earlier in this chapter the ability to use Subledger Accounting journal entries to represent accounting from legacy systems. Oracle provides an API allowing the import of journal entries into SLA, which could provide better visibility of information to the business users responsible for such application consolidation. The package is called XLA_JOURNAL_ENTRIES_

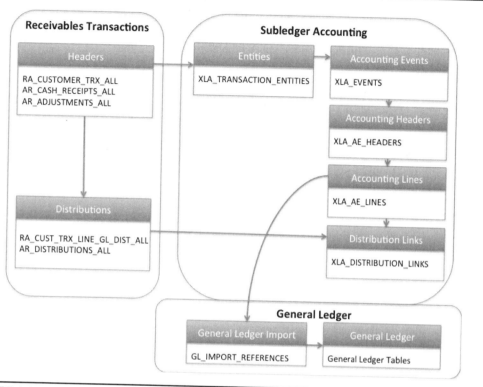

FIGURE 4-17. *Technical architecture of Subledger Accounting tables*

PUB_PKG, and has multiple subfunctions:Create_Journal_Entry_Header, Update_Journal_Entry_Header, Delete_Journal_Entry, Create_Journal_Entry_Line, Update_Journal_Entry_Line, Delete_Journal_Entry_Line, Complete_Journal_Entry, and Reverse_Journal_Entry.

Conclusion

Oracle Subledger Accounting offers unparalleled visibility into enterprise-wide accounting information with a single global accounting repository. It addresses the concurrent needs for centralized accounting processes with strong internal controls and diverse accounting treatments.

In summary, Oracle Subledger Accounting enables you to

- lower costs with streamlined accounting processes,
- meet diverse global accounting requirements and maintain internal controls, and
- access better information and provide better reporting.

The new Subledger Accounting engine represents a major shift in how accounting is performed. It is now possible to support multiple Enterprise Resource Planning systems in one corporation. With the new forms-based Accounting Method Builder, creating and maintaining accounting rules is more straightforward than utilizing Account Generator. Users can create new rules without knowledge of Workflow, without developing SQL code, and without access to the applications password. Users no longer have to account by exception. With the Accounting Method Builder, there is much more consistency and transparency to the accounting rules. With the new draft-accounting functionality, users can test the accounting-rule changes without impacting the General Ledger. User-defined accounting rules will be maintained in future patching and upgrades, giving more stability to the system. Because of these improvements over the Account Generator, transitioning your Account Generator to Subledger Accounting (SLA) should be a part of your postupgrade plans.

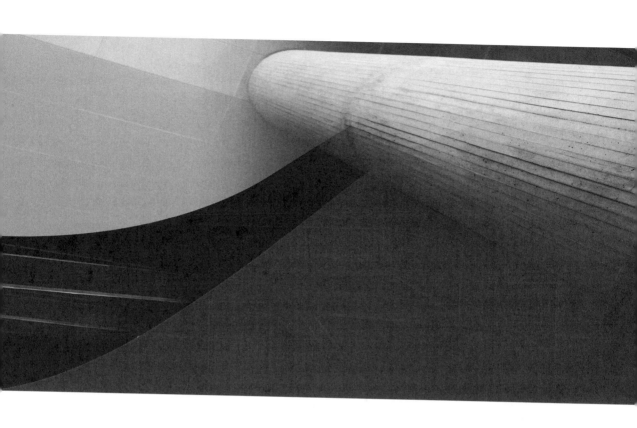

CHAPTER
5

Oracle Payables

payables system is the last stage of supply-chain management. It allows companies to pay suppliers for merchandise and services. There are several opportunities in Oracle Payables for automation, because the terms and conditions are known at the stage of the *purchase order* (PO); assuming that the goods are accepted, payment follows at a fixed time later.

The goal of supply-chain management is to keep stock levels low but have sufficient stock to meet demand. Stock sitting in a warehouse equates to money tied up unproductively—but only if you have paid for that stock. The goal of payables management is to postpone payment as long as possible and at the same time ensure that invoices are paid by their due date.

Payables controls are equally applicable to paying employee expenses and paying vendors for expensed and capitalized items. It is no more than prudent management to pay invoices only when they are due and, invoice or not, to be sure that payment is not made before delivery—unless it has been explicitly agreed to.

Receiving goods and paying for them weeks later amounts to an interest-free loan from your supplier. Supermarkets are champions at using the good terms offered by suppliers. Supermarkets might be operating on wafer-thin margins, but they regularly sell their stock days—if not weeks—before they pay for it. They have a surplus working capital, which they invest for profit. Supermarkets are an extreme example of investing other people's money wisely; however, managing suppliers' payment terms is a business practice from which all commercial organizations can benefit.

Purposes of a Payables System

The purpose of a payables system is to help you manage your procurement cycle, allowing you to process high transaction volumes and keep control over your cash flow. It also enables you to better manage your supplier relationships and make price comparisons. Oracle Payables can be configured to save your company money by enforcing your payment policies, such as

- paying suppliers on time, but no earlier than necessary,
- taking discounts when prudent,
- preventing duplicate billing or invoicing, and
- avoiding overdrafts of your bank accounts.

Because payables is only part of a complete cycle, it must be integrated with other modules. Oracle Payables shares purchase-order information with Purchasing so that you pay only for goods you ordered and received and do not pay more than the price quoted by the supplier. It shares receipt information with Purchasing so that you do not pay for items that are faulty, broken, or substandard. Oracle Payables is fully integrated with Oracle Assets in a way that allows you to account for fixed assets purchased. It is integrated with Human Resources to ensure that employee expenses are paid efficiently, and with Oracle Cash Management to enable you to reconcile your payments against a bank statement. Payables also integrates with Oracle Property Management to process lease payments to landlords as they fall due.

Innovative Uses of Oracle Payables

Open integration with third-party systems is a trend in the software industry and is becoming a standard business requirement. Oracle continues responding to this trend by continuing and upgrading functionality in Oracle E-Business Suite (EBS)—and specifically in the Payables application—with features such as Web-enabled commerce, E-Commerce Gateway, Evaluated Receipt Settlement (ERS), procurement-card integration, and attachments.

Web-Enabled Commerce

Web-enabled applications give access to any user with a Web browser and the appropriate security clearance. Oracle has termed these *Self-Service Applications*, as they allow users to access data directly instead of filling out a paper form and then having a payables clerk do the actual data entry, as previously required. Using a standard Web browser and the Self-Service Expenses application, described in more detail in Chapter 16, employees can enter their own expense reports.

Mobile employees can use the Expense spreadsheet to track expenses offline in *disconnected mode*, then upload their expense records into the Self-Service Expenses application to submit for approval. Once an expense report is submitted using Self-Service Expenses, Oracle Workflow routes the report for approval and automatically enforces company policies and business rules. Oracle Payables then processes the expense report and issues a payment to the employee.

E-Commerce Gateway

Oracle E-Commerce Gateway evolved from the Oracle EDI Gateway product, focusing on electronic data interchange (EDI), into a product focused on e-business integration. All the features and functions of Oracle EDI Gateway have been retained and enhanced to create the Oracle E-Commerce Gateway.

This product uses electronic messaging to communicate with trading partners. Instead of printing paper documents such as purchase orders, invoices, and remittance advisories, Oracle E-Business Suite uses the Oracle E-Commerce Gateway to send these documents to your trading partners. Oracle EBS uses international standards X12 and EDIFACT to ensure that recipients will be able to read the message, regardless of whether they are using Oracle EBS or not. These two standards are commonly used: X12 is sponsored by the American National Standards Institute (ANSI) and used in the United States, and EDIFACT is sponsored by the United Nations and primarily used in Europe. The Oracle E-Commerce Gateway extracts the data from Oracle EBS and delivers it in a common format to an EDI translator. The translator converts the common format supplied by Oracle EBS to either X12 or EDIFACT.

The actual mechanism for transferring the electronic document to the other party is not prescribed. In the same way that a paper document can be faxed, mailed, or sent by courier, electronic messages can be sent in a variety of ways:

- through modem links across phone lines,
- across the Internet using FTP or HTTP PUT, or
- on floppy disk sent through the postal service.

EDI transactions can be either *inbound* (data coming in from a partner to be loaded into Oracle EBS) or *outbound* (data that have been extracted from Oracle EBS and are now being sent to a partner). Support for new transaction types is continually being added; an outbound purchase-order EDI has been available since version 1 of the Oracle EDI Gateway product, and Release 11 of Financials introduced support for inbound invoices. Although you can write custom programs to fulfill any EDI need, some EDI transactions are available to use in combination with Oracle Payables (shown in Table 5-1).

The outbound application advice (824/APERAK) can be used to inform a supplier of a duplicate invoice or an invoice that does not refer to a valid purchase order. It can also be used to notify a supplier of invoice data rejected for any reason or to confirm that you have accepted an invoice.

Transaction	X12 Standard	EDIFACT Standard	Direction
Invoice	810	INVOIC	Inbound
Payment order/remittance advice	820	PAYORD/REMADV	Outbound
Application advice	824	APERAK	Outbound
Shipment and billing notice	857	No equivalent	Inbound

TABLE 5-1. *EDI Transaction Set Available for Accounts Payable*

Evaluated Receipt Settlement (ERS)

Traditionally, payment has been based on receipt of the supplier's invoice. However, recent innovations in workflow have led to evaluated receipt settlement. The receipt of goods drives payment under ERS; no paper invoice is sent to the accounts-payable department. Evaluated receipt settlement enables a user to automatically create standard, unapproved invoices for payment of goods. The invoices are based on receipt transactions that have been processed through Oracle Purchasing.

Creation of an invoice can be triggered by an *Advance Shipment Notice* (ASN) from the supplier (processed by Purchasing/Receiving under Oracle Purchasing) or a third-party receiving process. Invoices are created using a combination of receipt and purchase-order information; this process eliminates duplicate data entry and ensures accurate and timely data processing. Evaluated receipt settlement is also known as *payment on receipt* or *self-billing*.

Under the payables system, you choose which suppliers participate and you enforce matching rules to ensure that the proper payments are made to your suppliers. The system creates invoices with multiple items and distribution lines and automatically accounts for sales tax. The amount on the invoice is determined by multiplying the quantity of items received by each item's unit price on the purchase order. The payment terms on the invoice default to the purchase-order payment terms. The payment currency defaults from the supplier site. Sales tax is calculated based on the tax codes on each line of the purchase order.

The ERS process saves the supplier the expense of generating invoices and saves you the expense of matching invoices to receipts and processing payments. ERS imposes a measure of control in doing so. As the customer, you must be careful to accurately record what is received. Your business processes must absolutely minimize discrepancies between the purchase order and the receipt. The supplier must be equally vigilant in comparing your remittance advice with its shipments to you.

Procurement Cards

To simplify the administration of employee expenses, companies can offer their employees the use of a corporate credit card, which can be used to make purchases on the company's behalf. With the procurement-card integration feature, you can import the transaction detail from statement files provided by the card issuer. Employees are notified automatically of any transactions appearing on their card; they can use Oracle Self-Service Expenses to verify those transactions and override default transaction accounting. Once the transactions have been verified, invoices that represent the employer's liability will be automatically created to pay the card issuer.

Procurement cards reduce transaction costs in several ways:

- Obligations to many suppliers are consolidated into a single payment to the card issuer.
- The transaction description is already automated, to some degree, in the line detail provided by the card issuer.
- The employee is identified automatically.
- The accounting distribution often can be fully determined by identifying the employee and the supplier. If not, the number of choices usually is quite limited.

This process can empower employees to buy what they want, when they need to. In essence, it enables them to be more productive without creating additional paperwork or bypassing the business-approval and audit procedures. Items purchased using procurement cards generally are expensed. The card issuer knows nothing of your inventory item numbers, so it would be impractical to buy for stock; and the budgeting, approvals, and assets interfaces are not present to support purchase of capital items.

Attachments

You can link invoices to related data files, such as images, word-processing documents, spreadsheets, and video files. These attachments are stored within the Oracle database or on a secured network drive, and are accessible through the Payables screens. This new feature enables your payables department to build a better profile of your suppliers and trading partners, and makes the information readily accessible.

For example, you could attach to the invoice record in Payables a scanned image of the original supplier's invoice. Doing this would allow you to archive the paper copy and rely entirely on the application data and the stored image to resolve any future queries. This method is particularly suitable if you use a paper-based procedure for invoice approval and account coding. The invoice image can be scanned after the invoice has been forwarded to the buyer for approval and account coding.

With Release 12, buyers can communicate all necessary attachments to suppliers, including file attachments via e-mail. When you are trying to upload any attachment in EBS via Oracle Application Framework screens in iProcurement, iExpense, iSupplier, or iStore, there is no limit to the file size of an attachment; however, the limitation of 2–4 gigabytes for a LOB file type could be considered the limitation for an attachment file. If you do wish to limit the file size, you can do so by setting the profile option Upload File Size Limit. This option is interpreted in bytes rather than kilobytes by the Forms application but as is by the Oracle Application Framework.

An Overview of Payables in Your Business

As soon as a company agrees to purchase goods or services from a supplier, it has an encumbrance—whether the company chooses to account for it or not. As the goods or services are received, the encumbrance converts to a liability to pay the agreed price for the goods. The liability remains on the company's balance sheet until the goods or services have been paid for.

Payment terms will have been agreed upon at the purchase stage, and the supplier should quote these terms when sending an invoice for the goods. Typical payment terms might be 30 days net; better terms would be 90 days net or a 1 percent discount. The latter means the full amount is due by the 90th day but there is a 1 percent discount if the invoice is paid earlier. There is no limit to the range of possible payment terms; terms are separately negotiated either by individual supplier or by purchase order. After waiting as long as possible before sacrificing the discount or going into default, you pay the invoice. Payment can be made by check, bank-to-bank electronic funds transfer (EFT), or any of a range of cash and noncash payment methods. Once the invoice has been paid, the liability in the balance sheet is reduced to zero.

To explain the figures that appear on the balance sheet, you need to be able to list how much money is owed to each supplier and prove that the total money owed equals the liability shown on the balance sheet. This reconciliation of the Payables subledger with General Ledger (GL) should be performed regularly—at minimum once each accounting period. To start the reconciliation, compare the standard Oracle Payables Trial Balance report with the payables liability-account line in the appropriate Financial Statement Generator (FSG) balance-sheet report.

Timing Your Liability

Companies differ on when liability is first measured. Some record their liability from the day the invoice arrives or the date on the invoice, not the day the goods were received. The invoice due date has no bearing on the eventual liability—the due date is for operational control, not accounting. Organizations that automate purchasing and payables processes are in a better position to record liability for goods ordered but not received and for goods received but not invoiced. However, if you use Payables without the purchasing system, the best approximation is to record the liability when the invoice is received. Bear in mind that the decision on when to recognize a liability is a commercial accounting decision and should not be driven by system considerations.

Companies with a backlog of purchase invoices at period end will calculate the total amount owing from all the invoices that have not been keyed, then enter this single figure as an accrual journal in General Ledger. This allows the accounts to show an accurate liability figure and the accounting period to be closed on time. Once the backlog of invoices has been individually keyed into Payables, the accrual journal has to be reversed in the following period. The accrual journal also will typically include recurring expenses that have been incurred but not yet invoiced, such as telephone and utility bills and estimated procurement-card charges.

The Payables Workflow

Oracle Payables is tightly integrated with Oracle Purchasing and Oracle Cash Management. The close integration is dictated by workflow: purchase orders in Purchasing give rise to invoices in Payables; invoices give rise to payments, which will show as bank-statement entries in Cash Management. If necessary, Payables can be installed on its own without Purchasing or Cash Management, but you might not be able to take advantage of the full range of automation that otherwise would be available.

If you are not using an ERS process, suppliers will send you an invoice for the goods you have received. These invoices will be processed by your accounts-payable department, which ensures that the supplier is known and that the price, quantity, and payment terms match those on the original purchase order. Your business processes should specify how to deal with invoices from suppliers who are not in the system. This occurs commonly, even with a purchasing system in place. Many obligations, including withholding tax and property-tax payments, originate without a purchase order. In these cases, the user might have to do one or both of these extra steps:

- Identify and set up a supplier record in Oracle Payables.
- Determine which expense-account codes the items should be charged against.

Once entered and approved, the invoice is available for payment. Physical payment can take place in many different ways, including

- automatic or manual checks,
- wire transfers, and
- electronic funds transfer.

From the payables point of view, the invoice is considered paid and you have reached the end of the payables cycle. The payment eventually will appear on the company's bank statement, at which stage it should be reconciled within Oracle Cash Management. Reconciling the payment removes it from the list of payments issued but not yet cleared. Cash Management's reconciliation feature is powerful because it enables you to handle queries from suppliers much more effectively. You can bring up a record of the supplier's account online and identify previous invoices, their due dates, and their actual payment dates. If the check has been presented, you can see the date it was reconciled.

Sometimes suppliers mistakenly believe that a particular invoice has not been paid. Having crucial information at your fingertips (that is, the payment date, the check number, and the date on which the check was cleared by your bank) is a powerful way to quickly set the record straight, avoid making duplicate payments, and maintain better supplier relations. The bank-reconciliation functionality is part of Oracle Cash Management. Cash Management creates postings from a cash-clearing account to correspond to the reconciled payments. Bank reconciliation is described in more detail in Chapter 8.

Oracle Payables posts accounting transactions to Oracle General Ledger. It also integrates with Oracle Purchasing for invoice matching, with Oracle Fixed Assets for tracking fixed-asset purchases, and with Cash Management for enabling checks and payments issued out of Oracle Payables to be reconciled with your bank statement. In addition, expenditures can be transferred to Oracle Projects for project accounting, tracking, or billing; and lease obligations can be imported from Oracle Property Manager. Integration with Oracle Inventory helps reconcile inventory movements with European Union Interstat cross-border material-movement reporting requirements. An overview of the integration is shown in Figure 5-1.

The Payables Cycle

All payments pass through the same four-step Payables cycle, shown in Figure 5-2. An objective of your Payables setup is to reduce overhead costs by automating the cycle to the extent possible while still keeping all your controls in place.

The Payables cycle consists of the following four steps:

1. Enter invoices. (This process may or may not include matching each invoice to a purchase order.)
2. Approve invoices for payment.
3. Select and pay approved invoices.
4. Reconcile the payments with the bank statement (part of Oracle Cash Management).

The first three steps are discussed just ahead. Bank reconciliation is described in more detail in Chapter 8. Invoices and payments generate accounting entries that need to be transferred to General Ledger and posted. The General Ledger transfer process is described later in this chapter.

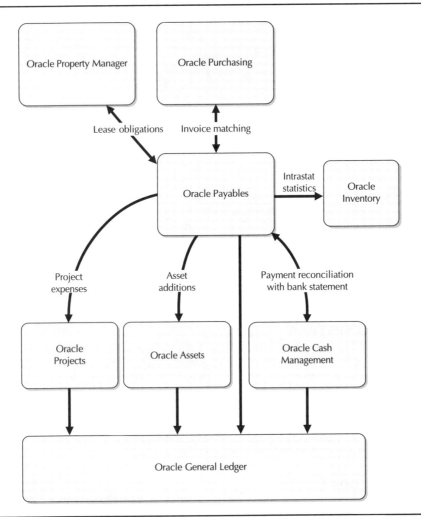

FIGURE 5-1. *An overview of Oracle Payables integration with other Oracle EBS modules*

Step 1: Enter Invoices

Invoices are entered in Oracle Payables using the Invoice Workbench. This form is at the heart of accounts-payable processing, allowing you to process all types of invoices and maintain accuracy and control over what you pay. The Invoice Workbench contains many different fields. Some of these are required for approval; others are derived or defaulted from supplier purchase-order information or from the supplier record, payables options, or batch options. Yet other fields are purely optional and might never be used by some companies.

As part of the new Release 12, Oracle has added several enhancements related to global organizations. One of them, mentioned in Chapter 2, is the Multi-Org Access Control (MOAC).

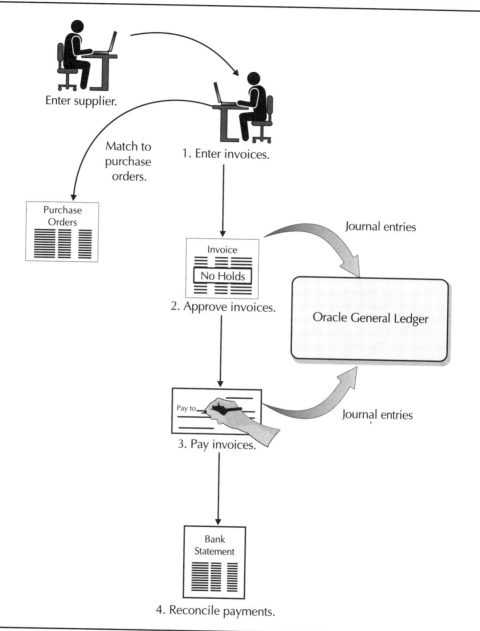

FIGURE 5-2.   *The Oracle Payables cycle*

It allows the users to work on the same screen for multiple organizations. Some of the benefits your organization can take advantage of with this feature are faster data entry, reduced setup and maintenance, more efficient transaction processing for companies that have centralized business functions or operate shared service centers, and a global consolidated view of information.

The details of the form—the data that must be entered and the cross-validation of related data—depend on the type of invoice you are entering. The various types of invoices are

- **Standard**   A regular supplier invoice. The invoice usually includes line-item details, including a description and price.

- **Credit Memo**   An invoice you receive from a supplier representing a credit for goods or services purchased.

- **Debit Memo**   An invoice that notifies a supplier of a credit you recorded for goods or services purchased.

- **Expense Report**   An invoice you enter to record business-related expenses for employees. The employee is the supplier.

- **PO Default**   An invoice for which you know the matching purchase-order number. Payables fills out as much information from the purchase order as possible: supplier name, supplier number, supplier site, and currency.

- **QuickMatch**   An invoice you want to match automatically to a specified purchase order and all the shipment lines on the purchase order. Oracle Payables completes the match automatically for each shipment line where the quantity ordered is greater than the quantity already billed against that shipment line.

- **Mixed**   A standard or credit/debit memo invoice that you want to match to a purchase order, another invoice, or both. You can enter either a positive or negative amount for a mixed invoice.

- **Prepayment**   An invoice used to make advance payments for expenses to a supplier or employee. In this case, you might not have actually received the goods or services yet.

- **Withholding Tax**   An invoice used to remit taxes withheld to the tax authority.

- **Retainage Release**   An invoice created for complex work and advance contract financing. It is the act of releasing, or paying, a portion of a payment that was withheld until a substantial portion or all of the service procurement work was completed.

NOTE
Once you have saved an invoice with the type of PO Default, Mixed, or QuickMatch, Payables will change the invoice type to Standard. You cannot later search and find PO Default, Mixed, or QuickMatch invoices in the Invoice Workbench.

Invoice Matching   Payables provides extensive purchase-order matching features to ensure that you pay only for goods and services you have ordered, received, and accepted. If a discrepancy appears between the figures on the supplier's invoice and your figures, the invoice should be put on hold and not paid until the difference has been clarified with the supplier. The matching process is highly integrated with Oracle Purchasing. If you are populating the purchasing tables with imported data, you also must populate the invoice and line-level match flags that allow the invoice to be paid.

When you match during invoice entry, you indicate whether you want to match to the purchase-order shipment, to specific purchase-order distributions, or to one or more receipt transactions.

By matching to receipts, you can more accurately capture and record costs for your material items. You then choose the shipment, distribution, or receipt you want to match and the quantity and price you are matching. Payables performs the following for each matched shipment:

- updates QUANTITY_BILLED and AMOUNT_BILLED in PO_DISTRIBUTIONS;
- updates QUANTITY_BILLED in PO_LINE_LOCATIONS; and
- creates one or more rows in AP_INVOICE_LINES and AP_INVOICE_DISTRIBUTIONS tables, which records the QUANTITY_INVOICED, the UNIT_PRICE, and the PO_DISTRIBUTION_ID, in addition to other columns with Payables information.

You have the option of setting up two-, three-, and four-way matching to ensure that you pay only for goods and services that have been ordered, ordered and received, or ordered, received, and accepted. Purchase invoices must be matched to a purchase order and, optionally, receipts and inspections before they can be approved for payment.

Oracle does provide an open interface for purchase orders, which will allow you to take advantage of matching by importing PO information from another purchasing system into the following interface tables:

- PO_HEADERS_INTERFACE,
- PO_LINES_INTERFACE,
- PO_DISTRIBUTIONS_INTERFACE, and
- PO_PRICE_DIFF_INTERFACE.

Invoice Import　The Invoice Import process allows you to create Payables invoices through an automated process. You would typically use this feature for established suppliers with a large business volume, for interfacing with external systems you might have, or for the initial data conversion to Oracle Payables. The import captures descriptions and prices at a line level. It can include either the accounting distribution or the information needed to have Account Generator determine the distribution. It can capture and carry supplier-specific information in Descriptive Flexfield (DFF) attributes.

Quick Invoices　The Quick Invoices form (shown in Figure 5-3) is designed for fast entry of large numbers of invoices. It is a simple form that does not perform any validation or generation of default values; those happen later when the invoices are loaded into Payables. The Quick Invoice form stores invoice header and line information in the Payables Open Interface tables. You then submit the Payables Open Interface Import program to validate your invoice records and create invoices with distributions and scheduled payments in the Payables system. Most validation and defaulting of invoice values occurs during the import process. Fields that are not needed for input can be hidden to make data entry easier, using standard folder technology, but some prevalidation is enforced by the form in the fields that use List of Values.

Step 2: Approve Invoices

Invoices must be approved before they can be paid. For efficiency, Payables can be set up so that most invoices flow straight through to payment. Holds, which require someone to act before the invoice can be paid, should be the exception—not the rule. Otherwise, a large number of invoices would require manual intervention at a stage in the cycle where it is not necessary.

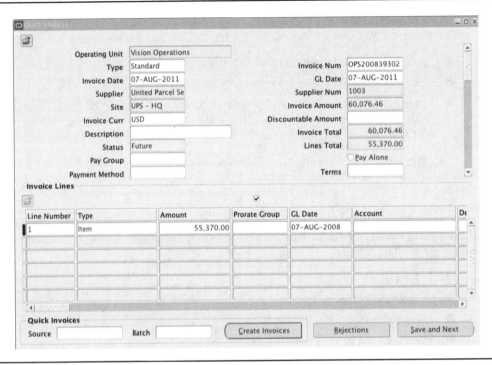

FIGURE 5-3. *Quick Invoices form*

An invoice can be approved one of three ways: through online approval, through the Approval Process, or by batch from the batch screen. Online approval is done on an individual-invoice basis and initiated from the Invoice Workbench. This is best used if you have a particular invoice that needs immediate approval and payment. The Approval Process is a concurrent program that scans all payable invoices and reassesses the system holds on each invoice. It produces a report showing which invoices have new holds placed and which invoices have holds released, and usually is set up to run in the background or is run manually immediately before the payment process.

During approval, validation occurs for matching, tax, period status, exchange rate, and distribution information for invoices; holds are applied to exception invoices. The approval process applies system holds to invoices. For new invoices, the approval procedure assesses whether any holds are needed; if so, the holds are placed on the invoice. For existing invoices with holds, the procedure assesses whether the existing holds are still appropriate and whether any new holds are necessary as a result of changes that have been made to the invoice. For example, when a tax variance is corrected, the tax hold is released. However, if after that change the invoice lines no longer add up to the invoice total, the approval process places a distribution-variance hold. Clearing holds on a batch of invoices is an iterative process, but user holds are always left unaffected and must be removed manually.

Holds Holds are placed by the system or a user on invoices that are not approved. Some holds prevent the invoice from being transferred to General Ledger. Users can place holds for any reason. System holds are used to enforce certain data-integrity and business-reality checks. An invoice cannot be paid or posted if the sum of its invoice lines does not equal the total invoice amount (DIST_VARIANCE is nonzero) or if the tax for a line does not equal the net amount multiplied by the tax rate (TAX_VARIANCE is nonzero).

TIP

For sites with a high volume of invoices, set up the Invoice Approval Workflow process to run two or three times during the day, or once during the night on new invoices. This relieves the burden of invoice-entry staff approving each invoice one by one online.

Holds are categorized according to the general reason for placing the hold. Table 5-2 gives an example for each of the different types of holds. The complete list of holds, along with their suggested actions, can be found in the Oracle Payables Reference Manual.

Whenever you have an invoice with a hold, you must remove the hold before the invoice can proceed to the next stage in the cycle. Certainly, all invoices with holds that prevent them from being transferred to General Ledger have to be cleared, and the invoices posted, before the accounting period can be closed. If you are still unable to resolve a hold and the period must be closed, you can sweep the invoice into the next period, then close the period after the sweep has been done.

TIP

Oracle Alert can be integrated effectively with Payables to streamline the Approval Process. For instance, an alert can be programmed to e-mail the buyer if there is a matching hold. The buyer then can research the hold and release it, if appropriate.

Type of Hold	Example	Reason	Remedy
Account	DIST ACC INVALID	Invoice was distributed to an invalid account.	Change the transaction or make the account valid.
Funds	INSUFFICIENT FUNDS	Invoice distribution amount exceeds funds available.	Manually override the hold or put more funds into the account.
Invoice	AMOUNT	Invoice amount exceeds amount specified for the supplier site.	Approve payment manually.
Matching	QTY ORD	Quantity billed exceeds quantity ordered by more than percentage tolerance.	Wait for the match to be satisfied or approve payment manually.
Variance	DIST VARIANCE	Sum of distributions is not equal to the invoice amount.	Resolve the discrepancy so that the invoice can be paid.

TABLE 5-2. *Examples of Payables Holds*

Step 3: Pay Approved Invoices

Once an invoice has been entered and approved, it must be paid in a timely manner to take advantage of available discounts and retain good relations with your suppliers. In Oracle Payables you initiate payment runs on a regular basis, say weekly or every second working day. The pay run will select all invoices that need to be paid, according to your criteria, and generate the appropriate payment documents. A single payment will be sent covering all of a supplier's invoices that are due to be paid. You can instead choose the Pay Alone feature to make sure that only one invoice is paid per payment document. This approach can be important for tax authorities, for example, who demand a one-to-one correspondence between payments and paperwork.

Oracle has introduced a new user interface in Release 12, called Payment Manager, that processes payments for multiple invoices, allowing the creation of a Payment Process Request (PPR). See in Figure 5-4 the home screen of Payment Manager. This new engine provides a huge advantage for the payables department with regard to manipulating payments and having a better understanding of the status of the process.

Payment Manager has introduced some new terminology:

- **Oracle Payments** An E-Business Suite module that Payables leverages to group invoices into payments, create instructions, and print or communicate with the bank. Payment Manager is the function you use to access it.

- **Pay run** A business action to select multiple invoices on a regular basis to be processed for payment. This may also be referred to as creating and processing payment batches and, in Release 12, managing a PPR through completion.

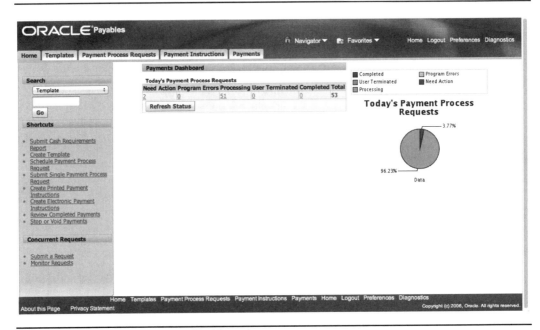

FIGURE 5-4. *Payment Manager dashboard*

- **Payment Process Request (PPR)** The selection of invoices into a group for payment processing.

- **Payment instruction** Information compiled from one or more PPRs that is formatted and either transmitted to a financial institution for payment or used in-house to print check documents.

- **Template** A way to store selection criteria, payment attributes, and processing rules that can be reused for single pay runs or scheduled pay runs.

The steps necessary to complete a pay run are initiated from the Payment Workbench. Once you enter the pay-run parameters and selection criteria, you are guided through the following five-step sequence:

1. **Select** Invoices are selected if they fall due on or before the pay-by date you specify and they meet all the other criteria you specify (such as pay group, method of payment, and currency). All payment batches for a single bank account can be initiated with a single payment-batch submission. You can leverage the templates and also schedule a repeating request to select the invoices for the PPR.

2. **Group into payments** You can prevent payment to a trading partner, prevent payment of a particular invoice, or add an invoice that Payables did not originally select.

3. **Format and print** The selected invoices are formatted either as checks (in which case Payables produces a print file containing remittance-advice information and the formatted check information) or as an electronic payment file, in which case a data file containing the payment information is formatted according to a particular bank or EDI format. Checks are printed onto the company's check-stock stationery, or a bank file is transmitted to the bank over a secure Internet connection.

4. **Confirm** You confirm to the system that each check has been paid. Confirmation releases a concurrent process that records the invoices as paid and marks the payments to be transferred to General Ledger. It also releases the bank account so it can be used for a subsequent payment batch.

5. **Deliver** Checks are posted to the supplier or a bank file is delivered to the bank.

At any time independent of your regular payment cycle, you can issue a manual payment (generated wholly outside the system but entered into Oracle Payables to ensure that the correct accounting entries are generated) or a Quick Payment (a payment for a single supplier generated within Oracle Payables, but outside of a payment batch run). Either method is useful, for example, if you are late with your payment and the supplier is pressing for payment before the next regular payment run.

On the whole, manual checks and Quick Payments should be discouraged because the administrative costs associated with a single payment are far higher than those for payments issued in a regular payment run. Oracle EBS recognizes that there will be circumstances in which a manual check is needed; the applications are flexible enough to cope with these exceptional situations.

Payment Methods There are a number of possible payment methods, including printed checks, printed transfer slips, and electronic documents such as EFT or EDI. The aim is to choose a payment method that the supplier accepts and that is inexpensive to operate, as your bank might impose different charges for various payment methods. Two are most commonly used:

- **Checks** Although check payment is readily accepted, it is also relatively expensive, considering the fees, time, and material required to print, mail, and reconcile checks. In addition to the payment document itself, Payables can be configured to generate *remittance notices*. A remittance notice is a letter informing the supplier of an imminent payment; it includes details of the invoices that are being paid.

- **Electronic funds transfer** EFT consists of a formatted file with payment information sent to your bank so it can disburse the payments directly into each supplier's bank account. Some countries have well-established EFT standards that are accepted by all their banks. In the United Kingdom and United States, the BACS (Bank Automated Clearing System) is commonly used; in Germany, the Deutsche Bank DTA (Datenträgeraustausch) format is widely accepted. Many country-specific formats are provided by Oracle; if your bank uses one that is not supported, you will need to write a customized EFT-payments program to generate the appropriate file layout. If the layout differs only slightly from a standard layout, it can be relatively simple to copy the standard program, reregister it under a different name, and make the necessary layout changes in Oracle BI Publisher. You will need to work with your bank to determine the required format.

General Ledger Transfer (Posting)

All subledger modules have a program that reviews all new or changed transactions (such as invoices, debit memos, and payments) and creates a batch of journal entries in the interface table that is ready to be imported into General Ledger as a journal. These programs are called Transfer to General Ledger.

The introduction of the Oracle Subledger Accounting (SLA) architecture to Payables in Release 12 provides the ability to create accounting entries based on a set of predefined accounting rules that SLA uses to create accounting, or your own customized rules using the Accounting Methods Builder (AMB). These definitions are grouped into Subledger Accounting methods and assigned to a ledger. See Chapter 4 for more information.

Each transaction in Payables that has accounting impact is called an accounting event. The steps involved in the accounting process are

- **Create accounting entries** Submits a batch program or, from the transaction window, individual invoices, invoice batches, payments, or payment batches.

- **Review accounting entries** Uses the View Accounting Lines window.

- **Update accounting entries** Changes accounts or corrects invalid accounts.

- **Transfer accounting entries to GL** Submits the Payables Transfer to General Ledger program to transfer entries to the GL_INTERFACE table.

- **Import and post journals in GL** Creates the journals in GL and updates the account balances to reflect the debits and credit in the journal.

The journals created from Payables are clearly identifiable in General Ledger according to their batch names and journal names. The logic behind the batch names is shown in Table 5-3,

Batch Name	Journal Name	Transactions Listed
user-ref Payables	Payments *CUR*	Payments transferred from Oracle Payables
user-ref Payables	Purchase Invoices *CUR*	Purchase invoices transferred from Oracle Payables

TABLE 5-3.   *General Ledger Batch Names from Payables*

where *CUR* is the currency of the payments and *user-ref* is the reference given to the transfer by the user who started it.

The View Accounting Lines window can present the journal lines in a graphical T-account format. You can view all the details in a T-account (or just the net total) and view T-accounts in detail by full Accounting Flexfield or summarized by account segment.

When you use accrual-basis accounting and submit the Payables Transfer to General Ledger program, Payables can transfer accounting information for both your invoices and payment transactions to the General Ledger interface table. When you submit the program, you can choose to transfer invoice, payment, or all (both invoice and payment) transactions. The accounting distributions for an invoice typically debit the expense or asset accounts and credit the AP liability account of an invoice. The accounting distributions for a payment typically debit the liability account and credit your cash or cash-clearing account. When you create payments, Payables may also create distributions for discounts taken and foreign-currency-exchange gains or losses incurred between invoice and payment time.

Processing Refunds from Suppliers or Employees

Using the Payments window, you can record a refund from a supplier or employee. This enables you to close an open credit balance and maintain a full transaction history for the supplier. When you record a refund, you link it to the associated invoices, expense reports, credit memos, and debit memos. Refund transactions appear in the supplier transaction history and are reflected in the supplier balance. Refunds are restricted to suppliers and employees; they do not integrate with Oracle Receivables.

Supplier Data

Oracle has made significant changes to the supplier data, starting with a new naming convention, in many screens, of the vendor as a Trading Partner.

The main change is the new representation of the suppliers in the Trading Community Architecture (TCA), which involves changes to the database model and includes other entities such as customers, banks, and legal entities, among others. This involves having a single model in the database, improving ease of data maintenance, data consistency, address validation, integrated enrichment capabilities (including Dun & Bradstreet), and important data-librarian functions and processes.

These suppliers or Trading Partners are uniquely identified by a supplier number (which can contain characters and numbers) and are associated with any number of supplier sites. A site is basically an address from which the supplier conducts some or all of its business. Sites are classified as Purchasing sites, Request for Quote (RFQ) Only sites, and—most important for Payables—Payment sites. A Payment site (shown in Figure 5-5) is where you send payment for an invoice. You cannot enter an invoice for a supplier site that is not defined as a Payment site. The supplier master tables

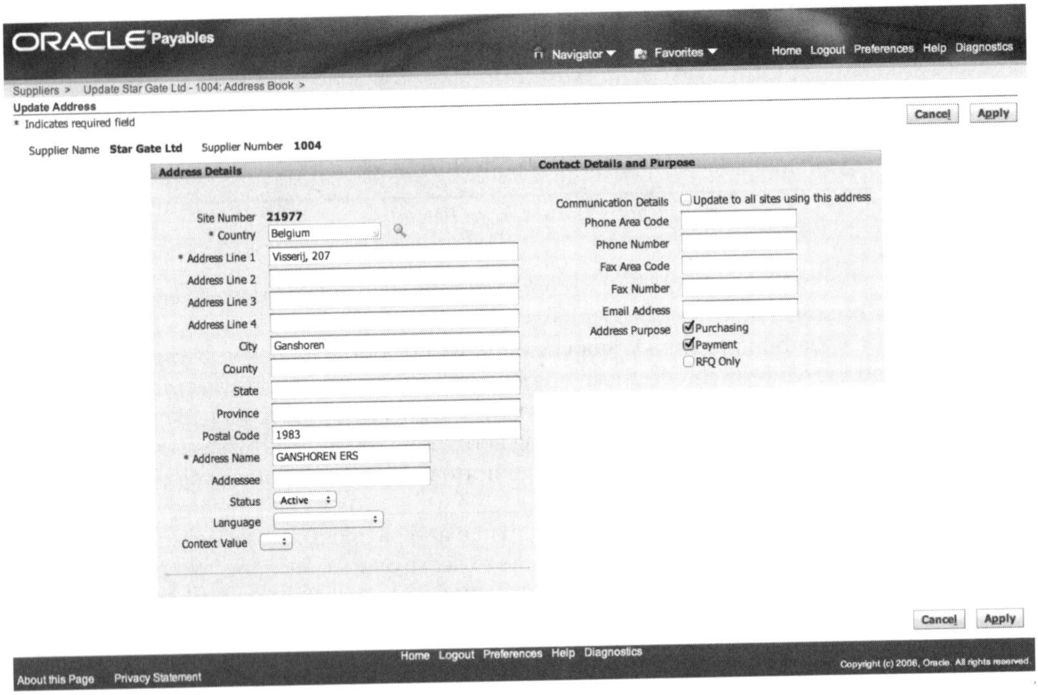

FIGURE 5-5. *Vendor site defined as a Purchasing and Payment site*

(often termed *vendor master tables* at the database level) are shared with Purchasing. Chapter 10 addresses the considerations involved in converting supplier information when you go live with Oracle EBS.

A schematic diagram of the supplier master tables is shown in Figure 5-6. Only the most important fields have been shown here; many more exist. Defaults are held at supplier and supplier-site level to speed up invoice entry. Incidentally, defaults are also held in the Payables Options form; these defaults are used when you define a new supplier. The defaults held at supplier level are used when you create a new site. The defaults at site level are used when you create a new invoice.

If you enable the Use Multiple Supplier Banks Payables option, you can enter your suppliers' bank-account information in the Banks window and then assign bank accounts to your suppliers and supplier sites. If you do not enable this option, you can continue to enter a single bank for each supplier or supplier site in the Suppliers and Supplier Sites windows.

CAUTION
The defaults held at supplier level are used when you create a new site. The defaults at site level are used when you create a new invoice. This arrangement might become confusing if you change the supplier's bank details at the supplier level and then pay an invoice for that supplier. When you create an electronic payment, the system will upload the bank details from the site level, which will show the original, unchanged bank details.

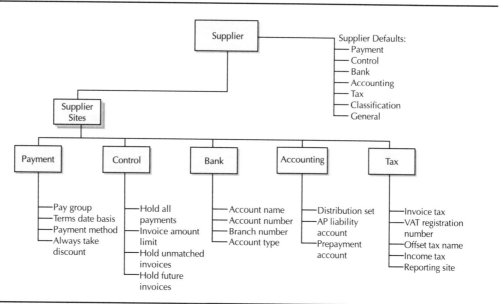

FIGURE 5-6.   *Schematic diagram of supplier master tables*

The Supplier Account

Each supplier in the supplier database has an account. The account is a record of all the transactions (such as invoices, prepayments, debit memos, and payments or payment reversals) that affect that supplier. The supplier accounts have little to do with the accounts stored in Oracle General Ledger or the Accounting Flexfield. The supplier account balance is calculated as follows:

>   *Inv* (invoices for this customer)
>
>   + *DM* (debit memos)
>
>   + *CM* (credit memos)
>
>   − *Pre* (prepayments)
>
>   − *Pay* (payments)
>
>   + *Refund* (refunds)
>
>   = Resulting Account Balance.

You can view the supplier's account balance on paper by running the Invoice Aging Report, which can be submitted for a single supplier. Alternatively, the Accounts Payable Trial Balance Report shows the account balance separately and in total for all suppliers. A snapshot of the supplier's account is available online from the Find Invoices window. Choose the Calculate Balance Owed button to see how much you owe a supplier and how many unpaid invoices you have in the system for that supplier.

Accounting Methods

Oracle Payables leverages SLA to define a primary and an optional secondary accounting method. The accounting method determines the number and nature of the journal entries Payables creates when transactions are transferred to General Ledger. There are three available accounting methods:

- **Cash** When you purchase an item, you recognize the expense (or, if it is a fixed asset, the increase in asset value) when you have paid for the item. You post only payments to General Ledger, not liability information for invoices. The payment distributions typically debit an expense (or asset) account and credit the cash or cash-clearing account.

- **Accrual** When you purchase an item, you recognize the expense (or, if it is a fixed asset, the increase in asset value) when you receive an invoice from the supplier. At that point you also record a liability to pay the invoice. You post accounting distributions for both invoices and payments. The invoice distributions generally debit an expense (or asset) account and credit a liability account.

- **Combined** You maintain one set of books for cash accounting and another for accrual accounting. You choose which will be your primary set of books and which will be your secondary set of books. Invoice distributions are recorded in your accrual set of books, and payment distributions are recorded in both your cash and your accrual set.

Accrual-basis accounting is used most often. The remainder of this chapter assumes that accrual-basis accounting is being used.

CAUTION
Once you have posted transactions, you cannot change your primary accounting method. To make such a change, you would have to define a new Accounts Payable organization and start over.

Accounting Entries for Payables Transactions

The introduction of SLA into Oracle Payables involves a change in how accounting is performed, compared to releases prior to Release 12. It introduces accounting events in Payables that are defined as transactions that have an accounting impact. A high-level overview of the process used to create subledger journal entries can be defined in three steps:

1. The Accounting Method Builder (AMB) tool is used to create and modify subledger application accounting definitions. In conjunction with these application accounting definitions, the Accounting Program uses the transaction-objects data to create subledger journal entries. For example, if an application accounting definition specifies that the Trading Partner name should appear in the description of a subledger journal-entry line, then the Trading Partner name is taken from the data provided by the transaction objects.

2. When transactions are committed in a subledger, accounting events are captured and stored in the Financial Services Accounting Hub. The Accounting Program identifies all accounting events eligible to be processed. For each of these events, the transaction-objects process provides the Accounting Program with transaction-objects data (source information). These are the contextual data of the transaction, such as amounts and GL dates.

3. When the Accounting Program is run, application accounting definitions and accounting transaction-objects data are applied to transactions to create subledger journal entries.

Subsequently, these entries can be summarized and transferred to General Ledger. Other activities, such as adjusting invoices, creating expense reports, and processing prepayments, also trigger accounting transactions.

In Oracle Subledger Accounting, as explained in Chapter 4, accounting events are categorized into event types. Event types are grouped into event classes that in turn are grouped into event entities. The overall grouping of these components is called an event model. The Oracle Payables accounting-event model is predefined by default and includes each Payables transaction type (event class) and its life cycle. It is important that the user responsible for the accounting within your organization understand the accounting-event model for Payables, because it classifies the accounting events—which is how the Subledger Accounting is created. The most relevant event classes and types for Payables are summarized in Table 5-4.

An event entity enables Oracle Subledger Accounting to handle the accounting for similar business events in a consistent manner. The event entities in Payables are invoices and payments.

The following sections describe the accounting entries that are generated for different transactions entered in Payables. In addition, there is an explanation of how Oracle Financials assigns account codes to the various accounting entries. During posting, entries are created as journal lines and batches; then they are placed in the GL_INTERFACE table, ready to be imported into Oracle General Ledger. Be aware that although transactions in Oracle Payables update the supplier's account within Payables immediately, they impact GL account balances only after you have run the Payables transfer process and posted the resulting journal within Oracle General Ledger.

Prepayments

A prepayment is a payment of a certain amount before you have received an invoice from the supplier. A prepayment could be sent with the purchase order as a deposit for goods or services. When you apply the prepayment to an invoice, you reduce the amount due on the invoice.

Event Class	Event Types
Standard Invoices	Standard Invoice Cancelled
	Standard Invoice Created
	Standard Invoice Distributed
	Standard Invoice Frozen
	Standard Invoice Reversed
	Standard Invoice Tax Holds Released
	Standard Invoice Tax Distributions Overridden
	Standard Invoice Redistributed
	Standard Invoice Unfrozen
	Standard Invoice Updated
	Standard Invoice Validated
Payments	Manual Payment Adjusted
	Payment Adjusted
	Payment Cancelled
	Payment Created

TABLE 5-4. *Some Payables Event Classes and Types for Subledger Accounting*

For prepayments, Payables creates distributions that debit your prepayment account and credit the supplier's liability account. Following are the journal lines that would be generated by a $20 prepayment.

Account	Derivation of the Accounting Flexfield	Debit	Credit
Liability	Defaulted from the supplier site; can be overwritten during invoice entry.		$20
Prepayment (asset)	Defaulted from the supplier site; otherwise entered during invoice entry.	$20	

Invoices

An invoice increases the supplier's account balance by the invoice amount. Invoices are entered in Oracle Payables either through the Invoice Workbench window or through the Invoice Open Interface (imported), where you are required to choose an expense (asset) and tax account for each invoice line. Once the invoice is completed, the corresponding journal entries will be posted to General Ledger in the next GL transfer. Following are the entries that would be created if an invoice amount of $235 were entered.

Account	Derivation of the Accounting Flexfield	Debit	Credit
Liability	Defaulted from the supplier site; can be overwritten during invoice entry.		$235
Expense or asset	Can be defaulted from the purchase order; otherwise, entered during invoice entry.	$200	
Tax	Defaulted from the Tax Name setup; can be overwritten during invoice entry.	$35	

NOTE
There might be multiple expense (or asset) accounts on an invoice if the invoice contains many invoice distributions.

The nature of accounting transactions for an invoice depends on whether you have posted a liability for goods received and, consequently, whether you have used Oracle Purchasing to initiate the invoice. The invoice will trigger accounting transactions, the net result of which is a liability to pay the supplier and a debit distribution to stock, fixed asset, or expense, depending on the nature of the purchase. If the purchase order and receipt were processed in Oracle Purchasing, there will be a liability for goods received related to the purchase as well, and the liability for goods received will be replaced by an invoiced liability. Because it is not required to use Oracle Purchasing with Payables, this transaction might not always take place.

Credit Memos and Debit Memos

A memo decreases the supplier's account balance by the memo amount. Credit memos and debit memos both have the same effect from an accounting point of view: they reduce the amount that you owe the supplier. Both credit memos and debit memos are used to record a credit against an invoice for goods or services purchased. Credit and debit memos are netted with the original invoice at payment time, resulting in a payment being issued for the reduced amount. Reductions to invoice amounts are distinguished according to their origin, either received from the supplier or created internally.

- **Credit Memo**   A negative-amount invoice created by a supplier and sent to you to notify you of a credit.

- **Debit Memo**   A negative-amount invoice created by you and sent to a supplier to notify the supplier of a credit you are recording; usually sent with a note explaining the reason for the debit memo.

Although the distinction between these two types of transactions is a reasonable one, the terminology is counterintuitive and confusing. Both transactions post a debit entry to the supplier's liability account and should perhaps be more correctly called *external debit memo* and *internal debit memo*. External debit memos are called credit memos because, as far as the supplier is concerned, they are credit memos in the supplier's accounts. Once entered to Oracle Payables, there is no difference between credit memos and debit memos; both are processed in an identical fashion. In broad terms, their effect is the opposite of that of an invoice. Here is an example of entries that might be generated for a $47 credit memo and a $47 debit memo.

Account	Derivation of the Accounting Flexfield	Debit	Credit
Liability	Defaulted from the supplier site; can be overwritten during memo entry.	$47	
Expense or asset	Entered during memo entry or defaulted from the invoice if the memo is matched to an invoice during entry.		$40
Tax	Defaulted from the Tax Name setup; can be overwritten during invoice entry or defaulted from the invoice if the memo is matched to an invoice during entry.		$7

Payments

A payment decreases the supplier's account balance by the payment amount. Payments can be generated in a variety of ways, depending on the urgency of the situation and whether you want to computer-generate the payment document or initiate payment outside of the Financials system. The available methods are summarized in Table 5-5.

No matter how a payment is generated or entered into Oracle Payables, the postings it gives rise to when it is transferred to General Ledger are the same. It credits bank cash or cash clearing, and it debits the liability account associated with the invoice being paid. Paid invoices show a liability of zero. Following are sample journal-entry lines generated by a $235 payment.

Account	Derivation of the Accounting Flexfield	Debit	Credit
Liability	Taken from the invoices being paid.	$235	
Bank cash account	Derived from the bank associated with the chosen payment document.		$235

Method Used to Enter the Payment	Method Used to Generate the Payment	Advantage
Automatic, in a payment batch	Computer	Mass payment of all suppliers who are owed money
Manual, from the Payment Workbench	Check is handwritten or typed; bank transfer is initiated by wire.	Flexibility to record payments initiated and completed outside of Financials
Quick, from the Payment Workbench	Computer	Ability to make immediate payments when speed is important
Quick, from the Payment Manager	Computer	Convenience; most payment information is entered for you and you skip the invoice-selection step needed in the Payment Workbench

TABLE 5-5.   *Available Payment Methods*

Payments do not generate tax postings, even when the supplier invoice carries VAT or sales tax. For instance, if the preceding sample payment were based on the sample invoice entries described earlier, the two liability accounts would now be the same, and the balance on this account in General Ledger would be zero. The invoice would now be paid and there would no longer be a liability to that supplier, assuming that this were the only activity on this account. (In any real situation, there would be other supplier liabilities posted to the same GL account, and it would be unlikely that the account would balance to zero.)

Refunds

Refunds are accounted for as negative payments. Therefore, they credit liability and debit the bank cash account.

Account	Derivation of the Accounting Flexfield	Debit	Credit
Liability	Taken from the invoices being paid.	$235	
Bank cash account	Derived from the bank associated with the chosen payment document.		$235

Recoverable Tax

Oracle Payables can automatically account for recoverable and partially recoverable taxes. Tax regimes such as value-added tax in Europe force businesses to collect tax on the goods and services they provide and then reclaim the tax they paid to produce those goods and services. In some cases the tax paid is either not recoverable or only partially recoverable. For example, when a large proportion of your own sales are tax exempt, you can reclaim only a proportion of the tax you paid. You can reclaim or recover tax based on a variable recovery rate, record the taxes for which you are liable, and ensure that you are recovering all allowable taxes.

Integration with Other Financials Modules

This chapter has already discussed Payables integration with Oracle General Ledger and Oracle Cash Management in detail. Payables is integrated with several other Oracle modules to complete the flow of the procurement cycle and prevent duplicate data entry. This interaction and sharing of information is what enables Oracle EBS to be a full working suite instead of several stand-alone modules. Data and processes flow into Payables from other modules, then back out of Payables into still other modules.

Integration with Oracle Purchasing

Payables shares supplier information with Oracle Purchasing. You can enter a supplier in either application and use that information to create purchase orders in Purchasing and invoices in Payables. The two modules completely share the database tables in the TCA model for vendors. There is no duplication of data; any changes made to the supplier details in one module are immediately available for use in the other module.

Once you have created and approved purchase orders in Purchasing, you can match Payables invoices to one or more purchase-order shipments or purchase-order distributions. When you do this during invoice entry, Payables creates invoice distributions using the purchase-order distribution accounting information.

Although it has no logic to compute them, Payables can discharge payment obligations for amortized loans. When you must account separately for the principal and interest elements of loan payments, the standard approach is to generate the payment stream in another system, then load the Invoice interface table with appropriate distributions.

Lease payments, with an unchanging distribution, are easier to handle. Payables will accept and store future transactions, known as *recurring invoices*, to enter into the payment cycle as they are due.

Integration with Oracle Assets

If you check the Track as Asset box in the Invoice Workbench or the Quick Invoice, Payables transfers this invoice line distribution to Oracle Assets when you submit the Create Mass Additions for Oracle Assets Program. The distribution must be charged to a GL asset-type account and assigned to an asset category; by doing so you can create assets in Oracle Assets from the invoice-distribution information in Payables. The asset value and date placed in service are derived from the invoice information. The number of units comes from the purchase order.

Integration with Oracle Self-Service Web Applications

The Self-Service Applications allow users to view and update data from a Web browser. They often simplify these processes; for instance, in the case of Self-Service Expenses, employees are able to do their own data entry for expense reports. The information they enter online is entered directly into the AP_EXPENSE_REPORT_HEADERS and AP_EXPENSE_REPORT_LINES tables. Workflow ensures that these expense reports are approved and routed according to the business rules that you define. For example, you can set up Payables to require a justification for specific expense types (for example, entertainment). You also can use Payables to review, audit, adjust, and approve expense reports.

Integration with Oracle Receivables

Trading partners who have a reciprocal relationship with you (meaning that along with selling you goods or services, they also purchase goods or services from you) are considered both suppliers and customers. In the Oracle E-Business Suite, these are treated since Release 12 as separate entities, but are modeled as part of the TCA. If information regarding this type of trading partner needs updating in Oracle Financials, you will have to do so in two separate screens.

The Payables and Receivables Netting feature enables the automatic netting of Payables and Receivables transactions. You can predefine a netting agreement that incorporates the netting business rules and transaction criteria needed to run your tailored netting process. The netting process automatically creates the Payables payments and Receivables receipts required to clear a selected number of Payables and Receivables transactions.

TIP

In order to proceed with Payables and Receivables Netting you'll have to create a new netting bank account, define the bank account at the legal-entity level, and create a netting control account.

Integration with Oracle Projects

Project-related information can be entered in Payables during invoice entry at the header or distribution level. Oracle Projects also can be used to pass charges from suppliers through to customers, a process that is a recurring task in business. Many companies are explicitly in the consignment or brokerage businesses, and other companies pass along some of the costs of providing service. Oracle Projects identifies recoverable expenses at purchasing time, captures the payment transaction, and passes the expenses on to Receivables. It has extensive logic for applying markups, accruing and grouping recoverable expenses, and presenting such charges on an invoice. Oracle Projects is a major system unto itself, and usually it is not worth the effort of installing it simply to rebill recoverable expenses.

Instead, you can institute a simple, straightforward customization that will work with any release of the products. You can structure a Descriptive Flexfield (DFF) to capture the customer data, such as the order number, as you process either a purchase order in Purchasing or a supplier invoice in Payables. You then can write a script to populate the interface tables for import by Receivables's AutoInvoice process, and thereby create sales invoices for each rechargeable expense.

Integration with Oracle Property Manager

The Payables Open Interface Import program is used to import approved scheduled lease payments from Oracle Property Manager. Export the lease-payment information from Property Manager by using the Export Payments to Payables window in Property Manager. This loads the invoice information into the Oracle Payables Open Interface. To import this information into Payables and create Payables invoices, use the Source of Oracle Property Manager when you submit the Open Interface Invoice program.

Integration with Oracle Inventory

From the Payables Invoices window you can access the Oracle Inventory Movement Statistics window. Here you can record the needed data associated with the movement of goods.

Other Integration

There are additional processes that can conceivably be integrated with Payables, depending on your business needs. These processes can be incorporated into future releases of Payables; however, generally current need is not compelling. Transaction volumes typically are small enough that they can easily be processed manually.

Oracle Fixed Assets computes the obligation for property taxes. Oracle Payroll withholds money for income tax, insurance, retirement, and other outside payees. Other systems, such as those used to compute corporate income taxes, usually present the payment obligation in report format. A common approach for paying the taxes is to set up the taxing entity as a supplier, generate an invoice for the amount due, and let Payables generate the check.

The Oracle Payables Data Model

Oracle Payables maintains data in a large number of tables. The data can be categorized as either reference or transaction data. *Transaction data* refers to invoices, credit memos, adjustments, and payments—the data that make up the supplier's account. *Reference data* refers to supplier information, a large number of lookup codes, and static information. The purpose of this section is to describe the transaction tables and how the accounting data are stored and processed.

Figure 5-7 depicts the main Payables transaction tables and their relationships to one another. The transaction tables fall into two groups: the Invoice Group, which stores all the data entered through the Invoice Workbench, and the Payment Group, which corresponds to payments raised either through the Payment Workbench or by an automatic payment run.

AP_INVOICES table stores invoice header information; it has one row per invoice, credit memo, or debit memo. As you would expect, AP_INVOICES's table carries the VENDOR_ID and invoice AMOUNT. The invoice lines, including tax lines if there are any, are in a new table AP_INVOICE_LINES. Each distribution, in the table AP_INVOICE_DISTRIBUTIONS, carries an amount and an account-code combination ID. The table AP_PAYMENT_SCHEDULES holds one row per invoice unless the invoice is due to be paid in installments, in which case there will be one row per installment. Each installment is characterized by a due date and an amount.

The AP_CHECKS table holds payment documents, including checks, EFT payments, and wire transfers. There is one row per document; the table stores information about the supplier who

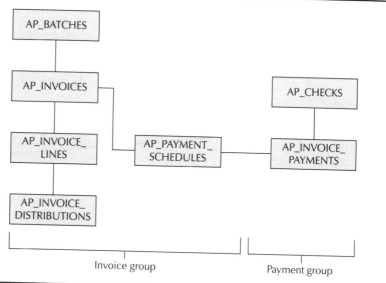

FIGURE 5-7. *The main Payables transaction tables*

received the payment (VENDOR_ID, VENDOR_NAME, and so on), the bank account that was drawn on (BANK_ACCOUNT_ID), and the AMOUNT and CHECK_DATE.

The AP_INVOICE_PAYMENTS table holds a permanent record of all payment documents that have been issued to pay invoices and invoice installments. If you need to account for a payment that is less than the total amount, you must create additional invoice installments in the AP_PAYMENT_ SCHEDULES table. Once a scheduled payment has been made, there is a one-to-one relationship between AP_INVOICE_PAYMENTS and AP_PAYMENT_SCHEDULES. The AP_INVOICE_PAYMENTS table holds the AMOUNT of the payment, the ACCOUNTING_DATE, and two account-code combination IDs. These are the asset account related to the bank account on which the payment is drawn and the accounts-payable liability account of the invoice that is being paid.

Technical Overview of the Automatic Payment Process

In Release 12, as described earlier, the payment process is initiated by a new PPR, which has four steps: Document Selection, Build Payments, Format Payments, and Confirm Payments. The Document Selection and Confirm Payments steps are handled by Oracle Payables, while Build Payments and Format Payments are handled by Oracle Payments (IBY).

Document Selection   This is the initial step, which happens when a PPR is submitted. A new record is created in AP_INV_SELECTION_CRITERIA_ALL populating a field consisting of the PPR name (CHECK_RUN_NAME).

At this stage the user does not have to specify the Payment Profile and Internal Bank Account for the payment. These parameters will be provided at a later stage.

The invoices are selected based on multiple criteria, such as due date, discount date, pay group, and others. This selection will populate the table AP_SELECTED_INVOICES_ALL; if the user wants to unselect invoices, those will be stored in AP_UNSELECTED_INVOICES_ALL. Once the selection has been made, the invoices are locked to prevent other check runs from selecting the same documents.

Build Payments   During this step, three main processes will occur, starting with the population of the IBY_PAY_SERVICE_REQUEST table. The first step is the Internal Bank Account/Payment Process Profile Assignment. If the PPR already has a bank account and payment profile assigned to it, this process will just assign those to all the documents. If the values are not provided, Oracle Payments will attempt to default the values; if they cannot be found, it might display a status of "Information Required."

During the second step, document validation, Oracle Payments validates all the documents based on payment method and then payment format.

In the third and final step, all the validated documents are grouped into proposed payments based on the grouping rules. These records are inserted into IBY_PAYMENTS_ALL, which holds the payment information for the selected documents. The build program then updates the IBY_DOCS_PAYABLE_ALL table with the PAYMENT_ID and FORMATTING_PAYMENT_ID values that corresponding to the payment that pays the document.

Format Payments   The Format Payments step has two options when a PPR is submitted: an automatic payment instruction or a standard request submission, in which the application waits for the payment instruction from the user. The table that stores the payment instruction information is IBY_PAYMENT_INSTRUCTIONS_ALL.

Once the instruction has been confirmed, the format processing occurs.

1. Payables numbers the payments.
2. Payables creates an XML extract message.
3. Payables passes the extract in XML format to BI Publisher.
4. Oracle BI Publisher applies the format template.
5. BI Publisher formats and stores the output.
6. Oracle Payments then updates the status of the payment instruction and the payments. If successful, the status of payments and instruction is "Formatted."
7. Payments prints checks.

Confirm Payments   This final process happens in Oracle Payables and closes the payment process by recording the Print Status of the checks to confirm the payments. The following steps will happen sequentially:

1. Sequences and values are assigned.
2. Data are created in AP_CHECKS_ALL with appropriate data from IBY tables.
3. Data are inserted into AP_INVOICE_PAYMENTS_ALL for the corresponding checks.
4. AP_PAYMENT_SCHEDULES_ALL is updated for each document in the payment process to indicate the payment details and status.
5. The documents paid in this PPR are released by clearing the CHECKRUN_ID column on the payment schedules.
6. AP_INVOICES_ALL is updated to show payment status.
7. Data are deleted from the tables AP_SELECTED_INVOICES_ALL and AP_UNSELECTED_INVOICES_ALL.

Technical Overview of General Ledger Interface

Transaction records that give rise to accounting events will record the essentials of the financial information: a currency, an amount, a date, and a corresponding code-combination ID. For invoices, credit memos, and debit memos, the two relevant tables are AP_INVOICES and AP_INVOICE_DISTRIBUTIONS. In accounting terms, the total supplier liability is held in AP_INVOICES and the expense, asset, or tax distributions are found in AP_INVOICE_DISTRIBUTIONS. For payments, AP_SELECTED_INVOICE_CHECKS carries both the bank-account code combination and the accounts-payable liability-account code combination.

There are two ways to create accounting entries for Payables accounting events:

- Submit the Create Accounting program.
- Create an online accounting entry for a single transaction or batch.

The Create Accounting program is useful when creating accounting entries for multiple transactions. It can help to determine errors when you cannot create accounting entries online. In both options you can create accounting in Draft Mode that will present the accounting results before the final accounting or Final Mode.

The Transfer Journal Entries to General Ledger program and the Journal Import program will create the final accounting in Oracle General Ledger. The Transfer Journal Entries to General Ledger program lets the user select how to transfer the information: in either summary or detail. If you transfer in summary, Journal Import creates summary journals. If you transfer in detail and submit Journal Import from General Ledger, then you can choose to submit Journal Import in either summary or detail.

The Transfer Journal Entries to General Ledger program transfers data from the Payables table for accounting-entry lines (AP_AE_LINES_ALL) to the GL interface table (GL_INTERFACE).

Journal Import then transfers data from the GL interface to GL tables including the GL table for journal-entry lines (GL_JE_LINES) and the GL Import References table (GL_IMPORT_REFERENCES).

Conclusion

The payables system is responsible for the payment of trade creditors. It is the last link in the supply chain. The importance of an effective payables system derives from its key position both in traditional cost control and in management accounting. Two trends in commerce are making payables even more central to a business: the growing dominance of supply-chain management in manufacturing industries and the gradual shift of commerce away from a static, supplier-customer model to an open, global, networked economy in which trade is initiated on the Web and conducted by electronic commerce. As both of these trends strengthen, Oracle Payables will prove an invaluable core application.

CHAPTER
6

Oracle Receivables

racle Receivables is a full-function accounts-receivable (AR) system that allows you to manage your customer base and invoice and payment processes effectively. Effective customer management is achieved through its sophisticated data model, user-defined correspondence, online memo pad for tracking customer interactions, and comprehensive reports. Powerful cash application tools and strong invoicing controls allow accurate processing of high transaction volumes with minimal manual data entry. In addition to supporting every Oracle module that generates customer-payment obligations—notably Order Management, Projects, and Customer Service—its open design supports non-Oracle systems and customer extensions within the Oracle product line.

Oracle Receivables and Your AR Business Processes

Most companies' policy is to take on new customers only after their account-receivable department completes a satisfactory credit check. They also review established customers' credit in the process of accepting new orders. After the order has been satisfied, the receivables function includes invoicing customers for sales and following up to ensure prompt payment. The Oracle Receivables workflow is shown schematically in Figure 6-1.

Companies sell their products either for cash (immediate payment in the form of a check, credit card, or notes and coins) or as invoiced sales on credit with specific payment terms. Invoiced sales create a *receivable* in the balance sheet (General Ledger), which represents the money due to the company. The financial health of a company depends on keeping track of its customers and ensuring prompt collection of the money owed.

Receivables produces three legal documents to notify customers of their obligations:

- An *invoice* is usually sent shortly after a sale has been made. It states the obligation and provides details.

- A *statement* is a summary of the transactions over a period of time. It shows all open transactions. It may also show payments made within the period.

- A *dunning notice* informs the customer of past-due obligations.

Companies can choose not to use both statements and dunning notices. However, because they are legal documents, most companies retain the ability to produce all three document types in a paper format. In the interests of efficiency, however, many now send invoices by EDI, fax, or e-mail, and they may agree with established customers to rely exclusively on electronic documents.

The customer can choose to pay the invoice in a variety of ways: by check or bank transfer, direct debit, or bill of exchange. When payment is received from the customer, you apply the cash to the customer account, reducing the amount owed and generating journals in GL. A partial payment will reduce the amount owed, but not to zero. The amount owed by each customer can be seen on the Aging Report and Account Details window.

Company policy establishes the steps to take when customers do not pay on time. Companies need to balance the risk of losing customers against the risk of being unable to collect debt. The process usually begins with a telephone contact, followed by dunning letters. Statements of a customer's account can be sent out periodically, and as a last resort, if the debt remains overdue, finance charges may be applied and the account may be referred to a debt-collection agency or the company's legal department.

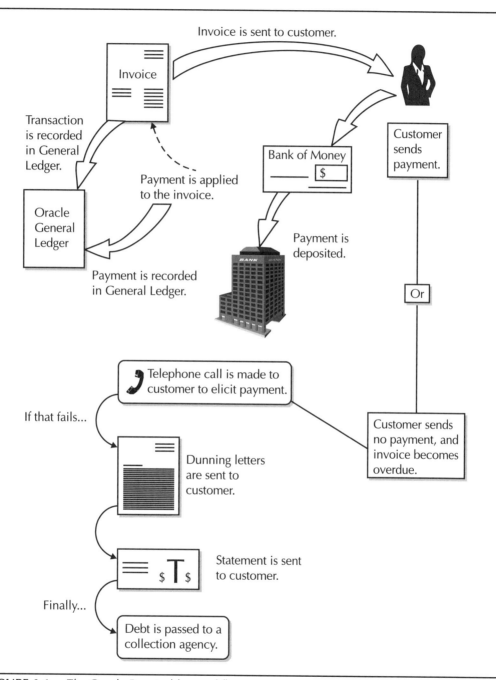

FIGURE 6-1. *The Oracle Receivables workflow*

iReceivables

Using iReceivables, customers get immediate secure access to their account details over the Internet. They can print copies of invoices or credit memos, dispute bills they disagree with, and review their current account balance. Access is available to anyone with a Web browser and the appropriate security details. All transactions accessible via iReceivables are protected by Oracle's standard application security as well as user authentication and the ability to define and limit user access. Oracle has enhanced iReceivables in Release 12 with new functionality and also enriched the user interface for a better user experience, providing high performance.

Creating and Managing the Customer Database

Accurate and up-to-date customer information is essential to many aspects of running a business: marketing, sales, and customer services, as well as receivables. The Oracle Receivables customer repository can hold and share an extensive range of customer data. Oracle's sophisticated data model, called Trading Community Architecture (TCA), supports the needs of customer relationship management and handles the many forms in which a company can relate to its customers. In fact, as detailed in Chapter 12, Oracle Receivables now uses only a simplified view of the total schema, which in Release 12 includes other entities such as vendors, banks, and legal entities. The terminology and structure of the customer model visible to a Receivables user is unchanged from prior releases. The description that follows of the customer model is as customer data appear to a user. A new user interface was created for Release 12 in Oracle Application Framework (OAF); that means that if you had extensions on the old Oracle Form for Customers, you will have to review the extensions and switch them into OAF.

In Receivables, customers are associated with any number of site addresses, and each address can have a list of contact names and telephone numbers. Each site can be designated for one or more functions, such as marketing, shipping, invoicing, and collections. You can designate contacts for each function. There is a Customer Type attribute that can be set to either "organization" or "person." The customer searches you perform, and the customer information you enter, vary depending on whether the customer is an organization or a person. The overall customer data scheme is shown in Figure 6-2.

As customers are entered into the system, each is given a customer profile. The customer profile is an essential concept in Receivables. Default data values are taken from the profile during data entry, and many of Receivables's reports use customer profiles as a selection parameter.

Customer Profiles

Customer profiles let you categorize customers into groups, known as *profile classes*. A profile class reflects several characteristics of each customer, including credit rating, payment terms, whether finance charges are calculated on overdue invoices, whether statements or dunning letters are sent, and the customer's credit limit.

While you should maintain a small, manageable number of profile classes, it is clear that each customer is unique, and a specific customer may not necessarily fit exactly into any one of the profile classes that you have set up. You can alter the characteristics of a particular customer's profile without modifying the profile for all the customers in the same profile class. When you make a change to a customer's profile and save your changes, the system asks you whether you want to apply the change to only this customer's profile, to all customers in the same profile class, or to all customers in the profile class who have not had their profile individually modified.

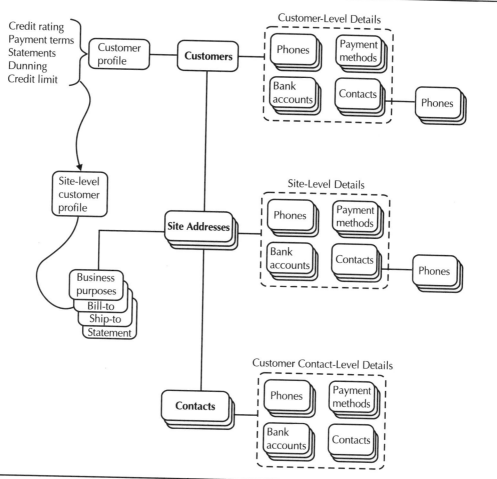

FIGURE 6-2. *Customer data*

Customer profiles can be assigned at the level of either the customer or the bill-to address. Because the credit limit is defined in the profile, it can make a significant difference whether you monitor credit compliance at the level of the customer or the bill-to address. Although it is not enforced by the structure of Oracle Receivables, which is completely flexible, it makes organizational sense to establish a policy of tracking customer profiles at one level or the other.

The Customer Account

Oracle Receivables enables you to find customer information using the customer name or various other criteria. Using the Find Customers window, you can look up a customer on the basis of a phone number or view all customers within a given city, state, county, province, country, postal code, or area code. Each customer in the customer database has an account.

The customer accounts in Oracle Receivables are not the same as the financial accounts stored in Oracle General Ledger. The customer account is a record of all the transactions—invoices, receipts, and so forth—that affect that particular customer. The account balance is calculated as follows:

> *Inv* (invoices for this customer)
>
> + *DM* (debit memos)
>
> + *Adj* (positive adjustments)
>
> − *CM* (credit memos)
>
> − *Rec* (receipts)
>
> − *Adj* (negative adjustments)
>
> = *Resulting Account Balance.*

You can view the customer account on paper by running a statement or the Aging Report, or you can view it online with the Account Details window, as shown in Figure 6-3.

Transactions in Receivables have an impact both on the customer account and on the financial accounts in General Ledger. There is no straightforward connection between the effects of a transaction on the customer account and on the postings to financial accounts. Some transactions, like the application of an on-account receipt to an invoice, have no effect on the customer's balance but do alter financial-account balances in the GL.

Business Purposes

Business Purposes identify the role played by each of the customer sites. A customer could be ordering goods or services from many different offices, for delivery at several other locations. Customers can ask for the invoice to be sent to any address they choose. Some have centralized accounts payable and offer one invoice address irrespective of the delivery address, while others want invoices sent to the relevant local administrative office. Credit control, statements, and

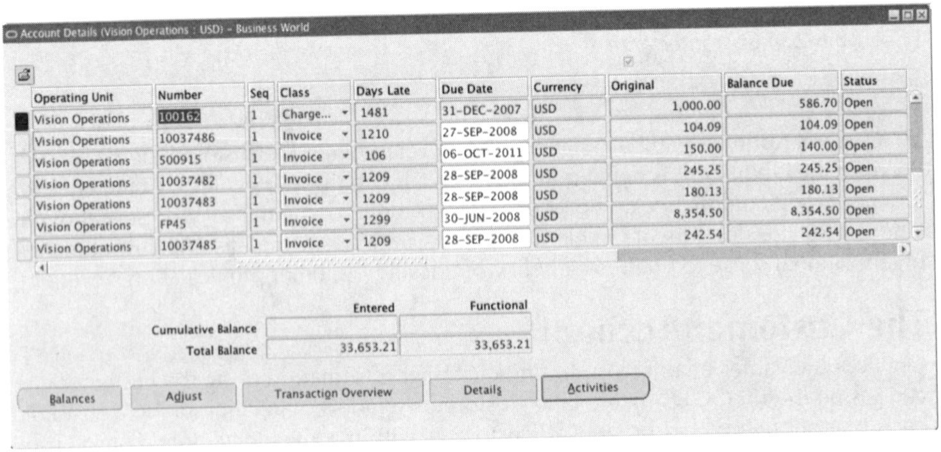

Operating Unit	Number	Seq	Class	Days Late	Due Date	Currency	Original	Balance Due	Status
Vision Operations	100162	1	Charge...	1481	31-DEC-2007	USD	1,000.00	586.70	Open
Vision Operations	10037486	1	Invoice	1210	27-SEP-2008	USD	104.09	104.09	Open
Vision Operations	500915	1	Invoice	106	06-OCT-2011	USD	150.00	140.00	Open
Vision Operations	10037482	1	Invoice	1209	28-SEP-2008	USD	245.25	245.25	Open
Vision Operations	10037483	1	Invoice	1209	28-SEP-2008	USD	180.13	180.13	Open
Vision Operations	FP45	1	Invoice	1299	30-JUN-2008	USD	8,354.50	8,354.50	Open
Vision Operations	10037485	1	Invoice	1209	28-SEP-2008	USD	242.54	242.54	Open

	Entered	Functional
Cumulative Balance		
Total Balance	33,653.21	33,653.21

Balances   Adjust   Transaction Overview   Details   Activities

FIGURE 6-3. *Account Details window*

dunning letters can all be produced at the level of either the customer level or the bill-to address. Oracle Receivables provides, among others, the following predefined Business Purposes:

- **Bill-to**   The address to which invoices are sent.
- **Ship-to**   The address to which goods or services are delivered.
- **Statement**   The address to which statements and dunning letters are sent.
- **Marketing**   The address to which marketing materials are sent.
- **Dunning**   The address to which reminder letters are sent.

Receivables offers the flexibility to define additional Business Purposes to assign your customer addresses. One typical use would be to carry additional addresses for shipping information, such as the freight forwarder, customs agent, systems integrator, or in-country agent for an overseas shipment.

Transactions

Transactions, such as invoices, credit memos, receipts, and adjustments, are entered against a customer account. Over time, the customer's account evolves as new invoices are raised, credits and receipts are applied, and adjustments are made. Paid invoices and their corresponding receipts are of no long-term interest in Receivables and disappear from the Aging Reports. However, each transaction will be posted to General Ledger and will have contributed to the receivables, revenue, tax, and cash balances.

Invoices

Each invoice lists what the customer has received and explains how the total invoice amount, which may include tax and freight charges, has been calculated. The standard printed invoice, while containing all the pertinent data, is commonly customized to alter the format and layout. Law dictates that certain data must appear on invoices—in the United Kingdom, a company's invoice must state the company name, its registration number, and its registered address. Tax requirements have to be observed, and certain customers may demand that you quote the purchase-order number on their sales invoice.

Invoices are entered in Oracle Receivables through the Transactions window or the Transactions Summary window, or they are imported through the AutoInvoice open interface. You must provide the customer number and bill-to address, the receivables account and freight account, and revenue and tax accounts for each invoice line. An invoice increases the customer's account balance by the invoice amount. Here are the accounting entries that would be created for a sample invoice amount of $125:

Account	Derivation of the Accounting Flexfield	Debit	Credit
Receivables	Defaulted from the transaction type; can be overwritten during invoice entry	$125	
Revenue	Defaulted from the item; can be overwritten during invoice entry		$100
Tax	Defaulted from the specified tax rate; can be overwritten during invoice entry		$15
Freight	Defaulted from the transaction type; can be overwritten during invoice entry		$10

TIP
You can use batch controls to ensure accurate data entry, and you can enter sales-credit information to compensate the salesperson. This accounting entry is the standard provided by Oracle Receivables and can be modified using the Subledger Accounting functionality, as seen in Chapter 4.

An invoice often has multiple revenue-account lines. For example, an invoice from a hardware reseller for a PC server and installation shows two separate lines on the invoice: the PC sale and the installation service are posted to different revenue accounts.

Recurring Invoices

Recurring invoices are useful for situations where you regularly deliver the same goods or services to a customer. You might need to bill for insurance premiums, a maintenance contract, or lease repayments once a quarter for three years, but you do not want to manually create a new invoice every time. You can quickly create a group of invoices that share the same characteristics using either the Transactions Summary window or the Copy Transactions window. All of the dates for the copied invoices (for example, transaction date, GL date, and due dates) are determined using a copy rule. You may specify any one of the following copy rules: Annually, Semiannually, Quarterly, Monthly, Bimonthly, Weekly, Single Copy, or Days.

The Single Copy rule creates one copy of your model invoice for the day you enter in the First Invoice Date field. The Days rule creates invoices at a fixed interval of days, based on the number of days you specify.

Tax Considerations

Tax is relevant in Oracle Receivables, as companies must bill their customers for tax on sales, collect the tax, and then pay the tax to the local fiscal authority. Oracle Receivables is integrated with the new Oracle E-Business Tax application, which allows the organization to have a single repository of transactions for global business insight, centralized rules applied to transactions to manage globally by reducing risk, and automation of tax processes on transactions to improve operational efficiency.

The Oracle Receivables setup is made completely on the Oracle E-Business Tax module. You can set up Receivables to use one of two basic types of tax: value-added tax (VAT) or sales tax. VAT is a fixed percentage rate and is primarily used in the European Union and parts of Asia (for example, Thailand and Singapore), while sales tax is levied in the United States and is based on the location of the customer. Both types of tax can be set up so that specific items or customers are exempt.

The tight integration between Oracle Receivables and Oracle E-Business Tax also provides a flexible tax-defaulting hierarchy that you can define at the system-options level. This hierarchy determines the order in which Receivables derives a default tax rate when you manually enter transactions or import them using AutoInvoice. Order Management shares the E-Business Tax configuration and has the capability to display taxes in customer quotes and orders. You have a choice of letting Receivables compute taxes or importing tax lines through the AutoInvoice import function. You can see in Figure 6-4 the default rules for tax calculation.

Value-Added Tax

VAT is imposed on the value added to goods or services at each stage of their supply. The VAT charged on a customer invoice is referred to as *output tax*; it is calculated by multiplying the

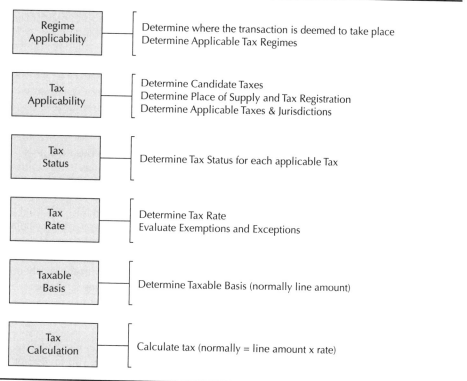

FIGURE 6-4. *Default rules for tax calculation*

value of the goods or services by the appropriate tax rates. Any VAT paid on a vendor invoice is referred to as *input tax*. The amount due each period, monthly or quarterly, is calculated as follows:

Amount Due = Total Output Tax – Total Input Tax.

VAT becomes due when the sale is invoiced, irrespective of whether the customer has paid the invoice or not. Depending on the payment terms you offer your customers, you may well end up paying the VAT to the tax authority before you have collected the money from your customer. Such sales have a short-term negative impact on your cash flow; you pay the government before the customer pays you. There is a provision to reclaim VAT if the customer persists in not paying and the debt is written off.

Whereas Oracle Receivables provides standard reports showing the total tax charged, the liability to pay the tax to the fiscal authority is not created in the Oracle Payables module. This liability should be entered manually in Payables, a task that is normally done at fixed intervals— that is, one Payables invoice is created monthly or quarterly.

VAT rates vary from country to country, and each country has exceptions for exempted sales— for example, zero rated and low rated. The rate is based on the type of goods sold, with low rates frequently targeted to support social ends. In the United Kingom, for example, books are zero rated, while children's clothing and heating fuel are low rated. You use the Tax Regimes, Taxes and Tax Jurisdictions window to define appropriate tax codes and rates in Oracle E-Business Tax.

Sales Tax

Sales tax is based on the location of the customer receiving your goods or services. The calculation of sales tax is based on the state, county, and city components of the customer's addresses and the tax rates assigned to each of these components. You can override any tax rate through customer and product exemptions, and you can compile periodic sales-tax returns using the U.S. Sales Tax Report. Many jurisdictions have different sales-tax rates for different types of goods as well. Groceries, for instance, are often taxed lower than other consumer goods, and to encourage the use of natural gas, the state of Maryland exempts gas appliances from sales tax.

Oracle provides a full schema for tax-rate structures. However, the process of keeping it populated with accurate data is truly onerous. It involves all kinds of taxing jurisdictions: states, counties, cities, and special jurisdictions. US companies that do business on a national basis usually find it well worth the price to subscribe to a service such as Vertex to obtain automatic updates. These vendors usually provide scripts to automatically post their data to the Oracle tables.

Taxware and Vertex Integration   A tax-vendor extension integrates external tax-calculation programs with Oracle EBS. This extension lets you perform complex tax calculations while retaining the full power of E-Business Tax and Receivables to create and store all other tax data. The tax-information service should be one of the super users' earliest considerations. It typically takes about three months to select a vendor and install the software. Usually it is best to use a single service for property-tax rates (fixed assets), payroll-tax rates (HR/payroll), and sales-tax rates (AR). It is not a secondary matter.

Tax Reporting Ledger

Taxable transactions are accounted for in Oracle Receivables, Oracle Payables, and Oracle General Ledger following country-specific rules that you define. The Tax Reporting Ledger, a functionality of Oracle E-Business Tax, provides a single tax-reporting solution to satisfy complex global tax requirements on sales and purchases by summarizing tax information from these applications and storing it in an interface table. You can then use a reporting tool, such as Oracle Reports, Oracle's Report Exchange (RXi), or BI Publisher to specify the information to include in your report and print it in a suitable format.

Revenue Recognition

Accounts receivable is designed to be the single source of revenue transactions for the General Ledger. It simplifies the accounting. A single set of numbers—amounts actually invoiced and received—drives the General Ledger, sales analysis, sales compensation, and marketing compensation.

Receivables may be set up with an aggressive revenue-recognition policy—billing orders as they are accepted and accruing revenue upon billing—or it may be set up with a conservative policy of not recognizing revenue until the money is in hand. Some businesses call for even greater restraint. Universities collect tuition in advance of delivering instruction, and a landlord may collect rents well in advance. The wisest policy for companies is to debit advance payments to a separate account, to be journaled into earnings at the time services are actually delivered.

A new feature of Release 12 is the inclusion of event-based revenue management. Receivables can automatically evaluate your invoices to determine whether to immediately recognize revenue or temporarily defer revenue to an unearned-revenue account. Revenue is subsequently recognized depending on certain events, such as customer acceptance or receipt of payment.

Receivables makes these automatic revenue recognition or deferral decisions based on your organization's established revenue policy and the existence of any revenue contingencies on the invoice line. Revenue contingencies are terms and conditions in a sales contract or order that prevent revenue from being immediately recognized, based on strict revenue-recognition requirements mandated by US GAAP and international accounting standards. Typical contingencies that can delay revenue recognition are fiscal-funding clauses (for government contracts), cancellation clauses, customer-acceptance clauses, customer creditworthiness, nonstandard payment terms, and nonstandard refund policies.

The extent of the revenue deferral, and subsequent timing of revenue recognition, depends on the revenue contingency. Each contingency has its own related contingency-removal event; for example, if the customer is not creditworthy, then you can recognize revenue on that customer's invoice only in the amount of any payments received. Or if the customer was offered a nonstandard refund policy on an order, then you can recognize revenue on that customer's invoice only after the refund policy has expired.

Receivables predefines a set of revenue contingencies that you can use with event-based revenue management. You cannot update or delete these predefined revenue contingencies, but you can create your own. Receivables also predefines contingency-removal events, which you cannot delete or modify.

Automatic Account Generation

Assigning Accounting Flexfield combinations to financial transactions is a major function of all the Financials packages. The assignments must be accurate for the financial reports to be meaningful. However, keying a multisegment Accounting Flexfield for every transaction would be incredibly time consuming. AutoAccounting is a mechanism for generating default Accounting Flexfields—for revenue, receivables, freight, and tax—based on other parameters associated with the invoice you are entering.

Oracle Receivables predefines setup in Oracle Subledger Accounting so that the Create Accounting program accepts the default accounts that AutoAccounting derives without change. However, you can optionally define your own accounting rules in Subledger Accounting to create accounting that meets your business requirements. In Subledger Accounting, you use the Accounting Methods Builder (AMB) to define the way subledger transactions are accounted. To do this, you create and modify subledger journal-line setups and application accounting definitions. These definitions define the journal entries that enable an organization to meet specific fiscal, regulatory, and analytical requirements. These definitions are then grouped into subledger accounting methods and assigned collectively to a ledger. See Chapter 4 for more information.

AutoAccounting and Account Generator are not interchangeable. Account Generator cannot be used in place of AutoAccounting in Receivables to generate default accounts for revenue, receivables, freight, and tax.

Account Generator is used in Receivables, but for the isolated task of assigning the correct balancing-segment value for finance charges and realized exchange-rate gain-and-loss accounts. For example, if you assess finance charges for an invoice that has a receivables account with a company-segment value of 20, and the balancing segment of your finance-charges account is 10, then Account Generator sets the balancing segment of the finance-charges account to 20. The finance-charges account and the exchange-rate gain-and-loss accounts are set up only once, in the System Options form, so it is not possible to set up different accounts for each company that is handled within one installation of Receivables.

While setting up AutoAccounting, you indicate whether to use a constant value for each of the account segments or to look up the value from another table. AutoAccounting can be directed to look up values in any of the following tables:

- Salesrep,
- Transaction Types,
- Standard Lines,
- Taxes, or
- Customer Bill-to Site.

Here are some examples of standard AutoAccounting table assignments:

Account to Be Generated	Table
Receivables	Transaction Types
Revenue	Standard Lines
Freight	Transaction Types
Tax	Taxes

Remember that each segment of each account can be generated according to a different rule. This is useful, for example, if you want the natural account for revenue to default from the Standard Line but you want the cost center to be derived from the Salesrep.

Oftentimes a company accounts for revenue based on the geographic location of its customers, or it uses lines of business to segment customers. In the first case, we would set up a "Sales Region" segment in the Accounting Flexfield, allocate appropriate region codes to the default revenue accounts in the customer bill-to site setup, and instruct AutoAccounting to use the customer bill-to site for the derivation of the Sales Region segment in the Revenue Accounting Flexfield combination. In the second situation we would define a "Line of Business" segment in the Accounting Flexfield. In addition, AutoAccounting can create accounts based on the warehouse and inventory item you specify when you enter transaction lines.

Limitations of AutoAccounting

AutoAccounting is limited to deriving the Accounting Flexfield values for revenue, receivables, freight, tax, and the less frequently used AutoInvoice clearing, unbilled-receivable, and unearned-revenue accounts. These are all the accounts required during invoice or debit-memo entry. You cannot use AutoAccounting, or Account Generator for that matter, to generate accounts used during receipt entry, such as unapplied receipt, unidentified, on-account, and so forth. In these scenarios, the customization of Subledger Accounting setup to create your own accounting is needed; then Subledger Accounting overwrites the default accounts, or individual segments of accounts, that AutoAccounting originally derived during transaction entry. However, you must still set up AutoAccounting.

Printing Transactions

The following four programs are provided as standard for printing accounts-receivable transactions:

- **RAXINV_SEL**   Prints selected invoices, based on parameters you enter.
- **RAXINV_NEW**   Prints all transactions that have not been printed previously.
- **RAXINV_BATCH**   Prints a batch of invoices.
- **RAXINV_ADJ**   Prints transaction adjustments.

The standard layout is intended to be a template, as no single invoice layout would satisfy all companies that use Oracle E-Business Suite. You will likely need to alter the layout to fit your organization's specific needs. Since the standard report already prints nearly all data that are relevant for these transactions, your customization will probably include removing elements you do not wish to print and changing the layout. Be sure to use a programmer experienced with BI Publisher and Oracle Reports, as the data model and functioning of the software are quite extensive.

TIP

Oracle has moved many Receivables reports into BI Publisher by creating templates and using Oracle Reports as the data source. This enhancement makes it easier to modify the look and feel of the BI Publisher templates by adding your company logo and changing fonts to meet the company's needs.

Transaction Printing Views

For more refined control over which transactions to print, and over the format and layout, you should build your own print program (using any SQL-compliant reporting tool) to assemble the data using the Transaction Printing Views provided in Oracle Receivables and format it as required. Those views are

- **AR_INVOICE_HEADER_V**   Retrieves the transaction-header information.
- **AR_INVOICE_ADJ_V**   Retrieves the details for an adjustment.
- **AR_INVOICE_LINES_V**   Retrieves the line items of each transaction.
- **AR_INVOICE_TAX_SUMMARY_V**   Retrieves tax-summary information.
- **AR_INVOICE_COMMITMENT_INFO_V**   Retrieves commitment information.
- **AR_INVOICE_TOTALS_V**   Retrieves the total amounts for all lines and associated charges for a transaction (for example, lines, freight, and tax).
- **AR_INVOICE_INSTALLMENTS_V**   Retrieves installment information for transactions with multiple installments.
- **AR_INVOICE_COUNT_TERMS_V**   Retrieves the number of terms for a transaction (that is, transactions assigned to split payment terms).

The Receivables Print Invoices programs (RAXINV_SEL, RAXINV_NEW, RAXINV_ADJ and RAXINV_BATCH) print selected transactions based on parameters that you specify at run time, such as transaction class, transaction type, or a range of transaction numbers. The Transaction Printing Views select all Receivables transaction information from the database. The programmer filters the pertinent information by entering parameters in the WHERE clause for each SQL statement in their custom report.

TIP
Developers should use the Transaction Printing Views rather than the Receivables base tables, because changes in the underlying table structures from one release to the next will be hidden in the views; the views join complex data structures correctly—reducing the debug and testing time.

Debit Memos

Oracle Receivables handles *debit memos* (DMs) the same way it handles invoices. A debit memo increases the customer's account balance by the debit-memo amount and is used to bill a customer for additional charges in relation to a previously invoiced sale. There is a whole range of situations where such additional billing is necessary. A debit memo would be handy, for example, when the freight cost has been left off of an original invoice because it was not known at the time of the earlier billing.

A debit memo is a legal document that you send to the customer, and it must comply with the same legal and tax requirements that are relevant for an invoice.

Credit Memos

A *credit memo* (CM) is used to alert a customer to a reduction in charges related to a previously invoiced sale. An on-account credit memo is a reduction in charges that is not tied to a specific previous invoice. There are many situations in which this is necessary. You create a credit memo when a discount is given at the end of a quarter for customers who have bought in excess of a discount threshold. Whenever possible, however, it is important to tie the CM back to the original invoice. That way you can assure that the proper GL accounts will be hit, and you will maintain a better audit trail. A credit memo is also a legal document that you need to send to the customer.

A credit memo decreases the customer's account balance by the credit-memo amount. Here are the accounting entries that would be created if a sample credit memo of $11.50 were applied to an invoice:

Account	Derivation of the Accounting Flexfield	Debit	Credit
Receivables	Same receivables account as the related invoice		$11.50
Revenue	Same revenue account(s) as the related invoice	$10.00	
Tax	Same tax account(s) as the related invoice	$1.50	

Here are the accounting entries that would be created for a sample on-account credit memo of the same amount:

Account	Derivation of the Accounting Flexfield	Debit	Credit
Receivables	Defaulted from the transaction type; can be overwritten during CM entry		$11.50
Revenue	Defaulted from the item; can be overwritten during CM entry	$10.00	
Tax	Defaulted from the tax rate; can be overwritten during CM entry	$1.50	

Receipts

Credit cards, checks, bank transfers, direct debits, and all other forms of payment received from a customer are collectively called receipts. A receipt is entered via the Receipts Workbench or the Receipts Summary window, or it is imported through the AutoLockbox interface. The acid test that all receipts have been correctly accounted for is the bank reconciliation.

Accounting for receipts depends on the extent to which the receipts can be identified. The ideal situation occurs when the customer clearly identifies the invoice or invoices being paid. Such receipts are entered and applied to the respective invoices, and no further research is necessary. These receipts are called *applied receipts*. When it is not possible to establish the invoice numbers, but it is clear which customer has sent the money, the receipt is entered and applied to the customer's account but not to specific transactions in the account. Such receipts are referred to as *on-account* or *unapplied*. Lastly, if it is not possible to determine which customer made the payment, the receipt is entered without specifying a customer account. These are known as *unidentified receipts*. The quantity, in terms of both number and value, of unidentified and on-account receipts should be kept to a minimum. With unidentified receipts, a continued effort is made to find the customer and record this in the system. On-account receipts are also researched to determine which invoices the customer had intended to pay, and then the receipts are applied to those transactions.

A new feature, the Line Level Cash Applications solution, was introduced in Release 12. It allows the application of receipts to specific transaction items such as individual lines, groups of lines, or tax or freight buckets. From the Receipts Workbench, you are able to choose whether to allocate cash to the entire transaction or to apply amounts against specific items according to the customer remittance.

Enter Receipt Actions

Oracle Receivables provides a powerful feature that lets you create item-level actions while you enter and apply your receipts. With item-level actions you can create adjustments, issue charge-backs, and apply receipts to credit memos and on-account credits to reduce the customer's balance.

Applied Receipts

An applied receipt decreases the customer's account balance by the applied amount. Here are the journal entries that would be generated by a sample applied receipt for $125:

Account	Derivation of the Accounting Flexfield	Debit	Credit
Cash or Bank Asset account	Taken from the payment method; cannot be overwritten during entry	$125	
Receivables	Taken from the receivables account(s) of the applied invoice(s).		$125

On-Account or Unapplied Receipts

An on-account receipt decreases the customer's account balance by the receipt amount. Here are the journal entries that would be generated by a sample on-account receipt for $125:

Account	Derivation of the Accounting Flexfield	Debit	Credit
Cash or Bank Asset account	Taken from the payment method; cannot be overwritten during entry	$125	
Unapplied	Taken from the payment method; cannot be overwritten during entry		$125

Unidentified Receipts

Unidentified receipts have no effect on customer account balances because the customer is not known.

Until the customer is known, the possibility remains that an unidentified receipt was sent in error and that the money will have to be paid back. This is represented by showing a liability in the balance sheet equal to the value of the unidentified receipt. Here are the journal entries that would be generated by a sample unidentified receipt for $125:

Account	Derivation of the Accounting Flexfield	Debit	Credit
Cash or Bank Asset account	Taken from the payment method; cannot be overwritten during entry	$125	
Unidentified	Liability account taken from the payment method; cannot be overwritten during entry		$125

Receipt Reversals

Oracle Receivables lets you reverse receipts when your customer stops the check or when the receipt comes from an account with insufficient funds. You can also reverse a receipt if you want to re-enter and reapply the receipt to another debit item. To reverse a receipt, you can create either a standard reversal or a debit-memo reversal. When you create a standard reversal, Oracle Receivables automatically updates your General Ledger and reopens the invoices you closed with the original receipt. When you create a debit-memo reversal, all previous receipt activity remains unchanged, but the customer account is charged with another receivable.

Application of On-Account Receipts

Receipts that were on-account when they were entered should be applied to their invoices once it is clear which invoice the customer wants to pay. The Applications window can be used to apply a receipt to an invoice or several invoices—or any combination of invoices, debit memos, and credit memos that belong together.

The credit posting is always to the receivables account of the invoice that is being applied. The debit posting hits the account that was previously posted in credit. This ensures that once a receipt reaches its final resting state as fully applied, the postings generated are always the same: a debit to the cash or bank-asset account, and a credit to the receivables account of the applied invoice. Whichever route the receipt has taken through being unidentified or unapplied, the unidentified or unapplied account is debited to cancel the credit that was posted when the receipt was originally entered. Here are the journal entries that would be generated by a sample on-account receipt for $125:

Account	Derivation of the Accounting Flexfield	Debit	Credit
Receivables	Taken from the receivables account(s) of the applied invoice(s)		$125
Unapplied or Unidentified	Taken from the unapplied or unidentified account for the payment method; cannot be overwritten during entry	$125	

Miscellaneous Receipts

The term *miscellaneous receipt* refers to cash received in respect to revenue that has not been invoiced. Typically this is revenue such as investment income or bank interest. Miscellaneous receipts are accounted for on a cash basis; the revenue is recognized when the money is received. To enter a miscellaneous receipt, navigate to the Receipts window and choose the Miscellaneous receipt type. There is no need to enter a customer account for miscellaneous receipts. The accounting for miscellaneous receipts is determined by the payment method and receivables activity you choose from a list of values. You can enter any receivables activity that has previously been defined as a Miscellaneous Cash receipt type.

NOTE
An unidentified receipt should not be entered as miscellaneous simply on the grounds that the customer number does not need to be entered. If it is originally entered as a miscellaneous receipt, you will not be able to apply the unidentified receipt once you determine the customer and invoice number.

Here are the postings that would be generated by a sample miscellaneous receipt for $342:

Account	Derivation of the Accounting Flexfield	Debit	Credit
Cash or Bank Asset account	Taken from the payment method; cannot be overwritten during entry	$342	
Revenue	Taken from the receivables activity selected during entry; can be overwritten		$342

Automatic Receipts

Automatic receipts are either bills of exchange or direct debits. *Direct debits* are a method of payment in which the customer authorizes you to debit the amount due directly from the customer's own bank account. You do this by sending your bank a data file via the Internet, which the bank processes. *Bills of exchange* are processed in the same way as direct debits, except there is an extra authorization step. Before you debit your customer's bank account, you must notify the customer that you intend to take a certain amount in respect of certain invoices. Once the customer has provided authorization, you can debit the bank account in the same way as for direct debits. Bills of exchange are clearly distinguished from other Receivables transactions to help with management and tracking. Transaction numbering enables you to link bills of exchange to the associated invoices and debit memos. To a certain extent, bills of exchange and direct debits rely on trust; if you habitually take too much money, or take money before it is due from a customer's bank account, the customer or the bank will withdraw your authority to directly debit the account.

Credit-Card Receipts

The procedure for processing credit-card payments in Receivables is similar to the procedure for creating automatic receipts. By providing a creditcard number as payment—you will also need an expiry date, possibly the start date, and the cardholder's name—your customers are accepting that their credit-card issuer will be asked to transfer funds to your acquiring bank (or service provider who has agreed to process your credit-card transactions), and from there into your bank account as payment for their open debit items. Used in this way, credit-card payments are treated in the same way as direct debits or bills of exchange. The following steps are required to process credit-card payments in Receivables:

- ■ Flag transactions to be paid by credit card.
- ■ Create a batch of automatic receipts to close transactions flagged for credit-card payment.
- ■ Approve the automatic-receipts batch to reserve the payment amount from the cardholder's account.
- ■ Create and approve a remittance batch to request transfer of funds from the credit-card issuer to your bank.

Lately, companies selling products via e-commerce Web sites have driven the demand for online credit-card capture, authorization, and settlement. This is achieved using Oracle iPayment. The "shopping basket" and "checkout" sections of the Web site are coded by the Web developer. If the customer chooses to pay by credit card (or bank transfer), control is passed to iPayment, which obtains authorization of the credit-card details. iPayment conducts an electronic dialogue with the computers of an electronic payment partner, such as PayPal, VeriFone, or CheckFree. You may chose to partner with another payment provider (there are several, WorldPay being a well-known one), in which case you will need to develop customized HTTP messages that conform to the standards of that particular payment provider. The authorization, or failure, is passed back to the e-commerce application, where the checkout process can complete or fail politely.

Bank File Formats

The transfer of funds occurs when your bank processes the remittance data file you send to them. The format of the electronic file has to be agreed upon with your bank. Each country tends to have its own standard for bank files: the United States commonly uses a US Treasury Format; the United Kingdom uses BACS (Bank Automated Clearing System); Germany uses the Deutsche Bank

DTA (Datenträgeraustausch). Many more formats are in use around the world, and an increasing number of these are covered by Oracle's Globalizations.

Multiple-Invoice Applications

You must be able to create complex cash applications that involve many transactions and that have the capability to either fully or partially apply to each transaction. Oracle Receivables provides this ability and thus allows your staff to be more efficient. To apply customer receipts to a group of transactions at once, navigate to the Receipts window, query or enter the receipt to apply, and then click Mass Apply. The customer's open items appear in a window. To apply the receipt, check or uncheck the Apply box next to each transaction. The Applications window is shown in Figure 6-5.

Cross-Currency Receipts Application

Oracle Receivables allows you to apply a cash receipt in one currency against one or more invoices in different currencies. You can also apply multiple payments in any predefined currency to a single invoice. For example, you create an invoice in Canadian dollars (CAD) but your customer sends a receipt in euros (EUR) as payment. Using the remittance information provided by your customer, you can either fully or partially apply this receipt to the invoice.

Oracle Receivables automatically calculates the open balance on the invoice (if any) and the foreign-exchange gain or loss (FXGL) for this application

Application-Rule Sets

Oracle Receivables supports a user-defined hierarchy of payment-application rules. You can define a set of rules to control how a receipt is applied against invoice lines according to their type (for example, revenue line, tax, freight, or charges). Within each rule set, you can specify the exact order in which Receivables applies the payment. Alternatively, you can define how the

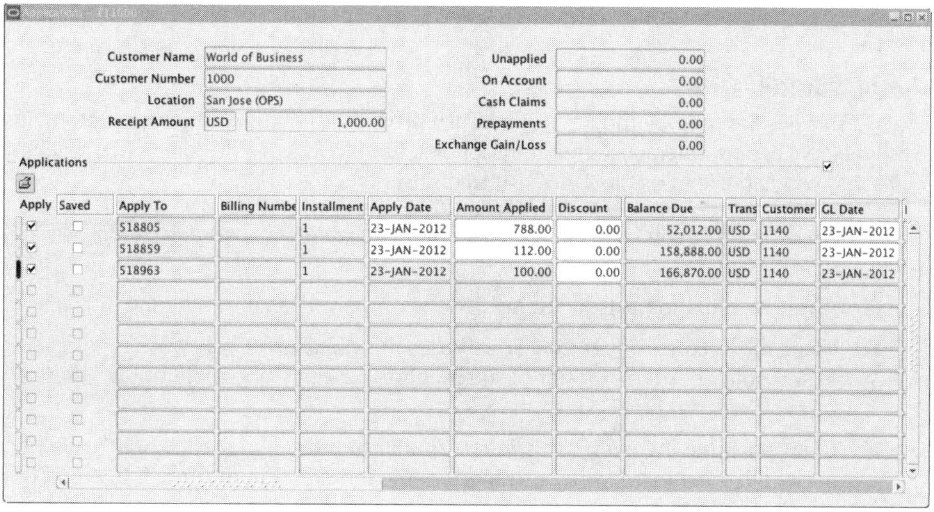

FIGURE 6-5. *The Applications window for applying receipts to multiple transactions*

receipt will be prorated among line types. The following application-rule sets are predefined in Receivables for use with manual receipt applications or the Post QuickCash program:

- **Line First – Tax After**   Applies payment to the open line amount, then the remaining payment amount to the associated tax amount.

- **Line First – Tax Prorate**   Applies a proportionate amount of the payment to the open line and the tax amount for each line.

- **Prorate All**   Applies a proportionate amount of the payment to each open amount (such as line, tax, freight, or charges) associated with a debit item.

QuickCash

QuickCash lets you enter your receipts quickly, with a minimum amount of information. QuickCash receipts are temporarily stored in two interim tables called AR_INTERIM_CASH_RECEIPTS and AR_INTERIM_CASH_RECEIPT_LINES. Batches of QuickCash receipts must be posted to transfer them from these interim tables to the regular receipt tables within Oracle Receivables. Posting QuickCash batches updates the customer-account balances and causes the receipts to appear on reports and inquiry forms within Oracle Receivables; it also realizes the applications specified during receipt entry. Once QuickCash batches have been posted, the relevant invoices will appear as closed in Oracle Receivables. The two interim cash-receipt tables are used by the AutoLockbox interface when receipts are imported from a bank file.

TIP
Because records are continually being inserted into and deleted from the two interim QuickCash tables, QuickCash online entry may slow down as the tables become fragmented. This may be a driving factor in setting your DBA's schedule to periodically rebuild these two tables, taking care to keep all the records in the tables at the time of the rebuild.

AutoCash Rules

AutoCash rules are used by the Post QuickCash program to determine how to automatically apply cash receipts against open customer transactions. Oracle Receivables offers five receipt-application rules that you can use to create AutoCash rule sets:

- **Apply oldest debit items first**   This rule matches receipts to debit items, starting with the oldest debit item first.

- **Apply receipts to past-due items**   Money received goes to overdue bills first.

- **Clear the account**   Post QuickCash uses this rule only if your customer's account balance exactly matches the amount of the receipt. If it does, the receipt is applied to all open transactions on the account.

- **Clear past-due invoices**   This rule is similar to the "clear the account" rule because it applies the receipt to your customer's debit and credit items only if the total of these items exactly matches the amount of this receipt. However, this rule applies the receipt only to items that are currently past due.

- **Clear past-due invoices grouped by payment term**   This rule is similar to the "clear past-due invoices" rule, but it first groups past-due invoices by their payment term, then uses the oldest transaction due date within the group as the group due date.

- **Match receipts with debit items**   This rule applies the receipt to a single invoice, debit memo, or charge-back that has a remaining amount due that is exactly equal to the receipt amount.

The rules you select affect the ease with which your receivables staff can apply cash and finance charges for your customers. For example, matching receipts to debit items tends to minimize the number of open items, making life easier for your accounting staff. On the other hand, a customer who just paid a recent bill might see finance charges for an old item that would not appear if the money had gone to the old item first.

It is well worth spending time on designing your AutoCash rule sets during the implementation of Oracle Receivables. The more applications that can be performed automatically, the less tedious work for your staff. In addition, fast and accurate application of cash dramatically reduces the number of payment inquiries from your customers.

Adjustments

Adjustments are alterations to debit items (invoices, debit memos, and charge-backs). You can separately adjust the tax, freight, lines, or receivables amount of a debit item, and the adjustments can be either positive or negative. You do not need to inform the customer about adjustments; they are internal corrections that do not materially affect the legal documents—invoices and debit memos—that have already been sent to the customer. Adjustments are commonly made for the following reasons:

- correcting a data-entry error,

- writing off a receivable item, and

- adjusting sales-revenue credit to your salespeople.

You create an adjustment in the Transactions Summary window by querying the transaction, selecting it, and then clicking the Adjust button.

Adjustments have to be approved. The person entering the adjustment can approve it, provided that the person's authorization limit exceeds the value of the adjustment; otherwise adjustments are authorized later by another user whose limit is sufficient. Unapproved adjustments do not get applied to the customer balance or transferred to General Ledger. The postings generated by an approved adjustment depend on what was adjusted—tax, freight, revenue lines, or receivables—and the contra account supplied by the user when the adjustment is entered. An unpaid invoice of $125 that was being written off as a bad debt would generate the postings shown here:

Account	Derivation of the Accounting Flexfield	Debit	Credit
Receivables	Taken from the receivables account of the adjusted invoice		$125
Adjustment	Taken from the receivables activity entered by the user; can be overridden	$125	

Writing Off Small Amounts During Receipt Entry

Often the receipt amount that the customer has paid does not exactly equal the invoice amount. This can result in either an underpayment or an overpayment. In the case of a substantial underpayment, the invoice is left open for the customer to pay the remainder. In the case of an overpayment, the difference is refunded to the customer. A common cause of overpayment is the customer paying the same invoice twice—such double payments should always be refunded.

If the overpayment or underpayment amount is small (in the subjective judgment of the person accounting for the receipt), the difference can be written off. Some common causes of small differences are listed here:

- The customer rounds the amount down to the nearest whole number.
- The customer remits the wrong amount by mistake.
- The customer pays a foreign-currency amount that does not exchange to the required amount of the invoice.
- A bank or correspondence bank has taken a handling fee for a bank transfer.

Experience shows that underpayments are more common than overpayments, so a degree of restraint should be instituted before underpayments are written off. However, there is a cost associated with chasing every last cent, and most companies accept that it is not economical to pursue small underpayments.

In Receivables, you handle these small differences by making adjustments and charge-backs against transactions to which you are applying a receipt. You create charge-backs and adjustments against each transaction, for positive or negative amounts, by clicking the Adjustment and Chargeback buttons from the Applications window.

Finance Charges

The Statement and Dunning Letter programs apply finance charges to past-due amounts. You set the finance percentages in each currency and give your rules for grace periods.

Finance charges are a frequent bargaining chip in collections and, as such, a frequent subject of adjustments. Many collectors will waive finance charges in exchange for prompt payment of past-due amounts. Setting up finance charges is an important aspect of setting up Oracle Receivables.

Commitments

A customer commitment takes the form of either a deposit or a guarantee. A *deposit commitment* occurs when the customer agrees to pay a deposit for goods that the customer has not ordered yet, while a *guarantee commitment* is a contractual guarantee of future purchases. Both of these are handled by Oracle. They give rise to unbilled-receivables and unearned-revenue account postings. Within Receivables, a separate commitment balance is maintained. Analogous to the account balance, it ebbs and flows according to customer commitments and transactions. The customer-commitment balance is available in several places within Receivables and is also available if you are using Oracle Order Management. You can see the balance for a particular commitment when entering an order (if you are using Order Management), a manual invoice, or a credit memo against a commitment, or by running the Commitment Balance Report. All transactions that reference a commitment or reference an invoice that references a commitment affect the balance of that commitment. The general formula for calculating the balance of a commitment at any given time is as follows:

> *Com* (original amount of commitment)
>
> − *Inv* (invoices against commitment)
>
> − *CMI* (credit memos that reference invoices that reference commitments)
>
> + *CMC* (credit memos against the commitment itself)
>
> = *Resulting Commitment Balance.*

If you were to enter a deposit of $1,000, Receivables would create the journal entry shown here:

Account	Derivation of the Accounting Flexfield	Debit	Credit
Receivables (deposit)	Derived using AutoAccounting structure	$1,000	
Unearned Revenue	Derived using AutoAccounting structure		$1,000

If you were entering an invoice against this deposit, Receivables might create these sample journal entries:

Account	Derivation of the Accounting Flexfield	Debit	Credit
Receivables (invoice)	Defaulted from the transaction type; can be overwritten during invoice entry	$1,100	
Revenue	Defaulted from the item; can be overwritten during invoice entry		$900
Tax (if you charge tax)	Defaulted from the tax rate; can be overwritten during invoice entry		$100
Freight (if you charge freight)	Defaulted from the transaction type; can be overwritten during invoice entry		$100
Receivables (deposit)	Taken from the commitment		$1,000
Unearned Revenue	Taken from the commitment	$1,000	

When you apply an invoice to a deposit, Receivables creates a receivable adjustment against the invoice. Receivables uses the account information you specified in your AutoAccounting structure. If cash were received against the preceding deposit, Receivables would create the journal entry shown here:

Account	Derivation of the Accounting Flexfield	Debit	Credit
Bank Cash account	Derived from the payment method	$1,000	
Receivables (deposit)	Taken from the commitment		$1,000

Finally, if you were to enter a guarantee, Receivables would create this journal entry:

Account	Derivation of the Accounting Flexfield	Debit	Credit
Unbilled Receivables	Derived using AutoAccounting structure	$1,000	
Unearned Revenue	Derived using AutoAccounting structure		$1,000

Entering an invoice against a guarantee and applying cash to a guarantee work in the same way as deposits; the receivables (deposit) account is replaced with the unbilled-receivables account.

Refunds to Customers

Customers who overpay an invoice, or pay one invoice twice, are due a refund. It is often easiest to simply absorb the overpayment as income if it is a small amount, but if customers demand refunds, as they will no doubt do for larger amounts, companies must be able to pay them. There are essentially three approaches for handling customer refunds:

- ■ Issue a manual check, record it in Receivables as a debit memo, and match the memo to the cash receipt.
- ■ Persuade the customer to leave the cash "on account" and apply it to the next open invoice.
- ■ Create cross-ledger postings to Oracle Payables, set the customer up as a supplier in Payables, and issue a check out of Payables in the normal way.

Which approach you choose will depend on considerations like the volume of refunds you have to administer and the impact on your bank reconciliation. The third option is more labor intensive, but it will make bank reconciliation a good deal easier, as all checks will be found in the same place. In order to create the cross-ledger postings, you will need to create a pair of transactions, one in Receivables and the other in Payables. Be sure to nominate a suitable cross-ledger clearing account to post through. Imagine starting off with an overpayment in Oracle Receivables. This would appear as follows in the customer Account Inquiry:

Receivables Transaction	Debit	Credit
Cash receipt		$12,000

The next step is to create a correlated pair of transactions, a debit memo in Receivables to clear the customer's account and a quasi-invoice in Payables to represent the fact that the customer (who must also be set up as a supplier) is owed $12,000. The Account Inquiry would now appear as follows:

Receivables Transaction	Debit	Credit
Cash receipt		$12,000
Debit memo	$12,000	
Payables Transactions	Debit	Credit
Invoice		$12,000

Finally, the Payables invoice would be picked up and paid in the normal way by Oracle Payables.

TIP

The combination of debit memo and invoice must be created in pairs. This requirement can be enforced by posting the contraposting of each through a clearing account. The clearing account should always show a zero balance.

Transfer to Doubtful Debt

Most companies track their overdue receivables diligently, requesting that customers provide full payment on the overdue amounts. Sometimes payment is unlikely, and the debt is classified as *doubtful*, meaning there is good reason to believe it will never be collected. Other times it will be written off completely as a bad debt. In Oracle Financials, handling bad debt is straightforward: you create an AR adjustment against the invoice, reducing the amount due on the invoice to zero, and then select an appropriate Bad Debt Write-Off expense account, to which you post the amount.

TIP

Set up a Bad Debt customer profile with a zero credit limit. Then, whenever you must write off a customer's invoices, immediately change his or her profile to "Bad Debt" to prevent further credit sales to that customer.

Doubtful debt, on the other hand, is somewhere between a healthy receivable and a bad-debt write-off. Doubtful-debt accounting—invoices remain open and show on the customer's account, no longer posting to the normal Trade Receivables account, but rather to a Doubtful Debt account— is hard to mimic in Oracle Financials. Some companies are content to change the customer profile to "Doubtful Debt Customer" and then use reports to track these customers. Doing this does not of course move the receivables from Trade Receivables to Doubtful Debt in General Ledger. One way to move the receivables to Doubtful Debt is to close the original invoice with a credit memo and enter a new debit memo for the customer with the Doubtful Debt receivables account. Manual controls must be put in place to ensure that the credit memo and debit memo are always created in pairs and that the same revenue account is used for both memos.

Customer Follow-Up

Collectors work constantly to collect debt promptly, to ensure that the customer-account balances in the system are up-to-date, and to chase past-due invoices. Oracle Receivables integrates with Oracle Advanced Collections to provide you with a complete collections-management solution. With this integration, all collections activities take place from within Advanced Collections.

Advanced Collections enables a simpler, more automated collections process flow for your users, yet also supports a more complex collections approach with many powerful features.

Customer Calls

The Interaction History window within Oracle Advance Collections is used to record the results of your conversations with customers. Customers may tell you that their invoice was wrong, that they dispute some of the charges, that they did not receive the goods, or that they have already sent payment for the invoice. You can enter follow-up actions on the basis of what you and your customer agree on. While you talk to the customer, you can quickly review all customer information and verify that the customer's record of the open transactions agrees with your record. It is good business practice to encourage a "one-stop" approach to customer service. That is, customer calls should be logged and the appropriate action determined at the time of the original telephone conversation. Any department that relies on written memos of the conversation or a procedure for passing action to other people within the organization is inherently inefficient, error prone, and slow to respond to customers.

Dunning Letters

Dunning letters are sent to remind customers of overdue invoices. Use dunning plans to manage your delinquencies if you utilize a simple collections process as part of your business practices. For example, if your collections user sends a letter to a customer regarding a delinquency and then follows up with a call if payment has not been received, you can use dunning plans. For complex collections processes, or multiple collections processes, you can use collections strategies.

When you use dunning plans, Oracle Advanced Collections selects delinquent customers and then—based on the oldest aging and the customer, account, bill-to, or delinquency score—automatically sends out the appropriate dunning correspondence. For each aging-bucket line, the system can send different dunning notices to different customers based on their scores.

Advanced Collections uses concurrent programs to execute the dunning process. Once you set up your dunning plans, you can schedule these programs to run automatically. It is recommended that you run dunning with the same frequency as your billing cycle. You must decide the data level for your dunning plan (customer, account, bill-to, or delinquency) and create a dunning plan before you can execute the concurrent programs for the dunning process.

Creating Dunning Plans

You can create dunning plans for each aging bucket created in Oracle Receivables. Each dunning plan is composed of one or more score ranges and correspondence templates associated with aging-bucket lines. For each aging-bucket line, you can send different dunning notices to customers with different scores.

After you select the scoring engine for the dunning plan, you can select a correspondence template for each aging-bucket line and optionally schedule a callback. Exclude any column of aging bucket by not adding, or removing, that aging-bucket row. Specify different ranges of scores for the same aging-bucket line and attach a letter to that range of scores.

You specify the data level at which to run dunning plans when you identify the level at which you do business with your customers in the Collections Questionnaire. This data level can be set at each operating level. Use the Define Operating Unit Collection Level page to define the collections for each operating level. The data level determines whether dunning notices are sent based on customers, accounts, bill-to locations, or delinquencies.

- **Customer level** Sends a single dunning notice detailing all delinquencies for a customer and optionally schedules a callback based on the customer score and the range specified in the dunning plan.

- **Account level** Sends one notice for every delinquent account and optionally schedules a callback based on the account score and range.

- **Bill-to level**   Sends one notice for every delinquent bill-to location and optionally schedules a callback based on the bill-to score and range.
- **Delinquency level**   Sends one notice for each delinquency that a customer has and optionally schedules a callback. Advanced Collections uses the transaction score to select the most appropriate configuration of dunning notice and callback.

In a dunning plan, you specify which correspondence template to use based on a score range for each aging-bucket line. You can have multiple score ranges for each aging-bucket line. Specify a correspondence template, delivery method, and optional callback for each range of scores.

If you used dunning functionality that was offered in a previous version of Receivables, then you can access those historical dunning letters by using the Dunning Letter Reprint – Historical Receivables Only program. This program reprints individual dunning letters that were created in earlier versions of Receivables, before the integration with Advanced Collections.

Before the integration with Oracle Advanced Collections was available, Receivables offered two dunning methods:

- **Days Overdue**   Letters were based on the total number of days that debit items were past due. This method generated letters for a specific customer based on a range of days overdue that you defined for each dunning letter set. Receivables considered the number of receipt grace days defined for a customer (if any) when calculating the number of days items were past due.
- **Staged Dunning**   Letters were based on the dunning levels of past-due debit items. This method let you send dunning letters based on the number of days since the last letter was sent, rather than the number of days that items were past due. For each dunning letter, you specified the minimum number of days that had to pass before Receivables could increment.

Dunning-Letter Customization

Oracle BI Publisher generates the dunning correspondence that you send to your delinquent customers. Advanced Collections provides seeded templates for correspondence, and you can create new templates to meet your business needs without programming.

You can send dunning correspondence as a letter, e-mail, or fax. Determine how many templates you need for your dunning plans. For example, a dunning plan could consist of the following:

- a polite reminder letter for a customer who usually pays promptly,
- an e-mail asking for payment for all past-due items, and
- a firmly worded letter demanding payment before legal action is taken.

Within the text you can embed field variables, which get interpreted and replaced with the appropriate information when the dunning letter is printed.

The integration between Oracle Advanced Payments and BI Publisher allows you to customize the letters without having a developer to code. You can see in Figure 6-6 how the template has to be uploaded into BI Publisher Administrator. Figure 6-7 shows how a prebuilt query can determine the set of customers that will be receiving the dunning letter.

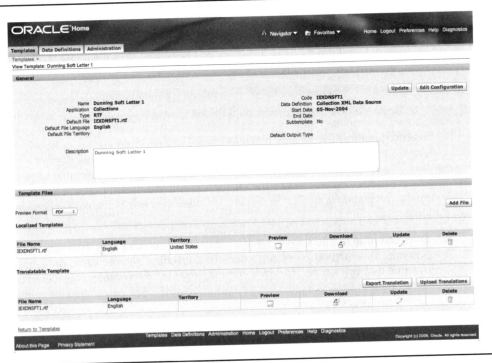

FIGURE 6-6. *BI Publisher templates for dunning letters*

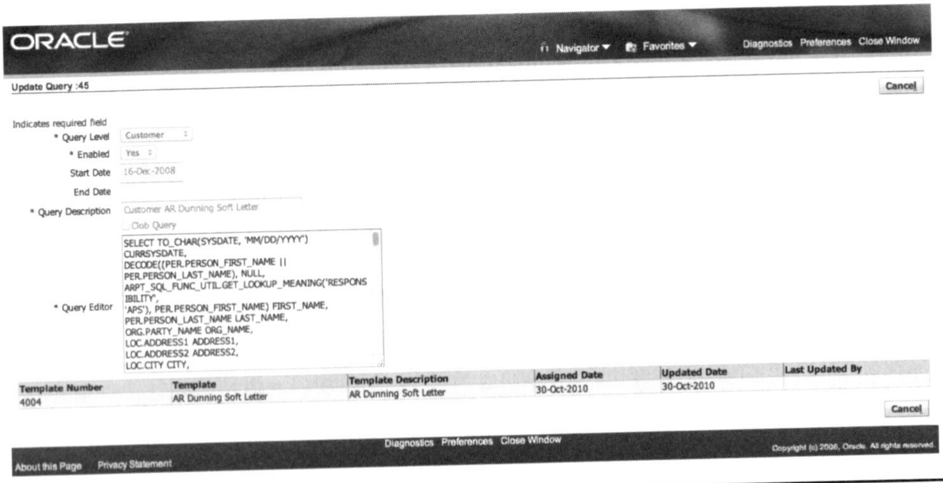

FIGURE 6-7. *Oracle Advanced Collections query template definition for dunning letters*

Statements

A customer statement shows all account activity in a particular time frame since the last statement. Statements are often sent as an alternative to dunning letters, although some companies send both statements and letters.

The statement differs from a dunning letter in that it shows all account activity (invoice, debit memo, charge-back, commitment, receipt, on-account credit, credit memo, and adjustment), not just the overdue items that appear on letters.

The following components of the statement can be customized:

- **Statement cycle**   Determines the frequency with which particular customers receive statements.

- **Statement-aging buckets**   Show how much of the debt is overdue and by how many days. The buckets are date ranges, such as 0–15 days, 16–30 days, and over 31 days, and can be set according to your preference.

- **Standard messages**   Printed text on the bottom of the statements.

You can define only one active statement address for each customer. Oracle Receivables produces one statement for the statement address. If you do not define a statement address, the system produces a statement for each different bill-to address on the customer's invoices. Because on-account or unapplied receipts are not associated with a site, they will not appear on any of the statements.

NOTE

In case you print statements for customers' locations by selecting the specific location, Oracle Receivables automatically selects the correct language in which to print the statements. If you are printing statements for all customers, you do not select the language in which the statements are generated: Receivables automatically prints them in the correct language as specified for each of your customers' statement locations.

Integration with Other Modules

Oracle Receivables integrates with several other modules in a way that reflects the fact that customers are at the center of your business. An overview of the integration is shown in Figure 6-8.

Receivables shares customer data with Order Management, Projects, and Service. The same customers are available in all modules, and they can be maintained from any modules. Updates made in any of the other modules are immediately available in Receivables.

Order Management

The shipping process within Order Management records products shipped to customers and updates the inventory. Shipment information, such as quantities, selling prices, payment terms, and transaction dates, are transferred into Receivables via the AutoInvoice interface. AutoInvoice creates the invoices for the sale in Oracle Receivables and accounts for the sales revenue. Invoices that originate in Order Management are printed in Receivables.

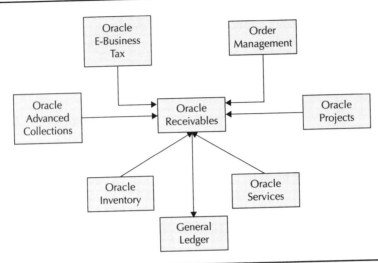

FIGURE 6-8. *Overview of Oracle Receivables's integration with other modules*

Creating Invoices from Orders

The AutoInvoice interface is a one-way process; there are no interfaces to post Receivables transactions back into Order Management or Projects. The sales records do not reflect discounts, write-offs, or other adjustments made in the collection process.

Set out your business processes to require that reversing transactions originate in the same place as the original transaction. Customer returns need to be entered into Order Management as RMAs (Return Material Agreements) to handle the inventory and sales compensation and other implications.

Despite the fact that it is a one-way passage, Receivables maintains somewhat informal links back to Order Management through the AutoInvoice open interface. AutoInvoice requires that you use the Transaction Flexfield, a 15-column Descriptive Flexfield (DFF), to uniquely identify invoice headers and lines in the import process. You do not have to specify all 15 segments, but must at minimum define the invoice or sales-order number and invoice-line number. Each line identifier has to be unique; each unique combination of header DFF segments represents one invoice.

The content of these columns is totally up to you. However, if you plan to use Oracle's standard invoicing programs, it is best to make the fields consistent with the fields in Oracle Order Management. The standard invoicing programs link back to the Sales Order tables through INTERFACE_LINE_ATTRIBUTE6, which is used for the sales-order line ID, and INTERFACE_LINE_ATTRIBUTE7, which is used for the picking line ID.

Projects

Projects invoices are imported into Receivables via the AutoInvoice interface. All the data Receivables needs to create invoices is supplied by Oracle Project Billing and are then processed by AutoInvoice to create invoices in Receivables. A further process then runs to tie back the invoices in Receivables to the original invoices in Project Billing. This process ensures that all the Project Billing invoice data are loaded successfully into Oracle Receivables. For successfully transferred invoices loaded into

Oracle Receivables, the tie-back process updates the project accounting data to reconcile invoices in Oracle Projects to Oracle Receivables. Rejected invoices remaining in the Oracle Receivable interface tables are updated so you can correct them and transfer them again to Oracle Receivables.

Inventory

Inventory items are necessary in Order Management to identify what has been sold. All Oracle products that reference inventory items do so by referencing the System Item Flexfield. The sales invoices imported from Order Management into Receivables also share the inventory information.

General Ledger

The GL transfer process reviews all new transactions in Receivables and creates the appropriate journal entries in Oracle General Ledger. These journal entries are imported to General Ledger via the Journal Import interface. The GL transfer process must be started by a human operator, as it cannot be automated. When it is submitted, the operator must choose to post in detail or summary mode. Summary mode produces one journal-entry line per distinct Accounting Flexfield combination. Detail mode creates at least one journal entry for each transaction in the posting submission. The operator should choose either one mode or the other, as a mix of summary and detail creates confusion for users. The benefits of each are discussed in Chapter 3.

Receivables Open Interfaces

Oracle Receivables provides four standard open interfaces:

- **AutoInvoice**   Used for loading invoices, debit memos, credit memos, and on-account credits.
- **AutoLockbox**   Used for loading bank receipts.
- **Customer**   Used for loading customers, addresses, contacts, telephones, and profiles.
- **Sales Tax Rate**   Used for loading tax-rate information.

The first interface, AutoInvoice, is used by other standard Oracle modules to import data into Receivables. But the other three are designed to allow you to build ongoing interfaces with external systems or to convert data initially.

AutoInvoice

The AutoInvoice interface lets you import invoice information from financial billing systems or invoices from Oracle Order Management and Oracle Project Billing. This interface is extremely powerful and complex, allowing the import of credit memos and debit memos as well as invoices. Because you can import only at the transaction level, grouping rules are used to determine which lines will be placed together on the same header-level transaction once they have been imported.

Oracle Receivables provides two windows to simplify the AutoInvoice process. The Interface Lines window displays all records in the interface tables that failed validation during AutoInvoice. The AutoInvoice Interface Exceptions window displays any errors associated with each failed record. Data-corrections tasks, which in the past had to be performed by technical staff with programming experience, can now be performed by business users without programming. The business users are the ones who typically know what values the data should take on, and these new windows bring the power to act closer to those who have the information to decide.

AutoLockbox

The AutoLockbox interface is used to load receipt information in Receivables. The primary purpose is to provide an automatic interface for receipts communicated to your organization electronically by your bank on a Lockbox tape or file. The AutoLockbox interface is quite general and can be coaxed into use for importing receipts from any external system, even if the data are not strictly a bank lockbox. You can define payment-application rules to control how the receipt is applied against line types (tax, freight, and invoice lines) and to predefine a sequence for closing transactions. You choose among a variety of rules, such as matching the oldest invoice first, matching on amount, or matching any user-defined hierarchy of rules. Application rules can be assigned to each transaction type, allowing you the flexibility to apply credit-card sales by exact match on amount while applying customer cash receipts on an oldest-first basis.

Customer Interface

The Customer interface lets you import new and update existing customer data from any feeder system and ensures that the data that you import are accurate and valid within Oracle Receivables. The Customer interface is essential during cutover for high-volume data conversion. The interface can be used on an ongoing basis when custom or third-party systems are the first to collect data on customers. Members of organizations such as labor unions are often customers in that they buy subscriptions or supplies. It is convenient to let the membership system collect member data and then import them into Oracle Financials as needed to support customer billing.

Sales Tax Rate Interface

The Sales Tax Rate interface lets you load sales-tax records—new locations and tax rates—into Oracle Receivables from a sales-tax feeder system. You insert records into the AR_TAX_INTERFACE table and then run the interface to validate and transfer the records to the underlying Receivables tables. The interface program lets you load one or more tax rates for the same location that cover different date ranges and postal codes. The records that you load into Receivables through the Sales Tax Rate interface update your existing sales-tax rates with the most current tax rates for each location. The Sales Tax Rate interface can adjust the active date range of existing tax rates as new tax rates are loaded into Receivables. Oracle Order Management also uses the Sales Tax Rate interface.

The Receivables Data Model

This section briefly describes the transactions in the Oracle Receivables module. The purpose of this section is to provide a high-level overview of the data structures and processing used by Oracle Receivables. Refer to this section if you are planning to write custom reports based on the Receivables data, or if you want to define alerts against actions or events triggered in Receivables. You should not plan to update or insert data, unless you do so via one of the standard interfaces.

The data model in Receivables has to cope with the conflicting needs of posting to General Ledger and providing customer-account balances. The transaction tables and their purposes are listed in Table 6-1.

At first sight the data model seems complex. It is based on a transaction view of Receivables, not an accounting or customer-reporting view.

The Receivables Aging Report, which is the central Receivables report, is large and complex, reflecting the fact that the AR_PAYMENT_SCHEDULES table is used for two distinct purposes:

Table	Purpose
AR_ADJUSTMENTS	Storing adjustments to invoices. The amount of each adjustment, the activity name, and the accounting information are held in this table. When an invoice is adjusted, the AMOUNT_DUE_REMAINING field in AR_PAYMENT_SCHEDULES table is updated.
AR_BATCHES	Grouping individual receipts; this table is optional. If it is used, a batch holds information about the batch source used, the bank account, and control totals.
AR_CASH_RECEIPT_HISTORY	Storing the current status of a receipt, receipt history, and receipt reversals. Receipts go through a cycle of steps that include confirmation, remittance, and clearance. Each step creates rows in this table. The CODE_COMBINATION_ID column stores the accounts that are debited and credited as part of these steps.
AR_CASH_RECEIPTS	Storing one row for each receipt. Invoice-related receipts have payment schedules and applications, while miscellaneous receipts (not related to the invoice) have distributions stored in AR_MISC_CASH_DISTRIBUTIONS.
AR_MISC_CASH_DISTRIBUTIONS	Storing all the accounting entries for miscellaneous cash applications. Miscellaneous cash is income that does not relate to a customer, such as stock dividends or bank interest.
AR_PAYMENT_SCHEDULES	Storing two types of records: invoice related and receipt related. The table contains one record for each invoice installment, or one row per receipt. Different transaction types are identified by the class, which can be invoice (INV), debit memo (DM), credit memo (CM), deposit (DEP), guarantee (GUAR), charge-back (CB), or receipt (PMT).
AR_RECEIVABLE_APPLICATIONS	Linking the receipts applied to invoices with the credit memos applied to invoices. This table holds the amount applied, the status, and the accounting distribution for the application.
RA_BATCHES	Storing information such as the batch source and control totals. Invoice batches are optional.
RA_CUST_TRX_LINE_GL_DIST	Storing all accounting records for a transaction. These are distinguished by the ACCOUNT_CLASS designation, which can be freight, receivable, revenue, tax, unearned revenue, unbilled receivable, or charges. The ARGLTP program uses GL_DATE and AMOUNT to post the correct amounts to GL for each transaction.
RA_CUST_TRX_LINE_SALESREPS	Storing sales-credit assignments for invoice lines.
RA_CUSTOMER_TRX	Storing header information for invoices, debit memos, credit memos, charge-backs, deposits, and guarantees. Each row includes general information, such as customer, transaction type, and printing instructions. This is a fundamental table in Receivables.
RA_CUSTOMER_TRX_LINES	Recording the quantities ordered, invoiced, and credited, as well as unit price. Each transaction line relates to just one transaction in RA_CUSTOMER_TRX. Lines may be either revenue-item lines, tax lines, or freight.

TABLE 6-1.   *The Transaction Tables in Oracle Receivables*

invoice installments and cash receipt payment schedules. It is a single table created from two subentities. The AR_PAYMENT_SCHEDULES table is used for many things, the most important of which is the record of the customer account. The Oracle Receivables module does not store the customer's account balance anywhere. Instead, the balance is calculated whenever it is needed. The sum of the AMOUNT_DUE_REMAINING for a customer for all confirmed payment schedules gives the current customer balance.

Technical Overview of the Application Process

Application is the process in which you match debit transactions with credit transactions. Debit transactions increase the customer's balance, while credit transactions decrease the customer's balance. Refer to Table 6-2 to see how transactions are classified into debit and credit transactions.

Application is the term for matching credit transactions to debit transactions in order to create a group of transactions that, taken together, have a zero effect on the customer's balance. The normal situation is for a receipt to be applied to an invoice. Both the receipt and the invoice are for the same amount, and together they cancel each other out. More complex applications involving multiple receipts, invoices, and credit memos can also be envisaged. The rule for determining a valid application is simple:

$$Inv + DM + Charge\text{-}backs + Deposits - Rec - CM = 0.$$

You can apply all or part of a receipt or on-account credit to a single debit item or to several debit items. When an invoice-related receipt is first entered, a row is created in the AR_RECEIVABLE_APPLICATIONS table with a status of "UNAPP" and an application type of "cash." Each subsequent application creates two new rows, one with APP status for the amount being applied, and another with UNAPP status for the negative of the amount being applied. When a credit memo is applied, a row is created in the AR_RECEIVABLE_APPLICATIONS table with a status of APP and application type of CM.

The rows in AR_RECEIVABLE_APPLICATIONS are a link between the transaction you are applying and the transaction to which you are applying. The PAYMENT_SCHEDULE_ID column links the receipt or credit memo to its payment schedule in the AR_PAYMENT_SCHEDULES table. The CASH_RECEIPT_ID column stores the receipt ID of receipt transactions, while the CUSTOMER_TRX_ID column stores the transaction ID for credit-memo transactions. The APPLIED_PAYMENT_SCHEDULE_ID and APPLIED_CUSTOMER_TRX_ID columns reference the transaction to which this record applies. The AR_RECEIVABLE_APPLICATIONS table resolves the many-to-many relationship between receipts and transactions as well as the many-to-many relationship between credit memos and invoices.

Debit Transactions	Credit Transactions
Invoices	Receipts
Debit memos	Credit memos
Charge-backs	
Deposits	

TABLE 6-2. *Classification of Transactions in Oracle Receivables*

On-Account Receipts and AR_RECEIVABLE_APPLICATIONS   On-account receipts are handled in a special way by Oracle Receivables. When an on-account receipt is entered, a row is created in AR_RECEIVABLE_APPLICATIONS in the usual way. However, there is no payment schedule to link the record to. On-account receipts do not relate to any particular transaction. There is a seeded shadow row in AR_PAYMENT_SCHEDULES identified by PAYMENT_SCHEDULE_ID = −1. All on-account receipts are linked to this shadow row.

TIP

If you write reports on receipt applications, do use an outer join to link the AR_PAYMENT_SCHEDULES table with the RA_CUSTOMER_TRX table. Doing so results in none of the on-account receipts being selected. There is no record in RA_CUSTOMER_TRX that corresponds to the PAYMENT_SCHEDULE_ID = −1 row in AR_PAYMENT_SCHEDULES.

Advanced Features

Receivables accounting periods control the dates that can be transacted, but do not affect how transactions appear in General Ledger. The GL date given for each transaction determines the GL period into which it falls. Invoices also have a transaction date, the date that appears on the top of the invoice. The transaction date determines when the invoice shows up in the customer account.

CAUTION

Because the transaction date is used for the customer account and the GL date is used for postings to General Ledger, you should ensure that these two dates are always identical; otherwise, customer balances in Receivables will not equal the accounts-receivable balance in General Ledger.

There are no account balances stored in Receivables. Account balances are calculated each time they are queried, either online or in reports. Online account balances are always as of today's date, whereas standard reports work on an as-of-date-supplied parameter. One advantage of Receivables working on a daily basis is that it is possible to request customer-account reports for any day of the year, not just for period-end balances. Without this capability, all statement and dunning cycles would be restricted to an accounting-period cycle.

Customer-account balances are not calculated at period end and brought forward to the next period. Oracle Receivables uses the same accounting periods that General Ledger uses, but it has no month-end process. Period statuses in Receivables can be opened and closed independently of General Ledger. A transaction cannot be entered unless the Receivables period is open. The period cannot be closed unless all transactions have been transferred to General Ledger.

The Customer Account and Balance Due

The following formula is used to calculate a customer's account balance at any point in time:

Inv + DM ± Adj − CM − Rec.

The calculation uses the original full amount of each transaction, whether it is an invoice, debit memo, credit memo, adjustment, or receipt. Throughout Oracle Receivables, you find another amount alongside the original amount; it is called the *balance due, outstanding amount,* or *amount remaining.* These three terms are synonymous. Look again at Figure 6-3, which shows the account details for the Business World customer. The rightmost column shows the balances due.

As noted earlier, accounts-receivable departments spend considerable time researching and applying receipts. They need a way of knowing when a transaction is complete. The balance due tells them when a transaction is fully applied: either the obligation has been paid in full or the credit has been totally applied to other obligations or refunded. There is another powerful reason for working with balances due rather than original amounts. If you replace the original amounts throughout the formula *Inv + DM ± Adj − CM − Rec* with the outstanding amount, the result does not change. Customer-account balances can be calculated from either the original amount or the outstanding amount of individual transactions.

Imagine a customer, Monolith Motor Company, which has two open invoices. One is for $5,537.50, the other for $1,170; the balance is $6,707.50. The balance due for both of these invoices is the same as their original amounts. Suppose that Monolith then sent us a check for $2,000. We might assign the receipt a reference, R1780, and enter it initially as unapplied. Here is how the customer account would then appear:

Number	Class	Original	Balance Due
10174	Invoice	$5,537.50	$5,537.50
10177	Invoice	$1,170.00	$1,170.00
R1780	Receipt	$2,000.00	$2,000.00
Monolith Motor Company Account Balance		$4,707.50	$4,707.50

The new account balance would be $4,707.50, which is the old balance minus $2,000. Note that the balance due for each transaction is the same as its original amount. If at some stage we established that the $2,000 receipt was intended to fully pay invoice 10177, and the remaining $830 to partially pay invoice 10174, we would enter the receipt applications in the Applications window. The customer account would then appear as shown here:

Number	Class	Original	Balance Due
10174	Invoice	$5,537.50	$4,707.50
10177	Invoice	$1,170.00	0
R1780	Receipt	$2,000.00	0
Monolith Motor Company Account Balance		$4,707.50	$4,707.50

Notice that none of the original amounts has changed; they never do. The receipt R1780 has been fully applied, the $2,000 has been "used up" paying invoices, and the balance due on the receipt is shown as zero. Invoice 10177 has been fully paid, which is reflected by the zero balance due. The remaining $830 has been used to partially pay invoice 10174, which is left with a balance due of $4,707.50. You have perhaps noticed that the account balance has not changed as a result of the receipt application; the sum of the original amounts is the same as the sum of the balance-due column. Applications are customer-account neutral.

Transactions with a balance due of zero are referred to as *closed*; otherwise, transactions are *open.* Closed transactions do not contribute to the customer balance. The work in a receivables

Increase Balance	Decrease Balance	Neutral
Invoice	Credit memo	Unidentified receipt
Debit memo	Applied and on-account receipts	Application of a receipt

TABLE 6-3.   *The Effect of Different Transactions*

department is directed towards reducing the balance due on all transactions to zero and closing each transaction. However, closed transactions can be reopened if, for example, an application is deleted (a check bounces) or a closed invoice is adjusted. Table 6-3 summarizes the effect of various receivables transactions on the customer's account balance.

Reconciliation

There are three types of reconciliation in addition to the bank reconciliation mentioned earlier. The types, which are distinguished according to what is being reconciled with what, are referred to generically as external reconciliation, internal reconciliation, and GL reconciliation.

- **External reconciliation**   The process of ensuring that all invoices have been correctly imported from feeder systems. The total revenue reported from your sales systems must equal the total revenue reported out of Receivables for any comparable time period.

- **Internal reconciliation**   The process of ensuring that the customer balance for each customer is the same irrespective of whether it is calculated using original amounts or outstanding amounts. Remember, the formula $Inv + DM \pm Adj - CM - Rec$ will give the same result whichever amount is chosen.

- **GL reconciliation**   The process of ensuring that the transactions in Receivables have been accounted for correctly and of verifying that the journal entries in General Ledger that have come from the subledger are all present and correct. A complete Receivables to General Ledger reconciliation is normally replaced by the reduced scope of a receivables "control" account reconciliation. That is, the subledger receivables total is reconciled to the Receivables accounts in General Ledger.

The timing of these reconciliations can be problematic. The logical sequence is to do the external reconciliation first, followed by the internal reconciliation, and then the GL reconciliation. If they are performed in some other order, any corrections you make will force you to repeat one of the previous reconciliations. For example, if you do the internal reconciliation first, before doing the external reconciliation, and then you identify an Order Management invoice that belongs in the period but has not been imported, you will have to import it into Receivables, and that will force you to repeat the internal reconciliation. Although the logical sequence is clear, the timing is not so obvious. It makes no sense to start the external reconciliation until the external feeder systems have completed their period end. Otherwise, further invoices can be generated after you start the reconciliation. However, you must keep Receivables open during the reconciliation, so that if discrepancies are found they can be corrected in the period in which they belong. That means that all three reconciliations should be completed after closing the feeder systems, but before closing Receivables. Not all companies are prepared to hold Receivables open long enough to rigorously complete all three reconciliations.

TIP
If you want to close the period to prevent further data entry, "soft close" the period by changing the period status to "Close Pending," which is similar to "Closed" but does not validate for unposted items.

The Purge Feature

Oracle Receivables includes an archive-and-purge feature. The purge is to recover disk space by archiving closed transactions. The archive process satisfies legal requirements imposed by various taxing authorities that accounting documents must be kept for a certain number of years before being disposed of.

If disk storage were unlimited and machine processing power arbitrarily fast, no one would need to purge data at all. But presently and for the foreseeable future, machine capacity is limited; after a certain amount of time your disk will be full and response times will suffer—no matter what size system you have. This is when a purge is needed. Space is more often a problem in Receivables than the other modules, because each transaction in Receivables eats up more space than a comparable transaction in the other modules—for example, a journal in General Ledger or an invoice in Payables. Another reason is that companies tend to have a higher volume of Receivables invoices than other business transactions.

Before implementing the archive-and-purge process, assess if you really need to do so by balancing the cost of buying more hardware with the cost of implementing and testing the purge. Users prefer having transaction history online, and it is difficult to put an economic value on the extra procedural effort needed to research an archived transaction compared to an online transaction.

The purge works by removing records of historical transactions—receipts, invoices, credit memos, debit memos, charge-backs, adjustments, and commitments—from the database. These can be copied onto tape or any other storage device and then deleted from the online database. Removing the records releases disk space for current data.

Groups of interrelated transactions are purged if all transactions in the group are closed and the youngest transaction is older than a certain age. You might want to purge all closed transaction groups that are older than one year. The ground rule for purges is that after the purge, none of the customer-account balances will have changed; therefore, any group of records that is purged must have the following property:

$$Inv + DM \pm Adj - CM - Rec = 0.$$

Receivables Conversion Issues

Conversion strategy is a trade-off between the effort involved and the completeness of the converted data. The minimum effort is no conversion: Customer accounts are "run down" or "run out" in the old system. Customer receipts for old invoices are entered in the old system, and new invoices are keyed into Oracle Receivables.

No Conversion

Not converting has serious drawbacks for users. The customer's actual balance at any point in time has to be assimilated from both systems. This means that statements or dunning letters cannot be produced throughout the duration of the rundown. Running two systems concurrently is particularly difficult if you cross a year-end, as all financial accounts will have to be summarized from the two systems.

Eventually you will want to switch off and archive your legacy system. At that point you will inevitably have some open items, and you will need to decide what to do with them. A no-conversion strategy often turns into a minimal-conversion strategy. With this in mind, you may as well anticipate doing some sort of conversion when you go live; then, at least you'll have the benefit from day one.

Minimal Conversion

A minimal conversion involves converting only outstanding balances. After the last month end in the old system, a list of customer balances is generated from the legacy system and used to create data for the Customer interface. A customer is created in the Oracle Receivables system, with one open invoice to show the outstanding balance for that customer.

Minimal conversion has the advantage that you can stop data entry into the old system immediately and switch all entry tasks over to the new system. The disadvantage is that there is no detailed accounting information in the new system, so no aging of debt is possible and the customer statements and dunning letters will contain no history.

Open-Item Conversion

The next step up is to convert open items. After the last month end in the old system, a list of open items—invoices, credit memos, and receipts—is generated. Each open item is then transferred into the new system. The customer should not be able to detect that you have migrated from one system to another. Statements and dunning letters will show all open items with the correct reference numbers and outstanding amounts.

Open-item conversion is the preferred conversion strategy of the authors of this book, because it is transparent to the customer and provides more detail than a minimal conversion.

Full Conversion

The last option is to convert all transactions from the old system. This involves doing a full conversion of all transactions (open and closed), and then reapplying receipts and credit memos to close items and re-create the account history. The extra effort required to bring across the closed items and the history is seldom worthwhile.

Choice of Mechanism—Manual, Interface, or Mix

The choice of what mechanism to use is independent of your decision on what to convert. You can decide to convert any particular data element either manually or via an interface, using a custom-built data-load program. Consider the effort required for each route: manual conversion costs are determined by (*time needed to manually key one data record*) × (*number of data records*), while program conversion takes the total effort involved in programming, testing, and running a migration from old to new. Manual conversion works well when dealing with a low volume of transactions, while programmatic conversion is justified with high volumes.

The more detail and history you decide to convert, the more interfaces you will need to program and test. Table 6-4 shows exactly which interfaces you will need to implement based on the range of data that you want to convert. You need not choose between an entirely program-based conversion or a manual one. For example, what if you wanted to convert only open items? Suppose your old system has a large number of customers and open invoices, but a low number of receipts and credit memos (as would be quite normal). You can convert customers and invoices using a program, and you can convert receipts and credit memos manually.

| Interface Data | Customer | > AutoInvoice | | > AutoLockbox | |
		Invoice	Credit Memos	Receipts	Applications
No conversion					
Convert only customer balances	✔	✔			
Convert only open items	✔	✔	✔	✔	
Convert open items and history	✔	✔	✔	✔	✔

TABLE 6-4. *The Range of Interfaces Depends on What You Choose to Convert*

NOTE
Make sure you convert the receivables account for each transaction correctly, according to an agreed-upon mapping between old and new systems. Although the transactions themselves do not need to be posted within Receivables, any applications that reference converted transactions automatically give rise to GL postings to their receivables accounts. An inaccurate conversion of Receivables accounts can cause headaches long after the conversion is completed.

Customer Conversion

Customers are the heart of corporate life, and life goes on during conversion preparation. The least disruptive approach to customer conversion usually involves some mixture of cleaning up data in the legacy system beforehand and using automated scripts to simplify the conversion process. The following factors are best addressed by knowledgeable people in advance of conversion:

- dividing customer records into customers and customer locations—the legacy system may not make the distinction;

- defining the activities at different locations, such as bill-to, ship-to, marketing, collections, and so on;

- defining which customer locations belong to each operating unit in a Multi-Org implementation; and

- entering address and contact data. The customer database is remarkably flexible; it can associate contacts with a company, with a site, or with a function. The same is true with addresses and telephone numbers. Doing this will force you to express relationships that are implicit in your legacy system.

Automated scripts can handle or at least support the following kinds of conversion activities:

- converting to uppercase and lowercase—using uppercase and lowercase makes more attractive invoices and order confirmation letters for your customers;

- validating postal codes, getting the full code (ZIP plus four in the United States), and getting the names of towns spelled completely and correctly (third-party mailing-list data are helpful for this task); and

- standardizing your use of salutations (Dr., Mr., Mrs., Ms., M., Mlle., Srta., Sra., Herr, Frau, and so on).

As noted, the Oracle Customer interface process is remarkably flexible. It can import the same data into a number of different table structures. It is wise to choose a few representative customers and import them repeatedly into the Conference Room Pilot instance in order to confirm that the data are being stored as you expect. The interface allows you to create new customers, addresses, contacts, and phone numbers, and also to update existing data.

The legacy system will almost invariably include some data items that do not appear to map to Oracle. You may not know immediately what they are for, but it is unwise to leave them behind. Consider, as a strategy, sticking them in a comma-delimited format into one of the many Descriptive Flexfield attributes (Attribute n) that you will not need for use with a real DFF. The import process handles this with ease. Then the data will be available for reference or as the source for SQL scripts if you need them in the future. You can always set the items to null when you are sure they will not be needed.

Conclusion

Oracle Receivables is a complete accounts-receivable system for managing your invoicing tasks and keeping track of customer data. Its powerful online collection tools help you track, monitor, and collect your receivables, thereby reducing your delinquent accounts. By implementing regular collection cycles, you can improve cash flow. Transaction efficiency with high payment volumes is promoted with cash-application features like AutoLockbox, automatic receipts, and iPayment. There are improvements on the user experience of three windows with which you can perform your day-to-day accounts-receivable operations. The Transactions window provides the functions you use to enter, credit, and adjust invoices, debit memos, credit memos, on-account credits, charge-backs, and adjustments. The Receipts workbench is used to record and apply receipts and to maintain up-to-date invoice information. The new Collections window from Oracle Advanced Collections simplifies communication with customers by providing information on outstanding balances and by generating dunning letters and aged balances.

CHAPTER
7

Oracle Treasury

reasury departments have two core functions: corporate finance, which is the process of raising long-term finance (for a company's expansion or acquisition program) and short-term funding, which is the art of understanding the company's cash flow; and managing surpluses and shortfalls, making use of capital markets to borrow or invest money.

The objective of corporate treasury operations is to optimize financial performance. Passive intervention works on the premise that financial markets cannot be predicted and seeks to neutralize the company's financial exposure; exchange-rate exposure is covered by foreign-exchange deals designed to eliminate risk. Active management assumes that market movement can be predicted; for example, a tire manufacturer predicts that rubber prices will rise in six months. Today's favorable price can be locked in by buying commodity futures.

In-house banking can save money. By borrowing from subsidiaries with surpluses and lending to those who need cash, in-house banking minimizes your overall borrowing requirements and thereby your interest charges. In-house currency swaps can be organized between subsidiaries when their currency positions are complementary. You save on currency-conversion fees. To recognize the opportunity you need a centralized, up-to-date, accurate picture of all positions, spot and forward. Oracle Treasury provides in-house banking features to coordinate liquidity, financing, and intercompany transactions. It allows cash pooling across bank accounts and lets you set interest rates for subsidiaries' transactions to accurately reflect the fair cost of funding.

An Overview of Treasury Operations

Treasury has to be part of an integrated software suite because cash forecasting depends on inflows and outflows generated elsewhere in the enterprise resource planning system: payroll, accounts receivable, accounts payable, and cash management. Treasury needs to be a separate subledger. Although the deals cast in Oracle Treasury are ultimately accounted for in General Ledger, the GL alone is not sufficient. Deals are opened, have a life, and are closed. One accounting journal reflects the deal value of the opening positions, and several additional journals can be generated to reflect interest payments or to revalue the deal throughout its life; a closing position is posted as a journal once the deal is closed. The deal is a single transaction (albeit financially complex), which will give rise to a minimum of two accounting journals, maybe more if revaluations are involved. Intercompany funding deals will generate journals in both companies' accounts, even though they are entered only once into Oracle Treasury. The treasury manager's prime concern is portfolio optimization, not accounting. He or she wants to be able to see the entire portfolio in one place and track its value over time.

Currency-Holiday Rules

Currency holidays are days in which the there is no settlement of prior transactions. The standard settlement period for most currencies is two business days, with some pairs (such as CAD/USD) settling the next business day.

In order for a date to be a valid settlement date for an foreing currency transaction, the central banks for both currencies must be open for settlement. If either currency has a 'holiday' on the target settlement date, settlement is deferred until the next valid business day for both currencies. In addition, intervening holidays—that is, holidays between the trade date and the standard two days later—may or may not defer settlement, depending on which currencies are involved.

Holidays can significantly affect the timing of your deal cash flows. To prevent your company from dealing with delayed cash flows, Oracle Treasury provides the Currency Holiday Rules window to define the holiday dates for each of your authorized currencies. If you enter into a deal that has a start, maturity, or settlement date that falls on a holiday, your company's deal cash flow could be delayed by one or more days because banks, brokerages, or counterparty offices are closed.

Treasury automatically checks the start, maturity, and settlement dates for each deal against the holiday dates for each currency in the deal. If any deal dates fall on a holiday, you receive a warning, which you can dismiss. The warning does not prevent you from entering the deal, but it does remind you that the deal date can impact your company's cash flow.

In Oracle Treasury there are three seeded types of holidays:

- **Constant holidays** Holidays that occur on a fixed date. For example, in countries using USD, New Year's Day is always on January 1.
- **Rule holidays** Holidays that change from year to year based on a rule. For example, in countries using USD, Labor Day is always the first Monday in September.
- **One-off holidays** Holidays that occur one time only. For example, in countries using GBP, the government may declare a holiday to celebrate the coronation of a new king or queen.

An example of how to set up the currency-holiday rules is shown in Figure 7-1.

Portfolios and Positions

A deal is a trade; it is a contractual agreement between two parties to exchange an underlying asset at an agreed-upon point in time. A portfolio is a collection of deals. A position is the total commitment in a particular market, the number of contracts bought minus the number sold. Oracle Treasury associates each deal—and therefore each portfolio and position—with a company or legal entity that enters into the trade. The company profile associates your deals with a set of books (the set of books within which the legal entity is accounted for) and with the related bank accounts and the contact staff for deals and settlement. Navigate to the Setup | Parties | Company Profiles window to set up companies.

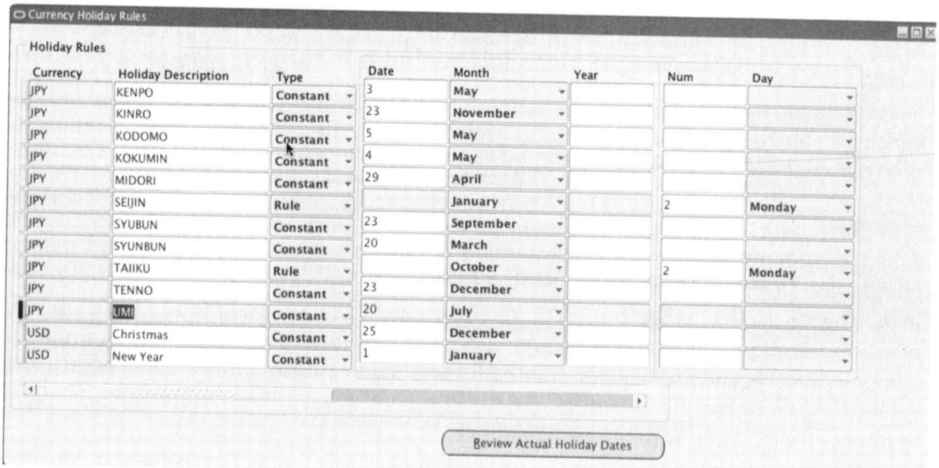

Currency Holiday Rules

Holiday Rules

Currency	Holiday Description	Type	Date	Month	Year	Num	Day
JPY	KENPO	Constant	3	May			
JPY	KINRO	Constant	23	November			
JPY	KODOMO	Constant	5	May			
JPY	KOKUMIN	Constant	4	May			
JPY	MIDORI	Constant	29	April			
JPY	SEIJIN	Rule		January		2	Monday
JPY	SYUBUN	Constant	23	September			
JPY	SYUNBUN	Constant	20	March			
JPY	TAIIKU	Rule		October		2	Monday
JPY	TENNO	Constant	23	December			
JPY	UMI	Constant	20	July			
USD	Christmas	Constant	25	December			
USD	New Year	Constant	1	January			

Review Actual Holiday Dates

FIGURE 7-1. *Oracle Treasury currency-holiday rules*

Counterparties are the organizations with which you enter into deals. Brokerages and banks are external counterparties, whereas subsidiaries of your own organization are internal. The counterparty may be one with which you enter into foreign-exchange or money-market deals; it might be a client and you the brokerage (you enter into deals on its behalf); it might be a legal or accounting advisor of yours; or it might be an asset valuer. Navigate to the Setup | Parties | Counterparty Profiles window to set up counterparties.

Different Types of Deals

Once you have set up your company and its counterparties, you are ready to enter deals. Oracle Treasury supports most of the deals that an organization's treasury administrator will be using. A brief description of each is provided in the following sections.

Quick Deals

A quick deal is a short-term money or foreign-exchange deal that is not yet complete. If your company utilizes short-term money or foreign-exchange deals, your treasury administrator can use the Oracle Treasury Quick Deals screen to enter principal details at the same time.

Exposure Transactions

Exposure is the risk faced by companies involved in international trade that currency-exchange rates will change after the companies have already entered into financial obligations. Such exposure to fluctuating exchange rates can lead to major losses for firms. Your company payroll, for example, is an exposure.

Oracle Treasury allows you to enter and monitor your exposures in the Exposure Transactions window or the Exposure Transactions Quick Input window. Use the Exposure Transactions window to enter the details for your actual or estimated exposure transactions. You can classify estimated exposures as either firm or indicative.

If you need to enter exposure transactions frequently and the details are available in an electronic source such as a bank file or a third-party application, you can use the XTR_DEALS_INTERFACE table and the Deal Interface Summary window to import the deal details into Treasury.

FOREX Spot and Forward Deals

A foreign-exchange (abbreviated FOREX) deal is an agreement to exchange certain amounts of currency at a specified exchange rate. Spot deals are for immediate delivery. Forward deals are for delivery at a fixed date in the future. A foreign-exchange deal can also be a *swap*, a transaction in which you and the counterparty lend to each other on different terms: either in different currencies or at different exchange rates.

Hedges

A hedge is an investment position intended to offset potential losses that may be incurred by a companion investment. A hedge can be constructed from many types of financial instruments, including stocks, exchange-traded funds, insurance, forward contracts, swaps, options, many types of over-the-counter and derivative products, and futures contracts. For example, a US-based company that receives revenue in a foreign currency has a foreign-exchange exposure against the US dollar. To manage this exposure, the US company would likely implement a hedging strategy to protect itself against foreign-exchange risk.

In Oracle Treasury, you can track your cash flow, fair value, net investment in foreign operations, and economic hedges as defined by the general de accounting standards.

Hedge policies are the first step in setting up a hedge; they define the exposure sources (known as hedge items) that you want to hedge and the financial instruments (known as hedge instruments) that you want to use to hedge those items using foreign-exchange spot and forward deals. Hedge strategies define the reasons that you are hedging your exposures. You can use hedge strategies to define all of the accounting-related reporting information that you require as well as to set up any default information that you want when you create a hedge. Every hedge must be associated with an underlying hedge strategy.

Once setup is complete, you can begin to create hedges. To create a hedge you must define the following:

■ **Hedge attributes** These define the basic information about the hedge, such as the company it is for and its start and end dates. The hedge attributes are where you select the strategy that determines the actual or forecast hedge approach.

■ **Hedge relationships** These define the relationship between the hedge items and the hedge instruments. The hedge relationship is where you assign the hedge derivative to the hedge item.

Rate Rollovers

A *rollover* is a loan that is periodically repriced at a fixed spread above an industry-standard rate such as the LIBOR.

Money-Market Deals

Money market became a component of the financial markets for assets involved in short-term borrowing, lending, buying, and selling with original maturities of one year or less. Issued initially to raise money for the issuer, the financial instruments or also called securities are bought and sold at exchanges until they mature, when the person holding the security gets the principal amount of the loan repaid. *Securities* are government bonds, treasury bills, or commercial paper issued by banks or other companies. Although called securities, the loans are unsecured and backed only by the reputation of the lender. Solid and reliable issuers such as the US government pay lower interest than commercial companies, which must pay higher interest rates to attract lenders. Money-market deals fall into one of the following types:

■ **Short-term money** Money borrowed for short periods of one year or less.

■ **Intercompany funding** The transfer of money from one company to another.

■ **Wholesale term money** Borrowing in large amounts from banks and institutions. These deals are rarely exchanged or traded.

■ **Retail term money** Mortgages, sinking funds, and hire purchases.

■ **Negotiable instruments** Unconditional promises to pay some amount of money. Negotiable instruments are easily transferred from one party to another by delivery.

■ **Derivatives** Financial securities that derive their value from the price of an underlying financial asset (a stock, bond, or commodity), or in some cases a market index. Options and futures are both derivatives.

The terms, conditions, and features of each of these deals are radically different, and each has its own dedicated window in Oracle Treasury to capture the deal parameters. Figure 7-2 shows the window where foreign-exchange deals are entered. The client field is not used at present but will be

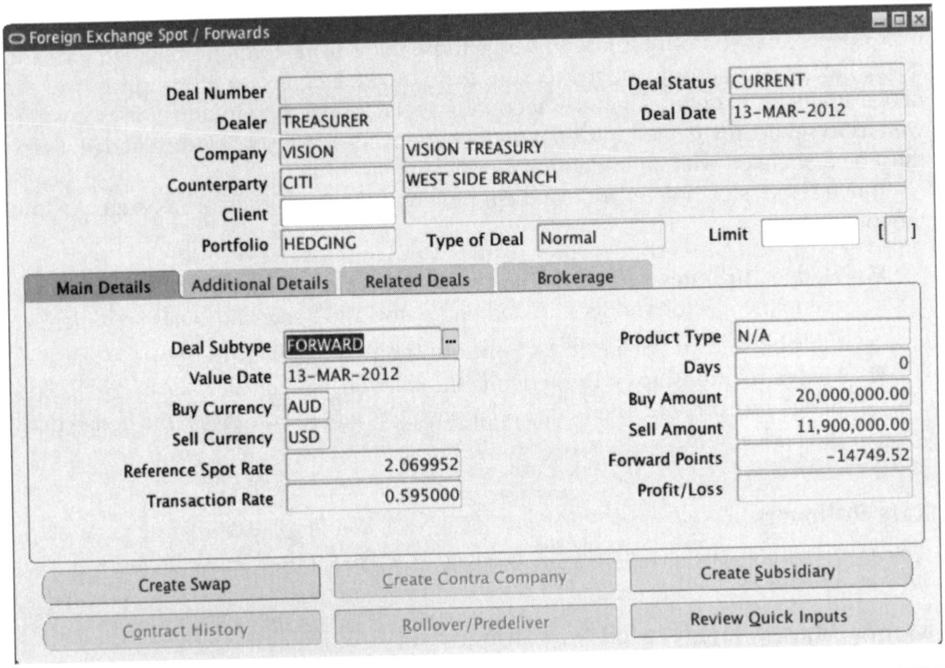

FIGURE 7-2. *The Foreign Exchange window*

introduced as more features are added to Oracle Treasury to enable brokerages to track deals against the clients who made them.

Using Treasury for Cash Forecasting

Enterprise resource planning transactions are either visible in the General Ledger, such as payables and receivables, or not yet visible, such as open purchase orders and sales orders. Both are imported into Treasury as indicative exposures. To get cash flows from the rest of the enterprise resource planning system, you first must define the cash-forecast template. Once you define this template, you can run the Cash Forecasting by Days or Cash Forecasting by GL Period concurrent programs. These programs compile data from Payables, Receivables, Purchasing, Order Entry, Payroll, and user-defined external sources. Any previous data retrieved through this process will be dropped and replaced with the current information. Make sure you have run the cash forecast for the correct date range and company.

Integration with Other Applications

Treasury generates journals that are posted to General Ledger. Both Treasury and General Ledger have interest-rate tables. Treasury has its own rates table, XTR_MARKET_PRICES, which is maintained separately from the GL rates table GL_DAILY_RATES. Treasury uses the rates from its own rates table for revaluations and tolerance-level checks. Treasury uses the GL rates table when transferring journal entries to GL, because Treasury requires both interest and foreign-exchange rates, and often requires these to be updated on a more frequent basis than GL. Due to the restriction that a company can be assigned only one legal entity, this module impacts the functional architecture.

Treasury Banks and Accounts Payable Banks

Treasury bank information is stored in a Treasury table (XTR_BANK_ACCOUNTS)—that is, a separate table from where Accounts Payable banks are stores—and reconciled in Treasury using a separate reconciliation process. All parties and banks used by Treasury need to be recorded in Treasury. The access to these data is limited to Treasury users because large amounts of money are affected. Treasury payments are more critical than Accounts Payable payments. They must be paid when due or serious penalties could result.

Cash Forecasting in Treasury and Cash Management

If you are upgrading your Oracle E-Business Suite release from 11i to R12, there is a change in the functionality of Oracle Treasury and Oracle Cash Management. These modules have a more integrated functionality, which makes some of the setups on each of them mandatory.

As explained in detail in Chapter 8, cash forecasting is a planning tool that helps you anticipate the flow of cash in and out of your business, allowing you to project your cash needs and evaluate your company's liquidity position. In particular, information is acquired from Payables, Receivables, Purchasing, Order Entry, Payroll, and external sources. Treasury summarizes the exposure information, which is then used to calculate Treasury's various cash positions in Oracle Cash Management.

Oracle Treasury Open-Interface Tables

Market Data Feed

Market Data Feed is feature in Oracle Treasury that allows you to automatically import critical market data such as foreign-exchange rates, interest rates, bond prices, and option volatilities. Because many Treasury operations require frequent updates to these market data, this automated method nicely complements the existing ability of manual entry. If you are able to receive an electronic flat file of market data from your bank, broker, or third-party rate-feed provider, you now can import the information into Oracle Treasury. You can either format the electronic flat file to conform with the sample SQL*Loader control file that Oracle Treasury provides, or create your own control file to import the data that are stored in another format. In the end, you will create a concurrent-request set that you schedule to automatically import your market data for your current or historic rates.

Oracle Treasury provides a standard concurrent program called Data Exchange—Market Data Transfer, which uploads the records of the open-interface table XTR_MARKET_DATA_INTERFACE.

Deals Interface Table

Oracle Treasury provides an interface table called XTR_DEALS_INTERFACE, as explained earlier in this chapter, that is used to import deals from external sources into Treasury. The XTR_DEALS_INTERFACE table is capable of holding data for many different deal types; however, since each deal type uses a different set of values (for example, foreign-exchange deals use two currencies, whereas intercompany funding deals use one), each deal type is imported into Treasury using a different deal-transfer package.

Transaction Interface Table

A table designed to hold common transaction information and also serving as a temporary staging area for deal data awaiting transfer to the actual transaction tables is provided. This table is called XTR_TRANSACTIONS_INTERFACE. This table is also used to store discounted securities (NI) deals.

Conclusion

Oracle Treasury is an integrated part of the Oracle E-Business Suite. The out-of-the-box integration with other modules within the suite presents a huge advantage for the MIS department reducing the total cost of ownership by not have to implement third party applications, that needs to be integrated either manually or custom built with Oracle E-Business Suite.

Oracle Treasury in conjunction with Oracle Cash Management forms a complete web-enabled treasury workstation solution for managing global treasury operations while improving visibility of all your enterprise-wide operational exposures, profitability and control with your treasury positions. The replacement of spreadsheets, emails, or faxes from throughout your organization to make timely and informed hedging decisions is the key for the decision making process.

CHAPTER
8

Oracle Cash Management

he purpose of Oracle Cash Management is to help you manage and control the cash cycle of your enterprise to ensure liquidity and improve profitability. The key benefits of this module include enterprise cash forecasting, efficient bank reconciliation, extensive multicurrency capabilities, and up-to-date cash-balance information. Cash Management is an enterprise-wide solution, providing comprehensive integration with other Oracle applications and open interfaces for integration with external systems. Cash Management supports two distinct but related business functions:

- bank reconciliation and
- cash forecasting.

Bank reconciliation determines whether the balance on your bank accounts in Oracle Financials is equivalent to the balance shown on your bank statements; cash forecasting uses the results of this reconciliation—a known and proven cash position—to predict your balance for next week, next month, next quarter, and so on. A fully integrated application suite is needed because cash flows are generated or identified elsewhere in the ERP system. Cash Management draws flows from the sources shown in Table 8-1.

Application	Cash Transaction Source
Oracle Payables	Supplier payments (future)
Oracle Payables	Supplier invoices
Oracle Payables	Supplier payments (historical)
Oracle Payables, Self-Service Expenses, and Oracle Projects	Expense reports
Oracle Payroll	Payroll expenses (historical)
Oracle Receivables	Customer invoices
Oracle Receivables	Customer receipts (historical)
Oracle General Ledger	GL budgets
Oracle General Ledger	GL cash position
Oracle General Ledger	GL encumbrances
Oracle Projects	Project billing
Oracle Projects	Project inflow budgets
Oracle Projects	Project outflow budgets
Oracle Projects	Project transactions
Oracle Purchasing	Purchase orders
Oracle Sales	Sales opportunity
Oracle Treasury	Foreign exchange
Oracle Treasury	Money-market transactions
Any external system	Expected cash flows

TABLE 8-1. *Cash Management Draw Flows*

When first introduced, Cash Management dealt primarily with bank reconciliation; it consolidated a range of banking features from Oracle Payables and Oracle Receivables and made them available in one place. Cash-forecasting functionality has been continuously enhanced during the product cycles of early releases up to Release 12. The capability to draw on relevant financial transactions from external systems on local and remote databases means that international companies with several Oracle databases around the world are no longer constrained to local cash forecasting. A company-wide forecast can now be compiled within a distributed database environment. Integration with Projects, Sales, and Oracle Treasury was introduced in Release 11i, and some new features were added in Release 12, including a new bank-account model, multiorganization access control, and subledger accounting (SLA).

The Need for Cash Management

Treasury managers are continually monitoring cash-flow details to ensure that the net cash inflow will cover the company's cash requirements. Managing cash in this way offers several benefits:

- **Improved overall profitability**   Surplus cash is quickly located and can then be invested.

- **Reduced risk of currency exposure**   Currency imbalances are quickly detected, and thus can be promptly resolved.

- **Prevention of finance charges**   Insufficient cash-flow situations are anticipated ahead of time, allowing for prompt adjustment.

Early predictions of insufficient cash flow give managers time to react. There are a variety of ways to steer a company away from a cash crisis—herein lies the expertise of the treasury department—but no department can respond appropriately or swiftly without having a sophisticated liquidity-analysis tool to prepare accurate cash forecasts quickly. Organizations that trade internationally have to manage their currency exposure by balancing their future inflow and outflow currency by currency, period by period. Large currency imbalances must be avoided to prevent exchange losses. Companies that undertake a large number of high-value treasury transactions (bonds, spot contracts, and so on) could consider the use of Oracle Treasury as an alternative to the more basic functions available in Cash Management. Oracle Treasury is described in Chapter 7.

The starting point for an accurate cash forecast is a proven cash position. The accounting process used to prove a cash position is *bank reconciliation*.

Bank Reconciliation

Bank reconciliation is an audit requirement; bank accounts are an asset of the company; and you must be able to explain all balances on the balance sheet. Bank reconciliation goes further than an audit and can reveal fraud as well as errors. To ensure that your transaction records match and that neither you nor the bank has made an error, you should reconcile your bank accounts each time you receive a bank statement.

Reconciliation is the process of explaining the difference between two balances. There are legitimate reasons for two balances to be different—for example, timing differences—but once the legitimate differences have been eliminated, the balances should be the same. Basically, bank reconciliation uses the following formula to ascertain that the balance on the bank accounts in Oracle Financials is equivalent to the balance shown on the bank statements:

Bank account balance in Oracle Financials

+ Items on bank statement but not in Financials

− Items in Financials but not on bank statement

= Bank Statement Balance.

At the most basic level, bank reconciliation is an exercise in comparison. We take an extract of the bank account in Oracle Financials and compare that to the statement provided by our bank. All transactions that appear the same on both lists are checked off. These are the reconciled transactions. We are left with two sets of entries: bank-statement entries that are not listed in Financials and Financials entries that are not listed on the bank statement. Both sets of entries require analysis to determine whether the source of the discrepancy was an error or a legitimate difference. This distinction is important; errors must be corrected.

The best method for dealing with entries that require correction is determined by the circumstances, but the essential purpose is to reverse the original (error) transaction and to enter a new transaction. Errors on the bank's behalf must be reported to the bank and corrected. Oracle Cash Management has the capability to reconcile bank corrections against the original bank errors.

Legitimate differences occur when the Cash Management bank account differs from the actual bank statement for the following reasons:

- timing differences due to checks in transit or other uncompleted items,

- bank charges and items that are unknown until they appear on the statement,

- fees for currency conversion, or

- transactions that have not yet been processed, such as payroll deductions from a service bureau.

The differences have to be eliminated; you do this by making appropriate account entries to explain them. The reconciliation process is diagrammed in Figure 8-1.

The Reconciliation Process

Oracle Cash Management is a collection point for bank transactions, regardless of where in the system they may have been entered. Bank transactions entered directly into Oracle General Ledger or generated from Payables, Receivables, or Payroll can be reconciled within Oracle Cash Management. Payments made to suppliers and recorded through Oracle Payables generate credit entries in the bank account; customers' receipts entered in Receivables post debit entries. Salary payments to employees are recorded in Oracle Payroll, and other bank transactions that may have been initiated from external systems, such as an EPOS (electronic point of sale) merchandising system, also can be stored in Cash Management. Transactions then can be reconciled either manually or automatically using the Reconciliation open interface.

Oracle Cash Management distinguishes between *clearing* and *reconciling*. You clear a transaction as soon as you have documentary evidence from your bank that it has processed the transaction and the funds have been moved into or out of your account. You reconcile a transaction once it has appeared on your bank statement. Reconciliation itself implies clearance.

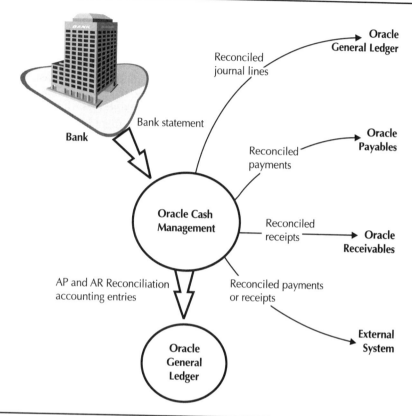

FIGURE 8-1. *Cash Management reconciliation process*

When you reconcile a transaction, the transaction is first cleared (the statement itself is the documentary evidence) and then matched to a bank-statement line.

Loading the Bank Statement

You can reconcile transactions manually or load an electronic bank statement directly into Oracle Cash Management, where the bank statement lines are reconciled automatically. The automatic reconciliation looks for certain match criteria to determine whether a transaction and a bank-statement line indeed are one and the same. When you use the Bank Statement open interface, flat file statements are uploaded into the Cash Management tables quickly and easily.

Bank Statement Interface Case Study

Bank-Statement Load

The UK subsidiary of an international company uses a PC banking package from NatWest called Bankline; most clearing banks provide something similar. You can download statements and transaction histories from the bank's mainframe computers to a text file on a PC. The company manually keys the bank-statement lines into Cash Management before they can be reconciled. In this case study, we see how a text file created from the Bankline package can be imported directly into Cash Management. Some of the reconciliation will be performed automatically. The process flow is diagrammed in Figure 8-2.

If your bank provides statements in a flat file format such as BAI or SWIFT940, you can use the Bank Statement open interface to load this information directly into Cash Management. This interface validates the bank account and currency code in the header information, and you can—if they are available in the bank file—cross-check against control totals.

Statement lines with errors can be corrected in the Statement Interface window. This feature can save hours of manual data entry and error correction. It is highly recommended that you negotiate a flat-file statement with your bank if you plan to reconcile your accounts within Oracle

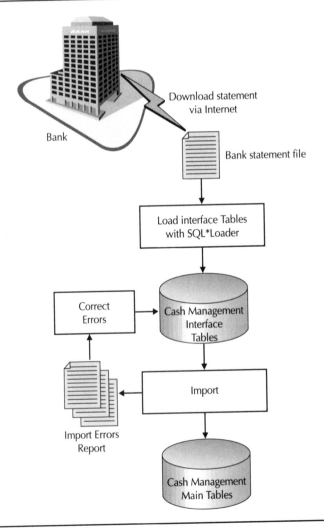

FIGURE 8-2. *Loading bank statements*

Cash Management. You always use the Bank Statement interface to load files of bank transactions. The procedure to load the bank statement is the same whatever format is loaded. During implementation the mapping will be easier if the bank provides either BAI or SWIFT940 format.

Format of the Bankline Statement File

The following code listing shows an example bank-statement format. Bank statements are not always in comma-separated (CSV) format, but are often in ASCII fixed format. The SQL*Loader program you develop will need to distinguish correctly between CSV and ASCII. For the purposes of this case study we have used the format supplied by the Bankline software from NatWest Bank.

```
"TransDate","ValueDate","InToday","Amount","Details","TransCode","RFR",  "CheckNo"
"2011-12-17",,"00","-82.25",,"CQ",,"003978"
"2011-12-17",,"00","-8614.09",,"CQ",,"003980"
"2011-12-17",,"00","-294.50","MRX987479","MSC",,
"2011-12-17",,"00","-459.70","RENTAL HIRE","DD",,
"2011-12-17",,"00","255117.51","TESSAFE UK - MANUAL","SO",,
"2011-12-18",,"00","-70004.44","600001 76702251","TR",,
"2011-09-29",,"00","33.54","INTEREST","IN",,
```

Field Mapping

The file contains vital fields such as the transaction date, amount, a transaction type, and some reference text. The Bank Statement interface relies on two tables being loaded: a header table and a lines table; the bank-statement file contains only statement lines. The mapping of the fields in the file to those in the interface table is set out in Table 8-2.

The InToday field in the source text file does not map to any column in the destination table. This field contains one of two values: "00" means the transaction belongs to today's statement balance, and "01" means the transaction does not belong to today's balance. Logic in the SQL*Loader control file selects only the "00" statement lines to be loaded to the interface table.

There are columns in the interface table for which no corresponding data are available in the source file. Suitable values have to be assigned to these columns during the load process, as detailed in Table 8-3.

Column Name in File	Explanation	Mapped Column in Interface Table
TransDate	Transaction date	TRX_DATE
ValueDate	Blank	EFFECTIVE_DATE
Amount	Transaction amount	AMOUNT
Details	Source or recipient of funds	CUSTOMER_TEXT
TransCode	Transaction code	TRX_CODE
RFR	Text information about the transaction	INVOICE_TEXT
CheckNo	Check number	BANK_TRX_NUMBER

TABLE 8-2. *Mapping of Bank-Statement Fields to Interface Table*

Column Name in Interface	Explanation	Constructed Value
bank_account_num	Account number of the bank account	98702245 in this example
statement_number	Statement number	SYSDATE
Line_number	Statement-line number	SEQUENCE(MAX,1)
currency_code	Currency code	GBP in this example

TABLE 8-3. *Unmapped Fields*

The values assigned in this example are highly specific and are unlikely to be relevant in any other situation. In particular, populating the statement number with SYSDATE (today's date) was a reluctant compromise. The statement number was not available in the file; yet statement numbers had to be unique and as meaningful as possible.

Application Setup Steps

The SQL*Loader control file must be registered within the Applications Object Library so that it can be made available to users. There are three steps involved:

1. Define the BANKSTMT program as an executable with the execution method "SQL*Loader."

2. Define a concurrent program based on this executable. The program has one parameter, which is the location and file name of the source data file.

3. Assign the program to an appropriate report group.

The SQL*Loader control file will need to be available to the concurrent manager. Assuming the executable was registered under the Cash Management application, the following copy command, or one similar, will copy the file to the correct place in the file system:

```
cp BANKSTMT.ctl $CE_TOP/bin
```

The bank account probably will already be set up as part of the Payables or Receivables implementation setup steps. If not, here are the steps to set it up:

1. Navigate to the Manage Banks and Branches window, select the Bank Branches tab, and select the "Create" button.

2. Navigate to the Manage Bank Accounts window and select "Create."

NOTE
You can define additional bank account types in the Oracle Cash Management Lookups window. For example, you could add Controlled Disbursement for your internal bank account.

Code	Description	Source
CQ	Check	Payables payment
DD	Direct debit	Receivables receipt
SO	Standing order	Payables payment
TR	Transfer receipt	Journal
CC	Credit card	Payables payment
CHG	Bank charge	
IN	Interest	

TABLE 8-4. *Transaction Codes*

Set Up Transaction Codes in the Application

Transaction codes for the bank should be set up corresponding to all the codes that might possibly appear in the data file. The codes have a type (Payment, Receipt, Miscellaneous Payment, Miscellaneous Receipt, Stopped, Rejected, Nonsufficient Funds), which determines how the statement line will be reconciled, and a source (Journal, Open Interface, Payables Payments, Receivables Receipts), which determines where the AutoReconciliation program looks for the corresponding transaction. When these codes are set up, the AutoReconciliation program will use them to help locate the source of the transaction. A code of payment can be a transaction that originates in GL or an accounts-payable payment. These are set out in the Table 8-4.

SQL*Loader Import Script

The text of the BANKSTMT.ctl control file is reproduced here:

```
LOAD DATA
INFILE 'NATWEST.txt'
APPEND
INTO TABLE ce_statement_lines_interface
WHEN customer_text = '00'
FIELDS TERMINATED BY "," OPTIONALLY ENCLOSED BY '"'
TRAILING NULLCOLS
(bank_account_num CONSTANT '98702245'
, statement_number SYSDATE
, line_number SEQUENCE(MAX,1)
, currency_code CONSTANT 'GBP'
, trx_date DATE "YYYY-MM-DD"
, effective_date DATE "YYYY-MM-DD"
, customer_text
, amount "TO_NUMBER(:amount)*(-1)"
, trx_text
, trx_code
, invoice_text
, bank_trx_number "LTRIM(:bank_trx_number, '0')"
)
```

```
INTO TABLE ce_statement_headers_int_all
WHEN (2:10) = 'TransDate'
FIELDS TERMINATED BY "," OPTIONALLY ENCLOSED BY '"'
TRAILING NULLCOLS
(bank_account_num CONSTANT '98702245'
, statement_number SYSDATE
, currency_code CONSTANT 'GBP'
, statement_date  SYSDATE
)
```

The control file will create a row in the CE_STATEMENT_LINES_INTERFACE table for each line found in the data file that is an "InToday" statement line. Today's date is used as the statement number. The check numbers provided in the file are left padded with zeros; the script removes these zeros.

The amounts in the bank data files are positive for incoming transactions on the account (cash receipts, direct debits, and so forth), and negative for outgoing transactions (such as checks and the like). Oracle Cash Management expects to see the bank-statement lines with negative numbers for incoming and positive for outgoing. Therefore, the SQL*Loader control script swaps the sign on all transaction lines.

One row is created in the CE_STATEMENT_HEADERS_INT table. The loader script uses the field name row (there should be only one of these present in any data file) to force the generation of the interface-header record.

Reconciling Journal Entries

Some journal entries in General Ledger will not have originated from another module; instead, they will have been entered directly into General Ledger. These transactions can be reconciled to your bank statement with Cash Management. The AutoReconciliation program will match the transaction if the journal-line description matches the statement-line transaction number and the two amounts match. There is no matching within a particular tolerance, as there is for payments and receipts.

TIP
This matching rule should be observed when entering data into General Ledger journals; otherwise the AutoReconciliation program will not make any matches. It is especially important to load the correct data into journal-line descriptions when converting legacy bank-account lines into Oracle General Ledger.

Reconciling Payments

Supplier payments entered in Payables can be reconciled to your bank-statement lines. When you reconcile payments using Oracle Cash Management, the payment status is updated to "Reconciled." There are two check boxes, both of which must be checked on the Account of Payment tab in the Payables options window: When Payment Is Issued and When Payment Clears. If you select both options, you have the same functionality as the Allow Reconciliation Accounting option provided in previous releases.

The AutoReconciliation program matches payments against bank-statement lines if the transactions meet certain match criteria:

- The currency is the same.

- The reference or payment batch name matches the statement-line transaction number.

- The transaction amount is the same as the statement amount to within the reconciliation tolerance.

Reconciling Receipts

Receipts created in Receivables also can be reconciled to bank-statement lines. Cash Management updates the status of the receipts to "Reconciled" and creates appropriate accounting entries to be transferred to Oracle General Ledger. Payables and Receivables can generate reconciliation accounting entries for cash clearing, bank charges, and foreign-currency gain or loss.

The AutoReconciliation program matches receipts against bank-statement lines if the following criteria are met:

- The currency is the same.

- The remittance batch deposit number or receipt batch name matches the statement-line transaction number.

- The transaction amount is the same as the statement amount to within the reconciliation tolerance.

Reconciling Other Transactions

Some transactions that appear on your bank statements are not initiated from the Oracle Applications. Such is the case when you are charged bank charges or receive interest, when the bank applies a specific exchange rate on foreign-currency transactions, or when a customer receipt is returned due to nonsufficient funds (NSF). Oracle Cash Management is the primary point of entry for these transactions. Used in this way, Oracle Cash Management becomes a subledger in its own right.

Reconciliation Tolerances

In the System Options form you can set reconciliation tolerances, which determine the size of the difference between the Cash Management transaction amount and the bank-statement amount that can still be acceptably reconciled. With a zero tolerance, both amounts need to be the same for them to be reconciled. Tolerances can be set as either percentages or amounts. Either way, they are relevant only for transactions sourced from Payables or Receivables; all other transactions have to have identical amounts to be reconciled.

Payables and Receivables handle the reconciliation differences differently. Using an option set in the Systems Options window, you can control whether the AutoReconciliation program charges differences (between the amount cleared by the bank and the transaction amount) to the Bank Charges or Bank Errors account. Receivables transaction amount differences are booked only to the Bank Charges account. This type of transaction, either positive or negative, passes through Receivables as a miscellaneous transaction and then into the General Ledger.

Cash Forecasting

Cash Management helps you analyze liquidity across the entire business. You can quickly prepare accurate cash forecasts and analyze your currency exposure, enabling you to make informed financing and investment decisions. You can forecast in any currency across different organizations in your enterprise, for multiple time periods. Cash forecasting is integrated with other application modules and with external systems through the Forecasting open interface. Figure 8-3 charts a cash position forecast.

Accurate cash forecasting depends on up-to-date banking information and relevant information from operational systems. The audience for the cash forecast is the treasury manager. The forecast is just that—a forecast; therefore, it does not form part of the statutory accounts of the company.

Cash forecasting takes today's cash position and attempts to roll the balance forward to a future period by adding predicted cash inflow and subtracting predicted cash outflow. The cash inflow and outflow figures are derived from the various sources shown in Table 8-5.

When producing a forecast, bear in mind the limited scope of the future-dated transactions stored in any accounting system. The money due from customer invoices over the next month can be judged accurately by looking at due invoices in Oracle Receivables. However, future sales that have not yet been invoiced will not appear in Receivables; a six-month forecast should include a sales forecast generated either from revenue budgets in General Ledger or from outside the system. You can base your forecast on future transactions such as orders and invoices, or historical transactions such as payments, receipts, and payroll.

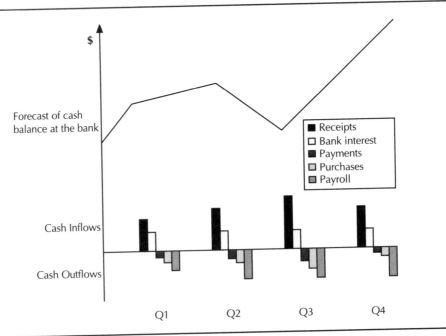

FIGURE 8-3. *A sample cash position forecast*

Cash Inflow	Cash Outflow
Customer invoices due in the intervening period (Oracle Receivables)	Invoiced liabilities due in the intervening period (Oracle Payables)
Receipts (Oracle Receivables)	Supplier payments (Oracle Payables)
Sales orders that have not been invoiced (Oracle Order Management)	Liabilities for goods ordered but not invoiced (Oracle Purchasing)
Budgeted revenue (Oracle General Ledger)	Unordered requisitions (Oracle Purchasing)
Inflow from external systems	Expense budgets (Oracle General Ledger)
User-entered inflow	Encumbrances (Oracle General Ledger)
Project billing (Oracle Projects)	Payroll expenses (Oracle Payroll)
Project inflow budgets (Oracle Projects)	Outflow from external systems
Sales opportunity (Oracle Sales)	User-entered outflow
Foreign exchange (Oracle Treasury)	Employee expense reports (Oracle Payables)
Money market (Oracle Treasury)	Project outflow budgets (Oracle Projects)

TABLE 8-5. *Cash Inflow and Outflow*

You can use the Forecasting open interface to view cash flows from external systems. Remember to include outflow generated by repayment of loans. Typically, this sum can greatly exceed the normal accounts-payable balances, but it is not tracked and accounted for in Oracle Payables, because the lender is not considered a trade creditor. In addition, look for capital expenditure that has been approved by directors but has not yet been put out to contract.

Forecasting is built around cash-forecast templates. A template determines whether to forecast by days or General Ledger periods, specifies which sources are included, and determines the level of detail. You generate periodic cash forecasts by projecting the cash position for each template. The forecast itself can be in any currency and, once generated, it can be modified or exported to a spreadsheet application. In a multiple-organization environment you can also forecast across organizations. For you to report a consolidated view across several ledgers, each must use the same calendar.

Cash Pooling

Organizations frequently use cash-pooling techniques to optimize funds by consolidating bank balances from across multiple bank accounts. By consolidating balances and minimizing idle funds, organizations may decrease external borrowing costs and increase overall investment returns.

Oracle Cash Management supports common cash-pooling techniques by allowing users to group bank accounts into different types of pooling structures and by managing the associated activity for either centralized or decentralized business environments. This functionality was originally made available to Oracle Treasury users in prior releases; it is supported via Oracle Cash Management as of Release 12. The following types of cash pools are supported:

■ **Notional cash pools** Organizations may choose to utilize notional cash-pool arrangements offered by banks that track not only individual account balances but also the net balance across all accounts. This technique is common in some countries and does not require physical cash transfers to be made between accounts for concentration purposes. The cash pool's closing balance for a day is calculated as a notional sum of the individual balances of the bank accounts included in the pool. The interest is calculated on the notional net balance of all accounts included in the pool and then paid out or charged to the concentration or lead account. The setup screen is shown on Figure 8-4.

■ **Self-initiated physical cash pools** Organizations may choose to monitor individual bank-account balances manually and then physically move cash to or from their accounts only as needed based on their particular preferences or objectives. Oracle Cash Management allows users to define and manage these types of bank-account structures, called self-initiated physical cash pools. These pools' definitions include rules to automatically determine when bank-account transfers should be made and for what amounts. Users are able to review transfer proposals from their cash positions based on daily activity as well as target balances, minimum transfer amounts, and rounding rules. Users are able to accept or overwrite system-proposed transfers, and Oracle Cash Management then generates all the bank account transfers automatically.

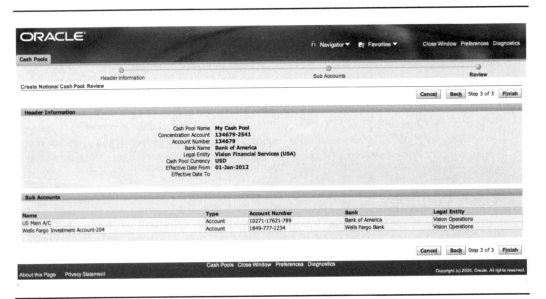

FIGURE 8-4. *Notional cash pool setup*

NOTE
Before creating physical cash pools, you have to decide how the physical fund transfers will be recorded in the system. If you are using Oracle Treasury, you can choose to create fund transfers in Oracle Treasury or Oracle Cash Management by choosing one or the other in the site-level system profile option CE: Bank Account Transfers. If you are using Oracle Cash Management only, you will only be able to create fund transfers in Oracle Cash Management.

Cash Management Interfaces

A great deal of routine and time-intensive work can be avoided by using the Cash Management interfaces. Interfacing bank data into Financials is a priority because a high volume of transactions regularly passes through your main bank accounts. The use of the Bank Statement open interface was described in the case study earlier in this chapter.

The Reconciliation Open Interface

The Reconciliation open interface is a powerful feature for enterprise-wide reconciliation. You simply define a database view or a table that Oracle Cash Management can use to access the payments and receipts in your external system. The Reconciliation open interface also is extensible. Oracle Cash Management executes your custom reconciliation logic when reconciling your external transactions.

The database view CE_999_INTERFACE_V forms a bridge between Oracle Cash Management and data held in an external transaction system. During implementation, you redefine this view to point to the payment or receipt transaction table in the external system. Each view column has to be mapped to the corresponding data field. You can use the reconciliation logic in the interface even if the external system data cannot be viewed dynamically across SQL Plus. To do this, create a table called CE_999_INTERFACE_V in the Financials database; then use SQL*Loader to populate the table with payment and receipt transactions from the external system.

The Forecasting Open Interface

The Forecasting open interface enables cash forecasts to be made using data assimilated from relevant transaction information in both local and remote databases. The information about future cash inflows and outflows can come from any application system; it need not be an Oracle Applications database. Provided the source system supports real-time access from an Oracle database (many databases are ODBC compliant), data integration is simply a matter of setting up a view (the External Source Transaction View) that will access the source application's database to include all transactions that you want to select for cash forecasting. The view will ultimately depend on a database link, a device which allows one database to select and modify the data in another database. Even if the source system does not support real-time access, you can create a table for the External Source Transaction View and use SQL*Loader or any asynchronous mechanism to populate the table with information about cash inflows and outflows derived from the source system.

There are a few steps involved here: Once connectivity has been established, a certain amount of setup is required in the target database. In particular, the Forecast Selection Criteria Descriptive Flexfield needs to be set up. This flexfield provides you the ability to filter and restrict the particular cash inflows or outflows that are to be included in the forecast. A certain amount of planning in close consultation with the business managers in the treasury department is worthwhile, to establish how they propose to operate their cash forecasts. For example, if several external source systems are to be integrated, one segment in the Descriptive Flexfield could identify the source system. That way you could run a forecast selecting only Payroll forecast transactions, for example. The database objects needed to achieve database connectivity are

- the table CE_FORECAST_EXT_TEMP,
- the index CE_FORECAST_EXT_TEMP_N1, and
- the package CE_FORECAST_REMOTE_SOURCES.

The SQL script containing the instructions to create these objects is available in the directories $CE_TOP/sql and $CE_TOP/admin/sql. In the target database, where the consolidated forecast is going to take place, you need to define external forecast source types (there is a form to do this) and corresponding database links to pull in the data from the remote databases.

The Cash Management Data Model

For bank reconciliation, Cash Management uses receipt and payment information held in Oracle Receivables and Payables. Cash Management has transaction tables of its own. Bank-statement details are held in the two tables CE_STATEMENT_HEADERS_ALL and CE_STATEMENT_LINES. Other tables, listed in Table 8-6, relate to the cash-forecast functionality.

Table	Purpose
CE_FORECAST_COLUMNS	Stores the forecast-period information of each cash-forecast template
CE_FORECAST_HEADERS	Holds header information of each cash-forecast template
CE_FORECAST_ROWS	Stores the source transaction information of each cash-forecast template
CE_FORECASTS	Stores information about cash forecasts; one row for each forecast run submitted
CE_STATEMENT_HEADERS_ALL	Holds one row for each separate bank statement
CE_STATEMENT_LINES	Holds one row for each line on a bank statement
CE_STATEMENT_RECONCILS_ALL	Contains reconciliation history and audit trail; each row represents an action performed against a statement line

TABLE 8-6. *Cash Management Draws Flows*

When payments or receipts are cleared or reconciled, Cash Management updates the flags in tables owned by Oracle Payables and Receivables. Refer to Chapters 5 and 6 for an overview of their data models.

Conclusion

Close attention to cash flow in a business is extremely important. Cash forecasts, predicated on a precise bank position, use forecasted cash inflows and outflows to estimate future cash positions. Through the last several releases of Oracle E-Business Suite, cash-management functionality has evolved from a single screen in Oracle Payables to a full-blown module of its own. It is now capable of managing not just bank data in Payables, but also transactions entered in General Ledger, Receivables, and Payroll, along with information from external systems. Cash Management is the prime point of data entry for bank charges and interest earned, as well as bank errors.

Automatic bank reconciliation can significantly reduce the chore of verifying individual transactions against the bank's statement of your account. Importing electronic bank statements will still further reduce the manual burden of processing statements. The cash-forecasting feature draws on transaction data throughout EBS to extrapolate future cash positions. The calculation is no longer restricted to money flows recorded in the local database. Using the Forecasting open interface, flows can be assimilated from remote databases, which need not be Oracle EBS systems.

CHAPTER
9

Oracle Assets

ixed assets constitute the durable capital base of an enterprise, traditionally the property, plant, and equipment necessary to deliver products and services. The concept has expanded over recent decades to include investments in nontangible assets such as software.

Asset management encompasses three primary activities: physical upkeep, asset tracking, and financial administration. Issues concerning the physical upkeep of assets include asset location, the condition of existing assets, and assignments of asset-management responsibility to various people within an organization. Tracking stores information to enable asset managers to follow leased, loaned, and consigned items from acquisition to disposal. Financial administration issues involve asset value, depreciation, and taxation. Capital assets such as buildings and machinery typically lose value over time. The loss of value during any given period is *depreciation*; it is charged as an expense in that period. The value of the asset at any point in time, usually the cost minus depreciation taken to date, is called the *net book value*.

Oracle Assets has always been a robust product. Users familiar with earlier releases will be pleased to find that now it is a complete asset-management system. Bar-code support for physical inventories makes it easy to reconcile the books with physical reality. The use of bar codes with Asset Warranty Tracking makes it much easier to take full advantage of the service due on a product, even as it moves from department to department.

The types of items tracked in Oracle Assets often require specialized financial consideration. Laws from different jurisdictions dictate how you can depreciate them, what investment tax credits apply, how you treat them in corporate reorganizations, and how you bring *construction in progress* (CIP) items onto the books. Oracle Assets allows you to attach notes in the form of spreadsheets, scanned documents, and other images to asset records. It is the best possible way to associate the online system with your offline business processes.

The introduction in Release 12 of Oracle Subledger Accounting (SLA) to Oracle Assets provides tools that allow users to meet multi-GAAP, corporate, and fiscal accounting requirements.

Oracle Assets provides several out-of-the-box sources and rules to derive account-code combinations and journal-entry descriptions. Users can use the seeded Oracle Assets accounting definitions or they may use the flexibility of SLA to create their own definitions with the Accounting Methods Builder. Users can also add detailed transaction information to journal headers and lines. Detailed subledger accounting journals are available for analytics, auditing, and reporting. They are summarized, transferred, imported and posted to Oracle General Ledger. For more details, see Chapter 4.

Registering and Tracking Assets

The identifiers of the physical items are assigned during the setup of the assets. There are several available identifiers to enable tracking from different perspectives, from the financial analyst tracking take-on, depreciation, and disposal transactions to warehouse staff and building managers tracing the whereabouts of equipment.

In the legacy-system environment you will often find several sources of information used to manage all aspects of assets. One reason for this is that there are distinct needs for the different strands of management, which rarely come together in a single software package. The E-Business Suite (EBS) has pulled these strands together. For example, you can schedule maintenance activities such as regular servicing for vehicles. You can also record insurance values against assets.

Such new areas of functionality combined with the appropriate use of Descriptive Flexfields bring more of the practical operational information into the ERP solution. The two main effects of this are to reduce dual keying, with the accompanying precision and time-saving advantages, and to bring more information into the relational database and within range of business intelligence tools.

The Asset Additions Cycle

Most fixed assets enter the system in batch mode through Mass Additions. You can use a custom program at cutover to populate the open-interface table with legacy data; or you can use the Create Assets feature to prepare the additions in spreadsheets, then use the Applications Desktop Integrator to import and validate your additions. After cutover, the data flow through existing integration from Oracle Purchasing and Oracle Payables. You can have Oracle Projects make entries into the Mass Additions interface as construction is completed on capital projects.

To set up Oracle Inventory and Oracle Purchasing to meet the requirements of Oracle Assets, you might want to assign inventory-item numbers to things you buy on an ongoing basis. You can then give them an asset category that will flow through to Oracle Assets.

You can assign items to a GL asset account as you enter invoices in Oracle Payables. The association actually takes place at the GL distribution level to account for the possibility that the expense for one invoice line might be distributed to multiple organizations.

Run the Create Mass Additions process in Oracle Payables periodically to send additions over to Oracle Assets. After they have been interfaced from Payables, use the Prepare Mass Additions form to fill in missing data. This might include physical attributes and descriptions as well as the location. If the asset does not originate from an item set up in Oracle Inventory with an associated asset category (which carries default depreciation method), you will need to assign one. You might also add other depreciation particulars, such as value, useful life, and how much the asset has already depreciated (for example in a legacy system).

TIP

If you can codify the business rules you use to assign locations and categories, you can save some work by automating this function. The purchase-order number and the accounts-payable (AP) invoice distribution line are available within Oracle Assets. A programmer can follow these items back to Descriptive Flexfield (DFF) entries in the Purchasing or Payables system and then use those DFF entries to fill in the required location, category, and depreciation information. You can make the system capture fixed-asset data from the best possible source, whether you are the requisitioner, buyer, AP clerk, or Oracle Assets administrator.

Tagging with Asset Identifiers

Oracle Assets associates four unique identifiers with each asset. Their names, uses, and sources are shown in Table 9-1.

The tag number relates items controlled by Oracle Assets to legacy and external systems. Oracle imports, accepts, carries, and reports on the tag number but does not generate or otherwise process it; there are several tagging systems. Scannable tags can be preprinted and positioned in the receiving area to be affixed to items as they arrive. Choosing scannable tags

Identifier	Optional?	Use	Source	Purpose
Asset number	No	External; forms and reports	User assigned or generated; can be imported. If generated, it is the same as the asset ID.	Identifies the asset in Oracle Assets forms and reports
Tag number	Yes	External; bar codes	User assigned; usually imported	Provides bar-code tracking of assets
Asset ID	No	Internal	Generated	Links asset records with depreciation and other transactions
Serial number	Yes	External	User assigned	Provides an additional asset identifier; usually assigned by the manufacturer

TABLE 9-1. *Oracle Assets Unique Identifiers*

requires a business procedure to get the tag number into the asset record. Alternatively, you can develop a system to print bar-code tags. If you have that luxury, it might be advantageous to use the asset number as the tag number.

Either alternative will require a moderate amount of third-party or *bespoke* (custom) code. If you are using preprinted tags, consider putting a scanner wedge on the receiving-area terminal. As they affix the tag during the receiving process, staff members can scan the tag number to a Descriptive Flexfield in the Asset Addition interface in Oracle Assets. A small bespoke program can get the tag number from there to the Mass Additions table. Going the other way, it is only a minor programming effort to pull the asset number or tag number out of the system and send it to a bar-code printer.

Oracle Assets includes full support for scanning bar-coded assets, including the capability for reports to reconcile scanned assets to those in the system. The process can drive additions, transfers, and retirements to bring the assets book in line with reality.

Major capital items often include components that need to be separately tracked and depreciated. For example, suppose a building includes an HVAC (heating, ventilating, and air-conditioning) system, which in turn includes compressors and generators. Oracle Assets can carry each device for depreciation purposes, but it will not record any configuration data. When planning your asset-management system, keep in mind that some trackable and depreciable items might be enclosed in or covered by other items—that is, their tags might not be visible.

The Asset Key Flexfield

The Asset Key Flexfield supplements the asset number with descriptive information that can be used to meet your organization's individual needs. Whereas the asset number uniquely identifies an item, the Asset Key Flexfield groups assets by nonfinancial identifiers. Given that important business dimensions such as company, account number, department, and product are often already encoded in the Accounting Flexfield, the Asset Key Flexfield can be used for more asset-specific information, such as a related project number.

The Asset Key Flexfield can include up to 10 segments. As with any Oracle flexfield, you define the number of segments and the name, format, and length of each of them. By taking advantage of Oracle flexfield-validation features, you simplify and refine your data-entry process. If the asset number, tag, and serial number are sufficient for physical tracking, you can use the Asset Key Flexfield instead to aid reporting. In fact, although it must be set up, it does not have to be actively used.

The Asset Key Flexfield plays no role in financial reporting, but is often used as the basis for custom reporting. It is designed to be used with the Descriptive Flexfield for storing information that will be used in custom reports. The standard forms support the complex functions of data capture and validation without the necessity of specific knowledge of the data. This leaves you the relatively simple task of preparing custom reports in the format that best supports your unique needs.

Web Applications Desktop Integrator (Web ADI) enables you to create custom reports for a number of Financials packages, including Oracle Assets. It lets you choose the columns to be displayed and used for selection and sorting in its variable-format reports. The Asset Key Flexfield provides an ideal framework for your custom ADI reporting. It has as many segments as you are likely to need, and the way in which you define it is not constrained by any predefined uses within Oracle Assets.

The Location Flexfield

The Location Flexfield is used for recording the physical location of assets and for property-tax reporting. Its segments usually include the country, state/province/department/land, county, and city in which an asset is located. To facilitate asset moves, you might want to add the addresses of facilities within a city. For example, you could define a Location Flexfield with these segments:

```
COUNTRY | STATE | CITY | LOCATION_CODE.
```

A data record for one of your assets might use those segments to store the following values:

```
USA | CA | Los Angeles | Jarvis House.
```

Oracle allows you to define up to seven segments. The number you decide is final, so you should be generous with your designation. Decide how Oracle's reports will support your property tax business operations. Consider your business processes for physically tracking assets. Plan for the future and define as many segments as you will ever need. You should include the following factors in your decision:

- **Your outside tax-rate services**   Get the tax package at the same time you buy Oracle EBS. Make sure the geography you define maps to the data you will integrate with EBS.

- **Your company locations**   How closely will you track assets? To the city? To a campus? A building? A floor? A room? Your business processes have to achieve a balance between the value of being able to locate assets and the cost of recording their movements.

- **Segment edits**   You will want lookup-table edits of country, state, and county. Which other segments will you want to edit? You probably will have names for your campuses, but can you anticipate every possible room number?

■ **Cross-validation rules** It would be painful to compile and write out the rules for numerous valid combinations of county, country, and state. Unless you can buy these rules through a service, having them all available is probably not worth the effort. On the other hand, you could set up cross-validation rules for your business locations; however, they particularly lend themselves to numeric codes, as they can validate ranges of codes. If you have decided upon regional zones, these could change, leaving you with a rule-maintenance headache; so use cross-validation rules sparingly.

The Category Flexfield

An asset's category determines its financial treatment within Oracle Assets, the way in which the asset is depreciated. The derivation process is illustrated in Figure 9-1.

The asset category specifies a default depreciation method to be used with an asset. You will usually want to set up categories so that you do not need to override the defaults they establish; this way, items can enter the system through Mass Additions without your having to deal with them individually. You can preassign the asset category for any item you buy regularly that is set up in Oracle Inventory.

The asset category specifies the General Ledger accounts to be used for the following:

■ asset-cost and asset-clearing accounts;

■ CIP-cost and CIP-clearing accounts;

■ depreciation-expense and depreciation-reserve accounts; and

■ revaluation-reserve and amortization accounts.

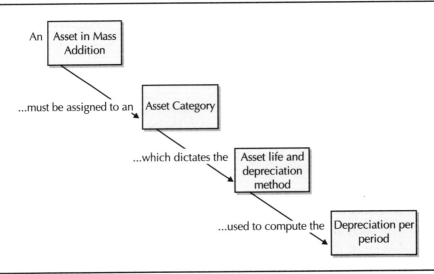

FIGURE 9-1. *Derivation of depreciation amounts*

Oracle provides up to seven segments for the Category Flexfield. You can use separate segments for concepts such as depreciation type, depreciation life, and method; or you can put them all together in a single segment. For example,

Segment 1: Vehicle | Segment 2: Owned-Luxury

or

Segment 1: Vehicle-Owned-Luxury.

Depreciation

Markets ultimately determine the value of any asset, but it would be impractical to survey the market every year to determine what each asset is worth. When an asset is acquired or built, accountants generally assign an initial book value, an economic life, and a formula to determine the depreciation and thus the value of the asset at each period during that economic life. An asset might have a *residual value* beyond which it will not depreciate. For example, a car is always worth one hundred dollars as scrap.

Each period's depreciation is booked as an expense in that period. At the end of the asset's economic life, the initial cost of the asset (less residual value) will have been expensed. The depreciated book value appears on the balance sheet as an asset. The asset is taken off the books when it is sold. The difference between the price received and the book value at the time of sale is posted to a Gain or Loss on Sale income account.

Depreciation is a "funny money" expense that lends itself to accounting tricks. Taking depreciation quickly has the effect not only of understating the value of assets but also of decreasing stated income (hence income taxes). Stretching it out can make a company's book value appear unnaturally healthy. For these reasons, governments and national accounting-standards committees (the Financial Accounting Standards Board, or FASB, in the United States) have standardized the ways in which companies recognize depreciation. The primary objectives of these groups include ensuring fair taxation and enabling shareholders to make meaningful comparisons between companies.

Ledger Accounting

The depreciation expense from each Oracle Assets depreciation book flows to a single ledger within General Ledger (GL). The flexfield combinations for the various asset, liability, and depreciation expense accounts are in the Accounting Flexfield structure that corresponds to that primary ledger. The relationship is many-to-one: many Assets books can be associated with one GL primary ledger.

There is an advantage to keeping the relationship one-to-one. Oracle Assets can easily handle transfers of assets between organizations when those organizations are in one Assets book. It generates intercompany journals to move the assets and associated liabilities between balancing segments within the one primary ledger in General Ledger.

To move assets from one asset book into an associated tax book, you can run the Mass Copy process, which will automatically migrate all assets and their associated transactions. There are also Initial Mass Copy, which copies new assets from a closed fiscal year to the open fiscal-year period in the tax book; and Periodic Mass Copy, which is run every period to keep the tax book in line with the corporate one—it just copies new assets.

You can avoid a lot of work by keeping all assets in a single asset book. During the setup of your book, define your various flexfields in such a way that you can create the necessary reports and journal postings through native Oracle Assets functions. As you weigh your various reporting requirements against keeping separate ledgers, be sure to favor the data over rigid adherence to a "pure vanilla" use of Oracle Assets. You will minimize maintenance effort if you keep the data structure simple and keep all of your records in one asset book.

Some businesses need to use multiple asset books to keep separate the assets of different divisions that share a single set of GL books. For example, a construction company might have a separate division to manage its plant and machinery and rent it out to other parts of the corporation. Oracle Assets in the E-Business Suite now makes use of the organization hierarchy to secure access to data by asset book. Security hierarchies are also a feature of Oracle Human Resources (HR); in Oracle Assets they are set up to associate organizations with asset books. Then responsibilities can be set up to use these security profiles, so that in the earlier example just the plant personnel can see the plant assets.

NOTE
Even if you do not buy a license for Oracle HR, some shared tables and forms are available in other modules, such as Payables, Purchasing, and Projects. This is because the employee and organization entities are owned by HR; therefore, there is no difference to the other modules whether HR is a full or shared installation—their use of HR tables remains the same.

Business Taxes and the Need for Multiple Asset Books

Many government bodies tax business assets. These bodies might have their own assessors—common for agencies dealing with property taxes applied to real estate and fixed plant assets—or they might allow the business itself to compute the tax based on a legislated formula. The taxing entities accept the company's own records (which are audited by outside auditors and, if necessary, by the taxing authorities themselves) as the basis for computing tax liability.

These government entities regulate and monitor the way in which assets are depreciated. The longer the life of an asset, the more the government will receive in tax revenue. Moreover, the less depreciation expense a company takes, the more revenue will be subject to income taxes. Governments set their own rules governing the depreciable life of different categories of assets and the depreciation formulas that apply to them. Not surprisingly, different taxing entities demand different depreciation schedules.

Oracle Assets helps you compute the most favorable taxation in areas over which you have some discretion. It has the capability to carry one asset in multiple tax-depreciation books for different taxing jurisdictions. The purpose is usually to carry varying net-asset-value figures in accordance with the different sets of laws, although depreciation and investment tax credits might figure too.

It would be impossible to achieve consistency between depreciation deductions (and the resultant net asset values) in one ledger and property-tax computations in another. If the depreciation schedules are different, the asset values will also differ. In the United States, most jurisdictions follow the federal government's lead regarding depreciation computations; otherwise, it would be much more difficult to reconcile state and federal tax returns. This arrangement means that it is usually adequate to maintain two depreciation books: financial and federal. States, counties, and cities are less concerned with whether the asset reports and property-tax filings they receive agree in value with the company's income-tax filings, as long as the two filings can be reconciled and each jurisdiction gets the tax computed by the formulas it dictates.

Merger and Acquisition Considerations

Tangible assets are a major factor in valuing corporate reorganizations. Assets that change ownership need to be fully identified by item, cost, and remaining depreciation. Because it is independent of financial factors, the Asset Key Flexfield is useful for grouping assets to be transferred. Once grouped, their value can be reported and agreed upon.

Oracle Assets carries all the data required to generate Mass Additions into a new system. In other words, the Oracle Assets module serves as a very accessible legacy system. Custom scripts to extract data for export are easy to write. The acquiring firm will find all the essential data regardless of whether it uses Oracle Assets.

Tax books shadow the actual asset books. Thus, the export procedure for *deacquired* assets (those that have been sold, scrapped, or transferred out) must ensure that the same assets appear in the financial and tax books after a reorganization. However, tax books require a separate export/import process using Mass Copy, because tax-book depreciation is independent of financial depreciation.

Taxes

Property tax is the major tax-reporting requirement addressed by Oracle Assets. The concerns are the location of each item and the value of each item in the eyes of the taxing authorities. The second major tax issue, income tax, is handled by General Ledger, which uses asset value and depreciation figures from Oracle Assets. Oracle Assets also carries the data to support other types of taxation, such as lease tax and use tax. Minor taxes can be handled by linking spreadsheets to asset records, but the system lends itself to custom-coded extensions where they are needed.

Property-Tax Calculation

Oracle Assets supports real and personal property-tax calculations through tax books and the Location Flexfield. The Property Tax report shows assets within a given geography. Real and personal property are distinguished by the property class assigned to the asset. You can use the desktop interface to pull these assets into a spreadsheet to compute tax liability.

Spreadsheets play a major role in most Oracle Assets property-tax computations. Although the rules are complex—different states and counties have their own rules for property classes and depreciation—the data are not highly volatile. It works well to have Oracle EBS serve as the repository for these handmade processes and the data that drive them.

Oracle EBS has been fully integrated with three specialized third-party property-tax preparation services. You send them data from Oracle Assets in their format: a Location Flexfield in the layout they dictate, identifying data for the taxable property, and your valuation data. The services will prepare property taxes for all applicable filing jurisdictions. They are simple to use and accurate, and saves significant amounts of time.

Income-Tax Calculation

Tracking depreciation is the primary means by which Oracle Assets can help you calculate your income taxes. Depreciation reduces taxes by reducing taxable income. Gains and losses on sales can be viewed as adjustments to depreciation. Investment tax credits, a tax-policy device used in the United States to favor certain types of business investments, affect the tax itself rather than taxable income.

Depreciation Methods

Depreciation is an instrument of public tax policy; depreciation regulations are designed to encourage investment. Allowing a company to *front-load* depreciation schedules (that is, to take more depreciation early in an asset's life) reduces the tax liability that results from a capital investment. The tax is made up in later years when less depreciation remains to be taken. Table 9-2 shows the effect that straight-line depreciation would have on a $5,000 investment for a firm in the 40 percent tax bracket. Table 9-3 shows the effect of accelerated depreciation on the same loan.

	Year 1	Year 2	Year 3	Year 4	Year 5	Total
Investment	−$5,000	0	0	0	0	−$5,000
Depreciation	$1,000	$1,000	$1,000	$1,000	$1,000	
Net cash flow before taxes	−$4,000	$1,000	$1,000	$1,000	$1,000	
Income-tax benefit at 40 percent	$400	$400	$400	$400	$400	$2,000
After-tax cash-flow effect of investment	−$4,600	$400	$400	$400	$400	−$3,000

TABLE 9-2. *Cash Flow for a Straight-Line Depreciation*

	Year 1	Year 2	Year 3	Year 4	Year 5	Total
Investment	−$5,000	0	0	0	0	−$5,000
Depreciation	$1,250	$1,900	$1,850	0	0	
Net cash flow before taxes	−$3,750	$1,900	$1,850	0	0	
Income-tax benefit at 40 percent	$500	$760	$740	0	0	$2,000
After-tax cash-flow effect of investment	−$4,500	$760	$740	0	0	−$3,000

TABLE 9-3. *Cash Flow Under Three-Year ACRS*

Whether or not you maintain tax books in General Ledger, the real-money implications of tax-book numbers must ultimately flow to the GL financial books. To account for the differences in depreciation recognized between the two books, follow these steps:

1. Within Oracle Assets, post depreciation from Assets's financial books to the set of financial books in General Ledger. The postings should look something like these:

Account	Debit	Credit
Depreciation expense	$20,000	
Depreciation reserve		$20,000

2. Use the tax books with Assets to compute the depreciation allowed for tax purposes. Subtract the depreciation listed in the financial books from the depreciation listed in the tax books to determine additional allowable depreciation expense. Suppose it is $5,000. To take additional depreciation in the current year but show that it must be paid back in future years, create manual journal entries like these:

Account	Debit	Credit
Net depreciation expense adjustment	$5,000	
Deferred depreciation expense		$5,000

3. Create a manual journal entry for the tax implications of the accelerated depreciation. If the rate were 40 percent, the entries would look like these:

Account	Debit	Credit
Income tax payable adjustment	$2,000	
Deferred income tax		$2,000

Accounting for Assets

The workflow-based Account Generator is the driver for accounting for assets transactions. The default accounts are retrieved from one of three sources: the asset book, the asset category, and the asset assignment. Different segments of the Accounting Flexfield can be generated from different sources. As this Account Generator method is used frequently across the E-Business Suite, it is an important area in which to have some skills and experience available during the implementation of the system, particularly if changes to the out-of-the-box default setup will be required. It is possible to convert the Flexbuilder rules used in earlier releases of Oracle Assets into Account Generator flows, to keep customized accounting that is already in place.

Depreciation Analysis

There might be different options available in the management of the asset base that affect the financial-accounting reporting. Should you lease or buy plant and machinery? What is the impact of selling off a vehicle that has become expensive to maintain, or of replacing the old, faithful printing press with a new, quicker model? You specify the asset category, value, and in-service date; the software calculates the depreciation into the future. This will be particularly useful for the more complex depreciation methods that are sometimes required by industry regulations.

To accommodate this, you can create formula-based depreciation methods as an alternative to the more normal ones such as straight line, reducing balances, units of production (for example, barrels per day for an oil well), ACRS, and MACRS.

NOTE
If you want to make an adjustment to the depreciation after you have run the depreciation program, perhaps to take account of a disposal that has happened in the meantime, you now have two options. You can run depreciation again, because running it no longer automatically closes the period in Oracle Assets. This will depreciate all the assets that were not depreciated in that period's previous run. Alternatively, you can roll back the depreciation run you have already done and rerun it from the start. A new feature introduced in Release 12 makes it so that Oracle Assets automatically rolls back the depreciation on just the assets that had changes (instead of the whole book) and allows the transactions to be processed normally. The assets for which depreciation was rolled back are automatically picked up during the next depreciation run or at the time that the depreciation period is finally closed.

Recoverability Ratio

Recoverable cost is the total amount of investment that can be recouped through depreciation over an asset's lifetime. Both the financial and the tax books carry recoverable costs. When the recoverable amounts in the tax and financial books are the same, usually the price of the asset minus its salvage value, there is no problem in computing depreciation. The total lifetime depreciation flowing from the tax books will equal the total flowing from the financial books. Accelerated depreciation will be recaptured within the asset's lifetime.

If the recoverable cost in the tax books exceeds the recoverable cost in the financial books, the full depreciation from the tax books could exceed the price of the item. Tax authorities do not allow this. The Oracle Assets topical essay entitled *Calculating Deferred Depreciation* suggests the following steps for handling this situation:

1. Run the Oracle Assets Recoverability report to compute the lifetime recoverable cost in the financial and tax books.

2. Compute the ratio between the two: corporate (financial) recoverable cost to tax recoverable cost. This recoverability ratio should be less than one.

3. Multiply the tax depreciation in each period by the recoverability ratio. This will force the total recoverable cost on the tax side to equal the total corporate recoverable cost. Financial depreciation will still have the shape of the tax depreciation curve, usually front-end loaded, with more depreciation in the early years. Each period's depreciation will just be proportionately less, so the total depreciation just equals the allowed amount.

Investment Tax Credit

An *investment tax credit* (ITC) is independent of depreciation. The taxing authority allows a company to reduce its tax obligation by a fixed percentage of a qualifying capital investment. The downstream considerations come into play when the asset is sold or retired. If the asset has not been in use for the prescribed period of time, the company might be liable for ITC recapture upon the sale.

Leased Assets

The physical handling of leased assets is similar to that of owned assets. The major difference is the need to track when the lease will expire, so that the lease can be extended or the item returned. Lease-expiration dates and lease terms must be carefully monitored.

Financially, leased items are more an issue for the accounts-payable department than for managers of fixed assets. The accounts-payable department makes the periodic payments. However, capital leases have an amortization structure with principal and interest elements. Oracle Assets carries and displays amortization data, which allows you to view the amortization schedule on a capital lease. The distinctions between an operating lease, which can be expensed, and a capital lease, which is treated as a sale or purchase from an accounting standpoint, are subtle. Oracle Assets applies an FASB13 test to leased assets in order to determine how they would be accounted for under US tax law. However, you can override Oracle's determination if your tax rules are different.

Capital Budgeting

Capital budgets are projections of capital expenditures and the depreciation expense flows that recapture those expenses. Oracle Assets includes reports to compare budgets and actual expenses on a yearly basis. Reports of projected depreciation are useful for General Ledger budgeting purposes as well.

Oracle Assets budgets follow groupings of asset books and asset categories. This arrangement offers a finer level of control than General Ledger budgeting, which must be done within the Accounting Flexfield structure.

Converting to Oracle Assets

Converting your assets correctly is a major challenge in cutting over from your legacy system to Oracle Assets. Testing—through repeated trial conversions—is the key to success. The critical determinants are whether the asset figures (original cost and depreciation reserve) and the future depreciation stream are correct. Your conversion test plan should accomplish the following goals:

- **Establish criteria for success at the balance-sheet level**   Start by comparing the legacy asset and depreciation reserve accounts stored in General Ledger to the legacy-system figures stored in Oracle Assets. Because some legacy assets and ledger systems are independent of one another, the figures might not match. On the other hand, Oracle EBS keeps the two in absolute agreement. You need to plan for a one-time accounting adjustment to bring assets and the ledger in line at conversion. The standard criterion for success in converting assets is that the totals of asset value, depreciation reserve, and residual value in Oracle EBS match the total in the legacy system. The test plan will specify that reports from the two systems match.

- **Establish criteria for success at the depreciation-expense level**   The standard criterion for success here is that the future depreciation cash flows are the same in Oracle EBS as in the legacy system. Again, specify the reports that should match between the two systems.

- **Define depreciation methods and categories to accommodate legacy assets** Each asset that enters Oracle EBS through Mass Additions will be identified with a category and, through the category, a predefined depreciation method. You cannot import a depreciation flow with an item; you must use an Oracle-assigned method. If there are assets in the legacy system that do not have a corresponding method in Oracle EBS, you can reach the required degree of accuracy by mapping them to one very close. You will pay in effort and time if you have to exactly match depreciation between EBS and the legacy system

- **Establish a strategy for assets that have remained on their original depreciation schedules** These are the easy ones. Oracle EBS can correctly establish the net book value and remaining depreciation flow given the original cost, current cost, recoverable cost, depreciation plan, and date the asset was placed in service. Your plan should call for importing these values; you can use them to run depreciation for the subsequent years. The legacy-ledger balances already reflect acquisitions and the prior year's depreciation, so the resulting journals would double the values. There are two strategies to deal with this issue: delete the journals before they can be posted or post them and reverse them (which shows a clear audit trail). The Oracle Assets book should reflect the same values as the legacy book, and it should generate the same depreciation going forward.

- **Establish a strategy for assets with depreciation schedules that have changed over time** Taking a simple example, suppose a $10,000 asset goes into service on a five-year depreciation schedule, but is changed after three years to a 10-year life, with the adjustment to be amortized. Give it zero residual value. Figure 9-2 shows the asset's lifetime depreciation; Figure 9-3 shows the residual value at the end of each year.

If the asset is imported into Oracle at the end of the sixth year, it will have a residual value of $2,283 and see depreciation of $571 per year. These figures ($10,000, $2,283, and $571 per year)

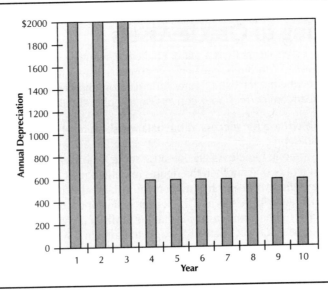

FIGURE 9-2. *An asset's lifetime depreciation*

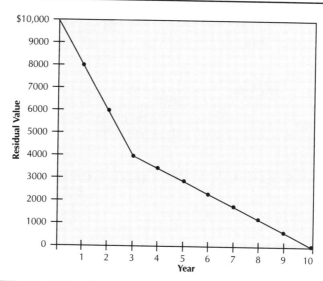

FIGURE 9-3.   *An asset's residual value at the end of each year*

are the original cost, residual value, and depreciation flow that would apply in the last three years of a $10,000 item depreciated over 17.5 years. The numbers in Oracle would be exactly correct if the in-service date were pushed back by 7.5 years, and the asset were depreciated on a 17.5 year straight-line plan.

However, this approach poses some difficulty. First, the in-service date might be important in the future; changing it misrepresents reality. More significantly, there is no standard depreciation schedule for a 17.5-year life. Oracle deals only with integers of years for asset life. The asset would require a handmade, one-of-a-kind depreciation plan; so would every other asset that changed plans or saw an amortized adjustment anywhere over its life.

- Oracle provides the tools you need to enter revalued assets directly. As you enter the cost data in the FA_MASS_ADDITIONS table, also enter the revaluation reserve and the revaluation-amortization basis. Oracle Assets will record the original cost in the books, but compute future depreciation using the revalued figures.

- There is a Mass Additions Upload feature in the Applications Desktop Integrator. You can purify and prepare your assets data in a spreadsheet, then have Web ADI load the data directly to the FA_MASS_ADDITIONS table. This is a good way of reducing the amount of development resources required, which enables you to concentrate your efforts on the data cleansing that is usually required. However, with this process there is no way of handling an asset that has a different cost in the asset book and its associated tax books. If accumulated depreciation is brought over this way, it only applies to the asset book. When you copy assets to tax books with Initial Mass Copy and run depreciation, Oracle Assets will calculate it based on category defaults. These defaults also define the remaining life in years of the asset.

Converting Tax Books

When converting your tax books, the preferred method is to repeat the tax-book depreciation process. First, add the item to the financial books; then move it to the appropriate tax books. Run depreciation against both the financial and the tax books.

The converted tax books might tie in to a set of tax books in General Ledger, but not all companies keep multiple ledger books. The conversion plan must include procedures for generating balance reports in the Oracle EBS and legacy assets tax books to show that both sides agree on the amounts being transferred within tax books. These amounts include acquisition cost, depreciation plan, accumulated depreciation, and residual value for tax purposes.

Trade-Offs Between Record Keeping and Reporting

The one parameter common to most of Oracle's standard reports is the asset set of books. Several reports group items by category and location, and only a few group items by Asset Key Flexfield. Unless you use desktop functions, your design of reports and sets of books must take into account two conflicting design points: *report structure* and *asset transfers*.

- **Report structure** Because most reports accept only a few parameters, reporting is easiest with multiple sets of asset books, each with relatively few entries. The easiest way to report on groups of assets within one primary ledger in General Ledger is to keep them in separate asset sets of books.

- **Asset transfers** Because the only way to transfer items between Ledgers is to remove them and then add them back in, the system structure favors fewer, more inclusive asset sets of books within a primary ledger in General Ledger.

Oracle Assets provides the necessary master record of which items the company owns and where they are. The master record is the thread that ties the systems together for audit purposes: the ledger agrees with the Oracle Assets books, and all Assets books carry the same assets.

The more than 100 standard reports in the Oracle Assets system are indicative of the variety of information needs. Even a thousand could not satisfy all users; yet each installation uses only a small fraction of those provided. Variable Format Reports, which you can access through ADI's Request Center, is a new feature that works with Oracle Assets. You can extract Assets data to be manipulated with whatever desktop tool you favor. Spreadsheets are the most common. You can also go to the Internet using HTML. Defining how to extract data for use in standard variable-format reports is a setup and programming task. From that point on, creating reports is strictly up to the Oracle Assets users.

The alternative to using desktop tools is to modify the standard Oracle reports, primarily adding additional selection criteria. Doing this is a much easier and less expensive task to manage than fragmenting the assets among many financial books.

Conclusion

Oracle Assets provides the essential record-keeping features for property, plant, and equipment, combined with the processing logic required to support almost every conceivable depreciation schedule. It will help you maintain accurate financial records of assets for financial and income-tax reporting purposes, and its design ensures the integrity of the journals it sends to General Ledger.

Improved integration with other systems—notably Projects and Payables—gives Oracle Assets more physical asset-management functions, along with the ability to handle leases and warranty information. You can take advantage of Oracle's partnerships with tax-information providers to compute your property-tax filings automatically. The open design of the module allows you to easily capture and work with custom data. You can add processes to manipulate and report on fixed-assets data through spreadsheets linked to the database, third-party software built to work with Oracle, or your own custom routines.

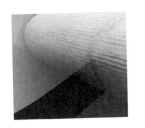

CHAPTER
10

Oracle Purchasing

urchasing is an integral part of the corporate supply chain. Among other things, it replenishes your inventory, fulfills customer demand, and helps control outside processing. Manufacturing and inventory departments base their purchasing recommendations on what goods are being requested and what goods are on order, as well as when they will arrive.

Purchasing Overview

Purchasing is usually considered the first phase in the supply-chain cycle. Its major functions are sourcing, requisitioning, purchasing, and receiving. The strength of the process lies in supporting operational rather than management decisions. For example, it can help personnel determine whether to approve an order or how much of an item to replenish, but it does not address such strategic questions as which suppliers should enjoy long-term contractual relationships. Oracle's Business Intelligence (BI) System completes the picture. It provides all levels of users with answers to questions across all Oracle EBS modules, including Purchasing. You can access information directly from the transaction system or from a central repository, such as a data warehouse.

Purchasing handles all acquisition activity within a company: goods and services, raw materials, capital goods, expendable supplies—everything the company needs. It captures task and accounting information that will be needed downstream by Project Accounting, Fixed Assets, Payables, and eventually the General Ledger. People and systems throughout the company use requisitions to tell the purchasing department what they need. Purchasing orders the requisitioned goods from suppliers; Receiving accepts delivery of items and delivers them internally to the requisitioner, or stocks them in inventory.

Approval policies are applied to all purchasing documents before the system acts on them. The document will be routed through the appropriate approval chain according to the type of document (purchase order or requisition), the accounts impacted, the amount ordered, its destination, and the type of material ordered. Oracle Purchasing efficiently determines the accounting distribution for each purchasing line by applying logic to the input provided by the requisitioner or buyer. The Workflow engine used to guide transactions through the routing and accounting-distribution processes provides users with excellent guidance and enables them to adapt the processes as necessary.

With Release 12 of the E-Business Suite, Oracle has made very good improvements in Purchasing functionality. Many of the changes add better user experience and tighter control. Oracle has introduced the Professional Buyer's Work Center, a next-generation interface that provides command and control for the procurement department, shown in Figure 10-1. Designed for contract administrators and procurement professionals, the Work Center combines ease of use with powerful capabilities to track, manage, and control all strategic and tactical activities.

In addition, due to the increasing share of budget allocated to services, procurement organizations are increasingly being given responsibility to control services spending. Much of services spending goes to complex services, such as outsourced high-value projects that require extensive collaboration between the buyer and supplier organizations. These services include consulting, advertising, construction, research and development, and professional services. These services require complex negotiated contracts that often include intricate payment arrangements. Oracle Procurement supports acquisition of complex services by allowing buyers to author, negotiate, execute, and monitor contract-payment arrangements like progress payments, advances, and retainage.

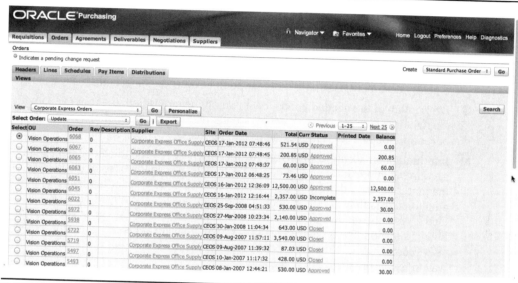

FIGURE 10-1. *New Professional Buyer's Work Center window*

Two other areas where functionality had to be customized in prior releases were attachments on purchasing documents to the suppliers and the approval process. Now buyers can communicate all necessary attachments to suppliers, including file attachments via e-mail and approval support for requisitions. Oracle Purchasing further expands and enhances integration with the Oracle Approvals Management product for approval routing of purchase requisitions. This integration gives enterprises even more flexibility to configure their business-approval processes. Key enhancements include parallel approvals and approvals based on position hierarchy.

The whole set of purchasing processes is now packaged as Oracle Strategic Procurement. It covers all the steps, starting with requests for materials from requisitioner to supplier (in Self-Service Procurement) and extending to incoming supplier catalogues. At the management level, Business Intelligence brings together the statistics to facilitate and monitor strategic procurement initiatives. BI can even provide cross-operating unit reporting, which is a useful feature for a shared service center.

The Purchasing module is the repository for all this information. It holds the documents including requisitions, purchase orders, and supplier price and item catalogs. It is where the approval hierarchy is set up, which is used by the workflow approvals. It can go live independently of the other parts of the procurement product set—and this might be a useful way to proceed, although the design should encompass the wider procurement goals.

Requisitions

The requisition form begins the procurement process. It says, "I want it." The requisition process traditionally has been a manual one, with a trail of paper forms and written approvals. Because they had to be relatively simple, the manual-approvals procedures were frequently inappropriately loose or restrictive for the requisition in question.

A manual process works well for some but does not take advantage of integration. Oracle Purchasing is flexible enough to support all kinds of business procedures. The objective of the requisition form is to efficiently capture everything from the eventual user up front. This user is the best source for defaulting the following information:

- **Requisitioner's identity and organization**   With Oracle Purchasing, capture of these data is automated, though the user has the option to override the defaults.

- **Description of the needed goods**   With an online requisition, the user can either choose the right item from an online catalog or enter descriptive information and a suggested buyer and supplier for nonstock items and services.

- **Information on accounts to charge for the purchase**   Depending on your setup, most accounting information will be derived automatically on the basis of the identity of the requisitioner and the item being requested. The requisitioner is a better source for additional data than people further downstream, such as the buyers and the payables clerks. Also, the requisitioner is the one who will know and care most about his or her budget situation. For users with lengthy Accounting Flexfields or significant project- and task-information requirements, capturing accounting data at requisition time is the only way to make sure the input is accurate.

Oracle Purchasing uses workflow technology to incorporate many requisitioning-related functions. The workflows that are delivered are flexible, rule-based processes that you can tailor to meet specific business needs. For instance, Purchasing can approve requisitions automatically and create purchase orders directly on the basis of factors such as the cost, item category, and requisitioner. It can automatically route requisitions through an approval cycle and prompt approvers to act. Approval does not have to be an approval of the cost of the material requested; for example, it can be to ensure that the technical specification matches the corporate standard. Purchasing can communicate by e-mail, over the Web, or directly through the applications.

With procurement cards (sometimes known as *P-cards*), you can bypass requisitioning altogether. Employees use their procurement cards to make a purchase; Oracle Payables derives the accounting information from data imported from the card issuer. Employees can verify their transactions, change the accounting data, and challenge any transactions on the statement that they did not make. Alternatively, you can still use a requisition but have the requisitioner put the card number on the requisition. Once the requisition is approved, the purchase will flow through on the card without the need for purchase-order or release transactions. As there is not always sufficient detail available from the card issuer about items bought, the use of requisitions can be a way of maintaining control and reporting while reaping the efficiency benefits of the card model.

The Inventory and Material Requirements Planning modules compute requirements by balancing *demand* (a combination of orders and forecasts) against *supply* (what is on hand, on order, and being manufactured). These systems can create requisitions to fill the difference between supply and demand. The generating systems populate all of the required data fields; these requisitions are usually converted to purchase-order releases that you can set up to pass straight to the suppliers without buyer intervention.

Approval policy for requisitions is defined at setup. Controls are imposed according to what is being ordered, who is ordering it, and how much it costs. These factors also determine which people appear in the approval chain or hierarchy. Even though just as many people might have to approve a requisition, the paperless approval process is usually quicker. Whereas a paper requisition might sit in an in-box for a week, Oracle Purchasing actively pushes actions awaiting approval to the approvers' attention when they log in. The automated system can have variable routing depending on who is available. As a last resort, Oracle Workflow and Oracle Alerts can automatically generate e-mail to nudge actions that seem to be hung up along the way. In theory, all this automation and notification should speed up the requisitioning process.

Requisition templates can also be set up to streamline the entry of requisition lines. Your Item Master might contain thousands of part numbers, yet most groups within your organization order only from a small subset of that large list. Requisition templates can be created from a list of frequently ordered items or even from an existing requisition, saving your employees time and preventing the mistakes and the resulting waste of time involved in searching the entire Item Master for the parts they need.

Suppliers

Successful buying entails satisfying the needs of the company at the lowest overall cost. This is often not the same as getting the lowest price. Buyers' time costs money, and unreliable suppliers can cost a company in terms of lost production, lost sales, and paperwork involved in tasks such as inspections, returns, credit memos, and invoice adjustments. Supplier relationships are a key element in purchasing strategy, and Oracle Purchasing is designed to manage these relationships.

Suppliers need to be set up before a buyer can create a purchase order. The essentials of supplier setup include name and address, site, terms of payment, and type (outside supplier, employee, or other types you have set up). Other information can be entered at the supplier level, saving keystrokes at the transaction level later on. There is usually a preferred ship-to address, bill-to address, mode of shipment, and so on associated with a supplier. Information entered for the supplier will become the default for all purchase orders entered for that supplier. Other data elements satisfy government tax and statutory reporting requirements. Payables and Purchasing share the same suppliers, and supplier sites and supplier maintenance screens can be made available in either or both of these applications. (Supplier access should be a secured process within any organization.) Responsibilities and business procedures should be in place to ensure that the supplier-update process is coordinated, and that only approved suppliers are entered and any duplication avoided.

Release 12 moves the Suppliers interface from Oracle Forms into Oracle Application Framework (OAF). This new user interface (UI) presents a clear distinction between the supplier's company details and terms and controls for the trading relationship. Managing the attributes specific to particular functional areas, such as Oracle Payables, Purchasing, and Receiving, can be controlled with the use of Function Security. The introduction of a quick update page allows tailoring of the screen with those values most often updated, for even faster maintenance.

Along with the many attributes that could be captured using the previous Forms-based user interface, the new Suppliers interface also includes a Survey section that provides administrators with access to the results of questionnaires that the supplier has been asked to complete, either during self-registration or as part of profile maintenance through iSupplier Portal.

NOTE
Since Oracle EBS Release 12 provides a new screen for vendors in Oracle Application Framework (OAF), if you had customizations or extensions on Oracle Forms in prior versions, you will have to reapply those in the new screen.

Supplier Relationships

Both buyers and sellers find it most efficient to set up long-term purchasing relationships. Sellers get business they can plan on, and buyers get the advantages of negotiated low prices, minimal paperwork, and the reliability that can only be achieved by sharing planning information with trusted suppliers. Both sides find it worthwhile to invest in establishing these relationships, and Oracle Purchasing provides several features that will help you manage them.

Contracts

Purchase orders and purchase agreements are the contractual vehicles recognized by Oracle Purchasing. Purchase orders (POs) are one-time affairs, complete unto themselves: They specify what to deliver, when, and where. POs might be adequate for all procurement activity in smaller organizations, and the 90 percent of the suppliers who account for 10 percent of purchasing volume in larger organizations. However, long-term supplier relationships usually involve purchase agreements.

There are two types of purchase agreements. The more basic, a *blanket purchase agreement* (BPA), specifies items and prices as negotiated with the supplier. A BPA usually applies for a given period of time; it also can stipulate minimum and maximum unit and dollar order amounts. Purchase-order releases referencing the BPA are created as required to tell the supplier how many to ship and where. A global blanket agreement is a special type of BPA in which buyers can negotiate enterprise-wide pricing, business by business, then execute and manage those agreements in one central shared environment.

A *contract purchase agreement*, the second type of purchase agreement, is really only an agreement to agree. It specifies terms and conditions but no items; other types of POs can reference a contract purchase agreement. A contract purchase agreement can also support competitive solicitations. First, there has to be an approved quotation through the request-for-quotation (RFQ) process, which is described later in this chapter; then buyers create purchase orders with lines referencing both the contract purchase agreement and the approved quotation under it. The introduction of a global contract agreement helps to centralize a supplier relationship. With this type of a contract agreement, buyers throughout the organization can reference the global contract agreement in the standard purchase order.

Planned purchase orders (PPOs) establish a vehicle to satisfy projected material and services needs over a period of time; they mix features of standard orders and BPAs. Like a standard order, PPOs specify accounting distributions for each line item. Like with BPOs, the lines are only tentative; a release is required for actual delivery. A PPO can be used to reserve funds under encumbrance accounting. For example, a school system, not knowing exactly how much heating oil it will require for the year or when the oil would be delivered, can use a PPO to protect that line of the budget with an encumbrance.

Solicitations

The process of establishing a relationship can be formal or informal. The United States federal government sets the standard for formal procurements; the European Union does the same for its members. The process also represents a maximum investment in establishing a supplier relationship. It is worth identifying each of the steps in the full process to see where the features of Oracle Purchasing can be useful:

1. A department within the company or agency drafts a requirement document, specifying what and how much is needed and when it is needed.

2. The buyers use their fund of experience and outside databases to assemble a list of potential suppliers.

3. Purchasing sends requests for information (RFIs) to the identified suppliers. It also might publish the solicitation. US public agencies use the newspapers and Federal Business Opportunities (FedBizOpps.gov). In Europe the solicitation must be advertised in the *European Journal of Purchasing and Supply Management* if the contract value is over certain monetary limits (depending on the industry sector).

4. Purchasing decides whether to do a formal procurement. If not, it skips to step 7 of this list and enters into negotiations with one or more suppliers.

5. For a formal procurement, purchasing writes a request for proposal (RFP) or a request for quotation. The RFP restates the requirement and specifies the format for a response. It might dictate some terms and conditions (T&Cs) and specify the format for adaptable T&Cs that must be stipulated in the bid. The request often spells out the criteria that will be used in evaluating the proposal. Purchasing sends the bids to all qualified parties who have expressed an interest and follows up with a bidder's conference.

6. Purchasing evaluates supplier proposals.

7. Purchasing asks the top bidders for best and final offers (BAFOs). The suppliers' BAFOs typically firm up terms and conditions.

8. The two parties complete a contract incorporating the RFP and BAFO documents.

The Purchasing RFQ process starts at step 5, with an RFP or RFQ. If the RFI needs to be communicated to a large audience, Purchasing could begin at step 3 by posting the requirement through Oracle Web Suppliers. Seen from another perspective, the RFQ itself serves as an RFI. It alerts suppliers to your need. The approved suppliers list (ASL) that Purchasing uses can carry source and price information item by item. An RFQ identifies a few suppliers from whom to request quotes on items that may or may not have been defined yet in the Inventory Item Master. (Items such as nonproduction purchases might never become part of the inventory system.) Purchasing provides forms for defining the RFP and entering bids. Once an award is made, the buyers cement the link between the procurement and the existing purchase agreement. They can then use Oracle's approved suppliers list and sourcing rules to indicate, by item or commodity, which contracts to source from.

A supplier list is a predefined set of suppliers that can be referenced when putting together an RFQ. A company might have contract purchase orders with Staples, OfficeMax, and Office Depot. To save time, it could put those three suppliers on a list called, perhaps, "Office Supply." Putting together an RFQ for printer cartridges would involve simply naming the item and the supplier list. You can then print out one RFQ per supplier on the list.

A competitive procurement can require a lot of time, which of course is not free. There are opportunity costs associated with the elapsed time, as the business might not be able to move until procurement is complete. Unless the business's policies absolutely require a competitive process, the purchasing manager might want to apply a cost–benefit analysis and limit RFQs to larger procurements. By posting solicitations on the Web, Oracle Web Suppliers can decrease the time and cost involved in a competitive buy.

Approvals

Separating the authority to initiate and approve expenditures is a fundamental accounting control observed by most organizations. The security controls define which types of approvals apply to each document type, and which people can view and modify each document type.

A setup parameter determines whether approval goes by individual (supervisor) or by position (hierarchy). Either way, approval uses human-resources tables, which are present regardless of whether you have Oracle Human Resources installed. If it goes by supervisor, the system looks at the supervisor link in a person's record. If it goes by position, the system finds the position each person occupies, links to the position hierarchy to find which position is next in the pecking order, and then links back to find the incumbent in that position, as shown in Figure 10-2.

Of course the next step up still might not be sufficiently senior to sign off on a large order. You can either set the system up to send that person the approval anyway, or find the level at which the approval limit is sufficient for the sum at stake and only send the approval notification there. If there are many holders of the position that has the appropriate approval limit, the system will choose the first person alphabetically and send that person the approval notification. Because an EBS user is linked to a person record, when you log on with your user name and password and respond to a notification, it is your electronic signature.

The overview presented here introduces the approval architecture and gives an idea of what can be done with the product's existing features. The discussion follows the setup sequence recommended in the *Installation Guide*. It ties in to Figure 10-3, which shows the major tables and the processes that populate them.

You must coordinate Purchasing with Oracle Human Resources (HR) if you are using both systems. When both systems are used, you can perform the following steps as part of the HR setup:

1. **Define jobs** A *job* is a set of responsibilities, such as those performed by a buyer or a receiving clerk. The people who create and approve purchasing documents have jobs. You need to define only those jobs that will be referenced in your approval process. Requisition approvals can involve most of the company, whereas purchase-order approvals are pretty much confined to the purchasing department.

2. **Define positions** This step is necessary if you are defining approvals by position hierarchies rather than supervisors. A *position* is a job slot—a job within an organization at a location. (Organizations and locations have to be defined earlier in the setup process.) Documents will be routed on the basis of the relationship between positions. This relationship is set up in the position hierarchy.

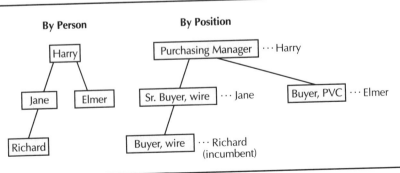

FIGURE 10-2. *Supervisor versus hierarchy approval structures*

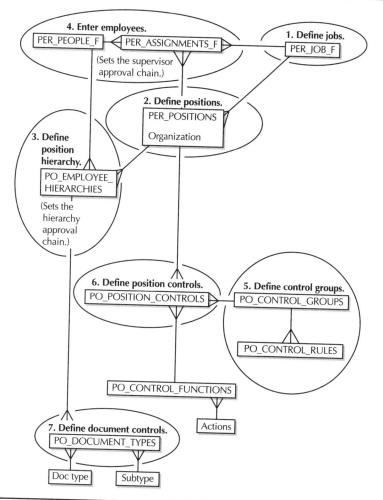

FIGURE 10-3. *Relationships among the major forms, procedures, and database tables in the approval process*

3. **Define the position hierarchy** Use the Define Position Hierarchy screen to indicate how positions relate to one another.

4. **Enter employees** Once you have defined jobs and positions for your employees, it is time to enter their names into the system. It helps to go from the top down, if you are using the supervisor-approval approach, so that the supervisors are already defined when you need to reference them as you set up the employees who report to them.

After you have defined the relationships among your employees through these setup steps, you define their actions and authority levels through a series of setup steps in Oracle Purchasing:

1. **Define approval groups** Use this function to give names to groups of things that need control, such as "Documents associated with Department XYZ for equipment-lease expenditures more than $1,000." A set of rules identifies all types of things in the group. Each rule can use a combination of total document amount, General Ledger accounts, item category, item, and location. The groups will be used later on to establish what needs to be approved and who can approve how much; each group has an approval-amount limit. Groups can overlap in instances in which larger orders require more approvals than smaller ones. These groups will later be tied to positions (if using a position hierarchy) or jobs (if using a supervisor hierarchy) for each document type. Higher approval-amount groups will be associated with higher-level positions or jobs.

2. **Define position controls** This step associates your approval groups with either jobs or positions for each document type. Positions are required if you are using hierarchies, but not if you are using supervisor approvals.

3. **Define document types** This step determines access to each document type. You can define who can access the document—the people in the hierarchy, everyone, or just the owner and subsequent approvers. You then give them a security level that says what they can do (view, modify, or full access).

TIP
If you use the position hierarchy, the Fill Hierarchy process can create a large number of hierarchy-relationship records in the PO_ EMPLOYEE_HIERARCHIES_ALL table, which makes the process slow. The Fill Hierarchy process has to be run every time an employee position changes. Therefore, to keep the number of records to a minimum, try not to have a large number of people occupying a single position (for example, do not have a default requisitioner position, because all who hold the position will reference all others and their approval managers, so 900 employees become 900 × 900 records).

TIP
The approval hierarchy and employees should be treated as standing data much like suppliers and customers, and be set up in each test cycle (with realistic data volumes). This will highlight inconsistencies and allow experimentation with position definitions before the system is rolled out to an expectant crowd of would-be requisitioners.

Globally Approved Supplier Lists

The approved suppliers list (ASL) relates items to your suppliers and the manufacturers who provide your suppliers, while providing information about the relationship between you and the supplier. For instance, the ASL will answer the following: Who is the preferred supplier? What agreements are in place? Which suppliers have been debarred and can no longer be used? The ASL carries practical information, such as vendors' part numbers and units of measure.

For some key suppliers you can be very specific in the information you hold. You can specify for each and any item from a particular supplier how many can be delivered in normal time scales, the length of the lead time, and other constraints. This information can be critical, for example in an assembly plant where virtually no stocks of expensive components are held. The planning function can see on Oracle Purchasing that a burst of demand will necessitate a change from the normal supplier, unless a certain lead time can be met.

This type of knowledge can reside on a legacy system or simply in the minds of the procurement staff. To put it into the E-Business Suite means that it is accessible by those who need it across the organization (even if the purchasing specialist is on vacation or leaves the company). Supply Chain Management also uses it to source supplies.

Large businesses do much of their purchasing at a global level, negotiating agreements that all operating units within the business can share. The process brings a number of efficiencies. Company-wide agreements offer better prices, and negotiating at a macro level cuts the overhead costs involved in buying.

Vendor Part Numbers, Substitutes, and Cross-References

Each supplier has its own part-numbering scheme and will likely use its own part number on invoices and shipping documents. Some suppliers might, as a courtesy, include your part numbers as well as the manufacturer's name and part number. You also might want to record this information for various reasons. For instance, you can store the vendor part numbers on requisitions, purchase orders, or quotations. Oracle Inventory keeps a cross-reference of manufacturers' names and part numbers. The ASL helps the buyer select a supplier and use the appropriate vendor part numbers and vendor units of measure on the PO.

Frequently, a supplier will want to substitute one item for another. Whether you allow the substitution depends on the context. In your business, you might be able to substitute Kleenex for Scotties tissues. The distributor cannot, but might be able to substitute boxes of peach-colored Kleenex for boxes of blue-colored Kleenex. The manufacturer, Kimberly-Clark, obviously cannot substitute one color for another. Substitution can be one way or two way. You can substitute bottled water for tap water, but not the other way around. Certain substitutions might be allowed only for a given period of time or for certain purposes. It would be logical to allow substitutions on issue but not on receipt.

The most elemental question when dealing with substitute items is whether to assign separate item numbers. If there is only one item number for Kleenex, peach- and blue-colored Kleenex will all be jumbled together on the shelves, with no separate accounting. When they have separate numbers, you can use the Define Item Relationships form to define substitution relationships. Inventory produces reports that might be useful in receiving, although there is not much logic to support substitution. These are simplistic examples, but they represent the need to distinguish between similar goods within your organization.

Purchasing offers a more general cross-reference feature for users to apply as they wish. A company that buys through distributors often has several part numbers to deal with—one for the original manufacturer and others for the intermediate suppliers. Add to that the fact that these sources might make substitutions upon occasion, such as satisfying an order for a 5 percent tolerance resistor with only a 1 percent tolerance resistor, because that is what they have in stock. The generic cross-reference function is a great foundation for custom code. Oracle provides the data-capture screens and some basic reporting. You can apply the relationships any way you need to meet your unique business requirements. This feature is often used to store an item's legacy part number, if your Item Master was converted.

Purchase Agreement and Catalog Import

When you purchase at a global level using an ASL, your supplier might have as much to do with the items on a purchase agreement as you do. When Dell or Staples gives you a corporate discount, they provide a catalog of the items they cover. You offer your employees and customers what the supplier offers you.

You can use the Purchasing Documents open interface to import prices and define the items in your system, either through electronic data-interchange transactions or by loading them directly from a flat file. You can automatically add the items to your price and sales catalogs, approved supplier lists, and sourcing rules. The Purchasing Documents open interface imports price- and sales-catalog information from the supplier into Purchasing directly as blanket purchase agreements and quotations. In addition to importing new and replacement documents, the interface now also imports updates to existing documents. This facility can leverage productivity tremendously. It cuts the administrative effort involved in using multiple suppliers and in changing suppliers. It integrates with Oracle EBS's quotation process, so the successful bidder's offerings can be incorporated quickly and smoothly into your business.

Communicating with Suppliers

Oracle Purchasing is designed to get complete information to and from suppliers quickly. Big money is involved in your communications with your suppliers. Having a product available where customers need it and when they want it will bring you a good price. Goods that cannot be sold or used are a liability. Information about what you can offer your customers might be the difference between success and failure.

Electronic Data Interchange (EDI)

EDI is a protocol for exchanging machine-readable transactions between buyers and sellers. There are standard transaction formats for orders, including headers, lines, and shipping information; order changes; order cancellations; order confirmations; and every other common transaction. EDI transactions parallel the transactions available in Oracle Purchasing, and the elements (header, line, and shipping) map closely to Oracle's data structure.

Business entities that participate in the exchange of EDI information have unique routing identifiers. Instead of having to initiate one-to-one communications with each seller, a buyer submits all EDI transactions to a network. The network sorts and forwards them according to the routing code. Value-added networks have historically filled this role. The Internet is evolving as the medium of exchange but does not replace EDI for high-volume transactions. In addition to the Oracle E-Commerce Gateway, there is an XML Gateway to enable organizations to exchange documents outside the EDI standards. EDI transactions are more batch oriented, whereas the XML counterpart is event based, real time, and based on a single transaction.

Automatic-Faxing and E-Mail

Faxing directly from Oracle EBS to your trading partners represents an intermediate level of automation: electronic on the sending end, paper on the receiving end. It accommodates suppliers whose internal processes depend on paper, yet it achieves the speed and cost benefits of electronic delivery. Although automatic faxing is not included as a standard feature of Oracle EBS, it can be accomplished through minimal customization. This very often also supports an e-mail gateway and e-mail documents in the form of PDF.

You will normally find that you will want customizations to the external document (the purchase order, requisition, and so forth) that you wish to fax or e-mail. However, some third-party software will take the output from a printer queue and run it through a formatting engine before passing it to a fax or e-mail server. Therefore, cosmetic changes can be handled by the formatting engine as long as the data are available on the document. If you advertise this service to sell the new system to users, remember that you might have to do some substantial data cleansing to have usable fax numbers and e-mail addresses when you convert your suppliers from a legacy system.

Oracle Supplier Portal

Supplier Portal is an Internet tool that provides your suppliers a controlled view of different aspects of their dealings with your organization. For example, you can post solicitations for your suppliers to review or you can let them preview your internal plans so they can provide you maximum service. Chapter 16 provides further details about this module.

Drop-Shipment Communications

Drop shipment eliminates the time and expense of routing goods through your warehouse en route to a customer. Although drop shipment enables you to offer better prices and service, you become dependent on your supplier and customer for information about the transaction, such as when to invoice. Oracle Purchasing has incorporated support for transactions that facilitate drop shipment. Drop shipment is further described in Chapter 12.

An advance shipment notice (ASN) from your supplier lets you know that an order has shipped. In a drop-shipment environment, a shipped order can trigger an ASN to your customer and/or send an invoice.

Supplier Acceptances acknowledges that the supplier has accepted the order and committed to a delivery date. This feature lets you know whether the supplier can meet your customer's needs. Use an alert to notify the buyer if there is no supplier acceptance within a predetermined period of time. You might want to have Order Entry forward the information as an acceptance to your customer.

Suppliers Under Multi-Org

Suppliers are best maintained in a global perspective. If Ford Motor Company were to negotiate a worldwide contract with Silicon Graphics International (SGI), every Ford division would need to recognize SGI as the same supplier, and the corporation would need to monitor total purchasing. Suppliers, therefore, are global within Oracle Purchasing and Payables, and supplier sites are specific to an operating unit. Ford of Germany may do business with SGI's office in Germany, but the system will recognize that office as part of SGI's global organization.

Inventory organizations within a company are connected by a transportation web. Factories or distribution centers ship to sales locations, or one sales organization that is long on product might support another that is short on product. Chapter 11 describes how to define freight carriers in the system, how to handle freight invoices, and how to account for the cost of freight.

The Implications of Multi-Org

Multi-Org functions make it possible for one installation of Oracle Purchasing—one set of software and tables—to handle multiple operating units. Within an operating unit there can be one or more inventory organizations. These are the two structures that affect purchasing.

- **Operating unit**   This structure is associated with log-in Responsibilities. It defines the scope of Purchasing activities available to a single user of the system.

- **Inventory organization**   This structure resides within an operating unit. It limits receiving to shipments destined for a specific inventory location within the operating unit.

Oracle introduced in Release 12 a feature called Multi-Org Access Control (MOAC) that enables companies that have implemented a shared-services operating model to efficiently process business transactions by allowing them to access, process, and report on data for an unlimited number of operating units within a single EBS Responsibility. This increases the productivity of shared service centers, for users no longer have to switch EBS Responsibilities when processing transactions for multiple operating units at a time. Data security is still maintained using security profiles that are defined for a list of operating units and determine the data-access privileges for a user. In Oracle Purchasing, the MOAC and preferences allow users to enter purchase orders for one operating unit and then seamlessly enter purchase orders for another operating unit. Setup is more manageable, and gathering information and running concurrent programs are more efficient.

Multiple Organizations in Inventory

Purchasing includes the Inventory screens necessary for creating and maintaining inventory items. This is an essential detail. Purchasing usually precedes Inventory in a phased implementation. Many attributes are associated with every item in a company's inventory. Some of these, such as description and size, are unchangeable. Most large companies allow other attributes, such as whether the item can be stocked, manufactured, or ordered, to differ between inventory locations within an operating unit. Not all inventory sites will need to store—or even see—every item of inventory.

Each inventory organization that handles transactions is associated with a master inventory organization. The master organization carries the definition of every inventory item available to the child inventory organizations associated with it. It provides a common reference for shared item numbers and carries values for item attributes that are the same across all the child inventory organizations.

In the simplest installations, the master is the only inventory organization; otherwise, the child inventory organizations each have some subset of the master inventory, with local settings for those attributes that are controlled at the organization level. The master organization can be shared as widely as needed within a company to ensure a common definition of parts and products. The only proviso is that every organization using the master has to have a common set of books. This is because several attributes, such as expense account, encumbrance account, sales account, and cost of goods sold, are Accounting Flexfields. They only make sense within the context of a single set of books.

A user logged in to a particular Purchasing Responsibility can order items for any inventory organization within the user's operating unit. Each shipment must be made to an inventory organization for which the item is defined. The Enter Receipts screen operates one level down, at the inventory-organization level. A receiving clerk can receive only shipments due into his or her location. A Purchasing Responsibility frequently accesses many inventory organizations, and therefore users use a Change Organization form to point the Responsibility at the one they want to define item attributes or perform receipts.

Receiving

Receiving is the function of accepting goods from a supplier and delivering them to their destination within the company. It usually involves checking the receipt and goods to make sure the quantity is correct and the quality is satisfactory, and then passing the information to Payables to use as the basis for paying an invoice. If you have enabled three- or four-way matching, the receipt of an item will be required before an invoice can be paid.

Oracle Purchasing continues to add features that reduce the amount of labor involved in receiving. Advance shipment notices received through EDI prepare the loading dock to process a receipt automatically. Oracle's Payment on Receipt option automatically generates an invoice in Payables, saving the vendor the effort of creating it and you the effort of keying it in—although it will still require approval and payment as normal. Drop shipments to support Order Entry eliminate the need for your warehouse to handle goods that would only have to be reshipped.

Exceptions

Usually a packing slip references the order number. The workers on the dock can compare the packing slip with the items received and the order, then enter the quantities received of each line item. The complexity is in the exceptions. To help when there is no packing slip, Oracle Purchasing lets the receivers scan by supplier, item number, and supplier part number to look for a matching order.

Quantities received do not always match quantities ordered, and the receipt date might not coincide with the required date. Purchasing uses a series of defaults—at the levels of system, supplier, and purchase-order shipment—to set tolerances for these variables. Purchasing enforces the business rules for dealing with exceptions, whether to reject the order or accept it with notification to the buyer that there is an exception. On a practical note, many receiving operations move so quickly that there is only a moment on the receiving dock for accepting or rejecting an order. A warning note is not much use to purchasing; it is more effective to write an alert that e-mails the buyer when the company accepts an out-of-tolerance shipment.

Additionally, the system needs to know when an order is closed. Most of the time Oracle Purchasing's native logic handles the situation. Once all lines are closed, the entire order will be closed. Lines, then, are the issue. What if 11 units of an item were ordered, 10 were received, and an invoice arrives for 10? There is a set of tolerance parameters to decide whether that line should remain open to receive one last item, or whether to assume that no more are coming. There are more tolerance parameters on the Payables side to reconcile prices and quantities invoiced with what was ordered and received.

Purchasing applies the logic of tolerances to order lines only; you will need to define processes to handle orders themselves. When do you close a PO with one line that has never been received? How about one with a line that was 80 percent received three months ago? Sometimes these matters take human judgment. Use Oracle Alerts to notify the appropriate buyer of POs that remain open but appear inactive, so they can decide whether to contact the supplier regarding the remaining items or simply close the PO.

You can set up Purchasing to allow suppliers to ship substitute items if the ordered item is out of stock or is unavailable. A default chain establishes whether the system will accept recognized substitutes for any given line item on an order.

Sometimes a receipt cannot be matched to a purchase order. The PO might already be closed, the items might have been order without a PO, or the supplier might have made a mistake. The setup parameters specify whether to accept such shipments or return them to the supplier.

Receipt Routing

Each purchase-order distribution line specifies one of three ultimate destinations for the item: inventory, expense, or shop floor. Business procedures establish the path that received items follow leaving the loading dock. They can go right to their destination or they might be inspected first.

A *receipt traveler* provides information regarding items in transit within the company in the same way a packing slip represents a supplier shipment. It indicates what the item is and where it is going. Inventory needs that information to stock items correctly. It helps people who order expensed items to reconcile what they get with what they requisitioned, and it informs inspectors what to do with an item after they accept it.

Drop-Shipment Receipts

A drop shipment, by definition, is never physically received in your warehouse. Therefore, it might be difficult to record information that would normally be picked up at the receiving dock: what was received, how many, and in what condition. The processing requirement depends on whether you or one of your customers is the recipient. Your customer is the recipient when you use the Customer Drop Shipment feature of Oracle Order Entry. As the recipient, your customer takes the lead in resolving quality issues.

You can assume the shipment has been received when the supplier sends you an advance shipment notice, or you can confirm the receipt by telephone. The customer is responsible for notifying you if the materials received are not those specified in the shipping notice or invoice that you have sent. The resolution between you and the customer is handled by Order Management; Purchasing handles issues between you and the supplier.

Productivity Versus Security

Companies with established supplier relationships often find that formal receiving does not add enough value to justify its cost. They might let the supplier replenish inventory and take the supplier's word for how much was sent; this offers maximum efficiency. Periodic audits and inventory out-of-stock conditions will reveal over the long term whether the suppliers' claims of quantities delivered are accurate.

Oracle offers options for receiving that support the various different receiving models. The model you choose depends on many factors, including the company culture, the value and volume of individual purchases, and the state of supplier relationships. The E-Business Suite offers the following features:

- **Web Confirm Receipts** Allows employees to confirm the receipt of shipments to company sites other than your warehouse.

- **Receiving Open Interface** Accepts scanned receipt data or receipt transactions prepared in an outside system. It lets you integrate Oracle Purchasing with new or existing applications such as Oracle Warehouse Management.

- **Advance Shipment Notice** Lets suppliers prepare you for a receipt of a shipment with an electronic packing slip, so your receiving dock can process an entire shipment with a single confirmation. The ASN is designed for use with bar-code scanning. The receiving dock can use handheld RF (radio frequency) scanners to record pallets or parcels being received. The notice can also include billing information (and be called an ASBN); this will cause the creation of an invoice in Payables.

- **Kanban Purchasing** Treats the presentation of a kanban card, or just an empty container, as an order to a supplier. The transaction is usually captured by a bar-code scanner. The system is most often set up to trigger an automated payment through Oracle Payables, and the transaction costs are minimal. Chapter 11 describes the use of kanban in inventory and manufacturing systems.

These electronic-processing alternatives enable you to control receiving at a minimal cost per transaction. Oracle EBS continues to offer several levels of receipt control in a document-oriented environment:

- No receiving is a very simple option. For services and kanban purchasing, the invoice alone may be adequate.

- Express receiving works on an exception basis. The receiving clerk notes that the transaction is an express receipt. Other than the entered exception lines, an express receipt considers the amount received to be the open amount for every line on the order. The process saves time by placing more responsibility on the receiving clerks. Finding what is missing takes more brainwork than finding what is there.

- Standard line-by-line receipt confirmation lets personnel check the quantities received against the packing slip and then enter quantities into Oracle EBS from the marked-up packing slip.

- Blind receiving offers maximum control—and a maximum of work. Because receivers do not know how much of each item to expect, it is impossible for them to dispose of a shipment quickly by just keying in the open amounts. It forces the receivers to count every item. This approach is most useful in operations with low volumes of expensive materials. Blind receiving does not use tolerances, making it an even more exact science.

Payment on Receipt

Rather than wait for your supplier to send you an invoice that you will need to either key into Payables or process through the E-Commerce Gateway, you can use the Payment on Receipt functionality. Payment on Receipt enables the user to automatically create standard, unapproved invoices for payment of goods based on receipt transactions. Invoices are created using a combination of receipt and purchase-order information, which eliminates duplicate manual data entry and ensures accurate and timely data processing.

After processing the receipts, you can run a batch program that creates the invoices and passes them to the Payables open interface. The invoices are then imported into Payables and matched to their corresponding purchase orders. After the invoices are approved, they can be paid the same as any other standard invoice.

Integration with Other Modules

Purchasing, being the initial process in the procurement cycle, is tightly integrated with several other modules. This integration serves as the foundation for the more extensive material management available through Inventory, Order Entry, Manufacturing, and Project Accounting. Because of this, purchasing analysts usually need to handle their implementation as part of a global vision.

Payables Integration

Purchasing and Payables share supplier data and generally work with the same transactions. As far as transactions go, most business that results in accounts payable is done through contractual vehicles established in Purchasing. During the invoice-approval process, Payables looks to Purchasing to validate payment obligations through a two-, three-, or four-way match process. The match process transfers the accounting from the purchase order to the invoice. If the item on the PO is an item that is flagged as an inventory item, the match process will bring over an accrual account. Otherwise, the match process will bring over an expense or asset clearing account.

Oracle Payables offers a number of options for matching:

- **Two-way match** Confirms that an invoice matches a purchase order in quantity and unit price (within the tolerance). This way the company does not pay for items it did not order. Two-way matches are appropriate for purchases of services and other intangibles that do not result in receipts of material goods. Rent and phone bills are two good examples.

- **Three-way match** Requires in addition to the two-way match that the purchase order matched to the invoice be physically received, all before payment. This prevents payment for items that were ordered, but for some reason were never received by your company.

- **Four-way match** Adds inspection to the process. Not only were the goods received; they also were accepted. Inspection is largely a matter of timing. Some items, such as electronic equipment, might take a while to check. The company does not want to pay for the equipment until it has confirmed that the items meet quality specifications.

In addition, other costs required to acquire the inventory can be matched to the receipt, even if they are not on the purchase order. For example, you can match an invoice for tax, freight, or miscellaneous charges to a material receipt. This step is required for accurate costing data if you use periodic costing. This kind of matching associates costs related to acquiring the goods that are on the receipt, but it does not affect the quantity and amounts billed on the receipt or the corresponding purchase-order shipment.

The Payment on Receipt feature consolidates the receiving and payables functions. It relieves the supplier of the need to invoice and you of the burden of processing the invoice. Instead, Oracle Purchasing creates an invoice automatically upon completion of the receiving, inspection, and delivery processes. It uses the payment terms and conditions set up for the vendor and automatically creates the match to the purchasing document. The supplier will have created an open receivable without ever issuing an invoice. Both parties use the price lists and financial terms in the governing purchasing agreement. The high level of trust in this business arrangement pays major dividends, significantly reducing paperwork for both buyer and seller.

Projects Integration

Purchases in a projects-oriented business can be coded to a project, task, and expenditure type. These details are then carried through the system to ensure that first the commitment (on the purchase order) and then the actual cost (from the invoice) are associated with the project. As far as a project is concerned, money is as good as spent once a requisition goes to Purchasing—it cannot be spent twice.

The Purchasing system gives Projects the information it needs to commit funds within the project budget. It provides Projects with up-to-date status and cost data as a purchase advances through the requisition, purchase, and receipt phases. Payables finalizes the cost when the invoice comes through. Note that an accrual journal for goods received but not invoiced is built in Purchasing and passed to the General Ledger; however, this accrual does not go to Oracle Projects so is not visible against individual projects. If month-end accruals are used, the customization required to put this into Projects as well is not prohibitively difficult. Project Manufacturing carries project identification through Inventory and Manufacturing. Purchase-order lines can include project and task data regardless of the destination: expense, inventory, or shop floor. See Chapter 14 for more on Oracle Projects.

Order Management Integration

User requisitions for internal stock items never go to suppliers. These requisitions are routed to Order Management through the Order Import open interface as internal orders to be satisfied from inventory once the requisition has been approved. Internal orders then proceed through the order cycle—Pick Release, Ship Confirm, and Inventory Interface—in a manner similar to that of an external customer order. Just as for requisitions that are satisfied through POs, Purchasing closes the requisition when the receipt is processed and the item is delivered to the requisitioner.

Inventory Integration

Many items handled by Purchasing must be identified by item number because the numbers are required for manufacturing, selling, and stocking items. However, Oracle Purchasing can handle orders for anything, regardless of whether it has an item number (and therefore whether it appears in Oracle Inventory). Using item numbers in situations in which they are optional offers a number of advantages:

- **Points of reference**   Each item is known by one designation throughout the company.
- **Consistency**   Suppliers always see the same description for orders of the same item. If they fill the order correctly once, they can be expected to do so again.
- **Recording usage**   Item numbers make it possible to track usage automatically.
- **Streamlining of accounting processes**   Each item number has an associated cost; this simplifies the processes of budgeting and paying invoices.

As mentioned earlier, many attributes are associated with an Inventory item—far more than are just needed for Purchasing. In fact many of the items frequently purchased never go into a physical inventory—they are expensed and consumed. Oracle sets attributes of all kinds as items are created; some of these attributes cannot be changed later and many depend on other settings. The purchasing analysts need to anticipate downstream uses of Inventory item data in their implementations. On a transaction basis, receipts of stock items from the Purchasing system bump inventory balances up. Purchasing puts records of open orders in the MTL_SUPPLY table to help Inventory plan its replenishment requirements. Requisitions for internal orders place a demand on items, which is relieved by Order Entry once the item has been shipped.

Units-of-measure conversion is another powerful feature of Inventory that makes it possible to buy an item by one measure, store it by another, and issue it by yet a third. See Chapter 11 for a more complete discussion of the Inventory integration considerations.

Accounting Issues

Purchasing has limited communication with the General Ledger, but as the first link in the supply chain it is the ultimate source of a great deal of accounting data. It prices requisitions based on the frozen costs in Inventory, then uses those extended costs to determine what approvals are needed to encumber funds, to accrue receipts, and to establish an expected price for Payables.

Average and Standard Costing

Oracle EBS allows you to choose between average and standard costing. *Average costing* is intuitive: if you have 10 baseballs in stock at $5 each and you receive another 10 at $7, your average price is $6. End of story. It is simple and it works.

Standard costing is the alternative. Under standard costing, you would put the $7 baseballs into stock at $5, keep the price at $5, and post the difference to a variance account. Then somebody would have to look into the variances to see what went awry. Who wants to do that?

Standard costing, it turns out, makes more sense than it would appear: it is highly advantageous for distribution operations (Chapter 11 explains this further). In short, average costing is not a true average. It averages only one thing—the price on the purchase order. There is still variance between the purchase price and the invoice price. Average pricing means the price changes all the time, making it harder for the tolerance process to highlight price changes. Most important, average costing supports the notion that purchase cost represents the total cost of an item, when the full cost actually includes purchasing, handling, storage, inspection, shipping, and a host of other activities involving the item.

In terms of accounting, there is always a need for an invoice-price variance account. A purchase-price variance account is necessary under standard costing. Management's objective is the same whatever the mechanism: to make sure that the company is paying what it expects to pay and that it pays a fair price. This concept is fundamental in dealing with suppliers and in product pricing. Chapter 12 describes how costs serve as the basis for setting sales prices.

Accrual Accounts

A receipt of goods represents an obligation to pay, whether or not the invoice is yet in hand. Receiving posts an expense to an accrual account, which Payables relieves when it actually pays the bill. Inventory receipts are accrued immediately, and a setup option governs whether receipts of expensed items are accrued immediately or at month end. Chapter 5 includes an accounting model that demonstrates how this works.

The process computes the accrual amount by extending the quantity on the receipt by the line-item price from the purchase order. It is only an approximation. Payables deals with discrepancies using its own tolerance logic. It posts acceptable differences to the invoice-price variance account.

Accrual accounting is a truer representation of a company's commitments than cash accounting in that it recognizes an expense when the items are received. That is not early enough for some entities, especially governments, which must adhere rigorously to their budgets. Encumbrance accounting goes one or two better. An encumbrance picks up expected expenses at the time a department makes a requisition or a purchase order goes to a supplier. These encumbrances are called, respectively, *commitments* and *obligations*.

Encumbrances are posted to the ledger to represent money under obligation to be spent. The Financial Statement Generator in General Ledger can report on encumbrances as a separate line or net them with accruals and actual expenses against the budget to see how much is left. Receipts relieve encumbrances—the actual obligation replaces the expected obligation.

Automatic Account Generation

It is convenient to say that Receiving posts to "the" accrual account. It is usually a single natural account in the chart-of-accounts structure, but it can exist in a great many Accounting Flexfield combinations, meaning the account can be broken down by other dimensions (segments), such as product line or region. Oracle Purchasing uses the accounting distributions from the purchase-order line to get the other segments.

It is worth discussing where those segment values originate. The requisitioner or buyer can enter them directly, segment by segment—although doing so is a lot of work. The originator of the transaction can use a one-field shorthand code (alias) for a full accounting distribution.

Additionally, there might be defaults associated with the supplier or item. The system might use Account Generator (which replaced Flexbuilder in earlier versions of the software) to apply user-specified rules to derive segment values from some combination of the requisitioner's department, item category, supplier, project, and other available data. It is based on Oracle Workflow and is easier to understand than previous incarnations and readily customizable. The graphical representation of the workflow process is a good visual aid for explaining the rules to business representatives.

The mechanisms described earlier are all used to generate individual flexfield combinations. Users often want to split the costs of a purchase over two or more combinations. Purchasing provides multiple accounting distributions for this purpose. Determining whether it is easier to do the distribution in Purchasing or in the General Ledger using allocations is a significant business-process decision.

Although Purchasing itself makes rather limited use of accounting data, Payables and Projects depend on the accounting data that are collected here. You can always demand that the users key in a full multisegment distribution, but a key task in setup is to devise a scheme that takes advantage of all Oracle EBS's devices for automatically populating flexfield values, thereby minimizing manual keying and maximizing both productivity and accuracy.

Implementation

Some users will bring up all the packages at the same time in a "Big Bang" conversion. The alternative is a phased approach. Though there is not a mandatory sequence for installing Oracle EBS, in general Purchasing builds on Payables, which builds on General Ledger. This sequence of dependencies is based on accounting information. On the materials side, Inventory builds on Purchasing, and the Item Master usually comes up as part of the Purchasing conversion (see Chapter 11 for detailed information on converting the inventory master). The scope of the Purchasing conversion depends on what has been done in previous phases.

Converting the Vendor Master

You can expect the legacy vendor master file to be cluttered with duplicate suppliers and ones that have not been used in years. You can also expect users to advocate converting the file as is because the schedule does not allow time to clean it up prior to conversion. This may or may not be true, but you can be confident that the users will never find time to clean up the data after they go into Oracle Purchasing. Oracle EBS does not allow deletions from some of its master tables, and it is quite exacting for those that are allowed—the master record being purged usually cannot have open, or even recent, transactions against it. Users will see the same stale and duplicate suppliers and incorrect data forever unless you cull them at conversion. Take the time to make sure you are converting clean data and only the data you intend to use.

Once you have extracted a list of suppliers from your legacy system, spreadsheets are a great tool to use for cleaning up supplier data. Most companies find that their supplier data fit comfortably within the 16,000 rows and 256 columns available in a spreadsheet. Sorts are useful for finding duplicate suppliers, and the word-processing features can be used to convert cases, translate abbreviations, and make other global changes.

Old mainframe systems did not deal well with lowercase letters. Keypunches and printers had a hard time with them. However, GOING TO UPPER- AND LOWERCASE LETTERS MAKES A HUGE IMPROVEMENT IN READABILITY. It makes a better impression on suppliers, and it makes it far easier for them to read purchase documents. Lowercase letters and proportional spacing also make it possible to fit much more information into your notes. The downside is that it is more difficult to police the standard.

Oracle EBS can assign vendor numbers automatically or accept user-generated ones. A common approach is to keep the old numbers for suppliers that are converted, and then make the new Oracle EBS vendor numbers one digit longer. After conversion, Oracle EBS's number generator is set one past the highest number of the old scheme. If the legacy system used five-digit numbers, the first new vendor number assigned by Oracle EBS would be 100000.

Purchasing and Payables share the vendor tables. A lot of the master data, such as payment terms, are intended more for the Payables system, although the screens are available in the Purchasing setup menu tree. In any case, the Payables setup has to be thought out prior to supplier conversion.

There is a Vendor open interface in Oracle EBS that will help you with importing suppliers. The open-interface table for importing suppliers from external sources is called AP_SUPPLIERS_INT and holds supplier information, which is loaded by the user for import. Since the change of vendors to the new Trading Community Architecture (TCA) data model, the columns in the table map to corresponding columns in the HZ_PARTIES and AP_SUPPLIERS tables. The Oracle Payables application uses this information to create a new supplier record when the Supplier Open Interface Import program is submitted. Each row in the table will be uniquely identified by its VENDOR_INTERFACE_ID value.

The Supplier Open Interface Import, Supplier Sites Open Interface Import, and Supplier Site Contacts Open Interface Import programs process the information that the user loads into the AP_SUPPLIERS_INT, AP_SUPPLIER_SITES_INT, and AP_SUP_SITE_CONTACT_INT tables, respectively. When all validations are passed, records are inserted into PO_VENDORS, PO_VENDOR_SITES_ALL, and PO_VENDOR_CONTACTS, respectively.

AP_SUPPLIERS_INT holds supplier information that is loaded by the user for import. The columns in the table map to the corresponding columns in the PO_VENDORS table. Payables uses this information to create a new supplier record when the Supplier Open Interface Import program is submitted. AP_SUPPLIER_SITES_INT holds supplier-site information that is loaded by the user for import. The columns in the table map to the corresponding columns in the PO_VENDOR_SITES_ALL table. Payables uses this information to create a new supplier-site record when the Supplier Sites Open Interface Import program is submitted. AP_SUP_SITE_CONTACT_INT holds supplier-site contact data that are loaded by the user for import. The columns in the table map to the corresponding columns in the PO_VENDOR_CONTACTS table. Payables uses this information to create a new supplier-site contact record when the Supplier Site Contacts Open Interface Import program is submitted. Each row in the table will be joined to the appropriate supplier site using the values for VENDOR_SITE_CODE and ORG_ID and/or VENDOR_SITE_CODE_ID.

Converting Transactions

Run-out, manual conversion, and programmed conversion are the main alternatives for dealing with open transactions in the cutover to Oracle Purchasing. Because different types of transactions have different life cycles, a combination of methods is often most effective.

Requisitions are easy to run out. They are not automated in most legacy systems, and if necessary, the company can forcibly clear the legacy system before cutover. Requisitioners are in house; you can tell them to hold their requisitions for a week or so, whereas it would be tough to tell suppliers not to send confirmations nor deliver their goods.

The Requisitions open interface provides an easy migration path for users converting from a system that already uses automated requisitions. You can write an extraction program to read the requisitions from legacy files and load them to the interface. The state of the requisitions is an issue; you should complete all the requisitions on which activity has started, so Purchasing can treat the imports as new transactions.

Purchase orders and PO releases are open until your suppliers satisfy them, which can take an indeterminate period of time. It might be possible, depending on the interfaces involved, to run out your POs and PO releases by using the legacy purchasing system in parallel with Oracle EBS. If so, you can continue to receive under the legacy system while placing new orders in Oracle EBS. The viability of this approach depends on the related systems: Can Receiving identify shipments as being from the legacy system or Oracle EBS, and can Payables match its invoices with POs and receipts from two sources? Have you accounted for accruals?

Another alternative is to start entering orders into Purchasing before cutover but not receive any goods or make any payments until afterwards. This strategy will hold the volume of open orders at cutover to a manageable number, which can be rekeyed into Oracle EBS after the legacy system shuts down. This approach requires that supplier data be converted early, with a manual process to coordinate supplier-data updates until cutover.

TIP
Purchase agreements are usually valid for long periods of time. Open agreements have to be rekeyed into Oracle EBS in any run-out scenario.

There are significant accounting implications in an automated conversion. The accounting data often have to be translated from a legacy accounting structure into Oracle EBS. The accounts might be different under Oracle EBS. Finally, Oracle EBS accrues upon receipt, expecting Payables to reverse those accruals. The automated conversion process has to generate the accruals accurately; otherwise the ledger will be thrown off.

Converting Purchasing History

Auditing requirements demand that records of closed purchasing activities be available for several years. It is almost never worth the effort to convert this data into Oracle EBS. The rather minimal advantages—supplier-performance tracking and online querying into old transactions—can be had more easily outside the Purchasing application. The reasons not to write conversion scripts for live data are given earlier in this chapter. Historical data are still more daunting, as they can incorporate old suppliers and accounting data, and require significant purification, translation, and normalization into Oracle EBS's data schemas.

There are several more pragmatic ways to store and access your historical data:

■ Microfiche or hard-copy transactions will suffice if the volumes are small. However, the time it takes to riffle through bankers' boxes of old transactions can mount up quickly.

■ Use standard query tools. Put legacy transaction data into a custom database on a PC or in Oracle EBS, and then access it using a standard tool such as Microsoft Access or Oracle Discoverer. This allows users to search by part number, supplier name, contact, and other useful data fields.

■ Put historical data in simple Oracle EBS tables. Put a bespoke form on the EBS menu so users can navigate to it easily. A simpler approach, if you do not need the access management afforded by the EBS, is to write a small program to deliver query results in HTML though the Web server.

Testing

Testing can verify that your setups will make Oracle EBS support your business procedures. Chapter 16 describes the testing process in detail. For Purchasing, you need business processes for most or all of the following tasks:

■ requisitioning expensed items, inventory replenishments, and capital goods;

■ creating purchase agreements;

■ approving through the approval hierarchy;

■ performing RFQs;

■ creating and sending purchase orders through the different means chosen—for example, mail, fax, and e-mail—for different types of suppliers and products;

■ creating accounting distributions using distribution sets, shorthand accounts, defaults, and automatic account generation;

■ ordering goods under purchase agreements; and

■ receiving goods under all possible exception conditions, including incorrect quantities, substitute items, unexpected receipts, unknown suppliers, and damaged goods.

TIP
Take the time and energy to plan thorough tests. To repeat the theme of this book, EBS works; the question is whether you have made it work for you.

Customization

Documents that go outside the company should represent the company well. Most companies add a company logo and return address to the purchase-order print program. Change orders and RFQs usually need the same type of modification. The alternatives for hard-copy documents are to adapt your purchase orders to preprinted forms, have a vendor provide a flash overlay for a laser printer, or create a bitmapped report that uses a PostScript printer.

Oracle provides about 100 standard reports with the system. Many of these are highly parameter driven, producing output in a number of different formats leveraging BI Publisher technology. Although the packaged reports might not be exactly what users would design, they satisfy most basic data requirements. Aside from external documents, the following are the most common custom reporting requirements:

■ Adapting high-volume internal documents, such as requisitions and receipt travelers, to precisely meet the company's needs. However, check whether you really need a requisition printed, given the workflow-managed process it will become.

■ Adding Descriptive Flexfield columns to reports. For example, defense contractors might accept a priority rating in a DFF and then print it on the purchase order.

■ Displaying vendor and manufacturer part numbers on reports, along with the Oracle EBS item number.

Conclusion

Oracle Purchasing improves all aspects of the process of acquiring goods and services. It manages what to buy through its links with Inventory and Material Requirements Planning (MRP). Inventory maintains the definitions of purchasable items and services and works with MRP in determining when and in what quantities to replenish stock items.

Electronic requisitioning and approval requires approvals consistent with the cost and nature of a user's request, and prompts approvers to move requisitions through the system quickly. Oracle EBS's sourcing rules usually make vendor selection totally automatic. Routine replenishments should require no user intervention.

There are many avenues available to inform vendors of your needs, including paper documents, the Web, EDI, and fax. Oracle Purchasing can manage complex solicitations and awards and use sophisticated sourcing rules to automatically select a vendor for each purchase.

By validating accounting and project data as it captures each requisition and purchase order, Purchasing ensures that the financial implications of its activity will flow accurately through Projects, Accounts Payable, Inventory, General Ledger, and Fixed Assets. Two-, three-, and four-way matching protect you against making erroneous disbursements through Oracle Payables.

Conversion is a major factor in installing the Purchasing module, especially since Oracle has yet to provide open interfaces for the Vendor and Purchase Orders conversions. Purchasing is often the first financial system with broad visibility throughout a company to go in. It requires a well-conceived access-security plan. Online requisitioning and approvals, when used, demand extensive planning and testing. The approval hierarchy should be treated as standing data, as much in need of testing as the suppliers.

By automating purchasing decisions that can be reduced to rules, Oracle Purchasing frees your staff to concentrate on more strategic objectives, such as building the best possible relationships with your suppliers. The full and timely information you can now provide might enable your suppliers to offer better prices and service.

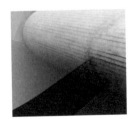

CHAPTER
11

Oracle Inventory

nventory is at the heart of almost any business and is central to the planning process. The considerations in setting it up are at least as complex as those for any other single application. Commonly, Inventory will be installed during the implementation of Order Management, Purchasing, Manufacturing, or Supply Chain Management, but it is an extremely complex module in its own right with several important setup considerations.

Overview of Inventory

An inventory system provides physical management of a company's stock until it is either used up or sold. It also performs a logical, cataloging function. Stock is referred to by its item number and has many attributes that affect the transactions that the modules can process against the item.

Every other module within Oracle EBS that needs to refer to things that the company buys, sells, or uses in its operation looks to the Inventory Item Master. These items include products ordered through Oracle Order Management, items invoiced through Oracle Receivables, items purchased through Oracle Purchasing, items paid for through Oracle Payables, items maintained through Oracle Service, and items charged against projects in Oracle Projects. Every module in the Manufacturing suite (Engineering, Bill of Materials, Work in Process, Master Production Schedule, Material Requirements Planning, and Cost Management) deals with items named in Inventory. Because many other modules need to access data in the Inventory Item Master, the Define Items form is found in the menu structure of most of the modules.

Inventory's ability to maintain items can extend further than its management of physical assets. Intangibles like magazine subscriptions or labor hours carry inventory names. The company can sell these items along with physical goods. Assemblies that are never stocked can also be defined in Inventory. A *phantom item*, for example, represents an intermediate step in manufacture, an assembly that is never stocked in inventory because it is used immediately in a higher-level assembly. A *planning assembly* represents a statistical average of parts requirements.

The stock-management function is unique to Oracle Inventory, as it manages physical instances of items that are available for sale, distribution, or internal consumption. Oracle Inventory's on-hand balance is increased when an item is bought or made. Inventory relinquishes control and decreases its balance when items are sold or put to their final use within the company. A pad of paper in the stockroom is inventory; the same pad of paper on somebody's desk is not—as far as the company is concerned, it is already used. A new desk in the warehouse belongs to inventory; a desk in somebody's office is no longer in inventory. Many major purchases, such as plant and equipment, never have an on-hand balance because they are put to their final use as soon as they are bought.

NOTE
Oracle Inventory is not a property-management or asset-tracking system. It is not well suited to keeping track of who currently has furniture, computers, or other assets that are in use within your company or on loan to customers. Oracle Assets is the package for managing such "inventory" of expensed and capital items, and Oracle Property Management is the package for tracking real property. You can, however, track capital items that have been returned to your warehouse awaiting reuse within the company in both Assets and Inventory.

The assets in inventory would not be worth tracking if they had no economic value, and Oracle Inventory recognizes that the purchase price is only part of the entire cost. There are additional costs associated with receiving, inspecting, manufacturing, storing, transporting to your other inventory locations, shipping to customers, and counting assets. Inventory is one of several systems that capture such costs. Wherever assets come from and however they are derived, Oracle Cost Management can store values for these cost types with each inventory item. Its cost-rollup function can sum the different cost types for purposes of analysis or to set a realistic frozen cost to use as a basis for pricing.

The science of managing inventory involves having what is needed, when it is needed, and no more of it than is needed. Oracle Inventory provides a number of different algorithms for projecting material requirements into the future. It has the ability to use these rules to compute future requirements, then recommend when, what, and how much to buy to satisfy the need. It coordinates with Manufacturing for parts required to build products. Supply-chain-management software coordinates with external suppliers to ensure availability of raw materials. As the pace of inventory movement has picked up, and companies have begun to keep ever tighter control over their stocks, Oracle Inventory has become increasingly proactive. It now has the ability to request action when it sees an imbalance between supply and demand and to request that assets be moved in anticipation of where they will be needed. It continues to increase support for kanban systems in which the presence of a physical signal such as a printed card or an empty container is enough to signal the need for inventory replenishment.

Large enterprises will have a number of physical warehouses stocking different items for different purposes. Setting up multiple inventory organizations that share one Item Master will provide the balance between global and local item definitions. Doing this allows local manufacturing- and distribution-center managers to control the operations they manage, while giving vendors and customers a common view of your company.

Integration with Other Modules

In the Oracle EBS scheme, modules other than Inventory are responsible for getting materials into and out of Oracle Inventory's custody. Purchasing and Work in Process are the primary sources of materials, which are either bought or made. Order Management and Work in Process are the primary consumers; material is sold, used internally, or put into products. These modules refer to Inventory master tables as they generate transactions that affect Inventory, notably receipts and issues. They perform their own work and then provide Oracle Inventory with the transactions needed to update balance records after the fact. This is important to conceptualize. Inventory does not issue stock to be sold. Instead, Order Management takes the material (via the pick-release process) and then notifies Inventory that the material is gone. Inventory does not receive stock. Purchasing brings it in, and then notifies Inventory to increment its records accordingly.

Internal to the company, these systems work as a troika. Even if a warehouse manager needs a chair from the inventory at that warehouse, the transaction needs to go through three systems to ensure proper accounting and replenishment. The manager submits a requisition to Purchasing, which sends an internal purchase order to Order Management, which cuts a pick slip and then ships the chair with a pack slip. Purchasing picks up the item with a receipt and then delivers the chair to the requester in the warehouse. This process may seem complex, but is necessary in order to retain control and record the proper accounting transactions.

Most transactions are processed in batch mode through open interface tables. Timing is critical. The concurrent processes must run frequently enough that the Inventory records are kept sufficiently accurate to support the target service levels.

Oracle's design anticipates integration with non-Oracle systems. Two tables, MTL_DEMAND and MTL_SUPPLY, provide Inventory with the information it needs to support replenishment processing. Outside systems as well as the E-Business Suite feed these tables. The only requirement is follow-through. The systems have to be conscientious about closure—relieving demand, for instance, when an order is canceled or shipped.

Item Setup

Inventory items are widely used throughout the Oracle E-Business Suite. You often have to set them up to be independent of the Inventory package itself. In fact, many users who need items will never use Oracle Inventory Responsibilities at all.

Item Numbers

You are probably surrounded by item numbers as you read this book. Look at the bottom of your keyboard, your mouse, your telephone, or your stapler. The numbers you find there uniquely identify types of items—parts, supplies, and products—to a company and its customers.

Part numbers can be made up of several segments, separated perhaps by dots, slashes, or dashes. One segment may identify the class of product (say, a mouse) and another may specify the type of mouse (wireless micro-USB). Segmented part numbers like this are called *intelligent keys*. They tell you something about the item in addition to uniquely identifying it. Oracle handles segmented identifiers through its Key Flexfield feature.

Choosing the System Item Key Flexfield scheme you will use to identify items is one of the first tasks you face in setting up Oracle Inventory. The scheme should be broad enough to cover every type of inventory in the company. A supermarket chain may have separate legacy systems to handle headquarters' stockroom inventory, produce division resale inventory, and produce manufacturing inventory for the store-brand pasta plant. Oracle Inventory will need to track them all.

Legacy inventory-numbering schemes are often constrained by design limitations from the era in which they were conceived. One notable limiting factor was the 80-column punched card. Designers often specified part numbers with eight to 10 characters so the remainder of the card would have room enough for a complete transaction. Many of the original intelligent-key features in such short numbers have become obsolete. For example, if a company established a system in which the first character of a part number indicated the product in which it is used, that designation will have lost its meaning when the company grew beyond 26 products. When the intelligent-key structure breaks down and the part number itself does not inform the user about the part, company operations become dependent upon people who know the numbers by heart.

Oracle item numbers have overcome several early design problems. Productivity in keying in a part number is no longer an issue: Oracle can complete the number automatically or present a short pick list based on the first few keystrokes. Self-checking numbers are of less use now that operators can visually verify a description on the screen.

The Oracle part number should satisfy the following criteria:

■ It should be unique across all operations within the company that uses item numbering. Often the easiest way to put this into effect is to let one segment of the new part number indicate what legacy system it came from or what group within the company defined it.

■ It should have an intelligent link with the legacy system. People who know the legacy numbers should be able to use Oracle without memorizing anything new.

- It should be short enough to fit conveniently into displays and reports. Although Oracle allows up to 20 segments of 40 characters each, for a theoretical total of 800 characters, a reasonable maximum is 3 segments and 15 characters, including separators. Otherwise, users may have to scroll through field contents in screens, and part-number fields may wrap on reports. Most users get by with one segment.

- It should not hinder performance or be difficult to support with bespoke (custom) code. Multiple segments add to the complexity of user-written reports and forms.

- It should anticipate reporting requirements. Many processes, in Inventory and other modules, have the ability to address ranges of items. Order Management maintains price lists by item range. Plan to take advantage of this as you lay out the first (or only) segment of the item number.

- It should anticipate flexfield security requirements. You may set up rules, in the same format as Accounting Flexfield cross-validations, to limit users to predefined ranges of items associated with their assigned Responsibilities.

- It should have some sort of validation plan. In a multisegment item number, you may want to confine every segment but one to a limited set of values. Most systems leave the last segment unconstrained so it can be chosen to make the number unique.

- It should have consensus. People identify with item numbers. You can expect resistance, rational or not, if the "headquarters MIS team" imposes a new numbering scheme without user buy-in.

Expect to spend a fair amount of time resolving the seemingly simple issue of what the item number will look like. The process presents a good opportunity to air everyone's expectations of the new system. It is useful to work through some complete scenarios with proposed new item numbers, including the use of the items in Purchasing and Order Management and in the pick-slip process, so that representatives of all the affected user communities see the impact.

As you design the part-numbering scheme, give some thought to the business process for assigning numbers. Implementing a global part-numbering standard can bring major benefits, but it also requires discipline. It is usually necessary to have a centralized cataloging operation that assigns numbers throughout the organization. Because there is no mechanism in Oracle Inventory to make mass changes to established items, it is best if all the master-level attributes for the item are set as the item is created. It is reasonable to limit the ability to create new part numbers to only one Responsibility, and assign only one person and a backup to that Responsibility. Establishing a "Request for New Part Number" document will help make this process more formal and ensure adherence to numbering and description standards.

Manufacturers and distributors have their own part-numbering systems, which are very significant in the Purchasing and Payables applications. Chapter 9 covers manufacturer part numbers, substitutions, and cross-references. Order Management supports customer part numbers and commodity codes.

Attributes

The Inventory master table, MTL_SYSTEM_ITEMS, is one of Oracle's largest master files, in terms of the number of columns. Some of the columns provide characteristics unique to the item, such as the Key Flexfield that identifies the item, its weight, and its volume. Most columns categorize the item in various groups: Is it hazardous material? Does it need to be cycle-counted? Can it be sold?

Columns equate to attributes in database terminology. A column in the MTL_SYSTEM_ITEMS table corresponds to an attribute of the item defined by a row in the table. For example, a "hazardous material" class might be an attribute of the item "turpentine." Attributes are organized in groups. The Define Items and Update Item forms put attributes in groups by business areas, such as Purchasing, Order Management, Inventory, Material Requirements Planning (MRP), Service, and so on. This system allows a user to review the settings of related attributes as a group. Attribute groups also support security. A Responsibility can be restricted to updating only those attributes within specified groups.

The setup of an item's attributes is critical to how that item will be transacted and processed throughout all the modules that access the Inventory Item Master. Several attributes cannot be changed once they have been set and transactions have run against them. This fact is particularly important for companies that implement Oracle EBS in phases. If, as is often the case, a company brings up Purchasing and Payables first, it may not appear to matter which way the Pick-to-Order or BOM-enabled flag is set. These settings become important as Manufacturing and Order Management are used. Getting them right when Purchasing is installed avoids the time-consuming and risky task of directly updating the database with SQL when new EBS modules come online.

Setting hundreds of attributes individually for each item would be a daunting task and would likely yield inconsistent results. The use of templates and user-defined statuses allows you to set these attributes en masse for like items. Custom conversion scripts can extend this same leveraging logic across all items being added as a group. It is essential to plan these group operators, templates, and statuses as an integral part of the inventory-conversion process.

TIP
Try to handle as many attribute settings as possible in the initial Item Master conversion—even for modules that will come up in later phases.

Attributes Within Inventory Organizations

Some attributes, such as item name and description, belong to the item itself. Others, such as whether the item is purchased or made, depend on the item and the inventory organization in which it is being used. You specify in setup which attributes will be controlled at the item level and which at item/org (item/organization). Attributes set to item-level control will have the same value across all inventory organizations. Attributes set to item/org-level control may have different values across the organizations. For example, Micros Systems manufactures its point-of-sale terminals in Beltsville, Maryland, but distributes them worldwide. Its 3700-series workstation is stockable in Beltsville, Los Angeles, Boston, Chicago, and many other cities; however, it can be built only in Beltsville. The Stockable and Build-in-WIP flags are both set at the item/org level.

It is essential that all organizations within a company share a common Inventory master. Otherwise there would be duplication of effort, with multiple part numbers for the same item and possibly multiple items with the same part number. Though it is not mandatory, you should usually associate every inventory organization within one set of books with one common master organization. This association does not require Multi-Org, nor is it restricted by organizational hierarchies defined in Multi-Org.

The master organization is usually not an operating organization. It does not maintain stock or execute transactions. It functions merely as a reference. It includes a record for every item used in any of the operating inventories as well as for intangible items used in Purchasing and Order Management that never appear in operating inventories.

Oracle specifies certain attributes that must be controlled at the master organization (item) level and a few that must be managed at the organization (item/org) level. The control level of the remainder of the attributes—a majority—is for you to determine at setup. Accounting fields provide an example of the way you determine the control level. If your automatic account generation takes only the natural-account segment from the cost-of-goods-sold account, it may be that one account will be sufficient for the item throughout the company. If, on the other hand, you need it to provide product-line or organization data, you might establish it as an item/org attribute.

Templates

Templates are used to set the attributes that determine how various applications will handle an item. Although it is possible to set the attributes individually when defining an item, the standard approach is to name the item, then identify one or more templates to set the item attributes. A template does not have to set all attributes. If only 10 specific attributes are defined in a template, applying the template leaves the other attributes unchanged. Used online, a template sets the attributes only in the Define Item screen, not in the database. If you apply several templates to one item, the settings overlay one another. The Define Item screen logic checks all the attributes at once, just before it saves them, to make sure they are consistent. The Item open interface can accept only one template name. The templates you define for conversion, therefore, each need to set every attribute that is not unique to the item and organization.

TIP

Be sure to debug your templates before putting them into use. To do this, use the template to create a phony item in a test instance. The Define Item screen will present an error if the attributes are inconsistent.

Oracle Inventory offers the Copy Item function, which is an alternative to using templates. This function copies all attributes of one item to those of another. It can be easier than using templates, but it risks compounding any existing errors. The best way to ensure consistent attribute settings is to make sure you have a well-planned, stable set of templates, then use those templates every time you set up an item. Address the risks of copying as you write business procedures for creating items.

You need templates at two levels for each type of item you will be defining: a master-level template to create a new item in the master organization, and at least one lower-level template to add the same item types to child inventory organizations. The master-level templates are the only source that will be used for attributes controlled at the item level. To avoid conflicts, only item/org attributes should be enabled in child-level templates.

There are several reasons to keep your templates in a spreadsheet as you develop them. You need to coordinate your master- and child-level templates. You frequently need to compare attribute settings in different templates and make across-the-board changes; for this reason, you will want to print your templates in a succinct form. If is often worth the effort to write code that automatically loads the templates from a spreadsheet, thereby ensuring that your templates remain identical across all environments.

Many users put the template name in the Item Type attribute. Though templates are designed in such a way that you can use many of them in creating one item, in practice you should use only one. That is all the Item open interface will accept. If you ever need to update item attributes after the fact using SQL, it is essential to know which template was used to create each item.

TIP
Your templates are not automatically updated when Oracle adds new attributes to the Item Master to support a new release. If your templates appear to work differently after an upgrade, check to be sure that the defaults Oracle generates for new attributes you do not set are consistent with the attributes already in your template.

Units-of-Measure Conversions

Warehoused items are stocked under units of measure (UOM). There are several possible conversions for Oracle to deal with:

- Your suppliers may deal in different units of measure than your company.

- Your external customers may use different units of measure than you use in stock.

- Your internal users may order merchandise by different units of measure.

Some conversions are universal, but others are item specific. A gross is always 144 of an item, and a dozen is always 12. However, a unit name may mean more than one thing. For example, a case of soft drinks contains 24 cans, but a case of motor oil contains 12. What is the conversion between *case* and *each*? And although a half pound of butter equals one fluid cup, the same is not true for water.

Oracle's conversion logic appears in the Inventory, Purchasing, and Order Management applications. The default for Purchasing is the primary unit of measure. However, most screens present the user with a quick pick of values to override the default. The quick-pick entries are the values within a UOM class. A UOM class is made up of related measures. Fluid measures would include milliliter, ounce, centiliter, teaspoon, tablespoon, cup, pint, quart, liter, gallon, barrel, and so on. Similarly, weights would run from microgram through ton and long ton; lengths would run from perhaps micron to meter. There is a base unit in each UOM class to which all other units are related. The base units are the basis for interclass conversions as well. To convert a tablespoon of butter into kilograms, the logic would find the equivalent measure in the base unit for volume, perhaps fluid ounces; then convert ounces to the base unit for weight, maybe grams; and lastly, convert to kilograms.

CAUTION
UOM conversions often work better in theory than in practice. They must be set up carefully, because technology can be more sophisticated than the people who have to use it. The US Army Depot in Long Binh, Vietnam, for example, once received enough telephone poles to build a log-cabin city as a result of a units-of-measure gaffe. A clerk had thought that the unit of measure was each, when it was actually something like a carload.

Used in combination, Oracle EBS modules impose checks that help validate unit conversion. It should be apparent when the unit is wrong on an order—the extended price for the order line will be way off. This check is absent for Oracle Inventory users who do not use Oracle Purchasing. The Inventory system will just as readily accept 10 pallets of copy paper as 10 sheets, and the problem may not be recognized until there is an out-of-stock condition or a wild variance in stock valuation.

The Inventory and Purchasing super users need to put a lot of planning into the UOM conversion plan. The first step is to research which measures are in use, then to set up appropriate UOM classes. After the classes are in place, planners need the right combination of business procedures and training to make sure that the requisitioners, buyers, and Order Management clerks are alert to the way conversion works and understand the units that are applicable to their operations.

You should usually choose your smallest common unit to be the primary unit of measure. This is ordinarily the unit of issue, or retail unit. Purchasing can place orders in the units most convenient to the supplier and they will be converted to stock units upon receipt.

Oracle does not allow you to change the primary unit of measure for an item. To do so would render historical transactions meaningless and change their accounting implications. That being said, it is worth the effort to fully understand units of measure and get them right in the initial inventory conversion. Figure 11-1 depicts the Oracle tables that are involved in UOM conversions.

The lines in the drawing represent the relationships between the tables, which are as follows:

- Every item must have a primary unit of measure. A dotted line in the figure means *may*, and a crow's foot means *many*. What this means in relationship 1, for instance, is that each UOM record may be referenced by zero to many material System Items records. A UOM class may have class conversions; class conversions must have a UOM class. (It is a mandatory field in the interface table.)

- Each unit of measure must belong to a UOM class. A class is made up of units of the same kind of measure. Inches, feet, and meters would belong to the length class. Each, dozen, gross, and ream would belong to the count class. Each class has a base unit of measure.

- Every unit of measure other than the base unit has to be convertible into the base unit. If the base unit is *each*, then a dozen is 12 times *each* and a gross is 144 times *each*.

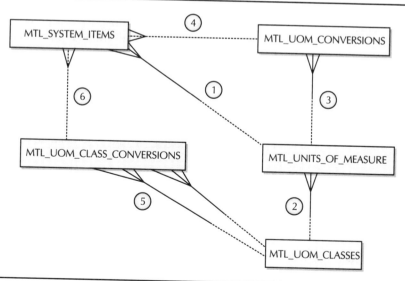

FIGURE 11-1. *Oracle Tables involved in units-of-measure conversions*

■ Optionally, the relationship can be made to apply only to a given item. Within the count class, if the item is *egg*, then a carton is 12 times *each*. If the item is *soft drink*, then a carton is 24 times *each*.

■ There may be conversions between UOM classes.

■ These conversions may be item specific. If the item is *butter*, for instance, then one pound (weight) equals two cups (volume). Oracle would use this conversion, plus two UOM conversions, to figure out what a tablespoon of butter weighs in ounces.

Setting Up the UOM Conversion for Your Inventory   Start by writing a script to find all of your legacy units of measure and their conversion factors. Draft your Oracle UOM setup procedures based on that list, correcting for whatever shortcomings you know to exist in the legacy system. Find out what manual computations purchasing or receiving and order management or invoicing have to do under the legacy systems, then set up Oracle to handle them automatically.

TIP

The only opportunity to correct ill-chosen legacy units of measure is upon conversion of the Item Master. The scripts that load the Item interface table have to be coordinated with the ones that load the Transactions interface to pick up on-hand balances, the Purchasing interface, and the Sales Order interface.

Status Codes

Inventory processes refer to eight status attributes to determine which processes can operate on an item within a given organization. These correspond roughly to master-level attributes that define whether the process is even applicable to the item. For example, an obsolete product may be an inventory item but not currently enabled for stock. On the other hand, a pick-to-order item could never be enabled for purchasing, because it has no physical reality; it is no more than a number given to a set of items that may be ordered together as one.

Table 11-1 shows the 10 status attributes. Where one exists, the table also identifies the base-attribute prerequisites for setting the flag to "enabled" status.

The value you enter for item status in the Open item interface overrides values you provide for the 10 status attributes. You usually want to use the following strategy at conversion time:

1. Define master- and operating-level templates for your different item types, including settings for the 10 enabled attributes.

2. Define a separate status code for each combination of the 10 attributes. There may be 10 to 20 different combinations.

3. Enter the name that represents the appropriate combination of enabled attributes as the status-code attribute in the template.

This approach simplifies conversion. All you need to do is associate a master- level template with each legacy item and an operating-level template with each item in an operating inventory organization. The 10 item-status attributes are set according to the status code in the template.

User Status Name	Meaning	Enabled Attribute	Base Attribute
Stockable	Item can be stored in inventory	STOCK_ENABLED_ FLAG	INVENTORY_ ITEM_FLAG
Build in WIP	Item can be built by manufacturing	BUILD_IN_WIP_ FLAG	n/a
Transactable	Transactions can be performed on the item in Order Entry, Purchasing, and Manufacturing	MTL_ TRANSACTIONS_ ENABLED_FLAG	n/a
Purchasable	Item can be put on a purchase order	PURCHASING_ ENABLED_FLAG	PURCHASING_ ITEM_FLAG
Internal Orders Enabled	Item can be ordered for use within the company; this affects Inventory, Order Entry, and Purchasing	INTERNAL_ORDERS_ ENABLED_FLAG	n/a
Customer Orders Enabled	Customers can order the item	CUSTOMER_ ORDER_ENABLED_ FLAG	CUSTOMER_ ORDER_FLAG
Invoice Enabled	Item can appear on an invoice in Oracle Receivables	INVOICE_ENABLED_ FLAG	INVOICEABLE_ ITEM_FLAG
BOM Allowed	Item may appear in a bill of materials, either as an item to be built or as a component on a bill	BOM_ENABLED_ FLAG	BOM_ITEM_ TYPE
Recipe Enable	A recipe or formula for the item can be created in Oracle Process Manufacturing	RECIPE_ENABLED_ FLAG	RECIPE_ITEM_ TYPE
Process Execution Enable	Item can be used in a production batch as an ingredient, product, or by-product	PROCESS_ EXECUTION_ ENABLED_FLAG	PROCESS_ EXECUTION_ ITEM_TYPE

TABLE 11-1. *Item Status Attribute*

Using status codes provides more control than updating the 10 attributes individually. The fact that you must name a predefined combination protects you from entering inconsistent settings. Item statuses give you the ability to plan and apply changes for groups of items at the same time via a batch process. They allow you to ensure consistency among your organizations and within your product lines.

Updating statuses through the combinations you establish in the Define Status form is a two-step operation. Users enter pending statuses for items via the Define Pending Status screen, then apply them using the Update Item Status concurrent process. Business procedures usually require that groups of related items, and items in multiple organizations, change status simultaneously.

Statuses are highly interdependent. Relatively few status combinations make sense in an organization, and individual items will go through a characteristic life cycle, such as from prototype to active to pending deletion. Plan to deal with statuses as a group using the Define Status screen to give your own name to combinations of all 10 statuses.

Revisions

Manufacturers change their products over time. They may change the components or the manufacturing process to reduce costs, improve the product, or reflect a change in suppliers. Identifying a revision level with the product helps move older versions out of inventory and allows customer service to provide better warranty and maintenance support to buyers.

You can update revision levels directly through Inventory screens. However, revision is usually handled through Oracle Engineering, part of the Manufacturing product suite. A revision usually corresponds to a change in the bill of materials for an item. Oracle Manufacturing associates item revisions with the engineering change orders (ECOs) that implement changes in the bill structure. The manufacturing plan coordinates parts and processes so that, as of the ECO implementation date, everything is in place and the stock of components no longer used is exhausted or returned to suppliers.

Bill of Materials

Inventory and Order Management use the manufacturing concept of Bill of Materials, even if you do not have Oracle Bill of Materials (BOM) installed. Bills play a role in the following situations:

- **Pick-to-order (PTO)** PTO items are defined to sell a number of items as a group. A computer retailer that carries monitors, keyboards, and system units as separate inventory items may find it convenient to give a separate inventory number to a complete system in order to ease the order-management process. The system will sell at a discount to its component parts, and the system will generally ship as a unit.

- **Assemble-to-order (ATO)** ATO items require a manufacturing step to create the ordered item. There is a work order associated with the order line, with a bill of materials to specify the components in the assembly. The assembled item goes from manufacturing into inventory to be held until it ships.

- **Configure-to-order (CTO)** Options are carried in the bill of materials for the saleable item. Order Management requires that users make all appropriate option selections before the order can be booked. CTO option selection applies to pick-to-order as well as manufacturing assemble-to-order operations.

- **Inventory replenishment** Material Requirements Planning, with or without Manufacturing, can use the bill of materials to determine what to reorder.

- **Costing** Costs of the individual components within the bill of materials (material, overhead, and so on) are rolled up to arrive at a proposed cost for a manufactured item.

- **Item revision levels** These are changes in the bill of materials for an item, usually corresponding to a new revision level.

Bill of materials are essential to manufacturing operations. Pick-to-order bills are surprisingly relevant for smaller internal and resale inventories. Many companies carry preassembled kits in inventory because they do not have PTO capability. Bill conversion adds a significant degree of complexity to inventory planning and setup.

TIP

Take an in-depth look at Oracle Bill of Materials features if you are planning to use Order Management. Most users have just enough kitting, subscriptions, and pick-to-order activity that they need it. It is far easier to implement pick-to-order initially than to convert later.

Grouping Items

A large inventory must be managed as much as possible through mass rather than individual actions. *Categories* are the mechanism for grouping items according to the way they will be handled internally. *Catalogs* group items by how they appear externally: what they look like, how they function, and how they are used. Leverage through groupings is one of the keys to Oracle Inventory's power.

Categories and Category Sets

A category set represents one way in which to divide items into categories. There is usually more than one category set, because it is useful to divide items up in different ways. Oracle's internal processes use categories in reporting within seven functional areas for which an item may be enabled: Inventory, Purchasing, Order Management, Service, Engineering, Costing, and Planning.

The Purchasing category set is useful to buyers. It splits all items up by their purchasing categories, which may include electronic components, commodity items, capital equipment, and packaged goods for resale. These categories would be useful for purchasing activities such as assigning buyers and tracking vendors. The Engineering category set, on the other hand, might divide items up according to the responsible engineering group.

Oracle's standard forms and reports in these seven applications accept categories as input parameters. For example, Order Management accepts a category as a parameter in its pricing, scheduling, and backlog-reporting processes. Categories give the sales department the power to discount computers differently from computer-printer cartridges. Oracle Applications forces a category for every enabled item subject to reporting within a functional area via a two-step process:

1. As part of setup, users must specify a default category set for each of the seven functional areas.

2. Each category set must designate a default category.

Users who do not want to take immediate advantage of categories—more probably, those whose conversion schedule does not allow for improving the business process at the time of cutover—can specify the same one or two category sets as the defaults for all seven functional areas.

The Open item interface process assigns default categories as it loads items. There is no facility to load category or category-set data. If there is any category information to be preserved from the legacy system, users should take the following measures:

■   Pass category names associated with each item into Oracle Financials as user-defined attributes in the Open Interface table. Since the system does not perform any validation on these Descriptive Flexfield entries, you can string together all your categories in a single 150-character ATTRIBUTE column.

- Use the online forms to define categories and category sets corresponding to the category information in the item import just mentioned.

- Write a custom script to read the categories associated with each item, look up the appropriate CATEGORY_ID and CATEGORY_SET_ID, and insert MTL_ITEM_CATEGORIES rows appropriate to each item.

Figure 11-2 shows the foreign-key relationships that have to be maintained as you add categories. The relationship between category sets and categories is complex. The most common usage is to choose your categories so that each category belongs to only one category set and to make an exclusive definition of which categories are within a category set. Doing so divides everything cleanly: Every enabled item gets assigned to one of the specified categories within a category set. However, Oracle allows categories to belong to multiple category sets and permits category sets to be nonrestrictive.

Categories are identified by flexfields, and flexfield formats can be different for different category sets. This degree of flexibility makes sense. The concept behind category sets is that the many different ways to group items have little to do with one another. In practice, most category schemes

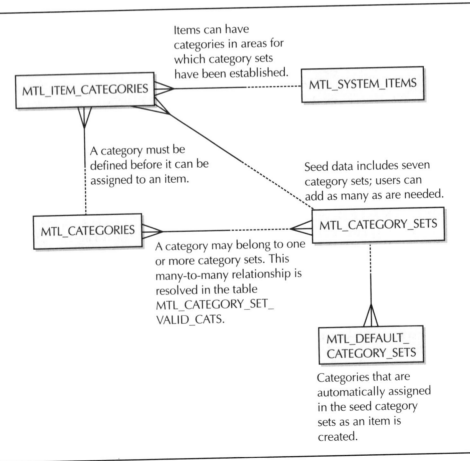

FIGURE 11-2. *Simplified category relationships*

can be satisfied by single-segment flexfields. Table 11-2 shows three categories that might be established if the item in question were a computer processor. Notice that two of the categories, Purchasing and Inventory, have two-segment flexfields.

TIP

Even though you may use only one or two unique structure layouts for your categories (a typical shop would have one- and two-segment structures), it is a good idea to define a separate structure for each category. Doing so provides you with a context field for any Descriptive Flexfields (DFFs) associated with the category. You might, for instance, want to carry the name of the person responsible for setting prices as a DFF for each Order Management category. The flexfield structure will tell the Define Category form to automatically present the appropriate DFF pop-up window; for other categories there could be a different DFF, or none at all.

The catalog scheme can be extended infinitely. Oracle Inventory often supports custom-written subsystems, which may have to categorize items in unique ways. For example, the Institute of Electrical and Electronics Engineers (IEEE) carries subscriptions as inventory items. One orderable item equates to a certain number of issues, or all issues of a publication for a certain time period. The IEEE has a custom-written subscription-fulfillment system that uses Oracle Order Entry and Receivables as a front end. It could, for the purposes of subscription management, develop a category set to categorize subscription items by periodicity: monthly, bimonthly, quarterly, semiannually, annually, and as required. Oracle's extensible functionality can minimize the amount of custom code needed in custom subsystems.

Some new features were introduced in Release 12; the item cross-reference type GTIN provides a place to record the global trade item number for an item. Cross-references can also be used to record the electronic product code. Walmart mandates that all pallets and cases must include RFID encoding of the GTIN, as well as serial numbers if necessary. Another introduction was the Charge Periodicity item attribute in the Order Management group, which supports recurring charges for the telecom industry. It represents a unit of time by which a persistent or recurring service or product is priced and billed.

Catalogs

Catalogs serve as indexes to inventory items. They help salespeople, customers, buyers, and engineers locate things by description. Each item can be cataloged by any number of characteristics appropriate to its type. A catalog group, defined as part of setup and associated with the item through the Define Items screen, establishes which descriptive elements apply to

Category	Category-Set Flexfield	Category Flexfield
Purchasing	Usage material class	Computer CPUs
Order entry	Order category	System components
Inventory	Storage type control level	Fragile packaged high dollar

TABLE 11-2. *Sample Flexfield Formats for Itemizing a Computer Processor*

the item. Each item is assigned to only one catalog group. Catalog entries for an item are free-form—that is, they are not required and are not validated against any list. They are in a table rather than a flexfield structure. Catalogs are nonintrusive and can be quite useful.

The Search Items inquiry screen handles catalog searches. You query using the catalog-group name and some combination of values and wildcards for the descriptive elements associated with that group. The form returns items that match the search criteria. Other forms, notably Delete Items and Item Cross References, allow you to link to the Search Items screen to pick items. A number of reports are able to select and sort information on the basis of catalog entries. Purchasing and the Manufacturing applications also take advantage of catalog data carried in the Inventory Item Master.

Issues of Volume

Inventory manages voluminous data in many ways. There may be large numbers of items and large numbers of transactions against those items. There are a great many attributes associated with each item and transaction. There are a great many different groupings of items. Finally, there may often be many locations, costs, prices, vendors, and so on associated with an item.

Oracle Inventory is designed to minimize the human effort associated with tracking the vast amounts of data associated with individual items and transactions. The power of its design is in the leverage that the following shortcuts provide:

- **Templates** Used as items are being created for assigning large numbers of attributes as a group.
- **Categories** Used for dividing items into functional groups for internal use and for organizing processes that address items by category.
- **Mass edits** Used for updating attributes that need frequent maintenance.
- **Multiple organizations** Used for controlling the many attributes that are common throughout all operating organizations at the item level, while letting attributes that affect site-level inventory operations be addressed by location.
- **Default chains** Used for broadly applying general rules while allowing specific exceptions; provided in all Oracle EBS applications.
- **Open interfaces** Used for embedding transaction logic in outside systems and importing the results into Inventory. The item-import process handles updates as well as inserts and so gives an alternative method for mass edits or updates sourced from third-party systems.

The US Bureau of the Census, which performs a small-scale manufacturing operation, is an example of the use of Oracle's open architecture and transaction import. The bureau presses CD-ROMs of census data on a make-to-order basis—a process too simple to justify the use of a manufacturing-software suite. To recognize the cost of manufacture, the bureau customized Order Entry to have it create a miscellaneous receipt of the ordered item in response to each customer order. That way, Order Entry has something to ship from inventory, at an appropriate cost, but Inventory shows it as stock-on-hand only for the brief period between Order Entry and the time the warehouse picks the order for shipping.

Physical Storage and Management

Physical storage of items is laid out to serve operational needs. The same type of item may appear in many places within the system. Oracle defines a hierarchical storage scheme, which breaks down as follows:

- **Inventory organizations**   Have different missions (for example, manufacturing versus sales) and different geographical locations.
- **Subinventories**   Reflect different storage areas within a geographical location. They are usually defined by the physical location and the nature of the items being stored.
- **Stock locators**   Are the addresses of storage locations within the warehouse. They are optional by subinventory.

Inventory Organizations

An inventory organization within Oracle EBS runs its own show. Although a single installation of Oracle Inventory can maintain Item Master records for an entire company, the people in each organization within the installation are responsible for managing their own stock. As indicated previously, many attributes of an inventory item can be different in different inventory organizations. Oracle Inventory moves stock between organizations by way of internal orders, using Purchasing on the demand end and Order Management on the supply end. Material does not move across organizations unless the people in the organizations allow it to do so.

Purchasing can support multiple inventory organizations. A single purchase order can handle deliveries to multiple locations. Its receiving operations support only one location at a time. People working at a loading dock only need to deal with receipts for their warehouse.

Manufacturing is oriented towards plants, which are associated with their own inventory organizations. A manufacturing plant draws raw materials from, and sends finished goods to, a single inventory organization.

Order Management has a customer's perspective. Just as customers hope to deal with the company without having to be conscious of its internal operations, Order Management maintains a global view. It accepts product orders on behalf of the whole company or operating unit, using customer data that are shared and consistent regardless of the organization. Order Management's concern with organization has to do with satisfying an order. It determines the plants or warehouses that will be used to make and ship products, and it provides for each operating unit to have separate customer addresses and contacts.

Individual employees normally belong to one operating organization, defined in the Responsibilities available in their user log-in menu. Oracle EBS hides its complexity from them. They see items, purchase orders, and other activity in light of their Responsibility in a given transaction, which handles movements between organizations using internal orders. Oracle Purchasing, which is associated with one organization, passes a requisition to Oracle Order Management. Oracle Order Management creates an internal order to fill the requirement from the source organization designated for the item in question. It is visible to the requesting Inventory or Purchasing organization in the same way a supplier order would be. The organization can see its open request for the item, and it can see the item as due into its organization.

Multiple inventory organizations serve different locations, corporate organizations, and purposes. Oracle EBS can handle many kinds of relationships among them. You may create a structure in which material flows in one direction, such as from plant to distribution, or in both directions. If the locations are close, you can have the system decrease stock in the source and increase stock in the receiving organization in the same transaction. If not, you can have the system track in-transit inventory. You can have Oracle EBS manage all aspects of your shipping operations.

The cost of an item may vary in different inventories. A markup can represent value added in freight or handling or within the company. Oracle can compute this transfer charge as a flat rate or a percentage. Or you may use a manual business procedure or custom software to establish costs in different sites, in which case the difference will be posted to a variance account.

Subinventories

The *subinventory* determines the uses to which an item can be put. For example, returned items awaiting inspection cannot be shipped to a new customer. The following questions should be considered when setting up subinventories:

■ Does the system track quantities for the subinventory? (Whether the quantity can be allowed to go negative is established at the organization level.)

■ Does the system track locations for the subinventory?

■ How available is stock within the subinventory to customers? Is it nettable against demand? (In other words, can it be shipped as product?) Is it reservable against customer orders? Should it be considered in available-to-promise (ATP) calculations?

■ Are items in the subinventory considered inventory assets, as opposed to expensed items?

The answers are generally yes for the major subinventories that support customers and manufacturing operations. They track quantities, have locations, are nettable, are "ATPable" and reservable, and are carried as assets.

Minor subinventories are convenient holding places for material in transit, such as returned goods or received goods awaiting inspection. Planning the major subinventories is an important part of setup. Make sure you split asset inventory into appropriate subinventories upon conversion, because it can be troublesome to redefine subinventories (and locations) after conversion. It is easy to add minor subinventories as required, as long as you do not have to move balances into them.

Subinventories are a useful tool for managing consignment goods. A procedure known as *vendor-managed inventory* (VMI) is a procurement and planning practice in which a company delegates key inventory-management functions to one or more of its suppliers. Oracle EBS provides integrated support for the VMI business process, but it is mandatory to have Oracle Inventory, Oracle Purchasing, and Oracle Collaborative Planning.

Locators

Warehouse locator codes usually include segments for aisle, rack, and bin corresponding to aisles on the long dimension of the warehouse, rows of racks across the warehouse, and stacks of bins from floor to ceiling. Large organizations may want another segment or two for building and room number.

Stock locators are a natural use of flexfields. Choosing your location-numbering scheme is part of setup. Oracle allows a large number of segments and characters, but short and concise is best, as in this example:

Building	One character
Aisle	Two positions
Rack	Two positions
Bin	One position

You can build the whole aisle/rack/bin structure into a single segment or split it into multiple segments. The benefits of a multisegment approach are modest. Using value sets to limit the valid entries in a given segment allows for expansion of any individual segment if a longer location code is needed. On the other hand, maneuvering through data-entry screens is faster with one-segment flexfields. Most companies combine all elements of the locator into a single segment.

Your location-numbering plan has to cover all types of storage. You might have to compromise, say, between an aisle/rack/bin scheme for packaged products, a rotating bin scheme for small electronic components, and a yard-storage scheme for lumber or quarry stone. Remember that Oracle Inventory, perhaps unlike legacy systems, will manage your entire inventory.

To allow for growth and promote ease of understanding, your numbering scheme must reflect an appropriate balance between brevity and content. Brevity is most important in data entry. It does not matter much if you scan most of your location codes, but it matters a lot to anyone who has to key them in. This example points up the need for a holistic approach to the applications—the need to plan setup, business procedures, and hardware at the same time.

Stock locators must be unique within an organization. Although some subinventories may not require locator codes, the numbers themselves are independent of the subinventory.

Locators may be specified or dynamic: either there is a preassigned place for everything, or you choose from available locations as items need to be stocked. In subinventories that use locations, each stock number may have one default location from which it is to be picked for shipment and another, possibly different, default location where it should be put upon receipt. Where the items are actually stored is quite independent of where they ought to be—Oracle Inventory records both. There may be multiple locations for a given stock number, each with a balance of individual units. Oracle Inventory can also track items by serial or lot number within each location.

TIP

Accounting considerations make it difficult to move stock locators from one subinventory to another. If you must do this, use miscellaneous transactions to bring the balances to zero, deactivate and then rename the locations in the old subinventory, define them in the new subinventory, and then pick up the balances through miscellaneous receipts. It is a good job for an SQL script.

Lot Processing

A *lot* is a group of units of a single type assumed to have the same attributes and to be controlled as a group. Lots are usually manufactured together and are subject to the same quality controls and handling. The major attributes of a lot are the lot number and expiration date.

Lots are useful in managing goods with limited shelf life. In general, the oldest merchandise not having reached its expiration date should be consumed first. There should be business procedures or subsystems to deal with stock that has passed its expiration date.

Lot numbers are associated with transactions affecting lot-number-controlled items. Lot numbers provide an audit trail through the system. Purchasing can receive items with lot numbers, Inventory can accept items with lot numbers from Manufacturing, and Order Management can pick and ship by lot number. This audit trail is essential in resolving problems such as finding where flawed components may have been used in manufacturing. Lot control must be a factor in planning business processes for discrete manufacturing. It demands a push-type inventory-management system that records part usage before the fact.

Serial-Number Processing

Tracking of serially numbered items can start at several points within the Inventory process: when the items are received into inventory, when they are received out of manufacturing into inventory, or as they are shipped. You decide item by item whether to use serial numbers and at what stage to start tracking them. Your choice will have a significant impact on the labor and processing involved in material-movement transactions and will depend on how much detail you need to track about each item.

Transactions for serially numbered items have to reference all the individual item numbers. The only economy available for data entry is that transactions can be entered by serial-number range. The labor impact of this requirement will depend on the level of automated data capture within the warehouse. Capturing movements through a bar-code scanner is, of course, more efficient than keying transaction data in through Oracle Inventory's online forms. The open design of the transaction interface process lends itself to the use of mobile devices. However, there are costs involved in implementing bar codes that should be weighed against the added benefits.

Oracle Service and custom extensions to Oracle EBS often take advantage of serial numbering. Service can associate original equipment manufacturer (OEM) warranty terms and conditions with components sold to customers. Test and inspection results are associated with serial numbers. Oracle Order Management controls RMAs (return material authorizations; for more on RMAs, see Chapter 12) of serially numbered items by serial number. That serial number may be useful in custom systems that track the costs of warranty support.

Configuration management, the tracking of serially numbered components within serially numbered assemblies, adds two more dimensions to the dilemma. The first dimension is depth. The system needs to track serial numbers at each level of nesting within the final product. The second dimension is time. Serially numbered components may be swapped in and out of an item. This can happen before shipment, in test and inspection, or through field upgrades and maintenance. An engineering change may change the structure—substituting one item for two, for instance. Configuration management is a widespread requirement, and one that differs significantly from industry to industry. Oracle has named its configuration management support Serial Number Genealogy. The support that appears in Inventory, the ability to drill down through the serially numbered components of an item in inventory, is only the tip of the iceberg. The modules that acquire materials for inventory, such as Oracle Purchasing and Oracle Work In Process, are responsible for maintaining the records.

Balances

Oracle Inventory provides inquiry forms for the various ways you need to look at item balances. View Item Quantities shows what is on hand, by subinventory, location, and revision level as well as by lot number and serial number. View Subinventory Quantities and View Locator Quantities give you inventory balances from a warehouse-storage perspective.

View Item Supply-Demand Information addresses a more interesting question: whether or not the warehouse can satisfy demand. It shows quantities on hand, due in by purchase order, due in from manufacturing, and reserved and due out on sales orders.

Inventory derives the quantity on hand from views instead of storing the information as a column in a table. MTL_ITEM_QUANTITIES_VIEW and MTL_SUBINV_QUANTITIES_VIEW sum across lots and serial numbers, and over receipts and issues, to present the figure of interest: how many of the item are available. The quantity can be used to satisfy customer orders if you have specified in setup that assets in the subinventory are nettable against demand.

An entry in the Define Organization Parameters form controls whether or not negative balances are allowed. Though it may be counterintuitive, allowing negative balances often improves accuracy. The premise is that Oracle Inventory's balance is not expected to be 100 percent accurate, but it should be accurate enough to assure a target level of support. The reasons for the discrepancies between what is actually in your warehouse and what is being reported in the application are timing and the economics of record keeping. Warehouse personnel might not record transactions as they happen, but instead may hold paperwork until a certain time of day or even day of the week. Additionally, Oracle Inventory processes some transactions in batch mode, another element delaying the process. Also, as described in the following section on inventory counts, the cost involved in achieving and maintaining complete accuracy is usually not justified.

NOTE
There may be accounting reasons for running a negative inventory. For example, during conversion, Micros Systems needed to make its legacy inventory available to be picked and shipped from Oracle Order Entry. Micros could not allow Oracle to value the inventory, however, because its legacy system already accounted for assets on hand. The solution? They set up two offsetting subinventories in Oracle: one with positive balances from which they could ship and capture the cost of goods sold, and an offset with negative balances. The result was an Oracle Inventory that could be used for shipping and would accurately record the cost of goods sold, but which appeared in the General Ledger as an asset with zero value.

Counting

The gap between ideals and reality can cause credibility problems in Inventory. The simple view is that the automated system should know exactly how many grommets, for example, are on the shelves. An answer like "3,285.32 grommets" will not make sense. How could there be .32 grommet?

It is a problem of volume. No operation of any size can be assured of knowing exactly how much it has of any item at any time. It does not pretend to try. It asks a more sophisticated question: how accurate do the data have to be to get the job done? Oracle EBS supports this statistical view. How accurate do the balances have to be?

Similar considerations apply in managing your checking account. You do not have to know exactly how much money you have at all times; you need to know only enough to make decisions. Can you afford the new suit? Do you have to draw on the credit union to make the mortgage payment? And you need enough control to make sure that nobody else is writing checks on your account and that the bank has not made any mistakes. The bottom line is that you need to know more or less what you have at all times, and you need to reconcile every now and then. You weigh the effort of keeping the balance totally up to date against the cost of an occasional bounced check, and on that basis you decide what level of accuracy is optimal for you.

Inventory balances have to be accurate enough that the warehouse finds sufficient quantity on hand when the automated system says to pick the item—not all the time, but a very high percentage of the time. Conversely, counting inventory costs money, often more than the items are worth. Management is the art of striking the right balance. Cycle counting with ABC analysis—counting the most important stock most frequently—gives the highest level of inventory performance for the counting effort invested. Cycle counting and ABC analysis are discussed in more detail in upcoming sections.

Manufacturing-Inventory Counts

Manufacturing operations assume that counts are approximate. Most of them do not actually count parts as they go into assemblies. Instead, they compute part usage by taking into account the number of items produced, the bill of materials for the items, and attrition factors built into the bills to cover waste. *Backflushing* is the name given to the process of updating inventory after the fact by this kind of deduction.

Attrition factors can yield fractional inventory balances. If one tube breaks for every 10 TV sets made, inventory should go down by 11 after a lot of 10. What about after lots of five? With rounding, two lots of five would reduce inventory by either 10 or 12, both inaccurate. The answer has to be to reduce inventory by 5.5 tubes after a run of five, despite the fact that tubes only come in integer quantities. The next inventory count will reconcile this estimate to the actual quantity on hand.

Physical Inventory

A physical inventory is a count of all items in some portion of an inventory. Oracle Inventory takes a snapshot of the balances as they exist at a point in time. Using the snapshot as a baseline, Oracle Inventory prints inventory-count tags for the warehouse staff, accepts its counts, and then requests recounts or makes adjustments. Your business procedures may allow inventory activity to continue throughout the count. Oracle Inventory does all its comparisons against the frozen snapshot. Allowing operations to continue, however, means that the counters have to allow for activity between the freeze and their count.

Though Oracle Inventory offers full support for physical inventory counts, most organizations find that cycle counting according to an ABC analysis is the most effective way to achieve their objective on a regular basis. The fact that Oracle Inventory lets you have both systems in use at once eases the transition to cycle counting.

ABC Analysis

ABC analysis divides stock into categories to be managed with different levels of intensity. There are typically three categories, though Oracle Inventory allows any number. Category A stock is high value, mission critical, or high volume. Category B is in the middle, and Category C is low value, low action, and low volume. It is worth a high investment of labor to keep the counts accurate for category A items. Category B and C items merit proportionately less effort.

Oracle Inventory lets you categorize your parts by on-hand quantities or on-hand item value; historical usage quantities, value, or number of transactions; forecast quantity or value; MRP demand quantity or value; or adjustment amounts. In the end, you can choose only one method of having Oracle Inventory automatically assign categories to your items. Run the analysis three or four ways to see which one appears to work best and note the exceptions. You may find that major finished goods represent the greatest high-dollar values but that the biggest adjustments are in items that regularly get broken or are subject to theft. Take the Oracle Inventory category assignments as a starting point, then use manual reassignments to take care of the exceptions.

Oracle provides two reports to help categorize items based on cost and activity in a given period: ABC Descending Values and ABC Assignment's reports. The ABC Descending Values report sorts items in descending order by the level of activity (monetary value, transactions, or quantity) and provides a cumulative total at each line. In other words, it highlights the items for which activity and cost show the most need for tight control. The Define ABC Assignments form assigns ABC classes to items; all you have to do is specify the cutoff points. Then, use the ABC Assignments report to show your assignments.

Many other criteria may be used to assign ABC categories. Users can buy third-party software or take advantage of Oracle EBS's open design to write their own ABC stratification logic. Standard cycle-count functionality will handle the assignments you have made using custom algorithms.

Cycle Counting

Cycle counting has replaced "wall-to-wall" counts as the preferred technique for managing warehouse stock. Shutting down operations just for a count is disruptive in small organizations and impossible in large ones. On top of everything else, complete inventory counts may be less accurate. People with little inventory experience are pulled in just for counting, and there is tremendous time pressure to finish and get back to business.

Cycle counting uses the ABC groups to establish how often items get counted. Users might specify that category A items get counted once a month, category B items quarterly, and category C items yearly. In setting up the count, the system divides the number of items to be counted by the number of workdays available to count them, so warehouse personnel count roughly the same number of items every day. The warehouse usually schedules an hour or two per day for counting, at a time when receiving and picking activity are low.

When the entered counts disagree with the computer count and the discrepancy is within a user-prescribed tolerance, the entered count is taken to be accurate; otherwise the system will request a recount. As with the physical-inventory process, although transactions can still be done during the count, they will complicate the process. Your business procedures should allow time for a count and a recount in a period when the items are physically inactive.

Cycle counting keeps average accuracy in the warehouse high and consistent. Management can devise reports (again, usually custom or third-party, using Oracle EBS transaction data) to monitor warehouse accuracy as measured by warehouse denials, stock shrinkage, and other parameters.

Many organizations converting to Oracle EBS have not implemented cycle counting. It represents a significant change in philosophy and business procedures, and it is usually best left until the Oracle EBS system is running smoothly. A gradual cutover is recommended, starting with the category A items. The warehouse knows the process is working when the number of recounts falls to an acceptable level, indicating that most counts agree with the automated records. Some items—and some subinventories—can continue under the old counting methods while cycle counting is being implemented.

The cycle-count interface makes it possible to use mobile devices to do the counting. You export the list of items to be counted and import the count results. This minimizes dual-keying errors (particularly if the counting device first reads the bar code and then the user types in the number of items present) and ensures that advanced warehouses already using this kind of counting equipment do not perceive that they are taking a step back with the move to the E-Business Suite.

Replenishment Counts

Inexpensive, expendable items may not be worth counting at all for financial purposes. If they are essential for the operation, however, they do need to be replenished. Oracle Inventory supports *replenishment counts*, in which the counter may either directly enter the quantity to be ordered or enter a count so Oracle Inventory can perform MIN-MAX computations to determine what to order, as described in the following subsection.

Managing Stock Replenishments   Inventory is responsible for the big picture of overall material requirements. In addition to its balance records, it maintains am MTL_SUPPLY table to record all items expected to be received into inventory. These include items on order from suppliers, items being manufactured, items in transit from other company locations, and items due back from customers. Inventory keeps a parallel MTL_DEMAND table with records of all material requirements for customer orders, manufacturing raw-material needs, and requisitions for internal use. Inventory is only the custodian. Purchasing, Order Management, and Work in Process (among other EBS modules) maintain data in these tables to reflect their operations.

Inventory's replenishment logic compares future demand against what is on hand and on order to determine what needs to be ordered. If there are customer orders for six of an item and two are on hand and two on order, the replenishment logic has to order more. It creates and sends a requisition to Purchasing.

Determining what to order is complicated by the time factor and ordering considerations. Suppliers and internal manufacturing operations need time to ship or make inventory items, and efficiency demands that items be ordered in rational units, like boxes or pallets. Using the actual need as a basis, the replenishment logic figures out how much to order and when.

Inventory uses forecasts to compensate for the fact that it cannot get materials instantaneously. It adds forecast quantities to actual demand to compute the most realistic estimates of requirements at each future point in time. The purchase requisitions it generates take into consideration the following lead-time factors:

- the time it will take to turn a requisition into a purchase order and get it to a vendor;
- the time it will take a vendor to ship the item; and
- the time it will take to receive, inspect, and deliver the item to its destination.

Oracle Manufacturing plans the production of manufactured items to meet firm (i.e., booked) and forecast demand. In addition to the preceding factors, it takes into account the time it takes to make items.

MIN-MAX Planning   Stock items may be coded for replenishment by reorder point (ROP) or by MIN-MAX logic. MIN-MAX logic is the simplest. It can base the replenishment decision solely on the amount of stock on hand and on order, or it can take demand into account as well. It takes minimum and maximum values from the MIN_MINMAX_QUANTITY and MAX_MINMAX_QUANTITY attributes in the MTL_SYSTEM_ITEMS record for the item.

MIN-MAX includes expected receipts (supply) and existing orders (demand) out to a cutoff date you specify. If the quantity on hand and on order falls below the specified MIN, it orders up to the MAX, as shown in Figure 11-3.

Demand data may at times be excluded altogether. They are not useful when lead times are longer than delivery schedules; in that case, parts could not be ordered from vendors in time to meet user needs. In addition, demand data may not be worth the effort for inexpensive items that experience steady consumption, such as paper clips or solder.

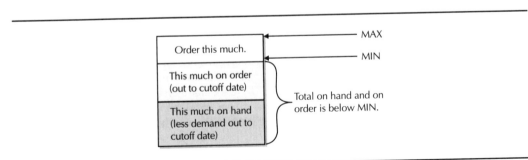

FIGURE 11-3.   *MIN-MAX reorder-calculation logic*

Using demand and forecast information and analyzing matching supply against demand by time period will usually provide a more accurate picture of requirements than will MIN-MAX point-in-time projection. Reorder-point replenishment, shown in Figure 11-4, uses future demand plus safety stock to compute requirements.

Reorder-Point Planning   Safety stock is a "fudge factor" to protect against the risks of a change in demand. Oracle Inventory supports two statistical methods for computing safety stock. It can use a straight percentage of forecast demand; alternatively, if there is enough history on the item, Inventory can compute safety stock as a factor of historical usage and the desired service level. Service level expresses, in statistical terms, the amount of time an item should be available when it is requested. It takes more stock to support a 99.9 percent service level than a 99 percent level. Businesses have to decide, by item, the trade-off between the cost of carrying stock and the cost of being unable to satisfy customers.

ROP incorporates the concept of an economic order quantity (EOQ). The EOQ formula balances the one-time costs of processing an order (cutting the purchasing order, receiving, and so on) against the ongoing carrying cost of keeping stock in the warehouse (cost of money, occupancy, overhead, and shrinkage). The item manager factors in the standard units for ordering and handling material (case, pallet, and so on) in setting the Fixed Order Quantity and Fixed Lot Size Multiplier attributes for the item. When the ROP replenishment logic determines that more stock is needed, it creates a requisition for some multiple of that adjusted EOQ.

Time is an important factor in balancing supply with demand. A carload of grapefruit next month does not satisfy shoppers tomorrow. You specify time buckets (days, weeks, or periods) within which Oracle EBS matches supply and demand. You set the parameters up item by item to meet your business needs. For a hospital, a can of Spam due this week will satisfy cafeteria demand next month. Milk due this week will not. If you are using weekly time buckets, you would say that the supply and demand for milk must match one another within each time bucket, whereas with Spam the demand in one time bucket can be satisfied by supply in any previous time bucket. You also specify how future supply may satisfy current demand. A pair of skis due next month may satisfy demand this week if the customer is willing to wait. Your company has to set the rules.

Material Requirements Planning   The Material Requirements Planning (MRP) application handles material planning across items and across organizations, using Purchasing and Manufacturing as sources for the items. Inventory handles replenishments at the item level only. In making its computations, it looks at supply due from purchasing or manufacturing and demand

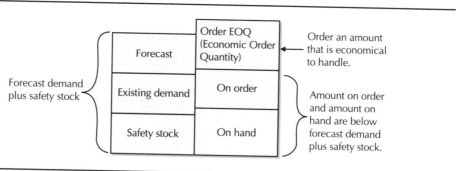

FIGURE 11-4.   *ROP replenishment logic*

for that item itself or as a component of a pick-to-order order line. In a manufacturing operation, however, the system needs to translate demand (in terms of shippable product) into requirements (in terms of components). MRP uses Bill of Material explosions to determine those parts requirements. MRP can also compute requirements across an organization, determining how much each factory must produce and each warehouse must ship in order to meet company-wide demand. MRP and inventory replenishment both calculate what is required and generate requisitions for Purchasing. Purchasing follows its setup rules to act on the requisition. It finds a source—either another organization within the company or a vendor—and places the appropriate internal or external purchase order. It advises Inventory of the state of the requisition through postings to the MTL_SUPPLY table.

Oracle Purchasing handles the receipt and inspection of items. It adjusts the inventory balances and relieves the on-order amounts appropriately. Users without Oracle Purchasing need custom programs to populate the MTL_TRANSACTION_INTERFACE and MTL_SUPPLY_INTERFACE tables with appropriate records to show purchasing activity.

Forecasting and Demand

Each installation needs to establish its own policies for recognizing demand and making forecasts to be used by the Oracle Material Requirements Planning application. Order Management is the primary demand driver. Establishing order cycles is a major part of Order Management setup, and the Demand interface is part of the cycle. In other words, a demand can be made visible to Inventory at several points in the cycle between the time an order is first entered and the time it ships. The earlier the demand is recognized, the higher the demand satisfaction will be; however, carrying costs will also be higher as a result of items held for orders that never firm up.

Demand, which is associated with *actual* customer requests, is firmer than forecasts, which are *estimates* of future requests. Forecasts have to be done by item, and they have to allow appropriate algorithms and parameters for each item. The algorithms take into account historical demand, trends, and seasonality and use mathematical smoothing techniques. You can make intuitive projections when past demand is nonexistent or would be a poor guide.

Actual demand places a reality check on a forecast. The forecast of what will happen has to be adjusted for what is actually happening. In inventory terms, demand *consumes* forecast. Subject to some exceptions, each order for an item lowers the forecast demand as it raises the actual demand. The exceptions follow:

- A given order that dwarfs the average is called an *outlier*. Suppose a Christmas tree lot forecasts selling 500 trees a week, one at a time. If it receives one order for 300 trees, this does not mean that the best guess is only another 200 will be sold. On the contrary, the best guess is that the order for 300 is a fluke and perhaps 495 more will be sold, one at a time. In Oracle EBS, the lot managers could reflect this by setting the outlier update percentage to 1, meaning that no single demand can consume more than 1 percent of a forecast.

- After correcting for outliers, if the forecast for a period can fully consume the new demand, it is consumed. Demand goes up, forecast goes down. Forecasts may be kept by demand class—groups of customers and types of orders. Oracle EBS then follows rules for consuming by demand class. For example, Schlage may not want OEM orders for deadbolts to consume the forecast for its wholesale-distribution arm. In other words, if OEM sells twice as many as expected, it will require more manufacturing instead of taking the pressure off the dealer sales force. Replenishment will buy the parts to make more deadbolts.

If the forecast for the period cannot fully consume the demand in that period, Oracle EBS follows the rules given for demand consumption. It may use up the demand by consuming forecast within a specified number of periods preceding the demand period, consuming forecast within a number of periods after the forecast, or "overconsuming" forecast in the current period. Overconsumption effectively ignores the impact of excess demand in one given period on the forecast. The replenishment algorithms use all the real demand, including that in the period of overconsumption, and add to it the forecasts for other periods that would have been diminished if the overconsumption had been applied to them. Overconsumption results in higher replenishment orders.

Different sources of demand require separate forecasts. Schlage's forecast for deadbolts will be the aggregate of direct-sales forecasts in the states and countries in which it markets, plus what it may manufacture for private-label sales. The forecasting system uses forecast sets to combine multiple forecasts into aggregate figures to plan manufacturing.

A *forecast* set is a group of forecasts that combine to give a complete forecast, as illustrated in Figure 11-5. A forecast must belong to one and only one forecast set. There may be more than one forecast set, each representing a different business scenario. You can have and maintain any number of forecast sets. A given run of the Inventory Reorder Point Planning Report or of MRP, however, has to use a single forecast set (or forecast) to calculate material requirements and create requisitions.

Multiple forecast sets are useful for "what if" projections. You can model different economic scenarios or determine what would happen if you acquired new customers or expanded your marketing territory. You can compare the results of different MRP runs. MRP runs do not order items; they simply create requisitions. Planners can look at different requisition quantities based on different forecasts and decide what to order. Once an order has been placed, the supply it represents will be taken into account by all MRP runs.

Forecast sets need to be consumed only if they are used in the replenishment process. Oracle EBS can consume more than one set, if you want to consistently generate material requirements for multiple scenarios.

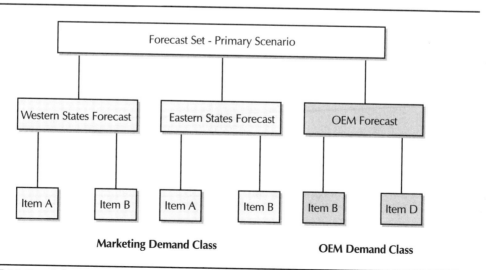

FIGURE 11-5.   *A forecast set*

Industry Efforts to Improve Stock Movement

The warehouse is the place where the information age confronts physical reality. It takes space to store things, money to carry them, and people and equipment to move them around. Warehouse operations are central to the whole supply-chain-management revolution. The objective is to avoid having things pass through a warehouse at all, whenever possible, and to move them with maximum efficiency when they have to be stored.

Several information technologies support warehouse operations. Just about everything comes marked with bar codes. Bar-code labels are about the only paper used anymore in warehouse operations. Portable RF (radio frequency) devices that combine scanner, display, keyboard, and radio functionality tell warehouse workers what to do, then accept their confirmation of what was done. Real-time two-way communications provide Oracle EBS's automated systems with the kind of information and quick response ability to increase efficiency significantly. Some of the areas of increased efficiency are:

- **Intelligent receiving**   Electronic advance shipment notices (ASNs) prepare Oracle Purchasing for a receipt. The automated system can decide whether to "cross-dock" part of the receipt to immediately fill back orders and where best to put it in the warehouse. After the warehouse worker identifies a receipt to the system, when possible by a bar-code scan, the system says what is in it, how much, what kind of inspection is required, and where to put each line of the receipt. It may have bar-coded labels printed to identify the materials as they are put into storage. The system can capture or verify serial numbers and lot numbers at the same time.

- **A choice of picking styles**   Options make it possible to find the best balance among speed, efficient movement through the warehouse, and accuracy. The options include order picking, cluster picking, zone picking, bulk picking, paper-based picking, and pick-and-pass picking. The newer approaches involve consolidating picking for multiple customer orders as well as warehouse movements, so that one pass through the warehouse, called a *picking wave*, satisfies many needs. The materials pulled in a picking wave are typically brought to a staging area where they can be sorted by order, container, and destination.

- **Multiple layers of containerization**   Inventory is often stored on the pallets or in the containers used to ship it, and these in turn usually carry bar-code identifiers. Oracle EBS now has visibility of inventory through the layers of shipping containers, and it has the logic to generate the inventory-movement transactions needed to build up and break down shipping containers.

- **On-the-fly decision making**   Oracle Workflow processes specify how much flexibility there is in choosing the storage locations to use for inbound and outbound goods. RF devices let the workers on the warehouse floor tell the automated system exactly what they have done, so the system does not get confused when they act on their own initiative.

- **Proactive material movement**   With visibility up and down the supply chain, the inventory system can anticipate where materials will be needed. It has the ability to initiate warehouse move orders to prompt the physical movement.

Most material movements are initiated by Oracle Purchasing (in the receiving process) and Order Management/Shipment Management (for getting goods out to customers). The few transactions described here are the ones that Oracle Inventory owns outright, the transactions that move material around within the inventory for the sake of inventory efficiency or in response to kanban requests.

Kanban

Kanban, which means *card* in Japanese, is a method to support pull-based replenishment in manufacturing systems. The manufacturing process takes materials as they are needed—that is, it pulls them—and a simple physical signal such as a kanban card or empty container triggers a replenishment. Kanban systems are self-regulating in that replenishments flow down to the point of use only at the rate they are needed. The immediacy of the kanban signals leads to shorter lead times and reduced inventory. Kanban is best suited for *flow manufacturing*, assembly-line operations that produce similar items on a continuous basis.

The production process is broken down into processing units (PUs). Each PU takes in raw materials, adds value to create an output, and passes the output to another PU. A kanban card, or even just an empty container, signals one PU to resupply the next one up the line. Presentation of the card takes the place of a requisition or a delivery order, depending on whether or not it goes outside the company.

The number of cards in circulation controls production; a PU is not allowed to make its product without a card. The simplicity of the system minimizes the cost of capturing transactions. It is easy to record that a kanban container passed from one station to another. A bar-code scanner is the preferred method, but a hand tally will suffice for most organizations.

Oracle EBS accepts kanban as an alternative to setting a release time fence for MPS or MRP within an organization. You have to define a pull sequence for every kanban item, showing the sequence of kanban locations (i.e., PUs) that models the replenishment network. The replenishment network includes locations on the shop floor, outside suppliers, other production lines, nonkanban organizations, and other, possibly remote organizations within the company. Because the PUs are represented by locations, Oracle EBS allows the use of stock locators for purposes of kanban definition, even if locator control is not in effect for the organization, subinventory, or item. The integration between Inventory and Manufacturing is such that Inventory can present a kanban card to initiate production when it projects a need for an item, eliminating the time it takes to go through a production-scheduling process.

The pull sequence provides Oracle EBS with the information it needs to automatically create kanban cards for each item, subinventory, and locator. Each card is uniquely identified by a generated kanban number. You have the option to ignore the pull sequence and manually generate kanban cards using numbers of your own choosing.

Automated support enhances the simple manual kanban concept. Bar-code scanning accurately captures shop-floor movement at very little expense. You can have Oracle EBS create nonreplenishable kanban cards to handle spikes in demand, and you can have Oracle EBS temporarily take cards out of circulation to hold down supply.

Warehouse Movements

Oracle Inventory has formal transactions to support movement of materials within the warehouse. Warehouse organization cannot be static. It has to continually respond to changes in demand and in what is actually in storage.

In arranging items within a subinventory—that is, items that are generally the same in terms of security requirements, handling requirements, special handling and the like—the optimum places to locate stock items in a warehouse depend on how frequently the items are picked, what else is commonly picked at the same time, how bulky the items are, and which shipping dock, staging area, or manufacturing location they usually go to. These factors need to be taken into consideration in initially assigning storage locations.

Warehouse organization is in constant flux. The important questions involve determining the optimal place to put each new receipt and deciding when it is worth the expense of moving items around within the warehouse just to tune the operation. Technology supports a more fluid organization. Programmed logic, from Oracle EBS and others, can pick optimal storage locations for receipts as they arrive and can periodically match the actual warehouse organization against past activity and future demand to figure out how it should be rearranged. Oracle Inventory includes alerts to determine when actions need to be executed and RF devices empower the warehouse workers themselves to make these decisions. They can tell the system what moves they have made, or want to make, in such a way that the automated records remain accurate.

Users previously accommodated rewarehousing transactions using miscellaneous issues and receipts or custom subsystems that fed the open interface tables. Oracle EBS now supports moves with a series of move transactions that are integrated into the stock-picking schemes, primarily pick waves. It directs the warehouse to pick materials to be moved in the same wave as material for customer orders. It all goes to staging areas, from which an item may go into a customer order through a standard pick release or be directed to another subinventory or storage location. Not coincidentally, staging areas work well in an automated warehouse operation. The picking apparatus and conveyor systems can bring stock to forward staging areas, from which warehouse workers can pick them again for packing. In this case, Oracle EBS's move transactions translate directly into commands to automated storage and retrieval systems, carousels, conveyors, and automated guided vehicles.

Conversion Issues

Oracle Inventory provides many open interfaces to assist with ongoing interfaces and initial data conversion. This section covers issues related to conversion, such as item, transaction (opening balances), and location conversions.

Item Master Conversion

Oracle Inventory provides the Open item interface to enable you to load new items into the Inventory Item Master. This program processes records that you have loaded into the MTL_SYSTEM_ITEMS_INTERFACE table, which has columns corresponding to those in the MTL_SYSTEM_ITEMS table. The load process cross-checks to ensure that the attribute settings are consistent with one another.

When converting from a legacy system to Oracle Inventory, it can be difficult to map all the item attributes one-to-one or even come close. Legacy items do, however, usually fall into groupings such as those defined by Oracle EBS templates. The recommended approach to conversion is as follows:

1. Define templates that can be used to set up every type of item in the organization. The Open item interface can apply only one template to set attributes for an item.

2. Associate a master-level template with each legacy item. If possible, expand the legacy schema to carry the template name, so you can prepare for Oracle EBS conversion as you maintain the legacy system.

3. Load the interface table with records in which the item-specific attribute columns (item number, weight, units of measure) are populated; name a template that will fill in all other needed attributes in the master organization. Typically, more than half the attributes will remain null; your testing will indicate which attributes need values.

4. Import the master items into Oracle EBS.

5. Populate the interface table with organization-level records. These usually include little more than the item number, the organization, and the organization-level template to

apply. The organization-level template must be compatible with the master-level template. You may find it useful to define the templates such that the name of one can be derived from the other.

6. Import the organization-level items into Oracle EBS.

Using templates does more than just simplify the conversion; it ensures that new items created after cutover will have the same characteristics as legacy items brought over during conversion.

TIP
The attribute names in the Define Item screen and the Define Item Template screen are not the same as the column names in the interface table. Use the following SQL routine to create a list of the correspondence between internal and external attribute names:

```
SELECT attribute_name, user_attribute_name

FROM mtl_item_attributes

ORDER BY attribute_name
```

Oracle EBS can carry multiple values for certain attributes that legacy systems define as unique to an item, such as cost, sales price, catalog, and category data. The interface program does not load these values. However, the Oracle EBS tables are relatively straightforward. Plan to write SQL*Plus or PL/SQL scripts to populate them as part of the conversion.

There is no open interface for batch updates of items. It is critically important to choose the right template at conversion. Make sure your test plan includes transactions from every business area—particularly Inventory, Purchasing, Order Management, and Manufacturing—that will use the attributes you set.

Transaction Conversion

Once the items and locations are in place, you can use the Open transaction interface to bring in balance data as miscellaneous receipts. The process is straightforward. The balances will be debited to the material account associated with the subinventory; the accountants will need to tell you where to post the credit.

Making the accounts balance between the legacy system and Oracle EBS takes some effort. The accounts will balance only if both the inventory balances and the item costs agree. Set up the Open Item Interface to bring in the frozen standard costs of each item. Reconcile the legacy inventory valuation that existed prior to conversion with the Oracle EBS's valuation. After you get the inventory-to-inventory conversion to balance, it should be a small matter to reconcile to the General Ledger. There should be no adjustment at all if the legacy inventory agrees with the legacy ledger (but it is worth checking whether that is historically the case).

Costs are more volatile than items themselves. Oracle EBS provides an online mechanism to update them. You use the Update Costs form to assign the new cost to the "pending" cost type, then run Update Standard Costs to have Oracle EBS apply the change and compute the accounting implications. Although you must let Oracle EBS apply the changes, it is quite easy to write your own script to create pending cost-type records. Use Oracle EBS's utility to delete pending costs, insert your new pending values into CST_ITEM_COSTS and CST_ITEM_COST_DETAILS, and then run the update. Oracle EBS does the complex work of revaluing stock, in-transit inventory, and work in process.

Location Conversion

Users can convert items and import balances via the open interfaces, but you still need custom scripts to set up stock locators. You set them up first because stock locators have to be present to accept balances.

There are usually so few subinventories that you create them manually. The major issue—deciding which subinventories to define for asset items—can remain unresolved well into setup. One of the first jobs in conversion will be to populate the location tables. Figure 11-6 shows how these tables relate to each other and the sequence of conversion within each organization. The tables with heavy borders are populated manually at setup. Those with medium borders are populated in the first automated conversion steps, and those with light borders are populated in the second phase of conversion.

MTL_SYSTEM_ITEMS master records need to be converted independently of locations and prior to loading any balance or location information for items. Load them through the Open Item Interface, as described earlier in this chapter.

FND_FLEX_VALUES may be used to validate some segments in the Location Flexfield, though usually not all. If you are going to limit the values a segment may assume, you have to set them up in advance. Most organizations develop a mass-load utility for flex values as part of General Ledger setup.

MTL_ITEM_LOCATIONS defines locations within the organization. These locations are independent of the items stored in them. There is no open interface to import these records. Write a script to create them from legacy location data. The script will perform the following tasks:

1. Create a master list of item locations from legacy files.

2. Perform the required translation from the legacy system into the Oracle Location Flexfield format.

3. Insert records directly into the MTL_ITEM_LOCATIONS table. Chapter 22 describes the process of analysis and programming. Be sure to do the following:

   ■ Validate the segments against any flex-value sets you may have defined for the Location Flexfield.

   ■ Use the legacy data to select a valid subinventory for the location. Subinventories can be assigned according to the type of item currently in the location, but inventory management is generally easier when physically adjacent locations belong to one subinventory. Recognize, however, that this may force some trade-offs between rewarehousing and assigning a less-than-optimal subinventory scheme.

   ■ Populate any other columns for which data are available from the legacy system, so that nothing is lost. Leave no legacy attributes behind. Map them into unused ATTRIBUTE1 . . . ATTRIBUTE30 columns if Oracle EBS does not have a place for them.

   ■ Populate the WHO columns with the date and the user ID of the author of the load script. Or better yet, create a conversion user and run all conversion programs from that account. Then, even years later, everyone can clearly identify records that were created during initial conversion.

- Use the Oracle-provided sequence MTL_ITEM_LOCATIONS_S to generate unique LOCATOR_ID values.

4. Test the validity of the conversion script by querying created locations and assigning items to them in the test instance.

Balance and location data are usually available in the same legacy file. Depending on the legacy system's sophistication or lack thereof, the data may be in the extract used to populate MTL_SYSTEM_ITEMS. Your first step is to write a custom script to populate the tables, shown at the top of Figure 11-6, that join to both items and subinventories. You add the balances after you have defined places to put them.

Chances are that Oracle Inventory admits more complexity than the legacy system. Your algorithms will have to define not only where items are, but also where they go when they arrive and where to look for them first. MTL_ITEM_SUB_INVENTORIES, MTL_SECONDARY_LOCATORS, and MTL_ITEM_SUB_DEFAULTS are simple tables. Generate entries for the mandatory columns and populate the others to the extent that legacy data are available.

Accounting Entries for Inventory Transactions

Inventory accounts for items and their costs. Its financial accounting is automatic; few organizations would bother to track items that have no monetary value. The money side flows to the General Ledger, where the financial operations of the whole enterprise are recorded and reported. Reporting follows the chart of accounts, discussed in Chapter 2.

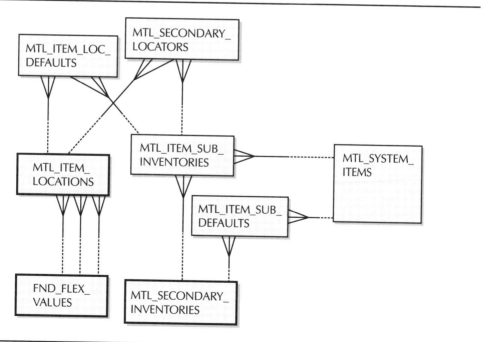

FIGURE 11-6. *Relationships among location tables in Inventory*

Inventory is carried on a company's books as an asset. The most fundamental accounting requirement is that the value of all the items in inventory sum to the amount carried on the General Ledger books. There can be more than one ledger and more than one inventory organization within each ledger, but they all need to balance.

In addition to the summary reports required by law, the ledger provides detailed information to support business decisions. The following types of decisions are made in Inventory:

■   What is the real cost at sale of an inventory item, factoring in the purchase cost, handling costs, storage, and everything else?

■   How can inventory costs be reduced? What are the optimal trade-offs?

■   Ultimately, what products are profitable for the company to manufacture or sell?

The Oracle Inventory setup requires many ledger accounts. These accounts are the basis for ledger reporting, of which the material managers will be the biggest users. They need to work with the accounting department and the software-setup team to make sure that the accounts will serve their own information needs.

Shaking down the accounting setups is a major part of the Inventory installation process. Setup would be simple if users knew how Oracle EBS worked and what they needed in the way of reports; unfortunately they usually do not have this information. Deciding what they want in light of what Oracle EBS can do is a matter of trial and error. There is a big difference between keeping the books in balance and producing information needed to manage the business.

Accounting models are an essential device for planning and communication. They show what information will flow to the ledger. The model is a kind of financial flowchart that accountants, functional experts, and the MIS staff can share in setting up the Oracle Inventory parameters.

The following accounting model is simple and accurate—but very incomplete. It exemplifies how to get the process started.

| Step 1 | Finance an inventory company by putting cash into the company for an inventory account: | | |

Account	Debit	Credit
Cash	$100	
Equity		$100

| Step 2 | Use $60 to buy some inventory: | | |

Account	Debit	Credit
Inventory Assets	$60	
Cash		$60

| Step 3 | Sell the inventory for $80: | | |

Account	Debit	Credit
Cash	$80	
Inventory Assets		$60
Profit		$20

Balance-sheet statements after each of these transactions would show the financial state of the company at that time:

After step 1			After step 2			After step 3		
Assets		**Liabilities**	**Assets**		**Liabilities**	**Assets**		**Liabilities**
Cash	$100	Equity $100	Cash	$40	Equity $100	Cash	$120	Equity $100
			Inventory	$60				Profit $20

Additional Accounting Transactions

The preceding model is overly simplistic, but it is financially accurate in that it balances, while not providing much useful information. The following paragraphs introduce some of the accounts that Purchasing and Inventory setup require. They make the accounting model and financial reporting more complicated, but they do a better job of reflecting the actual state of the business.

Most companies operate on an accrual rather than a cash basis. Their books show expenses as they are due, rather than when they are paid. They show income when it is earned rather than when the money is paid. Step 2—buying inventory— becomes two steps.

Step 2(a)   Buy the assets and incur a liability to pay for them:

Account	**Debit**	**Credit**
Inventory Assets	$60	
Accounts Payable		$60

Step 2(b)   Pay for the purchased assets:

Account	**Debit**	**Credit**
Accounts Payable	$60	
Cash		$60

The balance sheet statement after step 2(b) would look the same as that shown in the first example. After step 2(a), it would show the liability for accounts payable as follows:

Assets		**Liabilities**	
Cash	$100	Equity	$100
Inventory	$60	Accounts Payable	$60

Introducing the accounts-payable account increases the utility of the financial statement by adding new information. It tells management that there is $100 in the bank, but $60 of it is owed to suppliers. Oracle Payables requires at least one accounts-payable account.

This model still does not reflect how business really works. The verb *buy* in step 2(a) is too simplistic. Buying is really a process in which ordering, receiving, and paying the bill are separate steps. The company will issue a purchase order to the vendor. The vendor will ship the product, then send an invoice separately. The company actually owes for the goods when they arrive, regardless of when the invoice arrives. This calls for a receipt-accruals account. Sometimes the company wants to know how much (in monetary terms) has been ordered or even requested to be ordered, so it does not spend the same money twice. Still assuming that the exact cost of the assets is known from start to end, the accounting model would include the following steps:

Step 2(a)	Order the assets:		
	Account	**Debit**	**Credit**
	Assets on Order	$60	
	Purchase Obligations		$60
Step 2(a)	Receive the assets:		
	Account	**Debit**	**Credit**
	Purchase Obligations	$60	
	Assets on Order		$60
	Inventory Assets	$60	
	Receiving Accrual		$60
Step 2(a)	Process the invoice:		
	Account	**Debit**	**Credit**
	Receiving Accrual	$60	
	Accounts Payable		$60
Step 2(a)	Pay the bill:		
	Account	**Debit**	**Credit**
	Accounts Payable	$60	
	Cash		$60

Oracle Inventory uses all the accounts just mentioned, in addition to others, to account for such things as materials that have been received but not yet inspected. In addition to showing how an accounting model works, this example shows how accounts are used to provide the detail necessary to manage business operations.

Variances

Prices and costs are subjective. By convention, the term *price* applies to the seller's side of a transaction and *cost* applies to the buyer's side. Your supplier's price is your cost. Price and cost vary over time, and there may be several in effect at one time. In the course of a routine purchase there may be slightly different amounts at each step in the process:

- the amount the internal requisitioner expects an item to cost,
- the supplier price that the purchasing department enters on the purchase order,
- the invoiced price from the supplier, and
- the standard cost of the item within the inventory system.

Differences in price require adjustments in most of the steps shown in the accounting model used earlier as well as in many other places within manufacturing. The adjustments, called *variances*, are posted to variance accounts. Here is what happens to the buying segment of our accounting model when the system sees three different prices: $55 (standard cost), $60 (purchase-order price), and $58 (invoice price):

Step 2(b)   Receive the assets:

Account	Debit	Credit
Inventory Assets (at standard cost)	$55	
Purchase Price Variance		–$5
Receiving Accrual		$60

Step 2(b)   Process the invoice:

Account	Debit	Credit
Receiving Accrual	$60	
Invoice Price Variance		$2
Accounts Payable		$58

Passing the differences to variance accounts buffers the system from constant small changes in price. It is probably true that no two Ford automobiles rolling off the assembly line cost exactly the same amount to make. Ford, however, plans and prices as if they do. The company sets a standard cost, watches the variances closely, and then periodically adjusts the standard cost to bring variances back down.

Managing inventory and manufacturing processes is a matter of managing variances. They have to be kept small through periodic adjustments to standard prices, a process that brings them in line with actual costs for purchasing and handling.

Average Versus Standard Costing

Costing provides a system for judging success in many areas. At the highest level, margin on a product is the difference between price and cost. You analyze elements of cost and patterns of change to evaluate the performance of your purchasing, inventory, and manufacturing organizations. The choice of either average or standard costing is ultimately a business decision—Oracle Inventory can perform both.

Under *average costing*, Oracle recomputes item cost with every receipt. Under *standard costing*, the inventory-asset account is charged for each receipt at standard cost, with the difference posted to the purchase-price variance (PPV) account.

The similarities between standard and average cost are significant. Both cost methods recognize an invoice-price variance account (IPV) in Payables for differences between the purchase price and the invoice price. IPV picks up prompt-pay discounts and other charges and credits that affect the ultimate cost of purchased materials. Material is only one of the five cost elements for which average costing is an alternative. The other four, discussed in the section on standard costs, are treated the same under either system.

A change in the frozen cost of an item ripples through a number of inventory, purchasing, and manufacturing processes. Each issue to manufacturing is costed at the average cost in effect at the moment of the issue. The adjustments the system makes as you change the frozen cost are ultimately posted to variance accounts you have defined in inventory, purchasing, and manufacturing setups.

CAUTION
Converting from one costing method to the other is difficult. Take the time to determine your long-range needs as you initially install Oracle Inventory.

Nonmaterial-Expense Collection

Manufacturing collects expenses associated with producing individual products. Even in a manufacturing organization, there are a number of overhead expenses that cannot be pinned to one item of inventory. However, there is no tool provided for nonmanufacturing organizations to track expenses by item. Overhead expenses such as warehouse management generally have to flow to the ledger and be allocated back to individual items. Overhead costs associated with running an inventory system follow these paths into the general ledger:

- Overhead labor charges may be collected by a labor-distribution system; they flow from payroll to the ledger. They may be applied to the system via the Applications Desktop Integrator.

- Overhead resource charges (utilities and so on) are captured by Payables; they flow to the ledger.

- Overhead costs (occupancy, and so on) are captured by Payables and as depreciation flows from Fixed Assets and other sources; they flow to the ledger.

- Expenses associated with Inventory operations flow to the ledger using Accounting Flexfields defined in Inventory setup. Because the item number does not flow to the General Ledger, you need an allocation formula to distribute the ledger amounts to individual items.

The ledger postings are differentiated according to Accounting Flexfields associated with the items and the organizations, subinventories, and categories that apply to the item. The GL might capture, for example, inventory shrinkage for office supplies into one GL account. You can develop your own formulas to spread such overhead expenses over actual inventory items.

What you do with inventory overhead depends on the needs of the organization. If inventory is a major part of your operation and is held for resale, it makes good sense to compute the costs of purchasing, receiving, and managing it into the price at which an item is carried in inventory and eventually sold. If the inventory is for internal use, it may be adequate to absorb the cost of managing it as corporate overhead or use a high-level allocation to spread overhead to the organizations it serves.

Setting Standard Costs

Costs are usually set at two levels: *buy* and *make*. The cost of *buy* (purchased) items is easier to establish. The simplest figure is the average price recently paid to suppliers. The cost of *make* (manufactured) items equals the cost of the component items plus the labor, overhead, and outside processing that goes into them.

For users who need to establish costs precisely, Oracle EBS defines five cost elements for each item:

- material (the average purchase price),
- overhead (resource and department overhead),
- material overhead (also called *burden*),
- outside processing, and
- resource.

The total cost of an assembled item is computed as the sum of the five cost elements for the item itself and for the lower-level assemblies within it. In Oracle EBS's terminology, total cost is the *rollup* of the costs associated with the five *this-level* cost elements (those associated with assembling the item from its components) and the five *prior-level* cost elements (those same five cost elements applied to the creation of the lower-level items that make up the assembly).

Users who take advantage of these cost elements usually break down costs even further by defining cost subelements unique to the organization that rolls up to the cost. For example, the resources that go into the manufacturing of a part may include labor and utilities. Material overhead may include costs of purchasing and receiving.

Oracle EBS automatically computes and assigns the average cost of purchased items if you elect to use average costing. It collects the raw figures you need to compute all other types of costs, for both *buy* and *make* parts, but assigning them is up to you.

Oracle specifies five steps for setting standard costs:

1. Define pending costs.
2. Roll up pending costs.
3. Print and review pending costs.
4. Update pending costs.
5. Print new standard costs.

The end of the process, applying costs in steps 3–5 after you know what they should be, is straightforward. The art of pricing is in the first two steps, establishing pending costs.

Define Pending Costs

Pricing starts at the bottom, meaning the cost of an assembly depends on the cost of the components. The first step, therefore, is to establish costs for the lowest-level items: those you buy from outside suppliers. These items usually have the PLANNING_MAKE_BUY_CODE attribute set to "buy." You can, however, have a bill of materials for a *buy* part and specify that the cost be derived by a rollup in the next step.

To manually copy the frozen item costs into pending, use Copy Costs, and then use the Define Costs screen in Oracle Cost Management to enter or update pending item costs. You enter costs at the level of the five cost elements just described; the form displays the total as the pending item cost.

A large number of items and frequent changes would make a manual approach to setting pending costs impractical for most manufacturing organizations. If your organization cares only about material costs, Oracle EBS's average costing will satisfy your requirements. Otherwise you can write custom SQL scripts to insert pending costs into the CST_ITEM_COSTS and CST_ITEM_COST_DETAILS tables. Use the following guidelines:

- Define the costs of parts by user instead of basing them on rollup.

- Insert costs only for the elements you use. There is no need to insert zero values for cost elements you do not need.

- Tag the costs as being for *this level*. *Prior-level* costs would come from components, which a purchased item does not have.

CAUTION
Never insert frozen cost types (COST_TYPE_ID = 1) directly. Doing so will change the cost without adjusting the General Ledger, destroying the financial integrity of the applications. Instead, always create pending costs, and have the Cost Update process convert them to frozen.

Use these guidelines to apply the pending costs once you know what they are. Oracle Financials captures and carries a significant amount of data to help you compute the five cost elements, but it leaves it to you to write the equations to derive them.

Material cost, the price you pay for an item, is available from Oracle Purchasing. Oracle EBS's average costing sets the cost to a weighted average: the total on-hand quantity multiplied by the average cost equals the amount paid for stock on hand. It uses the purchase-order price, not the invoice price. You may want to use a different method, such as using the most recent price or the actual invoice price. Or you may want to use an outside source, such as commodity prices from the Internet.

Material-overhead costs are associated with the item type, not individual instances of an item. They can include the costs to procure, ship, receive, and warehouse an item. You can compute a figure from Oracle Purchasing's records of purchases and Oracle Inventory's records of stock movements. You need your own algorithms. The cost of receiving and warehousing 100 sacks of cement, for example, depends on the time it takes and the cost of labor, neither of which Oracle Inventory captures directly. Although you know it costs more to handle cement than nails, your company has to judge whether it is worth the effort to assign each item a material-overhead cost or simply charge all warehouse operations to overhead.

Overhead costs represent the costs of running a materials operation. Many companies do not bother to allocate them down to the item level. They collect the costs of the purchasing, warehousing, and shipping operations in the General Ledger and set margins high enough to cover them. If you have multiple locations, some more efficient than others, it may be worth allocating the overhead to provide a truer picture of cost of sales.

Resource utilization is usually not a factor for purchased parts. In discrete manufacturing, Oracle Manufacturing captures resource utilization costs, including labor, by work order. Its reports show the standards and variances. You can use the work-order-level data to compute new standard resource utilization.

Outside processing is also not commonly associated with purchased parts. It is captured by Oracle Purchasing on a Work in Process (WIP) job when a manufacturing operation is performed by an outside contractor. The cost is associated with the item being assembled through the WIP job.

In net, unless you use average costing, you always need a formula to compute the material costs of purchased parts. To reflect the differences among items and among warehouse operations, you may want to assign material-overhead and overhead costs. Manufacturing organizations use the data captured by Oracle Work in Process to compute costs for the resource and for outside-processing cost elements.

Roll Up Pending Costs

The cost of an assembly is the cost of its components plus the cost of building the assembly itself. *This-level* costs include the resources and outside processing that go into manufacturing the assembly, the material-overhead costs of handling the completed assemblies, the overhead costs of the inventory operation, and at times a material cost for shop stock, such as cotter pins, solder, and other materials that are not carried on the bill of materials. *Prior-level* costs are the totals of the five cost elements for the component parts of the assembly. If all you care about is a component's total cost, you may have Oracle roll up all *prior-level* cost elements into the material cost.

Oracle Cost Management's rollup process computes new costs for items flagged as Based on Rollup. To roll up pending costs, follow these steps:

1. Create "pending" cost-type records for the items to be rolled up in CST_ITEM_COSTS and CST_ITEM_COST_DETAILS. This step can be accomplished by using the copy feature, then updating the records through the Define Costs form. The alternative is to write scripts to update or insert the records directly. You need to set the Based on Rollup flag for the item to have Oracle EBS perform the rollup. You define *this-level* values for the five cost elements for manufactured items yourself. The rollup process itself will extend the standard cost of resources you specify on the bill of materials.

2. Configure Inventory to calculate component costs. You usually specify "frozen" as the default cost type in the Define Cost Types setup for the "pending" cost type. This instructs the rollup process to use frozen costs for an item for which no pending costs have been defined. In other words, use the old costs when you do not have new ones.

3. Run the rollup process. It uses the bill of materials to compute the *prior-level* costs for the assembly. A one-level rollup uses just the costs of the components on the bill, whether they are *buy* or *make*. A full rollup computes the costs of all intermediate-level assemblies, starting from the *buy* parts. In either case, the rollup creates CST_ITEM_COST_DETAILS records for every cost element in use. It adds the *this-level* and *prior-level* costs to get total costs by cost element, and it adds the five cost elements to get a pending item cost.

Print and Review Pending Costs

Oracle provides a costed, indented bill report that shows how the rollup cost of an item was derived. The report's detail is very useful in debugging your rollup procedures, though its size makes the report cumbersome for monitoring the whole costing process. You may want to use simple SQL*Plus scripts to analyze items with unexpectedly large differences between the old and new prices.

Update Pending Costs

The Update Standard Costs procedure is at the heart of costing. The frozen item cost is the single figure used for valuing inventory as well as the cost of goods sold and the default cost in purchasing.

Update Standard Costs copies costs and cost elements associated with the "pending" cost type to the "frozen" cost type. At the same time, it creates all the cost-adjustment transactions needed to make General Ledger's asset balances equal the extended value of material on hand, in transit, and on the shop floor in WIP.

Print New Standard Costs

The last step is to distribute these new costs within your organization via standard Inventory reports. They will automatically be included in Oracle EBS's costing computations.

The Costing Tables

Figure 11-7, complex as it may appear, is a highly simplified illustration of the data relationships involved in capturing and carrying manufacturing standard costs for labor and resource utilization.

The cost that is used throughout the E-Business Suite for a given item is carried in the CST_ITEM_COSTS record for frozen costs associated with that item. Other columns in that table, and CST_ITEM_COST_DETAILS, show how the cost was derived. Oracle EBS seeds two other cost types, "average" and "pending," both of which have assigned uses within the system. The rollup process will support any additional cost types your organization may add. The other tables in Figure 11-7 show where standard costs are carried and actual costs are collected in the manufacturing process.

Routings define the sequence of operations involved in making a product. Each operation may use any number of resources, among them labor, machine time, and commodity items like electricity. Which resources are used, and standard usage for them, are defined as part of the routing steps. The associated BOM_RESOURCES record gives a current cost for the resource.

Routings represent standards, or expectations, of how an item is supposed to be built and what resources it is supposed to take. In discrete manufacturing, these standards go into each job as a sort of budget. Then, over the course of manufacturing, the job records (shown in the upper right of Figure 11-7) capture what actually happens. The Shop Floor Transactions screen captures utilization figures associated with each resource used in each step of each job to produce one inventory item. This is far more detailed than most users can afford to enter by hand; most will capture it automatically, or not at all.

Direct jobs within Oracle Work in Process capture the cost of actually producing products. Oracle Manufacturing can set up overhead jobs to capture indirect labor and resource usage. Users can exploit the job data captured by Manufacturing to update standard resource utilization in the routings based on actual work-order experience. The cost-rollup process will extend the standard resource utilization by resource-unit costs to derive pending values for the resource cost element and subelements.

Determining Sales Prices

Oracle Order Management manages sales prices through the use of price lists and discounts, as described in Chapter 12. The frozen standard cost is the most common basis for setting prices, and the only one for which there is automated support. The mechanism favors a system that computes list prices, and uses them as the basis for creating different price lists for different customers.

Full knowledge of the cost factors involved in handling an item is essential to successful pricing. Order Management users need to plan their pricing operations with an understanding of the power of Inventory's item-cost processes. This pushes back, pyramid-style, into manufacturing. It is impossible to know the cost of an assembly without accurate costs for the subassemblies. Oracle EBS provides a robust mechanism to compute and maintain accurate item costs; and its cost system is the most convenient basis for computing sales prices.

Project Manufacturing

Oracle Projects casts a project-and-task perspective on your business activities. Whereas accounting budgets focus on accounting periods, a project budget takes a lifetime view of the tasks that make up a project. A project budget can assess *earned value*, weighing progress made against expenses incurred. The tasks within a project may be seen as milestones, not just steps to making a product. A project view can also put profit and loss into sharper focus.

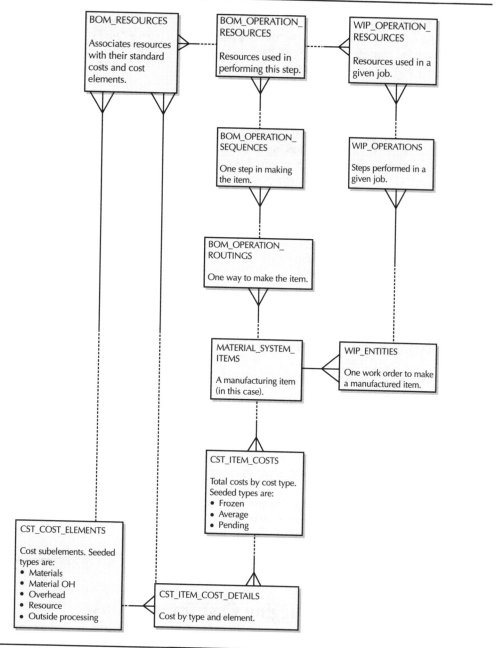

FIGURE 11-7. *Costing tables in Inventory*

Oracle Inventory lets you issue, receive, and track inventory quantities by project. It collects costs from Inventory for transfer to Oracle Projects. Project Manufacturing has a parallel capability to account for manufacturing expenses at a project level. Oracle Purchasing and Payables have long been able to manage project expenses. These packages combined give you the ability to maintain accurate records on the costs of prototype projects or work done for others on an outsourcing basis.

INTRASTAT Reporting

In the early 1990s, the European Community replaced individual countries' border inspections of individual shipments with a system of monthly reports of cross-border movements. The new system improves efficiency, allowing freight traffic to move unimpeded.

Cross-border movements of materials have major tax implications under the European Union's VAT system. A company is effectively taxed only on the value they add to a product. This is accomplished by taxing them on the entire value of their end product, but crediting them back for the VAT component of their raw materials. If a British company buys raw materials from France for 50 pounds, then combines them in a manufactured product which it sells in Germany for 100 pounds, it will pay the VAT on 100 pounds and be credited for VAT on 50 pounds. Needless to say, the tax authorities responsible for VAT collections watch cross-border movements and correlate them with tax returns.

Material movements visible to Oracle Inventory do not always coincide with the financial transactions managed by Payables and Receivables. They may take place in different periods, and Inventory manages some cross-border movements, such as the transfer of assets from a warehouse in one country to one in another, that do not have tax implications. Oracle Inventory's INTRASTAT reporting supports the reconciliation of financial to material transactions.

Activity-Based Costing

Activity-based costing, the second *ABC* acronym in Inventory, is not to be with ABC analysis used to support cycle counts. Activity-based costing assigns costs to activities based on their use of resources, and to cost objects based on their use of activities. Activity-based costing in Oracle Inventory means using the features of the whole E-Business Suite to capture the actual costs of doing business at a detailed level, taking advantage of the cost mechanisms shown in Figure 11-7 to carry granular cost data, and bringing standard costs in line with actual costs as often as required.

Only a minority of users will implement activity-based costing immediately upon converting to Oracle EBS. However, if you manage inventories of goods for sale, it may be a good idea to include ABC in your long-range plans. You want to optimize your margins at the lowest possible levels, and you cannot know your margins without knowing your costs. Analysis tools such as Oracle's Business Intelligence enable you to put ABC data to good use in support of management decisions.

Planning and Debugging Cost Transactions

The Oracle Inventory Reference Manual includes long, useful essays on average costing and standard costing. Diagrams show the debit and credit implications of many standard transactions. These diagrams are essential to your planning, but not sufficient. The diagrams do not begin to cover all cases, and the simple debit-and-credit T-bar diagrams apply only to the natural-account segment of the Accounting Flexfield. Your setup process has to ensure that the other segments—organization, product line, and the like—are also being generated correctly.

The situation calls for a common-sense testing scenario. After the accounting department has established a chart-of-accounts structure, you should run the following type of test in one of the early development environments:

1. Establish proposed natural-account values for inventory.

2. Set up test subinventories. They will need values for some or all the following, depending on whether the installation includes manufacturing: material accounts, material-overhead accounts, overhead accounts, outside-processing accounts, and encumbrance-account entries if you have specified encumbrance accounting.

3. Set up Account Generator (Flexbuilder prior to Release 11i) to generate the flexfield combinations for material expenses in Oracle Purchasing and the cost-of-goods-sold account in Order Management. These will use segments from the code combinations carried in Oracle Inventory to derive the segments used for the eventual General Ledger postings.

4. Set up one standard item of each major type in inventory. This would include items chosen from consumable supplies, manufactured, resale, consignment, nonstock, and whatever other categories make sense to the business. They may equate fairly closely to your templates. Assign account values for COST_OF_SALES_ACCOUNT, ENCUMBRANCE_ACCOUNT, EXPENSE_ACCOUNT, and SALES_ACCOUNT, consistent with your setup in step 3. Put them in the appropriate subinventories. If you are including Order Management and Receivables in the test, you may need to set up the AutoAccounting rules that will use segments of the sales account in creating the flexfield account to which it credits orders.

5. Set up or select master item records for other transactions, such as customers and vendors.

6. Refer to the *Inventory User's Guide* to set up default accounting information through the Define Organization Parameters screen. Specify Transfer Detail to General Ledger so you will be able to tie back any implications in General Ledger of a transaction to the transaction itself for the purposes of this testing. Note that you will almost certainly want to change this setting in production.

7. Create a list of transaction scenarios to be tested. These should include entries such as
   - cost change,
   - inventory adjustment,
   - cycle count,
   - complete from manufacture,
   - replenishment,
   - internal orders,
   - sales order and pick-release, and
   - PO receipt, inspection, and release.

The remaining steps of the test follow the plan set forth in Chapter 20. Once the test scenarios are laid out, you create test data for each transaction in the scenario, open a test accounting period, and run the test transactions (and only those test transactions) through the system in the chosen accounting period. You can examine the Accounting Flexfields as they appear in the MTL_MATERIAL_TRANSACTIONS table.

This catalog lists only essential steps. You need to elaborate on it, keeping in mind that thorough testing is the key to success in data processing in general, and especially in Oracle EBS. To repeat this book's central theme, the issue is not whether Oracle EBS's code works, but whether you have made it work for you. The only way to know is to test your transaction types, using your business procedures and your setups.

Operation of Oracle Inventory

Responsibility for running the Oracle Inventory system is best vested in one individual within a company, with operations within each inventory organization delegated to a person within that organization. Manufacturing concerns often give the responsibility to a materials-management group, sometimes shared with purchasing. Distribution companies may see it as part of operations. Whoever has the task, the system usually has more indirect users, through all the other EBS modules that depend on Inventory, than direct users.

Responsibilities

Defining jobs and limiting system access to the requirements of individual jobs are essential parts of Inventory setup. Chapter 21 describes how Oracle EBS uses Responsibilities to control access. The Responsibilities that Oracle EBS delivers with the package are user friendly rather than manager friendly, in that they offer a minimum of frustration by allowing a maximum of access. You will generally want to define your own, more limited Responsibilities, along the following lines:

- The super user has access to every process and every organization.
- Master item managers can create, update, and delete items and item attributes. They usually cannot set up catalogs, categories, or templates, but they can apply them to items. Business processes need to establish policy for deleting items and changing item numbers.
- Organization item managers in decentralized operations have the ability to add items and change attributes at the organization level.
- The warehouse manager can define subinventories, set up cycle counts, and manage the adjustment process.
- Line-level warehouse staff can assign locations, move inventory, and initiate and enter cycle counts.
- A Purchasing Responsibility has the ability to update Inventory Item Master attributes in the purchasing group, such as lead time.
- An Order Management Responsibility has the ability to update items, subject to the same limitations as Purchasing.
- Accounting or the warehouse manager has the authority to do the closing.

Although each attribute associated with an inventory item belongs to a certain attribute group, the Define Items form provides access to all attributes. Use the Function Security feature to restrict users' access to those attributes for which they are responsible. Use flexfield security as well, if different part-number ranges belong to different organizations.

Interface-Manager Processing

Inventory, like all of the EBS modules, has online screen operations and batch reporting. It has an intermediate layer, invisible to users, of *workers* that update Inventory transaction tables after the fact. These concurrent processes, executing in the background, are a concession to efficiency. They can be resubmitted at such short intervals that they approach real-time, but it would slow down the interactive processes if they were executed online. Instead, the online process writes the process to an interface table, and the workers awaken every few seconds to take it from there. This minibatching process has the added benefit of providing a natural interface into which user-written routines can insert their transactions.

The MTL_TRANSACTION_INTERFACE table is the major source of input for the Material Transaction Worker. It can be populated by user-written code as well as the standard Oracle online EBS modules. Oracle EBS's architecture anticipates integration with custom and third party systems. The Cost Worker checks a flag in MTL_MATERIAL_TRANSACTIONS to see whether a transaction needs to be costed.

At setup time, users can choose whether the Transaction Worker will run periodically as a concurrent process or immediately as a concurrent process. The greater the volume, the greater the advantage in periodic concurrent processes. The downside of periodic processing is that records are not totally up-to-date. It may take a minute or two for a pick or a receipt to be reflected in the database, raising (however minimally) the chance of a stock-out or unnecessary back order.

Use the Request Interface Managers form to start the background processes and specify how often they should run, how many can run, and how many transactions they should process at a time. It is more efficient to process a larger number at one time, but each process completes more quickly if the number is small. Whatever the number, as a concurrent process is initiated, it will spawn itself enough times to handle all the pending transactions. The workers behave like any other concurrent job, resubmitting themselves each time they complete, so there is always at least one active or pending job for each worker.

Because they work as background processes, it often takes a while to notice when the workers stop working. Inventory balances stop getting updated, or transactions stop being costed. Sometimes the workers are idle because the DBA has shut down the concurrent manager to which it is assigned. Occasionally, a pending concurrent process gets put into standby status and never starts.

The interface managers update transactions with error messages if they cannot be processed. You can view transactions that are in error through the View Pending Interface Activity form. Because errors are the exception, it takes discipline to remain in the habit of checking. The most common errors are caused by periods being closed within an organization before all the transactions were completed. However, there is the potential for numerous errors to occur, as these interfaces serve many different functions.

Periodic alerts are convenient for monitoring potential error conditions. They are easy to set up and efficient to run. Many users write alerts to check for an excessive number of records or the presence of error records in the MTL_TRANSACTIONS_INTERFACE table.

Archiving and Deleting Data

The Inventory system generates transactions at a tremendous rate. The Purge Transaction History process (an online form, initiating a concurrent process) deletes all transaction data prior to the given date. The only restriction is that the date must be in a closed period. Period purges are absolutely essential to holding down processing times and disk-storage requirements to acceptable levels.

Purged data are no longer available for any reporting purpose. Business needs define by policy what data, if any, must be kept for historical or audit purposes. You can likely satisfy any archiving requirements by running a concurrent process to generate detail-level transaction reports, which can then be copied from disk to a high-volume off-line medium such as tape or optical disk.

Deleting item records from the master is another matter. Items are the foundation of the inventory system. INVENTORY_ITEM_ID is a foreign key that permeates the whole of Oracle E-Business Suite. The first step towards deleting an item is to disable it for Purchasing, Manufacturing, and whatever other system might use it. Allow time for all the transactions that reference the item to be flushed through the system. After the item is no longer likely to appear in reports, it may be useful to change the item identifier to tag the item as awaiting deletion. For example, some organizations puts a "Z_" prefix on inactive items. Finally, the item can be deleted using the Delete Items form.

NOTE
Assemble-to-order manufacturing generates one custom item and bill of materials for each final-assembly (FAS) work order. These one-time items are usually most in need of deletion. They are also among the easiest to identify, because their item numbers have a characteristic infix. Such items are usually associated with one sales order and one point in time.

Advantages of an Open Design

One characteristic that distinguishes Oracle Inventory is the ease with which it can be extended using custom code. Oracle Corporation takes a keen interest in such user extensions. Its consulting arm, Oracle Consulting Services, will make such enhancements on a contract basis. If there is a broad enough community of interest, Oracle will incorporate the extension into its standard product. The Oracle Applications Users Group (OAUG) maintains an Enhancements Committee that works closely with Oracle on such requests.

NOTE
See Chapter 22 for details on the Oracle Applications Users Group.

Oracle EBS's RMA (return material authorization) processing is an example. The Order Management functions are fairly full featured; they can get the material back, put it into inventory, and issue a replacement or a refund. The RMA process does not extend to disassembly and restocking of configured assemble-to-order items. Users may need to develop their own business processes and custom routines to record the fact that configured items have been stripped to their components and to receive them back into the warehouse.

Conclusion

Part of the Inventory system is global, available to users of any product that uses items. Purchasing, Payables, Order Management, and Manufacturing need that function to define inventory items, to give them prices, and to assign them to categories and catalog groups. The part that is unique to Inventory, that you have to buy, has to do with running a warehouse. It includes subinventory and location management, warehouse counts, units-of-measure conversions, and replenishment.

Most users need to define Inventory items earlier in the implementation cycle than they need the functionality of the Inventory package itself. They need to look ahead to the total requirement, because some attributes cannot be changed. Inventory attribute settings and units-of-measure logic require close attention.

Oracle Inventory includes powerful devices for helping users cope with large numbers of items and transactions. Item templates, catalogs, categories, manufacturer's part numbers, customer part numbers, and cross-references all make it easier to locate items of interest and to deal with groups of items at one time.

Warehouses occupy a unique niche at the lowest level of Oracle's Multi-Org hierarchy. Inventory gives users the ability to manage activities in the areas of receiving, shipping, item cataloging, and warehouse operations at whatever level is most appropriate, from company-wide to highly local.

The cost data carried in Inventory support Order Management pricing. Inventory takes all costs into account; purchase cost is only the beginning. It can also carry cost elements for resource usage, overhead, handling, and many other cost elements. Although you can sometimes capture these costs directly at the item level, they are most often captured in the General Ledger, from which they must be allocated to individual items. Since margins drive profit, this planning is fundamental to most businesses. The best time to start is at initial item conversion.

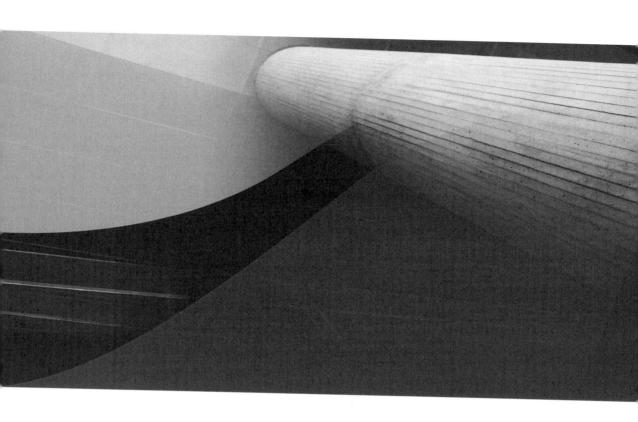

CHAPTER
12

Oracle Order Management

ustomers are the one thing on which every business depends. A business can ask its employees and suppliers to do things its way, but in general a business has to adapt to the customer rather than the other way around. Order Management satisfies customers' needs for goods and services. It qualifies buyers, provides product price and availability information, and accommodates orders and delivery arrangements.

Order Management is customer oriented, sharing custody of the master customer data with the other subsystems that deal with them:

■ Sales and Marketing, which manages initial contacts with customers as salespeople develop business;

■ Oracle Shipping, which handles the physical delivery of product to the customer;

■ Oracle Account Receivables, which invoices customer orders, creates credits for customer returns, applies invoice payments, and follows up with collections when necessary.

■ Oracle Service, which manages contracts and postsales service-related needs of the customer.

Oracle expanded the customer model after Release 11i to meet the needs of its Customer Relationship Management suite, primarily Sales and Marketing and Service. This model was also expanded in Release 12 into other modules and entities within E-Business Suite, such as vendors, banks, and others. It consists of the necessary attributes to support these areas. More difficult and far reaching, it went to the core of the question of what constitutes a customer. There is no correct answer: the people, addresses, and even organizations that the marketing, sales, shipping, and service organizations deal with are routinely different from one another. Although they are invariably related, the nature of the relationships is unique for every customer. Oracle EBS's customer scheme accomplishes the difficult task of managing this complexity while making it look (relatively) straightforward to the line-level people who enter orders and handle shipments.

The behind-the-scenes applications that support customer transactions include the following:

■ Oracle Pricing, which maintains the price lists available for an individual order and calculates the price of an ordered item based on sophisticated pricing strategies and rules.

■ Oracle Configurator, which provides guided selling, guided buying, and configuration capabilities to lead to an optimal product solution for the customer.

■ Oracle Bills of Material, which defines the components of pick-to-order kits and configurations and is needed to determine the availability of parts for manufactured items to compute an available-to-promise date.

■ Oracle Global Available-to-Promise, which seeks to optimize shipping plans, keeping shipping-related costs to a minimum while satisfying the customer's need for delivery of goods.

■ iStore, which is an electronic commerce application that provides a Web-based channel for unassisted selling of products and services directly to customers and business partners. It enables companies to bring products to market faster and to provide unique customer care. You can automate order fulfillment and order management and provide real-time feedback about order status and inventory availability while still leveraging the same business processes across channels.

■   Telesales, which is designed to meet the needs of inside salespeople in a call-center environment. It includes a versatile set of tools to effectively track, manage, and execute throughout the entire customer-sales cycle, including account management, opportunity management, contact management, quote generation, and order creation.

The nature of order transactions varies tremendously from business to business. Amazon.com processes thousands of orders per hour; Boeing might process a few per month for new planes and 100 per day for parts and service; and a shipyard might handle a handful of very complex orders per year, each with a large number of change orders. In Oracle EBS's parlance, these companies will use different order flows. In fact, almost all companies will have a number of different order-processing flows for different types of orders.

The order-processing flows define the stages of human and automated processes that orders and order lines can go through, and the actions that are allowed at each stage. It used to be that Order Entry handled them all; now they are split between Order Management and Shipping, and executed through Oracle Workflow. In any case, the seeded workflows predefine all the steps most businesses need, including the following:

■   **Order entering**   Get the details of what is being ordered, by whom, and where to ship it; and apply the prices. Return material authorizations (RMAs) are treated as reverse orders.

■   **Credit check**   Make sure the customer has sufficient credit for the order.

■   **Order booking**   Treat the order as firm, establishing a schedule date based on product availability.

■   **Demand integration**   Let your inventory department know about the demand. In businesses with long lead times it is a good idea to let the Inventory system know what unbooked orders are in the pipeline.

■   **Order confirmation**   Tell the customer he or she has a firm order.

■   **Pick release**   Tell the warehouse to pull, stage, and ship the order.

■   **Ship confirmation**   Confirm for Order Management that the items did in fact ship.

■   **Receivables interface**   Pass detailed order information to Receivables to create invoices and credit memos.

Not all actions apply to all orders. An order-processing flow defines the actions appropriate to a given type of order. To offer some examples from the computer business:

■   An order for freeware that has already been downloaded requires entry and billing but does not require approval or shipment.

■   An order for a free upgrade requires order entry, booking, approval, and shipment but does not require invoicing.

■   A drop-ship order has a purchase-release action in place of the warehouse actions of pick release, ship confirmation, and Inventory interface.

■   A phone order for hotline support service requires booking and invoicing, but not approval or shipment.

■   An internal order that will ship from one location within your company to another does not require Receivables interface.

At each point in the order process, the workflow defines a next step if all goes well, and one or more alternatives in the case of exceptions. You can define the order flow to ensure that an order is booked before being invoiced or approved before being shipped.

Oracle's Workflow product lets you construct customized paths through the standard program functionality in Order Management. That is, you build your own order-processing flows. As required, Workflow can lead the order-entry clerk through screens to enter a new customer, check credit, validate a credit card, configure an item, select shipping schedules for multiple delivery dates, and do everything else that a particular order might require. However, you provide rules to tell Oracle EBS when and what it can bypass.

Many companies add a user-defined credit-approval step to certain order types instead of using Oracle EBS's credit-hold mechanism. Credit holds are designed to work on an exception basis. If your business processes define every order of a given type as an exception, it becomes easier to define a new process-flow activity and then use the approval-activity step process rather than the hold-release process to move an order through the system. Once a customer has requested a purchase, the order can be available to other processes even if it remains unapproved for a while to come. By taking unapproved orders into account, you can get a more realistic demand forecast earlier on in the cycle.

When it comes to entering orders, speed is usually of the essence. The transaction for a returning customer ordering a handful of items through your call center should be as fast as possible. As part of setup, you can give Oracle Workflow rules that allow it to ask for only the necessary information, which makes for huge strides in the speed of order completion. The Order Entry process in Release 11i and prior was a masterpiece of programming, but it begged for a better tool. Workflow is it—a colossal improvement in functionality that is used throughout the E-Business Suite, but largely driven by the needs of Order Management.

Most businesses will find that Order Management achieves the threefold objective of being thorough, quick, and consistent with the rest of Oracle's E-Business Suite. Making the best use of such a powerful and nuanced tool takes some planning. Departing from the organization of other chapters, in this chapter we will focus first on the business of setting up Oracle Order Management, followed by the Order Management transactions, and then the support functions such as pricing and shipping.

OM Setups

Oracle Order Management (OM) has four major setup steps that are critical to any implementation: defaulting rules, processing constraints, workflow, and transaction types. This section outlines all four so you can understand the setup features and how they can be used to control sales-order management.

Defaulting Rules

Defaulting is the process by which values get populated into fields without being manually entered. In Release 11i and earlier, the Oracle Order Entry product contained a feature called *standard value rule sets* (SVRS), in which you defined how you wanted order attributes to be defaulted into sales orders. Since Release 11i in Order Management, there is a new defaulting paradigm called *defaulting rules*, which offers somewhat differing functionality. Defaulting rules were expanded in Release 12, providing more flexibility to the users and enhancing Order Management for a better user experience. This section outlines the key advantages of defaulting rules, with tips on how to use the new, more powerful features.

Functional Advantages of Defaulting Rules

With defaulting rules, you define a set of rules for each attribute (that is, each enterable data field) on the order header or line, then define the conditions for when to use each rule. This forces you to think of each attribute individually, instead of within the context of an order type. Once you think of attributes in this way, the framework seems more straightforward and intuitive. In addition, this framework brings more flexibility in where you can default data from and to, and enables you to invoke your own PL/SQL package to perform more complex logic.

Some benefits of this framework include the capability to default the order type, the capability to define defaulting rules for returns and return lines, and the capability to define formulas to create the defaulted data. It also provides a needed distinction between defaulting behavior and cascading.

Because defaulting rules are generic, and potentially can be used by other Oracle EBS applications, generic names are used for the things you default from and to. *Attributes* and *entities* are the things you default to; *sources* are where things default from. See the "Sources of Values" subsection later in this chapter, which discusses all the various places from which you can default.

Attributes and Entities in Order Management

An entity in this context is a group of related attributes that roughly correspond to an Oracle database table or a forms window in Order Management. So there are entities of Order Header, Order Line, Order Price Adjustment, Line Price Adjustment, and so forth.

An attribute is a field or column that belongs to that entity. Therefore, the *ordered unit of measure* is an attribute of the Order Line entity. When you query up the Defaulting Setup form for a particular entity, you will see a list of all the attributes for which you can define defaulting rules.

Conditions are rules you set up that will control when a particular group of default sources will be looked at. You define one or more *condition validation templates* based on whatever common business rules you might have. You define one or more of these condition templates *per entity*; then you can use them over and over for the attributes of that entity. For example, you might set up a condition template for all return lines and another one for all internal-order lines. The ALWAYS condition is seeded for each entity. If you are defining a set of conditions and using them in rules, be sure to place the ALWAYS condition last in the Precedence for Defaulting Conditions. An example for Order Header is shown in Figure 12-1.

Dependencies Among Attributes

Some attributes are dependent upon the values of other attributes on the same record. If an attribute is changed—either by the user or by the system—any other attribute that is dependent on it will be cleared and then redefaulted. For example, the Price List is dependent on Agreement. If the Agreement is changed, the Price List will be cleared and redefaulted.

Sources of Values

Sources are places where values can be defaulted from. Defaulting rules provide a variety of sources that you can use to build your defaults:

- **Constant Value** A text string that will be used.
- **Profile Option** The value of a profile option. This can be a system-provided profile option or a new profile option that you define just to provide a defaulting value.

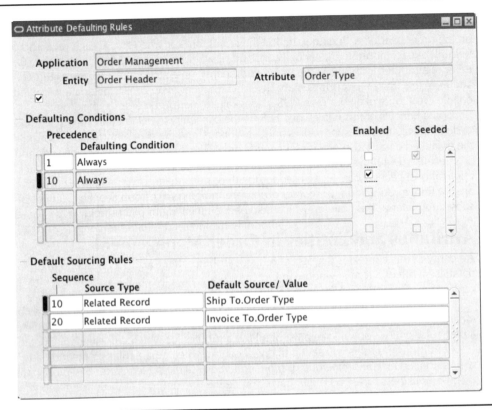

FIGURE 12-1. *Oracle Order Management defaulting rules*

- **Same Record** The value of another attribute on the same entity (or record) as the attribute you are defining the rule for. For example, you might set up the Promise Date to default from the Request Date on the same line.

- **Related Record** The value of another attribute on a related entity (or record). For example, you might set up the Ship Method on the line to default from the Ship Method on the header, or some attribute on the order header might default from an attribute on the related customer record.

- **System Variable** The value of a system (server) variable, such as System Date. For this type of source (and this type only), you can use an expression containing a formula, for example, sysdate + 7.

- **PL/SQL API** A routine you provide to provide the default. There are a few seeded defaulting rules that use this; for example, defaulting of the currency on the order header from the GL is seeded this way. You can look at this attribute for an example of how to specify a PL/SQL.

- **Others** Several esoteric source types relating to the Web App Dictionary definitions.

Detailed information on how to create, manage, and use defaulting rules can be found in the Order Management Implementation Guide.

Processing Constraints

Processing constraints allow Order Management implementers to control changes to sales orders. In Release 11i and earlier, the Oracle Order Entry product contained a feature called *security rules*, which allowed you to control whether changes could be made to certain characteristics of an order after certain cycle steps had been reached. In Release 12 of Order Management, there is a security paradigm called *processing constraints*, which serves the same ends by a somewhat differing mechanism.

Processing constraints are rules that allow you to control who can change what and when. You can control who can make changes based on Responsibility. A constraint (rule) can apply to all Responsibilities, to only a list of constrained Responsibilities, or to all except a list of authorized Responsibilities.

You can control more than just what can be updated. For the order-header, order-line, order-sales-credit, line-sales-credit, order-price-adjustment, and line-price-adjustment entities, you can control, create, delete, cancel, and split at the entity level. For example, given a set of conditions, such as the order being in a "booked" status, you may not allow a user to create a new order line. You can control the update operation down to the attribute level. For example, given a set of conditions, you could choose to allow updates to the warehouse field of an order line but not to the price-list field.

You can define rules such that a condition must be collectively true for a given constraint to fire and prevent the changes. This provides the granularity to be as precise as you want; for example, you could get down to the level of the sale of a particular type of cell phone for shipment to Long Island, perhaps to comply with a vendor-liability law. The conditions can be based on either the state of a workflow activity (where the entity is in the flow) or a value in a table. You also can base a condition on a custom API, which means you can call your own PL/SQL code to evaluate the condition. Multiple conditions can be combined using either AND logic (all the conditions must be true) or OR logic (at least one of the conditions must be true).

You can define a custom message that an Order Management user will see when they try to violate a constraint. The messages you set up might look like one of these:

"No one can change the customer purchase order at the line level; your company requires that one sales order relate to only one customer purchase order."

"No one can add a line to an order after any of the lines on the order have been invoice interfaced."

"Only the Customer Service Manager can change the discount percentage on an order line after the line has been shipped."

"You must provide a reason if you want to cancel an order line after it has been booked."

"Your company requires that all return orders, identified by the order type 'Return,' be shipped to a central returns-processing facility."

Functional Differences

To an Order Entry or Order Management user or implementer, the biggest difference between security rules and processing constraints is a philosophical one. The philosophy behind security rules was to prevent the user from doing anything that might cause inconsistency or confusion. As a result, the seeded security rules were very restrictive, and many companies did not need to create any more.

The philosophy behind processing constraints is the opposite. The designers decided that the implementer knows better than the developer what the user should be allowed to change.

Therefore, the seeded processing constraints are not very restrictive; they are designed to prevent only data-integrity problems; for instance, you cannot change the price on an order after it has been invoiced. The processing-constraints framework has many more features and is much more flexible than security rules; some of the enhancements that this framework allows are listed here:

- the capability to control changes based on who is trying to make them (by Responsibility);
- the capability to define constraining conditions based on the state of related objects (for example, define a constraint on a line based on the state of the order);
- the capability to control changes based on the value of a field;
- the capability to call custom PL/SQL code to determine whether a condition is true; and
- the capability to constrain operations at any point in the process flow. In prior releases you could control operations only for certain hard-coded cycle actions.

Workflow Integration

Order Management utilizes Oracle Workflow to provide you control over the sequence of events that occur in the processing of orders, returns, order lines, and return lines. Order Management provides the maximum flexibility to handle mainline revenue-cycle and exception-based business processes.

Oracle Workflow manages the state of all activities for an order, automatically executes functions and sends notifications, maintains a history of completed activities, and detects error conditions and starts error processes. The Workflow Engine is implemented in server PL/SQL and activated through a call to an engine API. (Refer to Chapter 17 for more discussion on the features and use of Oracle Workflow.) These notifications can be used to alert individuals to a situation that occurred within the process of the sales order or ask individuals to perform an action—for example, an approval. Oracle Workflow engine could send notifications to both external and internal individuals, if set up to do so. They can be sent to specific individuals or to a responsibility. You can view notifications that have been sent to you via numerous sources. When accessing your notifications, you can specify criteria with which to search them; for example, status, type, subject, sent, due, priority, if delegated. Once you have performed your search, you can view the details of each notification. If requested by the notification you might need to perform an action; for example, approve the sales order. When this type of notification is received, a small icon on the bottom of the notification will allow you to zoom into the required document for viewing immediately. You also have the option to forward the notification to another person if required.

Order Management enables you to model your business operation in terms of generic order processes. When defining a new workflow, you can start with the basic activities of order processing. You model your individual business processes by copying and editing seeded Workflow processes or crafting your business processes from the ground up using a mixture of seeded and custom activities. If you wanted to add an approval step to the order process, you would model your approval process in Oracle Workflow.

Order Management enables you to track the history of individual transactions by utilizing Oracle Workflow to control the execution of the order process. When Order Management begins an order-process step or sends a notification, the system records the event. The event is also recorded when the system has completed processing or the notification is answered.

Some of the features brought by the transaction-type and Workflow functionality are as follows:

- Each line on an order may follow a different flow. This allows you to have both order and return lines on the same order.

- You can create new workflow activities from custom PL/SQL code. This makes it very easy to extend OM.

- A workflow process can have subprocesses.

- A workflow process can have an unlimited number of activities. Order Cycles could have no more than 30 actions.

- There is no limit on the number of custom workflow activities that can be defined in Order Management.

- You can view the status of the workflow on an order or order line in either tabular or graphical format. In graphical format you can see not only the activities that the workflow has completed but also the activities that still require completion.

Cross-References

OM uses the standard Oracle Inventory cross-references associated with the Item Master to allow users to enter orders utilizing the cross-reference value instead of the item number. Some possible examples of cross-reference usages are old part numbers, UPC codes, manufacturers' part numbers, and EAN codes. You can set up any generic cross-reference types in the Inventory lookup tables to meet your business needs. Not only can your customers order using an identifier that is familiar to them, but you can have all related documentation (packing slip, invoice, bill of lading, and so forth) print the referenced value instead of your part number.

Customer Items

Extending the concept of cross-references, you can establish customer part numbers in Inventory and then use them within sales orders. By doing this, you establish specific item references for a customer that can be set at both customer and site levels. This comes in handy when you are required to fulfill orders in the customer part numbers in the case of OEM products. Once the customer part number has been established, you can take orders using that value instead of your actual part number. All related documentation (packing slip, invoice, bill of lading, and so forth) can now print the customer part number instead of your part number.

Folder-Enabled Forms

The sales-order pad and the Order Organizer (Summary Form) are both folder enabled. By utilizing standard Oracle EBS folder technology, you can customize the forms to meet your business needs. Folderizing the sales-order form is extremely valuable. Fields within all tabs of the sales order that are not essential can now be hidden from users' view. You can change field-name prompts and rearrange fields to meet your business needs without customizing the actual form. A key to remember is that each tab within the sales-order form can be manipulated; however, fields that reside in one tab cannot be moved into another tab's region. The capability to perform this functionality can be restricted by the profile option "Folders: Allow Customization," which is set at the user level in the system-administrator Responsibility.

Automatic Attachments

Controlled by the profile option "OM: Apply Automatic Attachments," users can predefine rule criteria in an effort to automatically attach required information based upon predefined setup requirements. Attachments can come in the form of short or long text; images (JPEG, GIF, BPS);

URLs; or files such as Word docs, Excel files, and so forth. This allows for easy application of critical information that might be needed to inform non-Order Management users, such as Shipping, Purchasing, or Accounts Receivable personnel.

Process Messages

When errors occur during the order processes (for example, order-import and order-booking abnormalities), the workflow engine looks for any error conditions and, if one occurs, generates messages to inform the user of the error condition. These messages are displayed in the View Message window. This window normally automatically opens to inform you of the condition when it occurs, but you can use the Find window to search for any new or previous messages that occurred.

From the View Message window, you can see the message details, save the output, forward to another user or Responsibility, or delete as required to meet business needs. This is a proactive response of the workflow process that occurs automatically. It differs from the notification process, as notifications are used to relay messages rather than error conditions. The two can be used in conjunction to inform the necessary personnel of any error conditions that occurred within orders, automatically providing notification and links to see the exact error condition that occurred.

Mass Change/Other Functionality

Order Management allows users to control changes across multiple orders or order lines by utilizing the function of Mass Change. Within the Order Organizer form, with a displayed query, users can select the orders or lines that are requiring the change. The user can select the lines (Ctrl + left mouse click) that require the change. Next, the user selects Mass Change from the Tools menu. The Mass Change form opens up to reveal pricing, shipping, and address details that might be selected for the change.

Once the required information is defined in the Mass Change form and submitted, the user will receive either a message that the Mass Change was successful or a process message informing the user of any problems that might have occurred during the process.

This same functionality can be leveraged to perform mass actions (using the Actions button) such as booking or performing Mass Cancels upon sales orders or sales-order lines. It is important to note that you will need to select more than one record to perform this functionality.

Integration with Order Capture

The integration between Order Management and Order Capture is controlled by an API. This provides the capability to integrate back-office modules (ERP) with front-office modules (CRM). Order Management is specifically tied to Quote Management, Service Orders, and Mobile Service Charges via Order Capture. Information from sales order is integrated with the Sales and Marketing modules. Information from sales orders also integrates with the Oracle Service's suite for installation details and service-program information into the Service Install Base module.

The Order Capture form is primarily used for a quoting mechanism. With it, users can provide a solution for entering and updating customer quotes and orders in the front-office environment. Order Capture provides real-time pricing, payment authorizations, reservations, available-to-promise (ATP), and payment methods. It acts as a single point of integration into the ERP applications to pass quotes as orders to Order Management. When the user is ready to process the order, the user simply clicks Book Order.

Numerous CRM modules utilize the tables associated with Order Capture to import orders and charges into OM for shipping, processing, and invoicing. These applications include Oracle Marketing Online, Mobile Field Sales, iStore, Telesales, Mobile Field Service, Field Service, Support, Customer Care, and Service Contracts.

Order Purge

Purging moves the information associated with old, completed orders out of your live files. Purged orders are gone. You need to make an archive backup before performing the purge. Oracle EBS itself will check to be sure there is no open activity against any of the purged orders.

Migration or Upgrade from Order Types

If you are a customer who is upgrading from a previous release of Order Entry to Order Management, your existing order types will be upgraded to new order and line transaction types. Your existing order cycles will be upgraded to new order and line workflow processes. However, you should not use these upgraded workflows for your new orders. They include many activities that check for status and are necessary for upgraded orders, but are very inefficient for new orders. As part of the upgrade, you should set up the flows associated with your upgraded transaction types as either seeded or custom flows, which were created for new OM orders.

Also note that your existing order-number sources are upgraded to document sequences. Document-sequence categories are created for your upgraded order types; these are assigned to the correct sequences, so you should not need to do anything to these.

The Customer Model

The customer model, also called Trading Community Architecture (TCA)—which has been available since Release 11i—provides capabilities needed to meet CRM and e-commerce requirements and provide a foundation for future enhancements that will benefit ERP applications.

The customer model is not a product; instead, it is the portion of the data model that stores customer information. All CRM modules utilize the customer model to store customer information, although the degree to which the customer model is utilized differs from product to product. The customer model is composed of the following:

- the data model (tables and the relationships between them),
- backward-compatible views (allowing ERP applications to have the same functionality as they did before, without being aware of the changed customer model),
- the upgraded customer screen in Oracle Application Framework (OAF),
- the upgraded customer interface, and
- upgraded customer merge.

A Single Source of Truth

Because all Oracle E-Business Suite applications utilize the customer model (ERP through backward-compatible views), Oracle EBS offers a single source of truth in viewing customer data. This means a customer record is the exact same record whether it is viewed through Oracle Sales Online, Oracle Marketing Online, Oracle Customer Care, Oracle Financials, or iStore.

The Party Concept

The party construct enables the customer model to treat all business entities equally. This means that regardless of the type of customer (organization, person, group, or relationship), each is handled in the same way by the data model: as a party to a transaction. Because all business entities are treated equally, the customer model can easily handle B2B, B2C, or mixed business models. Even though the model tracks different attributes for people than for organizations (such as, for people: date of birth, title, and gender; and for organizations: DUNS number, SIC code, and fiscal year end), both people and organizations are parties and are therefore stored in the same table in the database. This means that the same sort of business relationships that can be formed with an organization can be just as easily formed with a person. A key point is that the customer model was designed with B2B, B2C, and mixed models in mind.

The party type "Group" allows for the grouping together of any number of other parties into a single entity. This allows for the modeling of complex business entities such as households and buying consortiums. A group can be viewed as a single entity while still allowing for the members of the group to be viewed as stand-alone entities.

The party type "Relationship" allows for the relationship between two parties to be viewed as a party in its own right. For example, if Tony works at Oracle, this could result in three parties: Tony (party of type "Person"), Oracle (party of type "Organization"), and Tony @ Oracle (party of type "Relationship"). Because Tony @ Oracle is a party in its own right, addresses, phone numbers, and customer accounts can be directly associated with this entity.

A many-to-many relationship between parties and locations (as in addresses) allows for less duplication and easy update capability. Because an address can be associated to multiple parties, the address itself does not have to be duplicated numerous times. Additionally, if the address changes, it has to be updated only once.

The customer model separates the business entity (for example, party) from the business relationship (for example, customer account). This is an important concept because the separation allows for each party to have one or more customer accounts (thus it is possible to define multiple business relationships with the same party). Additional parties can also be associated to the customer account (for example, an authorized buyer or guarantor for the account).

The customer model allows for any number of user-defined party classifications that can be used for reporting and assignment purposes. A user might want to stratify customers by industry, size, and buying behavior. The user not only decides upon these categories; he or she can decide the classes (or values) within each category. Classes then can be broken down into subclasses, which allow for rollup and reporting at different class levels. Further, users can use this structure for assignment purposes.

A party is the highly generalized notion of a customer introduced in Release 11i. A party is defined as an entity that can enter into a business relationship. The new customer model supports four types of parties:

- **Organizations** Examples include Oracle Corporation, the US Department of Defense, and the University of Chicago.

- **People** Examples include Rhonda Cash, Lisa Dunning, and so forth.

- **Groups** A group is a party to which any other party or parties are associated. It is possible for a group to contain another group or groups. Examples include the Dunning Household (made up of John and Lisa Dunning and their children) and the West End Social Club (made up of Rhonda Cash, Lisa Dunning, Gina Gannon, and others).

- **Relationships**   In some instances, a party relationship can become a party in its own right. This, the most important conceptual leap in the new construct, will be explained further later in this chapter.

Any type of party can have one or more locations, phone numbers, and the like. A fundamental premise of the Oracle RDBMS is that such data should be normalized—put into separate entity types (such as tables) with no limit on the number of records associated with any given party. The entities associated with parties are as follows:

- **Locations**   This one is easy. A location is a point in geographical space usually described by an address.

- **Party Sites**   A party site links a party with a location. Parties can be associated to one or more locations, and locations can be associated to one or more parties.

- **Party Site Uses**   Party-site use describes the usage of a location (such as mailing address, billing address, home address, and so forth). Each party site can have one or more party-site uses.

- **Party Relationships**   A party relationship allows for the linking of any two parties, regardless of type. When two parties are connected through a party relationship, a relationship type is assigned, which describes the relationship (for example, "headquarters of," "employee of," "spouse of," "competitor of," "legal counsel for," "VAR of," and so forth). Once a party relationship is defined, it can become a party in its own right. For example, in the party relationship "John is the spouse of Lisa," both John and Lisa are parties and "spouse of" is the relationship type. However, the relationship itself can become a party record, which would result in three parties:

  - John (party of type "person"),

  - Lisa (party of type "person"), and

  - John is the spouse of Lisa (arty of type "relationship").

Even without taking relationships into consideration, it can get pretty complex. The party site in Figure 12-2 shows how things might be put together in Tony Cash's life, assuming that he shares a beach house with his cousin Rhonda Cash.

As with life itself, relationships can make things infinitely complex. Your business processes need to clearly define what you will do with the Oracle EBS customer model, despite the limitless possibilities of what you can do. The key is the way in which the data will be used. Order Management's transaction-processing requirements are rather straightforward. You need to define who places orders, who pays the bills, and where things get shipped.

The relationship-modeling concept can be extended to business-to-business needs as well. An example could be that Alcan outsourced its IT to Gemini; therefore, Gemini is entitled to a bulk-purchase discount on PCs that was negotiated for Alcan but is now executed by Gemini.

Relationships are somewhat more important in the Sales and Marketing and Customer Care modules. It is important for a salesperson to know all the decision makers in a chain and how they are related to one another; thus presumably the business processes for defining customer relationships would be established by the sales organization. The Order Management and Accounts Receivable setup teams would be lobbying to keep things simple enough that their reports make sense. Although Order Management is restricted to simplifying views of the customer schema, the simpler it is at the top level, the more likely it is that the data that percolate through the views will be consistent. It might be of interest to the sales department that the head

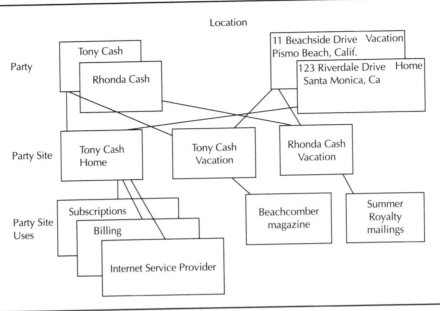

FIGURE 12-2. *Customer-model architecture*

buyer Rhonda Cash is a cousin to the IT department's Tony Cash, but that fact plays no role in the mundane affair of accepting orders and shipping goods.

Continuing down the path of defining entities, once a party relationship has become a party in its own right, it can have the same attributes as any other party, such as party sites, contact points, and customer accounts (see Figure 12-2). The following is a listing of relevant terms to the customer model:

- **Contact** A party that serves as a contact for another party. In most instances, it is a person serving as a contact for an organization.
- **Contact Point** An electronic method of communicating with entities such as parties and party sites. Examples of contact-point types include phone, fax, telex, e-mail, URL, and so forth. An entity can have any number of contact points.
- **Customer Account** A business relationship. When a party becomes a customer (purchases something), an account is created and associated to the party to track the attributes of the customer relationship. A party can have one or more customer accounts. Each account can have only one owner, but any number of other parties can also be associated to the account in roles other than owner.
- **Customer Account Site** A party site that is used within the context of a customer account (for billing or shipping purposes).
- **Customer Account Contact** A contact that is used in the context of a customer account.

Customer Agreements

Long-term agreements with your customers give both parties the benefits of a stable flow of business, predictable pricing and delivery terms, and decreased transaction costs. Order

Management does not demand agreements—it handles one-time orders quite smoothly—but using agreements makes the Order Management process significantly easier for established customers. Once the agreement is entered for a customer, multiple releases (sales orders) against the sales agreement are processed over a period of time within Order Management. Associating an order with an agreement automatically defines the following parameters:

- date range of the agreement,
- customer or customers covered by the agreement,
- price list,
- terms (when Receivables expects payment, and what prompt payment discounts apply),
- invoice rule (when and how Receivables invoices the customer), and
- accounting rule (when Receivables recognizes revenue).

A modification to the price of goods, such as a discount, can reference an agreement; an order placed under the agreement may get a more favorable discount than would apply otherwise. Customer agreements should be part of the business plan for most companies. They are a convenient vehicle for offering preferential treatment to steady customers, decreasing your workload, and preventing errors in data entry.

Sales Credits

Order Management's default is to assign the credit for an order or return to the primary salesperson assigned to the customer. The Enter Orders form allows you to override the default by explicitly assigning sales credit to one or more salespeople. The total sales credit within Order Management must equal 100 percent. Oracle Sales Compensation allows you to apply more complex credit-assignment algorithms by accessing your own PL/SQL modules through its APIs.

The sales-credit data captured by Order Management flow to Oracle Receivables through the AutoInvoice interface. Oracle Sales Compensation bases its commission computations on the records in Oracle Receivables. This process provides an important level of control: commission payment depends on realizing the revenue through billing or actual collection.

Using Credit Cards in Oracle Order Management

In this era of Web stores and business-to-consumer selling, the ability to accept and authorize credit-card payments has become vitally important. Oracle Order Management delivers greatly expanded functionality to handle credit checking and payment authorization. In particular, you can indicate that an order is being paid using a credit card and authorize those transactions through Oracle's Payments (formerly known as Oracle iPayment) product.

Credit checking and credit-card authorization are both ways of attempting to ensure that your company will receive payment for the goods that are being ordered.

One of the most important enhancements in Release 12 is the centralization and encryption of credit-card data and bank-account data in Oracle EBS. Information about credit cards, PIN-less debit cards, and bank accounts is encrypted and stored in the centralized payments model. Calling applications (such as Order Management and iStore) now simply integrate with the Payments model and do not store any payment-related data locally. In addition to these enhancements, there is support for capturing and validating the credit-card security code for credit-card transactions. The security code, however, is not stored anywhere in the database.

During order-header entry, the user chooses a payment type of "Credit Card" to enter one credit card that can be used as invoice payment on the order header and one credit card, which might be different, for the order line as invoice payment. You can enter multiple credit cards as prepayment; however, prepayment can be used only at the order-header level. The user enters the rest of the order information, including all the line information, and books the order.

Order Management calls the Oracle Payment server to obtain authorization for the full amount of the order, including tax and freight and other charges; Oracle Payment returns an approval or a denial, along with a risk code. Risk codes can also be assigned by outside credit-assessment services; evaluating such services is part of your analysis process. If all is well, the authorization code is recorded on the order header and the order proceeds in its workflow. If authorization is denied or an unacceptably high risk factor is returned, Order Management places the order on hold and selects the appropriate Workflow path to resolve the problem or deny the order. If the validation goes through, the order is picked and shipped, and during invoice interface the credit-card information is passed to Receivables. Accounts Receivable handles the funds capture and all accounting transactions.

Three types of credit-card authorizations can be done within Order Management:

- A credit card can be authorized automatically, which is what was just described. For this to occur, the order type must be set up for credit checking at booking or at shipping. The authorization will occur during the payment-verification processing, and the user will not have to do any action (other than booking the order) to make it happen. Your Workflow can call for credit to be reverified at shipment time, especially if the value of the order has changed.

- A credit card can also be authorized online, by the user choosing the "Authorize Payment Order" action from the Action button on the Sales Order form. If this is done, authorization is attempted using the Oracle Payment interface, and the results are processed the same as for automatic authorization.

- It might sometimes be necessary for an authorization to be done in an off-line or manual mode. This might be necessary because of hardware or software problems with the link to the Oracle Payment server or out to the credit-card networks. In any event, an authorization can be obtained through a telephone call or a dial-up device. In that case, the authorization code can be entered on the order header and the order will be considered authorized.

In Order Management, credit-card information is masked from view by unauthorized users, based on the setting of the "Credit Card Privileges" profile option. This protection applies to screens and reports only; credit-card information is not encrypted in the database.

The DBA must restrict direct access to the database to prevent access to sensitive information stored there. While there is no provision to encrypt just the credit-card information, it is possible, fairly common, and relatively quick to encrypt the whole database. That option becomes more and more compelling as data tend to be distributed far and wide over storage area networks and ASPs.

Because your DBA will almost invariably provide copies of your production instance for use by developers, you will need procedures to sanitize the credit-card data before releasing them, much the same way as you sanitize personnel data such as salary.

Risk Management

Oracle Payment has a risk-management feature that can help manage your exposure to questionable transactions. It allows you to define any number of risk factors to verify the identity of your customers, assess their credit rating, and manage risk in a secure online environment. You set up these factors and a risk calculation formula when you set up Oracle Payment. Authorizations from Order Management use the default risk-formula setup in Oracle Payment. Authorization returns a risk score in addition to an authorization code. The score can range from 0 to 100, with 0 referring to a risk-free transaction and 100 referring to a high-risk authorization. If the risk score exceeds the risk threshold you have set up in the corresponding profile option, the order is automatically placed on credit-card high-risk hold.

Oracle Payment uses a deterministic risk-management algorithm. It can be difficult to determine levels of risk in advance. Other vendors start with seeded rules for evaluating credit and then improve them based on experience using neural-network software. Although such an approach can require a substantial up-front investment and ongoing work to assess the results, it can be essential in a consumer-oriented business.

Oracle Configurator Developer

Oracle Configurator is used to manipulate models. A *model* is a combination of physical items (such as a 250- or 500-gigabyte hard drive) and phantom items (such as a "Hard Drive Option" class). When combined, they can now be leveraged to allow users to select between options and customize the product they want to order.

In OM you order and build configurations of a model, you do not order or build the model itself. The model can be a PTO (pick-to-order) or ATO (assemble-to-order) Bill of Material (BOM) model, or a configuration model based on a hybrid (ATO/PTO) Bill of Material model.

In Oracle Configurator Developer, you build the configuration model, which can include guided buying and selling questions in addition to the ATO/PTO BOM model. We need to identify some terminology within this process:

- *Configuring* is the process of selecting options to create a sales order of a configurable item.

- A *configurable item* is a model that represents what could validly be selected to create an orderable product or configured item.

- A *configuration* is a set of selected options that represents a valid, orderable product or configured item.

- A *configurator* is programming logic that enforces rules.

- *Instantiability* refers to an end user's ability to create and individually configure one or multiple occurrences (instances) of a Model or Component in a runtime Oracle Configurator.

- ATO BOM models represent product models that require assembly in Work in Process (WIP) and a downstream manufacturing process.

- PTO BOM models represent product models that require only a pick list.

- PTO BOM models that are configurable might consist of ATO BOM models. These are often referred to as *hybrids*.

Configuration models are compiled structure, rules, and User Interface definitions stored in the Oracle Configurator schema (CZ) in Oracle EBS. The configuration is orderable because it is a BOM based on an existing BOM model that is available in Oracle Bills of Material and is composed of Oracle Inventory items.

In Oracle EBS Bills of Material, you define the hierarchical relationship of items to create a BOM model. A BOM model consists of components, including other BOMs. All components in a BOM are also items defined in Oracle Inventory. You specify whether an item is required or optional when creating the BOM.

ATO and PTO BOM models list the available items in a BOM but enforce only minimum and maximum quantities and optional or mutually exclusive rules when adding items to the sales order. A configuration model is constructed using an existing ATO/PTO BOM model, but it can enforce many complex, user-defined rules that ensure that customers order only valid product configurations. An example of a rule is this: if you order word-processing, graphics, and Web-browsing software, you must have a minimum of 124 kilobytes of memory. Configuration models are created in Oracle Configurator Developer.

Not all BOM models are configurable. A BOM model that is configurable is an item defined in Oracle Inventory with the following attributes:

- User Item Type: ATO Model, PTO Model, or Model;
- Item Type: ATO Model or PTO Model;
- BOM Allowed: Yes; and
- BOM Item Type: Model, Option Class, or Standard.

The items that are components in an ATO/PTO model can have item attributes set for User Item Type and Item Type, but must have a BOM Item Type of "Option Class" or "Standard." Any item that is a BOM component that contains child components must have the BOM Allowed attribute set to "Yes." If a standard item has the BOM Allowed attribute set to "Yes," it can be a kit containing other standard items. Standard items within a kit are required (mandatory) and the BOM Allowed option must be set to "No" for the items in the kit.

For example, we might be configuring a desktop computer. The desktop is an ATO Model XSL-100 with the BOM Item Type of ATO Model. We might allow a user to select the amount of hard-disk space to be set into the desktop. We create an item for the varying types of hard drive from which the user can select (Hard Drive Option Class) with a BOM Item Type of "Option Class." We then create another item (HDD-6 Gig); this item will have BOM Allowed flagged to "Yes."

We also decide that a component of the desktop model will be a multimedia system. This will be optional for the user to select. The multimedia system (although an option under the desktop model) has a BOM associated with it. The BOM will include components for speakers, microphone, digital camera, and related software. The user cannot make option choices, therefore it is considered to be a kit. For the multimedia-system item, the BOM Item Type would be "Standard."

It all works like this: A run-time Configurator window is integrated (embedded) in Oracle EBS or in a custom Web deployment. There are three user-interface styles available for the runtime Configurator window:

- Java applet,
- DHTML window in a browser, and
- Custom user interface.

Oracle Configurator's development environment, Oracle Configurator Developer, is an application for creating configuration models that end users access in the run-time Configurator window. In Oracle EBS, the runtime Configurator window is integrated as an add-on to support configure-to-order functionality in the following modules:

- Order Management (Java applet or DHTML),
- iStore (DHTML),
- Sales Online (DHTML), and
- TeleSales (Java applet or DHTML).

Oracle Configurator is required for complex configure-to-order processes. In Order Management, you can configure any ATO or PTO BOM model regardless of whether a configuration model has been created for it in Oracle Configurator Developer. If not, the Java applet is available for option selection. Additionally, you can process simple option selection within OM without Configurator's use. This is known as the Options window. When orders are processed from Order Capture, both the DHTML and Java version are supported.

If a configuration model does exist, the run-time Configurator window is either a Java applet or a DHTML window, depending on whether the last defined UI style in is Model Tree or Component Tree, respectively. You specify the UI style in Oracle Configurator Developer. A configuration model for which no DHTML UI is defined will not be accessible from iStore or Sales Online.

In Order Management, configure-to-order functionality is only available if Configurator is installed and the profile option "OM: Use Configurator" is set to "Yes." For simple option selection, the profile option "OM: Use Configurator" is set to "No." This profile option can be set at the user and site levels. The default setting is "Yes."

Items in Order Management

Order Management handles orders for tangible and nontangible goods, services, and configurable items. Regardless of whether the item is physically in the warehouse, anything that can be ordered is in the Inventory master table. An orderable item can be a radio, a service, a subscription, or an hour of labor. Chapter 11 covers the topics of how to create Inventory items and refers to the correct item attributes needed to define an orderable product.

Order Management handles transactions other than sales that provide a product to a customer. Some obvious examples are leased items, promotional materials, and demonstration and loaned items. For example, Oracle Telesales and iStore can accept requests for product literature to be fulfilled through Order Management.

Assemble-to-order items are manufactured as needed. Either it does not make sense to build for inventory, or each unit is configured to order, incorporating customer-selected options. For example, you can usually select the CPU speed, hard-disk size, multimedia features, and memory when you buy a PC. An orderable item is defined as one item in Inventory, with a bill of materials describing how to build it. The bill structure includes option groups and optional items within the groups. Order Management presents these choices on the order screen and will not book the order until the item is fully configured. At that point the customer order is linked to a final-assembly work order to have manufacturing create what the customer ordered.

Oracle's Product Configurator expands the validation possibilities and extends configuration capabilities to untrained users over the Internet. Its indented-list presentation guides the user through the selection process. The user can click to a single-level view for a complete description of the option choices at that level.

While native Order Management is driven by table-based rules, the Product Configurator provides APIs to let you plug in custom-written PL/SQL code. It can manage whatever level of complexity exists in your business. It can configure groups of order lines that are identified as full systems. It can even handle upgrades to configured items that are already installed. By applying its rules to the current product configuration in Oracle Service, the Product Configurator is capable of determining which upgrade orders it can accept for an item.

Pick-to-order (PTO) provides convenient shorthand for combinations of products. Your company might sell cribs, mattresses, sheets, and mobiles to hang over the crib, each with its own part number. You also might sell these items as an ensemble, probably at a lower price than you would charge when selling the same items separately. This *ensemble*, or *kit*, would have its own part number. Order Management translates the pick-to-order part into its components and places a demand on Inventory for real items—the components—instead of the kit (see Figure 12-3).

An assemble-to-order (ATO) item is a product that is custom built out of standard components for each order. The system carries a bill of materials that defines how to make the product and how much time it will take to assemble. ATO order lines become linked to the final-assembly (FAS) work order created to have the item built under Oracle's Work in Process system.

Both ATO and PTO items can also be configure-to-order (CTO). A CTO item can be customized by selecting options. For example, when you buy a new car, you can select a larger engine or a deluxe audio system. Some options might have suboptions. What speakers do you want with the audio system you have selected? Or, now that the new parents have chosen blond wood over white finish for their nursery ensemble, do they want the pink, yellow, or blue fabric trim?

The structure of PTO and ATO products, options and all, is carried in Oracle Bill of Materials. An Inventory item with the Assemble-to-Order or Pick Components (that is, PTO) attribute will have an associated bill of materials. The bill is in the Order Management organization, which—in a Multi-Org environment—is usually not the same as the warehouse organizations.

The bill associated with a standard (without options) PTO or ATO item identifies its components. A PTO item might include other PTO items as components, as shown in Figure 12-4. An order for the top item is recorded as an order for all the real items that make up the bill.

The bill for a configured item can include optional items or optional groups. The exact configuration has to be defined before the order can be booked. In Figure 12-4, the bill for Option Group C will have a rule for optionally selecting Items E and F. Suppose the rule says only one of the two items can be specified. The order can be booked only when the customer has specified whether or not Item D is present, and has chosen either Item E or Item F.

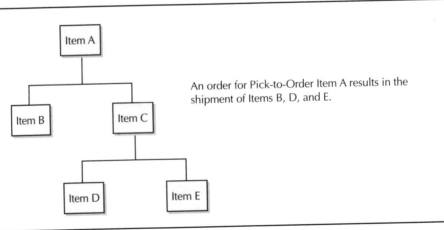

An order for Pick-to-Order Item A results in the shipment of Items B, D, and E.

FIGURE 12-3. *Bill explosion for a PTO item*

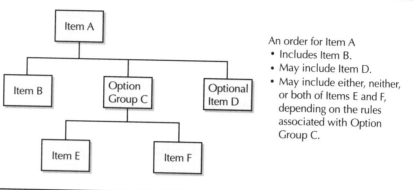

FIGURE 12-4. *Bill explosion for a configured item*

Suppose the customer wants Item A with optional Item E. If Item A is pick-to-order, this line will result in shipping Items B and E. If it is assemble-to-order, it will result in a manufacturing job to assemble Item A from Items B and E.

Option groups might appear within option groups, and ATO items might appear within PTO items. The system is extremely flexible—and complex. Powerful as it is, the Bill of Materials feature alone does not have enough scope to define all option combinations or to present them in a way that an untrained user can grasp intuitively. Oracle's Product Configurator adds rule-processing logic. For example, it can add the power requirements of boards within a computer to determine which power supply must be configured to drive the system.

An analysis of a company's Order Management business processes needs to determine whether Order Management is sufficient or whether the Bill of Materials, Engineering, and Product Configurator modules are needed as well. Oracle Bill of Materials defines the structures of bills and the resources required in manufacturing; Oracle Engineering manages the change in bill structure over time, reflected in engineering changes and item revisions; Oracle Product Configurator provides rule-based logic to support the selection of options in Configure-to-Order bills for both ATO and PTO.

The analysts need to look at recognized PTO and ATO operations, and also at *kitting*. Kitting—the process of assembling groups of items so they can be stored and shipped under a single part number—can often be eliminated by redefining the kits as PTO items. Changing to PTO saves the labor of assembling the kits and frees the inventory space that would otherwise be used for fully assembled kits.

Oracle Configurator

Oracle Configurator Developer is an easy-to-use, drag-and-drop graphical user interface (GUI) in which to create configuration models. It is also used to prototype, develop, unit test, and maintain configuration models used in Order Management.

Concurrent processes import BOM models into Oracle Configurator Developer. A particular configuration of the ATO/PTO model results from making selections of BOM model components that are optional in the BOM. The rule attributes on those components (such as mutually exclusive or minimum/maximum) are enforced by Oracle Configurator and result in a valid BOM.

If the ATO/PTO BOM has been imported into the Oracle Configurator schema (CZ) and further constrained with rules defined in Oracle Configurator Developer, it is considered a configuration model. In Oracle Configurator Developer, the imported BOM is a read-only structure and is exploded to show all optional components. Required components are not shown, because they are included in the BOM regardless of any changes made in Oracle Configurator, and do not influence the possible valid configurations that can be created for that BOM model.

Guided buying and selling provides a means of driving valid configurations from customer requirements or needs assessment. The user is presented with a variety of questions that automatically select items in the configuration model. For example, a customer is ordering a laptop computer. When you click the Configurator button, questions appear such as "What is your budget for this item?" and "What are the main tasks you will perform using this computer?" Based on the answers to these questions, the system adds items to the order to create a laptop computer that meets the customer's needs. Buying and selling questions are added manually to the imported BOM model structure in Configurator Developer.

Scheduling

The scheduling feature in Oracle Order Management consolidates the closely related functions of determining when items will be available to promise to a customer, scheduling the shipment or arrival of order lines based on this availability, and reserving on-hand inventory to sales-order lines. These scheduling activities can be performed on individual order lines or groups of order lines such as ship sets, arrival sets, and configurations.

Oracle Order Management works closely with Oracle Advanced Planning and Scheduling (APS) and Oracle Inventory to provide scheduling functionality. The features are provided in a variety of ways, allowing OM users to tailor their processes to meet the needs of their business.

Available-to-Promise

Order Management's Available-to-Promise (ATP) feature analyzes all transactions of a particular item in Inventory, Purchasing, and Manufacturing to answer one of the most fundamental questions of order management: when can the customer have it? Oracle provides a lot of processing to determine the answer, and at times the logic is complex. An individual order exists as part of a stream. For resale items, the ATP logic must go upstream from items in the warehouse and open orders that are already committed, to determine whether uncommitted units are available when the customer wants them.

ATP does an abbreviated bill-of-materials explosion to compute the availability of pick-to-order and assemble-to-order items. The availability of the product depends on the availability of its components. In the case of an ATO item, the time for final assembly must be factored in as well.

The ATP process follows rules that you establish as part of setup. These are similar to the forecasting rules described in Chapter 11. They define the sources that can be used to satisfy an order and order timing, such as whether an item available one week can be used to satisfy demand the next week. Complex as it is, the ATP process operates online to provide real-time information as you accept and enter orders. Your ability to provide and honor firm commitment dates is essential to maintaining customer confidence.

Shipment Scheduling

Shipment scheduling endeavors to give customers what they want, when they want it. Precise shipping dates are important: Some customers will reject shipments that do not arrive close to the specified date; others will at least note the inconvenience. Plan to use either Order Management's ATP inquiry feature or the link from the Order Entry screen to an Available-to-Promise query screen to ensure that you can satisfy the customer's request. If you are using ATP, you usually should enable reservation logic, so you can make sure the material is available to satisfy the customer order. A reservation directs Oracle Inventory to hold enough stock so that the order can ship on time. In practical terms, it means protecting the stock if necessary by refusing it to orders that attempt to reserve that same item later, even if they could ship earlier.

Customers can specify different shipment dates for different lines on an order, or multiple shipment dates or ship-to addresses for a single line. This results in a kind of matrix. On each of several different shipment dates, the customer wants some fraction of the ordered quantity of some subset of the order lines. Use shipment-schedule lines to break the order-line quantity out into the quantities to ship on different dates. It is most economical in terms of shipping costs—and most satisfactory to customers—if you ship everything that customers want together and schedule it to arrive on the day they want it.

However, other scheduling options are available. One option is to ship what you have and back-order the items that are not available, which probably increases your shipping costs. From the customer's perspective, it certainly increases the costs of receiving and handling the order. A partial shipment might not even be of use to your customers, if the items are related. To meet your needs and the customer's, you can specify groups of lines that must ship together. In Bills of Material, you can specify that kits and models for pick-to-order operations need to ship together.

With enhanced Schedule Order concurrent program a user can have the following:

- the capability to schedule at multiple points—either manually or automatically as the line is entered, when the order is booked, or later using a background process;
- the capability to determine the best warehouse for an order line using sourcing rules;
- the capability to define by customer whether the request date is the requested ship date or requested arrival date;
- the capability to automatically set the scheduled ship and arrival dates based on the calculated ATP date;
- the capability to define a shipping network and determine the number of days required for delivery based on the transit time;
- the capability to automatically reserve on-hand inventory to order lines;
- the capability to control, based on order-transaction type, the level of scheduling that should occur;
- the capability to view availability for multiple warehouses at one time; and
- the capability to group lines into arrival sets, which may be shipped from different warehouses on different days but should arrive at the customer site on the same day.

Calculating Available-to-Promise (ATP)

Oracle Order Management allows users to tell their customers when items will be available based on current on-hand inventory, expected incoming supply, and outgoing demand. Calculating ATP requires as input the item, the order quantity, the order-quantity unit of measure, and the request date. The user will enter the item and order quantity on every order line. The request date and order-quantity unit of measure can be defaulted or manually entered. ATP can be calculated for a single line, a group of lines, or a complete order. The results for a single line are displayed in a single column in a small window. The results for multiline ATP are displayed in a table. In both formats, the following information is displayed:

- **Warehouse** Either the warehouse on the order line or, if the warehouse on the order line was blank, the best warehouse as selected by the sourcing rules.

- **Available** The order quantity, if ATP was successful, or the available quantity (which will be less than the order quantity), if ATP was not successful.

- **On hand** The quantity that is currently in the warehouse.

- **Reservable** The on-hand quantity minus the quantity that is already reserved to other sources of demand.

- **Request date** The date on the order line.

- **Available date** The date that the ordered quantity will be available. It could be the request date if the order quantity is available on the request date, or it might be a future date when the order quantity will be available

- **Error message** Any error that occurred in calculating ATP. For example, if the Check ATP flag for the item is not selected then this field will display "ATP not applicable."

At the bottom of the Availability window there is a Global Availability button. Pressing this button will open the supply-chain ATP form, which has the list of warehouses where the item is enabled. The user can select the warehouses for which they would like to see the availability, and the system will return the availability in all the selected warehouses. This feature is available only if the APS module is installed.

ATP will be automatically calculated during scheduling and can be calculated manually by pressing the Availability button on the line-items tab of the sales-order form. The processes work the same. They use rules you have given in setup to decide what is actually available. For instance, you might decide to serve certain geographical areas or customers out of a select group of warehouses or decide not to commit shipment of items that you know to be in short supply unless your supplier has reconfirmed the delivery date.

Specific Order Types

Most often, orders are of a standard nature; however, occasionally you might need to process nonstandard orders. This section outlines specific order types and their common functionality. It also outlines a few of the more special order types that are typically used in business today.

Internal Sales Orders

Internal orders originate as requisitions in Oracle Purchasing. The requisitioner does not need to distinguish between stock items—which will be satisfied from inventory through an internal order that goes through Order Management—and items sourced externally from suppliers. The process for internal orders is as follows:

1. An employee (or an application) enters a requisition for a stock item.

2. The requisition goes through any necessary approvals in Purchasing.

3. The Purchasing system passes an internal sales order to Order Management.

4. Order Management imports internal sales orders through the Order Import process. Because the approvals have been done in Purchasing, internal sales orders move through without human intervention. They are processed at Inventory cost—there is no price list—and they

are open to changes as dictated by the processing constraints that have been set up for internal processing. Order Management creates a pick release when the item is available in the warehouse.

5. If the requisitioner is at another location, Order Management handles packing and shipping to that site.

6. The item is delivered to the requisitioner.

Internal sales orders are invisible to the requisitioner, who theoretically should not be concerned whether the material is being shipped from a vendor or from another warehouse within your own company. Passing these orders (however quietly) through Order Management fills several functional requirements. The orders use Order Management's picking and shipping logic, whether items are being released across the street or across the country. Order Management consolidates internal and external demand for the purposes of replenishment. It handles the accounting for the release from Inventory, and Purchasing handles the accounting for the issue to the requisitioner.

To state this from Inventory's perspective, Purchasing handles material supply. Its logic validates requisitions from within the company. It needs to see the order so that it can decide whether the order can be handled from Inventory or must go to an outside supplier. Order Management handles demand. It needs to see internal orders to make sure that the system orders or makes more of an item and to be sure that internal users do not consume materials that are reserved for manufacturing or customer use. Order Management generates the warehouse release and handles shipping.

Inventory balances supply with demand to determine when the item needs to be replenished. It needs an aggregate view of all internal and external demand, and all sources of supply, to determine when to reorder. Although it might seem unduly complex to thread through Purchasing, Order Management, and Inventory, consider the processing necessary to support internal consumption and the benefits of having each piece of functionality handled by only one application.

Several enhancements to internal sales orders were presented in Release 12 in order to offer additional and better change-management capabilities; among the most relevant are the following:

- changes to quantity and scheduled ship or arrival dates on the internal-sales-order line are automatically propagated to the internal requisition and vice versa;

- cancellation of an internal sales order or line automatically cancels the corresponding internal requisition or line and vice versa; and

- the urgent flag on the internal-requisition line flows onto the internal-sales-order line as the shipment priority.

Drop Shipment

Drop shipment allows you to reconsider the role of your warehouse in the supply chain and, possibly, bypass it by shipping directly from your suppliers to your customers. Sometimes the advantages of having material in your own warehouse are not worth the maintenance costs. A warehouse operation does provide the following benefits:

- You can quickly satisfy customer orders for a variety of goods from different suppliers in one shipment.

■ You can control quality by inspecting items before shipment.

■ You can handle customs, tariffs, and taxes at a wholesale level.

At times a warehouse is essential, particularly if you need to provide storage for materials you manufacture. On the other hand, having your warehouse handle goods en route from your supplier to your customer can add considerable expense, such as

■ occupancy costs for the warehouse itself;

■ labor in receiving, storing, and shipping goods;

■ inventory-carrying costs, shrinkage, and obsolescence;

■ additional time to satisfy a customer order as the merchandise passes from your supplier through you to the customer; and

■ the inability to receive and forward nonstock items, which might limit what you can sell.

Drop shipment is an attractive alternative when the costs of warehousing outweigh the benefits. You can even mix warehouse and drop shipments to satisfy a single customer order, drilling down to the point of splitting a single order line. This functionality provides a direct automated link between your suppliers and customers. The drop-shipment model is useful for intangibles and for brokered and consignment arrangements. Your organization might deliver service to your customers through an agreement with a third party. You convert the customer's order into a purchase order to the third party, then invoice your customer upon your receipt of the bill from the third party.

Oracle Order Management lets you specify, by the Line Sourcing field, whether the line must be a drop-ship item. It converts the drop-ship line into a purchase requisition, which it forwards to Oracle Purchasing through the open interface. The requisition carries the customer information needed to satisfy the order.

The full mechanics of Oracle Purchasing are available to satisfy drop-ship orders. To minimize the time and labor involved in purchasing, set up blanket purchase orders and outsourcing so the requisition is converted automatically into a PO release to a supplier.

Drop shipment depends on the supplier and customer for correct shipping and receiving information. The most automated approach is to have the supplier send an advance shipment notice (ASN) with information about the carrier and expected delivery date through EDI. The ASN might trigger an invoice; however, your business processes can make do with the supplier invoice or with telephone calls from the supplier or customer. Make sure you record any information you need for customer service, such as the serial numbers and warranty.

The drop-shipment business process must address any exceptions. What happens when the shipment is over or under, or when the customer wants to return it? Chances are you do not want it coming back to your warehouse. Spell out the details in advance with the supplier and the customer.

Return Material Authorizations (RMAs)

Sales orders get material out the door; return material authorizations (RMAs) bring it back in. Customers return material for a variety of reasons: the item was shipped on consignment, it was a demo, it needs service, it is defective and needs to be replaced, the customer got too much, the wrong item shipped, and so forth. Item attributes can define whether an item is returnable.

Oracle's RMA process flow basically reverses the order process: getting material in the door, putting it back in stock, and issuing a credit. There is also a corresponding Return to Customer transaction for getting the needed repair or replacement back to the customer. However, you will need to create a new sales-order line manually if you require a packing list or want to invoice for the repair or replacement. Dividing the process into a return and a reissue simplifies processing significantly. However, it does require some work on the user's part to retain the connection between the return and reissue parts of a transaction.

Oracle Order Management facilitates the link back to the original order through a Reference Source field on the return form that ties to a sales order or invoice line. Once the link is established, all the relevant information from the original order that shipped the item will be defaulted to the RMA. The Copy Orders form is also useful in RMA processing, because with the exception of the order type, an RMA is very similar to the original order. The Copy Orders form can provide the link forward by copying the RMA to the sales order that ships the repaired or replaced item back to the customer, or it can provide the link backward by copying an entire order to be returned.

Return receipts are handled by Inventory. An inventory API notifies Oracle Inventory of expected returns. As returns arrive, they are processed through the receiving forms (the same as Purchasing receipts). If you receive the return into your inventory, you can retain it or ship it to your supplier. If you pass the returned item to your supplier, you should notify the buyer and authorize the return by generating an RMA between your company and your supplier. The related Inspect Customer Returns form comes into play when returns are conditional based on the state of the returned goods.

You might have to interface Order Management's RMA process with custom-written or third-party software to handle back-end processing. Configured items are, by definition, assemble-to-order. Your company will have its own undoubtedly unique rules for deciding the extent to which you want to disassemble configured returns and put the parts back in stock instead of putting the configured item into inventory. Rules you establish for granting credit upon the return of individual components of a pick-to-order item will certainly be unique; some components might not even carry sale prices.

Your setup and testing have to ensure that RMA items are not treated as regular inventory. After defining your RMA business process for configured items, test and verify that Manufacturing does not see these units as demand and attempt to rebuild them. Also, you need to separate RMA items from regular finished goods by assigning them to a separate subinventory—for example, *REPAIR*—to hold them until they are certified for reissue.

Oracle Service provides postsales support for the products sold through Order Management. Service picks up product details such as the serial number and warranty when it ships. Order Management sometimes has a role as service is delivered. It handles orders for maintenance agreements and per-call orders for customers without agreements; it then forwards invoicing information to Oracle Receivables. Customer returns for depot maintenance (that is, factory repairs) are handled by the RMA process.

RMA activity generates credits and charges to be passed through to Receivables. You have to define business processes to deal with shipping charges (both ways) and parts and service charges for maintenance.

Oracle Release Management

Oracle Release Management, in conjunction with Oracle E-Commerce Gateway and the Oracle Order Management suite of products, enables you to perform release management of high-volume, highly configured orders while reducing cycle time and improving customer service.

The product cycle for many high-tech products is now measured in months, even weeks. Your profitability depends on your inventory management. You cannot afford to be stuck with obsolete components or finished goods. Release management reaches clear through the supply chain, coordinating engineering, customer demand, purchases from suppliers, and manufacturing to ensure that accurate, real-time product-delivery capability is managed effectively.

Demand-Management Flow

The demand-management business flow starts with an inbound demand schedule sent from your customer via EDI. The file is translated and received into the Oracle E-Commerce Gateway. It is then loaded into the Oracle Release Management Demand Processor interface tables and processed. After Oracle Release Management validates and archives the schedule, it manipulates the quantities and dates of the new requirements based on the parameters you have set for the trading partner. It then reconciles the new demand with existing demand and updates Oracle Order Management and Oracle Planning with the latest sales-order and forecast information. After the product is manufactured, it is shipped to the trading partner; the Oracle E-Commerce Gateway can then send a ship notice and an electronic invoice.

Your *planning schedule* provides forecasting and material-release information between trading partners. Requirements are posted in weekly, monthly, or quarterly buckets. The schedule typically is transmitted weekly.

Your *shipping schedule* provides precise shipping-schedule requirements from the customer to the supplier and provides requirements in daily buckets. It is typically transmitted daily and supplements the planning schedule. It also supersedes certain information transmitted on the previous planning schedule, which helps in facilitating just-in-time (JIT) manufacturing.

Your *production-sequence schedule* provides the sequence in which shipments of goods will arrive, the sequence in which they are to be unloaded from the conveyance method, or both. The schedule typically is transmitted daily.

Release Management gives you firm control over your planning, shipping, and production-sequence schedules. You can manage customer schedules based on sets of internal and external business rules that you have established. You have the visibility you need to match customer demand—both actual and forecast—with materials in your supply chain.

Oracle Shipping

The Order Management product is responsible for figuring out what is possible and committing delivery dates to customers. Oracle Shipping handles the physical tasks associated with shipping: picking materials from the warehouse, handling exceptions such as out-of-stock conditions, palletizing and containerizing materials, scheduling delivery by your own fleet or via common carrier, and managing drop shipments.

In a move to rationalize the product line, Oracle Shipping has assumed other functions that have nothing to do with the customer, such as interwarehouse shipments of inventory items. Chapter 11 describes how that works and how Oracle EBS is able to maintain visibility of inventory through various layers of containerization. The process needed generalization; custody and ownership no longer go hand in hand. You can continue to own materials that are on-site at a customer location, and conversely you might have custody of materials that are on consignment from your own suppliers. Oracle Shipping and Inventory manage the physical goods independent of the accounting notions related to purchase, sale, and ownership.

You can manage shipping information such as trips, stops, delivery legs, deliveries, and delivery lines in the centralized workbench called the Shipping Transaction window. In Oracle EBS's nomenclature:

- A *trip* departs from a particular location and must contain at least two stops for delivery along its route. It is specific to a carrier (think UPS, DHL, FedEx).

- A *stop* is a point en route where the carrier makes pickups, drop-offs, or both.

- A *delivery* is a group of sales-order lines for the same customer, at the same customer location, coming from the same location in your organization, organized to be delivered together. In addition to the preceding, you can group deliveries by freight terms, freight on board (FOB), intermediate ship-to location, ship method, FOB code, and carrier.

- A *delivery leg* consists of at least two stops. The bill of lading can represent one trip or a leg of a trip.

The shipping process starts with picking. Companies define release-sequence rules to control the order in which picking lines are allocated to inventory and the way in which picking lines are grouped onto pick slips. Your objective is to pull materials from the warehouse in such a way that you can easily group them into the shipping hierarchy of lines within orders within deliveries within stops within trips. Paralleling the shipment hierarchy is the consideration of grouping items within pallets within containers within vehicles or vessels.

The Shipping Transaction window provides a centralized workbench that consolidates three major shipping functions: Trip Planning, Ship Confirm, and View Shipping Information. It allows you to plan and organize trips, stops, delivery legs, deliveries, and delivery lines. The window consists of a Query Manager and Data Manager.

The lines that show up in the Shipping Transaction window have been through the pick-release process and are ready to go. You can indicate the shipped quantities, provide inventory-control information for delivery lines, and assign freight charges. You confirm whether the released picking-line items are being shipped or need to be back ordered. You can confirm an entire trip or delivery, or back-order an entire trip or delivery. You can also assign unplanned delivery lines to trips and deliveries during Ship Confirm.

Material-Picking Waves   Used throughout the shipping process, material-picking waves move product from a source subinventory (finished goods) to a shipping-staging subinventory. The staging subinventory acts as the destination subinventory on the pick-wave move order. Each organization should designate at least one staging subinventory; it will be the same location for each batch created. It is defined in Shipping Execution organization parameters, but can be changed at pick release.

The picking wave allows your shipping department to minimize the amount of physical movement within the warehouse. You can also take advantage of cross-docking opportunities, such as receiving dock right to the shipping-staging area. Even if you still create separate picking slips for each customer, Oracle EBS will create a move order to get the picked items into a staging area. Your setup determines how much you do there. You could merely box and ship individual orders, but the architecture allows you to do very involved groupings of deliveries and containerization. Figure 12-5 shows the typical shipping process.

Pick Release

Pick release finds and releases eligible order lines that meet the release criteria. In a pick-wave operation, the system creates move orders that move the inventory to staging areas, from which it

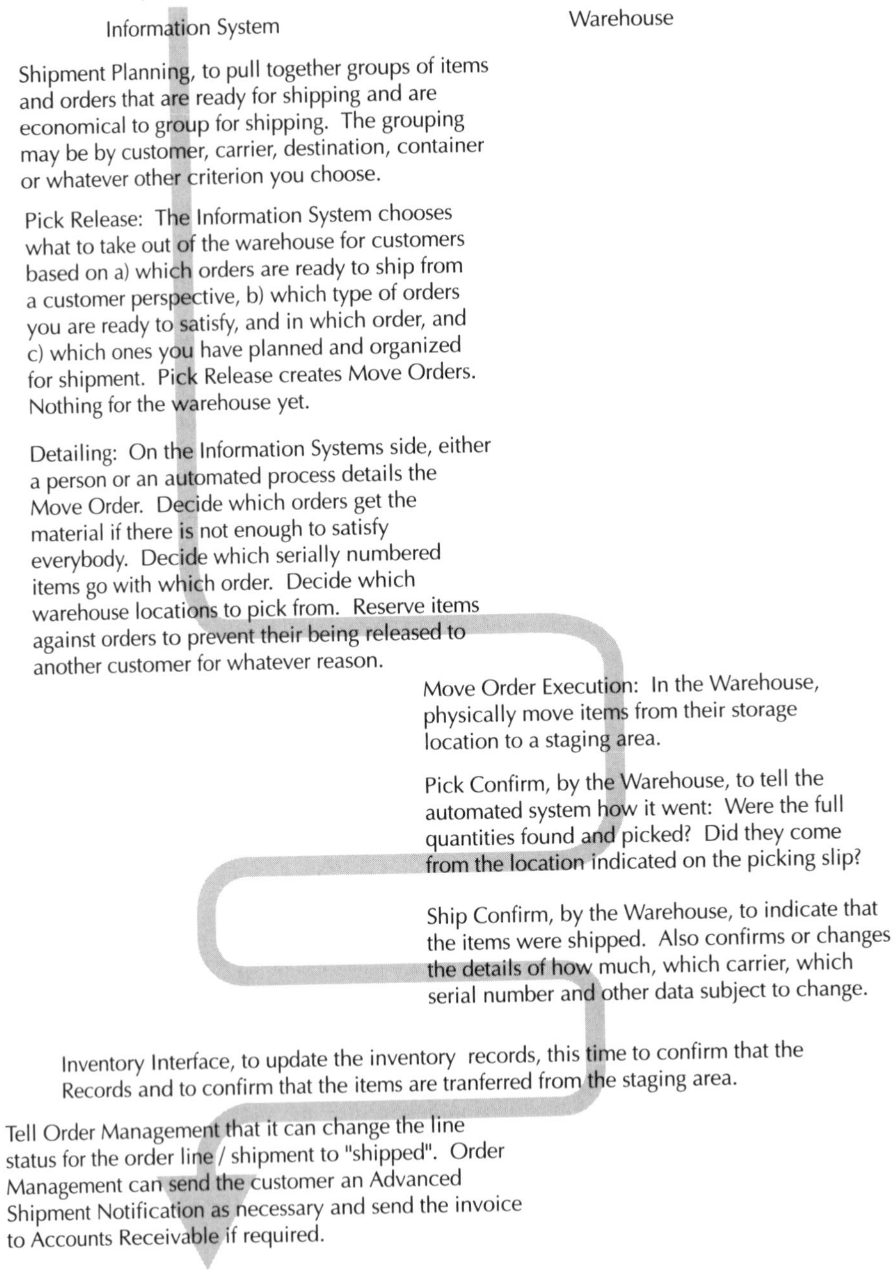

Information System   Warehouse

Shipment Planning, to pull together groups of items
and orders that are ready for shipping and are
economical to group for shipping. The grouping
may be by customer, carrier, destination, container
or whatever other criterion you choose.

Pick Release: The Information System chooses
what to take out of the warehouse for customers
based on a) which orders are ready to ship from
a customer perspective, b) which type of orders
you are ready to satisfy, and in which order, and
c) which ones you have planned and organized
for shipment. Pick Release creates Move Orders.
Nothing for the warehouse yet.

Detailing: On the Information Systems side, either
a person or an automated process details the
Move Order. Decide which orders get the
material if there is not enough to satisfy
everybody. Decide which serially numbered
items go with which order. Decide which
warehouse locations to pick from. Reserve items
against orders to prevent their being released to
another customer for whatever reason.

Move Order Execution: In the Warehouse,
physically move items from their storage
location to a staging area.

Pick Confirm, by the Warehouse, to tell the
automated system how it went: Were the full
quantities found and picked? Did they come
from the location indicated on the picking slip?

Ship Confirm, by the Warehouse, to indicate that
the items were shipped. Also confirms or changes
the details of how much, which carrier, which
serial number and other data subject to change.

Inventory Interface, to update the inventory records, this time to confirm that the
Records and to confirm that the items are tranferred from the staging area.

Tell Order Management that it can change the line
status for the order line / shipment to "shipped". Order
Management can send the customer an Advanced
Shipment Notification as necessary and send the invoice
to Accounts Receivable if required.

FIGURE 12-5. *Shipping process flow*

will be grouped into customer shipments. Pick release optionally calls inventory pick release to reserve items and print the pick slips.

Pick release may be done online, through a concurrent process or through a concurrent job. The process is managed by rules you establish at setup that govern

- the sequence in which you satisfy demand,
- how lines get grouped into picking slips, and
- how they are released.

The release-sequence rule decides who gets the goods if there is not enough to satisfy every order that is ready to ship. Among the criteria you can choose are order date, outstanding invoice value, schedule date, departure date, and shipping priority.

Pick-slip grouping rules can specify that pick slips are grouped by order number, subinventory, customer, ship-to address, carrier, delivery, shipping priority, item, location, lot, revision, or any combination of these. An example of a pick-slip grouping rule is by customer and subinventory. The grouping rules makes picking more efficient by putting logical lines to be picked on one pick slip. You choose your grouping rules to support the packing and shipping function: Do you want to sort orders out in the warehouse or in a staging area? Do you need to group shipments by destination for a common carrier or will you leave that to others?

The release rule establishes which among the order lines that are eligible to be shipped are actually to be released in a given operation. For instance, you could choose to set up specific runs to release back orders. It might be that you use expedited shipping for back-ordered items. You could want to set up a run to release only reserved items, or items ordered within a certain date window.

Move Orders

With Oracle Order Management, the pick-release process will now generate move orders to bring the material from its source location in stores to a staging location. This will be modeled as a subinventory transfer (the staging location is a subinventory that you set up in Oracle Inventory). These orders will be preapproved and ready to transact. Pick slips and other shipping and inventory reports will also be available.

First, the move order is created by the pick-release engine. Next it must be *detailed*. Detailing is the process by which Oracle EBS uses the picking rules to determine where to source the material to fulfill a request line (move-order line). The detailing process fills in the move-order line details with the actual transactions to be performed. If adequate quantity is not available to detail the move order, this process can be done again later.

The detailing process for a pick-wave move-order line also creates a high-level (organization-level) reservation on the material if no reservations previously existed. Users can choose to do this immediately after the move-order lines are created or to postpone this step until a later point in time. Postponing the detailing process might be employed by organizations that pick release across multiple warehouses but prefer to allow each warehouse to determine when to release its order lines to the floor. Detailing the order lines immediately after they are created is called *auto detailing*. Postponing the detailing process is referred to as *manual detailing*. Users can set up a default detailing mode in the Shipping Execution organization parameters. This default can be overridden at each pick release.

Before transaction, users can print a pick slip or push the move-order line details to mobile devices for transaction through the move-order APIs.

The user now transacts the move order to pick confirm. The order line can be transacted all at once, or users can transact one detail line at a time as the items are moved. The emphasis is on speed and ease of operations. Oracle EBS allows you to economize on data entry but go into detail as required to handle exceptions. If the user transacts less than the requested quantity, the order will remain open until the full quantity is transacted or the order is closed or canceled.

The move-order line details (transaction lines) created by the detailing process must be transacted to confirm the material drop-off in staging. This process is called *pick confirmation*. Pick confirmation executes the subinventory transfer that moves the material from its source location in the warehouse into the staging location. Pick confirmation automatically transfers the high-level reservation to a detailed reservation (including lots, subinventory revisions, and locators) in the staging location. At pick confirmation, a user can report a missing quantity or change the transaction line if the picker chose to use material from a different lot, serial, locator, or subinventory.

If an organization's picks rarely deviate from the suggested picking lines and the overhead of requiring a pick confirmation is unmanageable, the pick-confirmation transactions can occur immediately after the lines are detailed. This option is called *auto pick confirmation*. Users can set up a default pick-confirmation policy in the inventory-organization parameters. This default can be overridden at each pick release. Note that even if an automatic pick confirmation is employed, the material is only transacted to the staging subinventory and reserved. A user can still manage any discrepancies found by deleting the reservation and transacting the material back to its original subinventory. If mobile devices such as bar-code scanners are used to perform inventory transactions, you should use manual pick confirmation for greatest inventory accuracy and control.

If auto pick confirmation is used, then reservations are placed for each line up to the available quantity. If auto pick confirmation is not used, users have to query up the pick-release batch and confirm the quantities manually.

Shipping Tolerances

Some customers will be satisfied with more or less the quantity they ordered rather than the exact amount. This is especially true of businesses, which will be reordering the same stuff from you in any case. For example, they might order 12 tons of gravel but your trucks carry 11.5 tons. They might order 50 cases of Wheaties whereas you stock them 48 to a pallet. They might have placed an expedited order for 180 250-gigabyte hard drives whereas you have only 177 in stock and a no-back-order policy. Whether by an oversight in the Order Entry process or anomalies in the warehouse, Shipping will have to deal with small discrepancies in quantity. Your setup includes parameters to tell the system how to handle them.

At ship confirm, the shipping clerk can confirm a quantity greater than the quantity on the line if it is within the overshipment tolerance. If it is greater than the overshipment tolerance, a warning will be given. The actual quantity shipped is recorded on the line.

The undershipment tolerance works a little differently. At ship confirm, the shipper can confirm a quantity less than the quantity on the line; however, if the quantity shipped is within the undershipment tolerance, the line will be closed once the shipment is processed. If the quantity shipped is outside the tolerance, the line will split into two lines: one representing the quantity shipped and the other containing the difference. The point of using undershipment tolerance is to save the user from having to cancel off any remaining little bits of a line, if there is no intention or need to ship it.

Invoicing of overshipments is controlled by a new profile option called "OM: Overshipments Invoice Basis," which will control whether to invoice for quantity shipped or quantity ordered. There will be a corresponding new attribute on the customer and site level, which can be used if a customer or site needs to be treated differently from the global option. Undershipments are always invoiced at quantity shipped.

NOTE
Oracle Order Management does not support over- and undershipment tolerances for ATOs (models, kits, and all children).

Freight Costs

Many businesses consider their shipping operation to be a profit center. By tracking the shipper's freight cost (the amount the shipper pays the carrier), you can determine the profit margin between the shipper's freight cost and the amount a customer pays for freight. You can assign freight costs to trips, stops, deliveries, delivery lines, delivery legs, or containers.

You also can modify freight costs after ship confirm; however, you can invoice the customer for the modified costs only if you have not yet run the OM interface. Once you have run the OM interface, you can no longer pass modified freight-cost information back to OM. You can still modify freight costs, but you are not able to pass the information to OM.

You can apportion the freight costs on a per-line basis based on percentage of weight, volume, or quantity. If you have a weight defined for the items, the apportionment will be based on weight. If you do not have a weight defined, the apportionment will be based on volume. If you do not have a weight or a volume defined for the item, the apportionment will be based on quantity.

The currency of the freight costs will be automatically converted when you run the OM interface (pass freight costs back to OM). A primary ledger's currency will be used for the operating unit of the warehouse or ship-from location as the default currency. The currency will be converted to the currency of the sales order.

Shipping Exceptions

The Shipping Exceptions feature helps you identify and correct shipping exceptions that violate the requirements of your operation or of your carriers and customers. Users can use the Shipping Exceptions feature to do the following:

- define exceptions per business requirements,
- define handling processes for exceptions (through Workflow),
- record shipping exceptions during the shipment process,
- initiate exception handling, and
- view and track exceptions.

The Shipping Exceptions feature enables you to define exceptions and processes for handling them. You can record exceptions automatically from within Oracle Shipping Execution or you can log exceptions manually through the user-interface input forms. You can initiate exception handling and view and track the exceptions as you manage them to resolution. This helps you identify and correct shipping exceptions that violate the requirements of your operation or of your carriers and customers. It can be used to track carrier performance such as POD date and ship date and to analyze changes to orders after pick release. APIs are provided that allow you, with some custom programming, to use third-party applications to log exceptions.

European Reporting

Oracle Purchasing, OM, and Inventory enable you to support the automatic creation of the INTRASTAT and EXTRASTAT movement-statistics declarations to governmental authorities. You can compile all of the material-receipt (arrival) and shipment (dispatch) transactions for the given period and automatically create the Intrastat records. You then can review and validate the data using the movement-statistics exception report, update the information using the Movement Statistics window, and run the standard movement-statistics declaration report.

In addition, the Oracle E-Commerce Gateway supports the outbound EDIFACT INSTAT and EXSTAT transactions for electronic reporting to governmental authorities. The packing slip has been enhanced to support many of the requirements needed for shipments made in European countries. In Europe the packing slip acts more like a legal document, similar to how a bill of lading is used in the United States. For example, some countries require an audit trail of the packing slips created for a particular shipper, and the shipper must provide a gapless sequence of packing lists created. This requirement is supported with the current releases.

UPS Integration

Collaboration between Oracle EBS and UPS will benefit customers who use both Oracle Shipping Execution and UPS. The integration will be in the form of APIs. Oracle-UPS APIs is a set of programs that integrate shipping information, provided by UPS online tools into Oracle E-Business Suite to help customers streamline operations in the fulfillment cycle. Oracle-UPS integration will enable Oracle customers to do the following:

- verify address and postal code for shipments,
- inquire about time in transit for ground shipments,
- get shipping costs for deliveries, and
- track packages after shipment.

Oracle-UPS APIs will be used throughout the Oracle ERP application suite. OM and Customer Relationship Management (CRM) applications will use these APIs to verify address and postal code and to provide customers with shipping-service selections while taking orders. Shipping Execution will use these APIs to integrate UPS functionality seamlessly into the Oracle Shipping functionality. Negotiations with other carriers are underway, and integration will be released in the future.

Containers

Containers and vehicles are set up similar to items in inventory. They are controlled by the attributes found in the Physical Characteristics tab. The following is a listing of common terms used in the Shipping module:

- **Weight Unit of Measure**   Used for packing calculation.
- **Unit Weight**   Used for packing calculation.
- **Volume Unit of Measure**   Used for packing calculation.
- **Unit Volume**   Used for packing calculation.
- **Container**   Used to identify items that are containers used for shipping sales orders.
- **Vehicle**   Used to identify items that are vehicles used for shipping sales orders.
- **Container Type**   Used to identify the container type of items identified as containers.
- **Internal Volume**   The internal volume of the container or vehicle in the same UOM as the Unit Volume; used for packing calculation to calculate container-capacity restrictions.

- **Maximum Load Weight** Used to identify the maximum load weight of the container or vehicle in the same UOM as the Unit Weight.
- **Minimum Fill Percentage** Used to identify the minimum fill percentage under which the container or vehicle should be used.

Setting up containers and vehicles with this information allows full functionality of the containerization feature in Oracle Shipping Execution. Oracle Shipping Execution is not integrated with Inventory with respect to container management. Hence, this setup step is purely for the purposes of using the physical attributes defined for the containers and vehicles to drive the container functionality in Oracle Shipping Execution.

To effect inventory controls for containers, additional item-setup information would need to be completed, including making the container OM transactable. The container item would then need to be placed as a line on a sales order.

Container–Item Relationships Container–item relationships are set up only if you are using container management. They represent the amount of any given item that might fit into a specific container. They also can represent how many containers can fit into a master container. You can specify a preferred container-load combination for the system to use when calculating fill amounts automatically.

Pricing

Pricing is a complex art. Oracle Order Management in conjunction with Oracle Pricing gives you the tools to price goods and services with precision to meet your corporate objectives. The price a customer pays for an item is the product of the applicable list price and discount. Table 12-1 shows the computations and logic that take place at setup time and as an order is entered.

Oracle EBS's pricing engine receives transaction information, prepares pricing requests, selects price lists and modifier lists, and applies price adjustments (benefits) to the transaction. The pricing engine answers the following questions as it determines a price:

Price-List Setup Tasks	Order-Entry Tasks
Set the item price on a price list; base the price on the item cost, obtained from Inventory, and percentage or absolute monetary adjustment to the price list.	Choose the applicable price list for an order and then find the list price for the item or the secondary price list it designates.
Set up pricing rules for computing the list price of items with variable pricing, such as software licenses.	Accept any variables (such as number of seats or CPU size) that, in addition to quantity and units of measure, are applied by the pricing rules to identify the list price.
Set up automatic discounts as percentages, absolute monetary adjustments, or fixed prices.	Identify the best available discount.

TABLE 12-1. *Timing of Price Development and Application*

- Who qualifies for prices and benefits?
- What is the product hierarchy and what pricing attributes pertain to this item or service?
- How should the order price or order-line price be adjusted?

Order Management determines the price list and discount schedule at an order level. Upon entry of an order, the price list will be defaulted from the order-type, customer, invoice-to, ship-to, or agreement level. Depending on the setup, the specialist can override the price list for the order.

Oracle Pricing is defined as a separate product. It is responsible for maintaining price lists and the rules for applying prices, and Order Management is left to apply pricing to individual customer orders. Oracle Pricing supports e-business applications. Oracle Pricing provides an advanced, highly flexible pricing engine that executes pricing and promotional calculations for Oracle Order Management and other Oracle EBS modules. Oracle Pricing has the power and flexibility to meet the needs of complex pricing situations found over a wide range of demanding industry business requirements, which include the following:

- consumer goods, telecommunications, services, high technology, automotive, and aerospace and defense businesses that sell to other businesses; and
- telemarketing, mail-order, and Web-store businesses that sell directly to consumers.

Oracle Pricing delivers pricing capabilities for all applications and more by allowing you to efficiently set up your pricing information, then model the complex data relationships that determine the correct price. The concept of timing is crucial. Pricing is set up in advance of any customer orders. You must establish price lists. You can establish quite complex sets of rules governing their effective dates and the customers, items, and geographies to which they apply.

The productivity advantage of dealing with items as groups rather than individually is always a key consideration. Oracle Pricing gives you the power to deal with hierarchical groups of items, such as plastics, cleaning supplies, and so forth. It can deal with exceptions within groups—for instance, specifying a 30 percent across-the-board price reduction for a group of items, with the caveat that nothing be sold below cost.

Specifically, Oracle Pricing lets you set list prices for items or hierarchies explicitly or as a percentage or absolute change from the prior price. You can establish volume discounts based on quantity or usage. Some configured items are so complex that each one has to be priced individually: Pricing lets you provide base prices for individual features, arithmetic equations for computing feature prices based on quantity or capacity, and special prices for groups of features. The same kind of logic can be used for pricing-dimensioned items such as custom-built staircases or radio towers.

Currently, a much-needed enhancement in Oracle Pricing is the capability to import prices from an external source. Many commodities businesses peg prices to an external index such as the LIBOR interest rate or hog futures. Other businesses might leverage from their competitors' prices.

Oracle Pricing handles a wide variety of promotional-type prices, including buy-one-get-one-free, coupons, volume discounts by price, gift certificates, and cascading discounts. Oracle can handle most users' complete needs. Pricing is available throughout the Oracle CRM suite because salespeople can need pricing information at any point in the sales cycle and because pricing applies to service and products.

One of the features introduced in Release 12 is the price book, consisting of a robust self-service capability for users to manipulate list of products with their related prices. The key advantage is the ability to generate a price book showing list and net prices for a specific customer, even using the customer-item cross-reference number to make it easier to identify their items.

Oracle Advanced Pricing

Oracle Advanced Pricing is an extension of Basic Pricing that provides support for promotions and deals. Specifically, it lets you handle item upgrades (order one thing; get something better), tie-ins (order one thing, get a discount on another), free items, and favorable terms for shipping and payment (nothing down and no payments until 2015!). Advanced Pricing uses the same interfaces as Basic Pricing; you simply give it a more extensive set of rules consistent with its additional capabilities.

Price-List Elements

A price list is made up of item numbers and prices associated with them. Price-list lines carry the following elements:

- **Item**   The item to be priced.
- **Unit price**   The unit price of the item.
- **Selling unit of measure**   The unit of measure in which the item is to be sold.
- **Pricing rule and pricing attributes**   Considerations if the list price varies depending on usage factors.

Except for service items, price lists carry monetary values, not percentage figures. The formulas that update them can be expressed in terms of percentages, but a price on a list is fixed. The only computation at order time is discounting.

TIP

Inventory and other modules have the capability to capture costs in enough detail that costs can be allocated down to the item level with confidence. Inventory can carry all the components of item cost at the item level. You can improve control of your margins by having your business procedures use Inventory costs as a major determinant of Order Management prices.

Maintaining Price Lists

Once you have determined which group or individual within your organization will maintain the price lists, it is important to establish an approach to retain consistent data. Here is a common set of steps for maintaining price lists:

1. Create categories in Oracle Inventory to group items for the purposes of creating cost lists. Oracle Inventory categories are very flexible: They do not have to be mutually exclusive, nor must every item be assigned to a category.

2. Choose an Inventory organization to serve as the basis for pricing. In Oracle EBS's Multi-Org scheme, there can be many inventory organizations, each with different costs, within the scope of one Order Management organization.

3. Use Order Management's Add Inventory Items form to create a base price list carrying all items at cost for the current period. You might name it *COST_JUN_12*. This list will serve as the basis for other price computations, and perhaps also as the price list for internal orders. You can use Oracle Pricing's import features to easily import your cost data.

Once you have your costs in Oracle Pricing, you can use its suite of features to establish price lists for different promotions, sets of customers, and so on. Although it is not essential to start with your costs, if you do not you are liable to lose sight of profitability.

TIP
Compute standard prices as a function of cost and markup. It helps to have a relatively uniform markup, because other price lists and discounts will typically be set as percentages of the standard list cost. Uneven markups could result in sales prices set below cost.

GSA Pricing

The US federal government's General Services Administration (GSA) negotiates government-wide contracts annually with its major suppliers. The GSA sets a price list for the year, which contractors usually publish in book format and distribute to all potential customers within the government. One of the conditions the government imposes is that the vendor may not offer more favorable prices to any other customer.

Order Management enforces this rule by comparing the discounted price on an order line against the GSA price. Order Management will prevent the order—or, depending on the setup parameters, at least issue a warning to the effect that the GSA terms are being violated. GSA prices serve as a floor.

Companies with customers who are eligible for GSA prices allow these customers to order from the GSA price list. Even companies that do not do business with the federal government might want to put GSA pricing in effect to warn of sales being made with substandard margins.

Multicurrency Pricing

You can carry price lists in as many currencies as necessary. You can handle currency conversion and rounding as you establish the list—offering price stability to your customers abroad—or you can do spot conversions to set the foreign-currency amount at invoice time. Oracle Receivables has the complementary logic to account for multiple currencies, such as variance accounts for gain and loss on exchange.

OM Key Features

Oracle Product Development provided many new features in Release 12 that offer users an easy method of order-creation control and management. This section outlines some of the larger new features that have been created for Order Management.

Multi-Org Access Control

Multi-Organization Access Control (MOAC) enables organizations that have implemented a shared-service model to efficiently process sales orders by allowing customer-service representatives in a single location to accept and process sales for multiple operating units. This increases productivity by not having the users switch application Responsibilities when processing transactions with data secured based on security profiles.

Customer Acceptance

Companies in some countries and industries are forced to defer creating the invoice and/or recognizing revenue of the sales until the customer formally accepts the material—in other words, receives the shipment. For these scenarios, Oracle has built into Release 12 the customer-acceptance rules, which are defined in Oracle Receivables' Revenue Management module and enforced in Oracle Order Management.

There are several ways to capture the acceptance:

■ Customers can log into the self-service Order Information portal to perform the acceptance.

■ A user, typically a customer-service representative, can call the Order Information portal from a sales-order workbench and confirm the acceptance.

■ Order Import/Process Order API can import customer acceptance captured from an external system.

Item Orderability

Th Item Orderability feature allows companies to define which customers are allowed to order which products, and furthermore apply the business logic when the order is being created. One of the advantages is that users can define the orderability rule and apply it to items or item categories defined for an organization.

Accounting

Order Management is not a financial application; that is, it has no direct interface with General Ledger. It passes records of its revenue-generating activity with customers and items to Oracle Receivables via the Receivables interface and AutoInvoice open interfaces. Receivables is the eventual source of the revenue accounting logic that creates ledger-journal entries. Receivables uses the Account Generator and Subledger Accounting to determine the appropriate flexfield values for the revenue transaction.

Revenue comes at a cost. Order Management uses the Account Generator to create an Accounting Flexfield for the cost-of-goods-sold (COGS) account. It passes the COGS account via the Inventory interface program. Inventory uses the information to create a GL journal to debit the inventory-asset account and credit the COGS account.

Users define income reports using the General Ledger's Financial Statement Generator by subtracting COGS and other expenses from income. Most companies measure income by business unit, so it is important to have the Account Generator assign Accounting Flexfields in such a way that they can be easily compared. The item attributes for sales account, expense account, and COGS account are major inputs in determining the Accounting Flexfield associated with a transaction. To measure income accurately, expenses should be placed against cost, department by department and product line by product line, so that comparisons make sense across the organization.

The same logic used by the Account Generator is used to credit the appropriate organizations and locations with revenue through Oracle Receivables. It is critical to profit-and-loss computation that expense systems use parallel logic. Cost-accounting FSG reports lose their value as a management tool if one region receives credit for a sale but another is charged with the expense of servicing it.

Oracle provides considerable flexibility to define and control the interface process through various setup options. Because the interface is open, it is fairly easy to customize by updating the data in the open-interface tables between the Receivables interface and AutoInvoice steps.

The same elements of information are generally available to the Account Generator for revenue and cost of goods sold. These include the customer, salesperson, item, order type, and many others. You should ensure that the rules for generating all except the natural account and subaccount are consistent. The account values will naturally reflect revenue on one side and expense on the other.

In terms of timing, the order cycle establishes the point at which an order is sent to Receivables for invoicing and revenue recognition. The accounting rule passed from Order Management establishes when to accrue revenue and post it to the ledger. In computing income, the financial reports might have to recognize that there is a timing difference between expense and the associated revenue. This is a major issue in companies with small numbers of large orders, and such institutions as universities, in which revenue (tuitions) might precede expenses (faculty salaries). Use General Ledger accruals as necessary to put revenues and offset expenses in the same period.

Integration with Other Modules

Order Management communicates with other systems by sharing master data and exchanging transaction data through open interfaces and APIs.

Integration with Receivables

Oracle Receivables shares customers with Order Management, Sales and Marketing, Sales Compensation, and Service. The EBS applications share the function of maintaining these master tables. Order Management has the capability to import data to set up customers, a plus when integrating Oracle EBS with third-party systems that manage presales and sales activity. It is common to allow users to enter and maintain customer data through Order Management Responsibilities, as customer data play a major role in determining order defaults. Even if you do not have Oracle Receivables installed, Order Management will require use of its base tables.

Order Management passes Receivables the information it needs to bill the customer and collect. In a reverse process, it passes RMA information so customers can be credited for returns. This interface to Receivables is one way: adjustments to the invoice do not find their way back to Order Management. They flow to the ledger through adjustment accounts defined in Receivables. Order Management will never find out if a receivables clerk gives the customer a credit for a defective or missing product. A formal RMA, which originates in Order Management, is the only mechanism available to register an adjustment in Order Management. Receivables, because it deals with money actually invoiced and collected, is the authoritative source for completed sales activity. Order Management reports are the source for reports on future revenue from open sales orders.

Integration with Inventory

Inventory defines the stock items and their related costs that Order Management has available to sell. When order lines are demanded and reserved through the order screen and pick-release process, Inventory is updated to reflect the item's availability (affecting the MTL_DEMAND table). Once an order has been ship confirmed and Inventory interfaced, Order Management will write to the MTL_TRANSACTION_INTERFACE table, thereby allowing Inventory to decrement its on-hand quantities. Order Management can also take significant advantage of the categories defined in Inventory to ease data entry and reporting requirements.

You might be able to achieve a smoother workflow by using bar-code scanners in the pick-confirmation process. The Ship Confirm open interface offers a batch-mode alternative to the Confirm Shipments window.

Integration with Purchasing

Order Management links with Purchasing for internal orders and drop shipments. A requisition for internally sourced items will create an order through the Order Import open interface, then be processed through the full Order Management cycle. The Purchasing locations are translated into shipping and receiving warehouses. Requisition information is viewable in the Order Inquiry screens in these situations.

Purchasing is also greatly involved in the drop-ship order process. The sales-order criteria (ship-to address, item quantity, date required, and so forth) are passed to create a purchase requisition, then are eventually transposed into a purchase order for generating to the supplier, to ship the goods to your customer on your behalf. Once the goods have been shipped and validated, you can complete the process by completing a virtual receipt of goods, closing the PO, paying the supplier, and issuing an invoice for the goods sold.

Conversion Issues

In a phased implementation, the customer and inventory master tables that Order Management needs might have been put in place already for Receivables, Purchasing, and Inventory. It is up to the architects of those conversions to ensure that the attributes that Order Management needs have been loaded properly into the shared tables. Refer to Chapter 11 for conversion issues related to the Item Master and catalogs.

To minimize your work, plan for Order Management as you implement the earlier systems. For instance, it can be difficult to convert items to pick-to-order if they are being transacted already as prepackaged kits. Resetting the Order Management attributes on established items can be time consuming. It takes extra effort to compose a full implementation plan at the outset, but ultimately it saves a lot of time.

Order Import

Order Import greatly simplifies the conversion of orders by loading them into the five major Order Management tables that hold them. The open interface is as complex as the relationships among those five tables, and it can accommodate a wide variety of data conditions, although it does not support all of the functions that are available when data are entered through the screens. However, few organizations really need all of the features available in Order Import. Oracle Consulting, or another group with conversion experience, can often streamline an implementation by adapting conversion scripts that they originally developed for other customers.

You will need a strategy for handling conversion of incomplete orders. Good as it is, the open interface might have difficulty in dealing with back-order situations or partially filled orders. It raises questions of invoicing: what has the legacy system passed to Receivables, and what should Oracle EBS do? It is best to eliminate as much complexity as possible before the conversion. An optimal strategy might involve the following steps:

■ At some date just before conversion, complete booking and order-confirmation activity on in-process orders, and hold off entering new orders until after conversion. This will put all orders to be converted into booked status.

- Complete all open warehouse activity in the legacy system: picking, shipping, and ship confirmation.

- Use the legacy system to invoice for completed activity.

- Use an automated process to convert booked and approved orders for which there has been no shipping activity. These are the majority of the orders—the easy ones. Load them through the open interface. If the volume is enough, it might be sufficient simply to rekey every open order. The issues are labor and the time the operation can afford to be down for conversion.

- List the exceptions for manual entry into Oracle EBS. These will include partially shipped orders and held orders. Implement a manual procedure to deal with invoicing and cash application for orders that are satisfied under both the legacy system and Oracle EBS.

Responsibilities

Order Management is a large product covering functions that usually fall within several different departments. Most commonly the Responsibilities are divided as follows:

- Order entry is usually a department of its own, working closely with the sales department to enter and correct customer sales.

- The order-entry department enters price lists, discounts, and prices, with input from many departments throughout the company.

- Credit checking and approval is a financial function, often found in the accounts-receivable department.

- The item managers in the inventory department usually add new sales items and establish bills of materials for PTO and ATO items.

- Fulfillment is usually a warehouse function.

All constituencies should be represented among the super users who compile the Order Management setup. The department heads of each area need to define the different Responsibilities within their areas.

Conclusion

Productivity, flexibility, accuracy, and control are the major issues in order management; Oracle's product satisfies them well. Its integrated links through Inventory to Purchasing and Manufacturing ensure optimal availability of goods to satisfy customer demand. Its close relationship with Receivables means that customer invoices will be timely and accurate, and that each sale will be accounted correctly for the purposes of sales compensation and the ledger.

Oracle's CRM Sales and Marketing and Service product families are also highly integrated with Order Management, Pricing, and Shipping. This tight networking of applications allows a seamless integration of front- and back-office information to ensure that all of your business needs and the needs of your customers are met.

Order workflows give Order Management the power to address virtually any type of order; defaults minimize the number of keystrokes required during data entry. The hold mechanism and the approval steps you build into the order cycle ensure that orders that need special attention receive it while routine orders move swiftly through the system.

Pick-to-order, configure-to-order, and catalog functions make it easier for customers to decide what they need. They can make their choices on the basis of descriptions that are meaningful to them, not just your internal part numbers. They do not have to concern themselves with the details of what components you require to satisfy their needs.

The pricing and discounting tools are designed to leverage the cost data captured in Payables and Manufacturing and carried in Inventory. With Order Management you can easily implement strategies to meet your competitive and margin objectives.

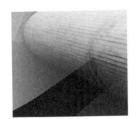

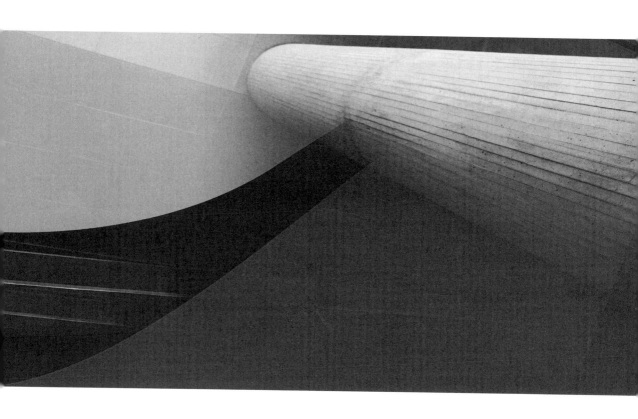

CHAPTER
13

Oracle E-Business Tax

ince the creation of the Oracle E-Business Suite, Oracle has provided robust tax calculation for each transactional module. This engine included calculations for almost every country with specific legal or government requirements. The path for this development has evolved in many ways, and as a result, Oracle introduced in the latest release a new application which consolidates the tax setups in a single location, leveraging the new Oracle Application Framework (OAF) look and feel.

In early versions of the E-Business Suite, the tax setups were made in each module and the implementation method included trial and error for each of the tax codes of regimes. From a global point of view, it was originated as customizations handled by each Oracle subsidiary or Oracle partner; later on, in Release 11i, Oracle included these patches into the product and shipped them with it. A few countries, such as Brazil, are still requiring the installation of products from Oracle partners (in Brazil's case, Synchro or Mastersaf) because of the complexity of their local government requirements and the integration points between the different modules within E-Business Suite.

The new E-Business Tax application is the result of many years of continued effort from Oracle to simplify the tax-setup process. It provides a single-point solution for managing your transaction-based tax requirements. By using a single OAF interface, E-Business Tax delivers tax services to all E-Business Suite modules and business flows.

This new module includes a data model comprising a system architecture that models all the aspects of the tax engine and allows global configuration and scalability for country-specific tax content.

This is a mandatory module if you are using business flows that are subject to taxation. The biggest advantage of using it is that you can model your tax requirements according to local and international tax requirements, including

- both simple and complex country-specific tax legislation;

- cross-border transactions;

- local compliance requirements for recording and reporting; and

- continual changes to tax legislation, such as new taxes, local law changes, special tax rates, and special exceptions for products and customers.

The entire tax configuration and maintenance is done through the E-Business Tax application, ensuring a uniform tax setup across applications, where the different tax areas within your organization can control based out of a centrally managed system of automated tax services.

This new application consolidates all the tax data from different modules; if your organization is using existing Release 11i tax data for tax determination and calculation, Oracle E-Business Tax provides a common model for setting up and migrating the tax data that were originally set up in Payables, Purchasing, Receivables, and Projects.

Oracle E-Business Tax and the Release 11i migration solution let your tax users begin using E-Business Tax according to your existing tax setup with a minimum number of changes. The purpose of this transition is to gradually adopt the new E-Business Tax setups and tax-determination process with no loss of service on your tax calculations.

The E-Business Tax solution for Release 11i migrated data includes these features:

- migration of application-specific ownership of tax setup to the E-Business Tax shared-ownership model for all procure-to-pay and order-to-cash transactions;

- migration of tax codes and rates (Payables tax codes and Receivables VAT taxes) to the E-Business Tax regime-to-rate flow;

- migration of existing tax codes and tax groups, as well as existing defaulting hierarchies, to E-Business Tax as tax-classification codes; and

- tax determination and tax calculation based on the tax-classification code.

NOTE
For a complete list of user tasks that are required to migrate tax data from Release 11i to Release 12 using the E-Business Tax user interface, please see the Oracle Applications Upgrade Guide: Release 11i to Release 12.

The main difference in tax calculation between Release 11i and Release 12 is that in the previous version, each application owned and maintained its own tax codes and rates. Since E-Business Tax provides a single source of truth for all transactions, the ownership of the tax setup is now modeled in the E-Business Tax application. On top of that, and based on the changes explained in Chapter 2 regarding the new model of legal entities and operating units, they will share the same tax setup, but it is possible to cover specific requirements defined by the tax authority for individual operating units.

Another important enhancement in E-Business Tax is the improved management of transaction handling and display. Release 11i, for example, did not show taxable-amount details or tax-line information. In the new application there is a single repository consisting on detailed and fully allocated tax lines. This common repository also serves as the source of truth for tax distributions for procure-to-pay (P2P) transactions. The Payables transactions are documented in this schema at the document level and the IDs for the tax lines and tax distributions are stored in Payables and also in Receivables tax lines for reconciliation purposes.

NOTE
Tax lines existing on a Release 11i item line that are migrated to Release 12 will be recalculated; however, no new tax lines can be added to the Release 11i migrated item lines.

Setting Up Taxes in Oracle E-Business Tax

Oracle E-Business Tax provides a single location to set up and maintain the E-Business Suite transaction-tax requirements in the global environment where your organization does business.

This new module uses tax configuration to determine the taxes, online at transaction time, that apply to each transaction and to calculate the corresponding tax amounts.

The scope of the setups within Oracle E-Business Tax includes:

- setting up and maintaining a tax configuration for each tax that your company is subject to;

- setting up and maintaining records for every legal entity and operating unit, and the taxes they are subject to;

- centralizing all the shared tax-configuration data for all the legal entities and operating units;

- setting up and maintaining tax registrations and classifications for legal establishments and third parties;

- setting up and maintaining classifications of the products that your organization buys and sells;

- setting up and maintaining classifications for all the transactions;
- setting up and maintaining tax rules and default values to manage tax determination and tax recovery on all the transactions;
- for simple tax requirements, setting up default values and a minimum number of tax rules;
- setting up and maintaining automatic accounting of all tax-related transactions;
- managing user control of updates and overrides of tax information on transactions;
- setting up and maintaining codes for tax-reporting purposes;
- running a full set of reports for your tax authority's tax requirements; and
- setting up and maintaining access to third-party tax-calculation services, such as Vertex or Taxware.

The Oracle E-Business Tax home page is a workbench designed for tax users to manage all the setup and maintenance of the tax data. It is a brand-new page in the Oracle Application Framework (OAF), with an easy-to-use interface (see Figure 13-1).

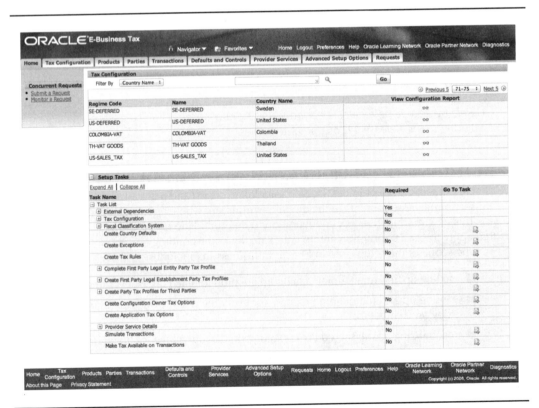

FIGURE 13-1. *Oracle E-Business Tax home page*

The order-to-cash and procure-to-pay business flows are covered by the application and its tax-content store. The following applications are included in the scope of E-Business Tax:

- Oracle Order Management
- Oracle Payables
- Oracle Projects
- Oracle Purchasing
- Oracle Receivables
- Oracle General Ledger
- Advanced Global Intercompany System
- Consigned Inventory
- Oracle Internet Expenses
- Oracle iProcurement
- Oracle iStore
- Oracle Order Capture
- Oracle Services Contracts
- Oracle Trade Management

NOTE
Oracle E-Business Tax in Release 12 does not provide tax services for Payables withholding taxes, Latin America Receivables transactions, or India transaction taxes. The setups for these transactions will have to be set up and maintained in the Oracle E-Business Suite using the functionality available from Release 11i.

The tasks involved in setting up a tax requirement in E-Business Tax fall into three general categories:

- understanding the organization's tax configuration for setting up transaction taxes,
- completing all of the setups and settings related to the processing of taxes on transactions, and
- setting up tax rules and defaults to manage tax processing.

Understanding Your Organization's Tax Configuration

The first step in your implementation is to answer some simple questions that will guide you through the entire setup process of the E-Business Tax application.

These questions are about your organization and the relationship between you and the legal and regulatory agencies that enable your company to operate in one or more countries.

You start defining in which countries your organization operates—and even more, in which countries you are legally registered—and the countries in which you have subsidiary companies that are legally registered or have a legal presence. By using the Legal Entity Configurator, available since Release 12, you capture information about your legal entities and legal registrations.

Each subdivision of a legal entity is called a *legal establishment*; that is the next level below the legal entities. Each legal establishment involves branches, divisions, and locations in the countries where you need to be registered for tax.

Next, consider the types of operations and businesses that your company is engaged in in the countries where you have legal entities or establishments. Some types to be considered include industries, kinds of operations, and scale of operations. Each of these factors may have an impact on your tax data and tax engine.

The step after assessing your company's operations is defining the main classifications of a transaction, also known as rules, which are the four Ps:

- **Party**   Who are your customers and suppliers?
- **Place**   Where do you perform the operations?
- **Product**   What products do you buy or sell?
- **Process**   What do you do?

The tax-processing overview for E-Business Tax is shown in Figure 13-2.

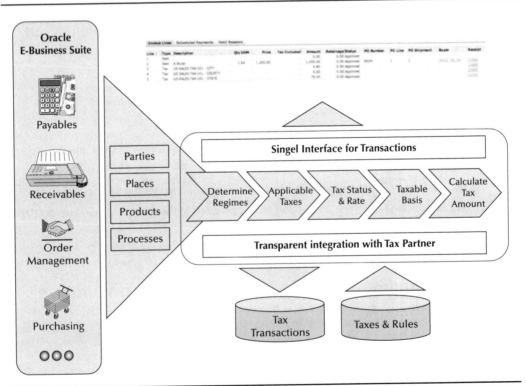

FIGURE 13-2.   *Oracle E-Business Tax tax-processing overview*

Defining Parties and Places

The first definition you must gather is the type of customers and suppliers your company is doing business with. This will have an impact on your tax requirements—for example the taxes that you are subject to or the tax status or tax rate that applies.

As simple example, which will help you to understand the combination of party and place, is to consider a company that you sell a product to that has a bill-to address in London and a ship-to address in Dublin. The tax should be 5 percent. The transaction rate for UK VAT is either the standard VAT rate or a zero rate, depending on whether the customer is registered for VAT in the country to which the supply is made. You can capture this information, for example, by classifying your customer as "Registered in another European country." You can use this classification in your tax rules to derive the appropriate status for this customer (and other customers similarly classified).

There are many examples where the parties or customers have a key value for the tax engine. For another example, imagine that your company is in Argentina and sells to customers that are not registered for VAT in the local country. In this case, per the local legal requirement, your company has to charge this customer another tax type, called additional VAT. You will apply the same solution as explained before, where you can classify this customer as "Not registered for VAT" and use this in your tax rules to charge the additional VAT.

A single system of taxation is called a *tax regime*. A tax regime is implemented by one or more distinct charges. Each such specific charge is called a *tax*. Therefore, a tax regime may include one tax only or several different taxes. The imposition of a tax is limited typically by a geographical boundary. In most cases, this geographical boundary identifies a contiguous political or administrative area, such as a city or a county. In some cases, a tax may be imposed or may vary according to a nonpolitical demarcation, such as a free-trade zone. The incidence of any tax on a specific geographical area is called a *tax jurisdiction*.

You can create a tax jurisdiction for a country, a state within a country, a county within a state, or a city within a county. In certain cases, a tax jurisdiction may need to encompass, for example, two or more cities, or an entire county plus one city in a neighboring county.

The details of tax regime and tax jurisdiction will be explained later in this chapter.

Defining Processes

The definition of the process is primarily the identification and classification of the transactions that you are creating in your E-Business Suite in the requirements-gathering phase for the tax-configuration definitions, such as: Is your company manufacturing items or buying and selling without any added process? Do you sell goods into another province, state, or country? There are other questions to ask, as well, about the process and how that can impact your tax data.

Oracle E-Business Tax leverages the Trading Community Architecture (TCA) to classify and categorize the transactions in a standardized format across the E-Business Suite.

Table 13-1 illustrates the top-level values of the structure—purchase and sale—which are seeded in the E-Business Tax application and are called *tax-event classes*. Within E-Business Tax you can define up to five levels of classification under the top levels.

The following step is the definition of rules at any level that your organization will need for a transaction business category described in Table 13-1.

Defining Products

The final definition is based on the products that you sell. For example if you manufacture goods for export, you may not be subject to taxes on the purchases that go into the manufacture of such

Classification	Level
Purchase	Top (0)
■ Purchase for manufacture of goods for sale	1
■ Purchase for manufacture for export sales	2
■ Purchase for manufacture for domestic sales	2
■ Purchase for resale	1
■ Domestic purchase for resale	2
■ Import of goods for resale	2
■ Import of goods for domestic resale	3
■ Import of goods for export	3
■ . . .	3
■ . . .	1
Sale	Top (0)
■ Goods manufactured by selling establishment	1
■ Domestic sales	2
■ Interstate sales	3
■ Intrastate sales	3
■ Export sales	2
■ . . .	2
■ . . .	1

TABLE 13-1. *E-Business Suite Transaction Categories, Using a Three-Level Classification Structure*

goods; but your organization will have to register for service taxes if you provide taxable services for collecting or remitting those services.

The tax users can reuse the classifications associated with the Inventory items through the Oracle Inventory application, using the Inventory item category for tax purposes. This allows better administration and control over the taxation of the products, reducing the complexity. But this is not limited to Oracle Inventory, because E-Business Tax provides a screen that allows users to create new item-category sets, restricted only for tax purposes. It is very important to set a clear strategy on how your organization will maintain the taxes for each product, taking into consideration these two options, of item category or item-category sets, and how the maintenance of tax for products can be affected with multiple sources.

In practice, you can implement a tax structure for your products using item categories, up to a five-level classification scheme, which can be linked to the tax rules.

Setups and Settings for Processing of Taxes on Transactions

Understanding the different setups of E-Business Tax sometimes requires some tax background; the purpose of this section is to present the different setup options and the ways you can use the different steps of this new module to adapt to the complexity of the tax within your organization. As mentioned before, E-Business Tax consists of a tax-knowledge base, a variety of tax services that respond to specific tax events, and a set of repositories for tax content and tax recording.

E-Business Tax has multiple components to model all the different tax complexities that can be presented in any country of the world.

Tax-Content Services

This component addresses the creation, maintenance, and management of tax content. Tax-content services store and maintain the master and reference data that are needed to support the other components in E-Business Tax. You use the E-Business Tax application to model the details of the tax setup for all of your company's tax requirements.

Tax-content services include these subcomponents:

- **Basic tax configuration**   Includes the regime-to-rate flow for each tax regime:

    - *Tax regime*   The set of laws and regulations that determine the treatment of one or more taxes.

    - *Tax*   A classification of a charge imposed by a government through a fiscal or tax authority.

    - *Tax status*   The taxable nature of a product in the context of a transaction for a tax.

    - *Tax rates*   The rates specified for a tax status for a given time period. Tax rates are expressed as a percentage, a value per unit quantity, or a fixed sum per transaction.

    - *Tax recovery rates*   The full or partial reclamation of taxes paid on the purchase or movement of a product.

- **Tax jurisdictions**   Provides the basis for defining tax jurisdictions. A tax jurisdiction is the geographic area where a tax is levied by a specific tax authority.

- **Party tax profiles**   Provides the basis for defining tax profiles for the parties involved in tax transactions that are set up through Legal entity and Trading Community Architecture. Party tax profiles contain all of the tax information for each party, including tax registrations and fiscal classifications.

- **Fiscal classifications**   Provides for the definition of tax fiscal classifications. A fiscal classification is a way that a tax authority classifies each part of a transaction:

    - parties and party sites involved in the transaction,

    - products involved in the transaction,

    - the nature of the transaction, and

    - documents associated with the transaction.

    Exemptions and exceptions   Lets you define a party, party site, or product as partially or fully exempt from a tax. Tax-exemption certificates from the tax authority normally support the details of tax exemptions. Tax exceptions let you define a special rate for specific products. This lets you define general rules for a wide classification of products while applying a separate rule to a subset of products.

■ **Country default controls**   Lets you specify certain defaults by country. These defaults are used during transaction entry.

Tax-Content Repository

This component contains master and reference setup data. Data created via tax-content services are stored in the tax-content repository. A list of the most important tables in the data model for the tax rules is shown in Figure 13-3.

Tax-Service Request Manager

This component manages the access to all tax data and services, including

■ integration with E-Business Tax services,

■ integration with tax-service providers such as Vertex or Taxware,

■ the standard interface for E-Business Suite, and

■ applications to add tax services to business-process flows.

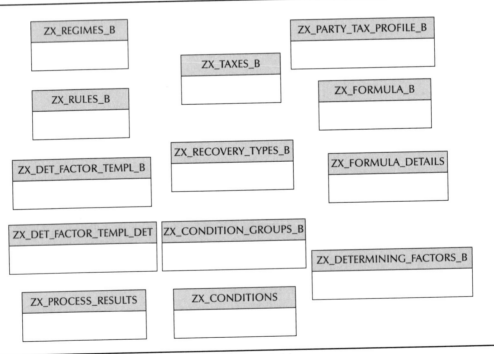

FIGURE 13-3.   *Oracle E-Business Tax most important tables*

Tax-Determination Services

The component of tax-determination services calculates transaction taxes based on transaction details and tax-setup information. This component is involved in the following:

- automatically determining which taxes are applicable for the transaction based on the place of supply, the tax registrations of the parties involved, and other applicability rules;
- determining how they should be calculated; and
- producing the results from the calculation.

The results are an ordered list of applicable taxes and associated details such as tax jurisdiction, tax, etc., which can be updated by the user. Depending on the complexity of the different regimes, tax rules may or may not be defined for all processes. If there is no complex rule associated with any process, then the default values, as specified during setup, are used during the tax-determination process.

Additionally, the user has the ability during transaction entry to

- enter or change additional tax-relevant factors—such as intended use, business-transaction category, and product fiscal classification—to ensure that the proper taxes are determined for special cases and exceptions; and
- view, drill down, enter, and change tax-line details.

Tax-Record Repository

This component contains the key attributes necessary to record a tax event. A single tax transaction can include over 600 key attributes.

Tax-Administration Services

This component manages the accounting for all tax transactions.

Tax-Reporting Ledger

This component manages access to the tax-content and tax-record repositories for tax-reporting purposes. Tax authorities around the world have promulgated a substantial variety of requirements pertaining to the communication of tax information, making tax compliance both varied and complex. The tax-reporting ledger is flexible enough to provide data in a user-friendly format that allows the standard and identified country-specific requirements to be met. Users are able to use the information in the centralized tax-record repository to create legal documents and reports that facilitate tax compliance. In Release 12, the existing tax reports are available as before, based on the new repository. In addition, new custom reports can be generated quickly from these templates using Oracle BI Publisher.

Helpful Features for Tax Setup

Guided Configuration

Oracle E-Business Tax enables a tax manager—i.e., an expert in the domain of tax—to configure the system to meet the tax requirements in one or more countries. An example of a tax configuration is shown in Figure 13-4.

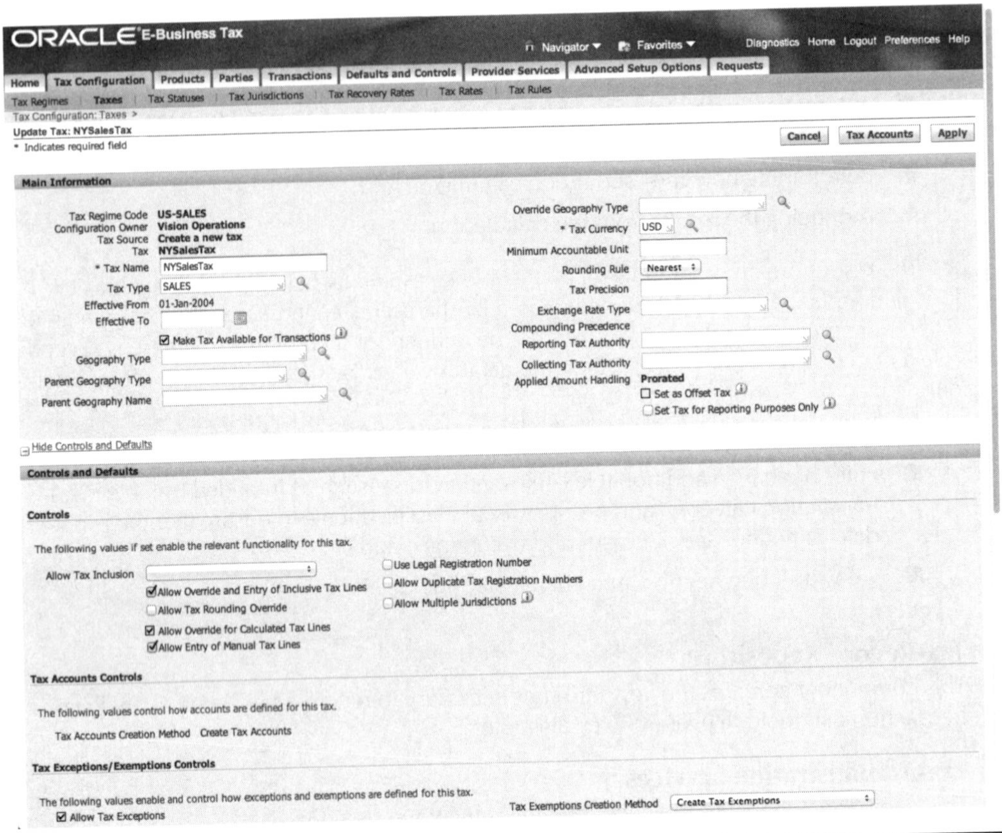

FIGURE 13-4. *Oracle E-Business Tax's intuitive user interface*

Oracle E-Business Tax provides features such as the following:

- a setup task list that lists the sequence of tasks that need to be completed, the order in which they typically need to be completed, and whether a given step is mandatory; where applicable, it also provides the user with a link to navigate to the UI where a given task can be completed;

- a guided rule-definition process particularly catering to first-time or occasional users whose primary expertise is in tax, not IT; this follows a step-by-step rule-definition process using terminology and concepts that a tax manager would understand;

- an expert-users rule-entry process that enables users familiar with the terminology and the process to quickly create tax rules;

- content containers that explain concepts and provide background information or information about related functionality; and

- information icons that alert the user in particular to seemingly innocuous options that may have profound downstream impacts.

Tax Simulator

A user interface is provided that allows users to enter a transaction, such as a purchase or sales invoice, and view the results of tax calculation. This is a valuable tool for tax managers, who can use this interface to ensure that the tax configuration—including any rules that have been set up—provides the expected results. The tax simulator can also help the tax manager simulate the effect of a new rule or of new incremental setup data, such as a new tax rate. A tax-simulator window is displayed in Figure 13-5.

The tax simulator enables the user to

- view tax lines for simulated transactions;

- drill down into an audit trail of information for each tax line, identifying the tax rules that were used;

- generate a log file that shows the tax rules that were found to be unsuccessful; and

- simulate the tax on stand-alone documents, related documents such as a payables invoice created by matching to a purchase order, documents to which another document has been applied (such as a prepayment applied to a payables invoice), adjusting documents such as a credit memo, and imported documents with tax lines.

Integration with Tax-Service Providers

Oracle has built a very robust solution to support the complexity of tax data worldwide, but companies will face multiple challenges—such as having to configure complex tax regimes or taxation rules from scratch—which add the time-consuming tasks of maintaining and testing every

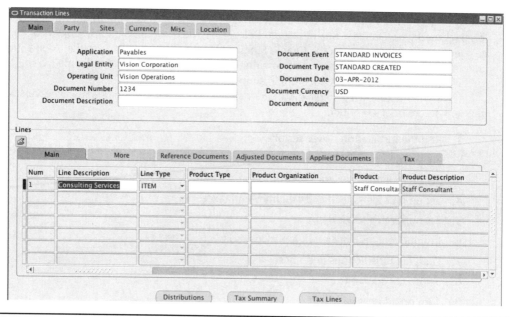

FIGURE 13-5. *Oracle E-Business Tax's tax simulation for Receivables transaction*

possible scenario. There are some important considerations that need to be evaluated from a tax perspective, such as local reporting requirements for countries outside the United States and the fact that E-Business Tax does not provide master geography data.

From an implementation perspective, there are many factors that will add pressure over the application, such as the automation. As mentioned previously, the time spent by tax experts on the configuration, maintenance, and test of changes on the tax-data attempts against the operational efficiency and also the risk of missing some tax-law changes might put your organization in bad position on an audit. In term of resources, during implementation you will be training some key users in the tax department; the knowledge transfer is key, as is thorough documentation of the setups and the changes performed, so that any changes within the organization do not increase the risk of losing the knowledge of how taxes are set up.

To respond to these challenges, Oracle has built inside E-Business Tax a bridge to use the tax services of external service providers for tax calculation on sales and receivables transactions. The integration between the external provider and E-Business Tax is transparent, and all the tax services are performed without any interruption to the E-Business Suite business flows.

Vertex and Taxware are two of the major providers of tax services. The setup for provider services is called a *service subscription*. A service subscription applies to the transactions of one configuration-option setup for a combination of tax regime and legal entity or operating unit.

Some of the advantages of subscribing to this type of service are the obtaining of out-of-the-box tax content and support for the major countries, constant automatic updates, and better audit support.

Before you can set up service subscriptions, you have to complete one or more of these tasks:

- setting up tax regimes,
- setting up party tax profiles, and
- setting up configuration options.

The two providers mentioned in this book offer a certified version of their products prepackaged with Oracle E-Business Suite Release 12. The product database objects of each tax-service provider reside on the Oracle EBS installation CD as a single zip file. A one-step automated process facilitates installation without any user intervention, replacing the multistep process previously required (which is still supported as an alternative).

Complete the following steps in the order shown to implement the prepackaged version of a tax-service provider's product:

1. Run the installation driver script.
2. Set profile options.
3. Set up lookup codes for tax-exemption reasons.
4. Set up provider-specific tax regimes and taxes.
5. Set up service subscriptions.
6. Install client-side tax-service-provider software.
7. Load tax jurisdictions and rates.
8. Set up tax accounts.
9. Turn on address validation.

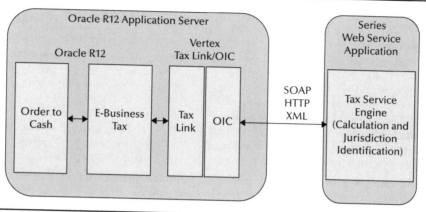

FIGURE 13-6 *Data flow between Oracle E-Business Suite R12 and Vertex*

10. Set up jurisdiction codes and other optional fields (if desired).

11. Verify the tax-service provider's implementation.

Figures 13-6 and 13-7 show a high-level overview of how these two tax solutions are integrated with E-Business Suite.

In Table 13-2 you will see some differences in how the two tax-service providers manage the information with E-Business Tax.

If your company decides to use the tax-service providers, you will have the ability to complete your tax returns using the out-of-the-box reports available within E-Business Tax. Reconciliation

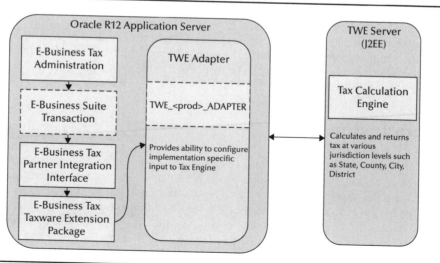

FIGURE 13-7. *Integration of Taxware and Oracle E-Business Suite R12*

Vertex

Vertex uses the term *geocode* for tax-jurisdiction codes. The geocode is an internal code that is understood by the Vertex integration. The geocode is a nine-digit numeric code that is composed of a two-digit state code, followed by a three-digit county code, followed by a four-digit code to identify a tax jurisdiction within a city; for example: 12-345-6789.

The Vertex integration uses the Vertex GeoCoder API to retrieve the geocode for a customer ship-to if a geocode is not available on the customer address and cannot be retrieved from the E-Business Tax jurisdiction setup. If the GeoCoder API cannot find a geocode, an error is raised.

Taxware

The Taxware jurisdiction code is a nine-digit alphanumeric code. It is composed of the two-character state code, the five-digit ZIP code, and a unique two-digit numeric code. For example, the code CA9411401 is composed of the state code CA for California, the zip code 94114, and the Taxware jurisdiction code 01.

The Taxware integration retrieves the jurisdiction code from either the customer address or the E-Business Tax jurisdiction setup. If a jurisdiction code is not found, then 00 is passed as the jurisdiction code to the tax-calculation API.

TABLE 13-2. *Integration Points Between Tax-Service Providers and Oracle E-Business Tax for United States*

among the different components of this tax footprint—including E-Business Tax, Oracle General Ledger, and the tax-service provider's repository—must be done.

The process for all Oracle Receivables transactions—for tax purposes—starts with storing all the transactions in the repository of the tax-service provider when the tax engine calculates the amounts. After that, the transactions are processed through the Subledger Accounting into General Ledger, which will allow users to reconcile total tax amounts of Oracle Receivables transactions by state to Oracle General Ledger. The total tax amounts by state reported by the Tax Reconciliation Report should reconcile to each state tax liability account held in Oracle General Ledger. Total tax amounts by state can be reconciled to the tax-service provider's repository by running the Vertex Sales Tax Register or Taxware Sales/Use Tax report.

Conclusion

Oracle E-Business Tax is a new application simplifying and improving the tax-setup process. This new application created with Release 12 continues Oracle's strategy of streamlining the setup process of E-Business Suite, providing non-IT personnel an innovative user interface capable of handling a single-point solution for managing transaction-based tax requirements.

The multiplicity of options to support the legal requirements for local organizations and companies with legal entities around the world is vast. E-Business Tax also includes a new data model comprising a system architecture that models all the aspects of the tax engine and allows global configuration and scalability for country-specific tax content.

The capability of subscribing to tax-service providers allows organizations the advantage of improving operational efficiencies, automating manual processes, and avoiding mistakes during the tax definitions, which can have important legal implications.

CHAPTER
14

Oracle Projects

he scope of information management for modern corporations is growing from the accounting core. Oracle Projects has been designed for a huge variety of project-oriented businesses. Key performance indicators such as profit margin are often measured by product, customer, or customer type and rolled up into division, region, and company. The project dimension allows a company to do the same by contract. It might sell a service such as facilities management or consulting. It might sell infrastructure setup such as optical-fiber laying. Projects also might not be billable to clients but rather be a way of controlling the cost of a program, perhaps retraining staff after a technology change or managing the commissioning of a new production facility.

The key dimension is time; a project is time bounded. It has an objective or set of objectives to which a value and usually a budget have been attached. The goals of using project costing and billing software are to

- monitor the costs against budget quickly enough that remedial action can be taken if necessary,
- account for direct and indirect costs,
- show the profit margin accruing from the project, and
- show costs and revenues accumulated to date (other subledgers and the General Ledger are limited to reporting by accounting period).

Enterprise project management involves the collection and coordination of corporate resources (such as people, money, and hard assets) to accomplish a predefined scope of work in a scheduled time frame and budget.

The Oracle Projects suite enables project managers to effectively oversee their projects, assess progress against predetermined milestones and budgets, staff their projects with appropriate talent, and quickly generate a wide variety of reports. It also helps virtual and globally distributed project teams to efficiently communicate, collaborate, and complete tasks in time. Oracle Projects also gives corporate executives the ability to quickly see how projects are performing across the enterprise.

Oracle has made a big investment in the Oracle Projects suite, combining all the needs into a set of products that can enable a company to track and manage its projects from different angles. Some of the modules that are part of the Projects suite are

- **Oracle Project Costing**   Provides an integrated cost-management solution for all projects and activities within an enterprise. Run across multiple currencies and organizations, it acts as a central repository of project plans and transactions, processes project costs, and creates corresponding accounting entries to satisfy corporate-finance requirements.

- **Oracle Project Billing**   Enables enterprises to simplify customer invoicing, streamline corporate cash flow, and measure the profitability of contract projects. It provides features to review project invoices online and analyze project profitability and corporate impact of project work.

- **Oracle Project Resource Management**   Empowers an enterprise to make better use of the single most critical asset: people. It enables efficient coordination of project resource needs, profitability, and organization utilization through the location and deployment of qualified resources to projects across the enterprise. It is integrated with Oracle HRMS to efficiently deploy human resources in various projects across enterprise.

- **Oracle Project Management** Enables integrated project planning, tracking, and real-time project-performance management. With Oracle Project Management, project managers can proactively plan and forecast their projects, manage change and performance in real time, focus on desired project outcomes rather than data management, and make better decisions with less effort.

- **Oracle Project Collaboration** Provides a secure and intuitive user interface through which a team member of a project can see assigned tasks, issues, deliverables, and other project-related information. It has structured workspaces such as the Team Member home page, with the help of which team members can work together more efficiently, make more effective decisions, and deliver superior results faster.

- **Oracle Project Portfolio Analysis** Leverages the rich project-management functionality of Oracle Projects to facilitate evaluation and collection of projects in a portfolio. It uses financial criteria, strategic goals, and information on available funds to help you evaluate, prioritize, and select the right projects to match your business objectives. It provides a full range of portfolio-analysis reports, charts, and graphs.

The Projects suite integrates with the other modules by sharing tables and through open interfaces. Shared information includes Human Resources organizations, employees, and Account Receivables customers. Cross-module exchanges include one concurrent process to populate the Oracle General Ledger interface tables with costs and another for revenue. Costs, which come primarily from Oracle Purchasing and Accounts Payable, can be recognized as commitments and obligations even before they are invoiced. Revenues can be recognized as they are earned, which can be earlier than they are billed. Costs that have been marked as project specific come into the module through the cost-transaction import interface.

Setup

Effort expended in the setup phase is well rewarded when the resulting business processes are straightforward and simple to operate. Ensure that you settle as many business requirements as possible early in the implementation, so that the subsequent test cycles have a solid base on which to start. The setup decisions you make determine the choices you have for the accounting and reporting. *AutoAccounting* is the automatic account-generation engine used by Oracle Projects to determine accounts for transactions that are imported into the module without accounts already attached and for transactions that originate from the module itself. In Release 12, with the introduction of Subledger Accounting (SLA), there is another level of accounting definitions that can overwrite the definitions of AutoAccounting, providing greater flexibility (see Chapter 4 for more details). The standard reporting tool for the module is the Project Status Inquiry screen. Both of these features are described in greater detail later in the chapter.

Organization Setup

Organization setup is one of the keystones of the E-Business Suite; Oracle Projects relies heavily on a carefully set-up organization structure. Organizations must be planned at a global level. They play a significant role in Oracle Human Resources, Oracle Inventory, Oracle Manufacturing, and several other modules. Oracle Projects uses the following types of organization classifications:

- business group,
- human-resources organization,

- operating unit,
- project/task-owning organization,
- project expenditure/event organization, and
- project invoice-collection organization.

The business group is the top of the organizational tree. There is a seeded Setup Business Group, which is best to use as the basis for the first real business group. There often is just one business group that represents the holding company. It holds the legislative rules (such as tax references) and terms of employment (such as default working hours) for employees.

For Oracle Projects, the business group is the owner of the *project-burdening* organization hierarchy, which defaults the *burdening multipliers* for an organization. Burdening is the process of allocating overhead costs to projects—for example, stationery or administrative office costs. One key constraint needs to be understood when designing the business-group structure: employees in one business group cannot charge cost items to a project owned by another. So in the case where employees charge their time to projects for other companies in the group, those companies need to be in the same business group. Employees are assigned to work in human-resources organizations. These can be one and the same as the project-owning organizations (which themselves may also be operating units) so that labor can be charged to projects without the need to set up cross charging.

Organizations can also be set up to own projects and tasks. This relationship can be used to drive the accounting (via AutoAccounting) and reporting. It is assigned to an operating unit (and therefore the user's Responsibility) through the organization-hierarchy branch. The introduction of Multi-Org Access Control (MOAC) in Release 12, enables companies that have implemented a Shared Service operating model to efficiently process business transactions for an unlimited number of operating units within a single application responsibility. By default, users can see a project only if they are set up as a key member of it. Project expenditure/event organizations can incur expenditure and create revenue events for a project. AutoAccounting can also use these organizations to derive account codes.

It is important to settle the organization structure across the whole implementation rather than on a module-by-module basis—it is a cross-functional exercise because organizations exist independently of their types. The organization setup resides in Oracle HR tables. These are accessible either through Oracle Human Resources (if it is installed) or through forms in the other modules if the install is set to "shared."

No license is required to use the HR shared tables when the other modules are installed. An organization is set up in the HR_ORGANIZATION_UNITS table regardless of which module's organization-setup screens are used, and organizations set up in one module are viewable in another, so that organization types can be added as shown in Figure 14-1. For example, rather than have two organizations set up—one by the Inventory setup team, the other as a project owner by the Projects setup team—which actually are the same business entity, set one up with both organization types assigned.

Once the organizations themselves have been created, the hierarchies can be put in place. This is important for Projects because it defines the relationships between business groups, operating units, and the project-specific organizations. For example, it is used to determine which projects a user can see from a Responsibility (which is linked to an operating unit). As with organizations, hierarchies are an HR concept that lives independently of any one module; thus they can be set up in either the Projects module or the HR module.

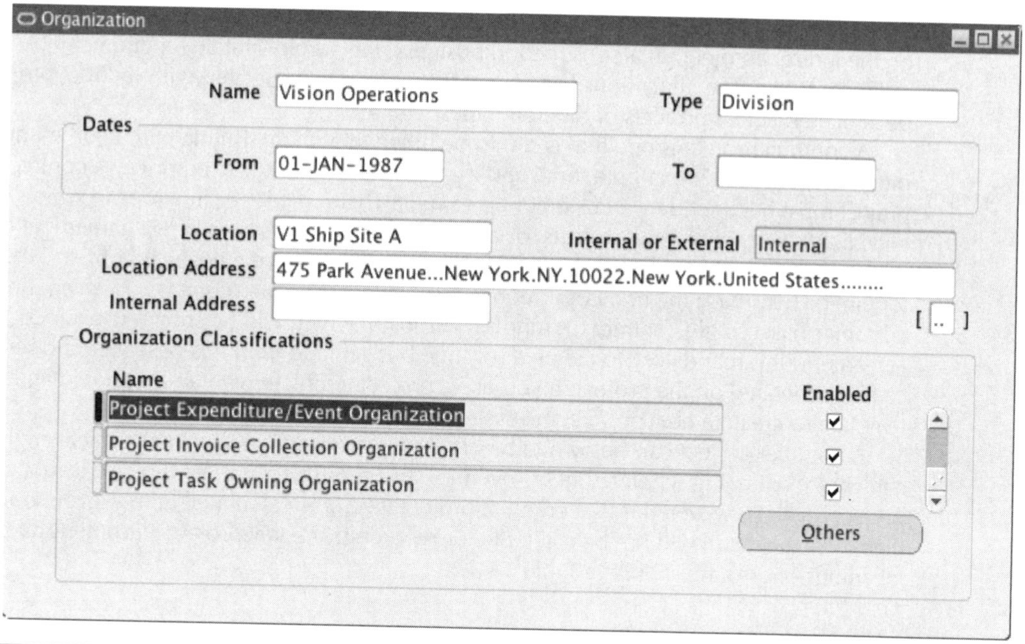

FIGURE 14-1.   *Organization-setup screen*

Oracle Projects uses employees as key members (such as project manager or quantity surveyor) and associates them with costs, which also need to be set up. There is an employee-and-assignment setup screen provided in the module in case HR is not installed. This version of the employee setup screen is more comprehensive than that found, for example, in Payables, because it can keep a history of the employees' assignments, which is significant for reporting. Employees are referenced in straight-time and overtime cost transactions; historic reporting of these could derive the position and job the employee held at the time.

Project Setup

A project can have one of three different type classes: capital, indirect, or contract. Project types can be user defined but must be associated with one of the three type classes.

A capital project is one in which the objective is to build something that will be capitalized as an asset. Oracle Projects is used to track your construction-in-process assets until you capitalize them by placing them in service, when they are interfaced to Oracle Assets. A project can result in one or more capital assets. These are defined at project level and then can be (but do not have to be) associated with tasks by using the grouping level. They can be associated with the whole project or with tasks at any level of the work-breakdown structure, so that expenditure items from many tasks will be included in the capital cost of a single asset when it is placed in service.

An indirect project is one to which overheads are assigned (which can subsequently be allocated to a number of other projects)—for example, a project office or depot. For example, in a consulting organization, an indirect project can be used to monitor sick leave, training, holidays, and other nonbillable activities. Each of these activities would be created as a task on the indirect project. In a construction business, the administrative function can be an indirect project. The allocations feature enables the costs associated with indirect projects to be allocated across projects of different types.

A contract project is one that is run to be billed to a client. Billing can be on many different models—for example, time and materials, cost plus, or fixed price. A contract project must be funded by a customer agreement. There might be situations in which it is expedient to set up several projects for a customer, in which case a single agreement can cover all of them. For example, a customer might want to have a hospital built and then run for him or her. These might be best reported on as two separate projects; however, the customer has a single contract for funding purposes, which will be shown in Projects as an agreement. It is mandatory to create a revenue budget, and until it is *baselined*, no revenue can be generated on the project. If you use a project template with an associated agreement template to create a new project, the system creates a Quick Agreement for you.

A contract project can be owned by one or more customers, either sharing a single agreement or having separate ones. Revenue can accrue either at the top task level or at the project level. However, if it is accrued at project level it is calculated at this level, too; therefore, the detail will not be available for reporting. The key project attributes and their meanings or uses are shown in Table 14-1.

Attribute	Meaning/Use
Project-owning organization	Organization against which revenue and expenditures are tracked.
Project type	Links to project-type class (indirect, capital, or contract); holds the costing, capitalization, and billing methods.
Status	User-defined statuses must be associated with one of six project-system statuses.
Start and completion dates	Period during which expenditures can be charged to a project.
Key members	Identified by role type, such as project manager or quantity surveyor; links to employee and identifies who can make changes to this project.
Customers	Links to customers set up in either Projects or Receivables.
Project classifications	Two-layer structure: class category and classification; used for reporting—for instance, for the category of "Public," classifications might be "Transport" and "Other"; can also used to determine accounting.

TABLE 14-1. *Key Project Attributes*

Task-Setup Attributes

Tasks are arranged into a multilevel hierarchical work-breakdown structure that is unlimited both in the number of levels and in the number of tasks. In practical terms, the depth of the structure is limited by reporting constraints: there are only 20 characters provided for reporting the fully qualified task number, including delimiters. Therefore, a construction project might have three top tasks of preliminaries, main building work, and retention-period activities. Under these there might be some middle-level tasks that group together the lowest-level tasks. It is these lowest-level tasks against which actual costs are accumulated. Revenue and billing only apply to the highest-level tasks.

The work-breakdown structure is a simple hierarchical list of tasks that make up the project. The top level of the structure is usually used to show the phases of the project, such as preliminaries, design, construction, testing, and commissioning. The lowest level is the level at which costs are collected. Therefore, this should be the level at which costs are realistically going to be managed.

Standardization in task numbering will help make project reporting more easily readable, because tasks will appear in alphanumeric order in the Project Status Inquiry screen and in standard reports. Task numbers such as 01 and 02 for top tasks, with 01.1, 01.2, 02.1, 02.2 as their subordinates, will add clarity. There is a 20-character task name and a 250-character description, so numbering tasks in this way does not have a detrimental effect on the richness of the information held. Note that task numbering might have an effect all the way through the business, in the case where project and task setup is pulled through from a third-party system; the naming and numbering conventions will have to change in the originating system.

Quick Entry Screens and Templates

Although a company might have only very few projects, the possible number in the software is unlimited; thus, efforts have been made to make the data entry as short as possible. Projects are entered using the Quick Entry screens, which derive much of the information from the project type and the template used. Projects can be created from another project or a template. The Quick Entry screens can be configured in the module-setup stage to suit the business; the use of templates adds defaulted values into many of the fields that have been chosen by the business as necessary.

A business that builds and maintains escalators may have two templates, one for new builds and one for maintenance, which default the Quick Entry screen data as shown in Table 14-2.

Note that Projects maintains the duration of a project in the template, so if the template project has a duration (end date minus start date) of 30 days, when a start date is entered in the Quick Entry screen, the end date will default to 30 days after it.

Transaction Setup

The crux of the Projects application is in tracking transactions against the project and tasks that are set up. There is a great deal of categorization required in Oracle Projects setup to support the wide array of project types and costing and billing scenarios. This makes the module extremely flexible, because reporting, budgeting, and accounting can all be tailored to business needs. Financial movements on a project are grouped as shown in Figure 14-2.

The bottom layer of this structure—event classification and expenditure-type class—are seeded values; the rest are user configurable (see the expenditure-type setup in Figure 14-3).

Quick Entry Field	New Build	Maintenance
Project Number	NB1	M1
Project Name	New Build	Maintenance
Project Start Date	Nov 2011	Nov 2011
Project Completion Date	Jul 2012	Nov 2016
Project Description	New Build	Maintenance
Project Status	Submitted	Submitted
Public Sector Indicator	No	No
Organization	Birmingham Engineering	Camberley Maintenance Depot
Customer Name	London Transport	London Transport
Key Members (by project role type)	Project manager—S. Jones Site manager—R. Atkinson	Project manager—R. Smith Maintenance manager—A. Capp
Project Classifications (by class category)	Contract type—new build Market sector—public	Contract type—maintenance Market sector—public
Distribution Rule (by project type)	Fixed Price—cost/event	Time and Materials—work/work

TABLE 14-2. *Quick Entry Screen*

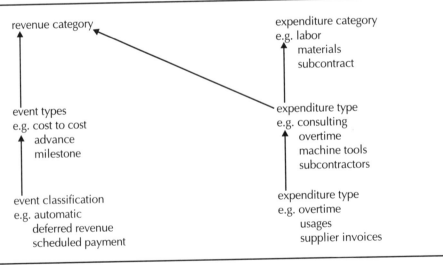

FIGURE 14-2. *Transaction categorization*

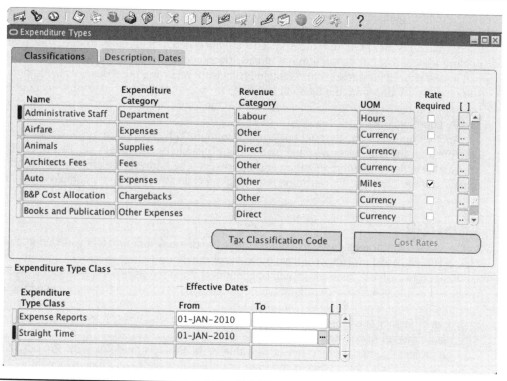

FIGURE 14-3. *Expenditure-type setup*

Transactions that come from other Oracle modules, such as inventory movements or supplier invoices, have expenditure type classes assigned. They will also have the expenditure type on them because project, task, and expenditure type are the three keys required on entry of these transactions in the source modules. Taken together, the six elements in this structure offer enough granularity to satisfy a rich variety of reporting needs.

An example of how part of this structure might be used is that straight time and overtime can be posted to the same GL account using the expenditure category of labor to determine the account in the AutoAccounting feature. In the Projects module, reporting by expenditure type can still allow effective management of the overtime bill.

One other part of transaction setup is resource groups and resources. This type of categorization is used for budgeting and for summarizing data for the Project Status Inquiry screen. There are three layers to this structure: resource lists, resource groups, and resources; resource groups are optional. When you undertake a project, you may use labor, services, materials, or equipment. Such expenditures can be reported in many ways. For example, you might report an invoice for materials by supplier, expenditure type, or organization; these are resource types, and the individual values are the resources (for example the suppliers or organizations themselves). You can optionally further group the resources into groups by expenditure category, revenue category, or organization. You can attach either the resources or the resource groups to a resource list. You attach resource lists to a project so you can use them to set the project budget and report actuals against budget in the Project Status Inquiry screen. You can use the same resource lists across similar projects to enable cross-project comparisons.

Transactions imported from other systems are allocated a transaction source. This source determines whether the transaction has already been accounted for in the GL. For example, you can import payroll transactions into Oracle Projects for reporting purposes but also import summary transactions into the General Ledger to be accounted. To avoid double accounting, set the transaction source to "pre-accounted" so that the transactions will not be picked up by AutoAccounting.

Another option on the transaction source is to import an expenditure organization that is different from the employee-owning organization. This means employees can be allocated to a project that is not in their organization and the cost can be tracked. The employee number is on the transaction record, so for reporting purposes you can still report on that employee's activities.

Costing

In the course of a project, costs accumulate; they are of many different types, depending on the type of project. Most projects will have the costs of purchases (whether bricks, subcontracted labor, or consumables). These costs will be identified at the requisition stage as being against the project (down to task and expenditure type). The Oracle Purchasing and Self-Service Procurement modules have the requisitioners enter project data in much the same way they enter General Ledger data. In fact, the project and task data, user identity, and type of goods are usually enough to generate the full Accounting Flexfield.

The project's commitment to buy is viewable in the Projects module, in the Project Status Inquiry screen. When the invoice is received, matched, and approved, the invoice lines are interfaced to Projects from Payables. At this point the commitment decreases by the amount of the invoice and the invoice appears in Projects as an expenditure item.

Many projects will use facilities such as computers and machine tools. The usage of these can be assigned to the project, task, and expenditure type. Usage logs can be prepared, signed off, and then keyed into Oracle Projects as expenditure items, as shown in Figure 14-4. Alternatively, they can be imported through the transaction-import interface. This is a standard Oracle open interface.

The same interface also supports the import of other types of costs—for example, labor costs. Very often these will be imported from a payroll or time-sheet system, which contains the project, task, and expenditure type that relates to each labor hour spent. These straight-time transactions are associated with employees who must be set up in Oracle's Human Resources tables (although they do not need to be linked to the project as key members). The HR tables are accessible through screens in Oracle Projects Responsibilities if Oracle HR is not installed as a full install. Unlike the HR screens in Payables, those in the Projects Responsibilities give assignment-history functionality so that the employee's job and location can be tracked (a useful feature for Projects reporting).

As the E-Business Suite is aimed at an increasingly globalized market, the capability to handle multiple currencies is important. Projects are no exception, and costs can be received in currencies other than the project currency (in which project reporting is done). There is a currency specified for the project (project currency), for the operating unit (functional currency), for the transaction (transaction currency), and for Self-Service Expenses (reimbursement currency).

Costs do not have to be just received or inputted to the system through the screen (shown in Figure 14-4). Oracle Projects can calculate indirect costs through the burdening concept. Burden costs are overhead estimates, as an alternative to allocating costs collected on indirect projects.

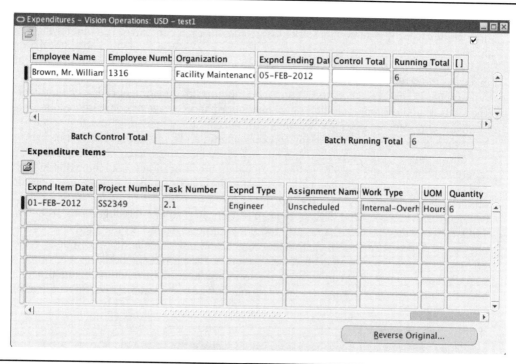

FIGURE 14-4.   *Expenditure input screen*

Burdening is sometimes known as *cost plus processing*. The burdened cost is the raw cost plus the burden cost. Raw costs, categorized by expenditure types, are grouped into cost bases.

For example, you can group expenditure types such as project management, consulting, and clerical into the office-labor cost base. Next, you define burden-cost codes to cover the types of overhead—for example, employee benefits and office space. Finally, you create a schedule to hold the multipliers for each of these cost codes—for example, 0.4 and 0.3, respectively. Say the labor cost base for a project amounts to 100; the system will calculate the burden cost as (100*0.4) + (100*0.3) = 70. Therefore, the burdened cost of the labor cost base will be 170.

You can account for burden costs separately, count them in with the raw costs, or not account for them at all but just use them as a management accounting tool.

Allocations

The burdening process estimates overhead costs and adds them to actual incurred costs. The allocations feature takes incurred costs that you decide are overheads (indirect) and allocates them to projects. Thus you can use the power of the Projects module to collect and report the details of costs on indirect projects, then allocate those costs to your capital and contract projects. You can also use allocations to charge specific fixed amounts or even General Ledger account balances. You can still use burdening even if you use allocations.

Take, for example, a telemarketing agency that has a four-floor office block. Each floor is dedicated to running marketing campaigns for different clients. The agency has set up a contract project for each client and a task under the project for each campaign. The rent for the office is posted to an account in the General Ledger. The agency defines a rule that allocates the rent paid on the office to the projects that use it. Cross charging has been enabled because the organization that rents the building is not the same as those that use it.

Another example is where the information-systems (IS) department runs as an indirect project. The IS costs are collated, including time-sheet information, usage of computer resources, and hardware and software costs. Only some of these costs are allocated—those that relate to the labor time of the support staff and the software-license costs, but not the hardware costs.

Allocations are rule based. You can create a number of rules, each of which performs a different set of allocations. Rules define from where the allocation is sourced, what its targets are, and how it is spread (see Figures 14-5 and 14-6). The source can be a project, just a task from a project—even restricted by resource—or a GL account.

Alternatively, a specified flat amount can be allocated among the target projects and tasks. The targets are specific projects or tasks (or whole projects excluding specified tasks). The allocation can be spread evenly across all projects and tasks specified or it can be targeted, say 80 percent to one project and 20 percent to another. The prorate method uses a resource as a basis for apportioning. This can be used to apportion the cost of a machine by the usage hours of each target project. If you want, you can set up an offset that creates a reversing expenditure

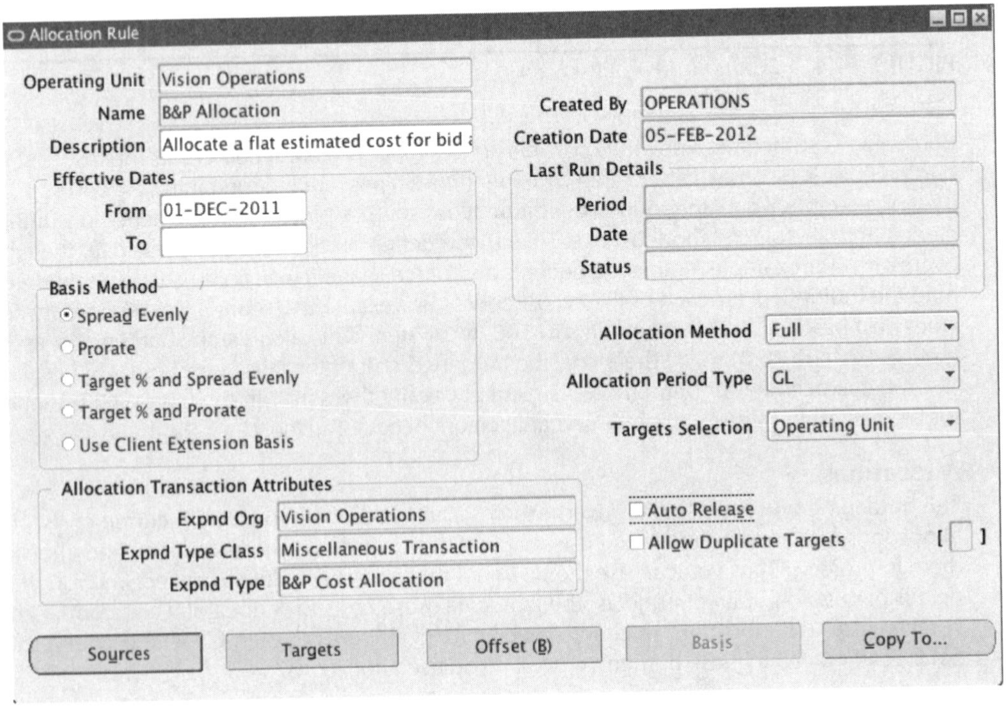

FIGURE 14-5. *Allocation-rule setup*

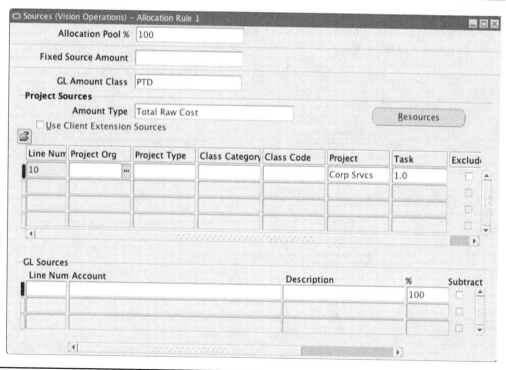

FIGURE 14-6.   *Allocation-rule-source setup*

(meaning a negative cost) on the designated project and task (which could be but does not have to be the same as the source). This can be useful to monitor the amounts allocated. (Note that it will decrease the total expenditure on the offset project.)

Once rules have been created for the allocations required, they can be built into Auto Allocation sets. A set is essentially a request set that can run a number of different project allocations, and GL mass allocations too. If you have many allocations in a set, you can have it run either in parallel or in a specific sequence as a step-down allocation set (aided by Oracle Workflow). When a set runs, it creates a draft release of allocation transactions for review. If you are not happy with the rule, there is an option to delete the draft, change the rule, and rerun. When you are happy with it, you run a release process that creates an expenditure batch with costs allocated to the target projects.

Billing

There are two functions that are only available to contract projects: accruing revenue and billing, for which the accounting flows are different. Accrued revenue passes from Projects straight to the General Ledger; the billing amount and details pass into Receivables on a draft invoice (which might be in the project currency or the project-customer currency). AutoAccounting provides the account-code combinations for both sides of the transaction. When the invoice has been processed in Receivables, the receivable amount is interfaced from there to the General Ledger.

Certain preconditions have to be met before revenue will be accrued on a project. Obviously it must be a contract project; it also needs to be in the correct status and have funding. It is possible to have a funding arrangement in place that imposes a hard limit, much like encumbrance does on purchasing, so no further revenue will accrue once the limit has been reached.

Revenue can be accrued against projects where billable work has been completed but not yet invoiced. Revenue accrual allows internal management reporting to show realistic figures for revenue and still honor the billing and invoicing schedule agreed upon with the project customer (see the following illustration).

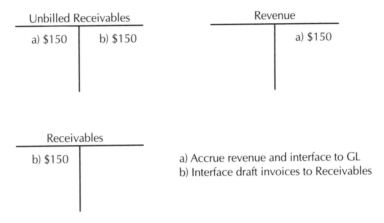

Contract projects can accrue revenue using several different models. You define which one is to be used at project definition by way of the project type and distribution rule, as shown in Table 14-3.

As you can see from the table, there are two different ways of accruing revenue: by expenditure item or by event. These methods map to the different types of project billing

Distribution Rule	Meaning
Cost/Cost	Accrue revenue and bill using the ratio of actual cost to budgeted cost (percent spent).
Cost/Event	Accrue revenue using the ratio of actual cost to budgeted cost (percent spent); bill based on events.
Cost/Work	Accrue revenue using the ratio of actual cost to budgeted cost (percent spent); bill as work occurs.
Event/Event	Accrue revenue and bill based on events.
Event/Work	Accrue revenue based on events; bill as work occurs.
Work/Event	Accrue revenue as work occurs; bill based on events.
Work/Work	Accrue revenue and bill as work occurs.

TABLE 14-3. *Distribution Rules*

available. Expenditure items on a contract project can be billable, and the system calculates how much revenue to accrue based on different formulas, which depend on the distribution rule.

Time-and-materials projects accrue revenue for the expenditure items (labor and materials) purchased. The amounts charged are determined by schedules of bill rates. These can be specific to employees, set up on the jobs they hold, or associated with nonlabor resources like machine tools or computer equipment.

Fixed-price projects can be set up to accrue as they spend. On the cost/cost rule, the project accrues a sum related to the percentage of total burdened costs that have been spent so far, calculated as in the following illustration.

Actual burdened cost to date = $5,000   Total budgeted burdened cost = $20,000
Total budgetet revenue = $100,000   Event revenue to date = $0
Revenue previously accrued = $15,000

The formula for calculating the increment of revenue to accrue would be:

(5,000/20,000 * (100,000 - 0)) - 15,000 = $10,000   (provided there is funding available if a hard limit is being used).

Percent-complete projects are another way of accruing revenue for a fixed price. You can enter percent complete against any task in the work-breakdown structure, but revenue accrues against top tasks or at the project level, whichever you have specified. You record the percent complete and the as-of date, and when you come to generate revenue, the system will calculate the percentage of the final budgeted figure based on the percent complete of each billable task.

Events can be used to do all or part of the billing for a project. Events can drive the revenue and billing for a milestone-driven project or can be used if the customer pays a performance bonus. They can be manually inputted and thus give control to the user over the revenue and billing amounts separately.

Intercompany Projects

Projects do not necessarily respect the organizational boundaries that divide a business. For example, you might have a contract with a global customer to do oil-rig refurbishment. You will resource the project from several regional offices but want to keep it as one project to manage the costs and reporting to the client. As you charge work from the regional organizations to the project owner (say, Engineering HQ), you can choose from two methods (if you want it done in Projects; otherwise it can be done in either the General Ledger or a third-party system).

The Eastern Region is in the same legal entity but a different operating unit from Engineering HQ. It does not want to invoice for the work it does, so it can use the borrowed-and-lent method. It sets up a transfer-pricing schedule for the work it does on the project. Eastern Region then charges its time and materials to the project, task, and expenditure type. The transactions will show Eastern Region as the expenditure organization. The Distribute Borrowed and Lent Amounts process determines the transfer-price amounts and the accounting entries. This process credits the Eastern Region costs and debits Engineering HQ's costs. Finally, as the provider, Eastern Region runs the Interface Cross Charge Distributions to GL process that interfaces those entries to GL.

The Central America Region is in a different legal entity from Engineering HQ. Note that it still must be in the same business group and share the same GL and project-accounting calendars. It requires physical invoices to be generated, so it uses the intercompany-billing method. Engineering HQ will be set up to allow charges from other operating units and to receive internal billing. You set up the list of eligible provider operating units. The transactions start life being charged by the region to the receiver organization, as with the borrowed-and-lent method.

AutoAccounting enables you to specify cost-reclassification accounts during the cost-distribution process. So for example, costs on the job charged by Central America go to a Work in Process (WIP) account but are reclassified as a labor expense, because this work in process is not an asset on the region's balance sheet. The Central America Region now runs the Generate Intercompany Invoices process. After their approval and release, the invoices are interfaced to Receivables (from where they can be printed).

The Tieback Invoices from Receivables process is used to create the corresponding supplier invoices in the Payables interface table for Engineering HQ, which can import them. After approval, these Payables invoices are interfaced to Projects, as they are coded to a project, task, expenditure type, and expenditure organization.

Interproject Billing

The principles of intercompany billing are also applicable to projects within the same organization. For example, a design house might want to manage individual design jobs as separate projects for cost control and reporting. However, their client might be a large automobile manufacturer that is unlikely to want to be billed for each one individually; therefore, the design house can either bill from one of the projects involved or set up a consolidation project. The project that bills the client is set up as the receiver, and the others as the providers. This is effectively a subcontracting relationship.

The providers generate Receivables invoices; then the Tieback Invoices from Receivables process creates payables invoices for the receivers. These payables invoices will be interfaced into the Oracle Projects module associated with the receiver project, task, and expenditure types. On the basis of these charges on the receiving project, external invoices can be generated to send to the customer that cover the activities of all the providing projects.

AutoAccounting

Oracle Projects is a projects subledger. It receives transactions from surrounding business processes that relate to the projects set up within it. These transactions might include the following:

- purchase requisitions for raw materials, consumables, or subcontracts;
- issues of the same from a warehouse;
- labor hours spent on project tasks;
- invoices received from suppliers for the supply of goods and services related to the project; and
- hours of use of a specialist machine—for example, to lay railway track.

Transactions that originate from outside Projects but within the E-Business Suite have their accounting set in the originating module. Purchase requisitions are accounted for by the account generator in purchasing. The account generator can use the project, task, expenditure type, item, and requestor to determine the accounts. Inventory transactions pick up their accounting when the transaction is created.

Labor hours generally come from a third-party product; they can be preaccounted, with summary transactions sent to GL separately, or can be accounted for by AutoAccounting. Oracle Payables accounts for supplier invoices. Usage logs can be preaccounted or you can use AutoAccounting, the automatic account-generation engine used in Oracle Projects.

Batch processes do the bulk of the accounting work in Oracle Projects. The main areas are distributing costs, accruing revenue, and creating draft invoices. These processes use functions to determine which accounts should be debited and credited for a given individual cost or revenue line. The functions themselves are further subdivided into function transactions. For example, there is a function called "Labor Cost Account Function." This is divided into function transactions, including

- private billable labor;
- all labor;
- private nonbillable labor;
- capital, all;
- public billable labor;
- contract, all;
- public nonbillable labor; and
- indirect, all.

Each of these function transactions relates to a single Accounting Flexfield combination. They are optional, depending on whether the business wants to distinguish between private- and public-sector work in the GL or report within Projects based on project classifications. If no distinctions are required, the "All Labor" transaction can be enabled, all the others disabled, and only that one mapped in AutoAccounting.

The structure used to determine the combination is rule based and user defined. It can use parameters (Rule A in Figure 14-7), SQL statements (Rule B in Figure 14-7), or constants (Rule C in Figure 14-7). You assign the rules to the function transactions; therefore, when Projects runs a process such as Distribute Labor Costs and it needs to find the labor-cost account for a labor-cost record, it uses one of the function transactions, which in turn uses rules to determine each segment value of the code combination.

In Figure 14-7, the business wants to determine the labor-cost account for all labor in the same way. It has a three-segment Accounting Flexfield (company, cost center, and account). Rule A derives the company segment from the expenditure organization on the labor-cost transaction. Rule B takes the value in a Descriptive Flexfield on the transaction and puts it in the cost-center segment. Rule C sets the account segment to a constant value of 5500.

This is undoubtedly a difficult structure to conceptualize; however, it is vital to do so because AutoAccounting is the engine that drives the accounting done by Projects. During the design phase of a Projects implementation, the challenge is to document the business requirements and the AutoAccounting solution so that business representatives will be confident in signing up to it.

By the time you perform integration or system testing, you need to decide the function transactions, rule assignments, rules, and segment pairings (associating rules with Accounting Flexfield segments). This way the test cycle will test the AutoAccounting functionality and you will have realistic postings in the General Ledger, which will provide a sense of security for the business representatives involved.

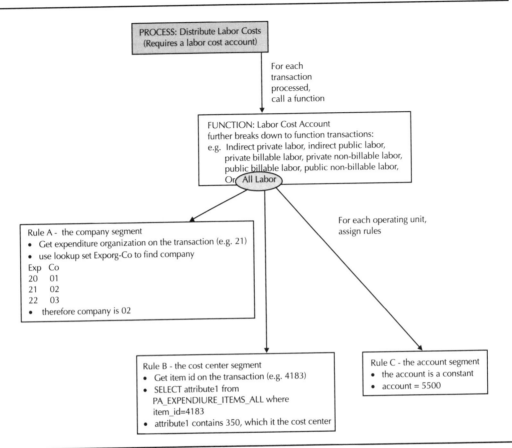

FIGURE 14-7. *AutoAccounting structure*

Project-Processing Cycle

The complexity of setup and the range of transactions that are inputted in Oracle Projects means the software has a great deal of number crunching to do to convert the raw transactions into costs and revenue. Therefore, it has been designed with a large number of batch-processing steps. For example, when an expenditure batch is inputted, it might include the number of hours of machine usage. The system records the raw data but the costs are not applied until the Distribute Usage Costs program is run to distribute usage costs; AutoAccounting determines the accounts required.

For example, the Distribute Usage and Miscellaneous Costs process takes the quantity on the transaction, applies the raw-cost rate from the nonlabor-resource setup, calculates the burden cost, and adds it to the raw cost to get the burdened cost. It then uses the usage-cost-account function to determine the appropriate cost account to add to the cost-transaction record.

The transaction sources for the costs being interfaced from other modules are seeded as preaccounted. However, if adjustments can be done in Projects (such as on supplier invoices), these will need to be accounted for by AutoAccounting; therefore, there is a Distribute Supplier Invoice Adjustment Costs process. Once the various types of cost are distributed and accounted for, they can be interfaced to the General Ledger.

The revenue side is also controlled by concurrent processes. Cost transactions can also be a source of revenue, so there is a Generate Draft Revenue process, which calculates the revenue available on each cost line and revenue event and determines the revenue accounts.

When the costs have been distributed and the draft revenue generated, you run the Interface Revenue to GL, Generate Draft Invoice, and the Interface Invoices to Receivables processes. These do the accounting for unbilled receivables, receivables, and unearned revenue.

The following is a list of some of the processes that use AutoAccounting. This is just a subset that is available to be run—it might be that a particular implementation will not use processes such as expense reports or burdening. The list shows the way the module is organized.

- Distribute Labor Costs

- Interface Expense Reports to Payables

- Interface Labor Costs to GL

- Distribute Usage Costs

- Generate Draft Revenue

- Interface Usage and Miscellaneous Costs to GL

- Interface Revenue to GL

- Distribute Total Burdened Costs

- Distribute Expense Reports

- Interface Total Burdened Costs to GL

Another process is required to populate the Project Status Inquiry summary tables. This should be done regularly (possibly every night), because runs will take much longer and use more computing resources if the frequency is reduced, therefore potentially squeezing the rest of your nightly batch-processing window.

The other regular set of processes is the interface between Oracle Projects and the other Oracle EBS modules. There is an option to submit processes together in a streamlined process, much like a request set. There are two types of these—"PRC:Submit Interface Streamline Processes" and "PRC:Submit Project Streamline Processes"—within which there are many options.

Reporting

To get the most out of the effort of loading all your data into a relational database such as Oracle's, think about reporting requirements early on in the implementation. You will gain the most from your information if it is in buckets large enough to give valid statistical comparisons. For example, if one of your lowest-level tasks in testing is called "client test" in some projects, "business test" in others, and "user test" in yet more, reporting on it will not reveal any trends. However, if you insist on one task name for all like projects (embodied in a template), the analysts or managers with responsibilities across several projects will soon see trends and exceptions.

Project Status Inquiry (PSI) Screen

One of the most powerful reporting utilities for everyday use is the Project Status Inquiry form. It is built to use a series of accumulation tables that are populated by a batch process called Update Project Summary Amounts. This means that although information on projects is not

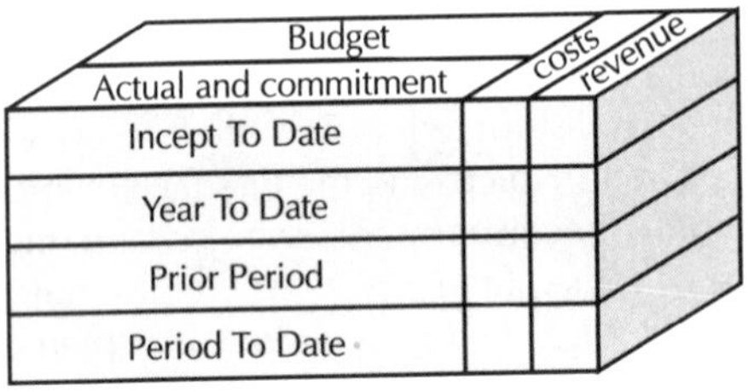

FIGURE 14-8. *Altering the PSI column definitions*

reflected in this screen in real time, the screen does not need to do online calculations and therefore is quick to use.

The process populates four time dimensions—inception to date, year to date, prior period, and period to date. In these dimensions, budget and actual figures are shown (and commitments), for both costs and revenue (see Figure 14-8). All of this is held within the structure of project, task, and resource. The power of the PSI screen is that it provides a drill-down feature from the project, through the task structure, to resources, even to the revenue and cost transactions themselves. The Export to Excel function makes this a good tool for analysis and presentation. You can use the folder technology on the PSI screen to alter the available data so you can focus the information for particular audiences.

There is a series of database views that display data from the underlying summary tables. The top layer of views is user customizable in the Project Status Inquiry setup screen (see Figure 14-9) by the use of SQL statements such as the condition-processing statement DECODE. Clearly this kind of customization should be constrained as far as possible to the implementation phase of a project; during live running, you need to provide consistency of reporting over time to make good use of comparative information.

In the default folders there are 27 columns for the project and task levels, and 29 columns for the resource. These include the database columns, such as actual and budget cost and actual and budget revenue, and calculated fields such as margin and estimate to complete (in financial and hours of labor terms).

Oracle Discoverer for Projects

Oracle Discoverer provides some pre-built business areas as a reporting solution for Oracle Projects, called Oracle Project Discoverer, which consists on:

- **Staffing** The staffing business area provides general staffing information about resources, projects, and organizations. From a supply perspective, you can identify information regarding resource and organization capacity, availability, overcommitment, and overall schedule through these folders. From a demand perspective, you can identify information regarding project and organization requirements.

- **Financials** The financials business area provides information about the project pipeline.

- **Competence** The competence business area provides information about the competence of the resources.

- **Utilization** The utilization business area brings a Business Intelligence model composed of dimension and data folders. Some dimension folders provided by Oracle Projects

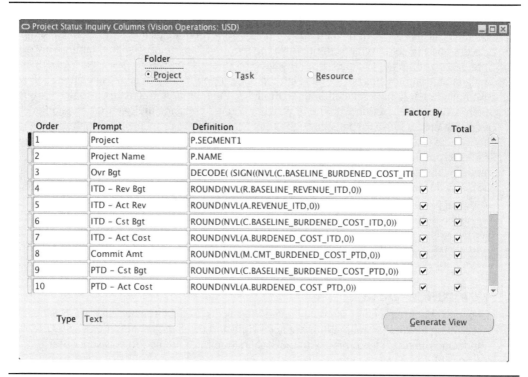

FIGURE 14-9. *PSI dimensions*

Discoverer are Person, Work Type, Job, Operating Unit, Utilization Organization, Supervisor Hierarchy, Time Periods, Number of Trend Periods, and Time Trend. Data folders contain the resource and organization utilization information. The following data folders are provided: Manager-Resource Utilization, Manager-Resource-Worktype Utilization, Organization Utilization, Organization-Job Utilization, Organization-Resource Utilization, Organization-Worktype Utilization, and Organization-Resource-Worktype Utilization.

These reports, or also called workbooks within Oracle Discoverer, use data from the End User Layer, which is essentially a series of database views that provide simplification of the transaction-processing tables for reporting. Because Projects tables have been included in the End User Layer, you can add your own custom reports to the workbooks without the need for a developer.

NOTE
The latest Oracle Discoverer release is 11g; some parameters in Oracle Projects Discoverer are only available when using Discoverer 4i, so you will have to validate the reports, and in some cases a customization will be needed.

Integration with Other Modules

Oracle Projects can be implemented as a stand-alone module, as it has sufficient GL setup screens and HR setup screens to populate the required data in those shared tables. However, its integration with other Oracle E-Business Suite modules is very strong (see Figure 14-10). It is this integration that provides businesses with the biggest opportunity to increase efficiency. For example, in a full implementation of all modules, the time used to create customers is reused on every separate transaction with them, whether you are checking their credit status in Receivables, receiving orders for spare parts through Order Management, or receiving a contract project.

Oracle Projects casts the additional dimension of project on the rest of the E-Business Suite. As noted previously, projects are different types of entities from those the standard financial-reporting tool—the General Ledger—is set up to handle. Projects are of limited duration; they can be divided into tasks that are far more granular than is usual in Ledger reporting; and inception-to-date reporting is very important for projects.

Integration takes two forms: some data are viewable from one module to another; some data are passed in batches between modules. All modules in the suite refer to Oracle Projects to validate project information. Many use project and task data as input to Automatic Account Generation. See Figure 14-10 for the complete picture of module integration.

Reference Data

General Ledger referencing is implemented in Projects as it is elsewhere in the E-Business Suite. Accounting Flexfield combinations are accessible and the standard APIs are used by the interfacing processes to comply with cross-validation rules. In the Projects super-user Responsibility you can see the GL setup screens.

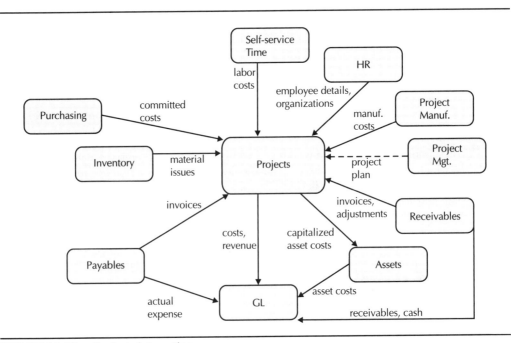

FIGURE 14-10. *Projects integration*

Human Resources information is referenced extensively in Projects, and you can see some of the screens in the Projects super-user Responsibility, although if you have HR installed you will not be able to use those screens, as more complete versions are available in the HR Responsibilities. The organizations, organization hierarchy, and employee setup are all shared between Projects and HR. It is particularly in this area that a coordinated approach in the implementation phase will have benefits.

In a business organized on project lines, it is important for the entry of data against projects to start right at the beginning of the transaction flow. Employees working on a project will book their time to it. They might use Oracle Self-Service Time to do that, in which case when they do their time sheet online they will specify the project details, which are validated on entry. Self-Service Time is a Web application that uses the same technology stack as Self-Service Procurement and Expenses. Users can book their time to projects either online or on an Excel spreadsheet that is subsequently uploaded.

Workflow is used to approve time sheets (or it can be set to automatic by a profile option, if preferred). The core functionality of the Workflow application has a long pedigree internally in Oracle and delivers significant efficiency benefits. Because it can be implemented across the Internet, there is no client software to maintain and it can be accessible from any Internet-connected browser, without the plug-in required when using the screens of the E-Business Suite professional interface.

While using Purchasing and Self-Service Procurement, users will make project-related purchases, such as materials or subcontracts. When the invoices are received for the materials or subcontracts, the users can match the invoice to the purchase order and the project-related information will be carried through (without the option to overwrite it in Payables). They will issue materials from an inventory to a project and might have manufacturing costs that are associated with a project. The standard key on these transactions is the project number, task number, expenditure type, and expenditure organization. This is because they all use the same entry point to Projects—the transaction interface.

The Transaction Interface

The same interface is used in the E-Business Suite to collate costs from other modules and external third-party systems. It distinguishes among the various sources by the transaction source. New transaction sources can be set up, but when you do that you will see that those used by the intermodule processes are seeded and unchangeable.

The main features of the transaction import interface are as follows:

- loads transactions to project, task, and expenditure type;

- can load transactions from different expenditure organizations;

- can reference, on transactions, employees set up in HR (the interface validates them);

- can load multicurrency costs; currency can be the same as the project or the functional currency of the expenditure operating unit;

- populates a single open interface table: PA_TRANSACTION_INTERFACE_ALL;

- loads by batches; if one record in a batch errors, the whole batch errors;

- can load transactions whether accounted or not (determined by transaction source); those accounted must have code combinations and will not be processed by AutoAccounting;

- can load transactions whether costed or not (determined by transaction source); costed transactions must have a cost, whereas uncosted ones have only quantities and will have costs calculated by the appropriate distribution process;

- can load costs whether burdened or not; a cost can be already burdened or a separate transaction can hold the burden cost to be added to the raw cost; and

- has a Review Transactions window in which errored transactions can be corrected for reprocessing (note that errors should be corrected in the source system wherever possible).

See Figure 14-11 for the whole process flow.

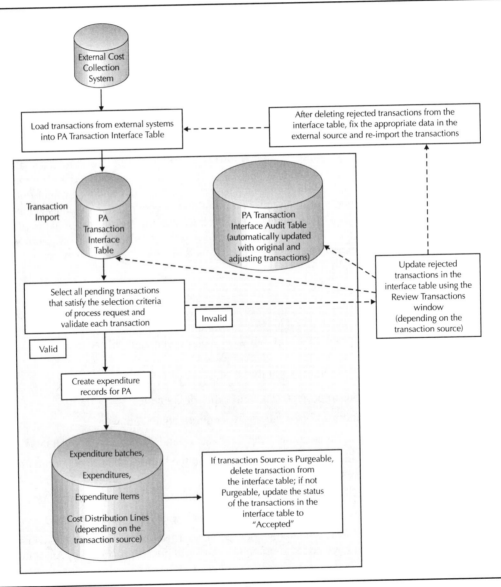

FIGURE 14-11. *Transaction-interface process flow*

Integration with Oracle Workflow

There are two workflow processes out of the box for Oracle Projects. One is to control the change of project statuses (see Figure 14-12), the other the baselining of budgets. When a user creates a project and submits it for approval, Oracle Workflow will route the approval to the user's supervisor (as defined on the employee record). If approved by the supervisor, Workflow changes the status. A similar process works for changing a budget from working to baselined.

Interfaces from Oracle Projects

Oracle Projects interfaces master data to the full E-Business Suite for validation. It passes transaction data to the General Ledger, Receivables, Assets, and Payables modules. To the General Ledger, Projects passes costs and revenue (including unbilled and unearned). There are three parts to the process: interface, import to GL, and tieback. In the interface process, Projects collects all the transactions that have been cost, revenue, or cross-charge distributed that are eligible for interfacing and loads them into the GL_INTERFACE table.

The GL date of the transaction is the end date of the earliest GL open or future period after the PA date. The PA date is the end date of the project-accounting period in which costs, revenue, and invoices are accounted for. AutoAccounting determines the relevant accounts.

Once transactions are in the interface table, GL import is run and creates GL journals, with a source of Projects and journal-entry categories of

- Labor cost,
- Usage cost,
- Total burdened cost,
- Borrowed and lent,

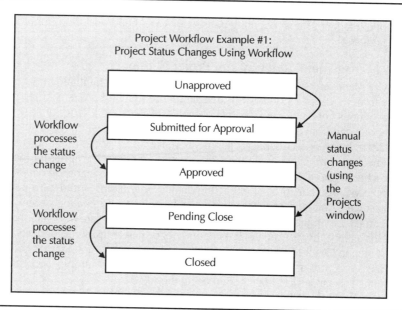

FIGURE 14-12. *The project-status workflow*

- Provider cost reclassification, and

- Revenue.

The tieback process is then used to print reconciliation reports to track the interfaced records. There are audit reports that can also help with this task.

The interface to Receivables works similarly in that there are three stages: the Generate Draft Invoices process, which populates the RA_INTERFACE_LINES_ALL table; the Receivables autoinvoice run; and a tieback process. All three can be run using a streamline process. Oracle Projects uses seeded values for the batch source, transaction types, and line-ordering and line-grouping rules; these should not be changed in any way. After the autoinvoice program runs, the tieback process reports back on which records were successfully interfaced and which not, and also creates the lines in the Payables interface tables for interproject and intercompany charges.

The interface to Oracle Assets takes the cost lines created in Oracle Projects against an asset and sends them to the assets module when the asset being constructed goes into service. All the costs associated with the construction-in-process item need to be interfaced to the General Ledger from Oracle Projects; then the date placed in service can be set in the Capital Projects screen (in the Projects module).

The minimum information for the asset is to have a corporate asset book associated with it. You can either assign the category, location, depreciation-expense account, and asset number in the Capital Projects screen or, after the next step—interface to Oracle Assets—in the Oracle Assets Mass Additions screen. The process credits the construction-in-process account (to which the asset-related costs had been posted) and debits the asset-cost account. Projects prints reports on the interface to Assets; however, after the Post Mass Additions interface has run, there is no tieback report. If further expenses attached to the asset come in after the transfer, you can post them to Oracle Assets separately and merge them there with the original asset.

As an alternative to using Self-Service Expenses, you can input expense reports into Oracle Projects. To track and pay these expense reports, Projects interfaces them to the Payables Invoice Import open interface. The accounting transactions are then transferred from Payables to the General Ledger.

Activity Management Gateway and Project Connect

The Activity Management Gateway (AMG) is a set of APIs that facilitate loading Oracle Projects with data from third-party systems. It is a separate product and is licensed separately. Unlike open interfaces, it does not have a separate set of tables; instead it is a series of package procedures a developer can call from a custom program, which provide the validation that is done in other circumstances by an open interface (like the Receivables Customer interface).

The developer still needs to do the work to create a custom wrapper for the APIs, but within it just passes the required parameters to the AMG procedure and loads the data into the application tables. The AMG also has APIs for extracting data for interfacing out to third-party systems. Thus percent complete and earned value can be sent back to the originating system.

You can create projects with or without agreements, or update or delete them (if there are no transactions against them). You can create, update, or delete tasks and budgets. There is a Control Actions screen in Oracle Projects that gives you control over which actions can be undertaken in the module on records imported from third-party systems; for example, you can prevent users from deleting tasks that have been added using the AMG.

The AMG can be used as a legacy-data conversion utility or in live running. For data conversion it is a useful way of quickly uploading a very large number of projects and tasks. It has been used in the field to load hundreds of thousands of tasks across thousands of projects.

You should remember that developer skills are still required to build the AMG APIs into custom programs. The skills required are PL/SQL and an understanding of the EBS environment.

Project Connect links Oracle Projects with Microsoft Project via the AMG APIs. This is often an enticing possibility, marrying the graphical representation of the popular project-management software with the ERP connectedness of the E-Business Suite. However, it must be approached carefully, because it requires disciplines in a PC-based environment that might not be currently prevalent. From Oracle Projects you can send a standing data catalogue including class categories and class codes, which the Microsoft product will then use during project setup. During the life of a project, tracking information can be sent from Microsoft Project to Oracle Projects, and the two can be periodically synchronized.

Client Extensions

Client extensions are PL/SQL packages that Oracle provides in the expectation that users will customize them. They are therefore supportable by Oracle Worldwide Support (unlike customizations). Some are specified alternatives selectable on screens; others are called by concurrent processes. There are 29 extensible PL/SQL packages, some of which comprise several extensible procedures, such as the allocations package. In that one you can specify how source, target, and offset projects and tasks are selected. Source, target, and offset are in separate procedures.

The procedures have sample code in them so you have a template from which to work. You will need to follow a normal system-development methodology to control the production of client extensions; analyzing and documenting the requirement, solution, installation, and use of the software created. It is recommended that you keep the modified code in a code-control system so changes can be version controlled. The packages will be replaced during upgrades, so you will need to go through and reapply changes you have made, using the code you have in your code-control repository. Although the extensions are already embedded in procedures and therefore have some of the structure preordained (such as the commit to the database), you will still need competent PL/SQL developers who understand the Projects application's table structure.

Data Conversion

Legacy projects and tasks can be converted either manually or through the Activity Management Gateway APIs. One common problem with data converted from legacy applications is the need for a substantial data-cleanup exercise. Because much time is spent cleansing each record, the incremental time required to type it in is not very significant until the number reaches the thousands. However, it should be remembered that data conversion is not a one-time affair. It should be done in test and live. The more test cycles you can process with real data, which cover all types of projects from all the different parts of the business, the smoother and surer will be your live conversion.

During the data-cleanup exercise, project classifications can easily proliferate, as each project has different characteristics from the last. Because the project owners see each one as unique, it is difficult for them to see the corporate view and the operational one simultaneously. Therefore, a positive commitment to a standard classification set early in the implementation by a senior manager will encourage a classification of projects that will go on to give meaningful management information.

To create cost conversions is not unduly difficult for a professional Oracle EBS developer. However, any revenue-events conversion would need to be directly to applications' base tables (PA_EVENTS), so is not supported by Oracle. The custom cost-conversion program will need to populate the PA_TRANSACTION_INTERFACE table. Once your custom program has done this successfully, you will be able to run the PA: Cost Transaction Import for the appropriate transaction source. This runs by operating unit, so you will need to run it once per operating unit. One quirk of this program is that it stops processing a batch once it has found an error in that batch. The standard work-around is to make each line into a batch.

The revenue- and billing-events conversion can be a relatively simple program that will insert into the PA_EVENTS table. When you design these programs, you will need to decide whether the records will be preaccounted. If they are preaccounted, enter code-combination identifiers in the relevant column and set up the transaction source as preaccounted. This way the records will not be interfaced to the General Ledger. Thus, if they are already included in a legacy GL conversion, they will not be double counted. Conversely, if you want them to go through the normal link to GL through AutoAccounting, leave the "Transaction Source Pre-Accounted" flag null (meaning no) and the code-combination identifier null, and the first run of the transfer to GL will pick up the transactions and process them.

Conclusion

Oracle Projects is at the vanguard of many of Oracle's visionary ideas. It demonstrates the big themes of that vision. The cost-collection mechanisms are increasingly self-service based; time-sheet information, employee expenses, and procurement all benefit from central control but enable distributed entry by the people who have the information required. Workflow and Account Generator work mostly outside Projects to ensure approval processes for the incoming transactions but are also used in project-status and budget management. Globalization is enabled by the strong intercompany and multicurrency features. The core accounting logic implemented in AutoAccounting makes flexibility the keyword and gives control to the business over the granularity of the information going to the General Ledger.

The variety of tools, from the Project Status Inquiry form to the Oracle Discoverer workbooks, illustrate the sharpening focus of the E-Business Suite on drawing data out of the system.

All these features work toward greater precision and visibility of transactions in Projects. They will attract a wide range of industries that might not have traditionally been project oriented, but can gain considerable control over costs and examine their margin in the project dimension.

CHAPTER
15

Oracle Credit Management

n today's global economy, many organizations have great challenges in managing credit decisions regarding customers and prospects. It is very common to have a manual approval process as part of credit approval, which does not always stays consistent over a period of time and creates difficulties such as shipping goods to bad-debt customers or producing delays in the shipment.

There are many ways of managing the key metrics for credit scoring; some are internal, such as checking the history of the customer, whereas for prospects, companies such as Dun and Bradstreet provide metrics that allow the credit-reviewing team to make decisions. This would also incur on different ways and locations to store the information of the client or prospect, creating a huge amount of information and in most cases redundant credit data, which can lead to mistakes.

Oracle Credit Management, an application in the E-Business Suite, provides a standardized system that lets you make and implement credit decisions based on the collected credit data of your business-to-business customers and prospects. By implementing this application, you will automate a periodic credit assessment, which includes the initial credit-review request and creation of the credit application, credit scoring and analysis, and final implementation of credit decisions.

It allows establishment of credit policies and standards for customers and prospects across the enterprise and a flexible credit-scoring model, including a seamless integration with Dun and Bradstreet.

An Overview of Oracle Credit Management

Oracle Credit Management empowers your organization's credit personnel to have a constant flow of monitoring and evaluation of the creditworthiness of your business-to-business customers and prospects. Thanks to its integration with E-Business Suite modules such as Order Management, Lease Management, and Oracle Loans, and external data, business users can create credit policies tailored to your company's business, balancing your organization's growth with a desire for financial stability.

Credit Management solution has four main process flows: credit policy management, completion of the credit application, credit analysis and implementation of decisions, and risk and revenue management.

Credit-Policy Management

Credit-policy management is how you model and define credit policies based upon two dimensions: the customer's credit classification or risk assessment and the credit-review type. The customer's credit classification is set to levels such as "High Risk" or "Low Risk" based on the credit relationship with customers and prospects of your organization. The credit types are the different reviews, such as credit checking, periodic credit review, and lease application.

The system provides multiple tools for credit personnel to determine which data points will be gathered from the different sources and combined to comprise the credit-review case folder. Some of the tools are credit checklists, scoring models, and automation rules.

Credit checklists specify which data points are required and which are optional during a credit review. Almost 200 preseeded data points are provided out of the box by Oracle; among the most common are Days Sales Outstanding (DSO) and Percentages of Invoices Paid Late. It is possible to define your own data point if you cannot find one that fits your needs.

Another tool is the scoring model. It is a combination of defined data points and the scoring method appropriate for a particular credit review. The definition has two steps: You indicate a score for each range of values and later optionally assign a relative weighting factor.

Automation rules govern the automation of the credit checking. They allow Oracle Credit Management to provide recommendations without a human interface. The automation rules in combination with the scoring model can automatically take actions such as releasing an order hold or approving a higher credit limit for a customer.

Credit Application

Credit Management provides a modular, online credit application. It can be completed by internal personnel on behalf of a customer or prospect, or it can be executed by business events that would drive the initiation of a credit review, such as an order being placed on credit hold due to the precalculated credit exposure or an externally defined user event.

Credit Analysis and the Decision-Making Process

Credit Management has a component in which the credit analysis can be determined through a manual intervention of the credit team. The introduction of the case folder allows the team to have a central repository for all the data, using an online case folder with analyst notes, calculated credit scores, and recommendations for making informed and documented credit decisions.

In Release 12, many applications are leveraging the Multi Organization Access Control; Credit Management takes advantage of accessing transaction counts and amounts for companies that have multiple operating units and performing the review in a cross-organization approach. Another huge advantage is the ability to consolidate customers using the new Trading Community Architecture (TCA) and to calculate for party and customer accounts at site levels.

The most common approach of implementation for Oracle Credit Management is through the automatic process, where credit recommendations are made through the use of automation rules. These automation rules—which include Oracle Workflow and Oracle Approval Management Engine (AME)—can recommend automatically setting a new credit limit or revising the current one, removing an order hold, or setting a customer account or party on hold.

Oracle Credit Management integrates with Dun and Bradstreet—a service that is not included in your Oracle EBS purchase but must be licensed separately. This integration will update the scores of your customers and speed up the automatic analysis of the credit application.

Performance, Risk, and Revenue Management

A constant request to credit departments is for key performance indicators and supporting references that the credit policies have adequately assessed the creditworthiness of the company's customers. Oracle Credit Management provides tools to help determine if the results of past credit reviews were under the policies defined within the module and manage the assumed credit accordingly.

Another important challenge many companies are facing today is revenue recognition and how it can be matched to the credit review. Organizations that do not have a credit-management system—or it is a third-party software—manage the risk through a manual process or a customization in Oracle EBS, which reverts the revenue entries for some customers until they proceed with the payment due to their credit rating. Oracle Credit Management has an out-of-the-box integration with Oracle Receivables within the E-Business Suite which makes this process much simpler and more transparent for users. This automation around revenue management has some integration points and setups that are performed on both modules (Credit Management and Receivables) where, based on the customer credit classification assigned by a Credit Management credit review, the revenue recognition will be achieved.

Credit Management Automation Tools

We have mentioned how Oracle Credit Management automates the credit-review process by using automation rules, Oracle Workflow, and Oracle Approval Management Engine (AME). In order to understand the workflow process, let's start by defining a role within Credit Management called the credit scheduler. This role has an active participation within the application, assigning credit tasks to the team of credit analysts.

As shown in Figure 15-1, the action (review, score and recommend) is performed in Credit Management and feeds the other E-Business Suite applications.

Oracle Workflow is how Credit Management automates credit decisions. A detailed description of Oracle Workflow can be found in Chapter 17.

Workflow attempts to make a credit decision; if it stops due to missing data, the pending action step is forwarded to a credit analyst. If Workflow cannot find a credit analyst, the pending action step it is routed to the credit scheduler for a manual reassignment.

Credit Management Key Definitions

In this section, an introduction of the key definitions of Oracle Credit Management is presented.

Defining Credit Analysts

In any credit-management process, one of the most important roles is that of the person who performs credit analysis. Credit analysis is the process of evaluating a customer's loan request or a corporation's debt issue in order to determine the likelihood that the borrower will live up to their obligations. In other words, credit analysts examine the financial history of an applicant in order to determine creditworthiness. In the case of an automated process, the credit analysts will assist in the resolution of credit-related issues and evaluate the creditworthiness of your customers and prospects. The functions of credit analysts within Oracle Credit Management are to view credit applications and case folders, and with this information to submit recommendations.

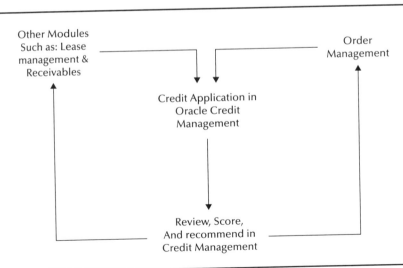

FIGURE 15-1.   *Oracle Credit Management high-level processes*

Oracle E-Business Suite makes it mandatory for you to define employees as credit analysts and managers even if you are not using the HR module. It is a simple process that is required for accessing the Credit Management application.

If your organization has client-facing representatives who might have to check for a credit analysis, then it is necessary to add the role of credit analyst—in this case it would be read-only, but it will be nice for those representatives to follow credit-application details without having to call a credit analyst to ask for an update.

Maintaining Customer Data

Oracle Credit Management has an open architecture that allows the use of public APIs (presented later in this chapter); it also has out-of-the-box integration with Dun and Bradstreet (D&B).

D&B is a service provider that has a very important database, with millions of businesses around the world. Without any doubt, the main benefit of acquiring the D&B service is that you do not need to have an internal history—specifically for prospects—of credit information; that information can be drawn from the D&B database and used to populate your Oracle E-Business Suite customer information with the metrics required for Credit Management. The information from D&B can be added to credit checklists as data points. In the definition of the checklist, users will select the score model; if that is set to "Customer Review with D&B data," the system will provide an overview of Global Access Data Products that you can purchase. As shown in Figure 15-2, you can select the data product whose data points you want to include on your checklist. You can select more than one data product, but you would typically include only one product on a checklist.

During credit analysis, Oracle Credit Management pulls the data points from D&B and checks if the data exist in E-Business Suite. If the data are not in EBS and are selected as required in the checklist, then Credit Management will pull the data from D&B and after that will complete the analysis. If the checklist has the "optional" box checked, the user will be notified that the data do not exist but the application will continue with the analysis and will make a recommendation.

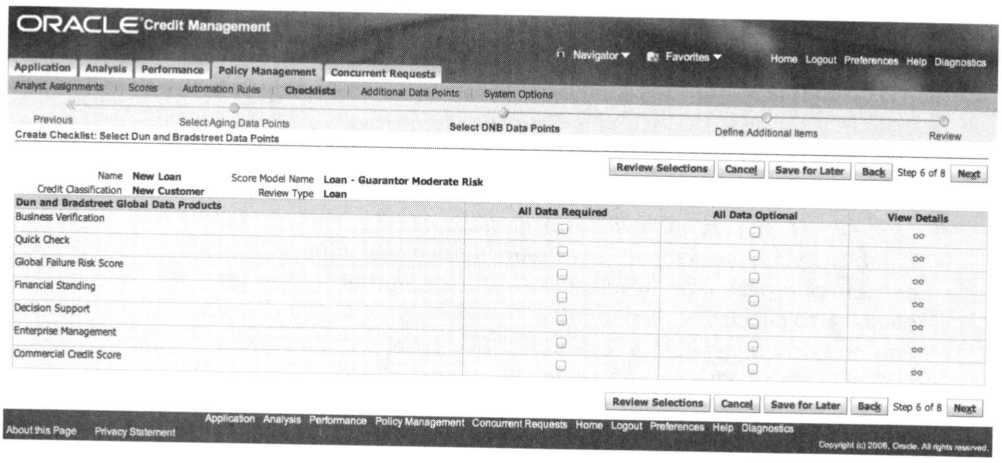

FIGURE 15-2. *Oracle Credit Management creating a checklist with D&B data points*

NOTE
If your company decides to purchase D&B service, you have to enable the integration between E-Business Suite and D&B and set the profile option "HZ: Allow Access to D&B Online Purchase profile" to "Yes" for the users that will be able to purchase D&B data.

Oracle Data Quality Management (DQM) is an application in the E-Business Suite's CRM family which has a set of tools and features that provide powerful searching and matching functionality for search, duplicate identification, duplicate prevention, and other data-management features. With a sophisticated matching mechanism, DQM can determine records that match specified search criteria or records that are potential duplicates of other records.

Oracle Credit Management employs DQM, which requires some setup. The usage of DQM is primarily in the function of matching rules to identify how search results should be displayed in Credit Management's search screens.

The performance of the application and the ability to produce a timely response are among the biggest challenges for any enterprise software. Oracle has created some summary tables that speed up the Credit Management analysis by having the application just examine these summary tables instead of do a full scan on the transactional tables.

The tables utilized by Credit Management are

- **AR_TRX_BAL_SUMMARY** This table stores the fields that summarize data across all timelines, e.g., Open Balance, Open Invoices Count, and Open Invoices Value. It stores the organization ID to ensure that data can be retrieved by account site. The lowest level of granularity at which the data can be stored and retrieved from this table is for a given currency at a specified bill-to location for a given account of a party. Balances are stored as current snapshots and are not dependent on any time parameter.

- **AR_TRX_SUMMARY** This table stores the fields—such as Total Invoices Value, Total Invoices Count, Total Cash Receipts Value, etc.—that require summarization for a specified period of time. The lowest level of granularity at which the data can be stored and retrieved from this table is as of a specified date for a given currency at a specified bill-to location for a given account of a party. A system option controls how the data are stored in the table, specifying the period of time, and reflects how your business wants to check customer historical data.

TIP
In order to have the summary tables refreshed, you have to set the "AR: Allow Summary Table Refresh" profile option to "Yes" and then run the Credit Management Refresh AR Transactions Summary Tables concurrent program for the initial load. Once it finishes successfully, you have to check that the Workflow Deferred Agent Listener, which runs on a scheduled basis, is executing the event subscriptions seeded by Credit Management by updating the summary tables.

Defining Credit Policies

Oracle Credit Management provides a very intuitive interface and a flexible setup, which will help the credit department to meet the needs of the credit policies of your organization.

The concept of the credit data point is how Credit Management takes the setup information that defines your credit policies and uses that for analysis, setting credit scores, and making recommendations. These credit data points are metrics which will allow Credit Management to determine the score of a customer or prospect. Some examples of these metrics are days sales outstanding (DSO), days payable outstanding (DPO), number of late payments, and accounts-receivable aging. The accuracy of these data credit points will lead to an accurate credit recommendation. Credit Management pulls the information from multiple sources.

Out of the box, Oracle Credit Management provides almost 200 data credit points extracted from other applications of E-Business Suite, such as Oracle Receivables, Loans, and Order Management.

Another option is to create your own data credit points, but this will require some skills in PL/SQL programming. It is also possible to leverage Web services to acquire these custom data points from other systems that are not integrated with E-Business Suite.

The last option, which has already been mentioned, is to purchase the information from Dun and Bradstreet, which is integrated with Oracle Credit Management, and include a number of D&B data points in credit reviews.

Defining Checklists

Credit checklists are the entities where your credit department documents the credit policies of your company. The creation of the checklist is performed through a wizard which guides users in selecting the necessary information step-by-step.

Figure 15-3 shows the first screen of the multistep setup process for credit checklists. The definitions required are shown in Table 15-1.

Oracle Credit Management uses these checklists on the credit application, determining the required fields, and during the credit analysis, where the data are automatically collected and displayed in the case folder. When defining a checklist, the user will select a combination of credit-review type and credit classification. During a credit review, Credit Management uses the intersection of the credit-review type and the applicant's credit classification to select the appropriate checklist to use for the credit analysis. The higher the customer credit-classification risk, the more stringent the credit policy. This is the scoring model described in the next section.

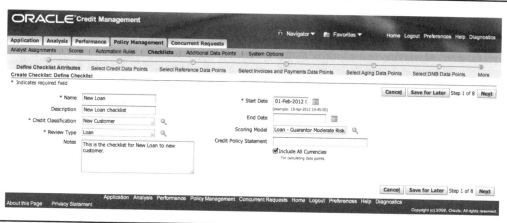

FIGURE 15-3. *Creating a credit checklist in Oracle Credit Management*

Checklist Definition Page	Data-Point Description	Data-Point Source
Select Credit Data Points	Indicates which credit-related data from Receivables and user-entered business information to include in the credit analysis	Receivables and user entered
Select References Data Points	Indicates the number of bank references and trade references to enter in the credit analysis, as well as guarantors, venture capital, and collateral	User entered
Select Payments Data Points	Indicates which historical orders and receivables data to include in the credit analysis	Order Management and Receivables
Select Aging Data Points	Indicates which aging data to include in the credit analysis	Receivables
Select Dun & Bradstreet Data Points	Indicates which data points from the specific Dun and Bradstreet Global Access Data Products report to include in the credit analysis	Dun and Bradstreet
Define Additional Items	Indicates if the credit analysis requires additional information from an outside source	User entered

TABLE 15-1. *Checklist Definitions*

Defining Scoring Models

E-Business Suite offers the ability to incorporate complex processes into business processes, with the ability to easily build in best practices. The definition of the scoring model is key to a true view of the customer or prospect across the organization. The scoring model is one of the primary credit-review tools that Oracle Credit Management uses to assess the credit-worthiness of customers and prospects.

Each credit review will have its appropriate scoring model, composed of data points and scoring method. In the definition of the data points the users will indicate a score for each range value and a weighting factor.

When Oracle Credit Management runs the credit analysis, it will analyze the scores assigned to each data-point range of values and will calculate a score and lower the result of the credit score, greater will be the credit risk assigned.

Figure 15-4 shows a case folder for the organization ABC Corporation Worldwide, with a credit score of 23.7.

Credit Management is a great tool for automating the complete process of credit review and recommendation. Once the credit score is calculated, the application will automatically generate the recommendation for each score range, improving the information delivered and decreasing the manual work almost to zero.

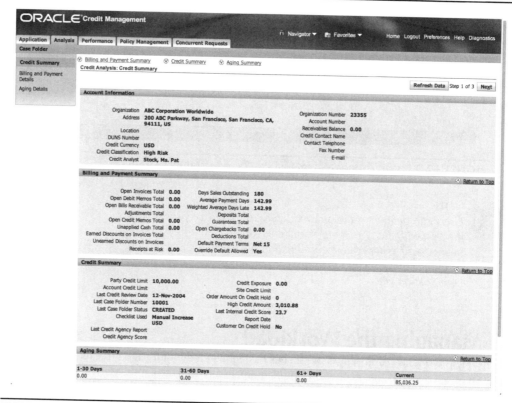

FIGURE 15-4.   *Credit Management case folder showing the credit score for an existing customer*

Assigning Automation Rules

During the credit review, having the automated workflow keep pace without interruptions is vital for a fast resolution on the recommendations. Oracle Credit Management's automation rules let a credit review proceed with the calculation of the scoring model selected and provide a recommendation without any disruption.

The purpose of the automation rules is that for any scoring model, you can have the system provide recommendations without an intervention from a user.

In Figure 15-5 you can see the details of an automation rule that is based on the scoring model "Low Risk Increase" and has two score ranges for recommendations.

A column defines the approval options for each decision. In the example, if the score range is between 0 and 35 then the automation rule will skip the required approval on a credit decision.

The automatic recommendation is performed based on the values entered in the recommendations screen shown in Figure 15-6. For example, if the credit score is below 35, the system will automatically recommend an overall credit limit of $50,000 and a transaction credit limit of $10,000.

From experience, we can say the automated process will work in an environment where there is a well-defined credit policy and a process in place to determine the different actions and reviews for the credit scores.

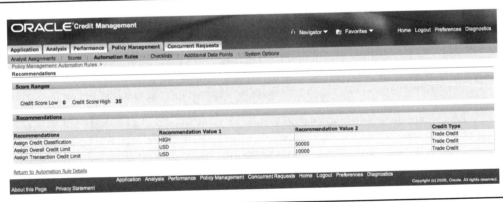

FIGURE 15-5. *Credit Management automation-rule example*

> **NOTE**
> *Users can define a set of automation rules for any of your scoring models, with the conditions that a checklist and scoring model are defined and assigned to a combination of credit-review type and credit classification and that there are no automation rules for that combination yet.*

Managing the Workload

Oracle Workflow runs behind the scenes during the credit application in Credit Management; if there is a decision that cannot be made automatically, it is the Credit Management application that assigns a credit analyst to resolve the situation through a manual intervention. The assignment of the credit analyst is based on a component of E-Business Suite called the rules engine.

In Figure 15-7 you can see the rules list, where users can define a sequence for assignment and a definition of who will be the credit analyst assigned for the case folder.

FIGURE 15-6. *Credit Management automation-rule recommendations*

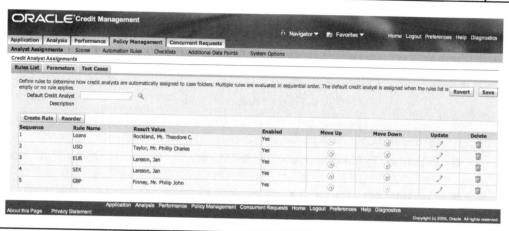

FIGURE 15-7.   *Credit Management rules list under the workload assignment*

When a credit analyst is required, the appropriate assignment is determined using the following sequence:

1. The assignment rules that you defined using the rules engine are executed.

2. If no credit analyst is identified, then the default credit analyst, selected on the Rules List tab, is used.

3. If no default credit analyst exists, then Credit Management uses the default credit analyst on the assigned customer-profile class.

If, after the above steps, Credit Management fails to identify a credit analyst, then it automatically routes the credit review to the credit scheduler. A credit manager must log on using the credit-scheduler Responsibility to manually select a credit analyst.

Credit Management Integration and Public API

Oracle E-Business Suite has multiple integration points. Credit Management is fully integrated with the credit-review process of Oracle Order Management, Oracle Lease Management, and Oracle Loans.

The Order Management credit-review process can be taken as an example to describe how the integration is performed between these applications and Credit Management. The credit-review process is initiated when a new sales order within the module violates the customer's existing credit limit and is set to pending credit review. Using a standard API called Create Credit Request, a credit-review request is created in Oracle Credit Management; later a credit application and case folder will be created. The case folder will follow the approval process within Credit Management, and when the recommendation is implemented, the closure of the case folder using the service-oriented architecture raises a business event indicating the recommendation. Oracle Order Management subscribes to the business event and, depending on the decision, does or does not take the order off hold or not.

There are five public APIs that are used by E-Business Suite and can also be utilized by the organizations:

- **Create Credit Request API**   The AR_CMGT_CREDIT_REQUEST_API.CREATE_CREDIT_REQUEST routine is used to create a credit request for initiating a credit review for a party, account, or account site. This API routine has four output and 35 input parameters. The API returns the CREDIT_REQUEST_ID value of the credit request created in Credit Management as one of the default output parameters.

- **Update Credit Request API**   The OCM_CREDIT_REQUEST_UPDATE_PUB routine is used to update an existing credit request for a party, account, or account site.

- **Withdraw Credit Request API**   The OCM_CREDIT_REQ_WITHDRAW_PUB routine is used to withdraw an existing credit request for a party, account, or account site.

- **Guarantor API**   The OCM_GUARANTOR_PUB routine is used to automatically submit a credit application for a guarantor that is included on a credit application or in a case folder.

- **Get External Decision API**   The OCM_GET_EXTRL_DECSN_PUB routine is used to bypass Credit Management's scoring functionality and extract case-folder contents for scoring by an external scoring engine. This API consists of four procedures: Get Score, Include Data Points, Get Recommendations, and Submit Case Folder.

NOTE
All APIs are PL/SQL APIs that create or update objects in the Credit Management system based on the specified parameters. The APIs do not cause performance degradation to the main flow calling the API.

Conclusion

Oracle Credit Management gives your organization the information and tools you need to monitor and evaluate the creditworthiness of your customers and make informed credit decisions faster. It provides a completely integrated credit review and approval process with a wealth of real-time internal and external data, minimizing data-entry errors and improving customer relationships. Automating the credit cycle process allows your organization to meet audit requirements (Sarbanes-Oxley, for example) by building and maintaining the relevant credit policies within Credit Management.

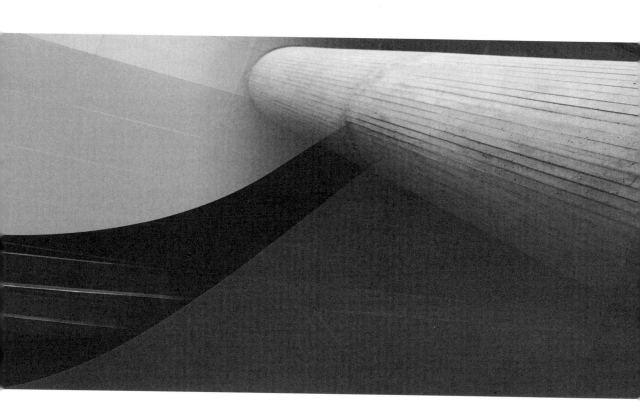

CHAPTER
16

Oracle Self-Service
Web Applications

ne important aspect of Oracle Corporation's enterprise resource planning (ERP) strategy is allowing the people with the information to apply it directly to the system with no intermediaries. The Web is an essential component in this vision, because it lowers the cost of rollout and has intuitive user interfaces. It has become a familiar tool to many members of the public—a familiarity gained at home researching a hobby or buying books or toys on the Internet. Therefore, the commercialization of the Internet has done much of the training and familiarization. The Internet paradigm is established and people are now happy to use it to transact business.

The move is therefore away from the paper-bound process flow. So, for example, a site manager on a building project will know what needs to be requisitioned to keep the job moving. In the self-service model, with little or no training the site manager can log on to a Web site and create the requisition, which then goes electronically to the appropriate approver. Progress notifications give notice of subsequent approval and ordering.

Two paper-based activities have been superseded by faster and more accurate electronic dialogue. One is the requisition, which is structured in the system to enable easy access to commonly ordered materials and ensures that the procurement department gets the details it needs; the other is the approval of the requisition. In the paper flow this might be a manager's signature on the original requisition, or none at all if the value is small. In the self-service model the requisition is automatically forwarded to the appropriate manager, using a set of definable rules.

Oracle's Self-Service Web Applications are being enhanced and augmented—the current product range for Financials includes Internet Procurement (including Self-Service Purchasing and Supplier Portal), Self-Service Time, Self-Service Expenses, and iReceivables. We will examine these in more detail later in this chapter. Other self-service functions, part of Customer Relationship Management and Human Resources, are dealt with briefly at the end of the chapter.

Oracle's Vision and Direction

Oracle's vision for its Web Applications is to extend the information input and output further among the interested parties. This reflects the direction of the commercialized Internet, which brings shops and services into our homes. It has as much a place in the business-to-business marketplace as it does in the business-to-consumer relationship. The drivers for this are:

- Shortening the links between the procurement and supply sides of the business to speed time to market. Internet Procurement puts people who need materials to get a job done closer to the procurement process. For example, through the Web a maintenance engineer can requisition the spare part needed to make a repair and then acknowledge receipt of it.

- Bringing external strategic partners closer to the business. Suppliers and customers can be given a view of the ERP system for the information in which they have a legitimate interest. They can see the status of transactions, which can reduce the burden on accounts-payable and receivable departments.

- Reducing the rekeying of paperwork. This reduces costs, increases accuracy, and reduces the time between steps in a process. An expense claim inputted by a consultant will go to the approval process immediately. Once approved, it will be immediately available for payment. All the input work was done in the first moment and so the claim will not sit in an in-box for any length of time—if approval does not happen within certain time limits, Workflow takes action to move it forward.

■ Relieving desktop users and network administrators of the need to maintain complex application-software desktop systems on a one-by-one basis.

■ Supporting low-cost global financial transactions.

Oracle Self-Service Web Applications Architecture

The Self-Service Web Applications appear on the same personal home page as the users' other Responsibilities, such as General Ledger, Purchasing, Payables, and so on. However, the applications themselves are built using a different architecture from those core applications. They do not use Oracle Forms. There are two styles currently in use in the Self-Service Web Applications, one for Internet Procurement and different one for the others. The Internet Procurement, also called iProcurement, user interface is more like a standard Internet shopping page than a "traditional" ERP. This is based on a technology difference—it uses JavaServer Pages rather than the PL/SQL cartridge used by the other applications. It is the way that other modules and screens are adopting.

These applications give Oracle great leverage on their investment in the building blocks: the Applications Server, the EBS open architecture, and Workflow. The Applications Server is the technology that drives the Self-Service Web Applications. It is one of Oracle's strongest product offerings and is on a rapid development path. The transactions created in Self-Service are interfaced to the core applications through either the open interfaces or specialist application programming interfaces (APIs), which validate the data and ensure data integrity. Workflow moves transactions through a process flow and generates accounting data in its Account Generator guise. It makes the process flows relatively easy to redesign to suit the purposes of the company (rather than force the company to change to accept the software).

Internet Procurement

Internet Procurement or iProcurement is a rapidly developing area of the E-Business Suite. That reflects the importance of procurement in moving to a successful e-business model. The rise of electronic catalogs and exchanges is based on the evident and direct relationship between savings in procurement and the sales margin. Savings can be in two forms: on the cost of materials themselves or on the process of procurement—less administration and quicker turnaround.

Self-Service Purchasing

Self-Service Purchasing (SSP) is a high-profile element of the E-Business Suite during an implementation purely because of the number of new users it impacts. From a user perspective, it has much of the same functionality as an Internet shopping site such as Amazon.com—it does not look dissimilar. You find what you want to requisition in templates or catalogs online, put it in a shopping cart, and submit it. Self-Service Purchasing supports the input of project details against requisitions so that these are reflected in Oracle Projects. The user is prompted for a project, task, and expenditure type and date. Lists of values are pulled through from the core application. You then receive notifications to inform you of the progress of your requisition. The setup tasks required to simplify and automate the process are substantial.

In the latest releases, Oracle has significantly improved some of the key features of this solution. One of the improvements is the content-management process with features such as online catalog authoring, difference summaries for catalog changes, and a new and improved catalog-security model. Another couple features are the functionality that allows requesters to suggest negotiation events when ordering goods and the provision of tolerance rules to automatically process minor changes without buyer involvement, providing more flexibility for the requesters.

Setting Up   It is not enough simply to export the full set of items to SSP and expect users to search through the entire list—even though the search engine is fully featured with numerous user-interface goodies, such as multiple search-results layouts and multiple favorites lists integrated into iProcurement to make the ordering process more intuitive. Two of the tools you can use to segment the items into sensible groups are item categories and shopping lists. Users can search for items, browse a shopping list, or browse by category. Shopping lists, as you can see in Figure 16-1 a list called "Personal Favorites," are a way of speeding up regular orders—users can create them themselves or buyers can create public lists. Employees simply enter quantities next to the items they need and add lines for items that are not on the list. Another way to speed up the process is Requisition Copying, which lets users copy, modify, and resubmit a requisition.

SSP has a range of catalog and content-management features. There is an API to load and update catalogs (using XML, which is growing in popularity as a standard for moving data across the Internet). Integration with Oracle Exchange and third-party integration with Requisite Technology and TPN Register can help by supplying preintegrated supplier catalogs. Of course, employees can enter special orders for items that are not in the catalog. Through Release 12 of Oracle Supplier Portal, suppliers can now author their own content either via file upload or online. Self-service authoring supports industry-standard formats for upload, including OAG XML, cXML, CIF, and text files. Any supplier-authored content is subject to buyer approval before it is made available to requesters.

An integration point that makes Oracle EBS a single source of truth is the single shared-catalog data model between Oracle iProcurement and Oracle Purchasing. The converged catalog combines the best features of both models, and provides a number of significant capabilities and benefits:

FIGURE 16-1.   *iProcurement shopping-list screen*

■ Automatically and perpetually up-to-date catalogs based on real-time data. The extractor process is no longer required to maintain the catalog. Instead, approved content is instantly available to iProcurement requesters.

■ Support for extensible base and category attributes to enhance the product data catalog. Oracle iProcurement customers can now define base and category attributes for their specific needs.

■ Support for price breaks based on quantity, shipping organization, and effective-date range.

Another key area of setup is the Account Generator. You need to decide on what basis the accounting will be determined. You also might want to cater for the situation in which multiple accounting distributions are necessary; for example, when a requisition is made on behalf of a number of departments, so the cost should be spread across those departments. You can switch this feature on or leave it off if you would rather enforce a business rule that a requisition applies to a single accounting distribution.

SSP in Use   The requisitioning process is well served by Oracle Workflow. The requisition goes straight into the application tables as it is completed. After the user submits it, Workflow records it and moves it onto the next approval step. The system can be set up to mail the requisitioner with each approval step. There is an out-of-the-box flexibility for several approval paths, such as approvals based on position hierarchy and parallel approvals. For end users, system administrators, and support there is a screen that allows a view of where transactions are in the process, as in Figure 16-2.

The budget can act as a control on requisitioning, especially in the public sector. *Encumbrance accounting* can prevent you from ordering something you do not have the budget to pay for. SSP can perform the budget check through its integration with Oracle Purchasing and General Ledger. It will advise an employee when the total of expenditures to date, open purchase orders, and open requisitions exceeds the budget.

You can use SSP to its logical conclusion by rolling it out to all employees in the company, or you might still have a limited number of requisitioners. It is important to understand the size of the task well in advance. Although the training requirement is limited, it is still advisable to give

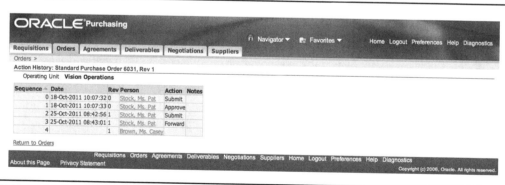

FIGURE 16-2. *Workflow approval-status control window*

some training. The other consideration with a very wide rollout is the scale of the work needed on the approval hierarchy. You can use a hierarchy based either on supervisors or on positions, as described in Chapter 10. The issue with SSP is one of scale if you roll out to the whole company.

Supplier Portal

Supplier Portal is a set of screens designed to give your suppliers a view of the transactions they have in progress with your company. It covers the whole procure-to-pay business cycle, from requests for quotations and forecasted planning schedules through purchase orders, advance shipment notices, receipts, and invoices. The benefits you derive from high-quality business relationships apply to you as both buyer and seller. Being a reliable customer by keeping your suppliers informed of your needs in a timely fashion reduces their costs and ultimately the prices they charge you.

Supplier Portal supports every phase of developing a relationship. Through online registration, you can tell who vendors are and what supplies and services they provide. You can have Workflow automate some decisions with regard to new suppliers, then call them to the attention of buyers for further action. You can provide approved suppliers with password access to projected requirements and upcoming requests for quotations.

Purchasing products and services from your suppliers involves complex judgments, balancing the quality and number of relationships you manage, any personal relationships, prices, and service. Supplier Portal can provide more information to support those judgments. It helps you maintain relationships with more suppliers, manages price and delivery information from more sources, and provides meaningful data on performance under your existing contracts.

Competitive Solicitations   Requests for quotations transfer extremely well to the Internet business model. Posting them publicly and e-mailing potential suppliers invites the broadest participation. You can let respondents download templates in word-processor or spreadsheet formats or a format to be sent back through the Oracle EDI Gateway.

Orders, Receipts, Invoices, and Returns   Supplier Portal does not alter the fact that purchase orders originate in Oracle Purchasing. You might still send them to the supplier in paper, fax, or EDI format. Supplier Portal enters the picture after the purchase order has been created. It enables your suppliers to look up the requirements you expect them to fulfill.

Using advance shipment notices, suppliers can inform you exactly what is in a shipment and when you should expect it. This information means your receiving dock can process against an expected receipt with no exceptions instead of against an order, wherein the normal types of exceptions are encountered (including back orders, short shipments, and substitutions). Advance shipment notices make the process more accurate and efficient. Billing information can be added to the notice to prompt Oracle Payables to create an invoice with no paperwork. The supplier can then see these self-billing invoices through the portal, and the payments made against them. Even more suppliers are allowed to submit invoices when a purchase order was not obtained up front. In this case, the invoice request first goes through an approval process. Along the approval process, users have an opportunity to add accounting information that is used when an approved request becomes an invoice. This will reduce the volume of inquiries and manual work for the accounts-payable department.

Supplier Portal supports your merchandise returns, usually controlled by a return material authorization number from the supplier. You share visibility of the return process until it is resolved by a replacement, repair, or repayment action.

Building Efficient Supplier Relationships

It is traditionally your responsibility as the buyer in a purchasing relationship to let the supplier know what you want through a purchase order and to keep the supplier apprised of changes in your needs through change orders. You sometimes lose track of your requirements, and suppliers might misplace an order in a complex and fast-changing environment. By providing your suppliers online access to open purchase orders, you allow them to see the status of open orders, recent PO changes, shipping schedules, and receipts. They can also update you with an acknowledgement of an order and propose a change in promised date (which is forwarded by Workflow for approval).

You might even structure your purchase agreements in such a way that your online posting represents your sole notification: Your supplier's obligation is to meet the requirements you have posted through Supplier Portal and to notify you if there is a problem. You can almost totally eliminate paperwork if you combine this approach with Oracle Purchasing's payment-on-receipt feature. Equally important, this approach offers your suppliers the most up-to-date information for planning purposes.

Forging tight links with your suppliers gives a new meaning to quality in a relationship. You elevate transaction-related measures such as timeliness and quality to the level of statistical measurement. Other measures, such as the accuracy of POs and invoices, become moot when both parties are working from the same database. You can add new parameters to your evaluation of quality, such as the vendor's resourcefulness in satisfying your changing requirements and in passing its transaction economies through to you in the form of favorable pricing.

Some manufacturers—notably carmakers—have their suppliers retain ownership of parts up to the moment they are consumed on the assembly line. The supplier accounts for the assets financially but the manufacturer has to account for them physically. In such cases, Supplier Portal can provide suppliers a window into a manufacturer's inventory operations so they can see and manage their own stock.

If you outsource manufacturing, you must inform the suppliers not only what you need but how to build it. They keep their manufacturing bill of materials in step with your changing engineering bill of materials. This arrangement works best as a collaborative process, because you need the suppliers' input to maximize profits. The total cost of the product includes component costs, which your engineering department can assess, and the costs of the resources your supplier will use in manufacturing. It is the kind of requirement Oracle's Concurrent Engineering workflow product is intended to support.

Supplier Portal provides links that can give you a significant competitive advantage. Proactively providing your suppliers with information adds value to their relationships with you. Sharing information and eliminating redundant transactions up and down the supply chain, from manufacturer to consumer, significantly reduces overall costs. You and your business partners benefit in proportion to the trust and support you offer one another by sharing information through the Oracle Web Applications.

Oracle Self-Service Time and Self-Service Expenses

Putting the recording of time and expenses on the Web shortens the time involved, which benefits both parties in the transactions. The company will be able to report operating and financial figures sooner, the individual will have a hassle-free process, and expenses are likely to be paid more promptly. Oracle allows its global employees to enter time and expenses over the Web so that even contract employees can be on the system with no need for software to be installed on their laptops.

Another advantage for organizations that have a shared service center or business-process outsourcing center in any location on the map is that they can retrieve time-and-expenses information and perform the verification of the information against policies and procedures with the digital copies of receipts attached to the system, reducing administration costs and leveraging a system to improve the efficiency of internal processes.

Avoiding the need to fill in paperwork and have it inputted centrally or even to connect to the head office to enter the information directly means there are fewer excuses for employees to not submit the information on time!

Self-Service Time

An increasing number of businesses orient themselves along project lines. Often the time spent by staff and subcontractors is the largest single cost on a project. Therefore it is important to have a slick and well-integrated time-recording process. Self-Service Time provides a matrix-style input screen for recording hours worked against projects. On-screen validation minimizes rejected time cards as the project, task, and expenditure-type information is pulled through from Oracle Projects. You define the length of the working day per project to validate the number of hours that can be allocated to it. In addition to time per day per project, task, and expenditure type, you can define flexfields to enrich the time cards with other information, such as percent complete or reason for overtime. Time-card entry can be made quicker by using aliases for common project combinations and copying time cards from previous weeks. You can see in Figure 16-3 that the user interface for entering time is very intuitive.

Of course not all your users will be able to get online at the right moment, so there is a downloadable Excel file that can be filled in off-line and subsequently uploaded. When it is uploaded, the entries are validated online in the same way as in the Web-driven process. The other option is for administrators to enter time cards on behalf of groups of employees. This has

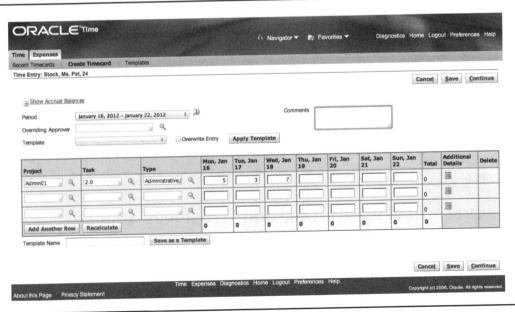

FIGURE 16-3. *Time-card entry in Oracle EBS*

all the same features as direct time-card entry and still goes through approval routing in the same way (distinguishing it from batch preapproved time-card entry in Oracle Projects).

Workflow takes care of the approval of time sheets—this is another approval hierarchy to be set up. This is a very direct way to enforce business policy, and can be combined with customized validation built into client extensions. These are slots into which custom validation PL/SQL code can be inserted without the usual concerns over protection from upgrade. The Self-Service System Administration Responsibility can review the progress of time cards through the approval routing in the same way as all the other Workflow-enabled transactions.

When a time card is approved, it goes into Projects through the transaction open interface. This does the final validation—there may have been changes between the creation of the time card and its approval and import. Employees must have valid assignments and jobs on their employee records to have time transactions registered against them.

Self-Service Expenses

Procurement cards give employees authority to "just do it," using a company credit card to buy supplies they need, within their credit limits, from authorized suppliers. For accounting, employee expenses usually take place after the fact. Oracle Payables imports a list of transactions in electronic format with the invoice from your card issuer. You distribute them to the individuals who made the purchases. These individuals confirm the transactions and provide whatever accounting data are needed. They might identify some transactions as personal and make provisions to reimburse the company.

Oracle Payables can assemble much of the necessary accounting information from the transaction itself using Automatic Account Generation. It will usually determine which department to charge by the procurement-card number. It might be able to deduce other Accounting Flexfield entries, such as the GL account, by applying logic to information provided by the card issuer. For instance, you might let the system assume that expenses on a corporate Exxon card have to do with cars, and hence go to the GL account for employee auto expenses.

On the other hand, there will be times when you need to provide account and organization data. Oracle Payables can pay the card issuer's invoice on time regardless of whether all the accounting distributions have been collected. As with all Workflow applications, you can monitor the process. You can spot bottlenecks in the process and pinpoint people and departments who are slow to identify their expenses.

Expense Reporting

Expense reporting can be a major burden, both for employers and for administrators. Expenses usually need to be entered very soon after they are incurred, so they can be accounted in the appropriate period and reimbursed. They need to be accurate, and at least some expenses will need to be approved.

To meet the timeliness requirement, as with time cards, your employees can fill out their expenses in disconnected mode on any computer by using a spreadsheet; a laptop on an airplane will work. Self-Service Expenses validates accounting distributions against information stored on the laptop, then double-checks them against the live database as the data are imported into Oracle Payables. You can ask employees to use Descriptive Flexfields to identify or categorize expenses below the level required by accounting. You might want to identify the mode of transportation (taxi, metro), airline ticket number, meal (breakfast, lunch), or type of personal service (dry cleaning, health club). For VAT recovery, the expense process can capture the tax amount for an expense item.

The employee has to make some network connection, usually over the Internet, to upload the spreadsheet expense report into Oracle Self-Service Expenses. The system does its own check against the live database and follows Workflow procedures to have somebody resolve any errors. After they are entered, whether online or in disconnected mode, expense sheets flow through a Workflow approval process. Your business rules will determine what levels of approval are required by the type and amounts of expenses.

You need to integrate Self-Service Expenses into the business procedures for managing receipts. You can set a threshold below which the employee need not bother with receipts, or you can define items that need no receipt. When receipts are required, the Workflow process has to define the form they will take: OLE objects, such as spreadsheets or scanned images, that are attached to the expense report or references to hard copy in a filing cabinet.

Your Workflow design has to take into account how receipt documentation will be used. Do approvers need to see every receipt or merely be able to look them up as needed? How will they be made available to auditors? Will any auditors need access to the hard copy? The answers to these questions will determine whether and where in the cycle to scan in hard-copy receipts and what to do with the paper after it is scanned.

Oracle iReceivables

In this do-it-yourself age, the biggest obstacle between you and your customers is often you. Customers want to do it themselves. Direct PC manufacturers are an excellent example of organizations empowering their customers, allowing them to configure and order products over the Web. Oracle iReceivables makes receivables information available over the Web that can be used internally or externally. Integration with iPayment allows credit-card authorization and collection; as with all the Self-Service Web Applications, it is developing fast.

Customer Relationships

You can measure the quality of a customer relationship by the success of individual transactions. You can use iReceivables to measure customer's performance: How often do they change and cancel orders? Do they pay you quickly? How good are their forecasts? It can also measure your performance in filling their orders and satisfying their service requests. Oracle iReceivables (formerly known as AR Online) gives you a handle on these relationships, which are the life of your business. The Workflow features let you devise special processes to address the unique needs of special customer relationships and give equal treatment to customers who enjoy equal standing.

Implementation Considerations

The whole concept of self-service systems is probably going to be quite new to many, if not most, organizations. It makes some demands during the implementation phase that need to be addressed in project plans. It might mean a much greater number of users than for your core Financials system. Testing might need to be extended beyond the realm of your own organization to a handful of carefully selected and willing customers and suppliers.

Typically, in this era of second- and third-generation ERP packages there will be a small, highly productive group of professionals taking care of accounting, receivables, payables, and so on; however, if you add SSP into the mix, suddenly a high proportion of the workforce is potential users. This means that you will need to ensure that all requisitioners are included in Oracle HR or the HR shared tables as employees. For initial data conversion, you can obviously choose to do this either manually or through an interface from your payroll system or legacy HR.

CAUTION
Although they are loaded onto the database, the HR APIs for creating and maintaining employees are supported by Oracle only if you install full Oracle HR.

The Workflow product makes good use of the e-mail system. This means that all the requisitioners need to have e-mail (loaded on their employee record) to exploit this functionality. There might be some staff members who share a computer (such as in the warehouse). Do you give them a group requisitioning authority or have a different strategy for this group, whereby a manager or administrator does any requisitioning for them? Delegated authorities and approval matrices can be tricky and time consuming to determine, and need to be thoroughly tested.

The Self-Service products are undoubtedly very easy to master; however, to incorporate them into the policies of the business or roll out new policies will require some training. Expect to hold some training courses for requisitioning, time recording, and expenses among the workforce. There are different ways to do this, depending on the culture of your organization. Web-based training will work in some environments, and video in others; direct classroom training should be a last resort, because of the cost (direct and opportunity).

One way of easing the training burden for requisitions, time cards, and expenses is to start well before go-live on a halfway-house approach that rolls out an interim paper-based system. This would aim to have on it all the items of information that will be required in the eventual computerized solution, to get users accustomed to the data required. It would also make administrator entry easier if you were to take a phased rollout approach in which core applications go live first, followed by Self-Service. In Self-Service Expenses, the downloadable Excel spreadsheet could be used for these purposes.

For those applications that have an external focus, think first about an internal pilot. There are doubtless some keen internal potential users for Supplier Portal and iReceivables—these applications can be used to see the external view of the relationships and the accompanying statistics. Following that, a limited external pilot will expose any issues with rolling out systems to users whose technical infrastructure you do not control and whose usage might be very different. For example, you could find that the customized front page with flashy graphics works perfectly on your PCs over your network, but your partners do not have the luxury of such a fast Internet connection and so suffer with poor performance. Managing expectations is clearly as important with your customers and suppliers as with your own staff, so communication needs to be carefully controlled by the implementation project management.

As you will be letting external parties look into your computer systems, there is sure to be close scrutiny of the security arrangements by the IT department. Security considerations, as described in Chapter 21, go way beyond a firewall and password control. Allow plenty of time for solution design and performance testing. These applications also have an effect on sizing— particularly on the Applications Server tier—and thus should be included in all sizing and performance estimates for the whole solution.

Other Self-Service Web Applications

The Customer Relationship Management (CRM) suite makes use of Self-Service to provide a typical Internet user interface. Using the same technology as Internet Procurement, iStore is a mirror module to SSP, aimed at customers wanting to purchase rather than at employees wishing to requisition. Customers can browse online catalogs, register as customers, and use the shopping-cart model to buy goods. iStore makes use of the latest Web technologies, allowing you to put multimedia clips into your "storefront" and present it in multiple languages to address the global market.

There is a series of Self-Service Web Applications that integrate with iStore to bring the full gamut of functionality that one expects of Web shopping. The task of taking customers' credit-card details is handled by iPayment, which can use third-party services such as PayPal and CheckFree.

For many sales—PCs, software, household goods, and so on—you might want to offer ongoing support. This is provided by iSupport, which allows online service requests and returns, and is a platform for added-value services such as knowledge bases and user surveys. These can lower your administration costs and help users help themselves.

Module integration is one of the key selling points of the E-Business Suite. This is where time and money can be saved in taking your business to the Internet. It is essential to have a professional, supported connection between the Web front end and the corporate back office. The suite of CRM Self-Service Web Applications is integrated to Order Management's Order Capture module to take the customers' shopping-cart information into the order system. It passes customer information to Receivables and Inventory provides item details. Oracle Configurator guides the users' choices and validates the contents of their shopping carts, and Alerts sends e-mail confirmations. Oracle MRP can be used to tell the customers whether the item they want is available.

The CRM suite of Self-Service Web Applications is functionally rich and will require skilled and committed resources to exploit fully. It is often a separate project from the other parts of the E-Business Suite. If this is the case, make sure there is coordination between them, particularly on the Order Management and Receivables setups, to ensure that orders and customers from the Web comply with business rules implemented during the core-applications project. Once established, your Web presence will give you cheap access to a world market and an easy way to collate information on your customers. You will be able to distribute more information about your products, reward loyalty, and proactively manage the customer base.

Conclusion

Self-Service Web Applications serve as a front end to many of the Oracle EBS applications. Their look and feel is more extended through the whole E-Business Suite since, in the latest release, many Oracle Forms were switched into HTML pages. Two premises underlie their design: They must support unlimited, universal access by untrained users; therefore, they require Oracle Workflow to make users productive and to protect the company from routing mistakes.

The Web dramatically extends the reach of the E-Business Suite with a relatively modest investment on your part. It can have a profound impact on an organization by removing perceived barriers to information. Strategic partners and your own staff are in closer contact with the business processes that make up the mechanics of the enterprise. Their inputs, whether they are a request for a credit memo, news of a delay in supply, or a time card loaded with overtime, will prompt rapid action that is made visible to them by Workflow. Expect Self-Service to continue on a steep development path.

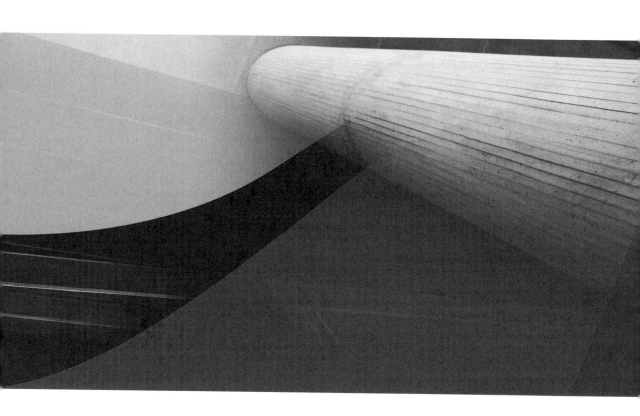

CHAPTER
17

Oracle Workflow

ll business processes involve information and people. People work with information, make decisions, approve expenditures, and monitor progress. The workflow prescribes how different types of information move among responsible people according to business rules. Oracle Workflow lets you automate and continuously improve business processes, routing information of any type—according to easily modifiable business rules—to people inside or outside your organization.

Oracle's Workflow technology sets the E-Business Suite (Oracle EBS) apart from other traditional enterprise resource planning (ERP) suites. Companies implementing other ERP systems must re-engineer business processes to fit the workflow inherent in their software design. Oracle EBS allows you to reconfigure workflows to fit your business; it also recognizes that best-practice workflows evolve and improve over time. Oracle Workflow accommodates workflow evolution without costly software changes using the Workflow Builder tool. You can define processes that loop, branch into parallel flows and then rendezvous, or decompose into subprocesses. The Workflow Engine decides which path to take based on the result of a stored PL/SQL procedure or the response to a notification. Oracle Workflow is embedded in Oracle E-Business Suite and Oracle Self-Service Applications.

Like flexfields, Oracle Workflow is an enabling piece of systems-level technology that Oracle is embedding throughout the E-Business Suite; it is fundamental to all the Self-Service Applications. Oracle also has implemented its Account Generator (AG) module using Workflow. AG permits your systems staff to define company-unique logic for selecting flexfield segments and at the same time give high-quality guidance to ensure that users do not get frustrated trying to produce intelligent accounting-key code combinations. Oracle E-Business Suite Release 12 comes with Oracle Workflow already installed as a part of the Applications Object Library (AOL).

Workflow Architecture

Oracle Workflow has a three-tier architecture:

- User Client tier,
- Applications Server tier, and
- Oracle Server tier.

The User Client tier consists of the Web Notification Worklist, the Web Process Monitor, the Web Analysis Tools, and an e-mail product. The Application Server tier has the Internet Application Server (iAS) and the Notification Mailer installed. The Oracle Server tier, where the database is installed, consists of the Workflow Engine, the Notification Services, and the Directory Services.

Developers who will be creating new workflows or modifying seeded workflows need the Workflow Builder installed on their computers. The Workflow Builder is a graphical process designer that can be installed on Windows-based clients. It uses a drag-and-drop screen to lay out how transactions will move through the system as they are being processed according to company-defined business rules.

User Client Tier

Users need only a Web browser to access the components of Workflow that they need. Workflow notifies people by electronic messages when their participation is required in a transaction, usually for an approval. The Web Notification Worklist allows users to see a list of their open notifications. Using this list they can read and respond to the notifications they have received.

You instruct Workflow to notify a specified *role* of the required action. One or more people can be assigned to a role. As they log in to Oracle EBS, Workflow notifies the people who occupy the role of all transactions awaiting their action. The notice for a transaction will remain in the personal in-box for everyone assigned to the role until someone has taken care of it. In addition, users can choose to receive their notifications by e-mail.

The Workflow Monitor displays a diagrammatic view of the process for a particular instance of a workflow process. The Workflow Monitor also displays a separate status summary for the work item, the process, and each activity in the process. These features comprise the Web Analysis Tools. Speedily moving their transactions through your system makes you a good partner for both suppliers and customers. The Workflow Monitor allows you to monitor individual transactions as they flow through and to analyze your overall activity. It is a great device for spotting bottlenecks, which Workflow enables you to quickly rectify at the Workflow level without affecting the underlying application.

Application Server Tier

The Application Server tier uses the Oracle 10*g* Application Server to interpret the HTML commands that create the information displayed through the browser. The Notification Mailer manages notifications and responses. Users receive notifications of outstanding work items and respond to those notifications using the e-mail application of their choice. Workflow can use either of two e-mail protocols: Unix Sendmail or MAPI.

Oracle Server Tier

The server-side components of Workflow are installed and run on the database server. These component process workflow activities, send out notifications, and provide a central repository of user names and roles. Business rules, which are defined using Workflow Builder, are enforced on the Oracle Server tier. The server-side components of Workflow are as follows:

- **Workflow Engine** Monitors workflow states and coordinates the routing of activities for a process.

- **Workflow Notification Services** Manages the notifications. It sends out notifications to a role and, when a response is received, returns that response to the Workflow Engine.

- **Directory Services** Defines the users and roles available to Workflow.

- **Workflow Definitions Loader** A utility program that moves Workflow definitions between database and flat-file representations.

Workflow Engine

The Workflow Engine running on the database server tracks all workflow-process activity. The presentation-level Workflow tools hosted on the Web server invoke PL/SQL routines to notify the Workflow Engine of changes in the state of a transaction. The Workflow Engine examines the rules and initiates whatever activities are eligible to run on the basis of the change. It supports a variety of logical constructs including branching, looping, simultaneous activities, and subprocesses. In addition, the Workflow Engine maintains a full audit trail of the Workflow process activities.

Workflow Notification Services

The Notification Services manage the information sent out by a workflow process. They route notifications to a role and enable users to receive and respond to notifications from the Notification Worklist or through the Notification Mailer. The Notification System also executes the notification functions that can be associated with a notification, allowing developers to validate user responses before it returns the responses to the Workflow Engine.

Directory Services

The Directory Services consist of three views, which provide Workflow with information about the users, roles, and relationship between users and roles. These three views amalgamate information available elsewhere in the application. Users, defined in the view WF_USERS, consist of people included in various application tables, such as PER_PERSON_F and FND_USERS. WF_ROLES contains information on the roles. This information is sourced from WF_USERS, the position information comes from HR, and the Responsibilities derive from the FND tables. WF_USER_ROLES provides information about which users belong to which roles.

Workflow Definitions Loader

The Loader moves Workflow definitions between database environments—for example, from the test database to the production database—and applies upgrades to existing definitions. In addition to being a stand-alone program, the Workflow Definitions Loader is integrated into Oracle Workflow Builder, allowing you to open and save Workflow definitions in a database or as a file.

Workflow Builder

Developers and implementation staff use the Workflow Builder to create new and modified *seeded* workflows. Workflow Builder manages the business rules, routings, and controls that characterize workflows and makes the necessary links to the application-specific code that processes transactions. In this sense, Workflow is a high-productivity development tool, a tool which business-process owners might not need the help of professional programmers to understand and use. It employs a user-extensible set of familiar or intuitively obvious flow-diagram symbols.

You should be able to change your Workflow processes without changing the application code. For example, the dollar level of an approval authority or the transaction routing can be changed right in Workflow. The application logic that is applied to the transaction once it is approved does not need to change. The way Oracle Workflow separates these processes allows you great flexibility in implementing your business rules without risk of compromising the integrity of the database.

Background Engine and Purge Obsolete Workflow

The Workflow Background Process concurrent request should be scheduled to process deferred and timed-out activities. Run the Purge Obsolete Workflow concurrent request to clear out-of-date workflow-status information from the system.

Embedded or Stand-Alone

Workflow is a core technology component that can be installed and run in conjunction with the E-Business Suite (embedded mode) or on its own as part of a custom-built application. In embedded mode, Workflow directories and files appear under the $FND_TOP directory. In stand-alone mode, these are placed in a wf directory under ORACLE_HOME. Oracle's development of Workflow continues apace; as new features and interdependencies are introduced, it is important to ensure that you are running the correct version of Workflow to embed within your release of Oracle E-Business Suite.

Currently, Version 2.6 is available only stand-alone; it is not and cannot be embedded in EBS. It will be included in future releases of EBS. Workflow version 2.5 is available both stand-alone and embedded in Oracle E-Business Suite Release 12.

The wfver.sql script can be used to display the version of the Oracle Workflow server, the status and version of the Oracle Workflow PL/SQL packages, and the version of the Oracle Workflow views installed. Use the script as follows:

```
sqlplus user/pwd @wfver
```

For Release 12 installations, this script can be found in the $FND_TOP/sql directory on the server or under $ORACLE_HOME in stand-alone installations.

Using Workflow

By default, the Workflow Administrator role belongs to the Oracle EBS System Administrator user rather than the Oracle EBS Workflow Administrator Responsibility. You can reassign this role to the Oracle EB Workflow Administrator Responsibility by logging in to Oracle EBS as SYSADMIN and performing the following steps:

1. Select menu options Workflow | Global Preferences.
2. Click Update, and then click the drop-down box for Workflow Administrator.
3. Select either Workflow Administrator or Workflow Administrator Web Applications, and click OK.

Creating a New Workflow

Launch the Quick Start Wizard from the File menu within Workflow Builder. (The Quick Start Wizard is available only in Workflow 2.5.) This will create a skeleton workflow from the file called wftemplate.wft. You will need to name a new item type and a new process.

- Item types are a collection of components that relate to a workflow process.
- Components are the characteristics that define the structure and behavior of an item type. These are item-type attributes, process activities, notification activities, function activities, messages, and lookup types.
- A process is a route map from a start activity to an end activity. The route may branch and loop but has to start and has to finish.

Once you have completed the Quick Start Wizard you will see the item type displayed in the Oracle Workflow Builder Navigator Tree and will display the Process Diagrammer window with an initial start and end node defined.

Within the Diagrammer window you can drag and drop notifications and functions from the Navigator Tree or create notifications and functions using the icons in the Process Diagrammer window. Putting these nodes into the process determines the behavior of the Workflow process.

Customizing the Account Generator Workflow Process

The Account Generator uses Workflow to populate appropriate values into the Accounting Flexfield. Because each company has a unique Accounting Flexfield structure, you are expected to customize the Account Generator seeded Workflow process to correctly populate the appropriate account values. You can do this by editing the seeded process or creating your own, provided the new process is within the seeded item type and is defined in the Process Property Page as "Runnable." Account Generator is used in several places throughout the E-Business Suite to generate accounts.

You can continue to use the old Flexbuilder rules as long as the business logic has not changed. You do not have to customize and use the Account Generator until your old Flexbuilder rules need modifying. Both the Account Generator and Flexbuilder can be in place together. You can pick and choose which processes use Workflow and which use the Flexbuilder rules.

To access a seeded process, pull down the File menu, select Open, and click the Database radio button. Select the appropriate process from the list on the right and move it into the window on the left. Click OK. This will retrieve the definition of the process from the database and bring it to the Workflow Builder, where it can be modified.

To activate the process you need to assign it to the Accounting Flexfield structure in the Account Generator Process window in Oracle EBS (log in as System Administrator, choose Application | Flexfields | Key | Accounts, and query up the required Accounting Flexfield structure).

Starting the Workflow Background Process

Sign into Oracle EBS using the System Administrator Responsibility. Take the navigation path Request | Run. Choose Workflow Background Process from the list of single requests. A background engine has to be running if the workflow is going to get past a deferred or timed-out activity.

To create a background process to run for timed-out activities, repeat the same steps but enter "No" for the "Deferred" parameter and "Yes" for the "Time out" parameter. Schedule this background process to run once every five or 15 minutes. To run the background processes in stand-alone installations you must schedule the execution of the WF_ENGINE.background application programmer interface using DBMS_JOB or a *cron job* program. Cron is a Unix/Linux-based system utility that schedules and runs background jobs. Another option to run batch process would be to schedule this as a concurrent request.

Prebuilt Workflows

Many of the EBS applications contain prebuilt seeded workflows. Some of these seeded workflows need to be customized before you use them; however, most are available immediately for use. Oracle continues to embed more prebuilt workflow processes into Oracle E-Business Suite with each new version or release. You can define your own new workflow processes or, provided you observe Oracle's policy on customizing standard workflows, you can modify the prebuilt processes.

Wizard Overview

The Implementation Wizard uses Workflow technology to guide users through the setup steps required to configure a fresh installation of the Oracle E-Business Suite. The wizard allows companies to implement EBS faster by improving project-team communication and ensuring that interdependent steps are achieved in the correct sequence.

Why You Need a Wizard

The wizard assists you in the setup and implementation of the Oracle E-Business Suite components. It walks you through the setup tasks and forms you need to complete in order to fully configure Oracle E-Business Suite. The wizard encapsulates the know-how and expertise that Oracle Consulting has developed over the years on the best approach to setting up and configuring Oracle E-Business Suite. The wizard enforces implementation rules and ensures that setup tasks are addressed by the appropriate staff.

Interapplication Dependencies

Many setup steps must occur in a specified sequence. As a couple examples, Human Resource (HR) employees need to be set up before purchase-order approval hierarchies can be defined; a General Ledger (GL) chart of accounts must be in place before the accounts-receivable system options can be set.

Intra-Application Dependencies

There are certain core tables within every application that underlie the application's basic functions. For example, the GL calendar must be defined before a General Ledger set of books can be established; accounts-payable tax codes are needed before suppliers can be set up. The workflow within the application-implementation wizard guides you through these steps in the correct order, allowing branching if several steps can be set up at the same time.

Assignment of Staff to Tasks

Throughout an implementation, focus shifts from the steps that key users do best to those on which consultants or the systems-department staff can take the lead. For example, during GL setup a consultant is best placed to configure the segments in the Accounting Flexfield, whereas users follow up by entering their accounting-code combinations. Following that, the consultant can complete the definition of a set of books that references account values (such as the realized gain and losses accounts and retained-earnings accounts) set up shortly before by the users.

Tasks Progressing in Parallel

To speed up implementation, setups can be taken on by different people and addressed simultaneously. The Oracle EBS applications have been categorized as follows based on their dependencies:

- common applications,
- common financials and their specific products,
- common manufacturing and their specific products,
- common distribution and their specific products,
- human resources, and
- sales and service and their specific products.

Apart from the common applications, which have to be implemented first, the other components can be implemented in parallel. This means you can assign different users to complete different processes and not worry about waiting for one part to be completed before the other completes.

Phased Implementation

Phased implementation is a strategy for reducing rollout risk by delivering chunks of business functionality on time and not before the business is ready. The totality of the project can be split into manageable phases, as follows:

- **Phase 1**   Financial applications covering procure-to-pay supply chain.
- **Phase 2**   Manufacturing, inventory, and financial applications covering sales to cash.
- **Phase 3**   Web store using Oracle iStore and CRM.

The Implementation Wizard allows you to structure the overall project into phases and requires you to perform only the necessary setup steps required by a particular phase.

Using the Implementation Wizard

A large implementation involves many processes and tasks. The wizard provides windows for the project manager to define project phases and to assign tasks to resources. The project staff can then use the wizard to drive the tasks that they complete. Using the wizard is very easy: you need only refer to three main windows—Process Group Selection, Process Overview, and Step Details.

Process Group Selection Window

In this window you can view the dependencies between process groups, select a process group to work on, and select tasks assigned to you using the Show My Tasks button.

Process Overview Window

This window allows you to view processes within a group, start a new task, close a completed task, and reassign a task to another user. The tasks within a group are displayed as a tree structure.

Step Detail Window

Here you can see the process diagram of the current implementation task and review your own progress through the task to completion. Each task links to online documentation and gives you a direct route to the application form corresponding to the task.

The project manager has access to additional windows and reports that show the progress of completed tasks, and all project team members can raise and resolve issues. The wizard automates many of the mundane chores involved in completing an Oracle E-Business Suite implementation. Project tasks are structured into their optimum sequence and the complexities of cross-product interdependencies are taken care of. The project manager has a ready overview of the progress through the phases, tasks, and steps involved; can review who is working on specific tasks; and see which of those tasks are taking time to complete.

New Features for Workflow with Oracle EBS Release 12

Oracle EBS Release 12 has introduced a number of enhancements to the Workflow Engine over Release 11i Financials. With better integration and functionality, Workflow setup and configuration is simpler and less error prone. The following items have been added for Workflow in R12:

- Workflow Notification Mailer,
- improved Workflow integration with Business Intelligence, and
- integration with Oracle R12 EBS Application Manager (OAM).

Conclusion

Workflow is a recent innovation in the E-Business Suite. Through the ability to reach into the internals of the applications and radically configure the software's behavior, customers can—without major reprogramming effort—accurately correlate the business suite to their needs and reconfigure on demand at low incremental cost when business processes need to change. Companies no longer need to ask Oracle how the software works; they ask themselves how they want to conduct business. The elements of functionality that each organization is expected to tailor are delivered using Workflow. This way, the application logic is protected from customization—business rules are implemented as data rather than program code—and the integrity of the database itself is isolated from the suite of forms, batch processes, triggers, and stored procedures that make up the E-Business Suite. Workflow makes the application software both adaptable and reliable.

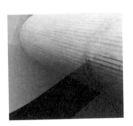

CHAPTER
18

New Applications in
Oracle E-Business
Suite Release 12

uch of the excitement surrounding Release 12 concentrated on Financials, with the new General Ledger architecture, Subledger Accounting, and the application E-Business Tax consolidating the tax setups. It also set a global business foundation for organizations of all sizes, across industries and regions with features such as Multi Organization Access Control, Advanced Global Intercompany System, and Subcontractor Payments for E&C.

One of the new additions to the E-Business Suite in this release was a module that helps organizations by providing greater insight into operations with actionable information to improve the decision-making process and facilitate improved profitability. It is called Oracle Profitability Manager and provides analytics across any enterprise in any industry sector by integrating Oracle Performance Analyzer and activity-based management.

Organizations running their business in a global, more competitive world need to have better visibility into the overall cost and tasks that are being performed outside the enterprise resource planning system; to calculate when a product is received needs to be integrated. The reply from Oracle was the addition of a new module in Release 12 called Oracle Landed Cost Management, which gives organizations financial visibility into their extended supply-chain costs. Landed Cost Management enables your company to manage estimated and actual landed costs for an item purchased from a supplier. Using Oracle Landed Cost Management, you can determine the real costs associated with acquiring items, including insurance, transportation, handling, storage, container fees, and import or export charges.

To further improve the integration and usefulness of data in the E-Business Suite, Oracle introduced Oracle Business Intelligence with the options of Standard Edition One and Enterprise Edition. In the past, Business Intelligence implementations, to complement the reporting requirements of Oracle EBS users, required a customized data warehouse. Now Oracle has released a product called Business Intelligence Applications that comes with a prebuilt data warehouse for most of the families of E-Business Suite, reducing the length of BI projects from months to weeks.

The Oracle Business Intelligence suite makes use of data from all of the E-Business Suite applications to provide performance measurements, operating alerts, and management reports. It provides key analysis across all functional areas—finance, manufacturing, purchasing, human resources, sales, service, call center, and marketing—delivered through a personalized home page accessed with a standard Web browser. The look and feel of the Oracle Business Intelligence applications is based on the new Fusion Middleware architecture, including WebLogic as the application server, which improves the user experience. In Chapter 26, a further explanation of Oracle Business Intelligence's tools is presented.

Oracle Profitability Manager

One of the main goals in investing in E-Business Suite—or any business software—is the ability to understand how the company is performing and how it will be performing in the future. This goal increases in complexity when the organization gets bigger, all the way up to global organizations with subsidiaries around the world reporting to a central world headquarters. Over the last decade, issues of corporate governance and close attention from governments have increased the focus on managing corporate performance.

Corporate performance management (CPM)—also known as business performance management—consists of a set of management and analytic processes, supported by technology, that enable businesses to define strategic goals and then measure and manage performance against those goals. Core CPM processes include financial planning, operational planning, business modeling, consolidation and reporting, analysis, and monitoring of key performance indicators linked to strategy. CPM involves consolidating data from various sources, querying, analyzing the data, and putting the results into practice.

Profitability ratios are financial metrics used to assess a business's ability to generate earnings as compared to its expenses and other relevant costs incurred during a specific period of time. For most of these ratios, having a higher value relative to a competitor's ratio or the same ratio from a previous period is indicative that the company is doing well. Some examples of profitability ratios are profit margin, return on assets, and return on equity. It is important to note that a little bit of background knowledge is necessary in order to make relevant comparisons when analyzing these ratios.

The key change as part of how the technology can bring value to the organizations is the way Profitability Manager is deployed throughout an enterprise so all the users have access to the information rather than only a few analysts. Information-driven organizations having access to information, and analytical capability can make the difference between being an unknown company and leading an industry.

An Overview of Profitability Manager

A common scenario in an executive meeting of an organization that does not have a clear strategy for business software and reporting is the CEO asking questions such as: Could you name the 10 customers that are more profitable? What is the true cost of a product or service? Which line of business makes the most money? The head of the line of business will answer, with some support, each of the questions, but the CFO will bring different answers, which will lead the meeting into a discussion of how these numbers were derived. The meeting will be completely diverted from its original purpose.

At first sight these are pretty basic questions, but traditional business systems fail to provide unique answers. Oracle Profitability Manager makes use of potent modeling techniques, enterprise-wide reports, and a tight integration with the E-Business Suite to provide true answers to these questions.

Oracle's modular suite of CPM applications integrates with both Oracle and non-Oracle transactional systems. This open environment accepts data from sources such as data warehouses, General Ledger (GL) systems, transactional systems, and spreadsheets. Each application can be deployed independently to deliver a high degree of value, but they work even better together, integrating strategic, financial, and operational management processes while delivering a low cost of deployment and ownership. Profitability Manager is a component of the CPM suite and since it uses the Enterprise Performance Foundation, data and metadata used in the other CPM products are also available within Profitability Manager. It is easy to reconcile between the source systems and other CPM applications.

Defining a Profitability Model

The Profitability Manager application was built on Oracle Application Framework (OAF), so the navigation is entirely on your Web browser. It will require some configuration on the source-data

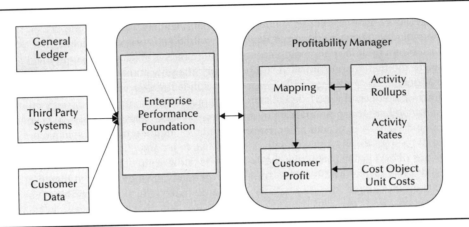

FIGURE 18-1. *High-level profitability process*

applications as well. The definition of a new profitability model to meet your business needs has these steps:

1. You start by analyzing the organization and determining the required outputs of the profitability model and the dimensions that will define the business environment of your enterprise.

2. Once you have defined the outputs, the next step is to select the source systems, which can be applications within E-Business Suite or external systems that will populate the dimension and fact data.

3. The following step is the creation of the metadata: the data about data content or a representation of dimension domains, dimension attributes, and dimension hierarchies.

4. The creation of business rules is a key step in the process because you define the data that will be stored in the dimensions of the profitability model.

5. The process continues with the integration of the data from the different sources selected in step 2 and the execution of business rules against source data.

6. The final step is reporting the results from the model calculations.

Figure 18-1 illustrates how the various parts of the Profitability Manager application are connected together.

Customer-Profitability Analysis

The profitability analysis is how you analyze the profitability of a customer. In general terms, this process does not differ from how it was done before Profitability Manager. The process has three steps:

■ **Account consolidation** The Profitability Management application has a single repository table called FEM_CUSTOMER_PROFIT which consolidates the information from all the sources that are defined.

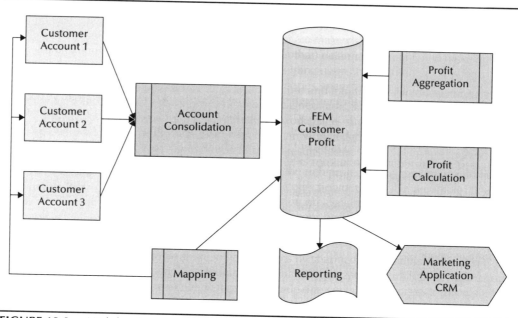

FIGURE 18-2.   *High-level customer profitability analysis*

- **Profit aggregation**   One of the challenges of an enterprise is how to consolidate information from a single customer within its hierarchy (parent company and subsidiaries). In this step, Profitability Manager aggregates individual customer accounts into a single customer-account record. It also consolidates customer-account records in relation to a customer hierarchy based on the definition of the customer.

- **Profit calculation**   In this final step, based on the user-defined formulas, points are assigned based on different attributes such as account, customer, and geographic regions. Profitability information is computed, including a value index score and profit percentile and decile rankings.

In addition, users have the option to use the mapping process to assign additional overhead to individual customer-account table records or to specific customer-profitability records.

This process is illustrated in Figure 18-2.

Implementation Overview and Considerations

Implementing Profitability Manager requires some technical skills because of the usage of terminology that is more related to reporting and Business Intelligence (BI). If your organization plans to include non-Oracle data sources, it will also require some knowledge of the source and how to define which fields will be feeding the tables.

A concept inherited from BI is that of dimension tables. Oracle Profitability Manager comes with some predefined dimensions and the ability to custom-define 10 new dimensions.

NOTE
Profitability Manager does not require the same dimensionality or processing keys on all user-data tables. This means that it is possible that transaction tables or account tables may have dimension columns that are not populated with a value.

The tables in Profitability Manager have some columns that are required to have a value and other columns that accept "NULL" values from the source table. The users building the design and mapping need to take this very seriously, because it can have an impact on the results. For example, in mapping to the table FEM_BALANCES, Profitability Management bases the calculation on some key columns, and values must be supplied by the source.

The Enterprise Performance Foundation has fact tables seeded that are leveraged by Oracle Profitability Manager. Some of the seeded tables that support profitability analysis, activity-based management functions, and data loading are shown in Table 18-1.

Profitability Manager allows users to create their own tables. It is strongly suggested that the following guidelines listed below be observed so that this does not create difficulties with maintenance.

- Naming conventions. Users will be selecting objects such as folders, conditions, and business rules in the Profitability Manager interface. They must be able to clearly identify available options.

- Processing frequency.

- Calendar periods needed.

- Financial-reporting conventions.

- Financial-reporting requirements.

A mandatory setup that needs to be performed before profitability matching is used is that of the signage methodology. The signage methodology indicates whether the data represent absolute values, GAAP signage, or reverse GAAP signage; it is how the application calculations store the results.

Source	Tables
Ledger	FEM_BALANCES
Account	FEM_MORTGAGES, FEM_CONSUMER_LOANS
Transaction	FEM_TRANS_CREDIT_CARDS, FEM_TRANS_MORTGAGES
Lookup statistic	FEM_ORG_STATS, FEM_CRNCY_STATS
Data loading	FEM_BAL_INTERFACE_T, FEM_MORTGAGES_T

TABLE 18-1. *Examples of Profitability Manager Sources and Tables*

The profile option "FEM: Signage Methodology" specifies the definition, and the account-type signage is defined in the "Extended Account Type Sign" attribute of the "Extended Account Type" dimension.

TIP

Once the setups are completed to fit your organization's needs, the process of validating the accuracy of the signage is accomplished by performing tests and validating the results. Once your business users have validated the results, this setup should never be changed within the profile options.

Cost-Object Dimension

Costs within Profitability Manager is defined by cost objects, entities that have components such as organization, product, and customer defining dimensions, with multiple dimensions intersecting to define the cost object.

There are three dimensions that are mandatory for the definition of a cost: a financial element, a ledger, and one selected by the user. As an example, if your organization would like to define cost objects based on the product master, then the dimensions would be financial element, ledger, and product. A required step to start calculating a cost is to freeze the definition; that converts it into view-only mode. The setup of the cost-object dimension is shown on Figure 18-3.

NOTE

Ensure that the processing key of the FEM_BALANCES table includes all of the component dimensions that you specify for the cost-object dimension definition. If they are not included, then the Cost Object Unit Cost rule will fail.

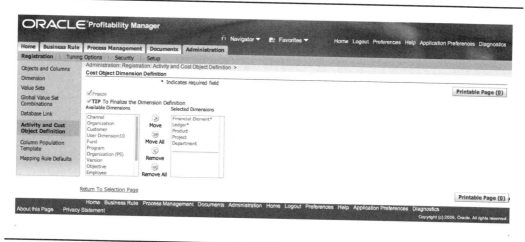

FIGURE 18-3. *Setting up the cost-object dimension*

Using Mapping Rules

Mapping rules are a very powerful tool within Profitability Management; they allow your users the ability to accomplish a wide variety of actions and reduce manual work. Some of the activities could be:

- moving data between different charts of accounts or products,
- generating data points that can be used for additional analysis,
- associating activities or expenses with cost objects,
- spreading costs to multiple cost centers based on a statistical driver,
- updating balances based on a lookup value, and
- reclassifying balances into different dimension values for better visibility.

Depending on the table classification type, the mapping rules are processed differently, as shown in Table 18-2.

Customer-Profitability Rules

The calculation of a customer's profitability is performed through Profitability Manager's customer-profitability rules. These rules offer a complete view and a flexible and adaptable calculation, by defining assumptions for both profitability measures and profitability reporting for customers and any user-defined customer hierarchy.

Challenges of the Customer-Profitability Analysis

In the current business world, organizations of all sizes are living in very competitive environments. As a result of the lack of business systems, covering every detailed aspect of the business to support with information at the right time for the decision making process, it is even more challenging having the top management making decisions based purely on information and not opinion.

Source	Target	Action
FEM_BALANCES	FEM_BALANCES	All rows that match the source criteria are passed through the rule formula, creating new rows in FEM_BALANCES as specified by dimension considerations in the "Debit/Credit" sections. The mapping engine processes the FEM_BALANCES table in a row-by-row manner.
Account or transaction types	Account or transaction types	Simple and field-type formulas update across the row in account tables. No new rows are created. These operations can be processed by the mapping engine using bulk SQL statements.
Account and transaction types are different	Account and transaction types are different	Only source rows that match the target table in all of the following columns are processed: ID_NUMBER, DATASET_CODE, CALENDAR_PERIOD_ID, and LEDGER_ID.

TABLE 18-2. *Processing Options for Mapping Rules*

After a customer makes a purchase, the experience of the product or service purchase, the service level, and the shipping time are metrics that will affect the customer's image of the company and produce a recurrent purchase or a negative experience. All these metrics are part of the customer-satisfaction or customer-service departments, which are loaded with surveys. Sometimes these departments cannot access the right information about what really matters to the people acquiring the company's service or products, or about the profitability of each customer and the services or products the customer buys.

By using the tools provided by Oracle Profitability Manager, organizations can analyze customers' profitability to help answer questions such as: What percentage of my business is relying on a few profitable customers? How many customers are profitable and unprofitable, and why? What is the attention that I am providing to the customers? Is it really worth providing this service to the unprofitable ones?

Oracle Profitability Manager has three main steps for the calculation of customers' profitability: account consolidation, profit aggregation, and profitability calculation.

The data model has a primary table called FEM_CUSTOMER_PROFIT, which is connected with some customer-account tables as a dimension.

Account consolidation is the initial step in the profitability process. It loads detailed customer-account records into the FEM_CUSTOMER_PROFIT table. The data can be loaded through inserting the records directly into the table with the interface table loader or consolidated from the specific customer-account tables using the account-consolidation rule.

The second step is profit aggregation, which aggregates the individual account records to the specific customer and then optionally rolls the aggregated customer records up into a selected customer hierarchy. It is necessary to specify how the source columns map to the target when performing the aggregation. If you are interested in rolling customer records up in a customer hierarchy, you will require a more advanced understanding of the profit-aggregation rule. We recommend referring to the Profitability Manager User Guide for further details.

The last step in the process is profit calculation. The previous steps must be completed successfully in order to have profit calculations completed. Profit calculation provides options to determine customer-profit percentile and decile and to calculate a value-index score based on a value-index formula that can incorporate customer-location information.

Activity Rules

Another important functionality of Oracle Profitability Manager is the support of different cost-assignment methods based on activity-based management methodologies. Other CPM products can leverage the results of this type of activity-based calculation, which utilize the Enterprise Performance Foundation data model, for other metrics and calculations.

NOTE
Before you can create and run activity or cost-object rules, a user with the Profitability Manager with Activity-Based Management Administrator Responsibility must define the dimensionality for the activity and cost-object dimensions.

Workflow Name	Description
dhm.dimension.event	Triggered when a dimension member is created by the Dimension Hierarchy Manager or loaded with the loader program
dhm.hierarchy.event	Reserved for future use
admin.prockey.updated	Triggered when a registered table's processing key is changed in "Administration: Tables and Columns"
ud.complete	Triggered when an Undo process is completed
ud.submit	Triggered when an Undo process is submitted
oglintg.balrule.execute	Triggered when an OGL integration balance rule is submitted
xgl	Triggered when an XGL rule is submitted

TABLE 18-3. *Oracle Profitability Manager's Standard Workflow Notifications*

Profitability Manager Workflow Notifications

Enterprise Performance Foundation and Profitability Manager use Oracle Workflow for notifications that can be adjusted to meet your business needs with regard to monitoring the progress of the analysis and taking action based on the result of the workflow. Table 18-3 shows some of the standard workflows.

Oracle Landed Cost Management

Another new application in the E-Business Suite complements Profitability Manager and allows your organization to go even further in the analysis of costs. Oracle Landed Cost Management enables you to manage estimated and actual landed cost for an item purchased. The different applications available in E-Business Suite for improving the purchase cycle and the supply-chain process needed a complete view of the cost of the items being purchased. With this new application, it is possible to determine real costs of acquisition of an item, including multiple details such as transportation, handling, storage costs, and container fees, among other charges. Many companies acquire niche products or produce work-arounds such as importing the expenses into Accounts Payable, but that also requires complex reporting to satisfy the needs of the controller or the supply-chain management. It is a common practice among corporations to analyze the replacement of an item in a production formula; without the real cost of the product, the decision can be misleading. Landed Cost Management provides visibility of these trade costs, allowing companies to have the right information for pricing and for negotiating with suppliers and customers.

Oracle Landed Cost Management allows you to have your purchasing department estimating the landed cost of an item before you know it. Once each of the item costs are known, you can update them with the actual landed cost.

The option of Landed Cost as a prereceiving application lets your users calculate estimated landed costs before the receipt of the items into your inventory. You can also use the option of Landed Cost Management as a service that will calculate the estimation after the receipt. The integration of Landed Cost Management is another key functionality, letting your payables department match invoices against the receipts which will be later used to calculate the actual landed cost of the item.

With the visibility provided by Oracle Landed Cost Management, viewing the estimated and actual cost side by side, your supply-chain team can see where cost improvements could be made. Landed Cost Management also provides valuable information for forecasting and budgeting by providing detail information of the expenses for reporting and regulatory requirements.

An Overview of Functionalities and Features

Oracle Landed Management provides multiple new functionalities and features with different purposes, which are described in this section.

The flexibility to configure charges that are applied to a shipment line or group of lines allows the application to collect a large number of estimated charges based on weight, volume, or quantity. Landed Cost Management will categorize these charges and indicate their calculation in the total landed cost of the item. Once actual amounts are received, Charge Management records the new value for reporting purposes and comparison with the earlier estimates.

Another option is to configure the charge lines that can be entered manually or allocated automatically. Oracle Landed Cost Management Calculation leverages this functionality to calculate the actual landed costs by prorating the actual invoices and proportional taxes to obtain the variances between what was estimated and what was charged.

E-Business Suite, as an integrated solution modeling business, processes tracks information on the financials and the supply chain, but these flows are usually running on different paths. Oracle Landed Cost Management was built to allow the linkage between them. Landed Cost Management's Shipment Workbench is a full tool that provides real-time accrual updates for a receipt or shipment. The different departments of the company can corroborate the accuracy of a supplier's estimate by comparing estimated and actual costs.

Among the many benefits of using these features provided by Landed Cost Management integrated with E-Business Suite are:

- understanding at a granular level all the acquisition costs that apply to a product, providing the visibility needed for budgeting and reporting purposes; and

- real cost of the items deriving on improvement on the profitability of the products by reducing the costs just by knowing them. Also intelligently source products and components to decrease charges, fees, and taxes.

Integration with Other E-Business Suite Applications

The integration of Oracle Landed Cost Management with other E-Business Suite applications is one of the biggest benefits, since all the information resides in a single location, avoiding customizations and interfaces.

Oracle Purchasing is the application which has the tightest integration and takes most of the benefit for the purchasing department. The purchase-order line provides the information about the expected shipment or receiving item, or services and charges that will be applied. The setups performed for Oracle Landed Cost Management regarding charges are available in Oracle Purchasing, where the procurement department supplies the information that is acquired, such as charge application and landed-cost estimations; and Oracle Landed Cost Management receives all the necessary information for calculation purposes. The information collected allows processes including matching the payable invoice to the purchase-order line. Additionally, Landed Cost Management recovers the tax lines associated with the purchase order that were originally calculated by E-Business Tax in order to include the nonrecoverable amounts in the landed cost.

When receiving is made, Landed Cost Management calculates the estimated landed costs for a shipment and these costs are then forwarded to Oracle Cost Management to update inventory valuations and accounting.

As mentioned before, after the actual values are received from invoices, if there is a variance between the actual and estimated landed costs, it is then passed to Oracle Cost Management for updates to the proper accounts and valuation.

By leveraging Oracle Advanced Pricing, you can enable options to have estimated charges applied automatically to a shipment.

Landed Cost Management Setup Process

Oracle Landed Cost Management relies on other Oracle E-Business Suite applications, which need to be implemented and set up first. The applications are Oracle Inventory, Oracle Purchasing, Oracle Payables (required for actual landed-cost calculation), and, depending on the functionality being deployed at your organization, Oracle Cost Management and Oracle Process Manufacturing. Once these applications are fully configured, several setups must have on them and some on the Landed Cost Management application itself.

As mentioned previously, Landed Cost Management can integrate with Oracle Advanced Pricing, but it is not required.

The Different Models of Landed Cost Management

Oracle Landed Cost Management has two different scenarios for how it can be used. It can be used as a prereceiving application or as a service. These two options are presented to reflect how your organization tracks and stores information about landed cost, depending on the goods or services.

- **Prereceiving application** Estimation of the landed cost is mandatory before the receipt. The information of the estimated landed cost is migrated to the receiving application during the process of creating the receipt of the item based on the Landed Cost Management shipment. Furthermore, the quantity received is passed and cannot be changed in Oracle Receiving, in order to ensure accuracy in the process. The receipt is performed using the known estimated landed cost, and the estimated landed cost is calculated based on the price and taxes for the item on the associated purchase order and the charges generated through the integration with Oracle Advanced Pricing or manually entered in Landed Cost Management.

  The process continues with the creation of the Payables invoice and the use of standard E-Business Suite functionality matched to the receipt. The concurrent programs Matches Interface Import and Submit Pending Shipments pass the information of the actual price to Landed Cost Management. If you are using Oracle Process Manufacturing, an additional concurrent program (Landed Cost Adjustments Import Process) needs to be performed so that Oracle Process Manufacturing can obtain the estimated and actual price information from Landed Cost Management for its processing.

- **Service application** In this scenario, the Landed Cost Management shipment is created automatically right after the receipt of items into Oracle Inventory. There are two concurrent programs, Landed Cost Integration Manager and Shipment Interface Import, that perform the estimation of the landed cost of the item automatically based on the purchase-order information and—if enabled—Advanced Pricing. All the information coming from the Payables invoices forms the actual landed-cost calculation; users are not allowed to perform changes at this stage.

The information provided in the Shipment Workbench for the landed-cost users is very rich and provides insight into the cost of the items. It makes it simple to compare and analyze the differences between the estimation and actual landed costs. The Shipment Workbench can be accessed to view the actual landed cost for the shipment after the Matches Interface Import and Submit Pending Shipments programs have completed successfully.

TIP
It is highly recommended to make a schedule of the concurrent requests for the chosen application and train business users to monitor their successful completion.

Landed-Cost Simulation

Estimation of the landed cost is a process that comes with experience and some certainty that a landed cost user can predict a very accurate estimation of the landed costs. This is not the case for the buyers that sometimes by not having the right estimations can mislead them to acquire products that might not be the most cost effective.

Oracle Landed Cost Management provides a simulation for the landed cost so that when the users are creating a purchase order—which can be a standard purchase order or a blanket agreement—they have the ability to simulate the landed cost of the items. This is a huge improvement if the organization does not have this in place, because the purchaser can compare overall landed cost instead of just item price. Users are able to review the landed-cost simulations by editing the charges automatically calculated; they can also delete them or create new ones.

Landed Cost Management Data Model

Oracle Landed Cost Management has a new schema called INL. Some of the most relevant tables in the INL schema created for the Landed Cost Management application are shown in Table 18-4.

Table	Description
INL_ALLOCATIONS	Stores all amounts of a shipment, prorated into shipment lines
INL_ASSOCIATIONS	Stores associations between landed-cost components of the same or different shipments
INL_MATCHES	Stores actual amounts and the shipment components they refer to, to be used in actual landed-cost calculation.
INL_PARAMETERS	Stores the general Landed Cost Management setup options by inventory organization
INL_SHIP_HEADERS_ALL	Stores header information on shipments
INL_SHIP_HOLDS	Stores information on holds that occur during Landed Cost Management shipment-validation process
INL_INTERFACE_ERRORS	Stores information on errors that occur during Landed Cost Management Open Interface Processor

TABLE 18-4. *Most Relevant Tables in Landed Cost Management*

Conclusion

Oracle Profitability Management and Landed Cost Management are an important step forward in the automation of manual and time-consuming tasks that every organization is performing nowadays. The tight integration with other E-Business Suite applications makes these products a very interesting choice to explore for large corporations, which typically perform these functions in-house or with third-party systems that require interfaces, increasing the total cost of ownership. Now with Release 12 they are available in one single, integrated suite, which brings the benefit of a single source of truth.

PART
III

Managing and Customizing an EBS Environment

.

CHAPTER
19

The Oracle Financials
Environment

racle Corporation is unrivaled when it comes to creating the environment in which its applications run. Its control of the technology stack extends from the database itself through to the application programming. With the acquisition of Sun Microsystems, Oracle became a vendor that provides a true end-to-end product stack, including not only the world's flagship suite of database and software products but also hardware, network, and storage solutions to power the largest mission-critical business systems. It provides a fully integrated suite of hardware, network, and storage solutions with Oracle Exadata, Oracle Exalogic, and Oracle Database Appliance. Furthermore, Oracle also provides the robust Oracle Enterprise Linux, with its unbreakable support option for a Linux-based operating system, in addition to the Oracle Solaris Unix-based operating system to run the Oracle E-Business Suite upon.

The unmatched level of integration in an Oracle solution offers significant benefits. You can be confident that the technologies needed to support the applications will evolve with them. The Application Server is a good example; it is evolving to build on the capabilities of the database and support ever larger applications with ever more users. Oracle's Business Intelligence System brings together reports created in Oracle Business Intelligence Enterprise Edition (OBIEE), using Oracle Reports, and even with the Oracle Data Integrator ELT (Extract Load Transform) tool and data warehouse to mine strategic information from the E-Business Suite.Much of the power of the Oracle E-Business Suite is realized through foundation features that are available to all through the Applications Object Library (AOL). These include built-in devices such as flexfields, folders, quickpicks, and the Concurrent Manager. The foundation software makes it possible for Oracle to make across-the-board improvements to the applications, increasing your capability to significantly customize the EBS without programming. Oracle Workflow and Oracle Alerts also provide a framework for customization without extensive programming (a little PL/SQL and SQL*Plus, respectively).

Because Oracle has created the languages in which the Oracle E-Business Suite financial applications are implemented, it can provide the well-defined integration points and interface specifications a programmer needs to modify or enhance the packages. Custom (bespoke) modules created by the development tools such as OBIEE and Oracle Fusion Middleware integrate naturally with Oracle EBS standard modules. Part of the effort that Oracle made to bring the Oracle E-Business Suite product up to date was to ensure that recent versions of the tools were used. Thus, for example, Forms 10g is used to create the screens (except for Self-Service products). However, there are many standard features of the E-Business Suite that are supported by the program libraries it uses. These make programming forms for the application quite a different experience from building "green field" systems using the same tools.

Oracle E-Business Suite is among the most significant suites of software in almost every organization that uses it. For this reason, most users have comparative freedom in selecting the hardware and operating-system environments used to support them. Oracle's open design means there are always a number of vendors competing for your business; it is important to appreciate the significance of different factors in the process of making decisions about hardware and software.

The topics touched upon here are covered in depth in the System Administration User's Guide, Flexfields Guide, NLS Installation Guide, Oracle Applications User's Guide, and Developer's Guide. This discussion introduces the topics and relates them to one another. It provides the high-level understanding of system features you need to make the best use of the Oracle E-Business Suite.

Online Operations

The E-Business Suite core financials user interface is handled through Oracle Forms programs. They have an up-to-date, textured look. One major difference between earlier Internet Computing versions and the E-Business Suite is that the forms are held together in a surrounding window; the toolbar is integral to this window, as opposed to the floating toolbar found in previous versions.

The forms' two basic modes of operation are *query mode* and *data-entry mode*. You use query mode to fetch data that have previously been stored in the database to be displayed or modified; you use data-entry mode to insert new data.

Query Mode

Oracle has designated query blocks in many of the forms. This reduces the confusion that might arise from the fact that the appearance of the form does not otherwise change between query and data-entry modes. Even experienced users stumble on error messages as they attempt to enter data when they are in query mode. You know you are in query mode when you are looking at a query block. The forms take you automatically to a data-entry block when the query completes, but the query block remains in an open window waiting for your next query.

Forms that include a query block usually allow you to query within the data-entry block. You press the Enter Query function key, enter data matching the record you want to find into the corresponding fields on the screen, and press the Execute Query function key. All rows that match your query show up in the screen. If you do not want to see the data but simply find out how many rows, there is a menu option called "Count Matching Records" that will do this much more quickly than you using the down arrow to get to the last record.

The underscore (_) and percent (%) signs are wildcard characters representing, respectively, one character and any number of characters. To query all customers whose names start with *Ab*, you would enter **AB%** in the Customer Name field and execute the query. To find all manufacturer's part numbers with a 2 in the second position, you would enter **_2%** in the Part Number field. You can have as many wildcards as you want in a query. Entering **A%B%C%** would fetch all rows having the letters *A*, *B*, and *C* in sequence.

Oracle*Forms recognizes a distinction between uppercase and lowercase letters, but the applications are sometimes programmed to ignore it. You generally have to query by upper- and lowercase in a field, such as a description, where you would commonly enter upper- and lowercase values. Queries on fields such as Warehouse Location or Employee Name do allow lowercase values, but they will usually translate for you.

You can recall the last query you made by clicking the Enter Query function key a second time. In one practical application of this feature, you will find that the system responds much faster if you provide a concurrent request number than if you do a blind query in the View My Requests form. The next time you want to check, press the Enter Query key twice. The job number will come back, and you can press the Execute Query key.

Oracle*Forms offers a powerful programmable query feature to users who know the names of the database columns. If in query mode you put a single colon (:) in one of the query fields and select Query Find, Oracle*Forms will prompt you to enter the text of an SQL WHERE clause. You can then make your query as complex as you like, within the limited size of the edit window.

You can query on attributes that are not otherwise available, such as the user attributes behind Descriptive Flexfields. For example, to query all invoice-line rows in Oracle Receivables that have been imported from your employee expense system and that reference customer ABC, you might enter the following in response to the prompt:

```
INTERFACE_LINE_CONTEXT = 'EXP'AND INTERFACE_LINE_ATTRIBUTE3 LIKE 'ABC%'
```

NOTE
The colon query is an Oracle*Forms feature. You can look in the Forms Operator's Guide for full details.

Data-Entry Mode

You enter data into a form by putting the cursor in a field and keying. Oracle EBS accepts data at the field level. It reads what you enter and provides immediate feedback in the form of validation-error messages and lists of values to choose from.

Many fields offer a limited number of valid entries. For example, when you enter a sales order it must be associated with a valid customer. The form gives you a visual clue that a list of values is available by highlighting a list icon and lighting a lamp at the bottom of the screen in character mode. It presents your choices when you press the List of Values function key.

Some lists of values are programmed to use an autocompletion function. When you have keyed enough that the form recognizes that there is only one valid entry, it automatically fills in the rest of the field, which saves you keystrokes. Some forms are programmed to pop up a list of values automatically as you enter the field; others if you enter an invalid value. List-of-values entries almost always handle case translation; you can key in **YES** when the form is looking for "Yes."

In data-entry fields where you are choosing from a list of values, there is no need to enter the entire value. Simply type enough to make your value unique, and Oracle EBS will fill in the rest for you. Using the yes/no example again, enter only **Y**; because "Yes" is the only value in the list that meets the criteria, the word *Yes* will be filled in as you move to the next field.

The E-Business Suite introduced color-coding of fields—yellow for mandatory, white for optional. This highlights the minimum data required to create a record. This is a very helpful feature, particularly for new and casual users such as developers on the implementation project.

Messages

The forms use the message-presentation system embedded in the Applications Object Library (AOL). Any routine, including stored procedures invoked by a form, can set a message. Processes native to forms management determine when a message has been set and must be presented, and whether a message is merely informational or indicates a condition that must be remedied. The most common use of messages is in field-level edits, when you receive an error message for entering an invalid value.

There is a national-language indicator associated with each online session. AOL's message-presentation routines select the appropriate message text, substitute variable data into the message if necessary, and display it at the bottom of the screen. The message stays until the user acknowledges seeing it.

Field-level edits can sometimes seem to trap you in a data screen. Even though you want to leave the form, it might not let you exit without entering a valid value. This is a frequent problem for new users in character-mode operations. Here are some strategies for escaping:

- Try to erase the field.

- If it is a new row, which is usually the case, try to clear the current row.

- Enter a valid value for the field, even though you want to leave the screen; then exit when you get to a field with more forgiving edits.

- When all else fails, use the File menu to close the form and return.

Oracle EBS uses a standard routine to present error messages. This device keeps the messages external and supports multiple national languages. Source text is kept in an AOL table, which is updated through the Define Text form in the Application Developer Responsibility. However, for the sake of execution speed, the generated message text for character-mode operations is kept in an operating-system file in the /mesg subdirectory of the application's root directory.

Navigation and Special Functions in Forms

Happily, all the terminal-emulation foibles are behind us, and whatever type of client PC you use, the navigation is the same. As frequent use of the mouse can slow high-volume input, there are still function keys to do the common tasks, such as F11 to enter a query, SHIFT-F11 to execute a query, and CTRL-L to bring up a list of values.

The navigator has evolved from earlier versions to give alternative views to the user other than the standard list of forms. One is a list of individual documents the user is working on and has placed on the navigator. The user can double-click the document to open it in the appropriate form. The other is a diagrammatic view of workflow-enabled processes such as payables-document entry or GL-journal entry. From this, the user can launch the relevant form for the part of the process currently being handled.

Display Formats

Oracle has applied consistent design standards to give forms throughout the Oracle E-Business Suite a consistent look and feel. Although you will soon develop an intuitive feel for how they work, the rationale behind the design merits some discussion.

Single-Row and Multirow Displays

Forms can display one or multiple rows per region. The formats are quite different. Oracle uses an entire region to display one row when there are a number of data fields to display. It puts the field description just to the left of the field itself. Labels go above the columns in a multirow display.

The multirow format provides information in a format that is extremely easy to grasp at a glance. It is so useful that Oracle uses it even when there is more information than can be displayed at once. It displays the key information on the left and allows you to scroll through the remaining fields on the right side of the window. Some screens allow you to define custom folders for the scrolled fields, eliminating fields you never need to see and shrinking the display width on others so they just fit your requirements.

Correspondence to Underlying Tables

Users see the applications as a collection of *screens*, each of which can have a number of *regions* (which are called *zones* in character mode), which contain a number of *fields*. A display or window incorporates one function—one entry on a menu. In rare cases, one screen may call another. A region frequently but by no means always corresponds to one database table, and there is never more than one base table to a region. A field within a region can be for display only or it might be part of the base table.

The organization of data displayed within an Oracle EBS form corresponds to database tables. Within a form, each window (previously called zones and regions; Oracle*Forms calls them *blocks*) usually corresponds to a database table, and fields in the zone correspond to table columns. However, there are some exceptions. A zone may not have a base table if none of its fields are stored in the database. An inquiry zone may correspond to a view that joins more than one table. Finally, the master-table zones can correspond to views that restrict the user's access to one organization within the underlying table on which the view is defined. The names of these tables end in "_ALL," such as PO_HEADERS_ALL, and the view name is the same, but without the "_ALL." So the Multi-Org view for the PO_HEADERS_ALL table is PO_HEADERS. The "_ALL" tables are owned by module schemas (such as Purchasing in the case of PO_HEADERS_ALL) and the views (such as PO_HEADERS) are owned by the APPS schema.

Forms are organized to present master data zones followed by as many layers of detail as are needed. For example, the Order Workbench form includes windows for querying orders, entering order-master data, and entering order-line data. This is the essential information: Who is placing the order and what do they want? There are supporting windows to capture pricing information at the header and line levels and shipping information at both levels; tax and payment information at the header level; and scheduling, project, and release-management information at the line level.

The zones are arranged such that you always see the context of your actions. Essential header information—such as order number and customer and line information, including the line number, item number, and description—is visible as you enter information about a shipment against that line.

One of Forms' strongest features is block coordination, a behind-the-scenes feature that manages context for you. Block coordination queries up only those detail records that belong to the higher-level records already displayed. Sometimes it does the query automatically as you bring up the master; sometimes it waits until you enter the block. Block coordination preserves the integrity of the database. It usually allows queries only within the context of a master record. For instance, you cannot query the open order lines for an item across all orders through the Orders Workbench. You might come across block-coordination activity in the process of navigation. When Oracle EBS asks you if you want to commit your work, the most common reason is that it wants to save the detail records associated with one master before moving on to the next.

Multiple Open Windows

Because productivity is one of the major reasons to use Oracle EBS, users find it annoying when the online system works slower than they do. However, it is a fact of life that some operations take time. By their design, concurrent processes leave you free to do other things as they execute. With a little planning you can achieve the same with online processes.

It is easy to keep multiple windows open in the E-Business Suite. All you need is to have your systems administrator permit multiple log-ins at the operating-system level. Having several sessions open can save a lot of navigation and keep several activities going simultaneously. It works because all the processing takes place on the host machine, which is designed to do several things at once.

It is common to have one window open for submitting concurrent processes, another for querying concurrent processes, and a third for making changes to the records used by concurrent processes. Updating standard costs is one example of an activity for which multiple windows are useful.

Oracle's Internet Computing architecture inherently supports multiple simultaneous processes. The real work is done on Application Servers, each of which is intended to support a large number of users. The Application Server does not know or care whether two or more of those processes represent different sessions for the same person.

The E-Business Suite has a useful feature that allows the user to take control over long queries. It is installed through a patch to the software that is downloadable from the My Oracle Support Web site at http://support.oracle.com. To use the My Oracle Support site to download patches, you are required to have a valid customer support number (CSI) with an Oracle support contract in place for your site license. When a user's query takes more than a threshold number of minutes, the application displays a dialogue box asking whether the user wants to continue. This is not only good for that one user's productivity, if he or she accidentally requested a huge number of rows from the database, but also protects performance for all users.

Although many users can read a database record at the same time, only one at a time can update a record. Oracle*Forms locks a queried row for the exclusive use of a user the moment that user changes a field. Other users are not allowed to update the record until the first user releases it. Because the system views you as more than one user when you are logged on multiple times, you have to be aware that what you are doing in one window might prevent you from doing something in another.

Batch Operations

Online processes take place (ideally) in real time. They progress at the user's pace, accepting data, updating the database, and presenting information as requested. An online process requires a full-time monitor that runs under the control of the operating system to respond to everything a user does.

A user kicks off a batch process, in effect saying, "Here's what I want. Let me know when you're done." Different operating systems vary in how they dispatch batch jobs and handle their output. The Concurrent Manager provides a standard user interface within the context of the E-Business Suite. It also imposes security and manages access, operating-system resources, and batch-process outputs. The Concurrent Manager is built to the lowest common denominator of operating-system function: it does not employ any features that are not common to all the operating systems it supports.

The Concurrent Manager

The Concurrent Manager is an EBS utility that oversees batch processes in Oracle E-Business Suite. It proceeds according to the following steps:

1. A display screen in the E-Business Suite gathers all the information needed to run the batch process. The Run Reports form captures run-time parameters from Descriptive Flexfields.

2. The online program submits the job by writing a row to the FND_CONCURRENT_ REQUESTS table.

3. The Concurrent Manager searches the table every few seconds. It determines which jobs are eligible to run and which of the eligible jobs should be executed.

4. The Concurrent Manager initiates job execution.

5. The Concurrent Manager uses operating-system-specific calls to track the status of its executing jobs until they terminate. It posts status changes to the table.

6. Users can submit queries to find the status of their jobs.

7. Users can have output printed or view it on their desktops.

TIP
Instead of constantly navigating to query the status of batch jobs, keep a second session open to the query screen (Navigate Other Concurrent). Reduce query time and clutter in the returned screen by querying on your user ID—or better yet, on the concurrent-job number itself. Click the Enter Query function key twice to automatically retrieve your last query.

Experienced Forms users sometimes enter a colon in one of the query fields. SQL*Forms then displays a window where the user can enter a precise query, as in this example:

```
REQUEST_ID 943124 AND (STATUS_CODE = 'E' OR PHASE_CODE = 'R')
```

This query would combine with any other query criteria (such as user ID) and return only jobs greater than 943124 that were running or had errored out. (See the AOL technical reference for the column names.)

The systems administrator can define multiple Concurrent Managers with different characteristics, all driven by a single Internal Concurrent Manager (ICM). Each of these ICMs is allowed to run no more than a set number of jobs at any time. The number of jobs that the ICM can handle depends on the number of CPUs available. Typically it is two jobs per processor. So just increasing the number of jobs in the ICM does not translate into more jobs processed by the ICM.

A Concurrent Manager might be specialized to run only certain jobs or to operate in a given work shift. The system administrator can use Concurrent Managers to control allocation of system resources, permitting more batch jobs to run concurrently at night than during the day, when they would take resources from online users. A Concurrent Manager can be specialized to run only certain high-priority tasks, which will therefore not have to wait in the queue with standard report requests.

The Concurrent Manager takes into consideration the characteristics of individual jobs and job steps as it determines which ones can be initiated. It uses information provided in the Define Concurrent Job and Define Request Sets screens to identify the following:

- **Incompatibilities** Some jobs cannot be run at the same time as other jobs or can only have one copy of the job running at a time.

- **Sequencing** There may be steps within a request set that have to run in a specified order.

- **Job priority** Jobs are normally scheduled according to the priority profile option for the user; however, the priority can be set in the job definition.

The Internal Concurrent Manager manages all of the existing Concurrent Managers, waking up periodically (as defined by an operating-system clock function) to ensure that everything that should be running is running. It identifies the jobs that are eligible to be started for each Concurrent Manager, then decides which, if any, will be started. "Eligible" means there are no conflicts, such as a dependency on an uncompleted job or a conflict with another job currently in execution, and that there is a Concurrent Manager eligible to run the job. There is a target number of jobs for each manager, representing the maximum number of jobs it can run concurrently, subject to the limitations on the Internal Concurrent Manager, as discussed earlier. The manager will initiate eligible jobs, based on priority and time in queue, until it reaches its quota of active jobs.

AOL does not manage the computer's internal dispatching priority. All active batch jobs have equal access to CPU resources. This architecture reflects the fact that not all the major operating systems function in the same way. Oracle's approach is to recommend that you define special Concurrent Managers for long-running or resource-hungry jobs, so they can be run in off hours, or that you limit the number of such jobs that can run simultaneously.

AOL spawns batch jobs as independent processes. It assembles the parameters in the FND_CONCURRENT_REQUESTS row into the standard operating-system format and includes them on the command line it passes to the operating system. The command line includes the schema name and password that Oracle EBS processes need to access the database. AOL invokes the process under an operating-system user ID associated with the current instance, so the environment variables are set appropriately. It uses standard operating-system procedures to pass the names of the log and print files to the background process.

The Concurrent Manager updates the appropriate row in FND_CONCURRENT_REQUESTS to show job status, setting a completion status when it finishes. Jobs might end on their own, successfully or not; the user might terminate them; or they might be terminated due to the failure of another related job. You specify when setting up a request set whether the success of the set depends on the success of each individual job. Often, one job will spawn other jobs. Update Standard Cost in Inventory spawns reports showing changes in inventory, Work in Process, and in-transit inventory; AutoInvoice Import in Receivables spawns a report on the success of the import process. The success of the parent jobs depends on the success of the jobs they spawn.

Third-party vendors, such as AppWorx, offer support for users who need to program complex intrastep dependencies and dependencies with non-Oracle systems, or for users with sophisticated load-balancing requirements. The third-party software usually interfaces seamlessly through the use of database triggers.

Concurrent Program Parameters

A concurrent job needs a group of parameters specific to the type of process and another group specific to the job itself. All Oracle*Reports jobs need a schema name and password, the name of the .rdf file to run, and the name of an Oracle*Reports profile file. AOL provides these parameters to the operating system—the user is oblivious to the details. Each individual report needs the parameters that were specified by the programmer. They are specified in the Define Concurrent Program screen. Different program types accept the parameters in different formats:

- SQL*Plus and Host programs accept positional parameters. The parameters must be specified in the Concurrent Program Details zone of the Define Concurrent Reports form in the same sequence they are expected by the program.

- Oracle*Reports accepts keyword parameters. The token name you give as you register the report must match the one the programmer used within the actual report as the user-defined parameter.

- SQL*Loader accepts all its parameters as a string in the Execution Options field of the Concurrent Program zone. You do not use the Details zone at all.

The parameters you specify in the Details zone are carried as a special form of Descriptive Flexfield (DFF), with each parameter acting as a DFF segment. There is a value set associated with each parameter, which prevents free-form entry and limits input to a predefined list of values. Each parameter can have a constant profile option or a SQL statement to generate a default value. You can also use the current system date or system time. The SQL code for value sets and default values can reference previous parameters, as described later in the "Flexfield Definition" section. For example, you could specify an item category in one parameter, then restrict the user's choices to replenishment orders for items within that category in a subsequent parameter.

Request Sets

It is common to need groups of requests to all run at the same time, especially for period closings and related processes. Request sets satisfy the need for reports to be produced and distributed together. They provide the sequence in which reports are to run and pass appropriate parameters to each report in the set. Request sets are assigned to report groups in the same way as individual reports. If you want, you can limit a user so that he or she has access to a report not by itself but only through a request set.

As you set up a request set, you specify the sources for the parameters for each separate step. You can set up defaults so the user who runs the request set does not have the same range of options as if he or she had run the report by itself. You can specify shared parameters, so that the same value is passed to two or more programs in the set.

Request sets are a convenient way to satisfy other common objectives. You can provide a given Responsibility with access to a report it does not otherwise have and limit the uses to which it can be put by predefining certain of the parameters. You can join a SQL*Loader step and a SQL*Plus step in tandem to load an interface table. The alternative—invoking them both from a Host script—is unattractive: You could compromise security either by hard-coding the password into the script or by passing the password to the script as a plain-text parameter. It would also require several lines of shell-script coding to attain the same results you automatically have by using a request set. The parameters for batch processes within a request set can be fixed at three points in time:

- as defaults (constants or profile parameters, or through SQL) when the report itself is registered,
- as defaults when the request set is established, or
- at run time.

The parameters for each report are presented separately, in the same DFF format that is used when initiating individual reports. Those that cannot be changed at run time can be displayed or hidden.

The Concurrent Manager treats a request set as a single job until it is initiated. At that point it creates one concurrent job for each step in the report. The request set is the parent of all. You can group requests into stages within the set. All the requests in a stage can run in parallel. The completion status of each request in the stage determines the completion status of the whole stage. That will be success, warning, or error. Dependent on that, you can have other stages started. The request-set job does not complete until all stages are complete.

Printing and Other Means of Output

An EBS environment can include many different kinds of printers. Some users do not want paper, at least not immediately; they want to preview report output online. The E-Business Suite output prints to a new browser window in HTML format. The EBS applications incorporate the output flexibility built into the Oracle*Reports and SQL*Plus programming tools. The user can specify printer characteristics at execution time.

The user can have the Concurrent Manager print any number of copies of the report automatically, as the job is executed, or after reviewing the report online. There are a substantial number of print styles available, beyond the normal portrait, landscape, and "landwide" (compressed to get 180 characters across the page instead of the normal 132). Many of the different styles are for specific documents such as checks or BACS (normally not actually printed but outputted to a print queue and redirected to electronic output). You also might want to define one to support very long records so that comma-separated files can be outputted to a printer queue. This printer queue can then be directed to a third-party output-formatting engine such as Bottomline Technologies's i-Point.

Most of the Oracle EBS reports are written in Oracle*Reports. Reports is a fully GUI-capable tool, with a word processor's flexibility working with fonts, text placement, and graphics. This GUI, or bitmapped mode of operations, is standard in desktop operations. However, for compatibility with older types of printers, Oracle*Reports offers a character mode of operation.

Oracle EBS distributes its reports using the character-mode option in Reports. Every platform is capable of handling character mode, and even though most modern printers can support some form of GUI operation, character mode is easier to maintain. You will probably want to customize documents that go outside the company, such as payables checks, purchase orders, order confirmations, packing slips, and invoices. You can take the opportunity to improve their appearances.

If you require graphics such as logos to appear on reports produced from Oracle EBS, you have several options available. You can add graphics directly to Oracle*Reports through preprogrammed printer cartridges or third-party software. Printer-level graphics can execute faster and be easier to implement. The Evergreen check-print program that Oracle delivers uses this approach to put MICR (magnetic ink) printing on checks. The character-mode report embeds HP PCL (Printer Control Language) control sequences in its text output. The printer interprets the control sequence to change fonts, in this case to MICR. Depending on the make of the printer, such control sequences can be used to include graphics or to invoke background masks that give the appearance of preprinted forms.

The limitations to printer-level graphics are these:

■ You cannot include graphic objects selected from the database.

■ You generally cannot mix fonts or use proportional fonts, because Oracle*Reports assumes fixed-space formatting when it operates in character mode. In other words, you can send font-change commands to the printer, but no Oracle process applies logic to protect you against running over the margins—you are on your own.

You can produce beautiful output with Oracle*Reports, but there are a few general limitations:

■ You must use a PostScript printer, and execution is usually a bit slow at the printer level.

■ If you want to see the reports on your client computer, the report-viewing agent on your desktop must be capable of presenting PostScript files.

■ You have to load the host machine, which generates the reports, with fonts corresponding to those on the desktop where you develop the reports. Because Oracle*Reports uses the font size to determine how much data will fit on a page, the fonts have to be available on the machine where the report is generated.

For these reasons, third-party options are becoming more popular. Many of them feature fax and e-mail output devices so that, for example, a purchase order can be e-mailed as a PDF file if an e-mail address is available; if an address is not available, the purchase order can then be faxed, and only printed if neither of these two methods is available.

Flexfields

A flexfield is a segmented identifier, like a phone number. An international phone number could include Country Code, Area Code, Prefix, Calling Number, and Extension segments. Each segment has its own meaning and can have its own rules controlling the entries that are valid for the segment.

Oracle defines Key and Descriptive Flexfields. Key Flexfields are used as unique identifiers and are predefined by Oracle, only requiring you to finalize the specific setup details. Ledger accounts, inventory items, and fixed assets are Key Flexfield identifiers. Descriptive Flexfields are Oracle's way of letting users add, fill, and view columns of their own data within the EBS database tables. Key Flexfields are usually required data elements within an application; Descriptive Flexfields are optional.

Key Flexfields

Key Flexfields allow Oracle EBS to use a single internal value to bind related records together and give users maximum flexibility in assigning external identifying numbers. For every Key Flexfield there is one master table with columns named SEGMENT1 to SEGMENT*n* and a key column named *something*_ID. In General Ledger, the column is CODE_COMBINATION_ID in the GL_CODE_COMBINATIONS table; in Inventory, it is the INVENTORY_ITEM_ID column in the MTL_SYSTEM_ITEMS table. Every other table that refers to an Accounting Flexfield carries a column, frequently also named CODE_COMBINATION_ID, which joins as a foreign key to GL_CODE_COMBINATIONS. It would be unwieldy in the extreme to have 30-segment columns in every table that joins to GL_CODE_COMBINATIONS, such as those carrying balance, budget, and journal details!

Oracle EBS uses number generators, called *sequences*, to generate unique IDs. Sequences are a feature of the Relational Database Management System (RDBMS). There is a naming convention for sequences—the sequence name is the table name suffixed with "_S." However, in several instances a single sequence is used to generate primary keys for multiple tables. Oracle EBS numbers can be as many as 22 digits long—enough to enumerate the grains of sand on the earth. The size of the generated key is not a limiting factor.

Using generated keys makes it easy to change the external identifier. An Inventory user can correct a part number without concern for any issue, receipt, or balance records that reference the part. The major issue in changing a part number is whether it still makes sense to the buyers and warehouse workers. Flexfield values are stored in the master table, but the juncture to a detail table is done through the generated key.

The EBS applications usually do not allow users to delete the records that define Key Flexfield combinations. Deleting them could orphan detail records, destroying referential integrity. Instead, many tables carry an END_EFFECTIVE_DATE column (or something similar) to indicate that the master record cannot be used for new transactions. Users sometimes rename items that are obsolete or have been entered by accident, giving them a "Z-" prefix or some other flag to indicate that they do not represent real items.

You define a structure for each Key Flexfield, naming the segments that make up the flexfield and indicating their length and format (alphabetic or numeric) and the value sets used to validate them. A single master table may include rows with different structures. For example, the ledger tables may support several sets of books, each with a unique chart-of-accounts structure. Each inventory category usually has its own structure. The master table that carries the individual segment values also carries a flexfield-structure identifier that tells AOL how to interpret the segments.

General Ledger's Accounting Flexfields make the most extensive use of the Key Flexfield structure out of all the applications. It is the only package to use three features of Key Flexfields, namely parent–child relationships, rollup groups, and compiled-value attributes. Chapter 2 describes these features in the context of implementation concepts.

Descriptive Flexfields

Descriptive Flexfields (DFFs) allow users to define custom fields into standard forms without modifying the system. Oracle includes a one-column [ ] "beer mug" device in regions that correspond to tables capable of carrying DFF data. When you navigate to the beer mug in a form where the DFF is active, a window pops up to display and capture DFF segments. Your DFF specification includes text to identify both a user-defined field in the DFF pop-up and a specification of the value set that is used to validate it.

A DFF exists as values in a series of columns usually named ATTRIBUTE1 through ATTRIBUTE*n* in the underlying table. There are exceptions; the Receivables interface uses two DFFs, a standard DFF on the ATTRIBUTE*n* columns and another on a set named INTERFACE_LINE_ATTRIBUTE*n*. Because there is no generated key before the rows are imported, Oracle Receivables uses the interface-line DFF to provide the foreign-key link among the interface tables RA_INTERFACE_LINES, RA_INTERFACE_SALESCREDITS, and RA_INTERFACE_DISTRIBUTIONS.

Oracle has established in advance which tables support Descriptive Flexfields. They include the ATTRIBUTE*n* columns in the table layout and a field for the DFF on the forms that maintain the table. Use the Define Flexfield Segments form to activate the DFF by defining how the segments will be used.

Programmers can populate DFF columns by other means, such as database triggers and stored procedures, which totally bypass the DFF validation. The concept of a Descriptive Flexfield is immaterial to pulling data out of the tables for character-based reporting; including them requires custom programming in any case.

A typical use of DFFs is in purchasing. Federal law allows contractors to request expedited delivery of materials to be used on defense contracts. The contractor passes the contract number and defense rating down to the supplier, which then lets them jump the sequential delivery queue for hard-to-get items. A federal contractor might define the following DFF in the header block of the Enter Purchase Orders form:

Column Name	Description	Format	Value Set
ATTRIBUTE1	Contract number	Alpha, 20 char	None
ATTRIBUTE2	Government priority	Alpha, 2 char	DODX

The value set DODX would contain two entries: DO and DX. As a result of this definition, a block containing the following fields would appear when the user entered the DFF field of the input form:

Contract Number _____
Priority _____

If the DFF were defined as mandatory, the user would not be able to exit the block without making an entry. "Contract" could be anything, but "Priority" would have to be DO or DX. The entered values would be stored in ATTRIBUTE1 and ATTRIBUTE2 of PO_HEADERS, the base table for the Headers zone.

Oracle EBS's standard report-submission form uses the Descriptive Flexfield device to accept run-time parameters, a usage that taxes the DFF architecture to its fullest. A range of value sets prompts users for beginning and ending values, such as a range of inventory items to include in a cost rollup. You can use special validation to have the user enter a Key Flexfield value as a parameter. It pops the Key Flexfield, guides the user through the entry of a valid value, and captures the generated key column as the parameter.

Contexts

Contexts enable you to have a different set of flexfields appear based on the type of record or the value of another field. In setting up Inventory, you might want the Purchasing category to carry flexfields naming the normal procurement vehicle and normal safety-stock percentage for new items in the category, but Order Entry might carry the normal order-ship time you quote for products in the category. As another example, Oracle Receivables handles invoicing for Order Entry and for Oracle Projects. Each system tags the invoices it passes to Oracle Receivables for billing with system-unique data fields. Projects uses a project number; Order Entry uses a pick-slip identifier. Receivables is *context sensitive*, meaning that it uses the context to determine what the fields mean. The DFF will react differently depending on the value of its Context field.

Flexfield Validation

Flexfield segments are more useful if they are validated, so that you give the user a number of values rather than a free text field. It might be necessary to make sure the country or area code in a telephone number is valid, or that Department 739 exists within a company. The structure of a list of valid values called a *value set*. A value set can be used in many different flexfield definitions; for example, a value set with two valid values: Yes and No. They can be handled in two ways. Oracle EBS provides tables and update screens for users to maintain smaller, not-so-volatile value sets. Alternatively, you can use SQL to select a column in a table anywhere in Oracle, inside or outside the EBS applications, in which valid values are to be found. A second column can be identified as the description to help the user choose a value.

Cross-Validation Rules

There are usually flexfield combinations that do not make sense and should not be allowed. The department number associated with asset and liability accounts in an Accounting Flexfield must usually be all zeroes. If the country code for a phone number is 011 (for the United States), area code 911 and prefix 555 are not valid. Cross-validation rules can prevent users from entering these combinations.

The values in a dependent value set depend on the value of another, independent segment. General Ledger subaccounts are commonly dependent on the account segment. Assume, for example, that the meanings you give for accounts 1001 (Cash in Banks) and 1002 (Money Market Assets) are always the same within the value set. However, in your subaccount value set you might define 01 to mean Citizens Bank when the account is 1001, but Rushmore Fund when account is 1002.

TIP
Make flexfield segments as independent as possible of one another. Most dependent-segment relationships, such as department within division, change over time. You have more flexibility if you use parent–child relationships in a flexfield segment instead of defining hierarchies into the flexfield structure itself. It is tedious to constantly maintain dependent value sets or cross-validation rules.

Cross-validation and dependent-segment validation are complicated to manage. They work best when the segment values do not change often. A flexfield that includes complex, volatile, and difficult-to-validate segment values merits re-examination. It might be possible to exclude segments or control them by administrative procedures rather than by automated validation.

Cross-validation rules follow INCLUDE/EXCLUDE logic. A simple rule that most companies use is to force the department number to the default on asset and liability accounts. Assuming a very simple three-segment Accounting Flexfield, the rules would be as follows:

Action	Company Low	Company High	Department Low	Department High	Account Low	Account High
INCLUDE	00	99	000	999	00000	99999
EXCLUDE	00	99	001	999	00000	19999

These rules are applied in sequence. The first one here says that all Accounting Flexfields are valid if the company is between 00 and 99, the department between 000 and 999, and the account between 00000 and 99999. That's everything; if you were to use only this rule, there would be no invalid combinations.

The second rule excludes combinations in which the department is anything other than 000, for all values of company and for values of account between 00000 and 19999. In other words, combination 01-010-05555 would be invalid. Although it is in the INCLUDE range for the first rule, it is also in the EXCLUDE range for the second rule, because 010 falls between 001 and 999, and 05555 falls between 00000 and 19999. The effect of both rules together is that only department 000 is valid with any account in the range 00000 to 199999.

Though these INCLUDE/EXCLUDE rules could be applied differently, Oracle recommends that you stick with their convention of defining one INCLUDE followed by a series of EXCLUDES. It is harder to debug and harder to maintain if you do cross-validation with a series of INCLUDES, such as the following—which is logically equivalent to the previous set:

Action	Company Low	Company High	Department Low	Department High	Account Low	Account High
INCLUDE	00	99	000	000	00000	19999
INCLUDE	00	99	000	999	20000	99999

The recommended approach favors leniency in that errors would result in failing to exclude invalid combinations rather than excluding valid ones. You can usually trust the system users to know their data. Their own caution usually keeps them from entering bad values, and you can be sure you will hear from them when they cannot enter good ones.

The EBS applications apply different edit mechanics as rows are created, updated, and queried. As you create a master record with a Key Flexfield identifier, all the segment values must be valid and the combination must pass the cross-validation check. This is the only time cross-validation rules are used. Changing them later has no effect on records you have already created.

If you create a row with a combination of valid segments but later disable an individual segment, the master record remains in the database and can be transacted. General Ledger allows you to disable account and department values, preventing their use in new code combinations, while still accepting journals to be posted against existing code combinations using those segments. The point to remember is that disabling an individual segment value does not prevent transactions against existing records. To prevent all transactions against a given GL account value, you would need to disable every existing code combination that uses the value.

Flexfield Security

Flexfield security enables you to control access to Key and Descriptive Flexfield combinations at the Responsibility level. It is often applied to the Accounting Flexfield to define different responsibilities for different GL companies and prevent companies from making entries in each other's books. You might apply it to the System Item Flexfield to reserve a range of item numbers for the engineering department and prevent manufacturing from creating or referencing items within the range, or to the Asset Flexfield if you want to distribute responsibility to different organizations.

You write the exclusion rules in the same format as the cross-validation rules. You give each set of rules a name, and associate the names with Responsibilities. As a flexfield is presented to the user, AOL filters out the values that the rules prevent the user from accessing.

Flexfield Definition

There are several reasons for having any complex flexfield structure laid out in a document: It documents the flexfield usage and provides a single source from which the flexfield can be copied identically into multiple instances. Additionally, because flexfield definitions persist in memory even after they have been changed in the database, flexfields are easier to debug if they are entered afresh for every test.

When you have multiple contexts for a flexfield, you usually need a separate series of segment definitions for each context. Although different contexts might have the same segment, the edits are often different. It is generally easier to define two distinct value sets, each of them simple, than to define a complex one to do double duty. The spreadsheet (or word-processor) columns for each segment within a context should include those covered in the following sections.

Flexfield Information

The power of flexfields is that you can define their appearance to the user, the relationships of the segments to each other, and their validation. The setup is through a set of forms, requiring an understanding of the concepts but no technical skills. The information required for the setup is as follows:

- **Segment name**   This is the label that will appear when the flexfield is presented.
- **Security flag (Y/N)**   Do you want flexfield security? If you define access rules, security can restrict the users who can access a flexfield. You can also use security merely to prevent users from changing values in a flexfield that is meant only to display information.

For example, Oracle Payables gives the option of importing the DFF values from employee expense reports as you convert them into the invoices used for reimbursement. You might want the DFF values to be visible on the invoice, but if you allow users to change them, they will become inconsistent with the expense-report values.

■ **Segment format (Char or Number)** This refers to the entered value; not the hidden value that will eventually be stored. Char is appropriate most of the time even when the values are numeric, such as for General Ledger accounts. You do need to define the format as number for numeric-range validation: 10 comes before 2 in an alphabetic comparison, but not in a numeric.

■ **Segment length** How many characters do you want entered? It is best to make segments equal to the length defined for the column returned by the validation and the default WHERE clauses. The flexfield-presentation routines will encounter errors that users cannot bypass if the results exceed the length you give. The size of the description plus 150 characters maximum for the value exceeds the width of the screen. Sometimes you have to specify a display length less than the segment length in order to fit the flexfield on the screen; in that case, the segment will scroll.

■ **Validation type** This is usually "None," "Independent," "Dependent," "Special," or "Table." Value pairs are used for specifying ranges, primarily as parameters. Special validation is useful for entering Key Flexfield values as parameters.

■ **Value-set name** This will tie the DFF to an existing value set, limiting the values available to only those in the standard set of user-defined values, known as a quickpick. Since value sets can be difficult to debug, because of the persistence of their values in memory, it is useful in debugging to define new value sets rather than fixing old ones. At least in your test instance, it is convenient to give value sets a suffix such as "_00," so you can change them globally within your word-processing source document, including all :$FLEX$.value_set_name references, as you debug them.

Value-Set Information

Value sets can be very sophisticated, incorporating SQL querying from several tables and able to populate the database with one column (such as an internal ID) and show the user a different one (such as the related description). Their design requires careful thought; the following information will need to be decided on before starting the setup through the forms:

■ **Tables** Make a list of the tables referenced in the validation SQL, each with a one-character alias. You can leave the Source Application field blank. Tables can actually come from multiple applications, or even from outside the E-Business Suite.

■ **Value-column name** This is what the user will see.

■ **Description-column name** This is what the user will see as confirmation. This also can be handled by additional columns, with the small difference that the description is presented even when the value is filled by default, which is not the case for additional columns.

■ **Hidden column** If you make an entry here, this column, rather than the value column named earlier, will be stored in ATTRIBUTEn. This is useful for picking up generated keys or code values.

■ **Additional column** These are values that will be shown to help the user make a selection when he or she is presented a list of values for a segment. For instance, it might help when asking a user to select a customer number to present the customer name and marketing contact.

■ **WHERE clause for the value set** Use the table aliases established earlier to keep this as short as possible. You can reference the value selected in value sets associated with prior segments by :$FLEX$.value_set_name.

Additional Flexfield Information

For the convenience of the data inputters, you can define a SQL default for the flexfield definition. The format for selecting the default value in the flexfield closely parallels the WHERE clause of the value set that validates it, so it is convenient to keep them side by side. Economy is important: The length of the SQL phrase is limited to 200 characters in the Default Value field of the Define Flexfield and Define Parameters screens. As with the WHERE clause earlier in the value set, you can refer to the values selected in prior segments by :$FLEX$.value_set_name.

Often, once an Oracle Form or Responsibility has loaded a value set, the value-set definition will persist in memory even after it has been changed in the database. The WHERE clause in a value-set definition often presents this problem. You will find it difficult to perfect your code by changing it in place and retesting, even if you navigate out of the form and change Responsibilities. You will usually find it easier to abandon and re-enter unsuccessful value sets than to try to fix them. The work goes faster if you can create a new value set for each test by updating the value-set names in a reference document, then copy and paste them into the application.

National Language Support (NLS)

Many companies that use Oracle E-Business Suite are multinational. Oracle's National Language Support (NLS) satisfies the need to operate your Oracle database and Oracle EBS applications in a language other than English. With the introduction of the UTF-8 character set, all languages can be supported in a single database instance. UTF-8 is a superset of other character sets and uses multiple bytes per character for some languages. This does have an effect on storage space required. The E-Business Suite supports the installation of forms, reports, messages, help, and some reference data in multiple national languages in a single instance.

AOL-Level Language Determination

A user's national language is under his or her control. The E-Business Suite uses the mechanism of profile values to control language, territory, radix, and date format. They can be updated in the course of a session through the Preferences screen in Self-Service Applications or the User Profile screen in the core application. This approach makes national language independent of security considerations, such as Responsibilities, and it means you do not have to confine a multilingual user to one language—for example, in an international shared-service-center environment.

Internally, the language is carried as a session variable. SQL's USERENV function can return the national-language attribute of an Oracle log-in session and the current form. Programmers can take language into consideration in PL/SQL routines and even SQL*Plus code. Specifically, it gives Oracle EBS a device to determine the language in which to communicate with any given user.

Literals in screen canvases are compiled into Oracle forms and reports. Oracle EBS handles the translation centrally; the installation provides forms generated in the necessary national languages.

A single Applications Server can handle multiple languages, but obviously must have the relevant files installed. The Applications Server directory structure includes subdirectories for each language; a structure to support American English and French would look something like the following:

```
APPL_TOP
  BOM
    12.1.3
    forms
      us
        BOMxxxxx.fmb (forms 10g portable source file)
        BOMxxxxx.fmx (forms10g generated runtime file)
      fr
        BOMxxxxx.fmb (forms 10g portable source file)
        BOMxxxxx.fmx (forms10g generated runtime file)
    mesg
us.msb (English messages)
fr.msb (French messages)
```

The Oracle E-Business Suite uses its own message format. Instead of having all possible messages and help text hard-coded into the forms, Oracle EBS puts in subroutine calls that name the message to be presented. The forms find the message in the appropriate national-language library. Oracle's device of staging the messages in operating-system files on the server, rather than storing them on the database server, makes the presentation more efficient.

National Language Support for Reports

Separate versions of reports programs are required for the same reason as they are for forms. Their boilerplate includes compiled literals in headings and field identifiers; they need to select the appropriate translations of lookup codes, flexfield values, and data fields, and use the right display format for numbers and dates. National-language versions of report programs are stored using the same directory scheme as for forms.

National Language Support for Flexfields

Flexfields are used to capture variable data and report run-time parameters. The prompts for each segment are in the Forms user's chosen language. As part of your setup, you need to translate your custom flexfields and value sets for the countries to be supported by your implementation. A user-profile option controls whether flexfield entries are keyed left to right or, as in Arabic or Hebrew, right to left.

National Language in Data

Data are defined here as information that your organization stores in the database. Perhaps the language is French, and you enter a description such as **Marteau**. When you click the translation icon on the toolbar, a form will pop up with the languages available for translation and allow you to make entries for those you wish. You might want to enter the English translation as **Hammer** and the Spanish as **Martillo**.

The form presents the translation that corresponds to the language of the session. If the user were connected through a session in French in the previous example, bringing up the record just entered in a query form would display only "Marteau."

Alerts

Oracle*Alert is licensed as part of the E-Business Suite, yet it functions more like an extension of AOL in that it supplements the features of all the E-Business Suite. An alert is essentially a single SQL statement or PL/SQL block and instruct what to do with the rows it returns. The most common action is to e-mail them to the people who need to take action. You can have an alert generate one e-mail per row or put all rows into a single e-mail. You can have multiple recipients. Alerts can be used in place of reports, with the following benefits:

- Alerts send information only when it is needed, whereas reports are usually produced on a periodic basis and might not always be promptly read.
- Alerts send just the relevant information; not a whole report.
- Alerts target just the people who need to know.
- Alerts are easy for programmers to implement. They justify their cost by making the business more responsive and reducing paper costs.

There are two types of alerts: periodic and event. Periodic alerts are fired by the clock, event alerts by a predefined change in a database table (such as an insert, update, or delete). Event alerts usually require more system resources than periodic alerts, because they have to execute every time the database changes. Unless the recipient needs to respond extremely fast, and you can count on the recipient to actively monitor his or her e-mail, a periodic alert that runs a few times a day should suffice.

The periodic-alert mechanism has a clock at its core. It wakes up on the schedule you set to see what needs to be checked. It executes a check for each alert whose time is due. If the check comes back positive, it takes an action. Sending an e-mail message is the most common action, but alerts can kick off virtually any kind of process within Oracle EBS or the operating-system shell, such as the following:

- Check the age and number of completed concurrent requests on the system. If the number is too great, kick off a job to delete the oldest ones or send a message to have the DBA do so.
- Initiate a process at the operating-system level to send or receive electronic data transfers. Though alerts have the power to handle such operations, most users implement them through the Concurrent Manager.
- See whether any tables or indexes are close to being out of space. Make a quick fix by allowing more extents and alert the DBA.
- Check for data exceptions such as a missing field value that might be optional in Oracle EBS but required by your business practice. You might choose an alert as an inexpensive alternative to modifying a form for the purpose of tightening the edits.

The real-time nature of event-alert triggers generally dictates that they work one row at a time. Periodic-alert triggers can be written either way. In general, a single message with multiple actions is easier for a user to deal with than many messages with one action apiece. You do not want to flood in-boxes.

Because they are written in SQL and not highly formatted, alerts are generally quicker and easier to write than custom reports. Oracle Alert is an end-user tool; thus individual alerts enjoy support from Oracle at the same level as, for instance, FSG reports in Oracle General Ledger. Oracle does not assume similar responsibility for custom code you write in Oracle*Reports or

SQL*Plus. Nonetheless, alerts do require knowledge of programming. The people writing them need the level of understanding of the Oracle EBS tables that is provided by the Technical Reference Manuals available for each module. An online electronic technical reference manual for the E-Business Suite (eTRM) also provides details on schema and table structure for objects that developers will need to understand while developing applications for the EBS suite. The eTRM is available at http://etrm.oracle.com or at the My Oracle Support site (http://support.oracle .com). Note: a valid My Oracle Support account is required to access the eTRM.

Event alerts can be CPU intensive, so you should weigh the gain versus the cost involved in developing these types of alerts for active tables. If used effectively, alerts are a great tool, but if used excessively, they become a drag on the system and fill up users' mailboxes with unimportant notifications. Testing the usage of new alerts in a sandbox nonproduction environment is highly recommended to avoid any potential issues with the current or future production environment.

TIP

Programming staff should consider whether an alert would do the job before undertaking a custom report.

Application Management

All the standard applications are preregistered in AOL. You register new applications that you build and install yourself under AOL using the same conventions. This knowledge is essential to developers writing enhancements to the system.

In upgrading or applying patches, the process might at times alter or completely delete and re-create AOL data that are owned by the standard applications. However, these processes will never affect data that are owned by your custom applications if they have been set up correctly.

Users and Responsibilities

In setting up an Oracle EBS user, you define the person in terms of his or her role in the business. Of course, the person needs a user ID and a password, the same kind of access control as for a network, an operating system, or Oracle. You also provide the user's name and e-mail address.

A person is linked by his or her name to the Human Resources system, which places the person in the hierarchy of organizations and managers. Systems such as Purchasing might require managerial approval for some type of transactions. The applications maintain a link between people in the HR master table (PER_PEOPLE_F) and system users (FND_USER). This link frequently determines access to Purchasing, Payables, and Human Resources functions.

Oracle Alert and Workflow processes use the e-mail address to notify a user of actions that need attention. E-mail is an especially convenient medium for getting the message to those users whose jobs do not require that they log on to the applications frequently.

Responsibilities are Oracle's device for giving and controlling access. Granting control user by user and process by process is infeasible. Instead, the systems administrator can do the following:

■   assign multiple functions to a form;

■   put every needed form on one or more low-level menus;

■   put low-level menus on one or more higher-level menus, working up to a top-level menu;

■   create a Responsibility name associated with that top-level menu; and

■   assign one or more users to the Responsibility.

Any user with the Responsibility can get to any process in the associated menu structure. Each user can have as many Responsibilities as necessary. However, as a matter of convenience it is useful to put all their commonly used functions into a single Responsibility, saving users from the effort of constantly changing Responsibilities.

The Responsibilities that Oracle delivers provide maximum access—and minimal control. The systems administrator's best course is to leave them alone and define new, more limited Responsibilities that suit the business and to deactivate the original Responsibilities, at least in the production instance. Creating new responsibilities can seem complex at first and involves developing new high-level menus to be associated with them. The most common need is to offer a more limited number of lower-level menu choices. However, you can also broaden menu choices, even including functions from multiple applications in the menu structure of a single Responsibility.

Your custom high-level menu will usually use the lower-level Oracle menus as delivered. For example, you will usually want to take the ability to create and update inventory items away from most users. However, users who have the privilege can usually both create and update items. Oracle's low-level menu offers those choices. You would place it, as is, on the higher-level menu you create for the inventory-item definition and Responsibility.

The wide-open Responsibilities that Oracle delivers with the system remain useful to the developers. They do not need to be restricted by the administrative controls imposed on production. The primary reasons a systems administrator might limit developers' activity to the development instance are to control system functions and protect sensitive data, both of which can be managed by granting or withholding Oracle Responsibilities. Because the only easy way to create a test instance is to copy production, and production Human Resources/Payroll is bound to contain sensitive personal and salary data for each employee, it makes sense to provide access to those systems on a need-to-know basis. The systems administrator might need to withhold Systems Administration privileges from developers to prevent them from modifying system security and granting themselves access to HR/Payroll.

Security

Encrypted passwords at the levels of the E-Business Suite and Oracle user IDs form the basis of security within the EBS. The system administrator assigns EBS user IDs and initial passwords to new users. The password assigned by the systems administrator is immediately expired. The new user is prompted to change it when he or she first logs on, after which it is known only to him or her. The systems administrator can change it but cannot read it.

The following steps show how a user moves through the two levels of security to get to the database. From left to right:

1. The user presents his or her user ID and password to AOL at log-on. This logon is done after the user has logged on to the operating system and network, which may or may not be password protected.

2. AOL presents a list of the Responsibilities authorized to the user. Each Responsibility is associated with a top-level menu, which branches down to a menu tree of EBS functions. The systems administrator custom-tailors the top-level menus to meet the needs of the installation. Most organizations stick with the submenus that Oracle distributes.

3. Each menu entry represents a lower-level menu or an Oracle Form. The bottom level is always a form (although it might be the form that invokes reports and other batch processes).

4. AOL looks up the Oracle user ID and password appropriate to the application to which the process belongs. There is a common view, the APPS schema, which has been granted the appropriate permissions on all the application schemas. AOL fetches and decrypts the password for the appropriate user ID, then activates the form in a session with that Oracle user ID. The form may go through this process again to kick off batch jobs such as reports.

5. The Oracle EBS user winds up using a form or batch process that has access to the Oracle RDBMS. Changes the user can make to the database are limited by the functions programmed into the process and the permissions the Oracle EBS has on database tables.

There is an added need for security with Internet Computing, because with the Internet you have no control over who will attempt to access your system.

Once a user is validated to EBS, the process is the same for all users. The menu structure provides functional security, preventing unauthorized access to processes. Oracle Responsibilities have the following two mechanisms to control access to data:

- ■ **Multi-Org**   Restricts users to a single organization or operating unit.
- ■ **Flexfield Value Security**   Blocks access to ranges of flexfield values.

Multi-Org cleanly segregates data through the use of views defined on major tables. Those views automatically limit access to subordinate tables, because there is no way to get to the detail except through a join on the master table. The tables on which views are defined have names ending in "_ALL."

The view definitions use an interesting device in the Oracle RDBMS itself. The applications set the organization ID as an RDBMS-level environment variable. Whereas views in the past have referenced only data in the database, these Multi-Org views apply this environment variable to determine which rows are included. They select from the "_ALL" tables where the organization ID in the data is equal to that attached to the environment variable derived from the Responsibility. Because the views are one-to-one with the underlying tables, the applications can insert and update through them.

Flexfield Value Security operates at a lower level, within an organization. You set up rules to apply to individual Key Flexfields, such as the Accounting Flexfield or System Item (inventory part number) Flexfield, and assign the rules to Responsibilities. AOL filters the rows it presents, on screens or in batch processes, through the rules for the current Responsibility. Here are some examples of the types of problems that Flexfield Value Security can help you prevent:

- ■ One organization creates ledger journals using another organization's accounts.
- ■ Unauthorized persons see budget and actual journals for personnel expenses.
- ■ Manufacturing uses a range of part numbers restricted for Engineering.

Instances

The Oracle E-Business Suite environment is built upon the Oracle Relational Database Management System (RDBMS). A high-level overview of the database structure is essential to understanding the applications and to providing a basis for communicating with DBAs and systems administrators.

Let's present a high-level view of the elements in the RDBMS. An *instance* is a complete Oracle database. There is usually more than one instance per environment. The project organization determines the number of instances, because you tend to use one per test phase and at least one for development. Four is probably a minimum: Oracle's Demo instance, the Conference Room Pilot, a Test instance, and Production.

The database stores the data and also is the repository for stored procedures and triggers that Oracle EBS uses to manipulate the data. The system tables that keep track of database objects, such as tables and users, are themselves data and therefore within the instance. Most of these core system tables reside in the APPLSYS or APPLSYSPUB schemas.

Keeping the Oracle database in sync with the software, which is maintained at an operating-system level, requires good configuration management. It is recommended to use a commercial-grade software-configuration management system to keep track of current patches applied as well as software code implemented between the various Oracle EBS environments. Patches come from Oracle and from any development work that may be underway on-site. Typically, these patches will introduce some new software and changes to the database schema. Although it is possible, it is safest not to have instances sharing the same software libraries (often known to DBAs as the *codeset*). You will have great difficulty maintaining them in sync, as there probably will be conflicting pressures from the users of each (because that is the reason for having more than one environment). Before you apply a patch to the Oracle E-Business Suite, make sure to test it out first in a nonproduction sandbox environment. Be sure to work with the functional and development teams to ensure that the patch resolves the issue and does not break any existing application functionality. You can apply application patches in hot mode, without taking down the application tiers, but in most cases you will need to bounce the application tiers—involving a short downtime when applying these patches. Notification should be given well in advance to the functional and development teams, so as to not impact project schedules.

Bringing the database up or down takes place at the instance level. Oracle expects all the EBS data to reside within a single instance unless you have a clustered environment with Oracle Real Application Clusters (RAC). For the purposes of the E-Business Suite, either all or none of the tables are available. The Order Entry process should never hang up, for instance, because Inventory is not available to validate the product number. There is a device called a *database link* that makes it possible to join tables across instances and interface data from remote systems. It is possible to distribute the processing across nodes in a network system, but Oracle EBS does not support databases distributed across machines.

The disk space for an instance exists in files at the operating-system level, usually several files spread on more than one hard disk. To Oracle, these are *tablespaces*; to the operating system, they are files. A tablespace can consist of more than one disk file. This allows for large tablespaces, spread over more than one hard disk, and for expanding tablespaces. Table placement in tablespaces and on disks can be independent of schemas. Tablespaces represent the outer limit of objects recognized by Oracle and the inner boundary of those recognized by the UNIX, NT, or other operating system. DBAs manage tablespaces. Users have no need to be aware of them. With Oracle 10g/11g as the standard database version for Oracle R12 EBS, you can also use new ways to store the Oracle R12 EBS database with bigfile tablespaces and also with Oracle Automated Storage Management (ASM). Oracle ASM is a volume manager that provides for striping and mirroring (SAME) of the database environment for better performance, availability, and scalability. Many new features exist for Oracle 11g to improve the storage, management, and performance of the database tier; we discuss these in Chapter 20.

Tables are at the heart of the relational concept. A table is made up of a number of *rows*, all of which have the same *columns*. A table is like a spreadsheet, which is the reason tables are usually shown symbolically as grids. *Relationships* make the difference between a database and, say, a collection of spreadsheets. Two RDBMS tables can be related to one another by a common column. The PO_HEADERS_ALL and PO_LINES_ALL tables in the Purchasing application have the HEADER_ID column in common. The database can use the relationship based on this shared column to find the customer associated with a purchase-order line or the items associated with a purchase-order header. Spreadsheets cannot do that.

Each table exists within one tablespace and belongs to one of the users defined to that instance of the Oracle RDBMS. A user is known by a user ID, or *schema*. Database users are distinct from the AOL users described earlier. The original notion was that a schema was a group of related tables—a database design. That concept became outdated, as the Financials design now integrates a large number of schemas. In any case, one schema, or user, can give permission for other users to read and modify data in tables it owns.

Oracle EBS concepts function at the table level. Key tenets of the architecture are as follows:

- Each application module within Oracle EBS is known to the Oracle RDBMS by one Oracle user ID or schema. Records of individual users are stored within the E-Business Suite applications themselves, and the EBS application users will not have corresponding database user IDs.

- Each application module owns tables through its Oracle user ID. The application modules achieve their integration by sharing tables with one another. They are written with the assumption that all tables are available all the time; that is to say, in the same instance.

- Every application module grants full permissions on all its objects to a single schema, named APPS. With more than 200 products now in the Oracle E-Business Suite, this simplification is essential. Every form and Concurrent Manager process initiated within EBS uses the APPS schema.

File Storage

Each application has its own root within the operating-system directory structure, and each kind of code and operating-system data has its own home within that root. The Database Server tier might have a similar directory structure in addition to the database files, as in some environments it will take over from the Applications Server if the latter fails; in that case the software has to be exactly the same on both machines.

The client side looks very clean in an E-Business Suite implementation, because with the exception of the required Java plug-in for the user's desktop client browser, there is no need for any software. Even reports tools such as OBIEE and Discoverer have migrated to a Web-enabled model. However, there are still some desktop products, such as Applications Desktop Integrator (ADI).

Quickcodes and Lookup Types

Oracle keeps data in the database, external to the programs. For the most part, Oracle-written programs use code values instead of literals. For example, an mrp_planning_code value of 3 means MRP planning; 6 means not planned. Using codes is a tenet of a properly normalized data architecture and is the only reasonable way to handle multilanguage implementations. It prevents data redundancy. The delivered databases are seeded with a number of such Oracle-provided data values.

Quickcodes support quickpicks. They offer users a choice of codes for values such as invoice type or payment terms. There are separate quickcodes tables in each application that uses them. Users are generally expected to modify and add to the delivered quickcodes.

A *lookup* is a combination of a code and a description. The code is stored in the database, and the description in a lookup table. Descriptions are carried in the user's national language. The lookup tables are generally populated by the scripts in the application's /install/odf directory. Whereas users are expected to customize quickcode values, they usually do not modify lookup-table values except to support custom extensions.

Managing the Oracle EBS Environment

Any group of Oracle EBS users will invariably have a number of copies of each package installed. Production always takes one copy. Obviously, developers and DBAs should never jeopardize production by testing their patches and improvements there; they need their own copies. Fixing what is and creating what is to come are two different jobs that usually need different environments. Successfully managing software multiplicity can be a challenge, but many strategies are available to DBAs and implementers:

- multiple host processors;
- multiple database instances in clustered configuration with Oracle RAC;
- multiple versions of the Oracle EBS software on quad-core processors;
- multiple versions by creating gold and cloned images in a virtualized environment with VMware;
- multiple installations of a product within one database instance;
- multiple organizations within a single installation of a single product, through the Multi-Org feature; and
- multiple currency reporting for a single package.

TIP
Just as there are different types of users, there are different paths to multiplicity. The strategies that succeed for one group may not be appropriate for another.

Multiple Environments for Development

DBAs use separate machines, database instances, and program-directory structures to separate testing and development from production. The DBAs will be a lobby requesting fewer environments during an implementation. There are always pressures to have more, from the functional consultants who want a play area (often called the sandbox) as well as one or two test instances. The development team would ideally like to have separate development instances for customizations (with test transactions) and data conversions (which should be empty of transactions). With the advent of cloud computing and virtualization technologies such as VMware vCenter and VMware ESXi Server, creating multiple environments is far easier and more economical than ever before. Rapid provisioning of additional environments can be deployed quickly and easily for the Oracle EBS at less cost and time than using physical bare-metal environments.

The normal convention is to talk about instances and environments. An instance is just the database, whereas an environment is the database plus the software libraries. Wherever possible, keep this a one-to-one relationship.

Code

The DBA and developers need separate code libraries and directory structures to test Oracle distributions of new versions of applications before putting them into production, and to test patches before applying them in production. Oracle builds the software-release level into the directory-tree name at the operating-system level. For instance, all the code for Release 12.1.3 of Purchasing will be in this directory:

```
$APPL_TOP/po/12.1.3
```

By this convention, the Oracle install scripts will know exactly where to put Version 12.1.3—and will create the new subdirectory.

```
$APPL_TOP/po/12.1.3
```

Patches are a different issue. Oracle patch distributions modify the code within a distribution library. Oracle emphasizes—and we emphasize—that patches must be tested before being put into production. The only way to do that is to have a separate copy of the code libraries for test purposes. Apply the patch in the DBA test library (and the associated test instance), test the patch, and then use the same Oracle patch procedure to reapply it in production (or the appropriate one in the course of an implementation) once it works. We highly recommend that you create and use a patch spreadsheet to avoid careless errors and to maintain the status for the patch(es) applied and test results.

Oracle's convention is to have developers define custom applications to own custom modules. Doing this works for the following reasons:

- The Oracle E-Business Suite applications are designed to share your data and custom tools with each other. It is easy; for example, say that you have designed an inventory form to use within your custom inventory application. You can easily include that form in a menu of standard Oracle inventory forms. It is just as easy to incorporate your customized reports.

- Oracle's upgrade scripts touch only standard applications. Putting custom code in a separate application protects it from upgrade and patch activity.

Database Instances

The high level of integration within the Oracle E-Business Suite can lead to unexpected consequences in development. Repeatable results have been an essential part of testing philosophy since Roger Bacon pioneered the scientific method. However, with the E-Business Suite a tester will often alter the database in a way that cannot be undone. Moreover, a tester cannot know, or take time to figure out, the full impact of testing; for instance, a functional test that generates purchase orders to test EDI can affect the General Ledger, Accounts Receivable, Inventory, and Manufacturing.

The ideal solution would be to create separate environments in which each developer could test in isolation. The disk space this would require makes it unfeasible, precisely because of Oracle's high level of integration. Each test environment requires data for all the E-Business Suite applications and the full software libraries. To stick with the previous example, Purchasing requires items from Inventory, code combinations from the Ledger, and vendors shared with Accounts Payable.

The reality is that Oracle Financials developers have to establish conventions that let them work effectively within compromised environments. These safeguards usually include the following:

- Keeping two or three Oracle environments for development, corresponding roughly to development, integration testing, and patch testing.

- Periodically refreshing the test databases, usually by restoring copies of production. You must take care with this, as some software is installed in the database and relates to some in the software libraries, as described earlier. The copy populates the test instance with real data, as distinguished from live data. They are no longer live because they are not being used to run the business. Real data are essential for test purposes. Users understand the real data, they explain their problems in terms of real data, and of course it would be a huge task to generate representative test data for all the Financials.

- Using custom scripts as necessary to sanitize the real data by scrambling salary, medical, budget, and other sensitive data.

- When possible, having developers use rollbacks or SQL scripts to reset the database to its initial state prior to their testing.

- Allocating ranges of data to different testing purposes. For instance, Accounts Payable testers might restrict themselves to vendors starting with A and stock numbers starting with 1. Purchasing testers might then use B and 2.

Whatever the compromises, the developers will always work with fewer environments than they would like. Two is the lowest number that is at all workable.

To refresh an environment, the DBAs can *clone* from another one. This is a process that copies the database, the software libraries, and all the database-specific setup files. There are a number of postcopy activities involved in a clone that make it a long, nontrivial exercise. To refresh a database is a simpler process: taking a backup and restoring it over the top of the database to be refreshed. It is well worth understanding the big picture of database-administration activities, as they are always critical to the success of a project.

Many organizations keep the Vision database that Oracle delivers available for developers to experiment with. It is easier to try screen processes with a fully populated system than with a new one, which would require setup and generation of master data before it could accept transactions.

Conference Room Pilot (CRP) instances are a useful testing device for setup scripts and data. A CRP is usually an uncontrolled environment, allowing developers and users alike to conduct experiments without being concerned about the impact their transactions might have on testing. Because CRP is uncontrolled, usually using the wide-open Oracle Responsibilities, it is important to maintain external documentation for the setup values used. You can use Oracle's Application Implementation Methodology or the approaches outlined in subsequent chapters.

Multiple Use of the E-Business Suite in Production

Most of the E-Business Suite applications were initially designed to support a single organization with a single set of setup parameters. It became common in earlier versions of the applications to see multiple installations of Fixed Assets or Accounts Payable within a single enterprise, each one supporting some portion of the organization. Oracle's Multi-Org feature now supports multiple organizations within a single installation of a package. Multiple installations are no longer supported in the E-Business Suite.

Multi-Org

Applications using Oracle's Multi-Org feature (described in Chapter 2) are able to physically combine the records of logically separate business units. Keeping all the records in a single installation of the E-Business Suite is easier from an administrative perspective. It also makes it possible to draw from different groups' information to produce higher-level reports, such as a summary of customer or vendor activity across the entire company. Online users, however, are confined to working only with data that belong to their own organization.

The user's log-in Responsibility is associated with a single organization. A PL/SQL function, created especially for Oracle EBS, sets an environment variable to indicate that organization. The environment variable can be referenced by an SQL/PL/SQL function call. Specifically, it can be included in the WHERE clause of a view.

Most processes as of 10.7 reference the master tables through a view instead of directly. They can update through the view because it uses only the one table. The WHERE clause will restrict the view to records belonging to the user's organization.

Some tables, such as the customer master, contain rows that are available to all organizations. The convention in that case is to leave the ORG_ID (or ORGANIZATION_ID) column NULL. The view uses convoluted logic with a series of nested NVL functions to select rows with either a NULL or the right organization code. The code that generates the views is available in the /install/ odf subdirectories of the various application directories.

Multi-Org poses a setup rather than an installation question, something for the functional users to decide more than for the DBA. It adds somewhat to the complexity of using the packages. Users are frequently prompted to tell the system which organization they are in. Moreover, they can become frustrated looking for a purchase order or an item that they know is in the system but cannot find. The application modules will not let them receive a shipment that is not due in to their organization or look at an item that is not defined to their organization. Using Multi-Org requires very well thought-out business procedures.

Multiple Inventory Organizations

Inventory has always had its own set of organizations, separate from those that figure in Multi-Org. A company may have inventory locations for manufacturing, sales, and distribution. The same items appear in each, but the item-attribute settings vary. One location holds items for sale, another holds them as manufacturing finished goods, and the distribution warehouse does neither. One can receive the item; another can order it.

Inventory provides the essential capability to define an item globally. This means that the $8 \times 3/4$-inch screw used to build tractors in Peoria and trailers in Tucson has the same part number in each operation. Or the waffle iron built by an overseas subsidiary carries the same item number there as in the United States, where it is sold. Managers can use the global definition to ask global questions: How many screws do we need to buy next month, and how many waffle irons must we make? At the same time, it can leave lower-level decisions, such as stockage quantities, make-or-buy, and manufacturing processes, to lower-level organizations within the company.

Profile Options

Oracle EBS applications need to know a lot about specific users. What printer do they use? What print style do they prefer? How many copies do they usually want of reports? Which set of books do they use? What menu style do they prefer? Rather than tediously asking each time, the E-Business Suite keeps a set of defaults for each user, maintained at different levels.

The systems administrator or DBA is responsible for setting appropriate higher-level defaults, so the users have to deal with real only choices. If there is only one printer in the fixed-assets department, the user should not be bothered having to name it. There are four levels of defaults within EBS:

- Site
- Application
- Responsibility within an application
- User

The systems administrator sets profile options at all four levels; however, users can update some of their own, less critical profile options themselves. Because users are at the lowest level in the default chain, whatever is specified in their personal profiles overrides all the other levels. Otherwise, what the systems administrator specifies for a Responsibility overrides the specification for an application module, and those for an application override the defaults for the instance of the Oracle EBS.

AOL enables you to set up profile options to be referenced by custom code. This is a convenient device for communicating the characteristics of individual users. There is no Descriptive Flexfield defined on the FND_USER table, so this feature can be used instead. It is a convenient way to give specific instruction to a generalized module. Some users of a bespoke form might be allowed to update it; others might have view-only capability. Some Responsibilities under which a report is registered might be restricted to viewing reporting data within a single organization. Profile options are straightforward to implement and well supported in PL/SQL. You pass the FND_PROFILE.GET procedure two parameters: the name of the profile option and the name of a field to put the profile value in.

If you are using custom Responsibilities and applications, which is very likely, you must define all the profile options that are set up under the standard Oracle EBS applications and Responsibilities for the custom application and Responsibilities as well. Without this setup, you might experience inconsistencies and data problems.

Oracle's Application Implementation Methodology (AIM)

Even the most limited implementation of Oracle E-Business Suite is a major undertaking. Whether you plan to change them or not, you have to define your business processes to Oracle as a part of setup. The information you assemble about your business processes will be in the hands of many people scattered throughout your organization. A lot of it will never have been committed to writing. Once you have it in hand, you use this information to establish setup parameters for Oracle EBS, devise tests to ensure that they execute your business processes correctly, convert your data over to Oracle, and train your users.

Oracle Consulting Services developed Application Implementation Methodology (AIM) for their installation teams to meet this challenge. They have packaged their expertise as AIM Advantage. Features of the package include:

- planning and management of the implementation project,
- predefined business-process workflows that can serve as your starting point for defining your company's operations,
- tools that will help you analyze and document your business requirements,
- design and development standards,
- conversion and bridging modules, and
- test plans.

The Workflow-based Application Implementation Wizard further automates the process of creating setup parameters. It operates within and supports AIM Advantage. The wizard guides you through a multipackage installation process, displaying the setup screens within each application as appropriate. It recognizes the interdependencies between applications, the sequence in which your setups have to be done, and which setup steps are not necessary based on previous setup decisions.

Oracle Consulting remains closely associated with the AIM products. Its consultants use AIM to achieve consistent results and high productivity across a highly diverse client base. Buying the products means you can make optimal use of Oracle Consulting to support your implementation and use their work products to maintain the system after they have completed. Conversely, other technical-services firms often favor their own tools. You should have *some* methodology, preferably only one. Your project manager will have to assess the productivity and training-cost trade-offs among your existing methodologies, AIM, and other contenders.

Hardware Considerations

Hardware selection for the Oracle E-Business Suite is a multitiered affair. All projects must decide on Applications and Database Server hardware, and determine whether their client PCs are sufficient for the job. Be sure to also verify the correct supported version and platform for Java and Web browsers used on client PC desktops and laptops to avoid problems with forms issues for the users who will be working with the Oracle E-Business Suite. My Oracle Support Notes 389422.1, *Recommended Browsers for Oracle E-Business Suite Release 12*, and 277535.1, *Recommended Set Up for Client/Server Products with Oracle E-Business Suite 11i & R12*, should be consulted to address these issues.

The database server is the largest machine in every configuration and needs to be the most reliable. Industry standards dictate that Unix and Linux are the best overall platforms for the database server with Oracle EBS. In essence, the best overall guideline is to choose a platform already used by a large number of Oracle EBS customers, such as Sun and HP Unix platforms or Windows NT. Linux is also a competitor of the Microsoft operating system in the smaller projects. These are the ones for which Oracle first tests the combination of hardware, operating system, RDBMS release, and Financials release. Oracle provides a certification matrix of hardware and operating-system platforms on the My Oracle Support Site that can give you a basic idea of what combinations are best suited for use with the Oracle E-Business Suite.

Equipment from the major hardware manufacturers is quite scalable. A new user's objective should be to get a platform big enough to start with and capable of growing with the applications. Capacity planning is a difficult and inexact science that has been made less critical by Moore's law, except that the back-end hardware needs to be capable of being upgraded to have more processors. The middle tier is easier to scale, although with a large-scale Self-Service aspect you would be well advised to build performance testing into the project plan. Machine capacity is cheap enough, and machines are scalable enough, that it is not worth spending lots of money analyzing the requirement. When you need more capacity and you cannot wring much more out of your existing system by tuning, you simply buy what you need. The one exception to this is at go-live. You need to ensure that you have sufficiently performance tested the production system to ensure that users have an adequate service. Friends lost in the user community at this stage will take a great effort to win back. Sizing exercises can be performed by consulting with hardware vendors such as Oracle, Dell, HP, IBM, and Cisco.

Other considerations when buying hardware are resilience, failover, and acceptable downtime. You can build resilience into the solution with redundant components. If your production environment is a global enterprise, scheduled downtime will be difficult to arrange and should, therefore, be minimized. Hardware and storage vendors provide solutions to these problems. For example, EMC and Sun provide backup/recovery and replication technologies such as Sun Cluster, EMC SRDF, and HP Service/Guard to perform server- and storage-level mirroring to do online backups of the database. Having multiple application middle-tier servers means a failure in one will cause only a temporary dip in performance rather than an outage. In addition, by implementing multiple application-tier servers, you can use a shared application file system to ease patching and other system maintenance. By implementing multiple database servers with Oracle RAC and Oracle Data Guard, you can scale quickly and easily, as well as have database and server redundancy to protect against a single point of failure.

Conclusion

The E-Business Suite represents the realization of a sweeping vision. Oracle developed general-purpose programming languages and communications, analysis, network, and database components to be sold in the market for custom development tools. At the same time, the company is its own best customer, making Oracle EBS a showcase for what can be done with their database and tools. Control of the technology stack gives Oracle significant advantages in product reliability and performance as well as the speed with which it can incorporate new technologies.

Many of the standard features described here have a long pedigree in the applications. They have, therefore, had time to mature, using feedback from implementations all around the world. There is a considerable body of consultants and independent contractors who have the skills and understanding necessary to exploit these features to the fullest extent. Any methods of reducing the customizations required, by providing built-in flexibility, are able to save time and money in the implementation project.

Oracle is taking advantage of the high level of productivity afforded by its tools to expand the features provided by its E-Business Suite. The new package extends the number of business areas it addresses, specializes the applications for the needs of specific industry segments, and makes Oracle solutions increasingly possible for businesses that have few staff available to manage an implementation.

CHAPTER
20

Oracle E-Business Suite
Technical Architecture

he architecture of Oracle EBS has evolved through four generations: terminal emulation, client server, network computing, and finally the Internet Computing architecture. The differences among them are evident, from the user interface through to the back-end processing. In their style and use of infrastructure, the network, and computing hardware, each reflected a phase in the evolution of corporate computing, in particular the evolution of enterprise resource planning (ERP) systems.

In the early to mid-1990s, many corporate-computing environments were moving away from the mainframe-dominated model. Smaller, Unix-based systems were easier to manage and quicker to implement. Packaged software was ever more popular, and sales of Unix-based ERP systems eclipsed mainframe-based financial-software offerings. SAP was the market leader, but Oracle Financials also fit the mold. It was normally hosted on Unix or DEC's popular VAX operating system. Much like their mainframe predecessors, these systems centralized the required computing power and used low-bandwidth networks to display character-based screens.

Around the mid-1990s, pressure had grown to use the plethora of personal computers that had proliferated in departments all over the corporate world. They were linked by relatively fast local area networks (LANs); this, along with the PC's operating system of choice—Windows—allowed the development of standardized graphical user interfaces. Oracle's database-management systems enabled the client-server revolution, but ironically Oracle chose to focus its energies on improving the functionality of its host-based applications rather than adapt them to the client-server plan.

SAP stole a march when they launched R/3; PeopleSoft soon followed. Oracle played catch-up with their Smartclient offering (from version 10.6). Smartclient groomed the coat of the Financials pedigree and gave it an updated look. It worked well on a LAN, with the client loaded either on PCs or a local server, but its WAN performance suffered by comparison with the terminal-emulation model. Despite distributed-configuration management tools, client-server software imposed a heavy administrative burden.

Oracle—and in particular Larry Ellison—had been an early espouser of Internet technology. The 10.7 NCA (Network Computing Architecture) and versions of the applications combined the ease of use of the GUI interface with the systems-management advantages of centralized computing. The client needed only a Java applet viewer or a browser with a plug-in that was downloaded and cached the first time a PC used the applications. The network-computing architecture, which metamorphosed into the Internet Computing architecture, enabled a swath of new functionalities. Chief among these were Self-Service, Workflow, and Business Intelligence.

Release 12—The E-Business Suite

Building upon the popularity of Oracle Applications 11i, Release 12 provides a complete redesign of the ERP architecture. Oracle R12 provides a new application tier composed of the Oracle 10*g* Application Server (10*g*AS) built upon the foundation of the OC4J (Oracle Containers for Java) enterprise J2EE Web-based technology. Furthermore, Oracle R12 EBS includes the latest versions of the Oracle 10*g*/11*g* Enterprise Edition (EE) database server software for storing and managing database transactions within the E-Business Suite for Oracle.

Architecture Components

So what is this entity known as the E-Business Suite? It comprises three tiers of components. The bottom tier is the database; it holds the structure into which all the data are put that you want to keep. It also holds some of the software—the behind-the-scenes software that delivers some of the business logic required to validate or manipulate the data. Next is the applications tier, which holds the bulk of the software components that communicate with the database (including invoking the software resident in the database) to accept data from and present them to the users. The top tier is the client tier, which holds no business logic but is a presentation tool; it ensures a standard look and feel to the applications. Binding the tiers together is the network, along which data travel.

You should look at the architecture initially in software terms. The word *server* is frequently used. A server is a piece of software that communicates with and directs client software. Whether it is located on some dedicated hardware or shares a computer with other software is an output of a capacity-planning exercise.

The Client Tier

The client tier can operate on a PC, a laptop, or even a palmtop through an applet viewer or a Java-enabled Internet browser. A standard browser such as Microsoft Internet Explorer (from version 5.0x) or Mozilla Firefox or Safari, installed as part of a corporate configuration, will be sufficient. In earlier releases before Release 12, a file called a *JInitiator* was downloaded and cached the first time the user logged on to the application. It performed the operation of Java applets on the desktop. The new architecture changes to Oracle R12 EBS have made JInitiator obsolete. In its place, Oracle R12 EBS clients use a version of the J2EE Java desktop client software to connect to the Web front-end interface of the E-Business Suite. This lightweight Java client provides additional functionality over the previous JInitiator technology without sacrificing performance.

Because of the use of Java, the Release 12 desktop client benefits from a fast desktop processor and must have sufficient memory. Therefore, it is recommended that a Windows client have sufficient memory and processing capability per the guidance provided in the Oracle documentation.

The Applications Tier

The applications tier is where the forms and reports that make up the applications software live. This is where most of the functionality required by the business operates. It also launches the concurrent processing (batch jobs) and can manage the load across multiple computers using load balancing.

The Forms Service

The forms server has been replaced in Release 12 by a forms OC4J component. It is the software that runs forms and retrieves data from the database server. These data can be cached on the forms server so that there is less call on the database to keep going back to the disks to get the next record. For example, if the user retrieves a multiline purchase order, the forms server will cache the lines so that as the user scrolls to the next record, there is no call on the database. Each forms server can be a metrics client. As an alternative, socket mode can be deployed instead of forms service to improve performance across the network for environments that suffer from network-latency issues.

The Application Server

The Oracle 10g application server runs a number of different services. It starts off the communications with the client because it handles the initial request sent when the user types in or chooses the URL of the E-Business Suite. It then hands over the communication to a forms server if the URL is for the professional interface. For the Self-Service Web Applications, it also runs the PL/SQL cartridge, which generates the pages of the application. There is a software-load balancer available on the application server, which allocates requests between a number of Java Virtual Managers (JVMs) to prevent overloading. This is useful for the Self-Service applications, given that you might have a large number of users logging on to create requisitions, perhaps with some particularly busy periods.

The Concurrent Processing Server

This server runs concurrent programs such as reports and interfaces, which keeps the required processing from interfering with online activities. They are often computer-intensive programs, doing many computations on the data they retrieve from the database. The Concurrent Processing Server moved from its position on the database tier in Release 11 to the applications tier in 11i. Therefore, you can use multiple machines to segregate queues and provide failover cover.

The Discoverer and Reports Servers

While these are still available in Release 12 to maintain backward compatibility for Oracle EBS, they have largely been replaced by the much-improved business-intelligence technology available from Oracle in the form of the Oracle Business Intelligence Enterprise Edition (OBIEE) server. The Discoverer server runs Web-based Discoverer 3i sessions; the reports server runs Business Intelligence reports. Discoverer is capable of querying and manipulating large data sets, either directly from the applications database or from a separate Enterprise Data Warehouse (EDW) database. The system caches the data on the Discoverer server that does all the work as the user requests different views or summations.

The Administration Server

The E-Business Suite database administrators (DBAs) use this server to run specialist utilities. They can install or upgrade the database by running the adaimgr utility. They can apply applications-database updates using adpatch and maintain the EBS data using adadmin. *Patching* is the commonly used expression for applying a fix to a problem with the software. The fix might be to forms or reports on the application tier, or to packaged procedures on the database tier. These are available through a download from Oracle's My Oracle Support (formerly Metalink). Some features, such as MultiLingual Support and Multiple Reporting Currencies (MRC), require regular maintenance.

The Database Tier

The applications-tier processes communicate with the database tier. The volume of this communication is substantial; hence the need for a high-capacity connection between the two tiers.

The Oracle 10g database comes with Oracle R12 EBS versions 12.0.x; the Oracle 11g database is standard for Oracle R12 EBS versions 12.1.1 and later. The Oracle database stores the business and setup data (and associated indexes). As far as the database is concerned, there is no difference between these. This is the reason setup cannot be ported from one database instance to another when a project goes from one phase to the next (for example, from system testing to user-acceptance testing). Instead, a master instance is normally retained and kept in sync with the test instance by having all setup, database patches, and custom-code patches applied periodically. This master instance has up-to-date setup but no business data, and is copied to create the new environment.

The database also contains the PL/SQL packages, procedures, and functions that are a substantial part of the way in which logic is imposed on the data. Forms and reports invoke these program units, and they are executed on the database server; the results are passed back to the relevant application-tier server. The applications also use triggers. These are units of PL/SQL that are executed when invoked by forms or on conditions on a particular table (on insert, update, or delete).

Release 12 takes advantage of some advances in database technology that came out in the 10*g* and 11*g* database versions, such as advanced compression and the latest version of the cost-based optimizer (CBO), which replaced the legacy rule-based optimizer (RBO) that was standard in the 11i version of the product.

Cost-Based Optimizer

When the database-management system executes pieces of SQL, it dynamically alters the way in which it executes the program to choose the most efficient way. Release 12 comes with some concurrent processes that gather statistics to enable the system to choose which database path to use to execute a SQL statement. Rather than having set rules that the system follows, it uses the statistics to determine whether, for example, for a particular SELECT statement it would be better to use an index, or which table should drive the query. The optimizer chooses the lowest cost, which means the quickest response time for a form or greatest throughput for a concurrent process, such as an interface. The concurrent processes also populate backup tables so that it is possible to return to the previous set of statistics if the new ones cause a degradation of performance.

CAUTION
Cost-based optimization might affect your custom application extensions. You will need to factor in some time for an upgrade to Release 12 to regression test any customizations. Because Oracle EBS R12 can usually be run with the 10g/11g database, it is possible to do this upgrade first and use the statistics packages.

Materialized Views

Normal views dynamically query the data from underlying tables, but materialized views are summary tables. When you create materialized views, you specify how often they are to be refreshed and how—either only changes, tracked by a view log, or all records. Their advantage over normal views is query speed, which is a trade-off for being updated only periodically.

Partitioned Tables

Very large database tables can be divided into several partitions. SQL statements can then address the data in the partitions rather than the whole table, speeding up queries. However, all database tables reside in a single Oracle instance. Physically, they can be distributed over multiple devices within a storage area network.

PL/SQL Load/No Compile

This feature, which allows PL/SQL packages to be loaded into the database without being compiled, is useful for applying interdependent custom patches to the applications. Until now, the packages compiled as you added them, so that if one relied on another they had to be applied in order; now they can all be compiled together.

CAUTION
When applying standard Oracle EBS patches, you must follow the instructions to the letter. Any attempt to shortcut the process could cause problems and would not be supported.

Communications for Each Type of Session

All types of users can have access to a personal home page that is the entry point to the E-Business Suite. The home page is presented by the applications server. In version 11.51, this was done by Oracle WebDB; now with Release 12, the Oracle HTTP Server (OHS), aka Apache server, has taken over the role. It uses the standard http protocol or can use https, which is the secure version for use over the Internet. It presents the professional interface, Self-Service Applications, Business Intelligence, and Workflow notifications, and requires the user to enter the username and password just once for all of these. As the user selects one of these services, it initiates a different set of communications.

Professional Interface

When access to the professional interface is requested from the home page for the first time, the applications server sends the applet in a JAR (Java archive) file. This file is kept on the user's PC and is not downloaded for every subsequent log-on. However, the applications server ensures it is the right version and automatically downloads a new version when appropriate. The applet is a part of the standard Oracle Developer tool set. It handles the interpretation of data it receives and their presentation to the user. It standardizes the look and feel of data validation, lists of values, and the coordination of multiple associated windows.

Once the applet is on the PC, it establishes a connection with the forms server directly. It can do this on one of three models. It can use a socket-to-socket model using the IP protocol; this is the fastest and is ideal for intranet access. It can also wrap the IP messages in http packages, which contain headers and trailers that allow the communications to be directed across firewalls onto the Internet. The third model is using https, which adds a security tag to each message and is ideal for secure business-to-business communication over the Internet.

The forms server connects to the database server and handles requests from the client. Periodically (by default, every three minutes), the forms server sends a *heartbeat* message to the client to find out whether it is still logged on. If it receives no *echo* from the client, it will end the connection, roll back any pending database transactions, and end that connection too.

The forms server will also communicate with the concurrent processing server if the user starts a concurrent process. It will communicate with the applications server to present online help or to save attachments, which are now held on the database as large object binary files (LOBs).

"Traditional" Self-Service Web Applications

Self-Service Web Applications do not use Oracle Forms. The traditional ones are those that have been a part of Oracle Financials since before Release 12, such as Web Employees and Web Expenses. They start by requesting the static HTML log-on page from the applications server, which then uses the PL/SQL cartridge to connect to the database and service the requests.

New Self-Service Web Applications

The new Self-Service Web Applications are ones such as iProcurement and iStore. After the initial sign-on, instead of using the PL/SQL cartridge, they use a process on the application server called Apache JServ. This uses Java Database Connectivity (JDBC), which is an industry-standard protocol, to connect to the database server.

Mapping the Architecture to Hardware

The various servers described in the preceding sections are pieces of software that run on computer hardware. You must make choices during the early part of the implementation project about the hardware configuration, which have implications for cost, complexity, and timescale. For any of the configurations, it is important to understand the significance of these core systems to the business and include a systems-disaster recovery plan in the overall business recovery plan.

Single Server

The database and applications tiers can both be on one computer. This takes fewer resources to manage than multiple machines, and communication between the tiers is as fast as the internal bus of the computer (meaning unbounded by network constraints). It might be that an existing machine can be upgraded to host both tiers. This would speed up and reduce the cost of the implementation. The capital cost of the machines is only one consideration; the cost of managing the purchase, the dovetailing of timescales with the overall project plan, and the setup costs (particularly if a new server room needs to be built) must also be considered.

One disadvantage is the lack of scalability. Should the number of users grow, the hardware will eventually reach a point where either the memory or the central processing units cannot be expanded to meet new demand. The one piece of hardware also presents a single point of failure. This can be mitigated by having a standby server ready to take over; there also is failover software available from hardware vendors that handles the process.

Multiple Servers

Most commonly, the applications tier is put on one computer and the database on another. Often the applications-tier software is also loaded onto the database-server machine so that if the middle tier fails, the database can take over the job temporarily. It is possible to use different operating systems, and it is, in fact, common to see Unix on the database machine and NT on the applications one, which might work out to a cheaper overall solution. However, if the machines share the same operating system they can potentially share the same disk array.

As the user base grows and the use of the E-Business Suite becomes more intensive and extensive, the number of machines in the applications tier can be increased. If necessary, separate machines can run as forms servers and others as concurrent processing servers, applications servers, reports servers, and so on. Given that these are all performing discrete jobs, the configuration will depend wholly on the relative dependency of the organization on Self-Service Applications versus professional-interface transaction processing versus business-intelligence analysis.

Apart from the maintenance and systems-management overhead of multiple machines, all the machines in the database and applications tiers need to be connected by a very fast network, as the traffic between them is very heavy. This will often dictate that they are in one physical environment (such as a server room) connected by a 100-megabit or even a one-gigabit link. Disaster recovery can be provided for by a range of measures, from storing backup tapes off-site to disk mirroring.

Database-Server Sizing: Your Processor, Memory, and Disk Space

The E-Business Suite is similar to other Oracle systems when it comes to main-memory and processor-power requirements. They are a function of the number of online users.

Oracle EBS's design allows the largest machine, the database server, to focus more exclusively on the database processes that require concurrent support for a large user community. Application servers and concurrent process servers handle tasks that, because they support a single user at a time, can be handled by multiple, smaller servers. These smaller servers offer better prices and performance, as well as built-in redundancy.

The client's processing requirement is for a fast processor, because Java is processor hungry. The memory should be at least 128 megabytes, which is now quite normal.

Processing power is the key factor for the middle tier. The amount of disk space needed for storing forms and messages is static—although you must take account of each language installed—and there is not a tremendous need for temporary storage. You multiply your estimated number of simultaneous users by the estimate that Oracle provides of the processing power required by each user.

Estimating requirements for the database is more difficult. Equations exist to compute memory and processor requirements, but they are rather arcane and they assume more knowledge about the application than a beginning user ever possesses. The best rule is to talk to others who have their packages in production in a similar environment. The Oracle representative or the local Oracle Applications Users Group is a good place to start. Use their experience as a starting point; then factor in measurable differences such as the numbers of users, items, customers, journal postings, and the like.

Disk-space requirements are easier to compute. Oracle's seed data take up very little space. The majority of tables in each application are temporary or are smaller tables used for reference purposes, containing setups, value sets, and lookups. Each application has a handful of major master and transaction tables that can be used to size the whole application. Two master tables in General Ledger are GL_CODE_COMBINATIONS and GL_BALANCES; Journal Lines is the most populous transaction-level table.

A user can make a rough estimate of journal-storage requirements by computing the number of characters in a journal-line record and multiplying by the estimated number of rows. Doing the same for balances and code combinations provides a baseline for estimating all of General Ledger. Multiplying the space taken by the major tables by a factor of three to account for Oracle's overhead, the space taken by other tables, reserves for growth, and the DBA overhead of padding tablespace allocations to allow for table growth will yield a very rough estimate.

This offhand method exceeds the level of planning actually done in most shops. For large, sophisticated users, it is worth the effort to make more accurate projections of space requirements. Oracle provides a space-planning spreadsheet for this purpose.

The capability to carry *binary large objects* (BLOBs) in the database with Internet Computing or Smart Client radically changes the equation. The storage required for images, sound bites, and movies will almost always eclipse that needed for character-mode data. There is nothing in the Financials to predict the size of a BLOB—each shop will have to make its own estimates. Many users use a two-tier disk-storage approach for BLOBs. They store pointers instead of the BLOBs themselves in the database, so the BLOBs can reside on cheaper, slower storage devices. Factors that make magnetic-disk storage less expensive are bigger devices, fewer controllers, and less built-in redundancy. A writable optical disk is a very inexpensive alternative if the volumes are large.

Other factors that expand the total amount of disk space required include the following:

■ The amount of RDBMS overhead space needed in each instance. This requirement includes temporary tables, sort areas, rollback segments, unrecovered extents, and space lost to inefficiencies in tablespace allocations and the like.

■ The number of database instances required for development, testing, and maintenance. Except for large shops, all test instances need to be the same size as Production because they will be populated with copies of Production. There is no easy way to reduce the space required in a test instance by deleting data; records within the database are too interdependent. Large shops can manage it to some degree by partitioning transaction tables by date. After you size Production, multiply by at least three or four to account for test and development instances.

■ The amount of operating-system storage space required for the Oracle distribution (at least two copies) for patches and bespoke code, and for Concurrent Manager reports.

■ The file space required to hold concurrent-job output and log files. Some reports run to thousands of pages. Bitmapped reports, especially if they include graphics, are many times bulkier than character reports. The space requirements mount quickly if you allow the files to remain on the disk more than a few weeks.

In deference to users who need a guideline on which to ground their initial estimates, a small installation on a single database server will need four instances at 40 gigabytes per instance, plus about 20 gigabytes for library, temporary, and other space—or a total of about 180 gigabytes on the database server. Be skeptical of numbers much smaller than that.

TIP

For more in-depth coverage of the topics presented here, check out two excellent references available from Oracle Press: the Oracle Database 11g DBA Handbook *by Kevin Loney, and* Oracle 11g Performance Tuning *by Richard Niemec.*

Windows and Unix Operating Systems

Although many platforms will support the Oracle Financials server requirements, the two primary alternatives for users without a prior commitment to an operating system are Unix and Windows (2003 and 2008). They generally offer the most performance per dollar. The three-tier Internet Computing architecture exploits the strengths of both operating systems. Unix, with its greater reliability and scalability, is usually the best choice for the database server.

Windows and Unix both work well as application and concurrent processing servers. The greater reliability of Unix can be offset by redundant Windows NT machines. It is not a disaster if a Windows system crashes or must otherwise be rebooted. Assuming there are several Web or concurrent servers to choose from, the load-balancing mechanism can simply bypass the failed machine until it is available again.

Windows appears to offer savings over a more traditional enterprise operating system, largely because of the reduced cost of the hardware it runs on. That hardware-cost equation is changing as Unix-systems vendors are supporting Intel-compatible platforms and bringing down the costs of their own hardware. The cost of ownership associated with the architectures of the two operating systems is the increasingly important issue in choosing between Windows and Unix. Estimate the cost of your support staff, focusing particularly on the assumption that Windows will require less maintenance than Unix. Both operating systems are nuanced pieces of software that will not perform well in the hands of amateurs. There are several significant areas for comparison, as discussed in the following sections.

User Interface

The Windows interface is a major attraction of Windows Server; the whole thing is Windows. There is a vestigial remnant of the MS-DOS command language, but Microsoft hides it fairly well.

The Windows format is excellent for running desktop software. Windows Server 2003 and Windows Server 2008 now have a long pedigree and converging architecture. Windows tools can handle all systems setup and operations, but the fact is, a Windows-based setup can be frustrating. Although the graphical interface does make the product relatively attractive to work with, the far more crucial issue is that many Windows functions are just as difficult to execute as they would be if you had to type them in as command lines. It can be annoying to guess which obscure path to take through the "intuitive" Windows icons to get to the function you want. To make matters worse, online help for Windows frequently is not that helpful, offering scattered fragments of the answer but no body of text to explain the whole scheme.

The more pedestrian approach you take with Unix, reading the many excellent hard-copy references and researching the online manuals to find a utility you can execute from the command line, is still easier for most programmers than navigating the Windows maze. In fact, even though Unix systems offer windowed interfaces, most systems programmers still perform setup and management through the command-line interface.

Utility programs in the Unix world show their origins. Those such as backup/restore usually have more features and are more powerful, but they tend to be inconsistent from vendor to vendor and are often more complex than their Windows counterparts. Windows has nothing to match the powerful command-line, character-mode tools, such as grep, sed, awk, and vi. On the other hand, the tools require precisely the kind of operating-system guru that Microsoft buyers want to avoid hiring.

Unix has the most powerful shell language of any common operating system. In contrast, the command line is antithetical to Microsoft's philosophy. Its shell language, inherited from MS-DOS, is comparatively weak and poorly documented. This will not affect "plain vanilla" users much, but it is often convenient to use operating-system shell scripts for custom programming. Some things are just not better with GUI.

Device Support

Device support is a major operating-system function. Printers and disks are the most important devices for a server in the applications tier. To be as universal as possible, the applications use printers in character and PostScript modes. Windows generally does a great job with printers. Unix always works, but it takes a bit more effort to install and maintain bitmapped printers. Unix has the advantage when it comes to disks. The industry trend is toward intelligent disk arrays, such as the EMC Symmetrix, with built-in redundancy and backup. These remain somewhat more widely available in Unix. They allow mirroring, which keeps identical data on two sets of disks. The mirrored disks can be temporarily split, so that the backup can be taken while the database server is still running, and then resynchronized—all invisibly to the user community.

Reliability

What does it mean that Unix is more reliable than Windows? It is not uncommon to find Unix systems that have not been rebooted for a year or more. Windows systems tend to go down, or need to be brought down, quite a bit more often. Not only has the Windows operating system not been as stable as Unix; the hardware it runs on has traditionally been engineered to PC and LAN server standards, which have been somewhat less exacting than those for enterprise servers. The differences are reflected in price. Windows systems have generally offered better price performance than Unix.

These generalizations are rapidly becoming less true. The two operating systems are both becoming available on each other's traditional platforms, and Microsoft is making great efforts to improve Windows's reliability. Linux has grown rapidly to become the most popular enterprise operating system for hosting mission-critical Oracle systems. With the power and performance of Unix, the Linux operating system provides the cost-effective solution of Windows with far superior stability and patching functionality. In fact, Oracle has rebranded the Linux operating system to contain additional new features and benefits, such as hot patching with Oracle Enterprise Linux, under the banner of Unbreakable Linux.

Redundancy is easiest to engineer for individual users or tasks. If a desktop browser fails, you can exchange the failed machine for a good one. Most users can afford to be out of business for the hour or so it takes for the exchange. Likewise, most shops can accept the delay as Oracle EBS reassign a task after an applications-tier server goes down. The machines that host these individual tasks can afford to be less reliable, and thus less expensive, because the impact of their failure is limited, though in a global single instance it might still be an issue.

Tasks on the database server support all users simultaneously. The entire organization suffers when they go down. Because keeping the database in a consistent state is imperative, recovering from a failure can take a significant amount of time. Redundancy and reliability therefore have more value in a database server. Redundancy can be built into the disk subsystems, in disk mirroring, in multiple processors, in multiple paths between processors and disks, and in multiple links out to the networks. Each element increases reliability and cost; yet even the most redundant systems can never be 100 percent reliable. They all need off-site backup systems to guard against the worst case.

The Linux and Unix operating systems and the hardware designed to run them are generally more reliable than Windows. The Linux and Unix file systems are simpler than the one used by Windows, and simpler is better when it comes to Oracle. It does not need much operating-system support for disk storage. The RDBMS takes big blocks of disk space from the operating system and does its own formatting and allocation. Having an additional layer of disk-space management at the operating-system level just confuses the issue. Windows systems programmers have observed that the best way to keep disk usage straight on Windows is to reformat and reload the systems every few months.

Scalability

There are so many variables in any Oracle Financials environment—the number of applications, the size of master tables, the number of transactions, and the number of other processes on the machine—that real precision in the calculation of machine requirements is challenging. Just to collate the data needed to make the decisions of how many processors are necessary and how powerful they need to be requires a project-wide exercise; the answers might develop during the course of the implementation. The alternative is to take out insurance in the form of scalability. You can afford to start with less hardware than you need as long as you know you can expand.

Linux and Unix systems from Oracle Sun, HP and other major vendors can be configured large enough to handle the largest enterprise's Oracle EBS database-server requirements. Windows solutions remain more limited, in terms of both the number of processors in a single box and the ways in which multiple boxes can be strung together to increase power and reliability.

The number of Linux, Unix, and Windows systems that can be linked by a network is limited primarily by bandwidth. You can add applications-tier servers as necessary. The trade-off involved in using Windows, Linux, or Unix processors in these server functions is a matter of the price and performance of individual boxes—keeping the total number of boxes to a manageable number—and the productivity of the network administrators, DBAs, and systems programmers managing them.

Available Talent

Oracle EBS users need systems programmers for the server, LAN, and PC administrators; Oracle DBAs; and applications administrators. Depending on the installation, these might be one or several people; they can be employees or contractors. The skills tend to come in groups, and it is common to find DBAs with Linux/Unix and Oracle experience; however, it is less common to find people with EBS experience as well. It is desirable to have these skills combined in one person, as those who have them need to communicate closely with one another.

On the other side, Windows, LAN, and client-side experience are often found together. It is less common to find extensive Oracle DBA experience in a Windows expert, because larger Oracle implementations have favored heavier platforms. EBS experience is still rarer, because Windows is such a new platform for the E-Business Suite. What is increasingly important on the client side is browser and connectivity knowledge. Problems that are pinned down to the client are often browser related, and an administrator knowledgeable in this area can make the most of the nuances of browser setup.

Vendor Support

Linux and Unix vendors have historically been geared to support their customers' mission-critical applications. Microsoft has had to evolve its customer-support model as Windows moved into the enterprise. It is now a serious matter when a Windows machine crashes.

Microsoft's support model has historically been passive, commensurate with the low price of the Windows operating system. They put bug information and patches on the Internet for customers to find and apply themselves. This level is inappropriate for Oracle EBS installations, which need a high level of support when their production systems crash. On the other hand, Microsoft's mass-market, passive support model has forced them to engineer a relatively high level of reliability into their product. Now that HP and even Sun support Windows, it is reasonable to expect that they will provide that customer base the same level of support that they do for Unix and Linux.

The Bottom Line

The best feature of Linux and Windows is price. The software and the hardware it runs on are inexpensive. Oracle's EBS architecture is designed to accommodate its weaknesses and allow users to take advantage of its strengths.

Windows's GUI interface has no significant advantage over the Unix command line for the DBA who supports the Financials. The supposed advantage that Windows requires less systems-programming support might not prove significant. Any server, no matter who the vendor is, will require tuning, backup and restore, disk-space management, user management, and a host of other functions. They are conceptually and practically not much simpler under Windows than under Unix or Linux; it is just a different interface.

Both Linux and Unix have more proven reliability and scalability and more universal networking capabilities. Most Unix/Linux vendors offer a level of technical support appropriate to the Oracle E-Business Suite; Windows users might have to make sure they contract for what they need. In the final analysis, small users will probably find the costs of ownership more or less comparable between the two operating systems.

Base Software and Communication Technologies

The E-Business Suite is built on the pedigree of the previous releases, and so Oracle has taken care not to throw out the baby with the bathwater. The move to new technologies has been evolutionary and will continue to be so. The basis of much of the E-Business Suite still consists of forms, reports, and PL/SQL packages and procedures. PL/SQL is Oracle's procedural language; it can be used to do complex manipulation of data within the database. It has been one of the core skills required by EBS technical developers for many years. However, PL/SQL is being supplemented and sometimes replaced by Java. Java can be used inside and outside the database, is popular with developers, and is becoming the ubiquitous language of the Internet.

Connected languages such as JavaServer Pages are also becoming more important. JavaServer Pages is a middle-tier environment where *servlets* (a form of program unit) hold the business logic required and they generate dynamic HTML (hypertext markup language) pages, with embedded JavaScript to send to the browser. The JavaScript makes an HTML page interactive by handling features such as screen input and validation. These are used in the new Self-Service Applications such as iStore. HTML is a long-established Internet standard and is used to present the majority of static information on the World Wide Web. It is a language that enables a page of information to be defined with tags onto which are attached text, images, sounds, or programs (*applets*).

One of the main advances of Release 12 over Release 11i is that the whole application supports the hypertext transfer protocol (http) in the new application-server architecture with enhanced performance and scalability. This is a set of messaging standards that enables the E-Business Suite to work over the Internet and over a corporate intranet. Extra security is implemented in the https protocol.

The Transition to Global Installations

Global businesses can keep their costs down and the value of their information up by having a single ERP system. Oracle themselves led the way up a much vaunted path with their internal project that combined a move to global business procedures, an upgrade to Release 12, and the move to a single database instance. Using a single production instance of the database to run the entire company rather than splitting it into separate instances by country or business unit is a bold move, but Oracle E-Business Suite makes it possible. The advantages that Oracle chased in the move to a single instance are ones that other companies should consider:

- Lower cost of systems administration. No database or hardware administration skills are required other than at the center.

- Hardware in one large data center rather than lots of distributed hardware. This is cheaper.

- A single set of standing data (for example, customers and suppliers) to maintain. Debtor and creditor relationships can be managed globally.

- Global reporting. Global standard flexfields allow your business-specific dimensions to be a part of standard reporting (you could add them to the Business Intelligence System End User Layer).

- Facilitated move to shared service centers for transaction processing.

The E-Business Suite architecture helps the move to a single instance because of the following factors:

- Scalability of the Oracle 10g or 11g database (these features are extended in version 10g).

- Support for the Unicode (UTF-8) character set. This means you can have multibyte character sets (such as Chinese or Cyrillic script) on the same database as Western European languages. Note that there is a limit of two multibyte character sets per instance.

- Extended Multiple Language Support (MLS) in Release 12. Multiple end user languages can be loaded on the same forms server (although each language must be patched separately).

Time Zones

A global single instance will demand 24-hour, seven-days-a-week working, as the Pacific Rim offices are in office hours while the European ones sleep; the North American zone overlaps both. Therefore, there will be a constant mixture of daily processing tasks and the jobs normally thought of as overnight batch processes. This is where the segregation of concurrent processing hardware and forms servers will help. The caching capabilities of the application servers will also help to reduce disk activity on the database server.

The other time-zone issue is that the database server provides the time stamp on records. There is only one time available, so if Australian users register Receivables invoices on the U.S.-based system when they arrive at work in the morning on April 15, the invoice date will be April 14. This might confuse the customers when the invoice is sent to them and they get one day less on the payment terms. There is no standard way of overcoming this problem—although you can, for example, customize your external-facing documents to show local time by organization ID.

Support Advances and Tools

The complexity of Oracle E-Business Suite has advanced with the increasing needs and dependence of users. Speed of implementation and reliability in production are essential. As the move to global instances has been used to drive down costs, the Oracle product suite has evolved.

Enhancements and Patchsets

Bug fixes and enhancements are normally released by Oracle as *patches*. A patch is a file with install instructions that the DBA will need to run on the applications or database server, or both. A patch might contain changes to database tables, procedures held in the database, or forms or reports in the applications tier. During the initial setup of a master database instance during an implementation project, there might be scores of patches to add to the base install, which might take a few days to complete. Oracle R12 EBS provides new online patching functionality and patch tools with the Patch Wizard to simplify patch management.

Oracle Enterprise Manager

Oracle 11*g* Enterprise Manager (OEM) Grid Control is a stand-alone tool and separate product for the database administrator. It can be used to monitor and control any Oracle database, but it is bundled with the E-Business Suite, with an Applications Management Pack. This allows an E-Business Suite DBA to look at processes on the applications and database tiers of the system. OEM itself has a multitier architecture, with an Internet-enabled browser front end, which enables administration to be carried out from a browser anywhere. The middle layer is the Oracle Management Server, which performs all the core management services such as job scheduling, event monitoring, and alert notification through e-mail or paging. There is a centralized repository that holds statistics.

The key parts of the E-Business Suite for which OEM provides management utilities are the forms servers and concurrent processing servers. The OEM console provides performance monitoring and management. Monitoring includes information on top processor-power consumers—concurrent requests, forms sessions, and users. Management facilities allow remote control of the server processes, with alerts directed to the database administrators through e-mail or pager. The OEM displays when a forms listener (the communications part of the server) is down or when a process is taking too much computer-processor time. It can show when a concurrent process is locking out others or when a predefined proportion of concurrent requests have failed or ended with a warning. On detecting these conditions, the software can start a fix-it job, such as bringing the Concurrent Manager down and up again (a process commonly called *bouncing*).

The third function of the software is to collate capacity-planning statistics. The OEM saves statistics used in performance management initially in its repository; it can load these data periodically into an Oracle database. Customizable charts can help extrapolations of future traffic on the applications tier and, therefore, give an early warning of extra hardware requirements.

Backups and Cloning Environments

The importance of backing up your data and the *code set* (software) cannot be overstressed. This is just one part of a business-recovery strategy, which must be addressed as part of the implementation program. There are several key elements to backups. Regular backups of the data files that comprise the database should be made (daily is normal) and removed to an off-site location.

It is recommended that you have archive running on the database when it is in production (or an official test phase). This takes a before image of a record before an update or delete and an after image, and stores them in an archive file. These files are appended to up until a certain size and are then closed and the next one opened (which should happen every 20 minutes or so). If your database is then somehow corrupted (although this is increasingly rare), it can be rebuilt using the point-in-time backup plus the addition of the archive files that were created up to the point of the incident. In addition, the software and other files (such as Concurrent Manager job output and interface files) on the servers also need to be backed up regularly.

There is an increasing need for high-availability systems, running 24 hours a day, which does not give an obvious window for database downtime for backups. One solution is online backups. There are many third-party software packages that handle this, such as Legator and Veritas's Netbackup. To keep the database running while the backup is taken, use disk mirroring. This means that while the database is running, all the data stored are mirrored from the main disks to a second set (which might be in a separate physical location). To do an online backup, the backup software temporarily stops the mirroring and backs up the static mirror copy (which can be to a separate disk copy that can then be put to tape) before resynchronizing the live and mirror copies again.

Not only must the production data be protected; you will also find the need to host several environments. Generally, even after implementation you will need development and training instances. The training instance should be as close a copy as possible to the production one, so that training can be done with realistic data and the most up-to-date software. On the other hand, by definition the development instance will be further advanced in terms of software than will the production instance. Unless there is a substantial change in the business processes that affects the way data are stored (for example, from two-way to three-way matching for invoices), the development instance is probably best not refreshed from production.

The database itself can be copied, but a copy of the whole E-Business Suite is more complex. Experienced E-Business Suite DBAs can perform an operation known as cloning or *Backup and Recovery Process* (BURPing) to copy a whole environment to a different one. It can take two to three days to complete. This was common practice for previous versions of Oracle Applications; however, for the E-Business Suite it is a more complex operation and is not supported by Oracle Worldwide Support. The method supported by Oracle Support is to install it using the rapid install feature, then copy the database to get the data.

Conclusion

The E-Business Suite has quickly matured into a stable, richly featured Internet application. It delivers much newer technology to the users than did previous versions of the Applications. This is important in terms of its availability for business-to-business integration because it uses technologies that are current standards on the Internet—such as Java and JavaServer Pages—for presenting and XML for exchanging data.

It will continue to evolve and can be expected to exploit new products such as the 11*g* database and Oracle 11*g* WebLogic Application Server. The multitier architecture is flexible and scalable enough to support the largest corporations on a single production instance of the database. This will become more common as companies go after savings, and this trend will drive further improvements in support tools.

CHAPTER
21

Security

he information managed by the Oracle E-Business Suite often is the most sensitive in any business. Losing or muddling customer, supplier, or financial records can put a company out of business—at least temporarily. Compromises of the data can result in fraud, privacy violations, and competitive disadvantage. Recently, security breaches have resulted in substantial financial costs to public-sector agencies, hospitals, and large corporations. This report from SecurityWeek (http://www.securityweek.com) highlights the gravity of securing Oracle EBS environments:

> A study released today by the Ponemon Institute and sponsored by ID Experts revealed that data breaches of patient information cost healthcare organizations nearly $6 billion annually, and that many breaches go undetected.

> (Security Week, November 9, 2010. www.securityweek.com/data-breaches-cost-hospitals-6-billion-study-says)

All users take advantage of the native security features of Oracle EBS. Responsibilities restrict access using customized menus, data groups, menu and function exclusions, and request groups. Customized menus and exclusions confine users to the forms (screens) they will need to see. The request group assigned to the Responsibility confines the users to only report and program processes they are allowed to run. Data-security rules associated with the Responsibility restrict users to selected subsets of data within the database. Security rules work with the values of the value sets. They restrict the values to those that belong to the users' part of the business organization. Users are only presented with those value sets, flexfields, and concurrent-request parameters that are valid for them.

Applications-level security is designed protect data against unauthorized users who attempt to access them at the Oracle EBS applications level. The access restrictions on processes and data are supported by processes that track unsuccessful user-account log-ins and monitor active user accounts while they are on the system. It is possible to know the user ID, Responsibility, and form that any user is accessing.

A *hacker* is somebody who gains access to your computer under false pretenses, usually with mischief or malice in mind. The E-Business Suite cannot defend against hackers who are able to circumvent applications software to access data directly at the network, database, or operating-system level. Security policy, therefore, has to address threats at all levels, visible and invisible, to the EBS.

Architecture of Oracle Release 12 EBS Financials

Oracle E-Business Suite is an n-tier web based client server architecture. All EBS users access the system through browsers on their desktops. The desktop machines are most frequently Windows based, although they can be Macintosh, Unix, Linux, or Network Computer devices.

Whatever the desktop operating system, Oracle E-Business Suite application logic runs as a Java applet under the browser. The browser handles the logical connection with the network, although it and all other programs that might be running in the system actually call on operating-system services for interaction with the hardware.

The only piece of software in the desktop configuration that Oracle provides is the Java applet. The user installs a local copy of the Java virtual machine (JVM) software that interacts with the Java environment on the application server. Although that might be stored on the desktop machine, originally it is supplied from a controlled Oracle environment at the Web-server level, and the Web server always checks the applet's validity before using it. The Oracle EBS applications assume that the desktop environment is insecure. Even if a hacker could get full control of the desktop machine, the Oracle EBS software is designed to prevent the hacker from compromising applications data.

The Web server serves as the middle tier in the Oracle E-Business Suite environment. It executes the Oracle Forms online programs that support the user. Stated as simply as possible, the dialogue between the browser and the Web server works like this:

- The EBS user navigates over the Internet (or intranet) to the log-in page on the EBS Web server, which is monitored by the Web Listener.

- The user provides his or her EBS log-in ID and password.

- The Web Listener verifies that the user is valid and that the Oracle EBS applet on the browser is authentic and has not been tampered with. This is a complex process, described in more detail later.

- The Web Listener establishes a session between it and the browser, so it will recognize each incoming message as part of an ongoing conversation.

- The Web Listener passes the browser's messages to Oracle Forms, which handles creation of menus and presents each applications form that the user selects.

- The Oracle EBS applet running under the browser decompresses and presents the form, and data within the form, as it is sent from Oracle Forms running on the Web server.

There typically are a number of Web servers in a large Oracle EBS environment. One of them handles all user log-ins, then appoints one of the pool of Web-server machines, possibly itself, to manage the session with the user. In a multilanguage environment the Web servers usually specialize by natural language. Operations can continue smoothly if a Web server goes out. The master server can rehost the session with a small loss of time and transaction data. Oracle R12 EBS uses a repackaged version of the popular open-source Apache Web server called Oracle HTTP Server.

Although Oracle database software runs on the middle tier, the middle tier does not host the database itself. A single Web server does not have to manage any data that are unique within the Oracle EBS architecture. The economics of Web-server operations favors multiple, inexpensive machines. Web servers tend to use Windows NT/Windows 2000, Linux, or Unix operating systems.

The database is unique as a matter of principle. The system achieves consistency by maintaining a single, shared copy of every database record. The database machine has to be highly reliable because the database supports the whole universe of EBS users. It usually runs on a separate machine from the Web servers, and might support many Web server machines. To achieve the necessary power, reliability, and redundancy, the database server might be made up of a cluster of processors and storage devices. For instance, Oracle Real Application Clusters can be deployed for such a purpose.

The structure of the Oracle EBS applications themselves favors a three-tier architecture. The database is massive and highly integrated. Just running database operations can require as much processor power as is available on a large machine. The database machine has to be unique and highly reliable—meaning expensive—whereas the Web servers can be cheap and redundant. Depending on the processor capacity of the database server, it might execute batch jobs itself or farm them out to Applications Servers so it can devote its processing power exclusively to database-related tasks.

To Oracle's internal logic, the middle-tier Web server looks the same as an Oracle*Forms user logged on through a dumb terminal. In either case, the user would need to provide an Oracle RDBMS-level user name and password. In essence, the operation is completely transparent to the user. Both this internal user name and the associated password are hidden from the Oracle EBS user. Only a trained Oracle E-Business Suite database administrator (DBA) can see these internal tasks, by running DBA scripts.

Although the user name is not kept secure, the password is stored in an encrypted format and usually is known only to the DBAs. The session-initialization process, running on the Web server, retrieves and decrypts the RDBMS password. The Web server has to use the RDBMS-level user name and password each time it initiates a form or concurrent process on behalf of the user. It is not at all apparent to the user that every batch and online Oracle process he or she executes under the EBS requires an RDBMS-level log-in name and password.

The network links that join the three (or four) tiers of the middle tier for Oracle EBS in most cases use the internet standard TCP/IP packet-switching protocol. Although the link between the Web server and the database server is many times faster than that between it and the browsers, their character is the same. The universality of the connection scheme is essential to the functioning of the Web.

Each node in the system has a unique IP (Internet protocol) address. Sending a message over the full Internet is the most general case. There is a worldwide master directory of registered Internet users, consisting of their logical names (such as Oracle.com) and their IP addresses, a four-segment number. When a (segment of a) message entered into the Internet reaches an intersection, a router looks up the destination address and determines the best way to get it there. The router has algorithms to choose among multiple paths, and to reroute a message segment when necessary.

A key concept in packet-switching protocols is to break long messages into many segments of a uniform length. Making the packets flowing through the network more or less the same size ensures a level of responsiveness. It puts an upper bound on the amount of time any device in the network has to spend on a single packet. Breaking a message up does impose on the receiving node the task of reassembling the message from the various packets, which might arrive over different network paths and out of sequence.

The multilayer makeup of the packet-switching scheme is reflected in the contents of each packet. Simplistically (and glossing over some of the seven layers in the scheme), from the inside out a packet is made up of

- a portion of the message content, with an identifier describing where the piece goes in the reassembled message;

- a session identifier, indicating which process on the destination machine gets the message;

- the IP address of the destination machine; and

- the address of the next node along the path to the destination machine.

By the architecture of the Internet, nodes along the way are responsible for forwarding packets toward their final destinations. As in local area networks, there might be many machines on a single physical path in the network. Each machine is responsible for dealing with only packets that are addressed to it. Good citizens do just that. However, every machine on the network has the opportunity to read whatever packets it wants to. There is no privacy inherent in Internet architecture.

Electronic eavesdroppers who do not even belong to the network can sniff out its traffic. Individual data links within the Internet physically traverse copper wire, coaxial cable, fiber-optic line, and wireless links. There is no way whatsoever to predict the path. Although fiber-optic lines are somewhat difficult to wiretap, the rest are easy.

The Universe of Threats

Your systems and users are strung out over a number of machines and possibly a wide geography, joined by inherently insecure communications links. You protect your data by secret codes: user names, passwords, and other validation techniques. People who want to steal your data have a couple of choices: they could do like the National Security Agency, scanning the huge mass of data that flows over the network to pick out interesting material; however, this approach is difficult. It takes enormous computers and lots of patience. Most hackers get at your data by obtaining your secret codes and passing themselves off as legitimate users of your automated systems at some level. Most security is designed to frustrate these impostors.

Unauthorized Activity by Authorized Users of the Applications

In the average organization, insiders are the greatest threat. These are the people to whom you have granted access to your systems and who choose to abuse the privilege. The following are common ways for them to gain access through the standard Oracle Financials security structure:

- The systems administrator assigns the user a Responsibility with more functions than are appropriate to do his or her assigned job.

- A user is assigned increasing Responsibilities over time without anyone noticing the number of Responsibilities the user has accumulated, nor the combination of modules (applications) to which the user has access.

- The user quits or is reassigned, but remains authorized to use the system.

- One user shares his or her ID and password with another.

- The system goes into production with the testers' open-access user IDs, such as TEST/TEST, still active.

- The DBA inadvertently leaves access to the Oracle Tools (such as SQL*Plus and the operating-system prompt) available in the production instance. (Usually the system administrator has access to the APPS password. The systems-administrator Responsibility does not work correctly without it.)

To be effective, administrative procedures have to be rigorously enforced. There is no automated way to detect most breaches. Systems administrators create and edit menus based on what other people tell them a Responsibility should be able to do, and Responsibilities cannot be deleted from a user once granted; they can only be end dated. The user's quitting or being reassigned can be caught only if somebody, presumably someone in human resources or the person's manager, is charged with letting the systems administrator know. Sharing of IDs and passwords is almost impossible to catch. The bottom line is that to be effective, security has to be part of the organization's culture.

Unauthorized Users of the Oracle Applications

It usually is not difficult for a determined person to get hold of a valid user-name/password combination. The following tricks are some of the more obvious:

- Original log-ins have not been changed. Usually the systems administrator uses a common password to set up a user's account, and when the user first logs in, the system makes that person change it. "Welcome" and "password" are always good guesses to start with.

- Make educated guesses from what you know about a user. The kids' names are Kevin and Karen? Try kevin1 and karen1 as passwords.

- Go through a user's desk drawers or scan the files on the desktop computer to see if he or she has written down the log-in information somewhere. Most users are burdened with so many access codes (networks, PCs, different application machines, security locks to the bathroom, and so forth) that they cannot remember them all. Somebody will have been careless and written them down.

For reasons detailed in the following, it is easier to log in as an impostor using an authorized user's own desktop machine. Physical security is an important adjunct to computer security.

Physical Security Threats

Keeping unauthorized people away from your data-processing operations is a vital first step in computer security. If they do not have physical access to your systems, they cannot have easy access to printouts that are lying around, peek as users key in their passwords, or make off with laptops containing sensitive information. Laptop computers, and employees' home computers, present significant security issues. Users might save sensitive information on their hard drives. These machines also might have the ability to access your secure systems through devices like wireless routers via a VPN tunnel network connection.

Dedicated communications links on your campus also can pose a security threat. The way networks are designed, every computer reads the traffic addressed to every other computer with which it shares a link. If physical access is not an issue, it does not take a genius to plug a new machine into the network.

Every installation keeps a library of backup tapes. The archives typically are sufficient for the DBA to restore the Oracle system as it existed at any point in time back as far as several months. There are similar tapes to restore at the operating-system level. For an intelligence operative these archives are the keys to the kingdom. If they can restore your system, they know your business. It is wise to keep some of these archive tapes at an off-site location so you can rebuild your system on totally new hardware in case you experience a disaster. You need to accord all your backups the same level of security protection as the computer itself.

Damage Caused by Fraudulent Users

Depending on his or her privileges, a user with inappropriate access can perform all kinds of traditional mischief: enter fraudulent payments, cover for stolen inventory, or discount customer invoices in exchange for a kickback. Oracle will not question these activities so long as you have given the user authority to perform them.

Unauthorized users can steal a lot of information. The easiest way to get data in volume is through reports. A competitor surely can make good use of a customer list, price list, or employee roster.

Most online processes update only one or a few database records per transaction. It is not tremendously fast, and the speed constraint can slow down a hacker bent on destroying your databases. Moreover, if the damage they do is so obvious as to be discovered, the DBA sometimes can restore the records.

The relative slowness of online transactions will not deter experienced hackers. They can use programs to simulate online activity. Oracle Corporation, like all software houses, uses regression-testing software for exactly this purpose. A hacker with a fast Internet connection could use a regression tester to, say, change the prices on all the items in your inventory.

The saving grace is that a hacker who uses standard EBS functionality to do this dirty work does leave a rich trail of activity. At the applications level, each record is marked with the identification, date, and time of the last update. At the RDBMS level, the system keeps before and after images of the records every time the database is updated. Audit reports and alerts put in place by the DBA are a good way to detect this type of activity. The reports that Oracle Corporation provides with the system are not terribly useful in the hands of inexperienced IT teams; they cannot anticipate the kind of activity that would be suspicious in any specific customer environment.

Even when they are in place, audit-trail devices are useful only if you react quickly. The scent goes cold when legitimate users update master records after the impostor. After a relatively short time, the RDBMS activity log loses its value. Restoring to clean up the fraudulent transactions might wipe out so many valid ones that it is not worth the effort. In any case, activity logs typically are overwritten and lost totally after a few days or weeks.

Threats Outside of the Oracle E-Business Suite Applications

Oracle EBS application data are stored on magnetic disks along with all other high-volume data that need to be readily accessed and updated. They are located in operating-system files, just like the .doc files Microsoft Word creates on a PC, only bigger and in a different format.

Following the Word-document analogy, anything that can go wrong with a Word-document file also can go wrong with the database. Without proper controls it can be read, erased, or corrupted by unauthorized people. Surreptitious reading of your data offers the greatest security risk. You will notice immediately if the database is destroyed; you might never know if somebody merely swipes a full record of your company's operations. It is alleged that the Chinese government did exactly that to steal secrets from the United States' atomic laboratories. There is no way to tell, and the damage can continue over a long period of time.

As always, threats can come from inside or outside your organization. If your systems programmer is lax in assigning security protection to the Oracle database files or in assigning operating-system-level access privileges to programmers, insiders can make unauthorized use of your data.

The "holy grail" of hacking is to gain total control of somebody else's machine. In Unix this is known as *root access*. In NT it is called *systems-administrator access*. Gaining this access almost invariably requires getting the password.

There generally are three user accounts defined to the operating system with access to the Oracle data. In these instances a user account does not correspond so much with a specific person as with a Responsibility, such as systems programmer or Oracle DBA. The first account is the administrator or root, which has access to everything. The second is the Oracle user, the account that owns the Oracle RDBMS program and data files. The third is the Oracle EBS user, which owns all the program files for the applications. Although this account does not own the Oracle data, compromising a program under its control can just as effectively compromise the database.

The files that belong to these system-level users are stored on the Unix or NT server, which should be protected by a password that real EBS users never know. When the systems are administered properly, the real users have no way of getting to the actual database files in which data and programs are stored. The same considerations apply to operating-system passwords as to Oracle EBS passwords. The difference is the level of exposure. If the systems programmer's passwords are compromised, the whole computer is exposed.

The mechanisms for destroying or compromising data correspond to levels of functionality within the operating system. Programming is most powerful. When possible, intruders will use their ill-gotten privileges to install their own programs on your system and let those programs do the dirty work. A program operating with full operating-system privileges has in effect hijacked the entire system. A program is quick and quiet, and it provides the hacker control over timing.

Easier but less powerful, each operating system provides users with a number of commands that can be misused to steal data or corrupt files online. The same commands generally can be invoked both interactively and through a program. It would be possible, for instance, to write a script using the FTP command to periodically steal a copy of system master data by sending them to another system via the Internet.

In practical terms, the Oracle system is hopelessly compromised if a hacker gets into any of the three operating-system-level accounts on the database server: root, Oracle, or EBS. Hackers can get control by obtaining the password or by finding a lapse in security that allows them to plant their own files in the directory structures of these accounts. If a hacker is able to replace a valid concurrent program with his or her own altered version, the Oracle E-Business Suite is pretty much open to that person once anybody executes the program.

RDBMS-Level Compromises

The Oracle database-management system uses a system of *schemas*, also called *accounts* or *user IDs*, similar to those of the operating system. There are two accounts with access to all the data within the database: SYS and SYSTEM. Oracle EBS application data area owned by a group of schemas that usually use abbreviations of the names of Oracle EBS applications: INV, PO, AP, and so on. To reduce confusion, Oracle has created a kind of super user, usually called APPS, which has access to the data in all of the Oracle E-Business Suite of applications.

The Oracle E-Business Suite of applications is built with programming tools native to the Oracle environment, among them the SQL and PL/SQL languages as implemented in Oracle*Forms, Oracle*Reports, SQL*Plus, and a number of end-user tools. In almost any Oracle environment, there are many users with access to the Oracle programming tools. For starters, the developers need them. An intruder enterprising enough to get one of the key Oracle user-ID/password combinations usually will not find it difficult to put it to use accessing the Oracle EBS database.

Database records that an intruder adds, changes, or deletes at the database level are not marked with the user's identity or the date. The Oracle programming tools operate at a lower level than the Oracle applications in which those audit-trail features are applied. However, changes at the RDBMS level do show up in Oracle's activity log, and they can be backed out of the Oracle database if they are discovered there.

Therefore, Web servers need the same level of protection as the database server itself. Several factors might make this harder to achieve—especially when the Web servers are hosted on the Windows platform—including the following:

- A major economy of Windows systems is that they supposedly do not require the same level of systems-programming support as other operating systems. Security management is a systems-programming task, and it requires knowledgeable people to administer it. It might be overlooked in a Microsoft Windows environment.

- Microsoft Windows has historically been easier to hack than Unix and other enterprise-level operating systems.

- Microsoft Windows' file-sharing and file-level security is very complex. It is liable to lapses and oversights on the part of the systems programmer.

- Web servers might be physically dispersed in areas without the same level of physical security as the database server. Custody might be lax as components are swapped in and out of the system.

A smaller number of machines obviously is easier to manage than a larger number. Taking administration and security considerations into the cost-of-ownership equation, it might make sense to use powerful Unix devices rather than smaller NT machines as servers.

Desktop-Level Security Considerations

Let us assume that the web based access on the client desktop computer is not secure. It validates the desktop applet every time it is invoked. However, there still is room for a hacker to play some tricks. If he or she were to get control of the desktop machine in any way, physically or by way of a virus, he or she could capture all of the data coming into and out of the machine. That traffic of course includes the Oracle user ID and password, and whatever transactions a legitimate user puts through the system.

Development and Production Environments

The freedom programmers need to set up and customize the Oracle E-Business Suite of applications in a development would be a license to steal in the production environment. Programmers need the capability to write programs and put them where Oracle EBS can run them. Such freedom would allow them access to all the data in the production instance.

The data-processing shop needs to build a gateway between the programmers and the production environment. The customary name for this is *configuration management,* and it might incorporate an element of quality control. Forcing all changes to the production environment to go through the hands of an independent body serves several purposes:

1. It ensures that the DBAs and others responsible for the production environment know exactly what is in it.

2. It ensures that all programs go through the established testing procedures before they are put into production.

3. It provides the security of a second set of eyes looking at code before it goes into production. The fact that a programmer's work might be reviewed for adherence to coding and testing standards likely will act as a deterrent to including "Trojan horse" code that could compromise the system.

There is no way to set up and test the Oracle E-Business Suite without a populated database. Most users find using real data to be the only practical recourse. All the developers have access to them. The point of a development environment is that it does not matter how they change and delete records in the database. However, the real data usually include sensitive information about your business.

You have the choice of trusting your programmers or sanitizing the data before giving them to the developers for use in development instances. Personnel data are a classic example. You almost certainly want to have the DBA write a routine to scramble salary, date of birth, and other sensitive data fields before releasing the data to the programmers. Depending on the nature of your operation, you also might want to scramble customer, product, pricing, and other data going into the test instance.

Network-Level Compromises

As previously established, the network is inherently insecure. However, you can use some combination of controlling your data lines, encrypting your data, and trusting that your data will be so lost in the cacophony of Internet traffic that it is not worth the bother of finding them.

A truly dedicated private line outside your own premises is hard to find anymore. The circuits you lease from common carriers are logical, not physical. They provide you with end-to-end connectivity, but along the way your data are sure to be mixed with those of others through multiplexing, packet switching, and the other devices that telecommunications companies use to squeeze maximum use out of their physical links.

Your only real protection is encryption. You can handle encryption yourself, although it is tough to administer, especially at the desktop level. The *virtual private networks* (VPNs) offered by common carriers encode your data to keep them away from prying eyes. Your protection is as good as their encryption.

You might choose to trust that your data will be so difficult to segregate from the torrents of traffic over any given part of the network that they are not worth the trouble. That probably is a good assumption once your traffic reaches the high-bandwidth Internet backbone circuits. However, it might be that your traffic makes up a significant portion of the traffic on the lines connecting you to the backbone. Somebody else on that network could read your mail fairly easily. They can steal your data without your knowing, or steal the passwords they need to hack the system and make their own changes to your database. Oracle's digital-certificate-verification system, described later, is designed to protect you against this type of intrusion.

You might depend on physical security on your own premises; however, the local area networks that connect users to your system probably are not secure. The traffic on them could be read easily enough by a computer that was physically tapped into the network, but you might figure that anybody who attempted it would be conspicuous in your environment. You have a choice to make: trust your physical security or provide end-to-end encryption between the Web server and the desktop.

A malefactor can initiate a denial-of-service attack (DoS) to bring your operations to a halt without ever penetrating your system. Your system is flooded with so many bogus messages that legitimate traffic cannot get through. The Serbian military attacked US intelligence sites this way during the Kosovo conflict. Security-software firms offer software antidotes to sophisticated attacks of this nature.

Countermeasures

It should be clear that there are many facets to the security issue. You have to trust your own people enough to let them do their jobs, but you cannot afford to trust them blindly. You must expect the worst from people outside your own community. You also must recognize that there are many user IDs and passwords in your organization, and the compromise of any of them could cause you serious problems.

There are trade-offs. Security costs money. It takes people away from other critical tasks. You have to balance the value of the assets you are protecting, the level of risk in each area, and the costs of countermeasures. Home security offers a good analogy. You need different kinds of protection against theft, robbery, and kidnapping depending on whether you have a Picasso or Elvis in velvet hanging on your wall, whether you live in Brooklyn or Sioux Falls, whether you are a carpenter or a Mafia don, and whether your income is $50,000 or $500,000 per year. Likewise, the risk profile of each business is different.

Security-Policy Definition

The trade-offs you make need to be expressed in a security-policy document. It needs to address the total needs of your enterprise, of which Oracle EBS is probably only one part. However, a global approach is essential because an attack through a weakness in another system easily could compromise your Oracle data, and there are a number of scenarios under which an attack through Oracle EBS could compromise other applications in your system. For example, somebody might introduce a Microsoft virus to the client desktop Windows PC system via an Excel spreadsheet attached to a budgeting system. Common elements of a security policy include:

- **A definition of the components to be protected**   This includes machines, network links, and software systems such as the EBS applications.

- **A definition of the classes of people who need access and the uses they will make of the system**   From the most privileges to the least, common classes of users include systems programmers; Oracle DBAs; systems administrators, programmers, configuration managers, and others who deal with installing the Oracle E-Business Suite; registered users; and groups of outsiders who do business with you over the Internet.

- **Password-management policies for each class of user**   The policies should address the format and length of passwords; the frequency with which passwords are changed; supplemental authentication such as fingerprint readers, voice recognition, and *strong authentication* by time-dependent passwords (described later); and administration vehicles such as *single sign-on* (also described later).

- **Physical-security policies**   These include access control for computer and Web components, access to terminal work areas and computers, policies for distributing passwords and for (or against) writing down passwords, policy for controlling information generated by Oracle EBS and other systems in paper and electronic formats that are no longer under the users' control, and physical control of backup tapes, test data, and the like.

- **Encryption policies**   These should define when and where data need to be encrypted, and the algorithms to be used. This might cover transmission over external (Internet) links or internal data links, and data stored in the database.

- **Security mechanisms to use, such as firewalls, antivirus software, and intrusion-detection software**   These tools are discussed later.

- **Development-environment policies**   You should define the steps required to purify real data for test purposes, and the ways in which development and test activity will be segregated from production. The configuration-management gateway should be defined by which setups, seed data, and program materials pass from development into production.

- **Monitoring policies**   A suspicious volume of apparently legitimate activities often means trouble. At an Oracle EBS level you can monitor activities such as the total number of log-ins by each user; log-ins at odd hours of the day; suspiciously large numbers of records modified by any individual user; and unusual numbers of reports programs, or output lines, produced by a given user. You can specify reports to track log-ins, usage, password changes, and activity by root-level users at the levels of the Oracle RDBMS and operating system as well. You can track network access, especially in the form of *pings* that appear to be feeling out your defenses.

■ **Defense and counterattack policies** What do you do when you detect an attack? Whom do you contact? How do you coordinate with law-enforcement agencies? The policies need to define which operations can be shut down and which will continue under different scenarios. The backup and recovery policies in place to protect you against normal software and hardware failures must anticipate recovery from security breaches as well.

Several security-policy aspects can be implemented through software. IBM and RSA are well-respected vendors for security-policy management. *SC Magazine* (www.scmagazine.com/) provides product evaluations.

Access-Control Policies

Just as burglars prefer unlocked houses and car thieves prefer to find the keys in the ignition, cyber bandits like to take advantage of easy targets. The easiest and most important first step toward better security does not take any software. All you need to do is implement common-sense security procedures.

Physical security is an obvious step. Anybody who can cruise through your offices is almost sure to find listings with company-sensitive data, notes about log-in IDs and passwords, and unguarded workstations. If you do not have access control, you have no security. You need to make it difficult for an outsider to get time alone in your shop.

Almost all software systems are protected by a system of log-in IDs and passwords. Human factors are their weakness. Most computer users try to keep them simple because among their banks, personal Internet accounts, and work life they have a large number of such ID/password combinations to remember. An administrator has a hard choice in the area of human factors. If you make the combinations difficult (like msmith/X5vV74a), the users are almost sure to write them down. If the users can make them simple (like msmith/msmith1), they are pretty easy to hack. Changing them periodically is important. Your shop is vulnerable to every password that has been compromised since the last time they were changed.

One recommended procedure is to generate new passwords for your users on a routine basis. Ones they choose themselves might be too simple. They might choose words such as their children's names. If the system will let them, users might rotate among two or three standard passwords. They carelessly use the same password for private activities where security really is not an issue, such as access to Internet sites.

The generated password has to be secure and memorable. The most appealing technique in general use is to run together two recognizable words, such as *bohemianblather* or *phoneticantique*. These are easy to remember, and much, much easier to type than something like X5vV74a. A vocabulary of 25,000 words yields 625,000,000 password combinations—certainly enough to discourage guessing.

Distributing new passwords in a secure manner takes some ingenuity. If you do it through a paper document, the paper itself opens you to compromise. If you distribute it by computer, you almost have to use a secure system separate from the one being protected. Even at that, people might be tempted to cut and paste from the screen. Depending on your situation, it might be appropriate to do it in person or by telephone.

A monthly password change gives you an opportunity to review usage. You might want to drop people who have not used the system recently, or at least make them come to you for a new password instead of distributing it to them. Infrequent users can be more of a risk than everyday ones. They are less likely to care deeply about the integrity of the system, more likely to write down their passwords, and less likely to notice unusual activity in their account.

People in the corporate IT environment typically need access to many different things. As a group, they need operating-system-level access to all the different platforms and all the Oracle instances in development and production. Because they have broader access to company data, tight management of their access is more important than it is for mere Oracle EBS application users. These people also are tempted to be lazy as they get overloaded. They might use the same account names and passwords in production as in test, or make up passwords that are simple to remember.

Single-sign-on products from security-software vendors address these problems. They enable you to define the types of access allowed for different classes of users, more or less like Oracle database or Oracle EBS Responsibilities. They recognize different types of access permission such as read, write, and delete. They provide a user with access to all permitted resources through a single sign-on that the user can be expected to remember and protect. It saves effort and reduces risk. Oracle provides a comprehensive suite of such products as an optional and additional licensed set of products called Oracle Identity Management. Further discussion of the Oracle Identity Management suite of products is provided later in this chapter.

Control of Internet Access

A Web presence is an invitation to the general public to visit your site. You have to expect hostile visitors when you implement Oracle Web Customers or Web Suppliers. At the Oracle EBS applications level, your concern is to limit any particular outsider to just the information that party needs to know, and to prevent anyone from obtaining company-confidential information. The Oracle E-Business Suite provides you with the mechanisms. You limit the types of information by the screens or Web pages you offer, and you control access by a system of user IDs and passwords.

The same sorts of password-management considerations apply outside the company as inside, except that you have even less control of what users do with their passwords. You can predict that another company's people will tell each other how to get into your system. Your security issues are not their problem. If you really need to impose tight security on outside organizations, you will have to use some means of strong authentication, as discussed later.

The second threat from the Internet vector is hackers, people who intend to compromise your Web site by introducing their own programs into your environment. The defenses against hackers tend to be generic; there is not much that is Oracle specific in their usual mode of operations.

An Overview of Public-Key Cryptography

Password schemes have inherent limitations. Anybody who knows the password can get into the system, often from another location. Once a password is compromised, the system remains exposed until the password changes. Several kinds of additional security devices offer additional protection. Most of them depend on secret coding techniques, called *cryptography*.

The simplest encryption codes work letter by letter. You can decode the secret message "Iwguu Vjku" as "Guess This" by figuring out that you need to replace each letter in the cypher code with the letter that comes two before it in the alphabet. In other words substitute G for I, U for W, and so forth.

Character-for-character encryption is easy to break; there are only 26 choices for each letter. Amateurs do it for fun with newspaper cryptograms. Computer encryption treats each message as a number, then uses complex mathematics to generate an encrypted version of the number. The mechanics are fascinating, although certainly not essential to an executive understanding of computer security. Skip this section if you are not fond of math.

Each letter, number, and special character is represented internally in a computer by an 8-bit byte, each bit being set to off or on to represent the value 0 or 1. The total number of values that can be assumed by one character in memory, represented by 1 byte, is 2^8 ($2 \times 2 \times 2 \times 2 \times 2 \times 2 \times 2 \times 2$), or 256. There are 256 standard character assignments to represent standard letters, numbers, and punctuation in English. For example the letter A is represented by the bits 01000001, equivalent to the decimal number 65. There is a 1 in the 64s place and a 1 in the 1s place; 64 + 1 = 65. Incidentally, all modern computers use 8-bit bytes. Computer makers and software writers use different methods to represent other character sets, such as Japanese, in combinations of bytes.

In the final analysis, every message can be treated as a string of bytes, and each string of bytes can be represented as a number. The following table shows how in our standard decimal system the number 1,132 is constructed.

Operator	Digit	Position Value	Position as Exponent		Extended Value
	1	thousands	10^3	which equals	1,000
plus	1	hundreds	10^2	which equals	100
plus	3	tens	10^1	which equals	30
plus	2	ones	10^0	which equals	2
Total					**1,132**

So the word "Guess" could equate to the decimal number 306912260979, as in the following table.

Letter	Numeric Value of the Letter	256s Position	Power of 256	Power of 256 Multiplied Out	Power of 256 Times the Value of the Letter
G	71	4	256^4	4,294,967,296	304942678016
u	117	3	256^3	16,777,216	1962934272
e	101	2	256^2	65,536	6619136
s	115	1	256^1	256	29440
s	115	0	256^0	1	115
Total					**306912260979**

As you can imagine, the numbers can get very large in a hurry. That may be a problem for people, but computers are designed to deal with large numbers.

We turn the number back into letters by repeatedly dividing by 256 and keeping the remainder, as in the following table.

Number to Divide	Number Divided by 256	Remainder	Letter Equivalent of Remainder
306,912,260,979	1,198,876,019	115	s
1,198,876,019	4,683,109	115	s
4,683,109	18,293	101	e
18,293	71	117	u
71	0	71	G

This is one way in which characters can be converted into numbers and numbers back into characters. The upshot of this is that any message can be sent as a number or series of numbers. Numbers are convenient because they are so easy to manipulate with arithmetic. Here is a code that would fool a Sunday crossword cryptographer, although perhaps not the CIA. What happens if you multiply the "Guess" number by 3 and turn it back into letters? Your code number is 3 × 306912260979 or 920736782937.

Number to Divide	Number Divided by 256	Remainder	Letter Equivalent of Remainder
920,736,782,937	3,596,628,058	89	Y
3,596,628,058	14,049,328	90	Z
14,049,328	54,880	48	0
54,880	214	96	`
214	0	214	Ö

The code for the word "Guess" becomes Ö`Z0Y. You could transmit it over the Internet and nobody would guess what it meant. However, the person on the other end would know what to do. Convert the characters to a number and divide by 3, getting back 306912260979, and then use the same rules to convert that back to letters. Pretty neat. This is a lot better than translating one character at a time. A code breaker who tried to deal with the characters Ö and Z individually would get nowhere. These characters only mean something in the context of the whole code, which in this instance is five characters long. For comparison, common units of encryption now in use on the Internet are 1,024 bits (16 characters) and up.

Most traditional data-encryption methods, such as the government-standard DES (Data Encryption Standard) use an approach similar to this, except that the technique they use to scramble the numbers is much more sophisticated than simply multiplying by a constant. The essential feature is that both people in a secure conversation use the same rules for encrypting and decrypting the message. They have to agree in advance on what codes, or encryption keys, they are going to use.

Agreeing in advance on encryption keys can be a problem. How are you going to exchange keys? Over the telephone? Over the Internet? That would require secure communications. But if you already had secure communications, you would not be bothering, would you? Historically, most organizations used code sheets that were distributed in advance, so the people on both ends would change them on a scheduled basis. Weaknesses in the system of physically exchanging codes compromised the German code system in World War II and the Soviet code system in the Cold War. Modern computers are a whole lot better at deciphering codes than the Cold War code breakers. There had to be a better way to distribute codes, and there now is: public-key cryptography.

The magic of public-key cryptography is that there are separate keys to encrypt and decrypt messages. The owner of the code generates two key: a public key (actually, two numbers) used to encrypt messages and a private key (again two numbers, one of them the same as for the public key) to decrypt messages. The owner of the code gives the public key to anyone who needs to send secret messages. Any person with the public key knows many things:

- the algorithm for encrypting messages,
- the algorithm for decrypting messages,
- the key for encrypting a message,
- the plaintext message before it is encrypted, and
- the ciphertext resulting from the encryption process.

Even with all that, the person remains unable to deduce the most crucial piece of information: the key for decrypting the message. How is that possible?

It is obvious that encryption and decryption cannot be mirror-image processes, like multiplying by 3 then dividing by 3 in the example earlier. The secret is in the numbers that the most common public-key algorithm, RSA, throws away. See www.rsa.com for an elegant description of how public key cryptography works. Bring a PhD in mathematics along for the journey.

The algorithm uses the plaintext message to create an immensely big number and then divide by a much smaller number. It throws away the dividend and keeps the remainder as the encrypted code. Anybody who had both the quotient and the remainder could decode the message just by going backward. The magic is that the remainder, even without the quotient that got thrown away, uniquely represents the encrypted message. However, the only way to decipher the message from the remainder alone is by using the private key, which only the owner possesses.

The RSA technique makes use of an elegantly simple formula known as Fermat's lesser theorem. For any number a and any prime number p, $(a^p - a)$ is divisible by p. As an illustration, here are two small examples developed in a spreadsheet:

- $13^5 - 13 = 371,280$; $371,280 / 5 = 74,256$; it is evenly divisible by 5.
- $5^{13} - 5 = 1,220,703,120$; $1,220,703,120 / 13 = 93,900,240$; it is evenly divisible by 13.

From this you can see that the algorithm can develop very large numbers even starting with small ones. As the numbers used in 1,024-bit encryption are about 300 digits long, you can imagine that the generated numbers get immense. They are far too large even for computers to deal with. The encryption algorithms depend on the fact that they can discard most of the intermediate numbers generated at each step in the process and still come up with an accurate result.

Of course there is a caveat. RSA codes are not unbreakable, just very difficult to break. The reason is that the algorithm for generating the keys depends on the use of very large prime numbers. Breaking a code is a matter of finding the prime factors of a very large number. So far, mathematicians do not have any approach much better than brute force for finding them. If you take a typical RSA key (300 decimal digits) and start trying to find prime factors (first try dividing by 2, then 3, then 5, then 7, then 11…) it will take a long time before you find all the prime divisors. The number of 300-digit numbers is astronomical. By way of comparison, the number of nanoseconds since the beginning of the universe can be expressed in about 25 digits. There obviously is no conceivable way to assemble the factors of all 300-digit numbers into a database ahead of time; likewise calculating them is a major challenge.

After finding all the prime factors used in an RSA public key, you have to plug them into the algorithm and see if the decrypted text makes sense. Just to be tricky, most computerized algorithms wrap multiple layers of public-key encryption, or mix public-key and other types of encryption, so even if you did hit on the right prime number you would not recognize the fact from looking at the decrypted results. No wonder the National Security Agency is a major purchaser of supercomputers. In *The Age of Spiritual Machines*, computer genius Ray Kurzweil says that quantum computers will make quick work of such problems by trying all solutions in parallel. Fortunately for the security community, they so far only exist in theory.

Implementation of Public-Key Cryptography

Public-key cryptography enables you to send and receive encoded messages. You tell your correspondents how to encrypt message traffic to be sent to you; they tell you how to encrypt traffic back to them. Traffic is secure in both directions, but neither of you knows how to decode traffic destined for the other. Although public-key cryptography is the big concept, it requires the support of a few smaller concepts to make it serve the needs of computer cryptography. These include *digital signatures* and *digital certificates*, as well as *digital key rings* to keep track of things.

Digital Signatures

With public-key cryptography, you can be confident that you are the only one who can read the message you receive. However, anybody in possession of the public key could have sent it. You can see how this would cause problems in an Oracle EBS environment. If anybody in the world could have your accounts-payable system write him or her a check for $1,000,000, the fact that nobody but you would fall for their request would be small consolation. Public-key cryptography requires two-way security. You need to get the message, and you need to be positive that the message came from the person who purports to have sent it.

Digital signatures complete the picture for two-way authentication. The process is the reverse of message encryption. With signatures, the sender of the digital signature has the private key and the receiver has the public key. The sender encrypts the message with the public key of the intended recipient. That way only the recipient can read it. The sender uses his or her own private key to encrypt a signature block saying it is from him or her. That proves that no one else could have sent it.

Upon getting the message, the recipient knows that the sender is who he or she claims to be, because only the sender has the private key to encrypt the signature block. The recipient, or anybody who has the sender's public key, could figure out who sent it. However, the recipient is the only person in the world who is in a position to use the sender's public key to confirm that the message is from the person who purports to have sent it, using a private key to read the message.

Key Rings

Each user (or at least, each desktop client) in an Oracle EBS environment has a unique public key for encrypting messages to the Web server and a private key for encrypting its digital signature. The public and private keys for traffic received from the Web server may be the same or different.

The Web server in an Oracle EBS environment engages in encrypted sessions with many different users. It needs to maintain a database of the public and private keys it uses for encryption and decryption with each of its opposite numbers. The device for doing so is called a key ring.

Needless to say, the key ring itself has to be encrypted, as it is written to local disk storage. Interestingly, public-key cryptography is not relevant in this application. Because the same modules both read and write the key-ring data, they can use traditional encryption techniques. There is no need for the server to keep secrets from itself.

Digital Certificates

Certificates are digital documents that confirm that a public key is uniquely associated with an individual or other entity. They prove who owns a specific public key. They help prevent someone from using a phony key to impersonate someone else. It is important in the Oracle EBS applications to make sure that people logging in through a browser are who they purport to be.

The most widely accepted format for certificates is defined by the ITU-T X.509 international standard. X.509 specifies the authentication service for X.500 directories, as well as the X.509 certificate syntax. The standard does not specify a particular cryptographic algorithm, but the RSA public-key algorithm is well suited because of the advantages already named for public keys. An X.509 certificate consists of the following fields:

- Version
- Serial number
- Signature algorithm ID
- Issuer name
- Validity period
- Subject (user) name
- Subject public-key information
- Issuer unique identifier (versions 2 and 3 only)
- Subject unique identifier (versions 2 and 3 only)
- Extensions (version 3 only)
- Signature on these fields

This certificate is signed by the issuer to confirm the link between the user's name and public key.

The desktop tier in the Oracle architecture is assumed to be insecure. That means that there should be no way for hackers to compromise the Oracle EBS applications even if they totally take over one of the PC workstations. To manage this, Oracle makes the single assumption that the Java applet it places on the desktop remains valid.

It does this by downloading the applet from the Web server the first time it is needed, or when a new version comes out. This takes time, but it means that the Web server can be confident in the applet. Once downloaded, the applet resides on the PC's hard disk, which is not secure. It uses a digital certificate to revalidate the applet each time it connects to Oracle. The applet has buried within itself, in encrypted form, all the information needed to confirm that it is what it thinks it is, and check sums to confirm that none of it has been tampered with.

The digital certificate guarantees the integrity of the Oracle E-Business Suite architecture. That means the applet is intact; it has not been modified to steal passwords or surreptitiously modify Oracle EBS application data. However, it does nothing to ensure that whoever logs in is not using a stolen password. Digital certificates do not reduce the need for policy in other areas of security.

Virtual Private Networks (VPNs)

Common carriers include encryption over their own networks to create virtual private network (VPN) offerings for clients. Although all customer traffic flows over a common network, the service provider ensures each customer's privacy. For customers, it is cheaper and easier than implementing their own encryption.

Oracle EBS users with geographically dispersed users often find it worthwhile to use VPNs. The desktop and network security systems complement each other. The log-in/password combination confirms who the user is, the digital certificate assures the integrity of the applet on the desktop, and the VPN protects data traffic between the desktop and the Web server.

The entire Oracle E-Business Suite is being enabled for operation with the wireless Internet. There is a rapidly evolving class of devices such as Apple iPads, Android tablet devices, and Internet-enabled cell phones such as the Apple iPhone that use Internet protocol over wireless connections. Some of the myriad terms for the wireless connections include 4G, 802.11 networks; Bluetooth, and W-CDMA carrier networks.

In concept, the security issues for wireless are the same as for the wired Internet. Packets have to be encrypted because they travel through a totally insecure medium, in this case the airwaves. In practice, the issues are somewhat different, because wireless links have less bandwidth, the connections have to be handed off frequently in a cellular structure, cellular transmission usually involves a long series of links that can include all the protocols named in the previous paragraph, and the connections tend to be shorter and more frequent. In addition, portable devices are easy to lose and often do not have enough of a keyboard to make it easy to enter log-ins and passwords, especially if you need multiple layers. A security consultant is almost indispensable in planning wireless applications at the current state of the art.

Strong Authentication

Passwords are second to physical security on the list of biggest single weakness in most systems. People get careless. Just as they might leave confidential information out where prying eyes can find it, they also leave passwords out where they can be found, lend them to someone else, forget to change them, or use ones that are easy to guess.

Strong authentication means using a different password each time a user logs on to the Web server. This usually requires a combination of something the user knows (the account number and password), something the user has (like a magnetic card device), and something the user does (like answer back to a challenge phrase sent by the server). Random-number generators are common in machine-readable devices. The random number changes every so often—perhaps every minute. The user's card and the server both contain clocks and random-number generators, and they both start with the same seed number. That way the server knows, depending on the minute of the day, what number is valid to authenticate a given user. Coupling the random number with an account number and password assures the system that the user is in possession of both the physical key and logical-access keys.

Each person on earth is unique in ways that can be detected to a high level of confidence by machines. Although they cannot yet check DNA samples, devices do exist to verify a person's identity by their fingerprints, their voice, the geometry of their face, or their retina. A retinal scan is the most secure, but the devices are a bit expensive and an eyeball scan may appear a bit intrusive. Fingerprint readers are less off-putting and commonly found in modern laptop computers Voice-recognition equipment requires only a microphone. These are becoming increasingly common on multimedia computers for taking dictation, making phone calls over the Internet, and attaching voice messages to records in Oracle. Most requirements for additional authentication can be satisfied by one of these types of device.

Strong authentication is a good idea for servers that are publicly accessible; that is, available from off campus. Weak or password-only authentication might be sufficient for on-campus local area network connections, provided it is reinforced by physical security and a policy of changing passwords periodically. The design of the Oracle E-Business Suite does not include provisions for strong authentication. An implementation in Release 11 or earlier would depend on extensions to the system written by a third party.

Virus Threats

Viruses are antisocial programs introduced onto your machines by stealth to compromise your secrets or create mischief. They usually enter a system carelessly through some common means of data exchange such as e-mail, file transfers, or removable media like diskettes. All viruses work by executing some type of code. The most common ones—the easiest to write and spread—are macro viruses that tend to affect Microsoft Office products. These do not have much impact on Oracle products. The more insidious ones execute compiled code, such as C programs.

Desktop machines are the most common targets for viruses. PC users have a lot of contact with the outside world through the Web, exchange of diskettes, and so forth, and often they are not terribly careful. The good news is that Oracle does not present much of a target for desktop viruses. The integrity of the Oracle E-Business Suite depends on only one desktop-level program: the Oracle EBS applet. The digital-certificate security used to protect the applet should certainly be proof against any virus that is sent over a network.

Although viruses are not much of an issue for the Oracle E-Business Suite, it could be made an unwitting vector for macro viruses hiding in Word and Excel files that are attached to database records. They would not affect Oracle EBS itself, but they could wreck the desktop machines of users who open the attached files.

Although viruses can be terribly destructive on a Web or database server, common-sense precautions are enough to keep them out. Programmers and systems administrators generally use desktop machines for ad hoc communications with the outside world. Communications to and from a server usually are between known and trusted parties.

Hacker Countermeasures

Almost all hacks require the hacker to gain control of the log-in id and password of a powerful user. In Unix, this is the root account; in NT, the administrator. Given enough time, almost anybody can guess a password. In the old days before hacking was commonplace, Unix used to merely present a user with a polite message when his or her log-in attempt failed, then let the user try again. Some hackers took a lot of time; more sophisticated ones wrote programs to keep on trying until they had success.

Unix is not so forgiving anymore. It usually allows a user three tries to get the password right, then breaks the connection. Moreover, it alerts the systems operator to the fact that somebody is trying to hack the system. Hackers have evolved other techniques.

A hacker wins if he or she can surreptitiously plant a program on the system and get it to run. The rogue program can either do its damage directly or sniff out log-in/password files and pass the information back to the hacker. The rogue program needs high-level permissions to do this sort of damage—exactly the kind of permissions that the operating system is designed to keep out of the hands of users. The hacker needs to find a careless user, such as one who accidentally allows general users to have write permission on system-level directories, or needs to know the holes in the security design of the target operating system. Often it takes both.

There is an ongoing game of fox and hounds among hackers, security-software vendors, and operating-system vendors. The hackers try to find the loopholes. Security vendors try to beat them to the punch and crow about their prowess in preventing trouble. Operating-system vendors test thoroughly before they release a new version, then develop and disseminate patches as quickly as they can when holes are discovered.

You need to defend yourself at several levels:

■ **Do not let hackers have access to your system.** The most common device for isolating your system from the outside world is called a firewall. Firewall systems act as an intermediary with the outside world. They accept packets from the outside world, inspect them, and reroute them to an internal server whose address is not known to the outside world. Firewall systems have enough intelligence to determine whether a particular packet belongs to an established session, a known application, and a known user. A firewall system should be able to hold hackers who are probing your system at bay, never letting them near.

■ **Acquire software or an outside service to probe your system for holes in your defense.** Proving a negative is a difficult proposition. It is hard to ensure that all your permissions are set properly to deny access to a hacker. The best way to find out is by testing.

■ **Do not make it easy when hackers do get access.** The password-management techniques described in this chapter for the Oracle Financials can be applied at all levels of your system. Strong authentication is especially necessary at the operating-system log-in level, for the root and Oracle manager IDs. If your DBAs can dial in from home or access the system across the Internet, you certainly need it.

■ **Use intrusion detection to find out when hackers have gotten in.** Prepare reports of successful and unsuccessful log-ins, especially for the most critical accounts. Take steps to change your passwords and, when necessary, the dial-in numbers for the modems, network paths, and other information the hackers might have in hand. At the Oracle EBS application level, keep track of who has logged in and how often. Audit for suspicious changes in critical tables, such as FND_USER (where the passwords are stored).

■ **Offer nothing useful if hackers do get in.** Encrypt sensitive data on your hard disks. You usually do this at the application level. This encryption can be fast. It does not need a public-key approach, because the same agent—the application itself—does both the reading and writing.

■ **Set up a "honeypot" to trap hackers.** A *honeypot* is a decoy machine, one that is relatively easy to hack, contains dummy data that will appear tempting to a hacker, and is loaded with tracking software that will lead investigators back to the hacker's lair.

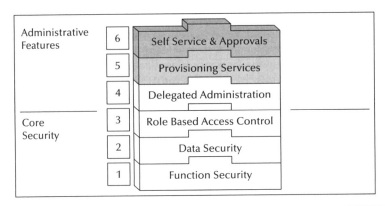

FIGURE 21-1. *Role Based Access Control for Oracle Release 12 EBS (Source:* Oracle E-Business Suite System Administrator's Guide—Security Release 12.1*)*

Functional and Application Security (RBAC)

Functional and application security with Oracle Role Based Access Control (RBAC) builds upon system, database, and network security protocols to provide finer-grained application security within the Oracle E-Business Suite. Figure 21-1 shows the topology for RBAC in terms of an overall Oracle R12 EBS environment.

RBAC began life in Release 11.5.10 of the Oracle E-Business Suite as part of the new mechanism to implement role-based user management. Roles are created and can therefore be assigned to users and groups to implement a complete functional-based security policy that is mapped out to the technical layer for application security within the Oracle R12 EBS environment. For instance, if you want to segregate users based on job function, such as payroll clerks, then you would create a role for that job function and assign the Oracle R12 EBS Responsibilities for access to read, write, and make changes to AR, AP, and GL modules as required. The beauty of RBAC is that you can segregate jobs by function and category, thereby fulfilling the auditing requirements for Sarbanes-Oxley and the Health Insurance Portability and Accountability Act as well as managing a secure environment. In addition, RBAC provides you with the ability to create a one-stop area for implementing user-based security with policies in a self-service environment. Role categories can be set up and managed as shown in Figure 21-2.

For instance, you can set up a role called Sales Manager and grant this role to sales reps and other users. By nature of how the role is set up and granted to users, the required user Responsibilities inherent in the role will be propagated down to users to whom it is granted. Process approvals are managed via the Oracle R12 EBS Workflow engine for roles created and granted to users within the Oracle R12 EBS environment. Oracle developers can customize RBAC to suite business needs by implementing use of the following Workflow business events.

Event	Purpose
oracle.apps.fnd.umx.rolerequested	Raised when a role is requested
oracle.apps.fnd.umx.accountrequested	Raised when an account is requested
oracle.apps.fnd.umx.requestapproved	Raised when an account or role is approved
oracle.apps.fnd.umx.requestrejected	Raised when an account or role is rejected

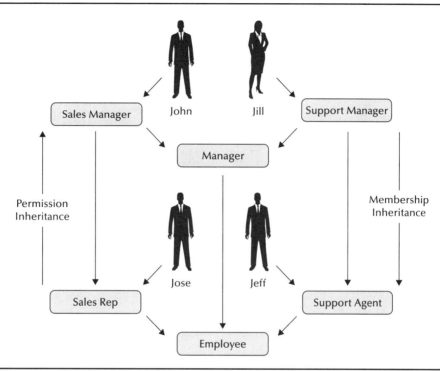

FIGURE 21-2.   *RBAC Hierarchy for Oracle R12 E-Business Suite (Source:* Oracle E-Business Suite System Administrator's Guide—Security Release 12.1*)*

Additional details on how to implement custom programs for these Workflow events with RBAC and Oracle R12 EBS can be found in the *UMX Developer's Guide,* Note: 399400.1 on My Oracle Support at http://support.oracle.com.

Oracle provides the following event parameters for implementing user Workflow security parameters.

Name	Description
REG_SERVICE_CODE	Primary key of the registration process
REG_SERVICE_TYPE	Registration process type
REQUESTED_BY_USER_ID	Identification of the user submitting the request
REQUESTED_FOR_USER_ID	Identification of the user for whom the request is submitted
REQUESTED_USERNAME	Requested user name
WF_ROLE_NAME	Primary key value of default role for account requests
AME_TRANSACTION_TYPE_ID	Primary key for transaction type in Oracle Approval Management
AME_APPLICATION_ID	Primary key for transaction type in Oracle Approval Management

These Workflow user-event-management business parameters can be customized with development efforts for Oracle R12 EBS environments.

The parameter WF_ROLE_NAME is an optional parameter and is not required for Self-Service Account Creation. You can use a null value for this parameter. A sample program is shown here that illustrates how you can implement the Workflow business-event parameters for user management with RBAC.

Sample Program

```
/**************************************************************
Purpose: enable subscription to user management for RBAC events

Function custom_logic (
p_subscription_guid in raw,
p_event in out NOCOPY WF_EVENT_T)
Return varchar2 is
l_first_name varchar2(30);
Begin
l_first_name := p_event.getvalueforparameter ('FIRST_NAME');

// Manipulate the data
End custom_logic;


**************************************************************/
```

Once you have set up the roles and Responsibilities within the Oracle E-Business Suite, you can access them from within the Oracle Application Manager graphical user interface.

New Security Features for Oracle E-Business Suite R12

With Oracle Release 12.1.1 as well as the updated Oracle 11gR1 and Oracle 11gR2 database for the Oracle E-Business Suite, a host of new security features provide you with additional security and auditing capabilities.

In summary, these new security features include

- Oracle 11g Total Recall and Flashback Data Archives and
- Oracle 11g Database Firewall.

If you have implemented later versions for Oracle Release 12 E-Business Suite, such as 12.1 and later, then you should have an Oracle 11gR1 or Oracle 11gR2 database tier. In order to implement these security features, you must either be on a later release of EBS or plan to upgrade the database tier to Oracle 11g or later; previous database versions before 11g do not provide these features. One caveat to keep in mind: these features are not included with the base Oracle R12 EBS licenses. You will need to purchase an additional license to implement these security products. Let us take a quick look into the features and how they may benefit your organization in terms of database and application security for Oracle EBS.

Oracle 11g Total Recall

Oracle 11g Total Recall is a new database feature available in the Oracle 11g database release. It provides functionality to flash back queries to view data in previous states by using a new mechanism called Flashback Data Archives (FDA) to interact with flashback database functionality in the Oracle 11*g* database. Total Recall differs from flashback query in that the Total Recall data are stored in an archive tablespace and will remain there until the user-defined retention period has expired. Total Recall is quite useful for auditing purposes to track critical data changes for various applications. For instance, you can archive data for security purposes by storing the flashback data archives on disk or tape. Please keep in mind that Oracle 11*g* Total Recall requires an additional and separate license cost apart from the core Oracle EBS and database licenses.

Let us look at a brief example of how we might use this feature.

Step 1: Create new flashback archive

```
CREATE FLASHBACK ARCHIVE DEFAULT myflash1 TABLESPACE fbarch1
QUOTA 30G
RETENTION 1 YEAR;
Flashback archive created.
```

Step 2: Enable flashback data archiving for tables

```
ALTER TABLE scott.emp FLASHBACK ARCHIVE fbarch1;
Table altered.
```

Now let us perform an update operation.

```
UPDATE scott.emp
SET salary = 90000 WHERE employee_id = 19;
1 row updated.
```

We can find the previous value before the table was changed.

```
SELECT salary
FROM scott.empAS OF TIMESTAMP TO_TIMESTAMP('2007-07-13 02:19:00', 'YYYY-MM-DD
HH24:MI:SS')
WHERE employee_id = 19;
```

As you can see, Total Recall and flashback data archives are a powerful tool for auditing changes made to your database environment, and are simple to implement.

Oracle 11*g* Database Firewall

The Oracle 11*g* Database Firewall is a new product feature to provide a secured DMZ zoning for hardening your Oracle infrastructure. It includes a policy analyzer for implementing new security policies as well as firewall-management reports for tracking security issues and alerts. In addition, there is a remote and local monitor that forwards network traffic based on access-control lists.

We recommend the new Oracle Database Firewall for large mission-critical Oracle R12 E-Business Suite environments that do not have a firewall product already in place. For instance, if you want to secure the entire Oracle infrastructure and have data warehouses running on Oracle in addition to Oracle EBS applications, and do not have a product in place such as a Check Point firewall, then we advise this as a possible firewall strategy to complement your current and future Oracle infrastructure. For environments that are Oracle-centric shops, we highly recommend that you deploy the Oracle database firewall product as part of your security infrastructure. Not only does the Oracle database firewall product interact more efficiently than a traditional firewall

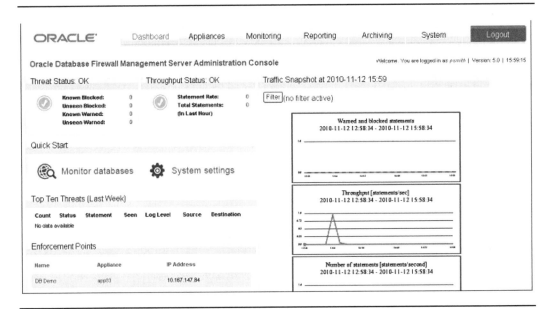

FIGURE 21-3. *Dashboard interface for Oracle Database Firewall with Oracle R12 EBS*

product, it may also be a more cost-effective approach when all software licenses are negotiated with your Oracle sales representative as a package deal for a complete end-to-end Oracle solution. In addition, with today's economic conditions, many corporations cannot afford to hire multiple workers in systems and databases to manage all facets of the enterprise. By deploying the Oracle Database Firewall product, the Oracle DBA can perform not only database-administration tasks but security-administration duties once reserved for IT security engineers. This maximizes the return on investment for budgets and increases the role and responsibility of the Oracle database professional. Figure 21-3 shows the useful dashboard functionality provided by the Oracle Database Firewall product.

The Oracle Database Firewall uses a central administration console similar to that found with other Oracle systems-management tools, such as Oracle Enterprise Manager Grid Control and Oracle Application Manager for the Oracle R12 E-Business Suite. Like other firewall-system products, such as Cisco and Check Point Firewall, the Oracle Database Firewall product allows you to set up and customize security filters.

Additional details on how to install and configure the Oracle Database Firewall product can be found online in the Oracle Database Firewall documentation at http://www.oracle.com/technetwork/documentation/db-firewall-268658.html.

Audit Vault for Oracle E-Business Suite R12

Audit Vault is a powerful database module that can be implemented for the Oracle R12 E-Business Suite to provide comprehensive monitoring and tracking of database changes performed within the Oracle R12 EBS environment. In particular, changes made to the Oracle database tier are captured by Audit Vault and stored for future auditing reports. Audit Vault can be used to configure policies

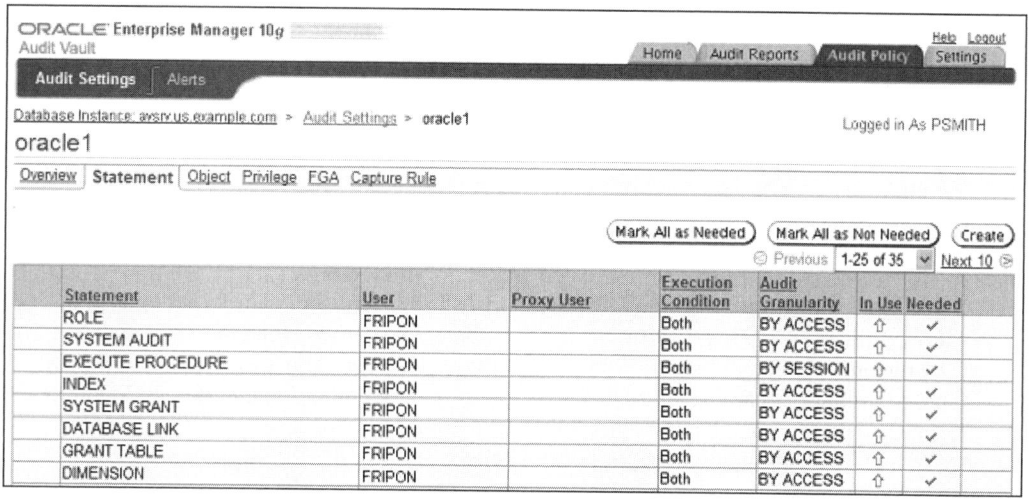

FIGURE 21-4. *Audit Vault FGA dashboard*

for tracking and capturing changes made to Oracle R12 EBS environments. Traditionally, Oracle DBAs would set up auditing via either file OS based audit files or to capture audit changes made to table data within the Oracle database server by configuring the database initialization parameter. Then the DBA would issue the Oracle SQL*PLUS database command AUDIT SESSION to capture changes made at a the level of a user database session or issue the AUDIT DELETE TABLE command to track any commands to delete a table within the Oracle database. With Oracle 11g, the Audit Vault product takes auditing to another level that allows you to graphically configure and manage auditing functions at an enterprise level for large Oracle infrastructures. For instance, the dashboard provides the database administrator with a central monitoring point for executing auditing tasks.

A configuration for fine-grained auditing is possible via a graphical interface in Audit Vault, as shown in Figure 21-4.

Identity Management for Oracle R12 E-Business Suite

Oracle Identity Management is a suite of robust security applications for monitoring and securing the Oracle suite of database applications. Originally intended at first for the Oracle database platform, the suite of products now has been extended to support the Oracle R12 E-Business Suite of enterprise resource planning applications. In summary, Oracle Identity Management includes the following products and applications:

- Oracle Internet Directory
- Oracle Access Manager
- Oracle Adaptive Access Manager
- Oracle Virtual Directory

Oracle Internet Directory (OID)

Oracle Internet Directory (OID) is a certified Lightweight Directory Access Provisioning (LDAP) server for managing security across multiple domains for Oracle-based applications. OID or Oracle Internet Directory is the Oracle LDAP implementation (Lightweight Directory Access Protocol) with Application Server. You might think of OID as Microsoft Active Directory on steroids for Oracle. LDAP has a naming structure based on an inverted tree, as shown in Figure 21-5.

LDAP uses a treelike structure similar to a B-tree algorithm, with a naming convention that uses relative distinguished names (RDNs) and distinguished names (DNs) to identify relative paths and exact paths to entries within the LDAP directory. It uses the common name (CN) to identify a specific value within the LDAP tree, such as Robert Smith, and a user id (UID) for a user account within the installation. LDAP provides you with fine-grained security to map relative and specific values within an Oracle environment across different platforms. For example, you can have an OID server on Linux authenticate against a Microsoft Active Directory (AD) LDAP server. Understanding OID and LDAP is fundamental to implementing Oracle Identity Management products with the Oracle E-Business Suite.

We will run through configuration for OID with Oracle 10g Application Server to see how it works.

We start a new session to configure OID. Of note: OID can also be configured for non–Application Server environments. For instance, we can set up OID with Oracle 11g. The OID security is available from the Network Configuration Assistant to set up the Oracle Internet Directory with Oracle database environments. For Oracle 10gAS, the method to set up and configure OID is to use the **oidadmin** utility. In the Oracle 10gAS environment, the **oidadmin** utility is located in the $ORACLE_HOME/bin directory. Make sure to correctly set your Oracle environment variables for your operating system. We start **oidadmin** and the welcome screen shown in Figure 21-6 appears.

We need to log in to OID as the default administrator. Since OID uses LDAP, we need to specify the log-in format based on CN. The user ID is cn=orcladmin, and the password is the password for the ias_admin account chosen during the Oracle 10gAS installation process.

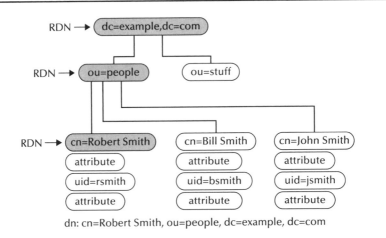

FIGURE 21-5. *LDAP directory structure*

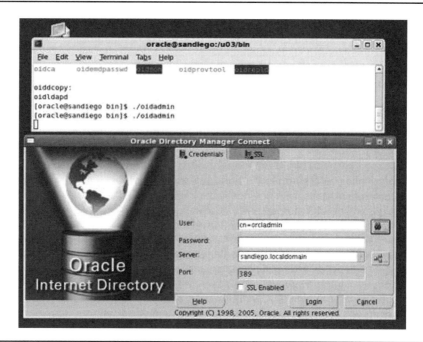

FIGURE 21-6.   *Oracle Internet Directory access*

After the log-in is complete, the welcome screen appears and shows the default OID environment.
The tree structures can be expanded to expose the various configuration details for OID in the
10*g*AS environment. Recall that Oracle R12 EBS uses an Oracle 10*g* Application Server as part of
the middle-tier server. You will need a separate environment for the OID server apart from the
Oracle R12 EBS middle tier.

As you can see, multiple tasks can be performed to administer users and servers within the
OID environment for Oracle 10*g*AS. Suffice it to say, it would require an entire book to detail all
aspects of Oracle Identity Management with Oracle 10*g* Application Server. For now, we will
provide a basic walk-through to get the baseline configuration up and running with the new 10*g*
Application Server. There are three divisions of OID configuration to consider:

- access-control management,
- schema management, and
- server management.

Access-Control Management
Access-control management is the process of granting and restricting access to a realm of Oracle
application or database servers within the OID environment for Identity Management.

Access controls can be managed and created via the OID interface for applications and users
based on the OID LDAP X.509 standard using cn (common name) and LDAP syntax. For example,
this image displays the cn=Reports details for access-control management.

Schema Management for OID and Identity Management

By default, OID stores all metadata about configuration details and users in a set of schemas within the Oracle 10*g* repository database, which is part of the Infrastructure component of Oracle 10*g*AS.

Each schema item is broken down into subitems such as object ID, class, and attributes based on the LDAP syntax for OID, as shown here.

Server Management for OID and Identity Management

OID provides various types of server configurations for Oracle 10*g*AS:

- directory server,
- replication server, and
- integration server.

These servers determine the specific type of security mechanism and configuration to be used with Oracle 10*g* Application Server. For example, to view, change and update settings for the directory server, the tree-structure menu item under Server management would be expanded.

There are also options to modify settings for SSL (Secure Sockets Layer).

To configure Oracle 10*g* Application Server with a basic Identity Management setup, you must begin with the Oracle 10*g*AS control window.

The settings for Identity Management are accessed on the Infrastructure tab in the Application Server Enterprise Manager. As expected, it shows that nothing has been configured yet.

The host-name details for the 10*g* Application Server must be entered, port number.

Recall that the user name has to be specified in LDAP format with cn=orcladmin and the password for ias_admin that was given during the Oracle 10*g*AS installation. Oracle then politely informs us that the entire tech stack for Oracle 10*g* Application Server will be shut down and restarted to complete the basic Identity Management configuration. We verify that all settings are correct.

Oracle Access Manager (OAM)

Oracle Access Manager (OAM) is Oracle's identity- and access-management product for authentication and authorization purposes with Oracle database and Oracle EBS. OAM provides a host of powerful features, such as single-sign-on authentication, and integration with other third-party identity-management products as well as Oracle Adaptive Access Manager.

Benefits of Oracle Access Manager

In the past, the Oracle E-Business Suite only supported single sign-on when an Oracle Single Sign-On Server was deployed separately. However this required the additional hardware to host an Oracle Single Sign-On Server as a go-between proxy-type authentication server, and it lacked many key features then available with the Oracle Access Manager product. With the arrival of the new Oracle E-Business Suite AccessGate product, these restrictions no longer exist for deployments with OAM and Oracle R12 EBS systems. The Oracle R12 EBS AccessGate product is a Java enterprise (J2EE) application, hosted on a separate application server, that provides you with a direct integration pathway between Oracle EBS and Oracle Access Manager. In addition, by using AccessGate for Oracle R12 EBS, you can leverage all of the authentication features now available within OAM. You can also integrate additional identity-management products, including Oracle Identity Federation and Oracle Adaptive Access Manager.

Requirements for Using Oracle EBS AccessGate

Before you can deploy OAM with Oracle R12 EBS, you will need to install and configure the following applications:

- Oracle EBS Release 12.1.1 or later or Oracle EBS Release 11i 11.5.10 CU2 (ATG RUP 6 or higher)
- Oracle Access Manager 10gR3 (10.1.4.3)
- Oracle Internet Directory 10gR3 (10.1.4.3) or 11gR1 Patchset 1 (11.1.1.2)
- Oracle WebLogic Server 10.3.1 or later version

Oracle EBS AccessGate is supported on any OS platform that supports the Oracle WebLogic Server 10.3.1. OAM is supported on most OS platforms. To verify, we recommend that you check the certification matrix available online at My Oracle Support (http://support.oracle.com).

Oracle Adaptive Access Manager (OAAM)

Oracle Adaptive Access Manager (OAAM) is the complementary identity-management solution in the Oracle Identity Management suite of Oracle Fusion Middleware products. It differs from its sister product Oracle Access Manager in several key ways. First of all, OAAM provides a suite of risk-management, fraud-detection, and fraud-protection functions for large enterprise environments. Whereas OAM is more of a security-authentication mechanism that behaves similarly to a firewall or proxy server, OAAM provides you with the ability to create risk-management policies for mitigating fraud activities against your Oracle environments. OAAM shares many features in common with another enterprise auditing product called Oracle Governance Risk and Compliance Manager (GRC), except that its functionality is broader in scope. GRC is more geared toward auditing, whereas OAAM is based on fraud and risk management. The main administration graphical console for OAAM is shown here..

In addition, you can set up biometric authentication such as fingerprint scanners to interact with OAAM. This is useful for top-secret and sensitive secured environments, such as those found in large investment banks and government organizations such as the Central Intelligence Agency or the United States Department of Defense. Detailed coverage on how to deploy and administer the OAAM product is complex and beyond the scope of this paper. For information on how to install, configure, and manage OAAM, we recommend that you consult the Oracle documentation for OAAM available online at http://download.oracle.com/docs/cd/E17904_01/im.htm.

Oracle Virtual Directory

Oracle Virtual Directory provides LDAP virtualization directory services with Oracle Identity Management products to authenticate LDAP resources between Oracle database and Oracle EBS applications. As such, Oracle Virtual Directory functions to integrate Oracle applications in a secure environment. It provides virtualization for resources to integrate various identity-management products and links the LDAP sources together for access under a unified directory structure. In a nutshell, it is a gateway-type product. Further details can be found online at http://download.oracle .com/docs/cd/E17904_01/im.htm.

Security-Patch Maintenance for the Oracle R12 E-Business Suite

Patch maintenance is a critical task performed by Oracle DBAs on a regular basis to ensure that bug fixes and security vulnerabilities are addressed and resolved for the Oracle R12 EBS environments that they support for mission-critical applications. Patches fall into two key types: bug fixes and security patches. For security patches, Oracle releases quarterly critical patch updates. Oracle highly recommends that these updates be applied as soon as possible to remedy current and new security issues discovered in the Oracle software environments. Oracle provides excellent guidance on patch-maintenance updates online at http://www.oracle.com/technetwork/topics/security/ alerts-086861.html. An example of the patch security matrix for the Oracle E-Business Suite is shown here.

We highly recommend that you keep your Oracle EBS environments up to date to mitigate the risks involved with the security assessments provided by Oracle in the critical patch updates and critical vulnerabilities.

Conclusion

The easiest and most obvious security measures also offer the greatest return. Take care in setting up your Responsibilities within the Oracle E-Business Suite. Give a fair amount of thought to the business procedures that your systems administrator must follow in assigning Responsibilities to users. Make passwords hard to figure out and change them periodically.

Oracle EBS security extends well beyond the application software itself. Every organization needs a comprehensive security policy that names and assesses every kind of exposure and provides for countermeasures appropriate to the risks. Physical security is first and most essential. All else is for naught if an intruder can simply walk in and grab a report or access a desktop computer. You need to carefully manage access at every level of the system, including communications links, databases, and operating systems. Oracle EBS security is no defense against intruders who are allowed to attack your operation from below.

Whether or not your most sensitive data are in the custody of the Oracle E-Business Suite, security usually needs to be managed at a higher organizational level. A uniform policy needs to coordinate activity in the information-systems department; telephone, wireless, and Internet communications; human resources; and plant security. Consider putting responsibility for the policy in the hands of a single individual and engaging an outside security consultant to help coordinate policy. Oracle EBS security is relatively straightforward. A security expert can learn how to incorporate the Oracle tools into a corporate plan much more readily than you can extrapolate your total corporate security needs from the Oracle E-Business Suite.

References

Best Practices for Securing Oracle E-Business Suite Release 12

Oracle Corporation-My Oracle Support (MOS) Note **403537.1**

Oracle® E-Business Suite System Administrator's Guide—Security Release 12.1

Oracle® Database 2 Day + Security Guide 11*g* Release 2 (11.2)

Oracle® Database Advanced Security Administrator's Guide 11*g* Release 2 (11.2)

Oracle® Audit Vault Auditor's Guide Release 10.2.3.2

Oracle® Fusion Middleware Administrator's Guide for Oracle Internet Directory11*g* Release 1 (11.1.1)

Oracle® Fusion Middleware Administrator's Guide for Oracle Virtual Directory 11*g* Release 1 (11.1.1)

Oracle® Fusion Middleware Integration Guide for Oracle Access Manager 11*g* Release 1 (11.1.1)

Oracle® Fusion Middleware Administrator's Guide for Oracle Adaptive Access Manager Release 11*g* (11.1.1)

Oracle® Database Firewall Security Management Guide Release 5.0

My Oracle Support (MOS) Note **975182.1**

Integrating Oracle E-Business Suite with Oracle Access Manager Using Oracle E-Business Suite AccessGate.

CHAPTER
22

Customization
and Modification

he Oracle E-Business Suite of modules offers great value, given the range of functions built into the modules and the ease with which you can extend them to meet your needs. Establishing custom applications is the first step if you want to customize EBS to adapt it to your business requirements. The installation process allows a remarkable degree of manipulation. Beyond that, the environments in which the Oracle E-Business Suite are written and executed are open to modifications at the program-code level. Oracle includes complete source code and technical documentation with your software purchase license agreement.

The challenge during implementation is to derive maximum value from the Oracle system. Meeting this challenge means making the best use of the standard features within each package and considering the most advantageous trade-offs between modifying your business processes and modifying Oracle EBS.

The architecture of Oracle EBS is open to configuration or modification at a number of levels. It is useful to start with a definition of terms:

- **Configuration**   The process of setting parameters within Oracle EBS to make them operate in accordance with your business rules.

- **Modification**   Writing or changing code and tables. Some modifications—very minor relative to the massive body of code that makes up each application—are usually necessary. Extensive modification is costly and risky, and might warrant writing a totally customized subsystem.

- **Custom code**   What you write in order to achieve a modification; known in Europe as *bespoke code.*

The size of your company weighs in the economic trade-off between modifying business procedures to fit the code and modifying the code to fit business procedures. Smaller companies—with fewer people to train and fewer resources to modify the package—tend to adapt to Oracle EBS as it is. They might find the cost to alter an existing process to be very low. Larger companies find it cost effective to invest in modifying the software to minimize the impact on their business practices, because larger numbers of employees and customers will be affected. Individual products have application-specific customization features, such as the Financial Statement Generator within General Ledger and the approval hierarchies within Purchasing.

Modifications are characterized by programming. Whereas all of Oracle's configuration features are supported directly through specialized online setup processes, you implement modifications by programming in standard tools, outside of Oracle EBS. Some custom code, such as for custom forms and reports, is programmed using Oracle EBS conventions and tools and is registered with Oracle EBS. Other custom code, such as for database triggers and stored procedures (PL/SQL program units), is totally outside of Oracle EBS, although it operates on the Oracle EBS application data.

Oracle's architecture anticipates modification better than do those of its competitors. The code is well documented and accessible. The applications are characterized by a generally thorough and robust data model that is capable of representing, or being easily extended to represent, most real-world situations. Although the applications always include forms written to capture transaction data, they cannot be optimally adapted to every business and workflow situation. Likewise, the standard reports provide a prototype of every report you are likely to need, but it would be impossible for Oracle to anticipate which fields are essential and which have no meaning for your business as they work within the maximum design limit of 180 columns. The architecture and documentation make it possible to create your own custom versions of Oracle's forms and reports to meet your business needs in a controlled fashion, with minimal risks to data integrity and minimal effort required for version upgrades.

Anticipating and Planning Customizations and Modifications

Executives who buy Oracle EBS are almost all of one voice: "Don't change the code!" It often takes the IT organization months to soften that stance, in which time they and the users might be forced into poor business decisions to avoid changing the code.

Here is what Oracle says; this standard disclaimer (taken from the preface to the *Oracle Inventory User's Guide*) is as interesting for what it says as what it does not:

- It says, "Do not use database tools to modify Oracle Applications data."

- It adds, "If you enter information into database tables using database tools, you may store invalid information."

- It does *not* say, "Don't modify the code or add your own code."

Rather than forbidding system modifications, it implicitly establishes a common-sense ranking, from those changes that are expected and pose little threat to those that are ill advised because of the risk. Oracle EBS implementers need to establish, from the inception of the project, that they have the authority to perform the implementation in the most effective way. That might at times include modifications and bespoke code. By the same token, management needs to make sure that each bespoke module is cost justified and carefully managed. There are predictable ways in which users modify the applications; the following sections examine them individually.

Risks and Costs in Customization

The database-integrity risks involved in the different types of customization sort themselves out easily into minor and major threats, depending on whether they update the database or not.

Here are some guidelines for assessing the risks from various types of modification:

- **A module that does not update the database can imperil only itself; the risks are easy to bound.** The example would be a report or query screen. A programming error can do no more harm than to produce incorrect information or possibly cause poor database performance from a long-running query.

- **A module that only updates user attributes (ATTRIBUTE1 to ATTRIBUTE*n*) can affect only modules that use those attributes.** This limits the impact of the Descriptive Flexfield (DFF) features and the reports that incorporate user attributes. Problems manifest themselves quickly, but without much serious impact. For example, the user might query a row on which a DFF has been defined, change something other than the DFF, and then not be able to resave the row because the value set imposed on the DFF does not allow a value that had been previously inserted by a bespoke module. Problems at this level are certainly annoying to users, but they do not compromise the system.

■ **A module that inserts rows into database tables as if Oracle had done so can affect the whole system.** The potential impact can even extend to Oracle-created rows in the same tables. Oracle has provided application programming interfaces (APIs) and the open-interface tables and programs to enable you to safely load major transaction tables and those master data tables with complex relationships. However, there inevitably will be some data you wish to interface that do not have any Oracle-written support. In these cases you should study records entered through the forms, and their tables and columns, using the trace utility.

■ **A module that updates Oracle's attributes in rows created by native Oracle modules can imperil every process that uses the updated material.** The risks are harder to assess. These modifications require thorough analysis to determine where the values are used, backed up by extensive testing to prove the underlying hypotheses. For example, there is no batch device to update inventory-item attributes. All Oracle provides is the Define Items form, which would be impractical to use when there are thousands of items to update. Oracle's form does extensive cross-checking to protect against inconsistent attribute settings. You would have to test any batch script to make sure you do not load attribute combinations that Oracle would not have allowed.

The most obvious advice is to do a thorough job of analysis before updating anything. Include a test plan as part of the analysis or design document, and make sure your programmers and users execute that plan thoroughly. Programmers must not modify code they do not understand. Developers often overlook the WHO columns (CREATED_BY, CREATION_DATE, LAST_UPDATED_BY, LAST_UPDATE_DATE) in a custom script, but these should always be set. It goes without saying that one should be extraordinarily careful deleting rows.

Custom code always involves a degree of development risk. The history of data processing is one of slipped schedules and cost overruns. Every implementation that involves an automated cutover from a legacy system requires some custom code just to handle conversion and bridging. The task might appear easy, given the existence of well-documented open-interface tables; however, looks are deceiving. Do not overestimate the quality of the data in your legacy system or underestimate the complexity of mapping legacy data to Oracle. Populating the interface tables in a way that is acceptable to Oracle is not a trivial task.

For accomplishing this you will want to use your most experienced in-house staff—or hire some good consultants. It is not a task for those inexperienced with the Oracle database, tools, or with Oracle E-Business Suite. This last item needs emphasis. Although a good Oracle developer can learn his or her way around Oracle EBS, the productivity brought to a project by people who have coded interfaces, reports, and data conversions in this environment before is significant. It will ensure that your code not only is delivered quicker but it is more likely to fit in with Oracle's own standards and make use of the myriad built-in features of the Application Object Library (AOL).

Writing the modules that are essential for cutover presents you with more than enough risk. Project managers are wise to keep functional modifications to a minimum at cutover. A good argument for postponing all but the most obvious requirements is that users cannot know exactly what they need until they have operational experience with the system. A large percentage of the developers' time after cutover will be spent fixing and writing custom extensions to the system. The implementation project manager has to balance the risks of the users' not being able to run the system because they do not have an essential modification at cutover against the risk of making unnecessary modifications because the users do not appreciate how they can do their jobs using Oracle's native capabilities.

Dealing with the expected but unpredictable requirements for system modification argues strongly in favor of a phased implementation approach. Even if they were able to communicate perfectly, users could never adequately voice their full requirements without actually using Oracle EBS.

The Oracle E-Business Suite applications are wonderful in that they come almost fully programmed—and very well programmed. For instance, a fully functional demo environment can be deployed instantly out of box, so to speak, by using the default Vision environment for Oracle Release 12 EBS. The applications are problematic in that an organization can never know exactly how this preprogrammed package will actually meet its needs. Oracle EBS customers have to acknowledge the nature of the bargain they make in buying licensed software. In exchange for the massive amounts of programming you avoid, you must be cautious about the effects of the minimal programming that you do perform, so as not to interfere with Oracle-designed functions.

Changing Oracle's Table Definitions

A cardinal rule is that you never change Oracle's table definitions. There is no assurance that Oracle will not change them from release to release, or even through the distribution of patches. A corollary is that you may break a lesser rule of database design: If you need additional columns beyond what can be satisfied using the user-defined attributes, you may implement a custom table with a one-to-one relationship with the Oracle table.

The Framework for Modifications

Custom code has to be kept separate from Oracle's standard code distribution to keep it from getting overlaid by patch and upgrade activity. It is also convenient for the developers to keep their code in a separate place and to know that place contains all the code for which they are responsible. The best approach is to place your custom code in custom applications (with their associated custom schemas in the database). The custom application should ideally only insert or update data held in the custom schema. (An exception to this will be a modified form which is in the custom application but still accesses the tables in the APPS schema.) Doing this does not limit access; any menu can be customized to include forms and programs that belong to any other application.

Similarly, the report groups for one application can include custom reports and batch programs from all applications. Locating your custom modules in custom applications or a custom schema for database objects makes them easy to identify without restricting the way you use them. It makes configuration management easy. Because all the code within your newly defined application is custom, you can easily compare the state of modules in your development and test environment against those in production.

Right at the start of the project, before any custom code has been designed, lay out the framework for modifications in document form. This can be split into five areas: custom solution life cycle, design standards, build standards, test strategy, and configuration management.

Design and Build Standards

Design and build standards need to ensure that the technical analysts and developers that join the development team adopt a consistent approach. The design standards define how the design specifications will be presented and what they will cover. The build standards define how programs will be coded and determine naming conventions and header and comment styles.

Programming and Documentation Standards

Each shop has its own approach to documentation and programming. The universal rules are few. Each piece of documentation should be self-explanatory, stating what its purpose is and naming the other documents and the code modules it references.

Code is an individual thing. The code examples here demonstrate standards used in one EBS shop, Watkins-Johnson, at one point in time. One of that company's best traits is that it never stops improving its development process. The following section of code and the subsequent analysis exemplify the kinds of issues you might want to address.

```
l_variable                          VARCHAR2(30);
l_counter                           NUMBER := 0;
CURSOR
  variable_cursor
IS
  SELECT
    substitution_constant,
    variable_name
  FROM
    wj_fnd_rt_constants
  WHERE
    regression_test_name = '&&regression_test_name';
BEGIN
 FOR parm_rec IN variable_cursor LOOP
   l_counter := l_counter + 1;
   v_constant (l_counter) :=
               CHR(39)||parm_rec.substitution_constant||CHR(39);
   v_variable (l_counter) := parm_rec.variable_name;
 END LOOP;
END;
PROCEDURE insert_quotes (

   l_in                             VARCHAR2,
   l_index                          NUMBER)
 IS
   l_open_bracket                   NUMBER;
   l_close_bracket                  NUMBER;
   l_length_in                      NUMBER;
   l_out_db                         VARCHAR2(500);
   l_out_char                       VARCHAR2(500);
   l_work                           VARCHAR2(500);
 BEGIN
   l_open_bracket := INSTR(l_in,'[');
   l_close_bracket := INSTR(l_in,']');
   l_length_in := LENGTH(l_in);
   IF (l_open_bracket = 0) OR
      (l_open_bracket = l_close_bracket)
   THEN
```

```
      l_out_db := """"||l_in||""""; /* Whole entry is a literal */
      l_out_char := insert_pounds(l_in);
    ELSE
      IF l_open_bracket  1
      THEN                   /* =========== Do the opening literal */
        l_work := SUBSTR(l_in,1,l_open_bracket - 1);
        l_out_db :=''''||l_work||''''||';
        l_out_char := insert_pounds(l_work);
      END IF;
      /* ========= Do the bracketed command ============ */
      l_work := SUBSTR(l_in,l_open_bracket,
                   1 + l_close_bracket - l_open_bracket);
      l_out_db := l_out_db || l_work;
      l_out_char := l_out_char||xlate_brackets(l_work);
      IF l_close_bracket  l_length_in
      THEN                   /* ======  Do the closing literal */
        l_work := SUBSTR(l_in,l_close_bracket + 1,
                   l_length_in - l_closing_bracket);
        l_out_db := l_out_db || '||''''||l_work||'''';
        l_out_char := l_out_char||insert_pounds(l_work);
      END IF;
    END IF;
  v_action_table_db (l_index) := v_out_db;
   v_action_table_char (l_index) := v_out_char;
 END;
```

Every piece of PL/SQL or SQL*Plus code has a header, similar to the following, that explains what the code is, where the specification is, who wrote it, and when it was written.

```
/*=========================================================================*/
/*                                                                         */
/*    Name:          Regressi.sql                                          */
/*                                                                         */
/* Description: Meta-code to extract regression test actions and create    */
/*              source code to include in custom programs to use RT        */
/*              for mass updates to the DB.                                 */
/*                                                                         */
/* Reference:     regressi.doc                                             */
/*                                                                         */
/* ----------------------------------------------------------------------- */
/* DATE      AUTHOR        VERSION        REASON                           */
/* ----------------------------------------------------------------------- */
/* 19/04/01 S. Russell  1.0           Initial creation                    */
/* 20/04/01 S. Russell   1.1           Changes for performance improvement */
/* ----------------------------------------------------------------------- */
/*                                                                         */
/*=========================================================================*/
/* Parameters: 1: Regression Test name, also constant name                 */
/*                                                                         */
/*                                                                         */
```

Watkins-Johnson has standard document templates for programs:

- The template they used to generate the preceding code sample specifies nine-point Courier type to get 80 characters in a six-inch-wide document (8½-inch paper with 1¼-inch margins). The code is easier to format when the word processor's line length is the same as that for the Unix vi editor. Lengths of 80 or 132 characters are standard.

- As shown in the preceding fragment of code, keywords are in all capital letters and variables in lowercase. It makes the code easier to read.

- PL/SQL and SQL statements are indented for greater readability. No universal rules can be written for indentation; these are complex, free-format languages. Generally speaking, though, the code is easier to read when loops and if-statements are indented to show levels of nesting, and SQL statements are indented to put the keywords on one plane and the variables on another.

- Comments are placed throughout the code. This author uses arrows made of equal signs and less-than signs to highlight the comments, making them easier for the eye to locate.

- In this code, standard variable names and variable types are aligned to make it easy to find variables. You can use a word processor to sort variable names so they are easier to find in a listing.

Code should never be data dependent. A statement such as the following is dangerous:

```
IF organization_id = 202 THEN
   v_switch1 := 'Y'
ELSE
   v_switch1 := 'N';
```

It represents a long-term risk, because it exposes the code to a change in organization codes. It would be tedious to locate every place where such data-dependent code appeared. A better approach is to set parameters externally or in a prologue to the module, as in the following example.

```
DEFINE BEM_ORG_ID=202
...
...
IF organization_id = &&BEM_ORG_ID THEN
   v_switch1 := 'Y'
ELSE
   v_switch1 := 'N';
```

This approach lets you collect all parameter settings at the beginning of a module, where they are easy to find and modify; their definitions are easy to find with a global search command. It also ensures that you give the variables a meaningful name. However, remember that customizing the application is different from developing a new application. Sometimes it is required that your code depend on setup of the application and that you reference a profile option or specific setup data. There are multiple places to document such dependencies—the setup documents will contain profile options, the functional and technical specifications will both refer to them, and the installation scripts will have prerequisite steps to ensure that all dependent setup has been done.

Each systems organization needs to establish standards to suit its background, tools, and needs. The examples here are meant only to show the kinds of things you want to consider when establishing standards.

Installation Scripts

As a part of your standards, you will need to address how software is installed. This can be either a manual or automated process. The components of the installation after copying the software to the bespoke directory are as follows:

- Create a custom schema and a custom top directory similar to an application top like AR_TOP or PO_TOP.
- Create bespoke tables and views and grant access as appropriate under the custom schema.
- Compile program packages if used.
- Create the program executable definition.
- Create concurrent-program definitions, including parameters.
- Create request sets if required (including stage definitions and dependencies).
- Attach to report groups.
- Create menus if required.
- Create Responsibilities if required.
- Create and populate value sets if required.
- Create and populate profile options if required.

If you use a set of scripts for at least some of these tasks, you will be able to ensure a consistent quality of releases, provided that you have strict standards and consistent quality in the scripts. Have the development team write programs that create the required installation scripts. They can use the following FND packages, which are supported for this purpose.

Package Name	Use
FND_PROGRAM	Setting up executables and concurrent programs
FND_SET	Creating request sets (including stages, etc.)
FND_USER_RESP_GROUPS_API	Assigning and updating Responsibilities against users

It is important that your scripts are always run in the same way; for example, always using the same user ID and password. If they require another user ID and password for some tasks, the prompt for the new information should be built into the script. Never build user IDs and passwords themselves into the script (they might change).

Planning a User-Defined Application

An application has its own library directories and its own Oracle schema, as described in previous chapters. The schema, associated with a user ID, owns tables and other database objects. All applications share their objects with the APPS schema through the use of grants and synonyms. A grant gives access (read or write) to an object owned by another schema; a synonym allows you to always call the object (for example, a database table) by the same name regardless of which schema you are using. Your custom applications should have their own schemas, which have access to all the objects that APPS does.

All tables will be owned by the custom schema and accessible by APPS. The conventions for views and package procedures are more flexible—they can be owned by APPS or by the custom schema (with appropriate grants and synonyms). Collaborate with the database administrators (DBAs) on the standards; they must be happy with the arrangements you make and particularly with the installation scripts you produce, as they will be running them.

Creating a custom application accomplishes one key objective: It keeps custom program modules separate from Oracle code. Users who are doing extensive modifications might want to define several custom applications, each corresponding to an Oracle standard application. Others might find that one custom application is enough. Then all custom AOL objects (forms, reports, menus, Responsibilities, and so forth) will be assigned to that custom application.

Creating an application of your own requires that you define the following elements:

- **Name**   Oracle's application names all start with "Oracle"; yours will probably start with a company or division name. For instance, Watkins-Johnson has defined the application WJ Purchasing for the extensions they have made to purchasing.

- **Root directory**   This directory must reside in the database or applications server operating system, and should meet the conventions for Oracle EBS. The directory names should be lowercase, as Unix is case sensitive (although other operating systems generally will not care). A typical root directory for custom code would be /oraappl/custom/ap, where /oraappl is the root directory designated at installation time for all applications, including Oracle's distribution; /custom is the root for all custom code; and /ap is the application being modified (Accounts Payable). This directory would have the standard subdirectories for custom code: /bin, /forms, /reports, and /sql.

- **Root directory on the Oracle EBS Applications server tier (for custom forms)**   The directory scheme will be similar to that on the database server. This becomes an issue when the middle-tier arrangement changes between phases. For example, in development you might have a single computer acting as the database and applications tier, but in user acceptance testing and production there might be two computers one for the database and one for the Application Server.

- **Base path**   This is an operating-system-symbolic variable name for the root directory. The reference to the base path is usually of the form $CO_AP_TOP, where *CO* is a company abbreviation and *AP* is the application in question. By Unix conventions it is in uppercase. Most other operating systems are case insensitive, so it might as well be uppercase. Watkins-Johnson, for example, has defined the base path $WJ_PO_TOP for its custom purchasing modules.

- **Short name**   This is used by programmers to identify modules, messages, and other components. Oracle EBS uses two or three letters, such as INV for Inventory or PO for Purchasing. The best bet is to add a one- or two-letter prefix to the Oracle short name and abbreviation.

- **Abbreviation**   This is used to prefix custom table names and other database objects. Form it using the same prefix as the application's short name.

- **Message prefix**   This will be important if you write custom forms using Oracle's message-presentation facilities. The major benefit of a message prefix is translation among multiple national languages. Use the application abbreviation as a default.

Registering a Custom Application

To create a custom application is not a difficult task. It is essential that once it has been created, all the development resources know about it and understand how it works and how they are to use it. To register an application, follow these steps:

1. Have the system programmer create the planned root directory with all the subdirectories. Make sure that the developers and the Concurrent Manager user are given the necessary read-write-execute permissions to access the directories. The Unix command for assigning full permission is

   ```
   chmod 777 directory_name
   ```

2. In Windows, predefine groups of users; then, after selecting the directory, navigate to File Sharing Security Permissions to grant access to those who need it.

3. Have the systems programmer modify the Oracle EBS applications log-in script to add the assignment statement equating the base-path symbolic variable to the directory named in step 1.

4. Log in using the systems-administrator Responsibility.

5. Navigate to the Register Applications form and enter the data and values, as previously planned.

6. Navigate to the Security menu and assign your new application to the custom Oracle schema you have created.

Custom-Code Conventions

The registration process starts with the operating-system file name for a form or report. The module name should do the following:

- uniquely identify the module within the Oracle EBS universe,
- identify the module as custom code,
- have an appropriate suffix for the module type,
- fit within operating-system limits on name length, and
- if possible, associate the code module with its design document.

The eight-character limit on file names does not apply in Windows, but it might still affect your developers as they transfer modules using e-mail and file-transfer programs. Most modules that Oracle delivers still adhere to an eight-character naming standard. You need to decide whether the eight-character limitation affects you. If you are free of it, the best bet is to use the 30-character convention that applies to database objects within Oracle. Even though some operating systems such as Windows are less restrictive, it is a good idea to require that module names start with an alphabetic character and do not include any special characters other than the underscore.

Modules have multiple names within Oracle EBS. A form has its module name, the name on menu lines to select it, and the name displayed by the form as it executes. The naming convention applies to the module name—the file with the .fmx suffix (or, in character mode, .frm). A report has three module names: the name of the operating-system file containing the report definition (with the suffix .rdf for Oracle*Reports or .sql for SQL*Plus), the registered name of the executable module, and the registered name of the combination of a report and a set of parameters.

It also has a name to select from the report menu and a report title. It saves confusion if you use the same name for the operating-system file, the executable, and the short name you give in registering a process, unless an executable will be tied to more than one process. It is usually best to name modified Oracle modules with their eight-character Oracle name plus the prefix that announces custom code. Totally new modules can have a unique name within the same convention.

It helps if the names of your design and user documents for a module can have the same name or at least start with a set of characters that relates them to one another. The .doc suffix will identify program documentation as such. It is convenient to keep the documentation close to the code. Some shops put documents in a LAN directory structure that parallels the Oracle EBS directory structure. Others actually put it in the same directories.

If you use configuration management, you will want to control release levels of the documentation by the same means as the modules it describes. The documentation should reflect each change you make to the code.

Custom Output

Reports top the list of essential modifications. Every business uses uniquely formatted external paper documents. Most Oracle EBS users find that the Oracle-designed reports are adequate, but there are instances in which it is worth a small investment to tailor them to the business.

Processes that run from the Concurrent Manager have two types of output by default: output and log files. Output is where the user-oriented information goes, whether that is a report such as an aged debt report or the interface error report for the customer open interface. The log is where the technical running details go, such as the parameters used for the run and any debug details, if debug is enabled for a particular run of the program.

Documents

The formatting possibilities of documents are endless. Oracle*Reports has the flexibility to print these documents in exactly the format any user needs. Oracle delivers stock print programs in the expectation that customers will use Oracle*Reports' flexibility to modify the output to correspond with their exact needs. This usually includes documents that will be distributed externally. Following are programs that are commonly modified from Oracle's standard output:

- AP Check Print
- PO Purchase Order Print
- AR Direct Debit
- AR Invoice Print
- AR Dunning Letters
- AR Statements
- SO Sales Order Acknowledgment
- SO Bill of Lading
- SO Pick Slip

These external documents usually carry the company logo and other stylized entries. They were traditionally produced on preprinted forms or generated with laser printers capable of flashing boilerplate text and images onto the forms.

Reports run on the database server, independent of the three client-side modes of operation. Oracle*Reports is a graphical, bitmapped tool. It is intended to design reports in a WYSIWYG (what you see is what you get) environment. Character-mode operation is no more than an overlay on its native GUI operation. Nevertheless, Oracle distributes its standard reports in character mode—the lowest common denominator—thus ensuring that all customers will be able to run them. Your customization will usually involve modifying the programs to change fonts and include appropriate graphics.

Previous chapters described the alternatives for bitmapped printing. One is to print to a PostScript device using the full GUI features of Oracle*Reports. The more common approach is to embed printer-command escape sequences in character-mode reports. Such embedded commands can invoke report masks to overlay the character printing and font changes within the print output. Although the escape-sequence approach is not as technically appealing as PostScript, it is well supported by Hewlett-Packard's PCL language and by a large number of third parties such as Unitask. The escape-sequence approach is fast and reliable; it is relatively cheap to get a third party to set it up for you.

Reports

Reports present information derived from data in the database. Oracle expects users to modify the standard reports and add their own. The facilities and documentation it offers for writing bespoke reports are excellent.

There is little risk in modifying the reports delivered by Oracle. Although the Oracle*Reports language can update data, few standard reports actually do so. As part of the analysis of the Oracle*Reports modules you plan to modify, look for update code in the PRE-REPORT and POST-REPORT triggers.

If there is not a standard report that satisfies your needs, there is usually one that comes close. It might lack a column or have the wrong sort order, or it might need to accept another parameter. The most common solution is to modify Oracle's program to meet the custom requirement. The usual approach is to do the following:

1. Analyze Oracle's code. Many reports are quite complex and appear to be case studies in the flexibility of the Oracle*Reports product. Some, such as the Bill of Materials Report, use PRE-REPORT triggers to populate temporary tables used in the report. Make sure you do not clutter such tables by failing to do a rollback in the postreport trigger. SQL*Plus reports can do the same, populating tables in one step and reporting in another.

2. Decide whether to modify Oracle's code or simply borrow its SELECTs to incorporate in a totally new module. The reports that Oracle delivers follow a consistent design. The PRE-REPORT trigger reads the parameters, performs any additional validation, sets internal-processing flags, and performs any preprocessing required for the report. Oracle usually incorporates major bodies of function in stored procedures rather than in the report trigger itself. It frequently composes WHERE and ORDER BY clauses as program variables in the PRE-REPORT trigger and references them as bind variables in the SELECT statements for the queries. It is often easier to deduce the essence of what they are doing and then incorporate queries based on their SELECT statements in new modules than to modify and debug code you do not fully understand.

3. Modify or create the report in a development instance. Compare the output of your custom report with the native Oracle report to make sure you are picking up the right rows and running the computations correctly.

4. Follow the procedures described in the next section to put the report into the development instance, define the run-time parameters, add it to a report group, and test it concurrently.

5. Migrate the tested report into the custom application in the production instance.

Almost all of Oracle's reports are written in the Oracle*Reports tool. However, SQL*Plus is adequate for many custom reports. The trade-offs for SQL*Plus are listed in the following table.

Advantages	Disadvantages
Every Oracle programmer knows how to use SQL*Plus, whereas many do not know or are not proficient in Oracle*Reports.	SQL*Plus cannot handle complex formatting. It is limited to printing columns across the page, with data directly under the column headings.
SQL*Plus reports are quick to write and simple to debug.	SQL*Plus cannot handle master-detail reports, except in a very limited way by doing page breaks at the master-control break.
SQL*Plus reports execute quickly.	SQL*Plus does not have any bitmapped logic for handling fonts and graphics.
SQL*Plus reports have access to the operating-system shell via the HOST command.	SQL*Plus reports are plain, and sometimes unattractive in comparison with Oracle*Reports output.
SQL*Plus modules can invoke PL/SQL routines. They can perform DDL (data definition language) commands such as creating and dropping tables.	The SQL*Plus devices for computing sums and showing control breaks are primitive. They make poor use of the column width available within a report.
SQL*Plus is all in ASCII. It is easy to scan your code to apply across-the-board changes.	Since most of Oracle's standard reports are written in Oracle*Reports, a custom modification might be easier than rewriting the report in SQL*Plus.

The cost-benefit equation usually favors using SQL*Plus for custom reports that are within its architectural reach. More complex reports require Oracle*Reports. All reports can be run from the Applications Desktop Integrator. This enables output to be delivered through Excel, Web, or text formats.

Registering Custom Processes

You register batch programs with the Application Object Library to make them eligible for AOL services. AOL will accept run-time parameters, initiate and manage program execution, spool print- and log-file output, and present output to the users at their desktop or in hard copy. The steps to register a report are as follows.

First, make the program available to the AOL by copying it into the directory structure for the application to which it belongs. The module name should conform to the naming standards discussed previously. Copy Oracle Reports modules to the /reports subdirectory of the application root, SQL programs to the /sql subdirectory, and Host programs to the /bin subdirectory.

Second, register the process executable in the development instance through the Define Concurrent Program Executable form. Registration establishes an internal database name that corresponds to the external, operating-system file name for the executable program. It is easiest to manage if they are the same. The executable-registration form also asks for the application, which is your custom application, and the execution method (that is, executable type: SQL*Plus, Oracle*Reports, shell script, or C) and a description.

Third, register the process through the Define Concurrent Program form. Registration associates a printer format with the executable module defined earlier. It allows you to define other programs (including itself) that cannot be run at the same time. An update process—especially if it commits its changes by stages—often should not run at the same time as another process that updates the same tables.

Last, define run-time parameters through the Define Concurrent Program form. Because you can use a single executable module in many concurrent-program definitions, you can provide different parameter settings for different sets of users.

Usually the original reports you write will have relatively few parameters. If you copy from Oracle, though, you will need to copy over Oracle's parameter definitions. Some reports have as many as 40 parameters. Oracle provides a facility to do this within one Oracle instance, but copying parameter definitions between instances as a manual process can be quite a chore. You have to either copy again from the native Oracle report in the new instance or create the parameters manually. The best way to copy parameter definitions is to open one Define Concurrent Process window for the new report and another for the existing report, then manually copy from the old to the new. You have to bounce back and forth between zones in each screen. As an alternative, have your development team create a script for extracting program data from one environment and inserting them into another using the FND_PROGRAM package. This package includes procedures for inserting concurrent executables, programs, and parameters.

The three procedures are invoked as follows:

```
-- create the executable
  FND_PROGRAM.executable('EXEC_SHORT_NAME'
      ,                  'APPLICATION'
      ,                  'USER_EXEC_NAME'
      ,                  'DESCRIPTION'
      ,                  'METHOD'
      ,                  'EXEC_FILE_NAME'
      ,                  'SUBROUTINE'
      ,                  'ICON_NAME');
--create the concurrent program definition
  FND_PROGRAM.register('USER_PROG_NAME'
      ,                  'PROGRAM_APP'
      ,                  'ENABLED_FLAG'
      ,                  'PROG_SHORT_NAME'
      ,                  'DESCRIPTION'
      ,                  'EXEC_SHORT_NAME'
      ,                  'EXECUTABLE_APP'
      ,                  'EXEC_OPTIONS'
      ,                  'PRIORITY'
      ,                  'SAVE_FLAG'
      ,                  'PRINT_FLAG'
      ,                  'COLS'
      ,                  'ROWS'
      ,                  'STYLE'
      ,                  'STYLE_FLAG'
      ,                  'PRINTER'
```

```
                ,                           'REQUEST_TYPE'
                ,                           'REQUEST_TYPE_APP'
                ,                           'SRS_FLAG'
                ,                           'DISABLED_VALUES_FLAG'
                ,                           'RUN_ALONE_FLAG'
                ,                           'OUTPUT_FILE_TYPE'
                ,                           'ENABLE_TRACE'
                ,                           'RESTART'
                ,                           'NLS_COMPLIANT'
                ,                           'ICON_NAME'
                ,                           'LANGUAGE');
--create the program parameters
  FND_PROGRAM.parameter('SCRIPTNAME'
                ,                    'PROG_APPLICATION'
                ,                     COLUMN_SEQ_NUM
                ,                    'END_USER_COLUMN_NAME'
                ,                    'DESCRIPTION'
                ,                    'ENABLED_FLAG'
                ,                    'VALUE_SET'
                ,                    'DEFAULT_TYPE'
                ,                    'DEFAULT_VALUE'
                ,                    'REQUIRED_FLAG'
                ,                    'SECURITY_ENABLED_FLAG'
                ,                    'RANGE_CODE'
                ,                    'DISPLAY_FLAG'
                ,                     DISPLAY_SIZE
                ,                     MAX_DESC_LENGTH
                ,                     CONCAT_DESC_LENGTH
                ,                    'FORM_LEFT_PROMPT'
                ,                    'SRW_PARAM');
```

The Define Concurrent Program form captures run-time parameters. You specify a prompt, a value set, and optionally a default for parameters that the user is allowed to enter. Parameters the user cannot change can be displayed or not. The default value can be a constant, a profile value, a system value such as the date, or a value derived from a SQL statement you provide. You can validate one parameter based on the entries for previous parameters. Oracle uses Descriptive Flexfields to validate and manage run-time parameters, as described in previous chapters.

If you are defining an Oracle*Reports process, you provide a keyword (or token) for each parameter. The sequence of the parameters does not matter, except to the extent that the value set you use to validate one parameter refers to the entry for a previous parameter. SQL*Plus and Host programs do not use keywords. The Concurrent Manager passes a list of parameters in the same sequence that you define them. In SQL*Plus, substitution variable &1 is the first parameter, &2 the second, and so on. For Host programs in Unix, the variables are $1 through $9, with the others available after you execute a SHIFT-COMMAND.

Registering parameters for SQL*Loader is different. You enter run-time keyword parameters such as DATA =, CONTROL=, and ERRORS = through the Execution Options field. It does not require any entries in the Parameters block of the form.

The Define Report Group form can be used to add the report to one or more report groups. This makes it accessible from the Run Reports form for every Responsibility associated with the report group through the Define Responsibility form.

The Execution Environment

Oracle's Concurrent Manager makes the bridge between online and batch operations. The Run Reports form writes a row to the FND_CONCURRENT_REQUESTS table as you submit the job. The operating system activates the Concurrent Manager at intervals to check the table. It initiates your request when it has worked its way to the head of the queue and there is an initiator ready. The Concurrent Manager submits the job to the operating system for background processing. The background process belongs to the applmgr user, just like the Concurrent Manager that spawned it.

The environment variables for your background process are established by the profile commands for applmgr. In most Unix systems the profile command file establishes the environment. Environment variables include the instance ($ORACLE_SID) and the top directories for each application ($AP_TOP, $GL_TOP, and your custom-application root directories).

TIP
It is useful to register SQL*Plus and Host utility modules with a name such as TEST to the systems-administrator Responsibility. You can then substitute any test code you need for these modules named $FND_TOP/sql/TEST.sql and $FND_TOP/bin/TEST. For example, when your concurrent jobs do not even start due to a "file not found" condition, check the environment. If you are in a Unix environment, put the env command in the TEST script, or Host env in the TEST.sql script, to verify the environment settings being used by the Concurrent Manager.

As applmgr executes your module, the default directory is the log-file directory. Depending on your installation options, this directory is usually either $APPLCSF/out*SID*, where *SID* is the name of your instance, or $*app*_TOP/log, where *app* is the name of your application. See the Oracle EBS installation references for more details. The log file (named l*request_no*.log, where *request_no* is the concurrent-request number) is written to this default directory.

The Concurrent Manager directs your spooled report to a subdirectory named /out or /out*SID* in the immediate parent directory of the log file just described. It uses different devices to get it there. For Oracle*Reports modules, the Concurrent Manager specifies this as the report-output file name on the command line used to invoke Oracle*Reports. This is not an option on the command lines to execute SQL*Plus and Host programs. Instead, under SQL*Plus, the Concurrent Manager will redirect the output to a SPOOL file as it invokes SQL*Plus; you cannot change it. Although you do not get the file name directly, you can use AOL-stored procedures to get your concurrent-request number and reconstruct it. If you direct output elsewhere through another SPOOL command, you cannot return to having it sent to the Concurrent Manager's intended file.

As the Concurrent Manager invokes a SQL*Plus routine, it runs a prologue that includes the following commands:

- SET TERM OFF
- SET PAUSE ON
- SET HEADING OFF
- SET FEEDBACK OFF
- SET VERIFY OFF
- SET ECHO OFF
- WHENEVER SQLERROR EXIT FAILURE

It sets the line size according to your report style: 80 for portrait, 132 for landscape, and 180 for landwide. It also invokes whatever SQL*Plus log-in script has been established for the applmgr user. This is the place to look if your SQL*Plus programs do not work consistently in all database instances.

Once your module has control, you can override the initial settings with a SET command. Two of the most common settings to override are PAGESIZE and NEWPAGE. If the output is going to a laser printer, you usually want SET NEWPAGE 0, to force each new page to go on a new sheet of paper.

It is a good idea to convert positional parameters in SQL*Plus into keywords immediately after the header block in your script. This will make your code easier to understand, as illustrated in the following example:

```
DEFINE P_USER_ID          = &&1
DEFINE P_REPORT_HEADING   = '&&2'
then
SELECT
  user_name
FROM
  fnd_user
WHERE
  user_id = &&p_user_id;
```

The Concurrent Manager uses the same spooling device for Host (operating-system level) programs as for SQL. If you could see the Unix command line used by the Concurrent Manager it would look something like the following:

```
your_program parm1 parm2 parm3 parm4 \
parm5  &  orequest_id.out 2 lrequest_id.req
```

In Unix, you can reconstruct the spool file name using the request-ID parameter within the command line, which is available to you as parameter $1. If you redirect the output, the Concurrent Manager will not be able to find it to print or display to the requester, unless you bring it back into the spooled output for your session with the Unix command cat or the Windows command type.

Overview of the Open Interfaces

Oracle does not want users bypassing the edits in its forms by using scripts to directly update the Oracle EBS applications table. This was a problem in earlier versions of the Oracle E-Business Suite, in which the online processes were the only means available for loading the database. Users had to decide between disregarding Oracle's stricture against modifications and rekeying data. Because rekeying destroys the integrity of the data in any case, not to mention being slow, most users chose to ignore the warning and load Oracle's tables through a batch process.

Recognizing the problem, Oracle has put emphasis on enhancing APIs in Releases 12. The open interface APIs serve as bridges between the Oracle EBS modules themselves and external systems, they serve installers in the conversion process, and they serve you in building custom extensions to the system.

Oracle's own applications communicate with each other through the APIs. The Financials applications place journals in the GL_INTERFACE table. Purchasing and Order Entry place transactions in MTL_TRANSACTIONS_INTERFACE to notify Inventory about receipts and shipments. Order Entry, Projects, and Service place invoice data in RA_INTERFACE_LINES and its related tables.

The Oracle EBS applications often have to interface with your company's third-party service providers. Those vendors, rather than either Oracle or the customer, define the interfaces. Oracle provides the generic programs or APIs so you can modify the programs or write code to load the open interface. Some examples are

- AR Lockbox,
- AP and Payroll Bank Reconciliation, and
- AP Electronic Funds Transfer.

Oracle's documentation is reasonably explicit about the values that need to be loaded, column by column, through the open interface tables. There is even more to be learned by referring to the Technical Reference Manuals: They tell you which lookup tables join to code columns. Often the value displayed in the screen or in a report is not the actual value stored in the base table. Instead, the base table stores a code that ties to a lookup table that has the full description of the value. You can use homemade lookup scripts, such as the one shown here, to find the valid lookup-code values.

```
COL lookup_code FOR 999 HEAD 'Code'
COL lookup_type FOR a25 HEAD 'Lookup Type'
COL description FOR a40 HEAD 'Description'
SET HEAD ON PAGESIZE 6000
SELECT
  lookup_type,
  lookup_code,
  description
FROM
  po.po_lookup_codes
WHERE
      lookup_type LIKE '&1'
  AND lookup_code LIKE '%'||'&2'||'%'
REM
REM:  Use similar code for MFG_LOOKUPS, FND_LOOKUPS and SO_LOOKUPS
```

The seeded values in the lookup tables rarely change, but the documentation describing seeded values is somewhat scattered within the reference manuals. Use the techniques described in the following sections to research the actual contents of rows inserted using the online processes.

Populating the Open Interfaces

The strength of the open interfaces is in their complexity. They are designed to validate and load every possible attribute value and data relationship. The major interfaces will use data from three or more interface tables to populate a half dozen or more Oracle EBS application tables. Their weaknesses also arise from their complexity: their performance might be slow and the error messages difficult to decipher.

Standardizing the Custom Load Process

You will often use open interfaces for data conversion as well as for any live-running interfaces with third-party systems. Therefore, the total number of times you will be populating open-interface tables might be tens or scores. In this case it might be worth looking at extending the build standards to create some common routines, which will ensure development quality and help users by always giving them the same approach when running interfaces.

Typically you will load data from a flat file into a staging table or a number of staging tables. Then another program will validate the data before loading it into the open-interface tables. When this is complete the open-interface programs themselves run to import the data into the Oracle EBS application tables. You can create a "wrapper" for the staging-table-loading programs (very often SQL*Loader). This can make the individual scripts either very simple to write or dynamically created from a file definition (entered into the database via a custom form).

File handling (in terms of archiving files loaded into the database), error reporting, and error handling can be integrated into this wrapper, so that the development team writes these components once. The users will always see an error report that looks similar. You can create a table to hold details of interface runs, so that there is an audit trail of successes and failures, which might be useful during live running for a shared service center to monitor performance and errors.

You can create a custom PL/SQL package into which often-used validations can be added, along with error-reporting and error-handling routines can be added. This package will grow as the project progresses, and might also contain procedures for other custom processes—for example, for file transfer used by outgoing interfaces. The configuration manager will also appreciate the effort put into this package, because it will reduce the total number of components that need to be released into production.

The actual data-validation and data-transformation programs are custom components that need to be written for each interface, although they will use elements from the common package. Another way to reduce complexity and avoid hard-coding validation into the program is to use a custom form to load lookup values for a lookup domain into a custom table structure. For example, the lookup domain might be LEGACY_PAYMENT_TERMS. For each legacy value of payment terms—which may be 0, 30 or 60—hold the Oracle value, which may be "Immediate," "30 days net," or "60 days net." This way, if new legacy values come to light later in the project, they can be added to the table with no changes to the custom code required; the code required to find a value in the table for a given domain and legacy value will be a procedure in the common package.

Another way to reduce custom code is to use standard gateways into Oracle EBS. You might be able to use the E-Commerce Gateway or the XML Gateway to import purchase orders or invoices without the need for custom code. This is more common for ongoing interfaces, as it is normal for companies not to want to invest in legacy systems to change them so that they support the required standards. Data conversion normally deals in flat files of data (unless it involves migrating from an Oracle system or upgrading from an earlier versions of Oracle EBS). With Oracle Fusion and BPEL, import and export of legacy-application data is much easier than what was required in the past. We discuss these topics, and how they can be leveraged to take advantage of Oracle EBS, later in the book.

Interface-Program Execution

The open-interface programs are executed as concurrent processes. You explicitly submit jobs to run most interface processes. Some, like the Material Transactions interface, do not have to be started because they are handled by worker processes that resubmit themselves every few minutes.

The interface tables include process flags to indicate the status of a row: not yet processed, in some state of being processed, and in error. Some interface processes will operate on every eligible row within a table; others will take no more than a maximum number you have established with a parameter. The first thing they do is to set the process flags of the selected rows to indicate that they have been selected. You are then free to continue inserting rows into the interface while the interface program processes those that have been selected. Unless otherwise stated, the rows will be deleted from the interface table once they have been successfully imported.

You will discover that some interface processes, despite the fact that they will select every row in the interface table, work more efficiently with small numbers at a time. Some even run out of system resources and end abnormally when they attempt to process too many records. In these cases, you can write your scripts to load a given number of records at a time into the interface tables. An easier alternative is to load all the records to the interface, but set the pending flag to a value the interface program does not recognize (−1,000,000 in the following example). You can then release rows in the interface table a few at a time with a script like this one:

```
UPDATE mtl_system_items_interface SET process_flag = 1
WHERE process_flag = -1000000 AND ROWNUM = 100;
```

Interface Errors

The open-interface programs process all the records they can and mark the rest with error messages. The messages might be in the failed records themselves or in an errors table linked to the interface. The message system is designed to indicate the column in error and the nature of the problem. One error may cause several messages, in which case you will need to investigate them all to determine the original problem. It is important to isolate the original error message and not waste time with messages that are only by-products of the original problem. Some messages will be too obscure to lead you to the problem. Some strategies for debugging your interface load script are as follows:

■ Develop your script in a test instance so you do not load invalid data into production.

■ First get it to work for a simple case. If you are loading customer master records, start with the simplest possible customer: one with one site and no ship-to or bill-to address, contacts, or other related records. Add in the complexity one element at a time.

■ Load one row at a time until the script works. Until you understand the process, plan to totally clear the interface tables after each unsuccessful test instead of trying to fix the failed rows in place. You can safely delete rows from the interface without destroying data integrity.

■ Reduce the processing that the interface program has to do. Look up and insert the primary keys yourself. Translate codes yourself. In doing this, you will encounter problems such as trailing spaces in a VARCHAR2 column in your own code.

■ Once the interface works, use an online process to query, update, and then commit the records you have inserted. This will cause the form to revalidate the record you created. In some instances, the online edits are different from the open-interface edits. You want to be sure the rows are acceptable to every module that will use them.

Occasionally, when you present the open-interface programs with a data condition they are not equipped to handle, they might experience an RDBMS-level error such as "Numeric or Value Error." In that case, they do not give you any help identifying the individual row in error, and every row selected will remain in the interface table. The problem is usually a data error on your part. You can usually find it by reducing the number of rows you are inserting and eliminating complexity until it does work. A careful examination of the most recently removed attributes should lead you to the cause.

It can be helpful to check with Oracle Support prior to using the open interface and obtain the latest version of the interface code. This can save time and frustration, as the initial versions of open-interface programs might contain bugs, and Oracle Support is likely to have patches that will resolve any performance problems.

In extreme cases, you can go to the code. Most open-interface programs are written in C, which makes them appear—on the surface—to be inaccessible. However, their table-processing logic is most often in PL/SQL stored procedures. Use a Unix grep or a Windows Find command to search the $*Appl*_TOP/admin/sql directory (/install/sql for Release 10.5 and earlier) for modules that work with the interface tables in question. Your programmers will find most of the modules less than 20 pages in length and fairly well commented. If need be, they can copy the modules, insert their own debugging code, regenerate the stored procedures, and then run the interface program again. Incidentally, the easiest way to log debugging data is to write your messages to a custom table.

Checking Interfaces

The applications use many of the open interfaces—among them, MTL_TRANSACTIONS_ INTERFACE, GL_INTERFACE, and RA_LINES_INTERFACE—for internal communications in daily operation. Although they rarely experience problems, your DBA needs to respond when they do. It is a good idea to monitor them with periodic alerts, reporting to the DBA when there are error rows in an interface or when records seem to be accumulating in the interface.

Most of the errors you experience in the interface tables will be due to data errors. Some of the interface tables are directly accessible through forms within the applications, thereby providing you a generic ability to update rows in the interface. Often, though, you need to do more. The best business practice is usually to fix data in the feeder system and resubmit records to Oracle. Doing that keeps the records in the two systems consistent. You need to consider systems and business processes for dealing with errors. Some elements to consider in a more extensive error handling process are

- an alert or a custom program, usually something simple written in SQL*Plus, to display the error record in the context of the originating system;

- a Descriptive Flexfield defined on the interface table to display pertinent data from the source system in a useful format;

- an established procedure for remedying the problem in the system that is feeding the interface;

- a standard Oracle process or custom program to clear erroneous records out of the interface; and

- instructions and processes for resubmitting transactions to Oracle, ensuring that each transaction is submitted once and only once.

The open interfaces are a powerful tool for communicating between other software packages and Oracle, but it takes a little planning to keep the channels open.

Application Programming Interfaces (APIs)

Increasing use is made in the E-Business Suite of APIs. These act differently from the open-interface model. They are used in customer creation (through Customer Relationship Management rather than the open customer interface), project and task creation in Oracle Projects, employee maintenance in Oracle Human Resources, and other areas. Instead of using an open interface table structure and a validation/insert program to load valid records to the application tables, these load data directly from a source into the application. They are coded as procedures within a package, to which you pass the data (in variables or PL/SQL tables). They validate the data and load it into Oracle EBS applications in a single step. The safest way to use these is to load a staging table in one step; then do your own validation and call the APIs in a second step.

The following extract from a PL/SQL script shows how an API call occurs within the script. This one is the CREATE_PROJECT procedure, which is a part of the Activity Management Gateway set of APIs for use in Oracle Projects. It uses the "_tbl" variable name to denote a PL/SQL table that holds a number of, say, tasks to create per project.

```
pa_project_pub.CREATE_PROJECT
    (p_api_version_number        = 1.0
    ,p_commit                    = v_commit
    ,p_init_msg_list             = 'F'
    ,p_msg_count                 = v_msg_count
    ,p_msg_data                  = v_msg_data
    ,p_return_status             = v_return_status
    ,p_workflow_started          = v_workflow_started
    ,p_pm_product_code           = v_pm_product_code
    ,p_project_in                = v_project_in_rec
    ,p_project_out               = v_project_out_rec
    ,p_key_members               = v_key_member_tbl
    ,p_class_categories          = v_class_category_tbl
    ,p_tasks_in                  = v_task_in_tbl
    ,p_tasks_out                 = v_task_out_tbl);
```

Scripts for Inserting Rows into Standard Tables

Even the latest APIs and open interfaces do not satisfy all requirements for loading Oracle master and transaction tables. Some users will still have to write scripts. Here are some common sense rules for writing these scripts:

1. Use the defined Oracle sequences to generate unique IDs. By doing this, you can be sure to avoid duplicating the identifier of a row generated by Oracle. For most tables, the name of the sequence is formed by adding "_S" to the name of the table. A typical script to get a sequence would be

   ```
   SELECT mtl_system_items_s.NEXTVAL from dual;
   ```

2. Research the actual contents of the tables by using the online screens to add the kinds of records you want the script to insert, and then printing them out. You can use the upcoming printtab.sql utility to display them in a useful format. Write your SQL or PL/SQL scripts to make entries similar to the ones that already exist in the database. An easy way to get around the SQL*Plus data-presentation issues is to use a third-party tool, such as Quest's Toad (Tool for Oracle Application Developers) or the free Oracle SQL Developer tool from Oracle. This will allow you to SELECT * from any table and will present the result in a columnar format that is easily copied into Excel. This is an excellent tool for developing SQL and PL/SQL, debugging, and running ad hoc queries (for example for reconciliation and testing).

3. If you are using SQL, create master table records first, so the detail records will have generated keys available to reference. You need your own, external unique key (such as the PO number) to relate master records to detail records. It might be helpful to carry that unique external key in one of Oracle's user-attribute columns, regardless of whether it is defined for use in a Descriptive Flexfield. If you are adding sets of related records using PL/SQL, put the master and detail records in the same commit group so there is no chance of destroying data integrity by getting only some of them. Consider adding table constraints to ensure the integrity of tables you address with custom code.

4. Use the systems administrator Responsibility to create an Oracle EBS user ID with no function other than to identify batch insertions. Populate the CREATED_BY and LAST_UPDATED_BY fields with the user ID associated with that user in the FND_USER table. Pull the date into a substitution parameter, so that all transactions created in the script have the same values for CREATION_DATE and LAST_UPDATE_DATE, as shown in this code sample. This process has a very important side effect: It rounds dates. Without rounding off the hours, minutes, and seconds, it is more difficult to construct a SELECT to locate the rows your process has inserted or updated.

```
COL c_date NEW_VALUE p_date NOPRINT
COL c_uid NEW_VALUE p_uid NOPRINT
SELECT
  user_id,
  TO_CHAR(SYSDATE)
FROM
  fnd_user
WHERE
  user_name = 'BATCH_USER'
/
INSERT INTO application_table (
    creation_date,
    created_by),
  ............
VALUES (
  TO_DATE('&&p_date'),
  &&p_uid),
  ............
/
```

5. Make sure you back up the tables that will be affected by your script, so you can restore the database to its original condition to rerun the test. Let other people who are testing in the same instance know what you are doing.

6. Do not leave legacy data behind as you convert to Oracle. If the staging tables you load from the legacy system include fields that do not map to Oracle columns, either plan to retain your staging tables permanently or concatenate the data fields and place them in one of the user-attribute columns. Doing this protects you against the risk that after conversion the users will recognize an oversight and refer to that data in straightening it out. It is common, for example, to need to modify the type attributes for planning, lead time, or work-in-process supply in the Inventory master table based on legacy settings. It is most convenient if the data are readily available.

7. Insert and commit the records.

8. Use Oracle screens to display and report on every record type and every relationship that should be observed among the newly added rows and between them and existing rows. Set up regression tests to do this automatically for large-scale modifications.

9. If there are any problems with the newly loaded data in your test instance, delete them all. The new rows will be uniquely identifiable by the WHO column values. You must never, of course, delete any rows other than the ones you added, and you hope never to have missed a problem in testing that would force you to delete from production.

10. The following script prints rows from a table, one column at a time:

```
REM printtab.sql.script ====================
PROMPT Enter table name
DEFINE table_name=&1
SET PAGESIZE 0 VERIFY OFF FEEDBACK OFF LINESIZE 100
SPOOL printtab1.sql
/* Generate SQL to read Varchar, Date and Number columns */
PROMPT SELECT
SELECT
   '"'||RPAD(column_name,30)||'="'||''||column_name||' '||CHR(10)||'

FROM
  fnd_columns c,
  fnd_tables t
WHERE
      c.table_id = t.table_id
  AND t.table_name = '&&TABLE_NAME'
  AND column_type   'L'
ORDER BY
  column_sequence
/
/* Generate SQL to read LONG column (if present)  ========*/
PROMPT "
SELECT
  ',"Long:",'||column_name
FROM
  fnd_columns c,
  fnd_tables t
WHERE
      c.table_id = t.table_id
  AND t.table_name = '&&table_name'
  AND column_type =  'L'
/
/* Run the generated SQL to print the table =========== */
PROMPT FROM &&TABLE_NAME
PROMPT WHERE
SPOOL OFF
SET VERIFY ON PAGESIZE 14 FEEDBACK ON
START printtab1

REM You may want to SPOOL the output of this utility and use a Unix
sed REM script to eliminate null columns.
```

11. This generates SQL that is missing a WHERE clause. You need to add a WHERE clause to select the one or two rows you are interested in. The script pauses just where you need to key one in. SQL*Plus cannot deal with a concatenation of more than about 60 columns, so you might need to edit the intermediate printtabl.sql. This script assumes only one LONG column per table; CHR (10) is a new line character.

Updating Standard Tables

Using Oracle programming tools to directly update the Oracle EBS application tables goes directly against Oracle's injunction against modification, discussed earlier in this chapter. It is a risky alternative, but sometimes the only one. For example, it might be essential to use an automated procedure to update lead-time attributes in Inventory or to set computed shrinkage factors. The volume would make it impossible to post such data manually through the screens. If you must "SQL the database," here are some essential precautions:

■ Look in the Technical Reference Manuals (TRMs) to see how each column is used. Do not ever update a foreign-key column.

■ Keep it simple. If possible, confine the update to a small number of related columns. Read the functional references as well as the TRMs. The TRMs are not intended to document the interdependencies among columns.

■ As part of your analysis process, use the Trace facility to see what SQL statements are executed in the course of the online update transaction you are replicating through batch codes. The DBA can set up Trace for you.

■ Read the SQL*Forms source code to see how each attribute you are updating gets edited by the native Oracle update or entry process. (The section of this chapter called "The Analysis Process" describes how.) Make sure you do not change data so that they do not pass the edits on the forms field. When necessary, trace the validation logic through to C-code exits and PL/SQL routines.

■ Check the DBA_TRIGGERS table to see whether any database triggers set or test the column value. Remember that it is possible that another related module can use or be dependent on data in other modules, so you must check them all.

■ Do not delete rows unless the Oracle forms you have analyzed allow them to be deleted and you are sure you understand the process. Use the Oracle purge process if there is one, or at least read that code to be sure you understand all the integrity constraints that Oracle observes in deleting records.

■ Use the WHO columns to show how the row was changed. Set the LAST_UPDATED_BY and LAST_UPDATE_DATE columns as described earlier for insertions into the database.

■ Save the old values in an unused user attribute in the table. If you have the old values and you can use the WHO columns to identify the rows that were updated by your custom process, you can reverse your update if necessary.

■ Thoroughly test every usage of the updated attribute and every online form in which it appears, to make sure the forms behave exactly as if the values had been set by native screen processes.

Batch scripts that update the EBS database are often one-time affairs used to correct oversights in setup or conversion. If the changes are at all extensive or the implications of the change cannot be fully assessed, consider creating Regression Tester scripts, as described in the upcoming "The Analysis Process" section to apply the changes through the forms. That will give you the benefits of Oracle's native edits.

Deleting records is permanent. Recovering from an accidental deletion might mean restoring the database. As an alternative, consider moving the "deleted" records out of the way by changing the sign of the ORGANIZATION_ID and generated-key values to negative. You can wait to confirm that getting rid of the records had no adverse effects before truly deleting them. A common example is moving inventory locations from one subinventory to another. Oracle does not allow you to make such a move once there are transactions in the locations. This restriction makes sense; the subinventories could have different material accounts, and moving locations could affect the ledger accounts. The following four-step script will accomplish the move.

1. Put a "ZZ" prefix on segment 1 of the MTL_ITEM_LOCATIONS records to be moved from the old subinventory. This will identify them as old. Changing segment 1 does not affect system integrity because the system uses the generated key (INVENTORY_LOCATION_ID) and not the segment values for foreign-key references. The "ZZ" prefix, incidentally, gets the old values out of the way by sorting them to the end of list-of-values selections.

2. Create new locations in the new subinventory by copying the old locations in the old subinventory, less the "ZZ" prefix. Use the sequence defined for the table (here, MTL_ITEM_LOCATIONS_S) to generate the primary key. The new records are accepted because they do not cause duplicates in either the primary-key index or the Key Flexfield index (on the segment values).

3. Insert transactions for the subinventory move into the MTL_TRANSACTIONS_INTERFACE table so that Oracle will make the moves and take care of the accounting considerations.

4. Once all the transactions for the old locations are complete, the balances are zero, and the period has been closed, get the "ZZ" prefix locations out of the way so they do not appear in lists of values or on reports. Do this by making the values of ORGANIZATION_ID and INVENTORY_LOCATION_ID negative. If you later find you have made a mistake in your analysis and these old locators are needed, you can put them back by making the key values positive again. You can delete them later when you are confident they are no longer needed.

You need to exercise several levels of caution in making a change like this. Start with a thorough analysis of the requirements; then test thoroughly in a development instance. Take a backup of the database before you run your update script in production. After your update, query the changed records immediately to ensure that they can be read and updated online. Then run concurrent processes against the changed records. Last, keep your old data in the database to ensure that the process is fully reversible at every step in case you have made a mistake.

This cautious strategy is effective for applying templates to existing items through open item interface. The interface does not directly allow you to update existing records. However, you can do the following:

■ Tag the existing items with the name of the new template. You usually put it in the ITEM_TYPE attribute or one of the user attributes.

■ Use the Open Item interface to create new records in the master inventory organization for the items you want changed. You can prefix them with some special character such as an asterisk or pound sign to avoid creating duplicate records; because they are new, they are automatically assigned new values for INVENTORY_ITEM_ID. Using the open interface ensures that the new attribute settings are valid and consistent.

■ Once the records are in place in the master organization, use new templates to create new records for the changed items in the other inventory organizations.

■ When all the new records are in place, move the old records out of the way by making their ORGANIZATION_ID and INVENTORY_ITEM_ID values negative and putting a prefix such as "ZZ" on segment 1. Then put the newly created records in their place by updating their INVENTORY_ITEM_ID values and dropping the special-character prefix from segment 1.

Any time you update inventory items, you run the risk that you might not be able to complete processing open transactions. As part of your analysis, you need to test every type of template change online to see what warning messages you get.

There are two primary reasons that this approach is less risky than simply applying SQL to the Inventory master table. First, it takes advantage of Oracle's native edits built into the open interface. Second, it is fully reversible if you find you have made an error, in that you can reverse the script to put the old records back.

Using Descriptive Flexfields

Oracle EBS gives you all the flexibility you need to capture and carry data that are specific to your needs. The major Oracle tables include user-attribute columns (ATTRIBUTE1 to ATTRIBUTE*n*) for your use. You can define Descriptive Flexfields to them, as described in previous chapters, or populate them directly with custom conversion, bridging, or forms modules you have written. Going further, if you need whole new record types, you can define your own tables to the applications and integrate bespoke modules to populate them.

It is good practice to define all uses of ATTRIBUTE*n* columns on the Define Descriptive Flexfields form, even those you do not use as Descriptive Flexfields. Define them, but set the "Enabled" value to "No." This provides a placeholder, which will prevent the next developer from defining a Descriptive Flexfield and overwriting an ATTRIBUTE*n* column that is being used behind the scenes.

Getting data into your tables and attributes is more of an issue. The advantages and disadvantages of using Descriptive Flexfields are described in the following table.

Advantages	Disadvantages
DFFs are easy to implement.	DFFs are limited to the validation checking provided through format checking and value sets.
DFFs fit into existing screens, zones, and tables.	Querying DFF values is an involved process, accomplished by by entering a colon in one of the enterable fields on a query screen, then typing the WHERE clause for SQL.
	DFF values are always stored as alphabetic.
	DFF attributes are limited in number (usually 15) and in size (usually 160 bytes).

Custom input forms, however, come with significant trade-offs of their own, shown in the following table.

Advantages	Disadvantages
Custom forms can handle any input requirement.	Custom forms require significant programming effort.
	Custom forms might damage database integrity if they populate native Oracle EBS table columns other than user-defined attributes.
	Custom forms must be integrated into the Responsibility and menu structure.
	Custom forms usually become release dependent.

It is usually easier to work around the shortcomings of Descriptive Flexfields than to create and implement custom forms.

- **Use DFFs, and accept the level of validation available through value sets.** It might not be necessary to go beyond the native capabilities of the Descriptive Flexfields. It is often not worth the effort. As you know from legacy experience, users can be good at following procedures even if the procedures are not enforced by the system. It works best, of course, when those users are the ones who have to live with the results of their own mistakes. As an example, it is usually not necessary to apply an edit to ensure that users do not embed special characters in part numbers. The few users allowed to create part numbers are smart enough to do it right.

  You can apply a separate edit to a segment within a DFF for each context you define for that DFF. Micros Systems uses a DFF defined on Employee Expenses to capture customer data when the expenses can be recovered. The context indicates whether the employee is providing a sales-order number or just a customer name. With a sales-order number there is nothing else to add; the SQL statements defined to generate DFF defaults automatically look up and display the customer, ship-to address, bill-to address, order type, and sales representative. However, with just a customer name, the segment values for ship-to address, bill-to address, order type, and sales representative have to be entered and validated. The DFF captures the same fields in either case, but the value sets used to edit them depend on the context.

- **Use the DFFs, but write alerts or batch reports.** Do this to perform editing beyond what is possible with native value set features. This approach is sometimes an acceptable compromise. It requires users to revisit their errors. Catching errors after the fact requires good procedures and discipline. It leaves a gap in time in which the system can continue to process with incorrect data in the database and leaves open the possibility that users will never bother to correct the errors.

- **Modify the Oracle screen.** You should add your own edits to the DFF fields and your own error messages. This approach does not require extensive analysis because it does not touch Oracle's logic. However, it does make the form release dependent.

- **Define custom database triggers to operate on DFF data.** Modify the Oracle forms. You can add your own edits and error messages for validating the DFF fields. Such triggers can modify the data, populate user-defined tables, or set user attribute values in other Oracle tables.

Database triggers cannot easily pass error messages clear back to the form. It is a matter of timing; users need feedback as they enter data, but the triggers fire only at commit time, when the user presses the SAVE key. Moreover, the database trigger applies to every row that is being committed. A standard error message cannot tell the user which row had the problem, or if multiple rows were in error.

The exception comes through the fact that database triggers can fail. When a trigger fails, it sends the user a message to the effect that the commit failed because of a trigger error. You can write a user-defined error code in PL/SQL that will provide a useful message. Because it is a database-level error, though, users have to know to ask for it to be presented. Nonetheless, despite these shortcomings and given the effort involved in modifying forms, database triggers are sometimes an attractive alternative for implementing custom edits.

Debugging database triggers can be frustrating. Until you become accustomed to Oracle's logic, "Mutating trigger" errors will often come up as a trigger working on one row attempts to select or update data from another row within the commit group. To give a simple example, you could not write a PRE-INSERT trigger on the PO_LINES table to keep the total PO value in ATTRIBUTE1 of the PO_HEADERS table. If you tried to commit two PO_LINES rows at the same time, the RDBMS could not decide whether to use the value computed by the first or the second execution of the trigger (row 1 or row 2 in PO_LINES). For the sake of consistency, the database-trigger mechanism will not ever let you do it, even in instances where you are only committing one PO_LINES record.

Customizing Workflows

Oracle is integrating the power of its Workflow tool to provide more and more flexibility within the applications. Workflow manages the interaction between users and the automated system in the course of processing a transaction. It handles transaction routing and lets you capture and attach information to a transaction in all media formats, including scanned images, voice, and video.

Workflow Builder is a separate Oracle product. The predefined workflows that Oracle provides allow you to provide parameters, such as approval hierarchies and threshold amounts, but the workflow decision logic within them is fixed.

Decision logic is an integral part of transaction routing. It is implemented in the Workflow Builder and can be supported by PL/SQL modules. This gives you all the power you need, in most instances, to customize the data-entry function. Workflow has the PL/SQL ability to query the database to validate data, the decision logic to test data conditions, and the ability to route the transaction to a user with an appropriate message when it finds an error.

Using Workflow to modify the applications makes modification of the online processes a much more attractive proposition than otherwise. It protects database integrity because your modifications do not affect the integrity of the lower-level validation within the EBS code itself. Configuration management is easier because you place your custom code in a predefined location, Workflow's PL/SQL API.

Custom Forms

There is less need to develop custom screens, or forms, than to develop bespoke reports. Descriptive Flexfields handle most users' needs in the way of entering additional data fields and, as described earlier in this chapter, you can manipulate data after the fact by custom code, alerts, triggers, or even reports. Despite all this, there are often good reasons to write custom forms, and Oracle delivers all the machinery and instructions necessary to do so.

The following table shows some typical uses for custom forms:

Requirement Solution	Requirement Problem	Example
Control	The Oracle-provided form gives the users power to see too much data or alter too many fields.	The Define Item screen in Inventory lets any user update all attributes in a group. A custom form might let users update only one field, such as lead time.
Efficiency	Standard Oracle forms require users to navigate through a number of screens, keying the same data multiple times.	Multiple related tasks can be accomplished on the same custom form, such as adding a new inventory location, moving all stock from an old location to the new one, and making the new location the default for issues and receipts.
Additional fields	Standard Oracle forms may not display or accept all of the needed data.	The Bill of Material Inquiry form can be modified to display cross-references and reference designators on the indented BOM explosion.
New subsystem	Totally new functions are needed, in a new application, against a combination of new and Oracle EBS tables.	A Proposal pricing screen can allow a user to enter prices, component sources, and modifications to standard Bills of Material for a custom bid.

Oracle EBS makes a distinction between inquiry and update screens. The worst a custom inquiry screen can do is confuse the user by displaying incorrect data. A form that only updates the user attributes (DFF segments) and custom tables does not jeopardize the integrity of standard Oracle data. The only forms that present major risks are those that affect the columns whose values Oracle sets and references within tables that belong to the applications. The updates they perform are on a par with scripts that "SQL the database."

The costs of analysis and testing mean there must be a significant business justification for writing a custom forms process that updates the Oracle EBS tables. The upcoming section "The Analysis Process" outlines the essential steps in analysis and design. The program-design documents should specify extensive testing.

Oracle*Forms programmers have the capability to customize any form according to their own needs without changing the form itself. Trigger code for forms is stored in a series of external libraries that are searched in sequence. Changing the code is a matter of placing your modification in the custom-trigger library, CUSTOM.pll, ahead of the standard library.

Developers of custom forms can use all of the AOL library routines in their custom code. These include flexfields, folders, quickpicks, and zooms. The AOL Reference manual describes the use of each. Developers might want to use Oracle Designer to lay out their screens, especially to take advantage of its ability to generate both Oracle*Forms and Web-based forms.

Modifications to Oracle EBS forms are release dependent because the tables they reference and the database triggers on those tables are release dependent. Their design documents should address the analysis requirements associated with release upgrades. You might want to specify regression tests in the design documents for more complex forms to confirm that their operation has not been affected by an upgrade.

Any custom tables used in a screen have to be registered before the screen itself is registered. Registration populates AOL's tables with the essential data needed to support field-level help. Use the Register Tables menu process within the application-developer Responsibility. You invoke the screen-registration process as a batch process under the application-developer Responsibility. Information about the screen, zone, and fields is placed in AOL tables. That makes the form available for the context-sensitive help, the EXAMINE function, and other internal uses.

One of the best references in Oracle's documentation suite for Smart Client/NCA is modestly entitled *Coding Standards*; however, it is more than that. It describes how to modify Oracle's Designer code and how to work with flexfields, zooms, and other AOL devices.

Messages

Message-service routines in the Oracle EBS present messages in the users' own national language (English, French, and so on). The program module—be it in Forms, Reports, or PL/SQL—invokes the Oracle EBS message routine, passing the message name as a parameter. The presentation subsystem returns the message in the appropriate language.

Predictably, the messages are stored in a database. Less predictably, AOL compiles them for use by the forms, according to national language, into an operating-system file on the Applications Server machine in the $*app*_TOP/mesg subdirectory. This approach eliminates the need for a trip to the database. The Forms program invokes a message by a subroutine call. It passes the internal name of the message to be presented, along with, in some cases, variables to be substituted into the message text. The message subroutine determines the national language, searches the operating-system file for a match on the internal name, fetches the associated natural-language text, substitutes in the replacement parameters, and presents the message.

You need to use Oracle's architecture if you are designing a bespoke form to be used in a multilanguage environment. You must do the following:

- Give each message an internal name.
- Translate each message into each national language.
- Maintain versions of the Forms boilerplate text in each national language you use.

It is simpler if you use only one national language. When messages do not need to be translated, you can embed them directly in the form itself and use the standard Forms messaging services to present them.

If you do use custom forms and they are registered under custom applications, you will need to take a step that allows your form to read Oracle's standard message file. To do this, in the Define Profile Option form, assign your custom application the profile option Message: Shared Application to have the value of the standard Oracle application it is matched to. For example, WJ Receivables will share messages with Oracle Receivables.

Sometimes highly used forms are called by another form, into which the application and form name are hard-coded. If you want to let users access your custom form from the native forms that include hard-coded references, you will need to create a link between your custom form and the Oracle form it replaces. Follow these steps:

1. Create your own module, giving it an appropriate custom name to distinguish it from modules written by Oracle.

2. Rename the Oracle distribution form according to your local convention. For instance, rename OEXOEMOE.fmx to OEXOEMOE.fmx.original. Repeat this for the .fmb files (source code). This makes the original name available for your use.

3. Create an alias using the appropriate operating-system feature, such as a soft link with the ln command in Unix or a shortcut in NT, linking the original Oracle module name in its native directory to your module in the custom directory.

This procedure satisfies the objective of separating Oracle from custom code without creating excessive work dealing with additional customizations.

It is often useful to set and retrieve messages in PL/SQL. The AOL Reference Manual describes the process reasonably well. However, the best way to understand the message process is to read Oracle's source code for the message-service routines. These, along with the Concurrent Manager routines and many others that are useful in modifying the system, are in the $FND_TOP/admin/sql directory. Find the message routines by navigating to that directory and giving the following command (in Unix):

```
grep -i get_message *
```

A Windows NT user, or any other user with NFS access to the server directory structure, can locate the files using the Word for Windows Advanced File Find facility, under File | Open | Advanced.

Performance Tuning

Database-performance tuning is a specialty unto itself. Additional tips and tricks on how to optimize performance within the Oracle E-Business Suite will be discussed later in this book. With that said, much of performance depends on table size, table placement, indexing, activity, and many other factors. The most significant factor in the performance of an individual program is usually how the SQL within the program is coded.

Most of the DBA's tuning activity takes place at the RDBMS level, invisible to the applications. The application designer's capacity planning will tell the DBA how much space is needed for each application and what the major tables are within each. The technical manuals provide the needed information about indexes.

The DBA might add indexes on the Oracle tables to meet local needs. For instance, it is common to add indexes on the user attributes populated by DFFs. Nonunique indexes can improve performance, and unique ones can constrain users from making duplicate entries.

Sometimes the Oracle indexes wind up missing after an upgrade or a patch. When performance seems to have degraded significantly on a given table, it is a good idea to check to see that the indexes are all there. The technical manuals list the indexes that are supposed to be on a table. The following script will read the metadata to do the same.

```
SELECT
    i.index_name,
    i.uniqueness,
    c.column_name ,
    ic.column_sequence
FROM
    fnd.fnd_indexes i,
    fnd.fnd_index_columns ic,
    fnd.fnd_columns c,
    fnd.fnd_tables t
WHERE
    t.table_id = i.table_id and
    ic.index_id = i.index_id and
```

```
  ic.column_id = c.column_id and
  t.table_name = '&1'
ORDER BY
  i.index_name,
  ic.column_sequence
/
```

Your DBA can compare this list with the indexes that are found through the USER_INDEXES view to determine whether any are missing.

Online Processes

In Internet computing, the performance issues are the speed and placement of the middle tier or Web server, the speed of its links back to the database server and forward to the client, and the speed of the desktop machine itself. Oracle recommends at least a medium speed (200 MHz or more) Pentium to drive the EBS applet running in your browser.

The performance issues with online processes often have more to do with user productivity than network or computer speed. The preceding section discussed situations in which it might be desirable to create one form that combines the function of several native Oracle forms. Workflow can be a very useful tool for streamlining the data entry process, allowing you to eliminate unneeded steps and providing default information.

Batch Processes

Oracle*Reports is a much more powerful tool than SQL*Plus, but it executes somewhat more slowly. There might be reports that run so frequently in the course of a day that it makes sense to speed them up. It can be a simple matter to pull the queries you need from an Oracle*Reports module and reimplement them in SQL*Plus or a simplified Oracle*Reports program.

Compiled programs, usually written in the Pro*C language, offer more programming flexibility and better performance than any other tools. They are also an order of magnitude harder to code, debug, and manage. Oracle itself is gradually replacing all the EBS logic now implemented in C with PL/SQL. Only large organizations doing major modifications will find it worth the effort to use compiled code.

The Analysis Process

You cannot modify a system without understanding it. You need a minimal understanding just to describe your problems to Oracle Support so they can fix them. How do you find out what goes on behind the scenes?

Analysts and designers fill the same role with the EBS applications as they do in custom development. They present user needs in a requirements document, then design a solution to the problem. The solution can be any combination of business procedures, configurations, and customization. An applications designer starts with a fully functioning, integrated system made up of a massive number of modules, whereas the designer of a bespoke system starts with no more than a legacy system and a concept of what might be.

Learning what the Oracle system does, and how it does it, is a challenge to which no analyst can fully respond. The packages are intricate, and the documentation about how they work internally is limited. An analyst always has to judge how much knowledge is enough for a particular job, and to weigh the risks associated with what he or she does or does not know.

User Reference Manuals

The User Reference Manuals frame the discussion between users and analysts about the requirements. Users describe what they want in terms of what the delivered system can and cannot do. Both the users and the analyst should read the relevant overview sections of the user references and the screen and report descriptions carefully. The analyst needs a test instance in which to practice using the native Oracle features before giving any thought to changing them.

Technical Reference Manuals (TRMs)

The E-Business Suite TRMs are organized by module. Each one starts with database-design diagrams that are broken down by functional area. They show the data entities and relationships, and are a useful starting point for any design work. Having said that, there is no replacement for actually talking to a functional expert on how the module hangs together—this kind of explanation needs to be combined with the TRMs, which give the link to database objects. The high-level design section goes on to list the tables, views, and modules (forms, reports, and concurrent programs) that comprise the EBS module. This is simply a list with a one-line description of each item.

The TRMs continue into a detailed design section, which concentrates on the database tables and views. This is extremely useful for developers, because it not only lists the columns but also has a short description of each and gives a raft of extra information. It shows

- foreign-key relationships with other tables (which are not always intuitive),
- values for lookup-code columns,
- indexes,
- sequences used on the table,
- database triggers on the table (for example, there is a series of data-validation triggers on the PA_TRANSACTION_INTERFACE_ALL table in Oracle Projects), and
- the SQL used to derive a view.

Reading Code

The only way to know for sure what a piece of code does is to look at it. The various applications are written in different tools, with different characteristics. This section explains how to read the code.

SQL*Plus and PL/SQL Routines

These are written in ASCII text. They are totally accessible and Oracle does a good job of commenting the code. The applications use these languages for relatively few reports. However, they have migrated more and more of the complex logic for routines such as Bill of Material explosion from Pro*C to PL/SQL. PL/SQL is the source language for database triggers, packaged procedures, Oracle*Forms triggers, and Oracle*Reports triggers. Stored procedures, triggers, and other PL/SQL routines that are executed at setup time are in the $APPL_TOP/admin/sql directory for each application. The directory $FND_TOP/admin/sql contains the AOL routines for concurrent-process submission, messaging, and the like.

Developer Code: Oracle*Forms and Oracle*Reports

This code has to be viewed through the appropriate Developer tool. Forms are organized into blocks, each one based on a database table. Reports are organized into groups based on SQL queries.

Each provides a number of ways for users to add asynchronous triggers where the most interesting code is often buried.

Your desktop environment might not enable you to view all reports. The PL/SQL buffer in Windows is only 64K. Several PRE-REPORT triggers, among them the ones for Bill of Materials explosions, are too large to display. A quick-and-dirty work-around is to bring a Forms or Reports module up in a word processor. Most of it will be unintelligible, but the SELECT, INSERT, and UPDATE statements are readable because they remain in ASCII. You might be able to do a find on a table or column name and get a quick idea of what the module does with it without laboriously examining its component parts in Designer. Some editors are better at this than others. Microsoft Word seems to pick up everything, whereas the Unix vi editor appears to impose a limit on the length of the lines it can handle; it drops material when the distance between carriage returns is too great.

C Code

C is still used, though Oracle is phasing it out. Application-specific C code is pretty much confined to Forms exits and concurrent processes; Oracle does not provide the source. One way to figure out what the code does is to bring it up in a word processor and scan to find the embedded SQL code. This task is especially difficult for Forms exits because all the logic for an entire application is compiled together into one module. Another way is to use a SQL trace. If you are dealing with attributes whose names appear in the C code, in a context that suggests they are being updated or they serve as the basis for decision logic, you will probably never fully understand exactly how the code works.

Laboratory Method

Working with the applications is a science. Some source code simply is not available; much of the rest will be just too complex, or at least too voluminous, for your programming staff to reasonably understand. After reading the documentation and as much code as possible, the analyst needs to apply classic laboratory methods to confirm theories as to how the various "black boxes" function.

The laboratory process generally encompasses these steps:

1. Define the process to be analyzed. Modules of most interest are those that update the database, both batch and online processes.

2. Determine by reading the User Reference Manuals, TRMs, and source code which tables are affected by the process and its subroutines.

3. Comb through the tables to see whether any database triggers defined on them affect other tables. For example, inserting new items into the MTL_SYSTEM_ITEMS table can fire a trigger that populates CST_ITEM_COSTS and CST_ITEM_COST_DETAILS. "Combing" is a science unto itself. The Unix command

   ```
   grep-i MTL_SYSTEM_ITEMS'find .- name "*SQL"-print'$HOME/msi
   ```

   will look for the table name MTL_SYSTEM_ITEMS in all files with a .sql suffix, in all subdirectories of the current directory, and put each instance found into a file called msi in your home directory. You can then look there to find database triggers affecting the table. Microsoft Word's advanced Fin utility (under the Open menu) will do the same thing.

4. Take a "before" image of the tables used by a process. You can usually confine yourself to the rows you know will be affected. The easiest way is to create a side table of just those rows with a CREATE *yourtable* AS SELECT * FROM *Oracletable* WHERE... You might want to use the printtab.sql routine shown previously to display the values in these rows beforehand. Needless to say, you do this in a test instance.

5. Execute the update process. This usually amounts to keying data into the screen and committing.

6. Compare the values in the tables before and after execution. The printtab.sql routine is useful for a visual comparison. If the data volumes are large, you may want to write a custom script to compare the before and after images of the database.

7. Establish the reason each changed value was changed and determine the significance of each change.

8. If you are going to repeat the analysis process, use a script to restore the test-instance tables to their original condition or pick another master record for the next test.

Some processes, especially database triggers, are easy to overlook. The database trace function is useful for determining exactly which tables are affected by an operation.

Detailed Table Analysis

The EBS applications' metadata tables can tell you more than Standard Oracle RDBMS functions. It is worth learning how these foundation tables can tell you what you need to know.

- **Columns in a table** The DESC function displays columns and data types. The fnd_col script shown here is a SELECT joining the FND_TABLE and FND_COLUMNS tables. It includes the column-description text used in the TRMs. It has the added virtues of presenting only columns that satisfy a LIKE clause, weeding out the predictable ATTRIBUTE*n*, SEGMENT*n*, and WHO columns and presenting the descriptions. It helps you cope with the large number of columns in the EBS tables.

```
REM fnd_col.sql script====================
COLUMN table_name  FOR a20   HEAD Table
COLUMN column_name FOR a20   HEAD Column
COLUMN col_type    FOR a4    HEAD Type
COLUMN descr       FOR a30   HEAD Description
SELECT
  t.table_name  table_name,
  c.column_name  column_name,
  c.column_type||SUBSTR(LTRIM(TO_CHAR(c.width)),1,4)  col_type ,
  c.description descr
FROM
  applfnd.fnd_tables t,
  applfnd.fnd_columns c
WHERE
      t.table_id = c.table_id
  AND t.table_name LIKE  '%&fnd_table%'
  AND c.column_name LIKE '%&COL%'
  AND c.column_name NOT LIKE 'ATTRIBUT%'
  AND c.column_name NOT LIKE 'SEGMENT%'
  AND c.column_name NOT EQUAL 'LAST_UPDATED_BY'
```

```
AND c.column_name NOT EQUAL 'LAST_UPDATE_DATE'
AND c.column_name NOT EQUAL 'CREATED_BY'
AND c.column_name NOT EQUAL 'CREATION_DATE'
/
```

■ **Tables where a column is used**   Using the LIKE feature and reading the column descriptions provided by the fnd_col.sql script make it fairly easy to find all the foreign-key joins on a column like INVENTORY_ITEM_ID. It would be a lot of work to dig that out of the TRMs. Want to know which tables use PO_HEADER_ID? Do a select entering that value for the column and leaving the table name blank.

You should be aware of some the weaknesses of this approach. Corresponding columns are not always named the same in every table in which they appear. In some cases, such as when more than one column joins to a single foreign key, the columns could not be named the same. For example, 17 columns within MTL_PARAMETERS join to CODE_COMBINATION_ID within GL_CODE_COMBINATIONS. In other cases nomenclature has changed as the system evolved. The primary key of MTL_ITEM_LOCATIONS is INVENTORY_LOCATION_ID. Most foreign-key columns that join to it are named LOCATOR_ID. The likely explanation is that the base table was in place prior to Oracle's decision to use the word *locator* to denote an inventory-stock location and the word *location* to mean a business location.

■ **Forms that use a table**   The form-registration process creates a record of the tables and columns used by a form in the FND_FORM, FND_BLOCK, and FND_FIELD tables.

■ **Menus on which forms appear**   Oracle's standard reports show a menu structure from the top down. It is sometimes handy to look from the bottom up, to find where a given form is used. The following is an example of a script to do this.

```
COLUMN menu_name for a20
COLUMN form_name for a14
COLUMN prompt for a11
COLUMN description for a30
SELECT
  fm.menu_name,
  fme.form_name,
  fme.prompt,
  fme.description
FROM
  fnd_menu fm,
  fnd_menu_entry fme
WHERE
    fm.menu_id = fme.MENU_id
  AND (UPPER(fme.prompt) like '%'|| UPPER('&1')||'%'
    OR UPPER(fme.form_name) like '%'|| UPPER('&1')||'%'
    OR UPPER(fme.description) like '%'|| UPPER('&1')||'%')
/
```

Regression Testing

New software releases are supposed to offer new functions and fix known problems without introducing new complications. Making sure that the old features still work requires significant effort. Oracle has a strategic partnership with Mercury to use their testing software Winrunner and Loadrunner (for performance testing).

The purpose of a regression tester is to apply identical tests to different modules of code—usually new and old versions of one module—and to compare the results. Most regression testers have similar architectures. Their major features include the following:

■ A means of capturing keystrokes and mouse movements. Most systems use operating-system files. Mercury uses a combination of database and flat files.

■ A device to edit the keystroke files so that tests can be copied and altered.

■ A device to play back the keystrokes, simulating online operation, and to save the results of the simulated online session. Two forms of output are of interest. There is a log file showing the interaction: the data provided by the test software and the response from the module being tested. The log file is the place to look when a test goes off track because the tested module does not receive data and commands in the sequence it expects. There is also a file containing effects of the program's execution, which in Oracle's case are changes to the database.

■ A program to compare the changes to the database resulting from different runs of the tester.

The objective of regression testing is to prove that the new, improved version of a program performs its old functions exactly as the previous version did. Each new release of a module should be accompanied by new regression tests to serve as the baseline for testing yet later releases.

Even though very few Oracle EBS shops are rigorous enough to implement automated regression testing, testing is important in managing release upgrades. Even though Oracle thoroughly tests its software before release, it is a good practice to execute all your major system functions in a test instance before putting them into production. Doing so protects against your own oversights in implementing the upgrade, against Oracle's in testing it, and against misunderstandings as to how the code has changed. The better defined the tests, the more successful they will be. All good tests are

■ defined in advance,

■ repeatable, and

■ thorough.

Whereas you regression test Oracle's code at an application level, you need to regression test each module of custom code individually as you do an upgrade. Examine the code, then run a test to see if it has been affected by changes to Oracle's schemas and code. Rather than use an automated regression tester, most shops can manage by including a written description of the tests to be performed as part of the design documentation for custom code.

Using a Regression Tester for Mass Updates

Regression testers, because they invoke online edits to Oracle EBS in a batch mode, can be very useful for applying complex changes to the system. Say for instance that you need to apply a new template to each of 1,000 items in the Inventory Master. The approach would be as follows:

1. Capture the keystrokes as you apply the change to one item through the online process.

2. Write a script to read the keystroke file, change only the item number, and rewrite it under a new name.

3. Run the script for each of the 1,000 items to be changed, creating 1,000 test files.

4. Run the 1,000 tests.

This method usually involves significantly more work than just SQLing the database. It is also significantly safer, because it uses Oracle's native edits and processing. Depending on the features of the regression tester, you can program each individual test to abort if it encounters an unexpected condition such as an error message returned from the online form.

You can also use the dataload program available free of charge at http://www.comstar.co.uk to apply keystrokes through a form. This works well for simple forms but needs constant user attention, so is not suited for large-scale inserts or updates.

Document Control

More is written and less done about methodology than any other topic in data processing. Documentation? Coding standards? Logs? Records? Most EBS shops do not see themselves as developers. They have little in the way of development procedures and do even less in the way of observing the ones they have.

Deadline pressure is the most frequent culprit. Consultants and employees scramble to get the system up, telling themselves that they will document after the fact. They are surprised to find themselves inundated with maintenance and enhancement requests long after the implementation, by which time even the people who are left on the project remember little about the implementation.

Minimalism is the key to success. People will adhere to methodologies if they are reasonable and understandable. Here are some general guidelines:

- Decide on your own methodology. A packaged system from a large consulting firm is almost always too complex, and usually is not appropriate to Oracle EBS. The best that can happen is that it will be honored in the breach. Second best, it will be totally ignored. Worst of all, some well-intentioned administrator will doom the project to generating nothing but shelfware by enforcing it.

- Let the programmers and analysts decide what they need. Experienced team leaders and independent consultants are often the best guides.

- Keep it simple and quick.

- Remember that quality has to be built in, not grafted on. Let the senior developers and consultants establish the culture and set a model for their peers.

- Keep standards and documentation close to the code. Programmers appreciate well-structured and well-commented code because it is useful to them as they maintain it. They do not care about what they do not use—and it shows. Paper documents have a tendency to stay in the filing cabinet. A better approach is to keep word-processing documents available over the network, if possible in the same directory structure as the code they describe.

The standards and procedures described here are minimal yet more rigorous than most organizations manage to sustain. Anybody who takes the issue seriously will find yards of shelf space in a computer bookstore devoted to books on the subject of standards.

Log Maintenance

It is essential to know what is in the EBS environment to maintain it. The E-Business Suite comprises many components, each of which will need periodic maintenance or enhancements. The whole software package works when the components are a valid, compatible configuration.

To ensure that the configuration remains valid, you must log the individual versions. The key logs are discussed here.

Oracle Release History

The DBA needs to keep a log of when each instance is updated to each new dot-point release. There are relatively few entries for each instance, because release upgrades are major events, occurring only every year or so. The log should indicate the levels of the RDBMS and operating system. EBS upgrades involve scripts to migrate data to new table structures; keep the output logs for the most recent upgrade. Because most test instances are created as copies of the production instance, be sure to copy the patch log as part of setting up the new instance.

Oracle Patches

DBAs apply patches with some regularity, and Oracle Support always needs to know which ones have been applied. DBAs are usually very conscientious about keeping records of their activity. Each patch generates a log as it is applied. Hang on to the output logs for patches to the current release in each database instance.

Setups (Reference Documents Used for Manual Setup)

Each application has a series of setup screens for the parameters that control its operation. The setups are in constant flux as the system's super users work out the business procedures appropriate to their installation. The setups invariably have to be keyed in a number of times, as in the experimentation phase of the project. Setup parameters should be organized according to the screen on which they are captured. Use one word-processor table per application, with these columns:

- screen name,
- field name,
- value,
- reason, and
- external reference.

The reason column is essential. The users should note why the parameter value was chosen and what other parameters are related to the setting. The external reference will link to spreadsheets where you keep those setups that involve a large number of values, such as Inventory templates and Fixed Assets categories.

Screen prints, often used to document the setups, fall short of doing the entire job for several reasons. The most obvious is that they can only be created after the fact. They take a lot of time and effort to create. Their natural medium is hard copy; when embedded in word-processor documents, they are bulky and slow to print. Most significantly, they do not carry the intelligence of the reason a value was selected; only what it is.

The super users of the individual applications most often key in the setups. This can be a lot of work, but it gives them a chance to review the values and ensure that they are keyed accurately. You can cut the work down using Oracle's Application Implementation Wizard. Power users might even consider using scripts or a regression tester to automatically key in the setups for multiple installations. The word-processor document describing the setups used in each Oracle instance should be referenced in the DBA's documentation for that instance.

Value Sets

Value sets are part of setup. Some, especially GL accounts and organizations, can be fairly large. You can choose to document small ones in the word-processor document with other setups. The best way to handle large value sets is in a separate spreadsheet. Some of these you can load through the Applications Desktop Integration tool. You might need scripts to load others from the spreadsheet into the FND_FLEX_VALUES and FND_FLEX_VALUES_TL tables.

Users may define value sets to validate DFF segment values and report parameters. Most such values are rather static and should be entered as part of setup. They deserve their own documentation. Larger and more volatile value sets are usually handled by, and documented as, user-defined tables.

Application-Specific Setup Documentation

Some applications have setups unique to themselves. Inventory uses item templates to facilitate setting up new items. Purchasing and Inventory share lists of buyers. GL uses Financial Statement Generator reports.

Oracle is designed to require users to key this customization into each new instance, except where it is propagated by the backup or restore process. The documentation should describe the entries and how to set them up.

Alerts

Alerts do not have source code per se; they exist only within the Oracle EBS tables. It is useful to keep a one-page document describing each alert and a list of alerts that relates their Oracle name to the document that describes them.

The alert description should include

■ the purpose and type of the alert,

■ the SQL code in the alert, which can be cut and pasted right into the document, and

■ the action the alert carries out (send e-mail, initiate a process, etc.).

The best practice is to set up and test alerts in a development environment. You key them into Production after they are debugged. They then migrate back to your test environments as they are periodically refreshed with copies of Production.

Alerts are a common suspect when system performance slows. The documentation will help the DBA in that regard. Aside from that, the documentation is useful in maintaining the alert and propagating it to new environments. The creator will almost always put it together in a test environment, document it, and then use the documentation to rekey it into production.

Responsibility Setup   The security plan for each instance deserves a document. It should name the different Responsibilities and specify who is expected to use each of them. It should name the top-level menu and report group. If the high-level menu structures you develop are not documented elsewhere, this is a good place for them.

You administer flexfield security at a Responsibility level. The documentation for the Responsibility should include the rules that restrict access to Key and Descriptive Flexfields. It can be useful to include printouts of the reports within the report group and the menu tree under each Responsibility. However, in many environments these change quite frequently. The best approach is to pull menu and report-group reports off the system as needed.

User-Attribute Usage by Table   Although the only support Oracle provides for user attributes is as Descriptive Flexfields, you are free to use them any way you want. You can populate them through DFFs, database triggers, custom-written forms, or batch processes. You can put them to temporary use as a record of changes to the database, as described in the section "The Analysis Process" earlier in this chapter.

The best practice is to define a DFF for each attribute field you use, regardless of whether you actually need to display it on a screen. Make the DFF segment inactive, but define it. This marks the attribute as taken, so no other programmer will attempt to put it to a different use. A DFF usage document also helps programmers know which user attributes are in use and which are available. For debugging, they need to know which processes set and use the attribute values. The table of attribute usage should include columns for the following information:

- Table name.

- Attribute name (ATTRIBUTE1 through ATTRIBUTE*n*).

- Narrative description of the way the column is used. Occasionally there are multiple uses, controlled by a DFF context segment.

- Name of the DFF using this attribute, if any.

- Context of the DFF using this attribute, unless it is global.

- DFF segment names for this attribute (if any). There can be one per context.

- Name of the value set associated with the segment and context, if it is used in a DFF and is validated.

- Column format as used. User attributes are almost always defined to Oracle as VARCHAR2(150) to VARCHAR2(240), but the DFF or other module that populates it determines the actual length and format of the contents. For instance, it is common to put the numeric values of generated keys in user attributes. Oracle Receivables links back to sales-order lines by this device.

- Modules and processes that set the value, such as DFFs, triggers, custom forms, inbound bridges, and conversion routines.

- Modules and processes that use the value, such as reports and outbound bridges.

Very often DFFs are listed in the individual, module-specific setup documents. This is a useful implementation method, but in production the list of DFFs will evolve and will be used by anyone producing reports, whether by building them with the Reports Designer or by using an end-user tool such as Discoverer. Therefore, you should write a publicly available but centrally maintained document that lists all the DFFs for all modules.

User-Defined Database Triggers by Table   Database triggers have to be re-established every time a new instance is set up. The DBA needs a list to make sure they are all present as needed. In fact, in most development instances and all production instances, it is the DBA who will implement the triggers using the developers' scripts.

Database triggers are also frequently the cause of data-corruption problems. There are tools to show the trigger names and whether they are enabled (this is, for example, a feature of the program Toad, mentioned earlier). It takes documentation for the DBA to decide whether a given trigger has anything to do with a given bug.

The list of database triggers should include the following elements for each trigger:

- trigger name,
- table name,
- brief purpose of the trigger, including reference to the design document that specified its need,
- columns referenced by the trigger,
- tables and columns updated by the trigger, and
- applicable design document.

There should be a design document supporting each database trigger. Triggers often do not have separate documentation when they exist as part of a larger suite.

User-Defined Stored Procedures   PL/SQL code in Oracle*Forms, Oracle*Reports, database triggers, and SQL*Plus modules can all call *stored procedures*. They represent "black box" procedures that can be separately tested and debugged, then used as needed.

The DBA needs to be able to implement stored procedures in each new instance and certainly needs to know what those procedures do to the database. The table of stored procedures should include these details for each procedure:

- owning subsystem,
- procedure name,
- purpose (two-sentence narrative),
- tables and columns updated by the procedure, and
- reference to the design document that specifies the stored procedure. Each stored procedure usually belongs to a suite. Stored procedures do not each need their own design document, but the should be covered by some design document.

Custom Indexes on Native Oracle Tables   Users sometimes put their own indexes on Oracle's tables to improve system speed or to enforce uniqueness. The DBA needs a list of such indexes.

User-Defined Tables and Views   Users often define their own tables in adding custom functions to the Oracle E-Business Suite. The DBA needs a list of these. The columns should include the following:

- **Owning schema**   There should be only one, or at most a few. Many organizations name it CUSTOM. At any rate, the objects you create should not be owned by the Oracle EBS schemas.
- **Table name**   As it appears in the custom schema.
- **Usage**   In two sentences or so.
- **Design-document name**   The design document will list the attributes within the table.
- **Indexes**   Index names and the columns to which they relate.

- **Grants and synonyms**   Identities to whom access has been granted and other schemas in which synonyms have been created.
- **Registration**   For example, is the table registered to Oracle EBS or not?
- **Whether the table holds a value set defined to the applications**

User-Defined Reports and Other Concurrent Processes   The AOL tables include entries for each registered report and concurrent process. The documentation lists what should be there rather than what is, and names the design document for each of them. The list of custom concurrent processes needs columns for process name, owning application, purpose, and design-document name.

Design documents for the individual processes tell what the report or process is for. They also describe the run-time parameters—how to set them up and which value sets are used to validate them.

User-Defined Forms   The list of user-defined forms is similar to the list of user-defined reports. AOL's tables have entries for all registered forms. The documentation list indicates which ones should be there and names the governing design document.

Customized Workflows   You should maintain a list of your modifications to the workflows delivered by Oracle and those you have designed to support custom processes. This list should reference the design documents.

Third-Party Setups   A record of the objects should be kept in Noetix Notes, Business Objects, Microsoft Access, Vertex, and other packages that reference and modify Oracle EBS tables. You need to apply regression tests to revalidate the integration after an upgrade of either Oracle or the third-party package.

Configuration Management

Matrixed into each of the lists of database objects is the concept of configuration management: what version of each module is in each of the different instances. Oracle Support, the DBA, and the developers need to have version information to support users in each environment.

Developers usually implement the EBS modules a suite at a time. They will put in a DFF, a database trigger, and two reports that use the newly defined user attributes all at once. To tell what is where, they need a matrix showing when each change is applied to each environment, with the following information:

- suite name, such as "Add Pick-to-Order unit pricing functions,"
- list of the modules within the modification suite,
- references to the design documents,
- implementation date,
- name of the person doing the implementation, and
- implementation notes.

The production environment needs tight control, imposed by the DBA or data administrator. The developers and DBA together can determine how much configuration management they need in the development and test environments. It depends on how big the systems organization is, how much modification there is, how many environments there are, and how likely the developers are to confuse themselves as to the state of their code in the multiple places it exists. They need to deal with the fact that the database typically migrates backward, from production to development and test, while code migrates forward, from testing to production. The code can get out of step with the database in a development instance.

There needs to be one master library for all source code. Custom code exists as operating-system files, but the setups exist only in documentation and the database itself. Other customizations, such as DFF definitions, value sets, and alerts, also exist as Oracle EBS objects for which there is no flat-file representation. A LAN server is usually best suited to hosting the mix of program documentation, source code, and code that exists only in documentation format.

Conversion code is generally not subject to configuration management. Its primary use after conversion is as a reference, as in "How did we get into this mess?" Putting conversion code in separate libraries keeps it available but out of the way. Sharing it might make you some friends within your local Oracle EBS User's Group. You might also find that you can reuse conversion code in interfaces. For example, calls to the Projects AMG APIs you used for converting projects and tasks from a legacy system can also be used for creating an ongoing interface from a third-party system that will continue to be used.

Many vendors offer configuration-management software—be cautious. Start with a discipline of setting up a library structure in which there is a place for everything, and get the developers in the habit of putting things where they belong. A packaged solution might be overkill and might not fit the requirements. Older configuration-management packages are designed to handle source programs in text format, for languages such as COBOL. Not many modules in Oracle EBS fit this description.

However, there are some packages that are more attuned to the requirements, such as Merant's PVCS. If you decide to use such packages, you also need to decide what will be source controlled, and by whom. You might decide it is just programs and that therefore only developers need access, but in this case you will still need a library for setup documentation, functional and technical specifications, and so on. If you also want to put documents in there (this is technically and practically possible), will you give access to the tool to the whole project team or create a potential bottleneck in a centralized configuration manager who would check out and check in the material? This will depend on the project-team culture, corporate culture, timescales, and experience of the team.

A major function of an automated configuration-management system is to force programmers to check software modules out before they change them, then put them back before they can be migrated into production. This is not terribly effective when much of what is being controlled is in the form of documentation—specifications, setup documents, instructions for setting up Descriptive Flexfields, test scripts, and the like. They tend to be worked on for long periods during the project. One solution is to ensure that they are checked in once per week. Build a foundation of good manual procedures, then move to an automated system only when you see where administrative procedures fall short.

Building Blocks of Configuration Management
There are three building blocks of configuration management. The first of these is the program header (and document header), which tells the author and, critically, the version history of the item. This was described previously in the "Programming and Documentation Standards" section. The system-release log (shown here) tells which versions of these programs and documents were released in which patch or release number.

Module	Program	Release 1	Release 2	Release 3
Plant hire items interface	Item_load.pls	1.0	1.0	1.1
	Item_staging_tables.sql	1.0	1.1	1.2
Custom certificates form and report	WJ_CERT.fmb	—	1.0	1.0
	Cert_profiles.sql	—	1.0	1.0
	WJ_CERT.rdf	—	1.0	1.1

The system-history log (shown here) tells which patches or releases went into which environments.

Release	INT	SYST	UAT	PROD
1	08-Oct-2001	15-Oct-2001		
2	20-Oct-2001	23-Oct-2001	30-Oct-2001	
3	07-Nov-2001	13-Nov-2001	16-Nov-2001	01-Dec-2001

Oracle CEMLI Standards—Customizations, Extensions, Modifications, Localizations, and Integrations
Oracle responded to criticisms and requests from the application-user community in terms of how to manage and deal with complex customizations and enhancements by implementing a new standard build process for changes made to the application code for the E-Business Suite. In a nutshell, this new paradigm—labeled Customizations, Extensions, Modifications, Localizations, and Integrations, or *CEMLI*, for short—remediated support issues that arose when customers opened new service requests with Oracle Support. Oracle provides this add-on service to streamline development and implementation efforts by Oracle EBS customers to stabilize both preproduction and postproduction environments before and after the go-live phase of a new Oracle EBS implementation. Furthermore, customers who host their environment with Oracle On Demand are required to adhere to the CEMLI standard established by Oracle. Additional details are available from Oracle on this service at http://www.oracle.com/us/support/library/cemli-services-e-business-suite-069223.pdf. Oracle recommends that customers avoid customizations and modifications whenever possible, especially for production environments.

Conclusion

There is no one-size-fits-all solution to a successful Oracle EBS implementation. Custom code for conversion is part of virtually every implementation. Most also involve some number of custom reports and bridges. Your implementation will go more smoothly if the project managers acknowledge the need for bespoke code and work with the data-processing shop to establish policies and procedures to manage it.

There is a spectrum of risk in modifying the applications. Reporting and inquiry modules are at the low end. Even if they produce incorrect results, they have no impact on other processes. Open interfaces require somewhat more analysis, because they do bring new data into the system. Although you often need to write custom forms, and bridge and conversion processes that directly insert rows into Oracle tables, invalid data you introduce in this way can affect other modules. Directly updating data in Oracle tables—and especially deleting rows—offers the most risk. Before writing scripts or forms that directly update Oracle's tables, you need to thoroughly analyze the native Oracle processes that create, reference, and further process the row.

There are circumstances that justify every one of these types of modification. They require an appropriate level of analysis, familiarity with Oracle's implementation tools and the Oracle EBS architecture, and testing commensurate with the level of risk involved. Analyzing and designing custom code is one of the best uses for consultants on an Oracle EBS project.

Development methodologies and disciplines are just as important for an Oracle EBS implementation as for locally written systems. The forms that testing, configuration management, and documentation take are somewhat different, but their importance is in no way diminished.

The open design of the Oracle E-Business Suite, the accessibility of the code, and the top-to-bottom integration of Oracle's technology stack tremendously enhance their value to you. Not only do you acquire the vast majority of features that your company needs with the price of purchase, you also get the industry's best architecture, tools, and resources for extending and molding what you have purchased to meet your exact requirements.

CHAPTER
23

Project Organization
and Management

mplementation of an enterprise resource planning product such as Oracle E-Business Suite is different from software development and implementation. The central task, coming up with reliable software, is accomplished through your selection of Oracle EBS. With the major issue of writing the application laid to rest, the implementation manager is left with a large number of smaller but still significant tasks: installing, configuring, testing, and maintaining the applications.

Functional users, often without much data-processing experience, lead or play a dominant role in an EBS implementation. Success depends on their extended teams. On the users' side, their role extends far into each of the affected functional areas. On the technical side, it usually reaches beyond the data-processing developers, systems experts, database experts, and communications experts to include outside consultants and vendor technical support. Most users still have their assigned jobs to do; thus they participate less than full-time. The project manager's task is to earn their goodwill, craft a mutually agreed-upon plan, and provide the team with the direction and support it needs to succeed.

Tasks in an Oracle EBS implementation are less dependent on one another than in a custom-developed system. The code Oracle delivers will be sufficient to support setting parameters, installing networks and clients, writing custom (bespoke) extensions to the system, and developing business procedures, test scenarios, and training materials. With some restrictions, these tasks can proceed in parallel. Unlike the case in custom development projects, it is usually resource constraints, not scheduling dependencies, that are the limitation.

TIP
Another limiting factor in an EBS implementation is experienced people—those who can effectively combine knowledge of your business, Oracle EBS, and programming methods in an Oracle environment. Scheduling dependencies and critical-path management are seldom major issues. Estimate the complexity of the modules in your particular case and use that complexity factor in staff planning.

Oracle Software as a Step Toward Corporate Maturity

The move to Oracle often coincides with a critical growth phase in companies with a billion dollars or less in sales. Young companies are often built around personalities and have limited need for systems and written procedures as long as the founding experts are available to answer questions as they arise.

The personality model stretches thin with a few hundred employees. The experts cannot be everywhere at once, cannot train every new employee, and cannot wrap themselves around every new development in the business. They need to be free from tactical decisions so they can focus on strategic directions. Tactical decision making has to be systematized by written procedures, and policy built into enterprise software. Oracle EBS is the catalyst for both.

Placing a value on the software's ability to enforce policy and procedures prompts the question, "What are the policies and procedures?" Employees and managers of young companies often resist the imposition of such bureaucracy. Cut-and-dried systems appear to cut down the company's flexibility. Reducing decision making to paper and code can be a personal threat: It makes the company's veterans less essential to day-to-day operations. They might not appreciate that it is essential to the growth of the company to apply their knowledge at a strategic instead of a tactical level.

Implementing the E-Business Suite represents an essential growth step. A foundation of sound systems must underlie future growth—but the problem is getting there. The project manager will find that the small circle of company veterans whose knowledge and support are crucial to success are, at the very least, highly occupied with operational issues. At worst, they might be indifferent to the project in the first place. Moreover, their lean staff usually cannot afford to lend people to the Oracle project.

Smaller companies are also characterized by some significant strengths: They are nimble and enthusiastic, and tend to make decisions quickly. Their lack of bureaucracy can be a decided virtue, with no organizational hierarchy to distance the EBS implementation team from the functional users. Certain critical success factors, applicable to all EBS installations, are especially important to managers in a younger, growing company:

- The executive sponsor—who is often fairly accessible in a company of this size—and the steering committee have to show visible support for the project.

- Management and data-processing methodologies must be simple enough for the in-house client to appreciate and understand.

- Each individual on the management information systems (MIS) team must be strong enough to earn the respect of his or her functional counterpart. Success will depend on personal relationships.

- The strongest functional people need to be named super users to define how the EBS applications will work in their areas.

- The super users' time must be respected. Most super users have two jobs: running the company and setting up Oracle. The MIS department and outside implementers must do their homework before any meeting and relieve the super users of as many writing, testing, and other functional-area tasks as possible.

When all is said and done, implementations at young, growing companies can offer the greatest satisfaction to the Oracle project team. The flexibility of such organizations ensures that the talent of all team members will be used to the maximum extent; they will grow outside their assigned areas and be visibly associated with the success of the organization.

Project-Management Software Versus Spreadsheets

When the data-processing department takes the lead, its first mistake is often to see the project-management job as a technical rather than a management challenge. Project management deserves tools appropriate to the task and to the sophistication of the broader team, but not just software tools for their own sake. Applying project-management software such as Microsoft Project to an Oracle EBS implementation without a commitment to the associated management disciplines is a misuse of technology. The best tools are those with which the project manager is comfortable, even if they are as simple as spreadsheets.

Critical-path scheduling is a key design feature of project-management tools. You enter an elaborate definition of the tasks to be done, the ways in which the tasks depend on one another, and the resources available to do them. The project-management software uses this information to compute when the project will be complete, on the basis of the given assumptions and how busy each resource will be at each point in the project.

Project-management tools depend for their success on several assumptions, most of which are met in prosaic projects such as home construction, but few of which are consistently met in an EBS project. Among the assumptions built into a critical-path-scheduling package are the following:

■ **Tasks are well defined.** This works in construction: experience is a good indicator of how many resources and how much time it will take to roof a house. It is much harder to determine how long it will take a committee to decide on a chart-of-accounts structure, or how many people are needed to clean up a legacy vendor file, or how much work it will take to normalize the legacy bills of material.

■ **Task sequencing is a limiting factor.** In home construction, the foundation must precede the framing, which must precede plumbing and electrical wiring, which must precede drywall, which must precede painting, and so forth. A separate type of worker does each task. However, in the E-Business Suite there are many more things that can be done in parallel, and each EBS implementer is generally versatile enough to handle multiple tasks. Although there will be dependencies, the lack of a particular resource is much less often a limiting factor than is a shortage of total resources.

■ **The project plan is updated frequently.** Project-management systems are built to provide management information. They assume that you can and will adjust the schedule periodically to reflect progress to date and revised estimates of work remaining to completion. A construction-project manager cannot afford self-deception. Even if it means acknowledging that the project is behind schedule, he or she cannot afford to have roofers show up when there are no rafters to nail shingles to; however, EBS projects admit of more self-deception. Regardless of the schedule, most of the staff members on the project will be flexible enough that they will find something to do. It is possible to avoid updating the plan until it confronts the reality of cutover, which includes fixing travel schedules for the training-and-implementation team.

In practice, project-management systems often turn out to be no more than devices to develop Gantt charts, which represent early hopes rather than present reality. If you are going to use project-management software—which should be the case for an effort involving 10 or more people—be sure to commit the resources it takes to manage the software. That means defining and redefining tasks as the project evolves and, most important, updating the plan with actual data and accepting what the tool computes as an estimated completion date. As the plan is used, make sure it is distributed widely and frequently, so that the people on the ground can make operational decisions based on an appreciation of the wider context.

Spreadsheets are appropriate for projects too small to justify the effort involved in using project-management software. All you need to do is identify the tasks to be done, estimate how long each will take, and assign someone to do the work. These are essential first steps in any system. Use the spreadsheet to total the work assigned to each individual and make sure there are enough people to do the job. If there are no major dependencies among the tasks, it might be all the management information you need.

Update the spreadsheet periodically, reducing the figures to reflect work actually performed, and recompute the amount remaining. This is easy enough to do, and it will accurately reflect the impact of decisions that are not made and tasks that go over budget. Replanning to move the tasks that have missed their deadlines should prompt serious analysis of the reasons for the change. Otherwise, replanning can become endemic, and the project will either gradually delay the go-live date or will shorten or skip some tasks (the user-acceptance test is a favorite for squeezing).

Using any project-management tool at all is a hard enough discipline. The project is better served with a simple tool used well than a sophisticated tool used haphazardly. In any case, simple tools are the best place to start. However, with the low cost and high availability of Microsoft Project, if it is there, use it. It is worth expending the small effort at the beginning of the project to avoid being harnessed to the labor-intensive plan updates of a spreadsheet system.

Developing the Project Plan

Any project plan, whatever the tool, is based on a *work-breakdown structure* (WBS). The rest of the functionality of the tool builds on the WBS, and the success of the plan depends on being realistic on the number of tasks and the length of time each will take. The steps for developing a WBS are as follows:

1. Outline high-level tasks straight into the planning tool. Include external tasks even if they are not part of the budget. Typical external tasks are installing computers, upgrading networks, putting browsers on desktops, conducting company reorganizations, and developing strategic business decisions. It would be useful to do a first draft and then take it to a workshop of the relevant team leaders to expand. You need input on solution architecture, technical architecture, functional configuration, development, user involvement, training, cutover, legacy systems, change management, and project management.

2. Keep reworking the outline until there is consensus among the business and technical leaders that it represents the tasks to be done. You might have to agree on which of several valid ways is best for structuring a WBS for a project. For example, you can choose between defining similar tasks for your different locations and putting all your locations under each task.

3. Use the project-planning tool to do resource loading and estimating. Figure 23-1 shows an excerpt from a project plan in a spreadsheet. The outline structure, indicated by indentation, is carried over from the word-processor outline. The number of days to be spent by the people in the project budget (the PW and Prog columns) is shown against each task. Other resources—in this case, user personnel who are outside the budget—are shown as notes. Project management needs a view of the project that covers resources beyond its control that nevertheless are essential to the schedule.

The computed duration of the effort shown in Figure 23-1 would be about 1.4 months, a figure obtained by dividing the greatest amount of work (27 days, by the programmer) by the work days per month (20). Such a figure typically would be about right for a bottom-up budget spreadsheet such as this. It usually works out that the individual task estimates, such as three days to define depreciation methods to Oracle, are high. However, it all works out because the excess time is eaten up by unforeseen tasks and the unbudgeted overhead costs of meetings and project coordination. If you use a simple task-estimating model to estimate the worker-days for a number of tasks, think carefully about overhead. There is often an overhead of 10–20 percent, made up of document and code reviews, system downtime and rebuild time, meetings, and training or coaching.

Task	Effort	Description	Days			
	Resource (initials or type)		PW	Prog	User	User Name
	Quantity of Resource	PW = Pete Prog = Sam or Carol	1	2		
1	Oracle Assets					
1.1	Assets Business Model					
1.2	Assets Mapping Leg. to Oracle					
1.3	Assets					
1.4	Oracle Assets Setup					
1.4.1	Asset Category Flexfield		2		2	Bobbie
1.4.2	Location Flexfield		2		2	Bobbie
1.4.3	Asset Key Flexfield		2		2	Bobbie
1.4.4	System Controls		1			
1.4.5	Locations	Develop spreadsheet of locations (or extract them from legacy); load to Oracle.		1	2	Bobbie
1.4.6	Asset Key Flexfields Combinations					
1.4.7	QuickCodes	Set up quick picks to use for manual entry of assets.	1		2	Bobbie
1.4.8	Fiscal Years		0.5		1	Bobbie
1.4.9	Calendars	Define the calendars over which items have been depreciated. These go back 30-40 years.	1		2	Bobbie
1.4.10	Journal Entry Sources	Done in GL.				
1.4.11	Journal Entry Categories	Done in GL.				
1.4.12	Book Controls		1			
1.4.13	Flexbuilder	Rules for automatically generating flexfields.	2		3	Bobbie
1.4.14	Depreciation Methods	Define methods to Oracle.	3		5	Bobbie
1.4.15	Depreciation Ceilings	Included in above.				
1.4.16	Investment Tax Credits	Included in above.				
1.4.17	Prorate Conventions	Included in above.				
1.4.18	Price Indexes	Don't use.				
1.4.19	Unit of Measure Classes	Use EA throughout.				
1.4.20	Units of Measure	Use EA throughout.				
1.4.21	Asset Categories		1		2	Bobbie
1.4.22	Financials Options					
1.5	Assets Scenario Development					
1.5.1	Develop asset scenarios.	Add assets, retire assets, adjust assets. Leases, expensed assets, capital assets, construction-in-process. Flow from FA through to GL, report from GL.	1		5	Bobbie
1.5.2	Test data to support scenarios.		0.5		2	Bobbie
1.6	Assets Conference Room Pilot I					
1.6.1	Set up (restore from clean setup).			1		
1.6.2	Run the scenarios.		1		3	Bobbie
1.7	Fixed Assets Conversion Dev.					
1.7.1	Map legacy asset fields to Oracle.			1	1	Bobbie
1.7.2	Write COBOL extract from MSA.			1	4	
1.7.3	Write Oracle Loader to staging table.			1		
1.7.4	Clean-up and Load	Write and test scripts to systematically clean up legacy data (duplicates, abbreviations, missing data, translations, etc.), and load to Mass Additions interface.		20	5	Bobbie
	TOTAL DAYS		20	27	43	

FIGURE 23-1. *Excerpt from a project-management spreadsheet*

Project Methodology

Implementing or upgrading your Oracle E-Business Suite requires a dedicated multidisciplinary team and a proven methodology. For projects of this nature, each big consulting firm follows its own methodology; Oracle has the Application Implementation Methodology (AIM) and, for upgrading, the EasiPath Migration Method.

The key phases for AIM are definition, operations analysis, solution design, build, transition, and production. The life-cycle methodology and documentation templates allow AIM to be a very useful tool for managing implementation projects successfully.

If your organization is considering an upgrade, the recommended methodology will be the EasiPath Migration Method, which differs from AIM in its simplified approach with four phases: migration assessment, update and test, transition, and production.

Oracle has adopted the new Oracle Unified Method (OUM) as a single integrated method to support the entire Oracle ecosystem across the complete suite of Oracle products. It supports current methods such as AIM, the EasiPath Migration Method, Accelerator for Business Flows (ABF) and Siebel, which makes for an easier transition. Taking into consideration that Oracle has been acquiring many companies in the past years, and with them their many methods and products—along with the legacy methods that existed before the acquisitions—it was necessary to provide a unique dictionary. OUM provides a common language across the entire Oracle ecosystem. While this seems like a very basic benefit, the value that it engenders is quite profound, especially with respect to the efficiency and interoperability of implementation teams. This common language helps to reduce the confusion that Oracle customers might experience if different methods were used to implement different portions of their Oracle software. OUM's common language allows customers to more effectively converse with their implementation teams and increases their level of comfort in understanding the progress and status of their projects. Also, by establishing this common framework and language, OUM allows Oracle to more readily accommodate and integrate acquisitions as they happen.

OUM also supports Oracle Fusion Technology Foundation—it has been built on a foundation of tasks that support the implementation of Oracle's Fusion Middleware and Fusion Technology, so it is "Fusion ready."

OUM is independent of any product release. The method does not have specific product information, templates, or samples; the guidance and templates are adaptable to the complete Oracle ecosystem.

This methodology provides a comprehensive toolkit, including:

- **Overview material** The overview shows OUM's approach to IT projects, including the industry standards upon which OUM is based.

- **Guidelines** Phase, process, task, role, and work-product guidelines cover every aspect of an Oracle-based business solution.

- **Templates** Templates enable fast and easy creation of high-quality work products.

- **Tailored work-breakdown structure** These standards enable an easy start in managing your project.

If your organization decides to leverage the Oracle Unified Method, you will be taking advantage of the methodology for a clear definition of the business scope control and business understanding. Statistically, success is improbable in more than half of IT projects, because of poor requirement analysis, which leads to a failure right from the start. If you can start with a

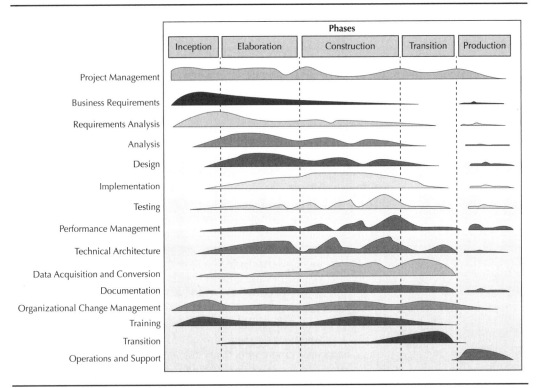

FIGURE 23-2.   *Oracle Unified Method guidelines*

solid scope and requirements planning, it establishes a clear connection between the business case, project goals, and project outcome.

Oracle E-Business Suite has many changes from prior versions. Since an implementation or upgrade project will include a multidisciplinary team, OUM provides a certain flexibility in allowing you to combine activities and tasks in different ways.

Another advantage of OUM is the iterative approach that incorporates testing and validation throughout the life cycle, rather than testing for quality only at the end of the project. This iterative approach reduces the project's risk. A key focus of each iteration in OUM is to identify and reduce the most significant project risks. This ensures that the most critical risks are addressed as early as possible in the project life cycle, which results in a measurable reduction of schedule and budget risks.

The Project Budget

A budget is a planning and measurement tool. It justifies the line items in your capital and operating budgets associated with the Oracle EBS project. The accuracy of your budget depends on several factors, including

- your level of experience with large data-processing projects, and especially package implementations;
- the level of confidence you require of the budget;

- the effort you invest in developing the budget; and
- the political realities of your company.

Your experience developing custom software will not apply directly to the Oracle E-Business Suite. The good news is that installing a package is cheaper and less risky than developing custom software. The bad news is that most of the tasks that remain are those involving users; these are even less predictable than software development. An experienced project leader can be of great help in developing a budget.

A budget is a tool for achieving your planning objectives, and planning objectives vary widely from organization to organization. Public-sector organizations tend to budget conservatively because it is difficult to get more if funds run out, and project managers tend to be measured by how well they succeed within the plan rather than whether the project is done in a cost-effective manner. Private-sector project managers might accept more risk in the hope of achieving a lower overall cost. Given two proposed budgets, a $3 million one with a 90 percent chance of success and a $1.2 million one with a 75 percent chance of success, a conservative agency would have more incentive to choose the former, whereas an aggressive company would more often choose the latter. Both approaches are valid; you need to know how much confidence is required in your environment.

The reliability of a budget reflects the effort you put into it. As always, it helps to have an experienced project manager familiar with the cost elements of a typical project. You can learn a lot by soliciting bids for the integration work from technical-services firms. Some companies need a detailed budget to justify the cost of implementing Oracle. Others see the conversion to Oracle as a strategic imperative and commit on the basis of a high-level estimate. The amount you want to invest to achieve an acceptably accurate budget depends on your situation.

The best approach would be to recognize the unpredictability of the process and budget incrementally by six-month periods, basing each step on the results and findings of the one before. However, most organizations do annual budgets and fix them a few months before the budget year. The Oracle project manager's strategy is usually to build a case for the maximum budget that will not kill the project. Few projects wind up giving money back; users always come up with out-of-scope needs—such as custom reports, Internet access, and so on—that truly are worth doing and manage to take up any slack in the budget.

The planning horizon for EBS projects is quite short. It is difficult to predict what people will be doing even six months in the future. It is important to apply actual figures to the schedule and budget spreadsheet at least monthly, to maintain an up-to-date estimate to completion. Expect this figure to change significantly as you learn more about the project. The most enlightened management approach is to be open about how much is unknowable and to react quickly as more becomes known.

The ultimate questions are, How much it will cost? and, How long it will take? The answers depend on many factors; among them are the amount of conversion and customization necessary, the company's ability to make decisions, the data-processing department's facility with Oracle, and the general level of talent among the business and data-processing staff. With all those caveats, you should start with an expectation that a $1 billion company will take at least four staff months of the functional-area users' time and four months of consultant time per package. Start with an estimate of $100,000 to $400,000 per package if you are using consultants.

The best average is six months' calendar time from when the team is in place until the first group of applications goes into production. Companies and packages are highly variable, however. The authors of this book have experience with packages being installed in as little as two months with little outside help and, on the other side, with a six-package EBS suite for a domestic company with two locations taking more than $20,000,000 and more than two years using a Big Five integrator. There is no substitute for doing your own planning.

The Project-Management Hierarchy

E-Business Suite software implementations apply data-processing equipment and disciplines to business requirements. Who should manage the effort—the business-area owners of the requirement or the MIS owners of the methodologies to apply the solution? Either approach can be successful. The key factor is that the technical and functional people have to work as a team, regardless of who is in charge.

Rarely is there a natural project leader within the company who has business experience as well as experience processing data and installing packaged software. There are several alternatives when no natural leader is apparent:

- Put the best person within the company in charge, trusting that he or she will learn on the job.
- Hire someone who has managed integration before.
- Entrust an integrator with project-management responsibility.

Using somebody within the company has major advantages. A solid manager, with knowledge of the business and the trust of people within the company, will usually learn enough to manage an integration project. This manager should usually plan to engage consultants to bring the needed functional-area and project-management expertise. However, it is important that the designated manager understand implementation of enterprise resource planning systems.

Hiring an experienced manager can be risky. It is difficult to learn a new business and a new company. Moreover, a new hire is likely to lack either management experience or detailed product knowledge; it is difficult for a candidate to have learned both on one project. Hiring to fill the project-management role involves risk, but it makes sense when there is no strong manager available internally.

It is tempting to offload the heavy responsibility onto someone who has done it before, such as a partner in an integration company, creating a reporting structure like the one shown in Figure 23-3. This alternative carries risks as well. It isolates company management from intimate familiarity with the project. It also creates a potential conflict of interest. The systems integrator might be tempted to let his or her own corporate goals, such as training new employees, overshadow the client's interest. Placing responsibility with an outside firm requires a good management-oversight plan.

In fact, there is no way for a company to totally pass off project responsibility to an outsider, whether that person is a new hire or an integrator. It can hire or contract for the functional, technical, and project-management skills needed to make the project succeed, but applications software invariably defines the way the business works, and management has to be closely involved in those decisions.

As noted, EBS implementation is really an exercise in management. The project manager has to get cooperation from an extremely broad group of people inside and outside the company. The manager needs to establish a vision and generate commitment if that critical part-time involvement is to materialize. The people behind the decision to use Oracle need to follow it through implementation.

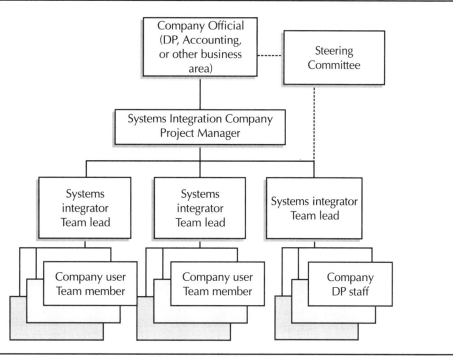

FIGURE 23-3.   *A systems-integrator management model*

Team Formation

The implementation team is a two-headed creature. If a functional-area person chairs it, the deputy should be from data processing. If a business-savvy data-processing manager leads the effort, the second-in-command has to be from the business area. Balance is critical. Because integration is one of the major benefits of a packaged solution, most implementations involve more than one package. Figure 23-4 shows a typical project organization for a 5,000-employee, billion-dollar corporation.

Your corporate officer in charge of an Oracle EBS project, often called the executive sponsor, is typically one of the three top people in the financial organization, with a title such as controller, chief financial officer, or director of finance. Chief operating officer and director of manufacturing are common titles for the nominee to head manufacturing and distribution implementations. The data-processing counterpart is either the chief information officer/director of data processing or a direct report to that position. It is important that these leaders carry enough rank to command resources and force decisions within the company, and that the two of them be of more or less equal rank.

The company project manager needs knowledge to act with authority. In addition to the MIS staff, it helps to have an experienced consultant aid with budgeting, staffing, scheduling, and the trade-offs between customizing the software and modifying business procedures.

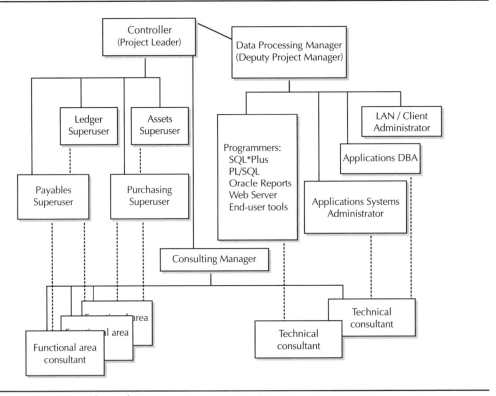

FIGURE 23-4.   *Typical Oracle-project team organization*

Functional-Team Leads

Few companies have enough staff to name dedicated team leads in each functional area. The work of the company must go on as Oracle is installed. The most common arrangement is for super users in each area to commit half their time to Oracle setup. The super users attend Oracle classes, experiment with the Demo instance of the Oracle products, work closely with on-site consultants, act as the representatives of their departments, research using My Oracle Support (formerly known as Metalink), and coordinate with other area super users. These super users must be well chosen; they drive the project and must be happy to be the owners of the process.

There is no substitute for experience. It is much more efficient to engage people who have worked with the Oracle E-Business Suite before than to learn the system through trial and error. A company can use business-area employees with Oracle experience, data-processing analysts with that experience, or outsiders. The need is for highly talented people over a short period of time—a definition that favors consultants. The organization chart shown in Figure 23-4 includes consultants in the project-team structure.

Database Administrator

Management information systems will bring technical talent to the team. The most obvious requirements are for programmers, a systems administrator, LAN and desktop experts, and a database administrator. Equally important and often overlooked are development disciplines: testing, configuration management, security administration, and continuity of operations are vitally important to the success of Oracle EBS projects. Many MIS shops have to improve their maturity levels in these areas to support the E-Business Suite.

An *EBS DBA* is an Oracle database administrator who is familiar with the special requirements of Oracle EBS. The DBA needs to be familiar with what is known as the Application Object Library, or Applications Foundation. It is the way Oracle has integrated proprietary C-language routines with programs written in the Forms, Reports, and PL/SQL development tools. Like any other application software, Oracle EBS applications need to be patched and upgraded at regular intervals; the DBA is required to understand patching procedure and ensure proper backup of the instance. Multilanguage Support has increased the responsibilities on the DBA.

A capable Oracle DBA on your staff can quickly absorb the EBS applications from a knowledgeable consultant. Technology transfer works well at the technical level.

TIP
The DBA's job is to create an environment in which other people can be successful; not one in which nothing ever goes wrong. An occasional failure is the price of success. The project manager must ensure that the developers have enough access and resources to get their job done. An overly controlling DBA, in eliminating personal risk, can doom a project.

Programmers

Not all Oracle developers are Oracle EBS developers. They might be familiar with the tools for building the customizations, but not know how to implement their changes within the application. The team can be staffed with programmers for Oracle Reports and PL/SQL who have no EBS experience. You will get better results if you support them with a consultant or senior programmer with experience writing code in an EBS environment.

The technology of Oracle EBS is moving towards the Oracle Application Framework (OAF) or HTML pages, gradually replacing all the Oracle Forms technology with this new technology. OAF is a model-view-controller framework built using Java EE technologies for application development within the Oracle E-Business Suite. The Oracle EBS developers have to learn this new tool in order to customize or extend the application.

The programming team as a group will be most effective with the following types of expertise:

Necessary

- Host operating systems: Unix, NT, Linux, or mainframe
- Oracle Forms and Reports
- Oracle Application Framework
- SQL*Loader

- SQL*Plus
- PL/SQL for Reports, Forms, stored procedures, and database triggers
- Oracle EBS programming skills: Key and Descriptive Flexfields, report-parameter definition, Oracle Alerts, interface programming, and related skills
- Shell-language programming (Unix, NT, or mainframe)

Desirable

- Oracle Workflow, including Workflow Builder (this is becoming increasingly important)
- Editors and utilities; in Unix these include vi, sed, and sort
- Client operating systems: various flavors of Windows, Mac OS, Linux, and others
- Browsers: Mozilla Firefox or Internet Explorer
- LAN server software: Novell, NT, and others
- Local area networks
- Oracle Application Server
- Applicable end-user tools (Oracle Express, Business Objects, ODBC interfaces to spreadsheets, and third-party reporting tools)
- Applicable desktop software, including word-processor macros and templates, spreadsheet macros, and presentation packages (while not essential, these tools can greatly improve programmer productivity)
- Methodologies such as AIM/OUM or some kind of documentation templates

There is nothing unique about the programming tools used in the E-Business Suite. Oracle programmers can write interfaces and enhancements without special training. The requirements for specialized knowledge are as follows:

- It takes more programming talent to understand and modify complex programs such as those Oracle delivers in the E-Business Suite than to develop new programs.
- It takes detailed knowledge of the EBS modules to write specifications for programs that will interface to EBS tables and processes.
- Someone, not necessarily the programmer, must know how to bring custom code into the E-Business Suite.

Sources of Staffing

Oracle's success is reflected in the marketplace. Oracle people are hard to find, and Oracle EBS people doubly so. This presents problems in staffing with employees, and the supply-and-demand equation makes consultants expensive.

It is almost always most efficient to staff with fewer and better people. Communication difficulties increase factorially with the growth of your team's size. It is easier to know who is responsible for each task on a small team, and to assess each individual's contribution. As every MIS manager knows, a good programmer can be 10 times as productive as a mediocre one.

The issue is where to find the good people. Do not plan on staffing an international implementation or international rollout without talking to somebody who understands the requirements of the countries under consideration.

Finding good employees is a matter of paying them and giving them incentives. The first issue is salary. You need to be sure your human-resources department's salary structures reflect the realities of the marketplace. Noncash incentives are important in hiring and especially in keeping your staff. Professionals want to be respected, and they want to work on successful projects. The job you do in managing the implementation will have a strong bearing on your employee retention.

There are similar issues in assigning strong people from within the business to the Oracle project. They become attractive to other companies—especially consulting firms—as they gain Oracle experience. The best place to look for functional-area talent is within your company, but you need to be willing to recognize the market value of the Oracle skills they will gain on the project.

Most projects need some outside consulting support. Here are the usual sources:

- Oracle Consulting Services

- Technical-services firms (such as Capgemini, Ernst & Young)

- Accounting firms (such as PriceWaterhouseCoopers)

- Regional technical-services firms (such as CMSI or Noblestar)

- Oracle EBS implementation specialty firms (such as IT Convergence, Allen-Sauer Consulting, Margaret Coleman Consulting, Seibert & Costantino, or Cornerstone Systems), and independent consultants

The larger firms tend to charge higher hourly rates for a given level of experience. The rates can be justified by the completeness of their offering: extensive marketing support prior to the engagement; experienced project management; and in the case of Oracle, outstanding training and a direct pipeline into the best sources of expertise.

There are many independent consultants, many of whom have worked for Oracle or one of the other integrators. These people are often talented individuals with good experience. They are a less expensive resource than consulting firms, but must be managed more closely. When it comes to the final push for the go-live date, particularly if that is a very tight deadline, you need to be sure that the whole team will pull as one and work the hours to get the job done. You need to recognize that independent consultants must feel a part of the team and that they are getting valuable experience. If there are niche skills to be learned, try to distribute these so you give appropriate incentives to all your consultants.

Smaller firms and independent consultants offer the most experience for the dollar. They are also somewhat harder to find. Whereas the larger firms will actively advertise and market to you, you might have to look to find small, new firms that are more focused on technology than marketing. You can go to Oracle's Web site (www.oracle.com) and search its lists of business partners. Try the search engines, using the keywords "Oracle" and "EBS." Alternatively, you can contact the Oracle Applications Users Group (c/o Meeting Expectations in Atlanta, www.oaug .org, or phone 404-240-0897) to find a local users-group chapter and ask informally for recommendations. You can also ask through the local chapter of the Independent Oracle Users Group, at www.ioug.org, or phone (312) 245-1579.

Choose a consulting firm appropriate to the size of your business and a consulting team appropriate to the size of your project. An inappropriately large firm or team can swamp a project by outnumbering and overwhelming the company employees assigned to the project, or reporting at a level above the decision makers within your company. Conversely, too small a firm might be unable to bring in additional resources when they are needed and might be unable to work essential communications channels within your company because it reports at too low a level in your management hierarchy. Your project manager as well as your programmers will benefit from outside advice. Your organizational structure might almost require that it come from different people.

In general, larger firms such as General Electric use larger integrators such as Oracle Consulting Services; smaller enterprises use regional firms and independent consultants. Your business should be significant enough to the consulting firm that they cannot risk giving you poor service.

Staff Size

Staff size depends initially on the scope of the project. Is it local or global? Are business processes to be changed and documented? Is it a new start-up or will it affect thousands of existing users? How tight is the go-live deadline? As a part of these scoping decisions, each company has to evaluate the trade-offs involved in project-staff size, some of which are listed in Table 23-1.

Regardless of its eventual size, a project team should grow incrementally. It is important for a core group to establish the project plan, environment, and methodologies before the main cadre comes on board. Overstaffing, evidenced by short workdays and a lack of a sense of urgency, makes project members feel superfluous and undermines their commitment. A team working overtime is more effective and certainly cheaper than an underworked one, but working overtime for too long will burn out the team members. Be realistic about the project plan so that when each group of new starters joins, you have work waiting for them to start. A couple of slack weeks at the beginning of a project assignment for anyone makes it more difficult for them to respond to urgency later with the commitment you would like.

Advantages of a Larger Staff	Advantages of a Smaller Staff
Opportunity costs. Quicker implementation means quicker realization of benefits.	Cost. Greater use out of employed staff and reduced use of consultants keeps costs down.
Operational impact. More outside staff means less disruption to continuing business operations.	Training. More employee participation means more knowledge transfer. An employed staff gains and retains Oracle knowledge.
Business tempo. You can demonstrate results within a matter of months of the commitment to Oracle.	Control. Intimate involvement in implementation decisions ensures that setup is appropriate to the company.
Opportunity to introduce new ideas. Outside staff come in with a different vision and can demonstrate how alternative procedures can benefit.	Esprit. Employees enjoy being empowered to define business procedures that affect them and playing significant roles in a major team effort.

TABLE 23-1. *Advantages of different project-staff sizes*

Types of Contracts

Cost and risk are key issues in contracting. What will the project cost, and who bears the risk? There are several risks in an EBS implementation. The most obvious is that the implementation is never completed. Your company spends money for the software, implementation services, and its own staff—and your implementation team can never bring the software to the point of being installed. The other risk is that the business suffers damage because you have not set the software up correctly.

It is tempting to try to push the risk onto a contractor, the possessor of expert knowledge in Oracle EBS, through a fixed-price contract. Oracle, its competitors (such as SAP and Microsoft), and major integrators are moving in that direction. They are all developing ways to make package implementation a more straightforward process. The OUM used by Oracle Consulting Services includes a project plan and techniques for managing setup, conversion, training, and all other steps in an implementation. The Workflow-based Application Implementation Wizard product leads you and your contractor together through the setup process. Oracle has products that handle data mapping for conversion and bridging.

It is possible for contractors to deliver all the components of a working system on a fixed-price basis: software installation, setups, conversion programs, bridges, training, and user documentation. However, they are reluctant to guarantee that it will work. The contractor may not always be able to prevent or offset failures on your part. Success depends on your ability as the client to define your business processes, test the system, absorb training, and operate the system. The contractor's technical knowledge might be essential to success, but it cannot guarantee success.

Vendors that do offer fixed-price contracts for Oracle EBS implementations usually word them in such a way that the client still bears the ultimate risk. The scope of the contract may extend through setup but stop short of cutover. It will not include postcutover support. The contract will specify a maximum number of reports to be modified. The terms will require that your key people be available to meet with their team for a given number of hours within a specified number of days of contract start. The terms are such that only a well-organized company can realistically meet them. However, a strong company that appreciates the risks will usually opt for a time-and-materials arrangement to save money.

You usually do best to recognize the need for a partnership between you and the contractor and to contract the work on a time-and-materials basis. Time-and-materials contracts can be structured to foster partnership. The client pays for services as they are needed, and the contractor serves at the convenience of the client. The contractor works knowing that it will be replaced if it is not delivering value.

You need to manage a time-and-materials contract closely to ensure that it does not get away from you. The data-processing press is full of horror stories about out-of-control projects in which the client no longer knows what is happening with a project, is bleeding money to a consulting firm, and is scared or unable to rein in the contractor. The following are some strategies to retain control:

1. Although a contractor may provide most of the project-management expertise, make sure that the de facto project manager is a company employee, not a consultant.

2. Develop a detailed project plan, with a work-breakdown structure and budget. Have the contractor report progress against the budget. Make sure there is an employee or independent outsider knowledgeable enough to assess the contractor's justification of budget overruns and slippages. Dedicate the resources it takes to make effective use of project-management software.

3. Define and enforce data-processing methodologies. Keep track of all contractor work products, so that in the worst case they can be given to another contractor.

4. Use two or more consulting firms, or incorporate independent consultants into the team, to obtain the benefit of independent points of view. Becoming dependent on a single source makes you vulnerable. No company owns any "magic bullet" technology without which other project members would be ineffective. Professional respect—not company loyalty—is the essential bond among members of your team.

5. Have the consulting firm staff up gradually. Make sure that you, the client, control when each new member joins the team and that you understand what he or she will be doing. Only bring developers on board when there are enough well-defined specifications to keep them working at full speed. If they start when there is only a sporadic flow of work and they are working under full capacity, it will be difficult to increase their productivity later—the expectation is set. If you have consultants from out of town, try to accommodate flexible working hours such as a four-day working week. That way the consultants can balance their personal and professional lives; at the end you get better results.

6. Staff the project with employees to the greatest possible extent to ensure that they learn the system for which they will be responsible and that the solution is based on employees' knowledge of the business rather than consultants' secondhand understanding. Keep reviewing their positions with those employees so they have a chance to raise concerns with you in time for you to respond (for example, if there is insufficient knowledge transfer). Their commitment is crucial to the smooth implementation of the project.

7. To the extent that you can, use consultants for advice and have employees do the work. This is especially important in the functional areas. After the consultants leave, somebody has to understand why the system is set up as it is.

8. Have team-leader and team meetings at least once a week to cascade news about progress and issues. Ensure that all the team members document their work. Because of their productivity, independent consultants usually offer good value as developers. You can afford to let outsiders do more in the realm of programming, so long as you can maintain what they produce. This means you need to plan knowledge transfer into their timescales and have an internal development-and-maintenance team skilled up to receive the consultants' creations.

9. Schedule deliverables frequently enough that the contractor has to show demonstrable progress. Look behind claims of a successful test phase to see what percentage of the functionality was actually tested. Note what issues are being carried forward into the next phase and ensure that the project plan reflects that.

Project Phasing

Most Oracle EBS projects involve more than one module. There is often a question of whether to cut them all over at one time—a "big-bang" conversion—or to convert in phases. There is no preferred approach, only a set of pros and cons that will vary from company to company. However, do not go for the big-bang approach without evaluating all the pros and cons of an implementation (see Table 23-2). Understand the critical success factors for your implementation and ensure that risk is minimized as much as possible.

Advantages of a Big-Bang Conversion	Advantages of a Phased Conversion
Less wasted effort. Converting all at once eliminates the need for temporary interfaces to the legacy system and puts all testing and cutover processing into one conversion.	Lower risk. There is less impact on MIS and the company at cutover.
Quicker total implementation. The full benefits of Oracle are available earlier.	Steady management attention. A phased plan can show progress every four months, building confidence along the way.
Better integration. Thinking through all system requirements at once eliminates re-engineering in later project phases.	Full testing. It is easier to test with a limited set of logic paths.
	Quick stabilization. The first packages in a phased implementation (General Ledger and Fixed Assets) typically affect few users. The impact of a rocky conversion is localized, and can be corrected before moving on.
	Lower overall cost. A longer implementation schedule means employees can shoulder more of the work.

TABLE 23-2.   *Advantages of different approaches to conversion to EBS*

Now that Multi-Org has to be setup for every Oracle implementation, the first step a manager should take is to define the multiple-organization structure and the ledger structure. Definition of the multiple-organization structure is irreversible and impacts all the modules. If you implement using a phased approach, your initial multiple-organization setup will impact the future phases. Initially, you should have a focused one- or two-week session to understand the functional architecture of the implementation and freeze that as early as possible. Involve consultants from finance, manufacturing, the supply chain, and customer relationship management in that session if possible. During that process, confirm how languages will be used and which country-specific globalizations and localizations are required. This will also be an opportunity to determine the requirement for accounting methods (generally accepted accounting principles, International Financial Reporting Standards) and reporting currencies.

Managing Your Relationship with Oracle

Oracle has a vested interest in your success. A successful customer is an ongoing source of business and of positive referrals. Just as Oracle will continue to sell you on the value of its new products, you need to sell Oracle on your value as a customer. Customers who develop a genuine partnership with Oracle have more say in how the products evolve, early access to products as beta testers, and more leverage in picking the Oracle people to provide them with support.

Oracle Releases and Versions

The Oracle products continue to improve over time. It is to Oracle's benefit that you continue to invest the time it takes to stay up to date. Oracle can provide better technical support to users of current-release software. Better support means that you are more likely to be pleased with the product—and more likely to buy more Oracle software.

Oracle assigns release numbers to the E-Business Suite taken as a whole and to each application individually. The scheme is universal; it also applies to the Oracle tools in which the EBS applications are implemented, the Oracle database on which they run, the operating systems that run the databases, and the hardware that runs the operating systems.

A software release is a set of modules proven to work together by design and testing. In the E-Business Suite it is identified by a triple-segmented number, such as 12.1.3. The first number represents a major change in functionality, with new screens, reference manuals, training materials, and table structures. The second number, called a *dot-point release*, represents a smaller increment in design, such as the introduction of a few new programs, without any profound change to the architecture. The third number identifies a maintenance release. The higher the third digit, the more bugs it fixes in the base release. Refer to My Oracle Support (formerly known as Metalink) for the latest details about new releases.

Each release of each application, and thus of the Oracle Applications, is certified to work on one or more releases of the Oracle relational database management system (RDBMS). The EBS applications exploit new database functionality as it comes out, and they depend on fixes to the RDBMS. The RDBMS in turn has a release-level dependency on the host operating systems that support it. Newer releases of the RDBMS require newer operating-system releases.

The interdependencies among the release levels of the operating systems (server and client), the RDBMS, and the EBS applications often force a stepwise upgrade path. Users who fall well behind might be forced into interim upgrades to achieve their final goal. Fortunately, the E-Business Suite is always available on at least two versions of the RDBMS, and an RDBMS version is usually proven on more than one release of the operating system. However, the best practice is to remain current within the past year. A shop should plan to hit all major EBS release levels (10, 11, 12 . . .), which come out every two years or so. Users who fall too far behind sometimes find it easier to reimplement, treating their old installation as a legacy system, than to go through an extended stepwise upgrade process. Reimplementation gives an opportunity to move the business-process design forward (including revisiting Key Flexfield definitions).

Oracle's customers are responsible for upgrading the operating system and the RDBMS to the version levels required to install the delivered version of the E-Business Suite. It is a job for the DBA or a consultant filling the DBA role. The entire combination of Oracle E-Business Suite, RDBMS, and operating-system version must be certified by Oracle Support. The DBA keeps a log of software-upgrade activity to provide release-level information to Oracle Support when reporting problems.

Resolving Errors: Service Requests and Patches

Supporting its customers is one of Oracle's most challenging tasks. The channels through which the company delivers technical support are under constant reorganization, yet the process is never as responsive as customers would like. It is a tough job. The good news is that Oracle customer support is usually ranked best among the major software vendors.

Oracle has put a great deal of resources into modernizing its support arrangements and tools. The results are beneficial to Oracle and its customers. There is a Web site, My Oracle Support (http://support.oracle.com), on which Oracle publishes a great deal of support information: other people's service requests (SRs), notes, and documentation. This is freely available (to customers using an access code and a user log-in and password). By logging in to this resource, a project staff member can see whether anyone else has had a similar problem and what the solution was. Usually this provides enough information to allow the issue to be resolved without resorting to Oracle Support.

It is useful to note that Oracle employees have access through My Oracle Support to more information than does the public. It is quite common practice on projects to have at least a minimal involvement of Oracle Consulting Services, and this is one of the advantages such a practice brings. However, if no resolution is evident, the same site is used for logging SRs. You can enter an SR on the telephone, but the Internet is normally an easier route, as you can immediately cut and paste error messages or log files into the request, and it seems to receive very prompt intervention.

Oracle's help desk may resolve an SR by explaining how to use the native features of the package, providing a work-around for the bug or shortcoming, or changing the software to fix the problem. Oracle creates patches to fix bugs. A patch may affect any number of modules and may involve seed data within the database as well. Oracle usually has to apply the same correction in multiple release levels of the software and on multiple platforms. It is a major configuration-management issue for them. It is not cost effective to maintain an excessive number of back versions of the software. Oracle will often ask users to upgrade to a more current software release rather than commit Oracle resources to fix a bug in an old release.

There are also feasibility and compatibility issues that can prevent Oracle from backporting certain fixes to previous releases, in which case having the customer upgrade to a current certified combination of releases would be the solution.

NOTE
The certification matrixes can be found on My Oracle Support.

It is important to understand that patches do not come with ironclad guarantees. They are unit tested to make sure they fix the stated problems in the stated modules. Some patches do not apply to all users. For example, a patch that applies to a standard-costing inventory operation might induce errors in an average-costing shop. That is not a problem, so long as Oracle controls who uses the patch.

Oracle cannot regression test to make sure each patch does not create problems in other modules. That is the reason Oracle is reluctant to provide patches on a wholesale basis. Applying them willy-nilly often creates more problems than it solves, and the problems are even more difficult to resolve because the patched software no longer agrees with Oracle's baseline.

Certain patches have widespread applicability. Oracle periodically assembles the important ones into *mega-patches*, *Cumulative Collection Patches*, *Family Packs*, or *Mini Packs*, which it does subject to regression testing. It distributes these widely and incorporates them into new shipments of the software. They are often available on My Oracle Support. A mega-patch often implements the fixes that are being shipped in newer dot-point releases.

If you have multiple languages installed on your application's instance, you need each patch for each language, unless it is a system patch. Other-language patches are available a few days to a few weeks after the English-language patch is released. Your DBA and functional super user should evaluate the impact of applying the patches in English only without applying them in all the languages.

Managing Bug Fixes
Oracle takes seriously its responsibility for making its software work correctly. It is organized to support a mix of weak and strong customers. However, it is no secret that stronger customers,

those who earn the respect of the Oracle help desk by making good use of their time, are more satisfied with Oracle support. They generally have more success overall.

Chapter 22 recommends that you maintain logs of SRs you place with Oracle and patches you apply to fix problems. You need to actively manage your open issues, making sure that Oracle understands the priority of each reported problem. It is a relatively unusual occurrence to report an unknown bug to Oracle Support. In most cases, the problem has already been identified and corrected. When contacting support, it is important to be concise and do your own research first. Has your organization customized the process that is erroring? Has the process executed successfully in the past? Does the process error only in production, or on your test and development instances as well? You should always have the log file available, and the exact program name, executable, and version available.

Oracle's help desk is much more responsive when your DBA is able to define a problem precisely when reporting it. Compare these two reports. First:

```
The PO Print program ended abnormally with error ORA-1800, Format Error
```

Second:

```
Program POXPRPOP got error ORA 1800 when it was executed under Concurrent
Manager, where it was executed with the Unix command ar25runb PROG=POXPRPOP
VERSION=2.0b P_PO_NUM='123' COPIES=3 DESFORMAT=PSHPL.prt.
```

It executed successfully from the command line after the following parameter change:

```
DESFORMAT=vinprn01.
```

The first message does not provide Oracle much information to go on; their recommendation may be only a guess. The second definition of the same problem is much more likely to exactly match a known bug and bring an immediate, correct response. The difference is the DBA's ability to communicate with Oracle, which requires knowledge of the architecture of the applications.

One of the biggest solutions that Oracle has put together for client support is a free tool called Oracle E-Business Suite Diagnostic, available through My Oracle Support in the format of a patch. The objective of this tool is to ease the gathering and analysis of information from your EBS application when diagnosing an existing data issue, transactional problem, or setup error through a complete setup Responsibility. The good news is that out of the box, Oracle provides more than 100 diagnostic tests that do not have to be run by a technical resource or DBA. They are part of E-Business Suite and can be run by a super user, with no technical skill required. It will also allow resolving problems without the need to contact oracle support, in some occasions or reducing the resolution time providing the Oracle support engineer the right information by uploading the results directly into My Oracle Support.

TIP
The Oracle E-Business Suite Diagnostic tool does not alter the data or setup in your system—no updates, inserts, or deletes happen. Sensitive customer information is not collected or displayed. The diagnostic tool's results are organized in the following groups: Setup, Activity, Collection, and Functional.

You have no contractual responsibility to diagnose or fix Oracle's bugs. You will eventually get a resolution from Oracle even if you do nothing to help yourself. However, shops that take a more holistic view are usually more successful. Taking into account the time you will spend updating the SR that educates Oracle about your unique situation, the time you spend testing the solutions they propose, and the costs to your business of waiting for a solution, it makes business sense for you to invest some of your resources to help Oracle. Your DBA and programmers are familiar with the programming languages Oracle uses, and you have the source code for most modules. With four hours' work, a good programmer will be able to positively identify perhaps half of the bugs you experience, and will at a minimum be able to provide Oracle with detailed information about those he or she cannot find. You will have more success if you cast yourself as Oracle's partner in resolving problems.

Reference Sources for Oracle E-Business Suite

EBS implementers need an overwhelming number of reference materials to do their job. Every project needs a librarian to make sure the necessary materials are on hand. The following sections outline the materials that should be available through the library.

Oracle Corporation takes pains to ensure that documentation is easy to get. They distribute books, CD-ROMs, DVDs of documentation with the software. They sell and sometimes hand out the CD-ROMs, each of which includes a complete set of user documentation for the E-Business Suite.

Application User References

There is a set of reference documentation for each application. Depending on the complexity of the application, the documents run from one to four volumes. All of the product documentation is organized the same way. The later documentation generally places the chapters in this topical sequence:

- Setup
- Descriptions of major functions
- Reports
- Batch processes

It used to be that the topical essays gathered into one chapter at the end of the reference described the major functions, while the rest of the reference focused more narrowly on individual forms and reports. Now, the discussions of application logic have been moved to the chapters on setup and individual system functions. The new organization appears better adapted for delivery by an online help system.

Online delivery has many advantages besides cost. Documentation is easily shared. It does not get lost. It is easy to do a keyword search of one or more documents. The HTML versions of the documentation include links. You can integrate Oracle's documentation with your own. It is possible to produce hard-copy printouts of individual sections as needed. The major advantage of hard-copy references is that they are easier for reading long passages. In the final analysis, you might need only about two sets of the books for each application: one for the developers and another for the super users. Everybody else can work from the soft copies. The HTML and PDF document formats are so universal as to present no problem; you can probably assume that desktop users can read them.

AOL References

There are a number of reference manuals that describe the technical architecture underlying all the applications. These are included on the CD-ROM, or located at the E-Business Suite documentation library at http://docs.oracle.com, although the DBA and development shop will usually want to have hard copies. These manuals include the following:

- **Oracle E-Business Suite Installation Guide: Using Rapid Install** A roadmap for installing the E-Business Suite

- **Oracle E-Business Suite Upgrade Guide, Release 11i to 12.1.3** A roadmap for upgrading the E-Business Suite

- **Oracle E-Business Suite System Administrator's Guide—Configuration, Maintenance and Security** A guide to user and technical application management

- **Oracle E-Business Suite Flexfields Guide** A handbook on the structure and use of flexfields

- **Oracle E-Business Suite User's Guide** A manual on development and personalization of the user interface

- **Oracle Alert User's Guide** A guide on how to set up alerts

- **Oracle E-Business Suite Multiple Organizations Implementation Guide** An explanation of Multi-Org setup, including details of accounting and technical implementation

- **Oracle Common Application Calendar Implementation Guide** An explanation of details of calendar setup and technical implementation

- **Oracle E-Business Suite Developer's Guide** A set of standards for developers writing extensions to the EBS applications

- **Oracle Application Framework Personalization Guide** A set of standards for developers writing extensions to the E-Business Suite on OAF

- **Oracle E-Business Suite Integrated SOA Gateway Implementation Guide** A guide on how to integrate data into the EBS applications using Web services

- **Oracle Workflow Administrator's Guide** A manual on setting up and customizing workflows

Online Help Within the Applications

The E-Business Suite offers an online version of the reference manuals through Windows help. Users can add their own text to Oracle's context-sensitive help messages for the forms, regions, and fields in the system. Larger users might find this degree of customization worth the investment.

The best approach for smaller users is to develop a comprehensive user's guide in document format. Such a guide can lead users through all aspects of a transaction, which may thread through many screens. Typical transactions could be adding a new item or ordering from a new vendor. This guide can be delivered in document format via a file server or in HTML format over the intranet or Internet.

Custom help, however it is delivered, has to be included as part of the test plan. It usually points to the logic paths that should be included in test scenarios in the first place.

A new, effective method for training and providing sustainable help to end users is the delivery of content through Oracle User Productivity Kit. This tool is an easy-to-use platform for content development, deployment, and maintenance. One of the biggest challenges in an EBS implementation is the training and end-user adoption; Oracle User Productivity Kit can mitigate the risk through all phases of the project. The abilities to offer multiple learning methods, produce test scripts, and integrate them to the online help are key advantages to this product that maximize the effectiveness of reference manuals.

Application Technical References

Oracle has put a great deal of resources into modernizing their documentation. As a result, the documents formerly known as Technical Reference Manuals have been converted into electronic Technical Reference Manuals, which are publicly available at http://etrm.oracle.com. These are an essential part of the development team's arsenal, and are inevitably sought after. Having them easily available electronically with a robust search engine and categorized by object type is certainly a significant benefit.

The manuals describe the databases and modules: forms, reports, packaged procedures, and compiled C code. Every shop should have copies of the technical references. Even users who have no intention of modifying the delivered code need them as an aid in debugging and understanding how an application works.

The Technical Reference Manuals all follow the same outline:

- A catalog of the modules within the application.

- Descriptions of the major tables, views, concurrent programs, lookup types, and workflow events within the system. The reference also shows the Oracle-created indexes on each table and the Oracle sequence (if any) used to generate the primary key of the table.

- Entity-relationship diagrams showing the foreign-key relationships among tables supporting the major functions within the application. This is essential knowledge for anyone needing to write reports or customizations.

The Technical References are the key that relates what a user sees on screen to the underlying Oracle objects. The user sees the external name of a form in its header; the Technical Reference provides the name of the form as found in the forms subdirectory. The user sees a record within a block on the form; the Technical Reference gives the name of the table.

TIP
The Examine and About This Record functions on the application menu are a quick way to find the name of the current table and column; however, they are normally views created specifically for use by the forms. With the introduction of many Oracle Application Framework (OAF) screens, there is an option within the About This Page section that mimics the Examine functionality for HTML pages. In order to enable the record history in Oracle EBS, it is necessary to enable a system parameter that can be found at My Oracle Support.

Another documentation tool that Oracle provides with E-Business Suite is called the Oracle Integration Repository. It is a compilation of information about the numerous interface endpoints exposed by Oracle applications. It provides a complete catalog of Oracle E-Business Suite's business interfaces and a comprehensive view of the interface mechanisms available. You can use this tool to easily discover and deploy the appropriate business interface from the catalog for integration with any system, application, or business partner. Some of the features of this API documentation are

- a unified repository from which all integration interface types are exposed,
- automated and documented updates;
- a catalog that is searchable on keywords and navigable by product family; and
- a powerful user interface to help you find the data you are looking for from the repository.

For more information about Oracle Integration Repository, visit My Oracle Support.

Oracle Tools and RDBMS References

It is essential for the DBA and programmers installing Oracle EBS to use SQL*Loader, SQL*Plus, data export, PL/SQL, and other utility products. The library must include copies of the appropriate reference manuals. Every user will need to have his or her own copy of the major ones. The essentials are the following:

For Each Developer

- SQL Reference Manual
- SQL*Plus User's Guide and Reference
- PL/SQL User's Guide and Reference
- Server Utilities Guide (Loader, Import/Export)

In the Library

- Server Administrator's Guide
- Application Developer's Guide
- Server Messages
- Server Reference
- Server Tuning Guide
- Oracle*Forms Library Set
- Oracle*Reports Library Set
- SQL*Net Library Set
- Oracle Web Server Library Set

Oracle8 versions and beyond of all the Oracle tools documentation are available in both HTML and PDF formats on a CD-ROM. By far the least expensive and most convenient way to provide library access to this material is online.

Third-Party Oracle References

Third-party books can never duplicate the detail of the Oracle references. They can offer insight into how the many pieces of Oracle's product line fit together and into making the best use of the features described in Oracle's references. They also collect essential reference material into a more compact format. The most useful reference topics usually include the following:

- database sizing and tuning, such as Oracle Press's *Oracle Database 11g Release 2 Performance Tuning Tips & Techniques* (McGraw-Hill Osborne Media, 2012);
- SQL and basic Oracle, such as *Oracle Database 11g SQL* (McGraw-Hill Osborne Media, 2007);
- production operation, including backup and recovery; and
- Web server/HTML references.

Operating-System References

The EBS applications make extensive use of their host operating systems. The systems programmer, DBA, and programmers need good reference materials on the following:

- command and shell languages;
- editors, such as vi in Unix;
- printers and PostScript printing (a tough subject in Unix); and
- utilities, such as sed in Unix.

User's Group Materials

The Oracle Applications Users Group and Independent Oracle Users Group hold meetings about twice a year in each major geographic region worldwide. The proceedings offer a wealth of practical information on installing the applications. The best investment is sending people to the conferences, where they can bring themselves up to date on Oracle's future directions as well as gain tips and techniques for the here and now. Second best is to buy a copy of the proceedings to put on the shelf.

The Oracle Applications Users Group provides support and services to geographic user groups and special-interest groups. This second classification is groups that are focused on one particular aspect of the family of Oracle EBS applications. Whether working with a particular application or in a particular industry, special-interest groups provide the specialized information to maximize your Oracle EBS investment. A comprehensive list of these groups can be found at the Oracle Applications Users Group's Web site (www.oaug.org).

Managing Implementation Activities

A project manager is constantly called upon to make trade-offs between meeting the deadline and doing a thorough job. Doing a thorough job means adhering to the essential data-processing methodologies of written analysis and design documentation, testing, coding standards, quality control, problem management, and configuration management. Although you pay in the long term for short-term expediency, a manager cannot successfully defend a systematic approach unless he or she knows the disciplines.

The right decision does not always favor more methodology. The project manager will be called upon to arbitrate between competing interests. Oracle Corporation and many large technical-services firms protect themselves by defining methodologies that might be more rigorous than is required. Clients sometimes complain about contractor methodologies that take large amounts of time and generate volumes of documentation that they, the clients, can scarcely use or understand. Because they must apply a consistent standard to all customers, Oracle's position for even its most sophisticated clients is that they must wait for Oracle Support to fix software bugs rather than do it themselves.

On the other hand, an experienced independent consultant might just fix the problem and move on. The project manager has to weigh cost and business necessity against the benefits of the methodologies. He or she has to know the methodology well enough to be its advocate most of the time and to know when it can be abbreviated. Equally important is good communication among the teams involved, with well-managed team meetings and briefings. These can maintain motivation and focus.

TIP
Applications software is no exception to the rule that poor methodologies cause software implementations to fail. These prosaic disciplines are more significant than hardware, staffing levels, or budgets. Good methodology answers the most essential question: How do I know that it works?

The Solution Definition

Requirements for configuration changes and customizations to the E-Business Suite will occur throughout the implementation project. The program charter outlines the solution in response to the requirements and will list any customizations identified at this early stage. The solution might include a list of modules required, the organization setup (or at least some options), and some discussion of key process flows (such as invoice-matching choices). Customizations can include external-facing reports, significant internal management reports, programmatic data conversions, and interfaces.

The program charter or other scope document is the starting point. There are different ways of taking it forward: through workshops, a series of prototypes, or pilot implementations. Whatever method you choose, you will need to document the solution. This minimizes the interruption caused by losing project members and helps forward momentum, as it prevents decision-making processes from being repeatedly reopened. You will need to manage the process so that all the members of the project team know their way around the documentation. As the solution develops and there is pressure to change the scope, there must be procedures defined that everyone knows and accepts and that the project office can police.

The solution is multifaceted, and can be owned by many different teams. They might refer to it in different ways—to the business, it is the system and procedures; to the functional teams, it is those plus the setup; to the DBAs, it is a series of environments; to the development team, it is a portfolio of working software. There needs to be a common thread that keeps these teams pulling in the same direction. A methodology provides this thread. We will use the Oracle Unified Method to illustrate the elements needed for a usable framework.

The OUM Project Life Cycle

OUM has three focus areas (Manage, Envision, and Implement), and within them a number of views that are designed to provide an initial tailoring of OUM or a starting point for using OUM to accomplish different types of objectives for the project life cycle. The Implement focus area illustrates through views the progression of tasks required for a successful implementation.

This methodology provides a comprehensive toolkit, including the following:

- **Overview material**   The overview shows OUM's approach to IT projects, including the industry standards upon which OUM is based.
- **Guidelines**   Phase, process, task, role, and work-product guidelines cover every aspect of an Oracle-based business solution.
- **Templates**   Templates enable fast and easy creation of high-quality work products.
- **Tailored work-breakdown structure**   These standards enable an easy start in managing your project

In addition to these flows, there is a project-management stream through the Manage focus area that provides a framework for monitoring progress and agreeing to changes (via a change-request procedure). In an implementation involving external and internal resources it is important that the business understand and own the solution. The progress of the solution definition along the clear path of a methodology increases the visibility of the implementation process.

Configuration of the package is an organic process: you set up the parameters, settings, and profile options, then test the solution and adjust them as required. As you dip further into the details of the processes and discover the exceptions, you will need to keep making adjustments to the solution. It is essential that you retain control over these adjustments, because the system is so integrated that a change can affect multiple modules.

There are natural points within a project executed under a methodology such as OUM that act as freeze points for the design. For example, the business must sign off on the high-level solution-design documents. Therefore, after that point, to keep control of the scope you can put in place a change-request process. This process ensures that any changes to the functionality will be considered in the light of the original charter and the project plan, and have their impact assessed. Impact can be on functionality, technology, budget, or timescales. A strong project office will enforce this rigor through the life of the project and be careful not to stifle changes that could significantly impact the business—this is not a layer of bureaucracy, but an imposition of discipline.

Written Business Procedures

Testing and training are based on business procedures that describe how the business works using Oracle EBS: this is how we process orders from established customers; this is how we process orders from new customers; this is how we handle customer returns; this is what we do when a longtime customer owes on invoices more than 90 days old; this is how we define tasks within a project.

The procedures for Oracle are based on the needs of the business, which are represented by existing procedures. These are just as often embodied in company culture, handed down by oral tradition, as they are written. Even in companies that do have written procedures, as encouraged by ISO 9000 and modern management science, actual practice often elaborates on or differs from the written procedures. The analyst's challenge is to define what current business practices are and then how they will be done in Oracle.

The greatest part of the business procedures usually addresses exceptions. It is relatively easy to describe the normal flow of a transaction such as a customer order. The complexity is in the exceptions: What orders should go on credit hold? Who releases them? When? What if the ordered item is not in the warehouse? Can we honor an order for an old release level? When do we partially fill an order? Can we fill a pick-to-order order from multiple warehouses? One of

Oracle's great strengths is that it will apply your business rules for you. To take advantage of Oracle, you have to define policies that might have always been made on an ad hoc basis.

Oracle's Tutor product gives you a head start when writing business procedures. It is software based on Microsoft Word that contains templated documents for many of the procedures you will need. The templates give a framework that includes navigation through the screens. The documents are designed to be printed and also published onto an intranet so that users have easy access to them and they can be easily and cheaply updated.

Testing

Business procedures describe how the Oracle system will be used. Each procedure needs to be supported by test scenarios to prove that it does work. The system is supposed to accept prepaid orders in foreign currencies? Manufacturing should be able to handle assemble-to-order jobs with outside processing in the final assembly step? Prove it!

Levels of Testing

Testing is a traditional data-processing discipline, which Oracle of course performs extensively before shipping its software. Steps in the testing process take on somewhat different meanings for the E-Business Suite.

Unit Testing and Link Testing   Making sure that individual modules of code really work is applicable to custom programs that are written for extending the system or for converting and bridging to outside systems. Unit testing is the best description to apply to shaking down EBS setups, flexfield rules, Oracle Alerts, and the like in test instances. Most software does not comprise a single module that does all the work. Therefore, link testing is essential to ensure that the solution works in a stand-alone test. This should include any steps required for installation. Typically the running of unit and link tests does not involve anyone other than the implementer (whether that is a functional consultant or developer), but you might want to insist on documentation that can be reviewed by the relevant users.

Integration, or System Testing   Also known as *string testing*, integration confirms that individual modules of code work together as a unit. In the case of custom code, such testing demonstrates that the custom code interacts properly with the native Oracle code. At a pure EBS level, it means making sure transactions flow through all the Oracle applications as expected. As an example, the testers need to confirm that accounting data entered on a sales order or requisition result in the expected ledger postings.

Acceptance Testing   Acceptance testing is part of a process in which the users agree that a system is ready to put into production. If the system implementers are outside contractors, bonuses or contingency fees may be tied to passing the acceptance test.

Parallel Testing   The necessity of parallel testing is an old data-processing shibboleth that needs to be raised to be dismissed. It is the concept that the Oracle E-Business Suite will run live in parallel with the legacy systems for a period of time, after which it will be decided whether or not Oracle meets the test. Here are the flaws in the parallel-testing concept:

- ■   There is never enough time or enough staff to run two systems at the same time, keying in all the transactions twice.

■ Business processes invariably change with Oracle. It is unreasonable to expect that the Accounting Flexfield, item numbers, invoicing policies, replenishment computations, and so on will be identical. It is a given that the outcomes of the two systems will be different— and it would take an impossible amount of time to reconcile the two at a detail level.

■ Some transactions can afford to take only one path, such as warehouse releases. Whose pick slips would the warehouse recognize—the legacy system or Oracle? Items could not be double shipped. Inventory records would be bound to disagree with the actual warehouse counts.

The best use of parallel processing is before cutover. It is entirely appropriate to convert legacy balances for the General Ledger, as well as prior months' journal postings, to confirm that Oracle's ledger reports agree with those from the legacy system. This is a totally adequate test of the Oracle ledger, but with crucial differences from real parallel processing. Testing with historical data removes the need for dual input, removes the time pressure of closings, and guarantees that the results are indeed comparable—because the transactions are identical. In fact it amounts to running test scenarios that happen to use real, historical data.

Regression Testing   Regression testing is a rigorous discipline to prove that the software still performs old functions properly after being enhanced with new features. The test system maintains a set of test data and test results as described in Chapter 22. The expectation is that the enhanced software should produce exactly the same results as the original.

Oracle developed its own regression tester, called Oracle Application Testing Suite (OATS), which is supported for use with Oracle EBS. OATS is composed of the following:

■ **Oracle Load Testing** for scalability, performance, and load testing;

■ **Oracle Functional Testing** for automated functional and regression testing; and

■ **Oracle Test Manager** for test-process management, test execution, and defect tracking.

Oracle E-Business Suite Accelerators are add-ins to OATS to enable support for automated functional testing and load testing of E-Business Suite screens based on both the Web and Oracle Forms.

Oracle Load Testing uses automated scripts created in OpenScript that can simulate hundreds or thousands of concurrent users to test application performance under load and identify bottlenecks. Your business users can record automated test scripts by stepping through Oracle E-Business Suite business transactions, mimicking normal business operations. You can use the same interface to run scripts, parameterize script inputs, add custom test cases to validate content, and extend scripts programmatically in Java. The Functional Testing product is a Web-based test-management solution that allows your company to plan, organize, document and manage the entire application-testing process. It can document and run both manual and automated test cases, track defects, and manage test requirements. Finally, the Test Manager allows management of users, roles, projects, and fields.

In an upgrade context, you could use the OATS tool to load test your new release test system to ensure that it adequately scales to the volume of transactions you anticipate in production, including worst-case peak loads.

Stress Testing   Stress testing ensures that the technical configuration of the implementation is acceptable to the end users. It demonstrates how the production system will perform under a normal production load. You can use a tool such as OATS or arrange for a large number of users to log on and follow set scripts. If you have a global implementation, you will need to load the system with concurrent processes and online ones, because the batch window could overlap with office hours in some countries.

Test Scenarios

A test scenario is a sequence of related tasks, not necessarily automated, each described by business procedures. For instance, there might be procedures to describe how to do the following:

- enter requisitions in Oracle Purchasing,
- approve requisitions,
- generate internal orders for release from the warehouse,
- pass internal orders to Order Entry,
- release the material to the requisitioner, and
- replenish inventory.

A typical test scenario would require a series of related transactions to test all these procedures: create a requisition, approve it, get it issued, and replenish to replace the materials that were issued. Another scenario would specify a requisition for a stock item with zero on hand. Yet another would specify a requisition for a nonstock item. Another would specify a requisition for a magazine subscription, for outside services, for a high-dollar item requiring special approvals, and for a purchase that requires competitive bids. Each scenario would trace the transaction through several business procedures: requisitioning, purchasing, receiving, and whatever else is relevant.

The test scenarios specify expected results: requisition denied, replenishment order generated, overshipment refused, and so forth. The scenarios need to be specific about financial outcomes. Automatic Account Generation includes some of the most complex setup logic in Oracle. If you have defined rules to have the cost-of-goods-sold account use the warehouse's company and location, the product-line segment associated with the item, and the natural account associated with the customer, you need to confirm that the system is generating what you expect.

Your super users should start to develop test scenarios as they test Oracle's functionality in the Conference Room Pilot. Testing will confirm their understanding of the effects of setup parameters on system operations. Keeping formal test scenarios will make it possible for them to confidently repeat a test after they have changed the parameters. For example, consider a company that deals mainly in prepaid orders and receives a small volume of customer returns. Is it worth using Oracle's Return Material Authorization feature, or should the business procedure simply specify a miscellaneous receipt into inventory and miscellaneous payment through Payables? The super user can test the alternatives; then write up the most logical approach as the agreed-upon business procedure.

Test Data and Test Scripts

Test data and scripts give substance to a test scenario. The test script for the preceding test scenario might be:

1. Log in with the Responsibility CATALOG_MANAGER.
2. Create an item with the identifier TEST_ITEM*nn*. The *nn* makes the item unique; this way the test can be repeated. Use template EXPENDABLE_SUPPLY. Give it a requisitioning objective of 8.
3. Do a miscellaneous inventory receipt to give TEST_ITEM*nn* an onhand balance of 6.
4. Log in with Responsibility ENGINEERING_USER.

5. Create a requisition for 10 of TEST_ITEM*nn*.

6. Allow the Order Entry import concurrent process to run as scheduled for the test, every minute.

7. Run the Pick/Release process.

8. Process the partial issue.

9. Run the Demand Interface process.

10. Run the Inventory replenishment process.

11. Confirm expected results: issue of 6, back order of 4, replenishment requisition for 12 sent to purchasing, issue charged to engineering department—expendable supplies.

Test data and test scripts need to run against master data. In this instance, one master record (the part) is entered as part of the script. Doing this ensures that there are no open orders against it. The other master record (requisitioner) is assumed to be in the system.

Testing has to be repeatable. The test scenario needs to specify the initial and final states of the database. A test scenario may restore the database to its initial state. This one might require canceling the back-ordered portion of open requisitions before it is run. Alternatively, the script may be repeatable through slight variations. For example, you can repeat the preceding script by changing the part number.

Acceptance tests are the most thorough applications of the testing methodology. They precede the trial cutovers; the base process is the same for both acceptance and cutover:

1. Create a new instance, keying in fresh setup parameters for each application.

2. Convert data into the new instance.

3. Run a full suite of test scenarios in the new instance.

4. Confirm the expected outcomes of the test scenarios.

You should consider the test unsuccessful if the expected outcomes are not achieved and the discrepancy cannot be explained. If a test reveals flaws in the setup parameters or conversion processes, it generally means that the whole test needs to be run again. This is hard medicine, but it is the only way to demonstrate conclusively that the setups are consistent.

Unscripted testing is one factor that distinguishes acceptance testing from trial cutovers. The functional users perform acceptance tests. After they confirm that all the tests in the test design work as expected, they usually want to enter transactions of their own to logic paths they might feel were not addressed by the test scenarios, and just to get the feel of the system.

CAUTION
Testing is inherently destructive. Test data corrupt a database. That is why testing has to be done in a test instance, prior to cutover. Spot-checking live data after conversion is never an adequate substitute for testing.

Configuration Management

An Oracle EBS environment is made up of a tremendous number of objects. Oracle delivers thousands of modules and tables; there are usually three or four database instances. Including a minimal amount of custom code, you add 30 or 40 different types of objects to those databases and program files. If you follow any development discipline, you will also develop a large number of specifications documents, test scripts, and other documentary support for the implementation. Configuration management is the discipline that keeps you from getting swamped.

Chapter 22 addresses configuration management for custom code. It boils down to version control—knowing what versions of programs and setups are current in which environments.

Configuration management for implementations without custom code boils down to controlling

- business procedures,
- test scenarios,
- test scripts and data,
- setup parameters for each application,
- value sets for each application,
- flexfield setups,
- attribute usage,
- alerts, and
- responsibilities and menus.

Almost all of this information exists in document format. The major need is for a shared document library on a LAN server, with a subdirectory structure that gives a home to every document type.

Oracle has a free configuration-management tool for E-Business Suite that allows the organizations to overcome maintaining current and consistent configurations across all supporting instances. Oracle iSetup reduces configuration time and effort—because manual configurations can be applied to one environment and migrated to others—and increases the accuracy of configuration documentation, because standard reports can be executed against current extracts and comparison reports can be executed to uncover and resolve differences.

Problem Management

The project manager's job can be defined as solving problems. Most projects have a systematic treatment of the following:

- **Logging and resolving user problems** Prior to cutover, these are problems that the functional users have in setting up and testing Oracle software. Afterward, they are live production problems—some processes will not do what they need to do. These problems can be resolved by the super users, the programmers, or the DBA. They are linked to SRs when they require Oracle's help.

- **Logging problems reported to My Oracle Support through SRs** The SR log will show when the problem was reported, how the report was phrased, when Oracle responded, and what they recommended. The actions can be implementing a patch, using a work-around, or discovering that it is not a problem but a misunderstanding.

- **Logging project issues that require management decisions** An issues log should give the issue a short name, indicate who is managing the issue, give the status, show a deadline date, and reference an issue paper that goes into the details. The setup document for the application in question should also reference the issue paper.

Open issues on these logs are perennial agenda items for project-status meetings, along with tasks from the work-breakdown structure that are started, completed, and stalled for one reason or another.

Quality Assurance

You ensure quality by adhering to established processes that yield predictable results. Some hallmarks of quality are an established planning process, well-defined methodologies, metrics for measuring performance against the plan, and a system for improving methodologies based on measured results.

One of the project manager's roles is to make sure the team agrees on adequate and appropriate sets of standards and methodologies. The team members are the ones who will live with them, so they should be the ones to develop them. The project manager's job is to encourage, lead, and sometimes push them to get it done. He or she should have sufficient resources in the project office to police the standards and methodologies. The project manager needs to ensure consistency of approach when there might be pressures to take shortcuts (often with documentation or testing) that will adversely affect the long-term quality for a short-term advantage. Quality assurance is making sure that the project team agrees about quality, what it is and how to create it, and that they are committed to producing it.

Conclusion

The project manager cannot mandate success. He or she has to provide the leadership and environment in which his or her team can succeed. The success of an EBS project always depends on outsiders and people who do not fully belong to the project. The project manager needs to convince the team that installing Oracle is worthwhile, that there is a workable plan, and that the project will be a success.

The project manager needs the discernment to recognize appropriate methodologies and the discipline to apply them. It takes leadership as well as a fair knowledge of data processing. The de facto methodologies are whatever the team implements in its work products. The project manager needs to convince the team of the need for a systematic approach and lead them to select techniques that they can apply successfully. Approaches adapted from the mainframe, from custom code development, or even from other EBS implementations might not be appropriate. The team will not understand them—much less buy into the concepts—unless they contribute their own ideas.

Testing is the most important of all the disciplines. Each component of the system, and the system as a whole, has to be proven to work before it goes into production. You know the Oracle software works, but that fact is of no value unless you have defined the business processes you need to make it work for you. The consequences of going into production without proving that you know how to execute all major business functions can be disastrous.

The project manager's responsibilities span the range of classical management functions. He or she must have management adopt achievable plans and budgets. He or she must bring together a staff with the best mix of functional-area specialists, data-processing staff, implementation contractors, and consultants. He or she must lead by vision and decision making. Lastly, the project manager must see that the methodologies essential to quality, and hence success, are defined and observed. However, attainment of success depends on how success is defined. Expectations should be managed for all the parties. The project manager plays a key role in defining success and managing expectations.

CHAPTER
24

Performance Tuning for
Oracle R12 Financials

ne of the greatest challenges of large corporate information systems—aside from security and disaster recovery—lies in the performance of the mission-critical applications that run as part of the Oracle E-Business Suite. Performance optimization is a large and complex subject that requires a book in itself to explain in depth. We will provide a set of best practices and tips to help you gain the most performance from your Oracle E-Business Suite environment. We will explain how to tune the overall environment with a focus on the following key areas:

- methodologies for performance tuning,
- a holistic tuning approach,
- system performance optimization, and
- application and database performance tuning.

First we will discuss how to implement an effective method to optimize performance with the Oracle E-Business Suite of applications, since without a solid framework, you will be constantly in reactive "firefighting," mode which is both ineffective and counterproductive over the long term.

Methodology for Performance Tuning the Oracle E-Business Suite

Establishing a method of best practices for performance tuning the Oracle E-Business Suite environment requires that you adopt a framework in concert with the key stakeholders of your IT organization. At a minimum, it is wise and prudent to examine the following topics in developing a roadmap for performance analysis with Oracle EBS:

- load testing before, during, and after go-live;
- functional requirements and testing;
- map the business and functional environments to the technical environment;
- the thinking of businesspeople compared to that of technical people;
- the goal of unify to resolve tuning issues (Method R);
- stress testing;
- integration testing; and
- unit testing.

Load Testing for Oracle E-Business Suite

Unfortunately, the subject of load testing is rarely if ever given consideration during the implementation of Oracle R12 EBS environments in most organizations. It is an afterthought—that is, until major performance issues appear to adversely affect the operational aspects of the Oracle Financials production systems. At this point, it places the organization at risk and forces the IT staff to react to the issues at hand, which causes stress, frustration, and an end result of just a temporary solution rather than a root-cause analysis and solution to the fundamental problem. It is wise to implement load testing at all phases of the project, from initial deployment of the Oracle E-Business Suite through go-live.

Why Do We Load Test?

Load testing provides numerous benefits as part of a performance effort to develop a proactive approach to highly optimized Oracle EBS systems. It allows you to generate metrics before, during, and after go-live to optimize performance and availability for Oracle EBS applications. For example, you can understand how long the Oracle GL batch jobs take to run on average at peak hours versus during the night. It also helps to create an accurate baseline of performance so that when changes are made to the environment, you can assess why performance has changed. For instance, if you determine baseline performance via load testing and then apply a new patch to Oracle Financials, you can truly know whether or not the patch has adversely affected performance for the Oracle EBS environment.

TIP
You really do not know the true performance until you test!

In order to measure load performance for Oracle EBS, you can use third-party load-generator tools such as HP LoadRunner to create custom scripts to simulate a real user environment and measure application response time based on a set number of users logged into the Oracle EBS environment. You can also use the Oracle 11*g* Real Application Testing Suite, which is excellent for database-tier load-testing scenarios, or the Oracle Application Management Pack, which is useful for measuring application-tier performance metrics.

Now let's discuss how to apply a methodology for functional and technical aspects of performance-test analysis.

Functional to Technical Specifications and Testing

Oracle database administrators have the challenging task of mapping business requirements onto technical results to optimize performance for the Oracle E-Business Suite environment. Part of the difficulty is due to the gap in understanding between the various parties and stakeholders within the IT organization who are responsible for the care and feeding of the Oracle E-Business Suite. Businesspeople such as financial analysts, project managers, and CFOs do not think like technical people. They live in a completely different world, apart from the technical staff. This creates unintended consequences leading to conflict, confusion, and unique problems in the operational aspects of maintaining a high-performance environment with Oracle E-Business Suite applications. The first step in the mapping is to eliminate the disconnect between the functional, development, and technical teams as soon as possible in the deployment process, to reduce bottlenecks in performance. We recommend that you do the following to bridge this gap in knowledge and communication:

- Establish stakeholders to review and test the business requirements from the functional and business units mapped out to the technical teams. Involve all parties from the users, developers, and functional users in regularly held staff meetings and review sessions.

- Document and review the business requirements for modules deployed (e.g., Accounts Payable, Accounts Receivable, and General Ledger) to really understand what to test and measure for performance tuning.

Now that we have given consideration to the functional aspects of performance for the Oracle E-Business Suite, the next logical step is to decide exactly what we need to tune.

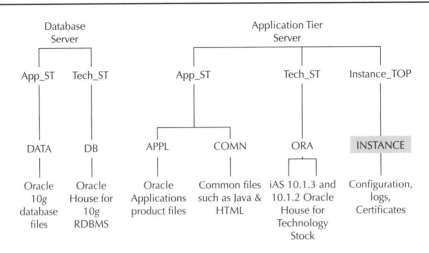

FIGURE 24-1. *Oracle R12 EBS architecture and file-system layout*

What to Tune?

Understanding where performance tuning needs to begin is paramount to successful optimization of the Oracle E-Business Suite. As the saying goes, "Knowing is half the battle."

There are two situations that affect how and when to tune. We recommend that you start with the initial business problem at hand and work out an action plan toward remediation. For instance, if the Oracle EBS database administrator receives a phone call from a user complaining about slow response time for invoices processed with Oracle Financials, then it warrants a closer look at tuning efforts regarding the Accounts Payable and Accounts Receivable modules within the Oracle E-Business Suite. It is useful to drill down from a macro level to micro areas of the environment to identify the low-hanging fruit for optimizing performance in such a situation. Never assume that it is the database or another technical component until you have completed a root-cause analysis. We will use a holistic approach to performance tuning as the capstone for performance optimization of the Oracle E-Business Suite.

Figure 24-1 shows the architecture for the Oracle Release 12 E-Business Suite.

Holistic Approach to Performance Tuning

There are various methods to performance tuning the Oracle E-Business Suite. By adopting the holistic method, you will use best practices in a proactive manner to alleviate the majority of performance issues before they become major headaches. This will save the technical and functional staff many sleepless nights and ensure a healthy environment. Figure 24-2 shows the overall picture of holistic tuning for Oracle.

By understanding the real problem first, you can drill down from the macro level to micro layers and arrive at root-cause solutions. Experts in the Oracle field, from Cary Millsap and Method R to the OakTable Network and the Battle Against Any Guess movement, agree that it is critical to identify the real business problem first before leaping to illogical conclusions. This avoids the fallacy in the fable of the blind men and the elephant, which would otherwise

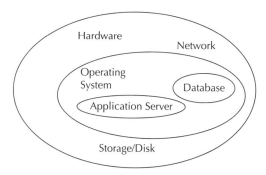

FIGURE 24-2. *Holistic view of performance tuning*

convolute the issue at hand. A holistic approach to tuning allows you to drill down to the root cause and perform useful and interesting analyses while filtering out any white noise. It is also important to develop test cases so that you can duplicate the identified performance problem. We are focused on methodology and not silly "silver bullets." In fact, Oracle recommends that you apply the holistic approach to tuning Oracle E-Business Suite via the My Oracle Support Note 69565.1: *A Holistic Approach to Performance Tuning Oracle Applications Systems.*

System-Performance Optimization

Many Oracle database professionals jump to application and database performance tuning before looking into system-performance analysis. This is a fatal mistake because many issues that cause performance degradation occur at the hardware, system, network, and storage layer. For instance, the Oracle application tier requires solid network connectivity to access the database-tier server. Therefore, if network latency is severe, application performance will suffer because the application services will hang during batch processing. In addition, if the disk setup is flawed on the storage-area network, read and write performance will be poor, causing slow application performance as a result. In this case, it behooves the application and database team to establish a close working relationship with the system and network infrastructure team to perform effective design and proactive tuning activities that can remediate performance issues before they occur. In summary, you should consider the following areas carefully for performance optimization with Oracle infrastructure:

- hardware server configuration,
- storage configuration, and
- network design and configuration.

First let's take a look at hardware performance.

Hardware Performance Considerations

One area that is frequently overlooked in sizing Oracle R12 EBS environments is the hardware server components. Most vendors such as IBM, Dell, Cisco, and HP have sizing tools available to plan for new Oracle R12 EBS environments. These give a starting point for sizing hardware for a new deployment of the Oracle E-Business Suite. We recommend that you obtain sizing recommendations from different vendors and compare benchmarks for performance to arrive at the best decision for your particular Oracle EBS implementation. One of the most frequently asked questions regarding hardware is whether to use a big centralized server or smaller blade-type servers. For the application tier, we recommend multiple smaller servers with a hardware load balancer to best distribute performance across the tech stack. For the database tier, we recommend a large single server or multiple large servers in clustered configuration for scale-out requirements via Oracle Real Application Cluster. More memory is not always better, but you do want to ensure that you have enough. How do you know how much memory and CPU resources to use for the servers? Initial load testing is your best bet to assess if you have sufficient memory and CPU resources, along with sizing estimates from hardware vendors to determine the sweet spot for your hardware server configuration. Tools such as top, sar, vmstat, iostat, and Oracle Enterprise Manager are useful yardsticks to measure resources and consumption during load testing and operations after go-live. As a parting statement regarding hardware server sizing, multiple cores (quad-core configurations) are excellent for CPU performance, but as a downside, they may have additional Oracle licensing requirements.

Operating-System Tuning

Tuning the operating system (OS) is an area that is commonly neglected during Oracle EBS implementation. As a result, performance problems occur because key operating-system parameters are not tuned. The approach for performance tuning the OS varies based on the platform. For example, Linux, Unix, and Windows have different requirements and items that are unique to each platform and must be tuned correctly. We recommend that you consult the My Oracle Support Note 224176.1: *How to Use OS Commands to Diagnose Database Performance Issues?* to identify the specific tools for measuring OS performance. As a general rule of thumb, for Linux and Unix platforms we recommend that you start with the following steps:

- Measure overall system performance with top and iostat.
- Check memory and configuration for kernel settings with dmesg and sysctl commands.
- Drill down if necessary with the strace utility.

Linux Performance Tuning

Linux is a popular operating system used in many large Oracle E-Business Suite deployments. Oracle has migrated from development on Solaris Unix to Linux recently as the chosen platform for testing applications. Since a complete treatment of performance tuning with Linux is beyond the scope of this chapter, we recommend that you consult the following My Oracle Support notes (http://support.oracle.com) to tune Linux issues:

Network Performance

- Note 274953.1: *Tuning TCP/IP Parameter in Linux Box for SQLNET*
  Use netstat and ping to identify latency issues with networks.
- Note 560590.1: *How and When to Use the net.ipv4.tcp_rmem and net.ipv4.tcp_wmem Linux Kernel Parameters*

Kernel Tuning

- Note 434351.1: *Linux Kernel: The SLAB Allocator*

Disk Tuning

- Note 175980.1: *Tuning Disk Throughput Using hdparm in Linux*
- The sar and iostat tools are your friends for identifying disk I/O contention issues.
- Also check for disk I/O issues with SAN tools (varies by vendor, such as EMC, Hitachi, etc.).

Unix is one of the most popular operating systems in production today for large mission-critical Oracle E-Business Suite systems. In general, Unix shares many of the same tools and design in common with its close cousin Linux as a multitasking and multithreaded enterprise operating system. Performance tuning of Unix is a complex and large subject also beyond the scope of this book. The following My Oracle Support (http://support.oracle.com) notes provide insight into usage of the tools and techniques for performance optimization of Oracle EBS on UNIX platforms.

Unix Performance Tuning

- Note 144638.1: *Relationship Between Common Init.ora Parameters and Unix, Linux Kernel Parameters*
- Verify that kernel parameters are set correctly and verify with the vendor platform.
- Assess performance with top, iostat, vmstat, and sar.
- OS Watcher tool

  Note 301137.1: *OS Watcher User Guide*

TIP
Find the performance bottleneck with top and ps to drill down to the root cause.

- Solaris: use truss and DTRACE for tuning system calls and processes

  www.sun.com/bigadmin/features/articles/dtrace_truss.jsp
- HP-UX: use the same utility for tuning

  http://docs.hp.com/en/B2355-90692/sam.1M.html

  IBM AIX: SMIT (System Management Information Tool) is useful tool for performance tuning

  www.ibm.com/developerworks/aix/library/au-smit/index.html

NOTE
You may need root OS privileges to run these tools or elevated privileges.

```
top - 15:05:08 up 33 days, 21:49, 10 users,  load average: 0.09, 0.05, 0.01
Tasks: 492 total,   2 running, 490 sleeping,   0 stopped,   0 zombie
Cpu(s): 16.9%us,  1.1%sy,  0.0%ni, 81.2%id,  0.7%wa,  0.0%hi,  0.0%si, 0.0%st
Mem:   4044596k total,  3683136k used,   361460k free,   272104k buffers
Swap:  2064376k total,      76k used,  2064300k free,  1488836k cached
  PID USER      PR  NI  VIRT  RES  SHR S %CPU %MEM   TIME+ COMMAND
 9455 applmgr   15   0  219m 112m  13m R 27.2  2.9 6233:08 npviewer.bin
10914 applmgr   19   0  546m  50m 7704 S  1.9  1.3  0:28.01 java
13701 applmgr   15   0 13020 1316  720 R  1.9  0.0  0:00.01 top
    1 root      15   0 10348  704  588 S  0.0  0.0  0:01.51 init
    2 root      RT  -5     0    0    0 S  0.0  0.0  0:00.00 migration/0
    3 root      34  19     0    0    0 S  0.0  0.0  0:00.23 ksoftirqd/0
    4 root      10  -5     0    0    0 S  0.0  0.0  0:01.17 events/0
    5 root      10  -5     0    0    0 S  0.0  0.0  0:00.00 khelper
   46 root      10  -5     0    0    0 S  0.0  0.0  0:00.00 kthread
   50 root      10  -5     0    0    0 S  0.0  0.0  0:05.01 kblockd/0
```

FIGURE 24-3. *Using top for Linux performance and Oracle R12 EBS*

Figure 24-3 shows an example of how to use the top command for Linux to view Oracle system performance.

The Linux and Unix top command is an excellent starting point to understand the current performance of a running Oracle EBS environment. You can then quickly drill down into storage and disk performance by using the iostat tool.

```
$ iostat
Linux 2.6.18-194.8.1.0.1.el5 (app01.ben.com)        09/19/2010
avg-cpu:  %user   %nice %system %iowait  %steal   %idle
           0.29    0.00    0.13    0.37    0.00   99.22
Device:            tps   Blk_read/s   Blk_wrtn/s   Blk_read   Blk_wrtn
sda               0.08         0.29         1.79   21019459  131483716
sda1              0.00         0.00         0.00       2496         28
sda2              0.08         0.29         1.79   21016659  131483688
sdb               0.00         0.00         0.00      23141       5072
sdb1              0.00         0.00         0.00      22253       5072
dm-0              0.23         0.29         1.79   21000250  131361616
dm-1              0.00         0.00         0.00      16120     122072
$ iostat -x
Linux 2.6.18-194.8.1.0.1.el5 (db01.ben.com)        09/19/2010
avg-cpu:  %user   %nice %system %iowait  %steal   %idle
           0.29    0.00    0.13    0.37    0.00   99.22
Device:         rrqm/s   wrqm/s   r/s   w/s   rsec/s   wsec/s avgrq-sz avgqu-
sz   await  svctm  %util
sda              0.00     0.15  0.01  0.07     0.29     1.79    26.25     0.00
3.77   2.05   0.02
sda1             0.00     0.00  0.00  0.00     0.00     0.00    23.37     0.00
3.22   2.70   0.00
sda2             0.00     0.15  0.01  0.07     0.29     1.79    26.25     0.00
3.77   2.05   0.02
```

Virtualization and Cloud-Computing Considerations

Cloud computing and virtualization are the hot technology in vogue today with data centers looking to consolidate hardware and reduce operating costs (CAPEX/OPEX) for Oracle applications. However, while the benefits of the cloud are magnificent, they also come with additional challenges and risks to address in order to avoid pitfalls. These risks include the time and opportunity cost of training existing and new staff on how to implement and administer the new virtualized cloud based environments. In addition, substantial time is required to migrate legacy environments to the virtual data center. The two major players in the cloud marketplace for Oracle EBS are VMware and Oracle. VMware is the market leader in virtualization, with VMware vCenter and vSphere for virtualization of Oracle applications. Oracle has a hypervisor product called Oracle Virtual Machine (VM) which consists of the Oracle VM Manager and Oracle VM Server. VMware has the advantage over Oracle in that its vCenter and vSphere hypervisor products can run nearly any application, including Oracle, in a virtualized cloud environment on server hardware. Oracle VM is limited to running only Oracle applications at this time. For customers with mixed workloads and mixed-application environments—such as a business requirement to run additional applications like Microsoft Exchange and SAP on the same server environment with Oracle—we recommend that you implement VMware for your private–public cloud solution. Listed here are some key considerations to keep in mind when virtualizing Oracle EBS.

- Virtual servers with VMware and Oracle VM require additional hardware resources to optimize performance compared to physical bare-metal implementations.

- Oracle and VMware have best practices you should be familiar with. For example, both offer DRS and clustering to optimize virtual-machine performance.

- VMware provides tools available with vCenter for provisioning, cloning, and deploying virtual machines as well as migrating physical servers to virtualized environments. Oracle provides similar features for these tasks with Oracle VM as well as template design with Oracle Virtual Assembly Builder.

Storage and Disk Considerations

- Solid-state disks offers the best overall performance, but are more expensive.

- Performance can be optimized with Disk I/O with RAID 0+1 or RAID 1+0 and Avoid RAID 5 for best overall disk performance.

- Automatic Storage Management should be implemented for Oracle 10*g* and Oracle 11*g* on the database tier for performance and availability.

- Usually vendor centric depends on storage vendor, e.g., EMC, SUN, HP, Hitachi, etc.

Areas to Tune—Start Here!

1. Oracle R12 EBS Technology Stack
   - Concurrent Manager Tuning
   - Oracle R12 EBS Module tuning: AR, AP, GL, HR, etc.

- Oracle 10*g* Application Server Tuning—Apache, Java tuning
- Servlet vs. Socket mode (11*i* versus R12 EBS)

2. Database Tuning
   - Instance tuning: SGA, PGA sizing is critical for database-tier performance
   - Statistics—FND_STATS

3. Tune server, operating system, storage Oracle R12 E-Business Suite Performance Tuning
   - Focus on methodology
   - Best practices
   - Holistic tuning approach
   - Proactive versus reactive tuning methods
   - Basic techniques to advanced tuning

TIP
Do not mistake the forest for the trees and avoid tunnel vision!

Application and Database Performance Tuning

Now that we have discussed methodologies and initial performance-tuning considerations, let's delve into core tuning areas for the Oracle E-Business Suite. Application and database performance tuning is the heart of challenges for Oracle professionals tasked with optimizing performance for Oracle Financials applications.

Application Tech-Stack Tuning

The Oracle EBS technology stack is a robust and complex set of application servers embedded within the Oracle E-Business Suite. In contrast to a non-Oracle EBS system, it poses unique challenges to optimizing performance and availability. The Oracle EBS application tier consists of multiple application JVM containers, an HTTP Web server based on Apache called Oracle HTTP Server, and the Concurrent Managers. Figure 24-4 shows the architecture of the application technology stack.

Tuning Concurrent Managers

Best practices:

- Useful My Oracle Support Notes: 104452.1: *Troubleshooting Concurrent Manager*
- Note 1057802.1: *Best Practices for Performance for Concurrent Managers in E-Business Suite*
- Myth: More Concurrent Managers are better
- Keep it simple and use only a few Concurrent Managers
- Tune queue size
- Tune sleep cycle (PMON)
- Tune number of processes
- Check for high number of requests

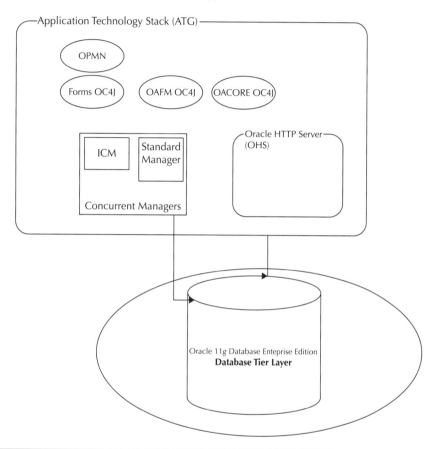

FIGURE 24-4. *Oracle R12 EBS tech-stack architecture*

- Use the following script to find high numbers of concurrent requests.

```
SELECT v.USER_CONCURRENT_QUEUE_NAME,COUNT(PHASE_CODE) v1
   FROM  APPS.FND_CONCURRENT_QUEUES_V1 v,
         APPS.FND_CONCURRENT_WORKER_REQUESTS r
  WHERE r.queue_application_id = 0
    AND r.PHASE_CODE = 'P'                 -- Pending Concurrent Re-
quests
    AND r.HOLD_FLAG != 'Y'                 -- Concurrent Requests not
on hold
    AND r.REQUESTED_START_DATE <= SYSDATE -- No Future Concurrent jobs
    AND r.CONCURRENT_QUEUE_ID=v.CONCURRENT_QUEUE_ID
```

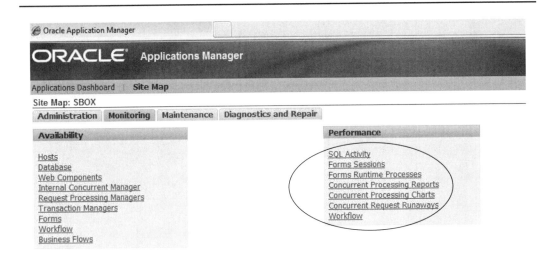

FIGURE 24-5. *Using Oracle Applications Manager for performance tuning*

```
        GROUP BY v.USER_CONCURRENT_QUEUE_NAME
        HAVING COUNT (PHASE_CODE) >=20
    /
```

■ Use Oracle Application Manager (OAM) charts to measure performance.

OAM is an excellent starting point to find performance bottlenecks for Concurrent Managers and other tuning issues with Oracle R12 EBS. Figure 24-5 shows the main tuning screen for examination of Oracle R12 EBS performance.

Figure 24-6 shows how to check for long-running concurrent requests for potential bottlenecks by using Oracle Application Manager.

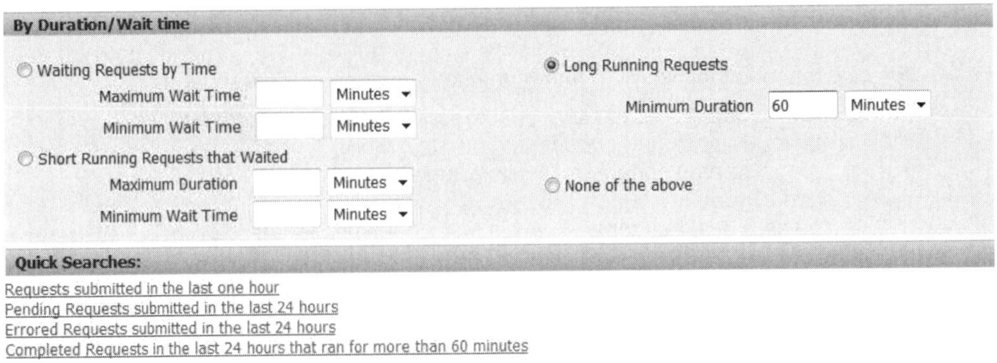

FIGURE 24-6. *Finding long-running concurrent requests with OAM*

You can use OAM to measure performance of Concurrent Managers for throughput to get the big picture. Figure 24-7 shows how to use OAM to examine database and concurrent batch-processing performance.

Tuning PMON Sleep Cycle

How to set value for PMON sleep cycle?

- Start-up parameter in adcmctl.sh script for Oracle R12 EBS

  Located under $INST_TOP/admin/scripts/ directory in applications tier.

- Parameters

  adcmctl.sh {start|stop|abort|status} [<APPS username/APPS password>] [sleep=<seconds>] [restart=<N|minutes>] [pmon=<iterations>] [quesiz=<pmon_iterations>] [diag=Y|N] [wait=Y|N]

- Tune by modifying the pmon and sleep parameters.

- You can also use OAM to set these values.

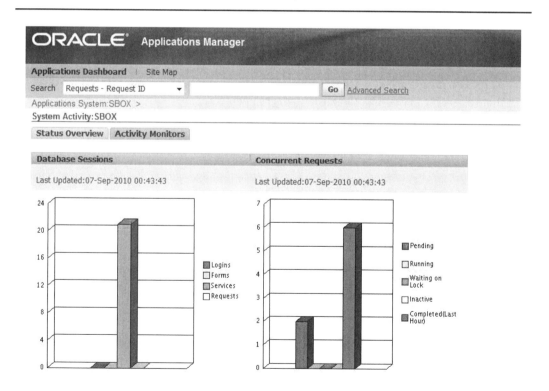

FIGURE 24-7. *Oracle R12 EBS performance analysis with OAM charts*

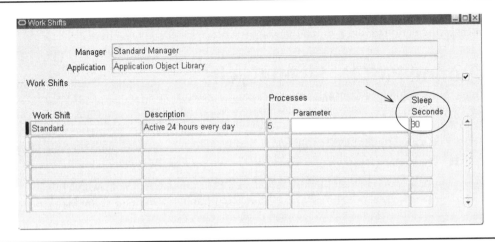

FIGURE 24-8. *Finding the PMON sleep-cycle value for Oracle R12 EBS concurrent requests*

Finding Value for PMON Sleep Cycle

Log in to OAM as SYSADMIN and systems-administrator Responsibility, then navigate to System Administrator | Concurrent:Manager | Define | WorkShifts.

Figure 24-8 shows how to locate the sleep value for the PMON process.

Cache Size and Performance for Concurrent Processing

Tune by setting in OAM for Oracle R12 environment.

The cache size can be tuned via the OAM menu as shown in Figure 24-9.

Tuning Number of Processes for Concurrent Managers

- Examine the number of processes for Concurrent Managers.

- Check the columns for actual, target, and running in OAM.

- Log in as SYSADMIN and then navigate the path Concurrent:Manager | Administer. See Figure 24-10.

Specialization Rules for Concurrent Manager Performance

- Use INCLUDE and EXCLUDE rules to optimize performance, since Concurrent Managers are batch-type processes.

- Log in as SYSADMIN and navigate System Administrator Concurrent:Manager | Define in OAM. See Figure 24-11.

The above menu item is located under Specialization Rules section in OAM.

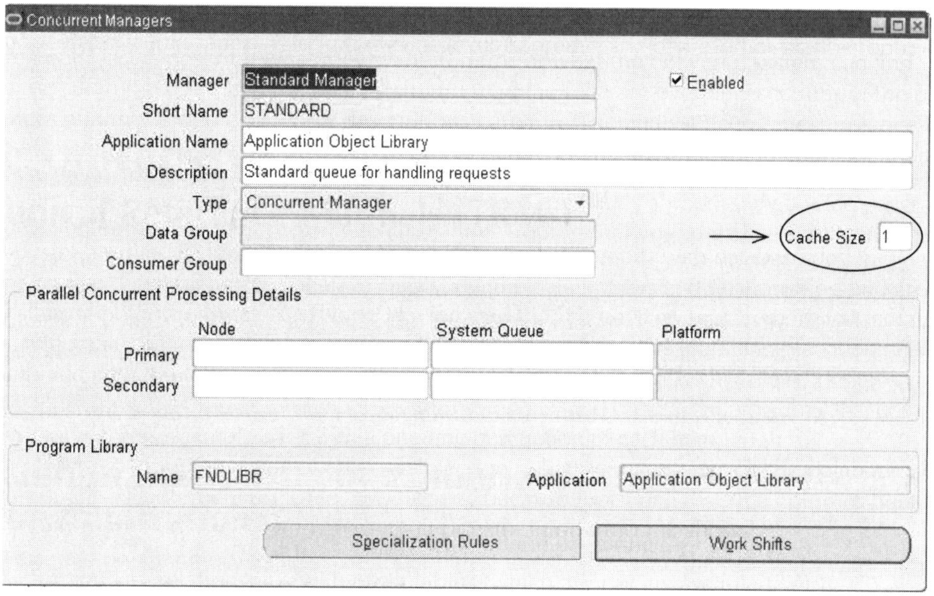

FIGURE 24-9. *Setting cache size for Oracle R12 EBS in OAM*

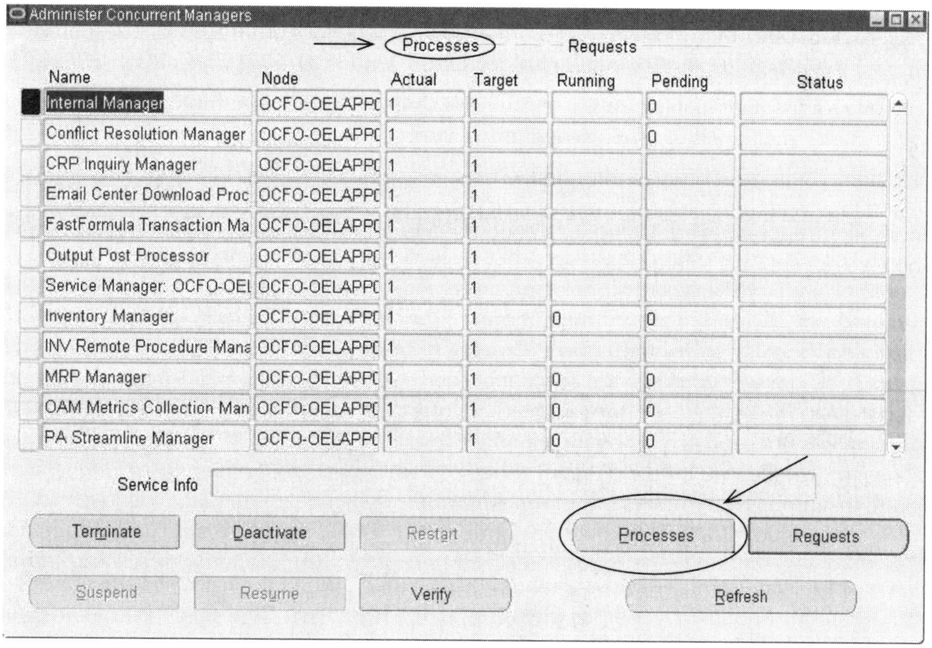

FIGURE 24-10. *Tuning the number of concurrent processes for Oracle R12 EBS in OAM*

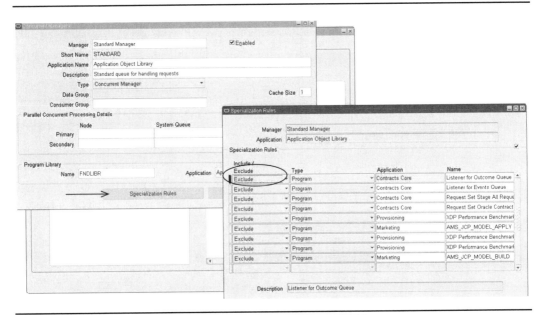

FIGURE 24-11. *Specialization rules for Oracle R12 EBS via OAM*

Setting Values for the Number of Processes with Concurrent Managers

- Located in OAM under the navigation path System Administrator | Concurrent:Manager | Define | WorkShifts. See Figure 24-12.
- Use combined specialization rules for complex tasks. See Figure 24-13.

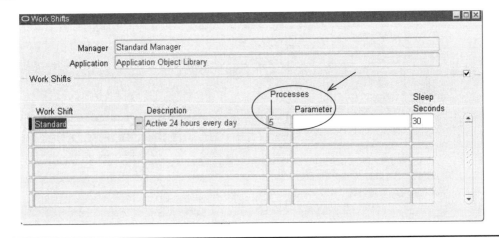

FIGURE 24-12. *Work shifts in Oracle R12 EBS via OAM*

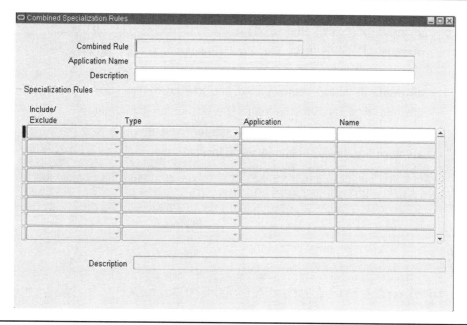

FIGURE 24-13. *Combined rules for work-shift specialization with Oracle R12 EBS*

Work Shifts for Performance with Concurrent Processing

- Set up different work shifts for balancing performance load with different critical tasks.

- For example, you can schedule AP to run during day and nightly processing on different work shifts.

- Log in to OAM as SYSADMIN and then navigate to System Administrator | Concurrent:Manager | WorkShifts. See Figure 24-14.

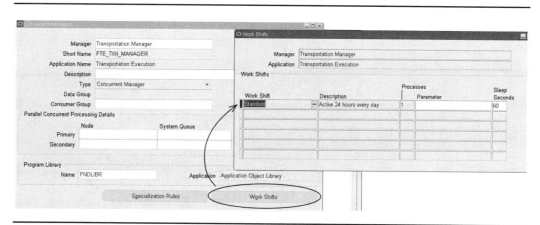

FIGURE 24-14. *Scheduling work shifts in Oracle R12 EBS*

The following are some key scripts for monitoring the Concurrent Managers:

afcmstat.sql   Shows all defined managers, capacity, process ID, etc.

afimchk.sql   Gives status for Internal Concurrent Manager and PMON

afcmcreq.sql   Shows Concurrent Manager basics

afrqwait.sql   Shows pending, held, and scheduled requests

afrqstat.sql   Lists concurrent-request execution times and status

afqpmrid.sql   Identifies the process IDs for FNDLIBR processes

afimlock.sql   Finds concurrency and locking issues

These scripts are located in the $FND_TOP/sql directory. You can execute them while connected to SQL*PLUS as the APPS schema.

Below are some additional scripts that can be used for tuning the Oracle EBS concurrent managers.

```
select
    f.application_short_name app,
    substr(p.user_concurrent_program_name,1,55) description,
    substr(p.concurrent_program_name,1,20) program,
    r.priority,
    count(*) cnt,
    sum(actual_completion_date - actual_start_date) * 24 elapsed,
    avg(actual_completion_date - actual_start_date) * 24 average,
    max(actual_completion_date - actual_start_date) * 24 max,
    min(actual_completion_date - actual_start_date) * 24 min,
    stddev(actual_completion_date - actual_start_date) * 24 stddev,
    stddev(actual_start_date - requested_start_date) * 24 wstddev,
    sum(actual_start_date - requested_start_date) * 24 waited,
    avg(actual_start_date - requested_start_date) * 24 avewait,
    c.request_class_name type
from fnd_concurrent_queues fcq,
     fnd_concurrent_queue_content fcqc,
     fnd_concurrent_request_class c,
     fnd_application f,
     fnd_concurrent_programs_vl p,
     fnd_concurrent_requests r
where r.program_application_id = p.application_id
  and r.concurrent_program_id = p.concurrent_program_id
  and r.status_code in ('C','G','E')
  and p.application_id = f.application_id
  and r.program_application_id = f.application_id
  and r.request_class_application_id = c.application_id(+)
  and r.concurrent_request_class_id = c.request_class_id(+)
  and r.request_class_application_id = fcqc.type_application_id(+)
  and r.concurrent_request_class_id = fcqc.type_id(+)
  and fcqc.queue_application_id = fcq.application_id(+)
  and fcqc.concurrent_queue_id = fcq.concurrent_queue_id(+)
```

```
group by
   c.request_class_name,
   f.application_short_name,
   p.concurrent_program_name,
   p.user_concurrent_program_name,
   r.priority
/
TOTAL   AVG    MAX    MIN    RUN    WAIT   #WAITED      AVG REQ APP    DESCRIPTION
PROGRAM               PRI    R                   UN    HOURS  HOURS  HOURS  HOURS
STDDEV  STDDEV  HOURS     WAIT TYPE
------  ----------------------------------------  --------------------  ----  -----
-                      --  -------  ------  ------  ------  -------  -------  ---------  ------
--  -------------                  --
SQLGL   Periods - Open Period: Child Process      GLOOAPC            50     1
2      .00    .00    .00    .00    .00    .00      .10    .01
BOM     Cost Manager                              CMCTCM                   50
1 ###### ###### ###### ######     .00      .00 -16403.89 ########
ALR     Check Event Alert                         ALECTC             1
8      .02    .00    .00    .00    .00    .01      .16    .02
OFA     Asset Inventory Report                    FAS410             1
2      .01    .01    .01    .00    .00    .00      .01    .00
SQLGL   Open Encumbrance Year                     GLEOYR             1
2      .09    .05    .05    .04    .01
```

Statistics Collection for Oracle R12 EBS

There are two fundamental reasons why you need to update statistics for Oracle EBS environments.

- Cost-based optimization requires the best execution path with current statistics.

- Second, it improves overall application and database performance because the execution plans are stabilized for queries issued against the database tier. Below is a reference point on how to collect statistics:

My Oracle Support (http://support.oracle.com)

Note 419728.1 *How to Gather Statistics on Oracle Applications* 11.5.10 (and above)—Concurrent Process, Temp Tables, Manually, which provide details on how to collect stats for the Oracle EBS environment.

Do not use DBMS_STATS with Oracle R12 EBS to collect statistics! The reason why you want to use the FND_STATS or concurrent program to update and collect statistics is because of the integrated nature of ERP systems of which Oracle R12 EBS is a part. By using the FND_STATS method for collecting statistics for Oracle EBS, you will ensure that all of the application schemas receive the best execution plan. If you run DBMS_STATS it will only update the internal database stats such as those for SYS and SYSTEM and will fail to grab the latest optimizer statistics for application schemas such as APPS.

Be sure to gather table statistics on CM tables:

- FND_CONCURRENT_PROCESSES
- FND_CONCURRENT_PROGRAMS

- FND_CONCURRENT_REQUESTS
- FND_CONCURRENT_QUEUES

The above Oracle EBS concurrent manager (CM) tables need to be updated frequently in terms of gathering statistics to maintain performance. Below are the two key methods to gather statistics for Oracle R12 EBS:

- Manual
- Concurrent job for gather stats

FND_STATS for schema statistics collection

Example
Collect statistics for AP schema:

    exec fnd_stats.gather_schema_statistics('AP');

Collect stats for all schemas for Oracle R12 EBS:

    exec fnd_stats.gather_schema_statistics('ALL');

How to gather stats for temp tables with Oracle R12 EBS:

    exec fnd_stats.gather_table_stats('<schema>','<temp_table_name>');

Collect stats for temp tables in AR schema:

    exec fnd_stats.gather_table_stats('AR','temp_ap');

Using OAM to gather stats for Oracle R12 EBS.

    Use the following navigation path within the Oracle R12 EBS menu from OAM:System Administrator | Concurrent Requests |

See Figure 24-15.

Application Tech-Stack Tuning

- Tune values for timeouts to prevent and resolve errors in performance for network delays for forms, oacore, and OC4J.
- Avoid and resolve the infamous "Uninterrupted Exception 150 error" when starting and stopping application-tier services.
- Values to check in Oracle R12 EBS Content file
- Consider shared APPL_TOP and staged APPL_TOP for performance.
- Implement Parallel Concurrent Processing to distribute the performance load for concurrent processing.
- Configuration settings for JVM with OC4J under both the Oracle R12 EBS Context file for application tech stack and opmn.xml values.

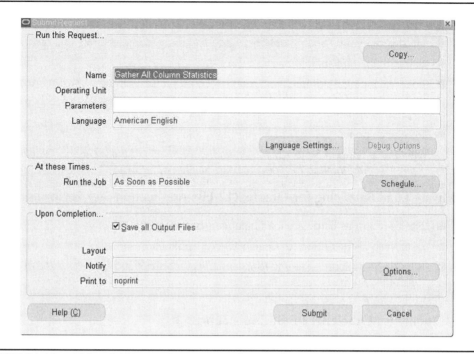

FIGURE 24-15. *Using OAM to gather statistics for Oracle R12 EBS*

Additional Considerations for Tuning the Application Tier with Oracle R12 EBS

- Performance metrics for OC4J groups
- Use server for concurrent processing server, application server in split-tier configuration to provide more performance and availability.
- Consider load-balancing hardware or software to improve performance and availability.
- Consider deploying Oracle RAC for scale-out and scale-up in performance if you need it for large deployments.
- Oracle 10*g* Application Server tuning issues
- Oracle HTTP Server: Apache Web server
- Timeout settings for Apache
- Under http.conf file under IAS_ORACLE_HOME and Oracle 10*g* AS home directory

Load Balancing for Application-Tier performance

■ Hardware load-balancing options: Cisco and Big IP some vendors that offer solutions

■ Software load balancing

■ Load balancing is complex and requires coordination with network, security, and systems-administration teams, as well as the database team, for successful implementation.

■ Reference point:

My Oracle Support Note 727171.1: *Implementing Load Balancing on Oracle E-Business Suite - Documentation for Specific Load Balancer Hardware*

Software Load Balancing for Oracle R12 EBS Application-Tier Performance

■ Not as robust as hardware load balancers but more cost effective

■ Uses Web cache option for Oracle 10*g* AS application server

■ My Oracle Support Note 380486.1 *Installing and Configuring Web Cache 10*g *and Oracle E-Business Suite 12*

Java Tuning for Oracle R12 E-Business Suite

■ Tuning Java components is essential for performance with Oracle R12 EBS.

■ Oracle R12 EBS is dependent on Java technology.

■ Default values are too low for Java with OC4J settings.

■ Watch for issues with garbage collection.

■ Avoid full garbage collection, as this impacts performance.

■ My Oracle Support Note 567551.1: *Troubleshooting: Configuring Various JVM Tuning Parameters for Oracle E-Business Suite 11i and R12*

■ My Oracle Support Note 362851.1: *Guidelines to Set Up the JVM in Apps E-Business Suite 11i and R12*

■ http://java.sun.com/javase/technologies/hotspot/vmoptions.jsp#BehavioralOptions
http://blogs.sun.com/watt/resource/jvm-options-list.html

Tools for Measuring JVM Performance with Oracle R12 EBS

■ Excellent free tool to graph performance for JVM with Oracle R12 EBS and garbage collection

■ www.tagtraum.com/gcviewer.html

See Figure 25-16.

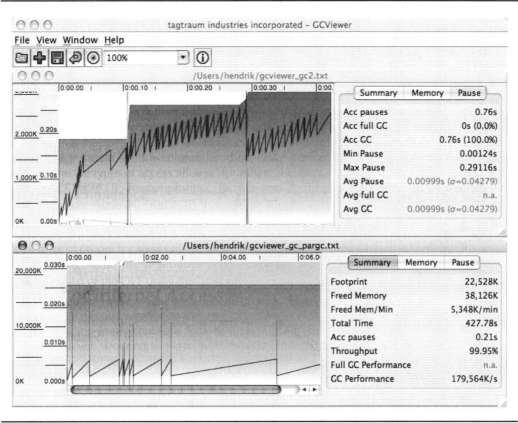

FIGURE 24-16. *Using JVM tools to optimize Java performance with Oracle R12 EBS*

Monitoring Java Performance: Oracle R12 EBS

■ Oracle 10*g* Grid Control (OEM) with Application Management Pack (AMP)

NOTE
These items require additional licenses.

■ My Oracle Support Note 557194.1 provides a script called monitor_jdbc_conn.sql to monitor JDBC connections.

■ Collect metrics to analyze current performance

■ Good information from ADDM and AWR in 11*g*. Below is the output from an AWR report from the database tier for *Oracle R12 EBS*:

```
Statistic                        Total              per Second      per Trans
-------------------------------- ------------------ -------------- -------------
java call heap collected bytes        683,300,160        1,300.0         877.8
java call heap collected count          3,693,358            7.0           4.7
```

```
java call heap gc count                          356           0.0          0.0
java call heap live object count              24,810           0.1          0.0
java call heap live object count             142,439           0.3          0.2
Instance Activity Stats           DB/Inst: SBOX/SBOX Snaps: 274-420
java call heap live size                   2,358,144           4.5          3.0
java call heap live size max              33,260,184          63.3         42.7
java call heap object count                   56,992           0.1          0.1
java call heap object count max              345,992           0.7          0.4
java call heap total size                 42,729,472          81.3         54.9
java call heap total size max            115,343,360         219.5        148.2
java call heap used size                   6,144,496          11.7          7.9
java call heap used size max              72,864,528         138.6         93.6
```

Database Tuning for Oracle R12 E-Business Suite

■ Similar to tuning regular Oracle 11*g* database, but unique in how statistics collected

■ Remember to use FND_STATS rather than DBMS_STATS to collect and update statistics.

■ Watch out for concurrency and locking issues for runaway user processes.

■ Schedule backup jobs during off hours to avoid impact on business users.

■ Suggested values for database initialization parameters for Oracle R12 EBS

■ My Oracle Support Note 396009.1: *Database Initialization Parameters for Oracle Applications Release 12*

■ Oracle R12 by default installs either a 10*g*R2 or an 11*g*R1 database for each fresh (new) installation.

■ For example: Oracle 12.0 to 12.04 uses 10.2.x database

■ Oracle 12.1.1 and later install Oracle 11*g*R1 database (11.1.x).

■ Watch out for upgrade issues from 11*i* to R12 EBS for database.

■ Suggested values for database initialization parameters for Oracle R12 EBS

Database Parameters for Oracle R12 EBS Sizing Chart

Table 24-1 shows the recommended values for the Oracle database-initialization parameters to use with Oracle R12 E-Business Suite.

Upgrade Performance Considerations for Oracle R12 EBS

■ When you upgrade from older releases such as 10.x and 11*i* to Oracle R12, you must account for performance items.

■ Rule based Optimizer (RBO) in 10.x and early 11*i* releases to the Cost Based Optimizer (CBO) in R12

■ Different way of tuning for stats and database

Parameter Name	Development or Test Instance	11–100 Users	101–500 Users	501–1000 Users	1001–2000 Users
processes	200	200	800	1200	2500
sessions	400	400	1600	2400	5000
sga_target	1G	1G	2G	3G	14G
shared_pool_size (csp)	N/A	N/A	N/A	1800M	3000M
shared_pool_reserved_size (csp)	N/A	N/A	N/A	180M	300M
shared_pool_size (no csp)	400M	600M	800M	1000M	2000M
shared_pool_reserved_size (no csp)	40M	60M	80M	100M	100M
pga_aggregate_target	1G	2G	4G	10G	20G
Total Memory Required	Approximately 2 GB	Approximately 3 GB	Approximately 6 GB	Approximately 13 GB	Approximately 25 GB

TABLE 24-1.   *Sizing chart for Oracle R12 EBS database-initialization parameters*

- Consider changes for SGA and PGA sizing.
- Migrate from old tablespace model to Oracle Application Tablespace Model (OATM)
- My Oracle Support Note 761570.1: *Database Preparation Guidelines for an E-Business Suite Release 12.1.1 Upgrade*

Conclusion

Oracle performance tuning is a massive discipline that crosses multiple business and technology areas. Tuning begins with a holistic approach to correctly implementing key business processes that map to the technical aspects of hardware, storage, network, and application processes, so that performance analysis is conducted in a proactive rather than a reactive manner.

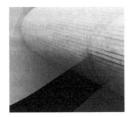

CHAPTER
25

Oracle SOA Suite
and BPEL for Oracle EBS

OA, or service-oriented architecture, is a software paradigm and methodology for creating content-rich applications based on business logic that can be quickly mapped to technical environments. In the past, millions of lines of complex application code were required to develop and implement Web-based client server applications for enterprise resource planning software packages, including Oracle E-Business Suite. Business Process Execution Language (BPEL), based on the XML standard, is used for mapping flowchart business logic to reverse engineer data-processing environments.

SOA Suite Integration with Oracle R12 E-Business Suite

SOA Suite can be used with the Oracle Financials to integrate Web services with all of the Oracle R12 EBS modules via the use of custom interfaces. These interfaces are developed by application teams to process data integrations with various functions such as AP and GL, as shown in Figure 25-1.

Web services are created via development tools available from Oracle, such as JDeveloper in Java, PL/SQL, and BPEL constructs. The Oracle 11*g* SOA Suite provides an integrated development environment for creating Web services, including Web service descriptive languages (WSDLs) to interface with Oracle R12 E-Business Suite. The key component that is used to rapidly implement SOA Web services with Oracle R12 EBS is the Oracle SOA Suite adapter.

In order to use the Oracle SOA Suite to develop your own custom integrations with Oracle E-Business Suite Release 12, you can use versions 10.1.3.5 or higher.

To use the SOA Suite adapter with Oracle R12 EBS, you must

- have Oracle E-Business Suite Release 12.0 or later, and
- enable the "Native E-Business Suite Connectivity Using J2EE Data Sources" feature.

There are no additional dependencies with Oracle EBS if custom integrations are used with the Oracle Fusion Middleware Adapter. Custom integrations developed with the SOA Suite adapter are executed against standard Oracle EBS Web services that are available and published in the Integration Repository.

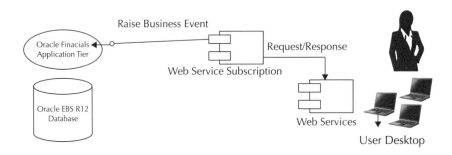

FIGURE 25-1. *Web-service integration with SOA Suite and Oracle R12 EBS*

Additional information about using the generic SOA Suite adapter for Oracle EBS can be found in the Oracle Fusion Middleware Adapter for Oracle Applications User's Guide (http://docs.oracle.com/cd/E12839_01/integration.1111/e10537/T430238T430241.htm).

Prebuilt BPEL Templates for Oracle R12 EBS

The Oracle EBS R12 product team has developed custom prebuilt BPEL business processes for the following modules:

- Oracle Price Protection
- Complex Maintenance, Repair, and Overhaul
- Oracle Transportation Management
- Supply Chain Trading Connector
- Advanced Supply Chain Planning
- Product Information Management

These prebuilt BPEL processes have been certified with Oracle BPEL Process Manager 10*g* version 10.1.3.5 (in Oracle SOA Suite 10.1.3.5) for Oracle E-Business Suite Release 12.1.1 and higher.

Information about using these prebuilt SOA integrations can be found in My Oracle Support Note 755067.1: *Using Oracle BPEL 10*g *with E-Business Suite Release 12.1.1 or Higher* (http://support.oracle.com). Oracle support is available with a valid customer support contract for issues that arise in integrating the SOA Suite adapter with the Oracle E-Business Suite.

Using Oracle BPEL 10*g* with E-Business Suite Release 12

Oracle BPEL Process Manager in Oracle Application Server 10*g* Release provides the tools and services into meaningful business processes for management and orchestration of complex business processes. Specifically, it allows you to perform the following tasks:

- configuring application software adapters to work with SOA Suite and Oracle E-Business Suite environments, and
- deploying Oracle E-Business Suite BPEL business processes with multiple BPEL domains.

The Oracle BPEL Process Manager software be licensed, obtained, and installed separately from the core Oracle R12 EBS applications.

NOTE
The tools in BPEL and SOA Suite have been tested and supported by Oracle, but they are not the only methods for integrating Oracle EBS with third-party and legacy applications.

Installing and Configuring SOA Suite

The first step in the setup and configuration process for the Oracle SOA Suite and Oracle EBS is to review the product documentation from Oracle. The following guides at the Oracle Technology Network (OTN; http://otn.oracle.com) are recommended to familiarize you with the architecture of SOA and BPEL, as these topics cover a wide scope beyond the context of this book:

- Oracle BPEL Process Manager and
- Oracle AS 10*g*/11*g* deployment guides.

Install Oracle SOA Suite, Including Oracle BPEL Process Manager

You must install Oracle SOA Suite 10*g* Release 10.1.3.1, followed by an upgrade to Patchset 10.1.3.5. This installation must be performed outside of the core E-Business Suite instance. It can be performed in it's own $ORACLE_HOME directory or on a separate stand-alone server.

- Download and install Oracle SOA Suite 10*g* Release 10.1.3.1 from the Oracle Technology Network at http://www.oracle.com/technology/software/tech/soa/index.html.
- Download and install Oracle Application Server 10*g* Patchset 10.1.3.5 at https://updates .oracle.com/download/8626084.html.

Be sure to take note of the host name and port number displayed at the end of the installation process.

Verify Successful Installation

Verify successful installation of BPEL by invoking the Welcome Page and the BPEL Console:

- Application Server Welcome Page: http://*hostname:port*/
  BPEL Control Page: http://*hostname:port*/BPELConsole

Configure Oracle SOA Suite to Integrate with E-Business Suite

Perform the following steps on each E-Business Suite instance:

- Register the current Oracle 10*g* Application Server (10*g* AS) instance against each Oracle R12 EBS environment by generating a new dbc file. The dbc file will be used for connecting from the Oracle 10*g* AS instance and the EBS instance.

NOTE
Every time that a dbc file is created on the Oracle R12 EBS environment from the registration process, any previous dbc files for the connection with the Oracle R12 EBS instance will be invalidated. Therefore, the dbc file on the BPEL server will need to be replaced with the new dbc file.

- Collect and bundle the Oracle R12 EBS artifacts required for the BPEL deployment and copy these over to the BPEL server via FTP.
- Create a new shared library instance on the Oracle 10*g* AS instance using the fndds.jar utility.

These steps will need to be performed once per Oracle R12 EBS environment that you plan to integrate with the Oracle SOA Suite, except for the last one—the shared library only needs to be created once per Oracle 10*g* AS instance.

Create BPEL Domains

For each of the Oracle R12 EBS instances, you will need to create a BPEL domain to be used for managing and orchestrating business processes. It is advised that you use the naming convention Ebs*SID*domain (e.g., EbsPRDdomain) for the domain name. Here are the specific steps for this task:

- Using the URL http://*hostname:port*/BPELAdmin/server.jsp, log in to the BPEL Administration screen as an OC4J Administrator with username oc4jadmin.
- Select the BPEL Domains tab.
- Select Create New BPEL Domain from the left column.
- Enter the domain ID.

Create JDBC Connection Pools

For each E-Business Suite instance, create a JDBC connection pool. Use the naming convention JdbcConn*BPELdomainname* (e.g., JdbcConnEbsPRODdomain) for the name of connection pool.

- Log in to Application Server Management (http://*hostname:port*/em), click on the OC4J instance where SOA Suite is installed, and navigate to the Administration screen.
- Click the Go to Task icon for Services and JDBC Resources.
- Under Connection Pools, click the Create button.
- Accept all defaults and click Continue.

NOTE
It is recommended that the JDBC connection pool bed created using the dbc file created for the E-Business Suite instance. Any other mechanism will only be a work-around. Since the dbc file already contains key connectivity parameters for the E-Business Suite instance, some of the values are not required.

Back on the main page, a "successful connection" message is displayed. If you see an error message, check the URL and credentials to ensure that you have entered the right information.

Define and Configure Data Sources

For each E-Business Suite instance, define and configure a data source. Use the naming convention DataSource*BPELdomainname* (e.g., DataSourceEbsPRODdomain).

- Above the Connection Pool section, under Data Sources, click Create.
- Accept the defaults and click Continue.
- On the next screen (Create Data Source), enter the values for your data source and leave default values for the rest of the parameters.
- Restart the appropriate OC4J instance after creating the data source.

Create an Oracle EBS adapter connection:

- At the top of the page, click the OC4J:home (or OC4J:Application server name that has the orabpel process running) breadcrumb link, then the Applications link.
- In the tree of applications, click the Default link.
- Under Modules, click the AppsAdapter link, followed by Connection Factories.
- Under Connection Factories, click Create.

NOTE
Use the Create button near the top of the screen, not the one in the Shared Connection Pools section.

- Accept all the defaults and click Continue.
- Enter the following values and restart the appropriate OC4J instance:

Field	Value
JNDI Location	eis/Apps/AppsAdapter*BPELdomainname*
xADataSourceName	jdbc/DataSource*BPELdomainname*

Define and Configure Database Adapter Connections
Configure the Database Adapter similarly to the Oracle EBS Adapter. Specify the following values:

Field	Value
JNDI Location	eis/DB/DbAdapter*BPELdomainname*
xADataSourceName	jdbc/DataSource*BPELdomainname*

Define and Configure AQ Adapter Connections
Configure the AQ Adapter similarly to the Oracle EBS and Database Adapters.

NOTE
Remember to repeat these steps for each E-Business Suite instance you want to integrate with the Oracle SOA Suite installation.

Deploying Oracle E-Business Suite BPEL Business Processes
Once you have configured the SOA environment and BPEL server and applied the required patches for Oracle R12 EBS instances, you can setup the BPEL processes with the EBS. This requires that you follow these steps for each EBS environment and corresponding BPEL domain:

- Unzip the copied files into an Oracle R12 EBS staging directory.
- Update the configuration in the common properties file.

- Use a centralized ANT build script provided by Oracle to deploy the desired BPEL business processes into the desired BPEL domain.

Preparation Steps Prior to Deploying BPEL Artifacts to Oracle SOA Suite

Perform the following tasks before deploying any BPEL business processes to the Oracle SOA Suite:

- Transfer the EBS_BPEL_payload.zip file from the EBS instance to the $ORACLE_HOME directory for the Oracle SOA Suite installation.

- Unzip the file $ORACLE_HOME/EBS_BPEL_payload.zip.

- Ensure that the environment variable PATH contains the complete path to the jdk/bin and ant/bin directories that are included in the Oracle SOA Suite 10.1.3.5 installation.

- Ensure that the environment variable ANT_HOME is set to the ANT root directory included in the Oracle SOA Suite 10.1.3.5 installation ($ORACLE_HOME/ant).

- Ensure that the environment variable JAVA_HOME is set to the JDK root directory included in the Oracle SOA Suite 10.1.3.5 installation.

- Ensure that the environment variable EBS_SOAHOME is set to $ORACLE_HOME/appsutil/ *EBS instance name or DBSID*/bpel.

The staging directory contains the following:

- $EBS_SOA_HOME houses the EBS central deployment ANT script and property file.

- $EBS_SOA_HOME/*EBS product short name* subdirectories contain artifacts for each individual product.

NOTE
You will need to figure out which BPEL business processes to deploy in each BPEL domain. This is dependent on your business needs and specific Oracle EBS products used in your environment, as well as the topology of your EBS environment.

Be sure to review My Oracle Support Note 755067.1: *Using Oracle BPEL 10g with E-Business Suite Release 12.1.1 or Higher* on a regular basis when performing the configuration tasks for Oracle SOA Suite with BPEL and Oracle R12 EBS.

The Central ANT Property File

The master BPEL deployment script uses an ANT properties file ($EBS_SOAHOME/EbsBpelGlobal. properties) for key environment-configuration values. The table for the configuration shows the values, the sample values of the properties, and a brief description of each. Review and update the values with the configuration information that reflects the topology of your software installation. However, do not update the property values of some of the ANT properties, as these are updated automatically by the master ANT script.

NOTE
The owner of the property indicates that the value is needed for that particular product installation; you only need to update the properties for the products being installed. Properties with the owner SYSTEM need to be filled out. In addition to the central property file, each of the EBS products to be installed may have its own local property files that may need updates. Please follow instructions in the product-specific documentation.

Run ANT to Deploy BPEL Business Processes into Oracle SOA Suite 10*g*

The following steps deploy the BPEL business processes into the target BPEL domains. The E-Business Suite product-specific steps should be completed successfully before executing the ANT commands.

■ You can run the ANT script in test mode to see if the key property values have been created correctly:

```
% ant -Dbpel.domain=BPELdomainname -Dstage.dir=<$EBS_SOAHOME> -f
EbsBpelMasterBuild.xml test
```

This will show the critical global properties that have been set in the EbsBpelGlobal.properties file correctly.

■ The following command will deploy all of the BPEL business processes for all product teams into the specified BPEL domain:

```
% ant -k -Dbpel.domain=BPELdomainname -Dstage.dir=<$EBS_SOAHOME> -f
EbsBpelMasterBuild.xml all
```

NOTE
The "-k" flag tells ANT to execute all targets that do not depend on failed targets.

■ All BPEL business processes for a particular product team can be deployed using the following variation:

```
% ant -Dbpel.domain=BPELdomainname -Dstage.dir=<$EBS_SOAHOME> -f
EbsBpelMasterBuild.xml product_short_code
```

■ You can also use the central ANT script to build product-team-specific targets from the product-team-specific ANT scripts. For example, the following command will build the ANT target dpp.deploy.all from the Price Protection ANT script:

```
% ant -f EbsBpelMasterBuild.xml dpp -Dadmin.password=helloworld -
Dbpel.domain=default -DEbsAppsAdapter=eis/Apps/AppsAdapterdefault -
Ddpp.target=dpp.deploy.all
```

NOTE
Oracle Price Protection requires the command-line parameter —
DEbsAppsAdapter=eis/Apps/AppsAdapterdefault in the ANT command.

Run-time status and execution logs will be displayed as the script is run; the output can be redirected to an output file to be examined.

The ANT targets can be executed to build the processes for each of the following E-Business Suite product target names:

- dpp: Oracle Price Protection

- msc: Advanced Supply Chain and Planning

- msc_otm: Advanced Supply Chain and Planning

- wms_otm (wms): Oracle Warehouse Management
  wsh_otm (wsh): Oracle Shipping Execution
  po_otm (po): Oracle Purchasing

- ahl: Complex Maintenance, Repair, and Overhaul
  cln: Supply Chain Trading Connector

NOTE
Price Protection and Supply Chain Trading Connector are not included in the ANT "all" targets and need to be executed separately.

Verify a Successful Deployment

Once the BPEL process is deployed, it can be seen in the BPEL Console. Verify that the processes were successfully deployed to the corresponding BPEL domain by viewing the processes from the BPEL Console in the respective domain.

Troubleshooting Tips for Common Installation and Deployment Issues

Deployment of BPEL and SOA Suite with Oracle R12 EBS presents additional unique challenges that may arise during the initial configuration phase. The most common issues are due to the instance for the BPEL domain or SOA Suite domain being off-line or not currently running. Since Oracle 10g AS uses an Oracle database for its repository in addition to OC4J processes, you need to verify both that the database repository is online and functional and that all of the J2EE processes are online (via the opmn commands). Also check to ensure that firewall rules and the proxy server are not blocking access between the EBS instance and BPEL/SOA Suite environments.

Additional tips are available in My Oracle Support Knowledge Note 797596.1: *Troubleshooting Tips and Known Issues for EBS SOA Suite Deployment in R12.1.1.*

Oracle SOA Suite Integration with E-Business Suite

Now that we have discussed how to integrate BPEL with Oracle Release 12 Financials, let us discuss how to integrate the Oracle SOA Suite with EBS. First, download the SOA Suite files from OTN (http://otn.oracle.com). We will use supported configurations, as such SOA Suite 10.1.3.5.0 with Oracle Release 12. In the following examples, Oracle Enterprise Linux 5.2 will be used as the platform for SOA Suite 10g with Oracle EBS 12.0.1.

Preparation

Download SOA 10.1.3.1.0 from OTN or Oracle E-Delivery. It is recommended that you first review the *Oracle Application Server Enterprise Deployment Guide 10g Release 3 (10.1.3.1.0), B28939-03,* available at http://download.oracle.com/docs/cd/B31017_01/core.1013/b28939.pdf.

In order to save you time and the 200-plus pages of documentation, we can simplify the steps for installing the Oracle 10g SOA Suite.

First you will need to install and configure the schemas for the SOA Suite. These schemas are deployed via the irca.sh script located under the $ORACLE_HOME directory for SOA Suite after you unzip the files for SOA Suite.

1. **Install schemas for SOA.**

```
$ cd /install/soa_schemas/irca
./irca.sh
```

Verify that the SOA schemas have been created without errors.

The irca.sh script will generate a log file that outputs schema-object creation. For example, this installation created a log file called irca2010-02-10_07-19-43PM.log.

Now that we have created the schemas for SOA Suite and populated them with the required metadata, we are ready to install the SOA Suite. Unzip the files that you downloaded earlier and start the installation by executing the runInstaller script.

2. **Install SOA Suite.** The splash screen will appear as long as all prerequisites have been met.

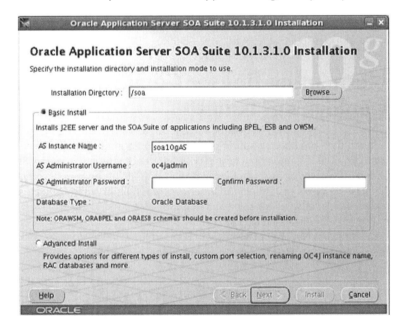

For the test SOA Suite deployment, we used the following entries for the 10g AS instance and administrator account (oc4jadmin):

```
AS instance name: soa10gAS
AS administrator: oc4jadmin

Schemas

orabpel
oraesb
orawsm

Oracle:

sys
system/manager

EBS R12:
apps/apps
sysadmin/sysadmin
```

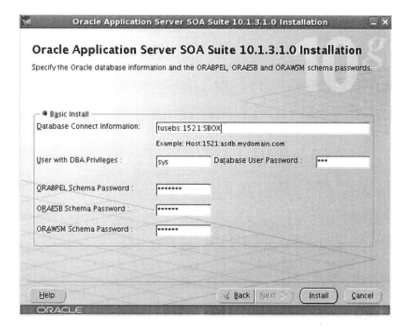

Next we need to enter details for the orainventory location.

After this runs, we need to run the orainstRoot.sh script as the root user in another terminal window.

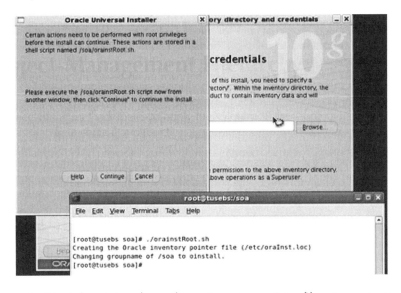

After the orainstRoot.sh script performs the oraInventory pointer-file setup, we are ready to kick off the installation for SOA Suite.

Now the Oracle installer for SOA Suite runs the prerequisite checks before installation begins. Since we are running an instance of EBS already on the same server for test purposes, these already comply with kernel and system requirements for SOA Suite.

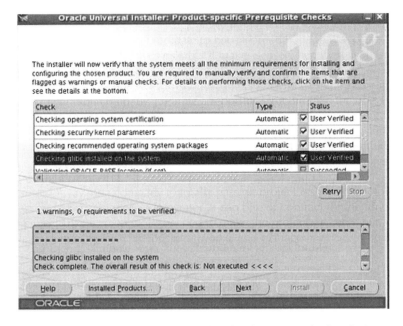

The installation begins after we confirm that the checks are satisfied with the settings for the installation.

SOA installation will process the setup details to build the environment. The last step is to run the root.sh script in another terminal session as root.

Enter the prompts for the directory and take the defaults.

After a while, the installation process completes. However, we have it fail at the end on configuration assistants during opmn on a timed-out process error. The solution to this issue, which most likely is a bug in 10g AS, is to stop opmn gracefully and kill any open opmn processes. Now that the installation has completed for SOA Suite, we need to apply a patch.

3. **Install patch for SOA Suite.** Download the patch from OTN or My Oracle Support. You will need to unpack the files as shown below:

```
$ unzip ias_linux_x86_101350.zip
Change to the directory and start the installation:
$ cd Disk1
./runInstaller &
```

Complete the installation of the patch and manually kill the opmnctl processes for SOA Suite.

NOTE
Be careful to kill only the opmnctl processes for the SOA Suite, not those for EBS.

Use ps-ef|grep opmnctl to find the process IDs and kill them. Then start opmnctl processes manually from the SOA Suite ORACLE_HOME directory.

Run the following opmnctl commands from the SOA Suite ORACLE_HOME/opmn/bin directory:

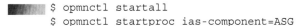

```
$ opmnctl startall
$ opmnctl startproc ias-component=ASG
```

```
[oracle@tusebs bin]$ ./opmnctl startproc ias-component=ASG
opmnctl: starting opmn managed processes...
[oracle@tusebs bin]$ ./opmnctl status

Processes in Instance: soa10gAS.tusebs.localdomain
-------------------------------+--------------------+---------+---------
ias-component                  | process-type       |   pid   | status
-------------------------------+--------------------+---------+---------
OC4JGroup:default_group        | OC4J:home          |  23833  | Alive
ASG                            | ASG                |  24395  | Alive
```

Now we need to restart the patch installer from the SOA Suite ORACLE_HOME directory and enter the password for the oc4jadmin screen.

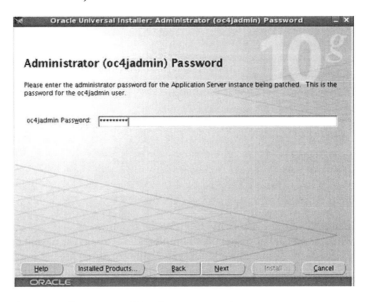

Next we need to enter the password for the OWSM schema.

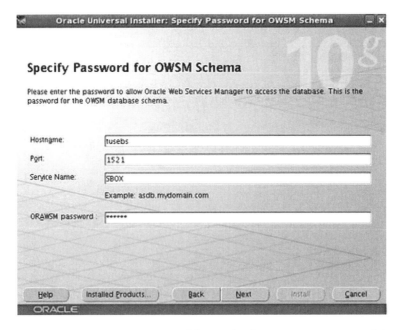

Click OK to shut down the application middle tier for the SOA Suite as part of the patch-configuration process.

Now you will see the preview screen, listing details for the patch with SOA Suite. For the summary page, you just need to review and click OK to install the patch for the SOA Suite.

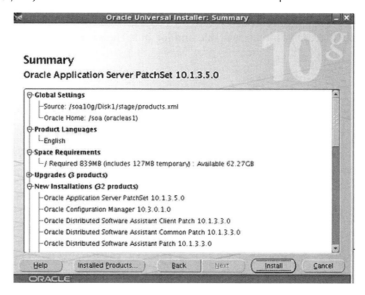

The patch takes about 30 to 90 minutes to run, depending on server performance.

As part of the final configuration for the SOA Suite patch, we need to run the root.sh script as root user.

```
# cd /soa
# ./root.sh
```

The root.sh script configures privileges required for the SOA Suite installation. The patch installation completes successfully.

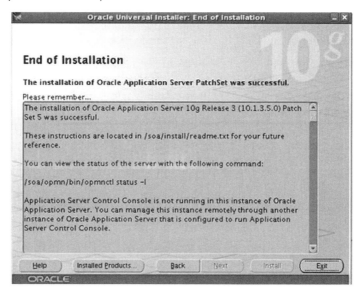

However, we need to check and—if required—start the processes for SOA Suite for 10*g* Application Server.

We use opmnctl to start and validate that all processes for SOA Suite are back online.

4. **Verify that SOA Suite is available and log in to the welcome page.** Oracle 10*g* SOA Suite uses the URL http://*hostname:port* for default installation. For example, http://tusebs:8889 will show the 10*g* AS site. You can access BPEL and other SOA Suite tools from this page.

We need to verify that single sign-on is working for SOA Suite. Navigate to http://tusebs:8889/ BPELConsole.

After we login to BPEL, we can check the settings for the SOA Suite. These settings will be used at a later point to configure SOA Suite for BPEL with Oracle EBS.

Now we also want to verify that all is functioning with the Oracle 10*g* AS environment, since this plays a key role in SOA Suite operations. We navigate to the main 10*g* AS console site. By default this is at the URL http://*hostname:port*/em. For example, our test server uses http://tusebs:8889/em. At this point you should be able to verify and check to see that all of the BPEL and SOA services are functional and online.

Configure Oracle R12 EBS with SOA Suite

Part A: Enabling Oracle E-Business Suite Integrated SOA Gateway Release 12.1

1. Apply the Oracle E-Business Suite Patch 9060361:R12.TXK.B: FSG: Log Location and Level Properties Not Accessible from OAFM.

As with all EBS patches, you will need to verify that all prerequisite and corequisite patches have been applied successfully without errors to the E-Business Suite via Auto Patch. Be sure to review the instructions!

2. Set the applications environment and stop all application-tier processes. From the applications instance $APPL_TOP, set the environment by running the APPS.env script.

3. Shut down the application-tier processes for your EBS instance by running $ADMIN_ SCRIPTS_HOME/adstpall.

4. Run the TXK development script to install Oracle Application Server Adapter for Oracle Applications as shown here:

   ```
   $FND_TOP/bin/txkrun.pl -script=CfgOC4JApp -applicationname=pcapps -
   oracleinternal=Yes -oc4jpass=welcome -runautoconfig=No
   ```

5. Run the TXK deployment script to install forms-c4ws.ear and configure the container Forms-c4ws J2EE group correctly, as shown here:

   ```
   $FND_TOP/bin/txkrun.pl -script=DeployForms-c4ws
   ```

6. Enable the new container forms-c4ws. (By default, the new OC4J container forms-c4ws will be disabled.) To do so, modify the following values of context variables in $CONTEXT_FILE:

```
Set "s_forms-c4wsstatus" to "enabled."
Set "s_forms-c4ws_nprocs" to 1.
```

7. Run AutoConfig. For information on how to run AutoConfig, see My Oracle Support Knowledge Document 387859.1: *Using AutoConfig to Manage System Configurations in Oracle E-Business Suite Release 12.*

8. Start all application-tier processes for the instance by running the script $ADMIN_SCRIPTS_HOME/adstrtal.

9. Enable the ASADMIN user per details in the Oracle Metalink support notes referenced earlier.

10. Log on to Oracle E-Business Suite using the user ID sysadmin.

11. Bounce the middle tier for the EBS environment

Part B: Configuring SOA Suite with Release 12.1.x for Oracle E-Business Suite

A recap of the earlier discussion of how to set up SOA Suite and BPEL with EBS will refresh your memory on the summary tasks. The following steps are required to configure the Oracle SOA Suite for Oracle EBS:

1. Register your installation of SOA Suite with the R12 EBS instance per details from My Oracle Support Note 755069.1: *EBS R12 Packager and Adapters for External Application Servers.* This involves generating a new dbc file to use with SOA Suite and your EBS instance.

2. Create BPEL domains in the SOA environment.

3. Create JDBC connection pools in the SOA instance for OC4J to access each EBS instance.

4. Define data sources between the SOA instance and EBS instances.

5. Create the Oracle adapter connection between the SOA instance and EBS instances.

Conclusion

Fusion Middleware is a rich set of development tools based on Web services that provide feature-rich integration for third-party applications and legacy systems with the Oracle E-Business Suite. By using graphical language constructs based on XML and Java, BPEL developers can use the SOA Suite to create powerful interfaces for managing data flow between EBS and Web-based applications as well as legacy mainframe servers to process data quickly and effectively.

References

My Oracle Support Note 755067.1: *Using Oracle BPEL 10g with E-Business Suite Release 12.1.1 or Higher*

My Oracle Support Note 556540.1: *Installing Oracle E-Business Suite Integrated SOA Gateway, Release 12.1*

My Oracle Support Note 755069.1: *EBS R12 Packager and Adapters for External Application Servers*

CHAPTER
26

Disaster Recovery and Business Continuity

ith the complex assortment of mission-critical applications running corporate financial systems via the Oracle E-Business Suite, executive managers need a way to safeguard the availability and stability of the data that are the lifeblood of the business environment.

In this chapter, we will discuss the following topics:

- disaster-recovery concepts and design,
- implementation of business continuity for the Oracle E-Business Suite,
- Oracle Data Guard, and
- Oracle Real Application Clusters.

Disaster-Recovery Concepts and Design

Before we provide the insights into how to apply technical methods to Oracle E-Business Suite for disaster recovery, it is useful to first review concepts of how to design a solid plan for high availability. Disaster recovery is a complex topic that is often misunderstood and confused with subtopics such as high availability, fault tolerance, and business continuity. **Disaster Recovery** is the process, policies, and procedures related to preparing for recovery or continuation of critical technology infrastructure after either a natural or human-caused disaster.

Disaster-recovery planning (DRP) is a subset of larger processes such as business continuity, and should include planning for resumption of applications, databases, hardware, networking, and other IT infrastructure components. A business-continuity plan includes planning for non-IT-related aspects, such as staff-member activities, during a major disaster, as well as site-facility operations, and it should reference the disaster-recovery plan for recovery of IT-related infrastructure and for business-continuity procedures and guidelines.

High availability provides data-center environments that run mission-critical database applications with the resiliency to withstand failures that may occur due to natural, human, or environmental conditions. For example, if a hurricane wipes out the production data center that hosts a financial application's production database, high availability would provide the much-needed protection to avoid data loss, minimize downtime, and maximize availability of the firm's resources and database applications. As part of disaster recovery, you need to keep in mind the two essential concepts of downtime and time to recovery from failures. Downtime consists of planned and unplanned downtime. Unplanned downtime includes outages that are unexpected due to power failures and natural disasters as well as human error. Planned downtime involves maintenance activities required for production systems, such as database patching of the Oracle E-Business Suite, where a short maintenance interval is required to apply a bug fix and resolve an application-related issues. For example, when the Oracle database administrator has to run Autopatch to apply a Fixed Assets patch, the applications middle-tier services must be shut down and restarted to complete the maintenance activity.

Implementing Business Continuity for Oracle EBS

Business-continuity planning (BCP) refers to the creation and validation of a rehearsed operations plan for the IT organization that explains the procedures of how the data center and business unit will recover and restore, partially or completely, interrupted business functions within a predetermined time after a major disaster. In its simplest terms, BCP is the foundation for the IT data center's operations team to maintain critical systems in the event of disaster. Major incidents could include events such as fires, earthquakes, or acts of terrorism.

BCP may also encompass corporate training efforts to help reduce operational risk factors associated with the lack of IT management controls. These BCP processes may also be integrated with IT standards and practices to improve security and corporate risk-management practices. An example would be implementing BCP controls as part of **Sarbanes-Oxley** compliance requirements for publicly traded corporations.

BCP standards arose from the **British Standards Institution** in 2006, when that organization released a new independent standard for business continuity called BS 25999-1. Prior to the introduction of this standard, IT professionals relied on the institution's information-security standard BS 7799, which provided only limited standards for business-continuity compliance procedures. One of the key benefits of this new standard was to extend additional practices for business continuity to a wider variety of organizations, to cover needs for public-sector, government, nonprofit, and private corporations.

Business-Continuity and Disaster-Recovery Guidelines

The following recommendations will provide you with a blueprint to formulate your requirements and implementation for a robust business-continuity and disaster-recovery plan.

   1.   Identify. the scope and boundaries of your business-continuity plan.

This first step requires you to define the scope of your new business-continuity plan. It provides you with an idea of the limitations and boundaries of the plan. It also includes important audit and risk-analysis reports for corporate assets.

   2.   Conduct a business-impact analysis.

Business-impact analysis is the assessment of financial losses to institutions, which usually results as the consequence of destructive events such as the loss or unavailability of mission-critical business services.

   3.   Obtain support for your business-continuity plans and goals from the executive management team.

You will need to convince senior management to approve your business-continuity plan so that you can flawlessly execute your disaster recovery. Assign stakeholders as representatives on the project-planning committee team, once approval is obtained from the corporate executive team.

   4.   Understand its specific role.

In the event of a major disaster, each of your departments must be prepared to take immediate action. In order to successfully recover your mission-critical database systems with minimal loss, each team must understand the BCP and DRP plans and follow them correctly. Furthermore, it is important to maintain your DRP and BCP plans and conduct periodic training of your IT staff members to have successful response time for emergencies. Such "smoke tests" to train and keep your IT staff members up to date on the correct procedures and communications will pay major dividends in the event of a disaster.

One useful tool for creating and managing BCP plans is available from the **National Institute of Standards and Technology (NIST)**. The NIST documentation can be used to generate templates that can make an excellent starting point for your BCP and DRP. We highly recommend that you download and review the NIST publication *Contingency Planning Guide for Information Technology Systems* (at http://csrc.nist.gov/publications/nistpubs/800-34/sp800-34.pdf), on creating and evaluating BCP plans.

Additional NIST documents may also provide insight into how best to manage new or current BCP or DRP plans. A complete listing of NIST publications relating to computer security is available at http://csrc.nist.gov/publications/PubsSPs.html.

Fault Tolerance and High Availability

Fault tolerance is that attribute of data-center technology that enables a system to continue to function correctly in the face of a failure involving one or more faults within any given key component of the system architecture or data center. If operating quality experiences major degradation, the decrease in functionality of a fault-tolerant environment is usually in direct proportion to the severity of the failure, whereas a poorly designed system will completely fail and break down with just a small failure. In other words, fault tolerance gives you that added layer of protection and support to avoid a total meltdown of your mission-critical data center and, in our case, Oracle servers and database systems. Fault tolerance is often associated with highly available systems, such as those found with Oracle Data Guard and Oracle RAC technologies.

Data formats may also be designed to degrade gracefully. For example, in the case of Oracle EBS environments, services provide for load balancing to minimize performance issues in the event that one or more nodes in the cluster is lost due to an unforeseen event.

Recovery from errors in fault-tolerant systems provides for either roll-forward or rollback operations. For instance, whenever the Oracle server detects that it has an error condition and cannot find data from a missed transaction, rollback will occur at either the instance level or the application level (a transaction must be atomic: all elements must commit or roll back). Oracle takes the system state at that time and rolls back transactional changes to be able to move forward. Whenever a rollback is required for a transaction, Oracle reverts the system state to some earlier correct version—for example, using the database checkpoint and rollback process inherent in the Oracle database engine and moving forward from there.

Rollback recovery requires that the operations between the checkpoint (implicit checkpoints are *never* required for transactional recovery) and the detected erroneous state can be made transparent. Some systems make use of both roll-forward and rollback recovery for different errors or different parts of one error.

For Oracle, database recovery always rolls back failed transactions and restores the state of the rollback or undo, from which it then rolls forward using the contents of the rollback or undo segments. However, when it comes to transactional-based recovery, Oracle only rolls back. Within the scope of an individual system, fault tolerance can be achieved by anticipating exceptional conditions, building the system to cope with them, and, in general, aiming for self-healing so that the system converges towards an error-free state. In any case, if the consequence of a system failure is catastrophic, the system must be able to use reversion to fall back to a safe mode. This is similar to rollback recovery, but can be a human action if humans are present in the loop.

Requirements for Implementing Fault Tolerance

The basic characteristics of fault tolerance are

- no single point of failure,
- no single point of repair,
- fault isolation to the failing component,
- fault containment in order to prevent propagation of the failure, and
- availability of reversion modes.

In addition, fault-tolerant systems are characterized in terms of both planned and unplanned service outages. These are usually measured at the application level and not just at the hardware level. The figure of merit is called *availability* and is expressed as a percentage. For instance, a *five-nine* system would statistically provide 99.999% availability. Fault-tolerant systems are typically based on the concept of redundancy. In theory, this would be ideal; however, in reality this is an elusive and impractical goal. Due to the time required to fail over, re-establish middle-tier connections, and restart applications, it is not realistic to have complete availability. We can obtain four nines as the best goal for high availability with Oracle systems. For Oracle RAC, you can deploy a fault-tolerant environment by using multiple network-interface cards, dual **host bus adapters**, and multiple switches to avoid any single point of failure.

Fault Tolerance and Replication

By using spare components, we address the first fundamental characteristic of fault tolerance in the following two ways:

- **Replication** This provides multiple identical instances of the same system or subsystem and directs tasks or requests to all of them simultaneously. Oracle Streams and Oracle GoldenGate, as well as third-party solutions such as Quest SharePlex, are replication technologies.

- **Redundancy** This provides you with multiple identical instances of the same system and switches to one of the remaining instances in case of a failure. This switchover and failover process is available with standby database technology with Oracle Data Guard. Oracle Real Application Clusters (RAC) also provides node and server failover capability with the use of services by using **fast connection failover** and **fast application notification**.

At the storage layer, the major implementations of **RAID (redundant array of independent disks)**—with the exception of disk striping (RAID 0)—provide you with fault-tolerant appliances that also use data redundancy.

Bringing the replications into synchrony requires making their internal stored states the same. They can be started from a fixed initial state, such as the reset state; alternatively, the internal state of one replica can be copied to another replica.

One variant of **data-mirror replication** is pair-and-spare. Two replicated elements operate in lockstep as a pair, with a voting circuit that detects any mismatch between their operations and outputs a signal indicating that there is an error. Another pair operates exactly the same way. A final circuit selects the output of the pair that does not proclaim that it is in error. Pair-and-spare requires four replicas rather than the three of data-mirror replication, but has been used commercially.

If a system experiences a failure, it must continue to operate without interruption during the repair process.

When a failure occurs, the system must be able to isolate the failure to the offending component. This requires the addition of dedicated failure-detection mechanisms that exist only for the purpose of fault isolation.

Recovery from a fault condition requires classifying the fault or failing component. NIST categorizes faults based on locality, cause, duration, and effect.

Recovery-Point Objective (RPO) and Recovery-Time Objective (RTO)

With respect to disaster recovery for Oracle EBS, the two additional considerations that must be factored into a disaster-recovery plan are the recovery-point objective (RPO) and recovery-time objective (RTO). The RPO is the point to which recovery is performed to minimize data loss before the moment at which the failure occurred. For instance, if an earthquake strikes the Santa Clara Oracle data center at 1 a.m. on Friday, then the RPO would be as close as possible before 1 a.m. to lose as little data as possible. In comparison, the RTO is the smallest downtime required to perform the recovery from the disaster or outage. For instance, if the EBS Financials brokerage system in San Diego crashes at midnight on Sunday, the RTO would be to bring the environment back up before the financial markets open at 5 a.m. on Wall Street, so that trades can be resumed and minimal downtime occurs. Both RPO and RTO dictate the core of a disaster-recovery plan and are based on corporate service-level agreements determined by executives with regard to business requirements for the corporate information-systems environment.

High-Availability Solutions for Oracle R12 EBS

Oracle introduced the concept of **Maximum Availability Architecture (MAA)** as the foundation of the high-availability architecture for mission-critical applications and databases that run in large corporate data centers. It is a comprehensive end-to-end solution developed for large, mission-critical data centers that require all layers of the application, data, and system environment to be fully redundant—for example, fault tolerant with zero data loss and maximum uptime to protect against losses in system performance and availability. Moreover, it provides application-server protection with the Oracle Application Server topology, which includes middleware services, the database tier with Oracle Data Guard, and system availability with Oracle RAC.

There are four high-availability solutions for Oracle:

- Oracle Data Guard
- Oracle Streams
- Oracle Application Server Clustering
- Real Application Clusters

Oracle Data Guard

Oracle provides a true disaster-recovery solution with Oracle Data Guard. Data Guard provides a standby database environment that can be used for failover or switchover operations in the event of a database failure at the primary database site.

Implementing a disaster-recovery environment for Oracle EBS with Data Guard imposes additional configuration requirements that are not present in a non-ERP Oracle environment. Data Guard uses a primary site that contains the production source environment with the database server and the secondary disaster failover site, which may be active or passive, based on its configuration and business requirements. Data Guard relies upon the mechanism of archive-log shipping to transfer archived redo log files from the primary site to the standby site, and uses redo apply processing to capture changes made on the primary site to the secondary disaster-recovery site.

Oracle Streams

Another option for implementing the MAA blueprint for high availability is to use Oracle Streams or Oracle GoldenGate for replication between Oracle EBS environments.

Oracle Streams and Oracle GoldenGate are replication technologies that allow you to replicate your database or a subset of database tables to another site. Oracle Streams is not a true disaster-recovery solution or high-availability option; it is more of a complementary solution to enhance the availability options provided by Oracle Data Guard and Oracle RAC. One of the most common ways to use this technology is with large Oracle data warehouses and data marts, to replicate a subset of the source data to another environment for testing and verification purposes. A better solution would be to complement the replication technologies with transportable tablespaces to enhance performance, as they have robust performance advantages over replication technologies. Oracle Streams uses **advanced queuing** as the foundation of its model for propagating changes between master and target replication sites.

In addition to Data Guard and Streams, as part of the Oracle MAA solutions we also have failover and clustering with Oracle Application Server Fusion Middleware servers.

Oracle Application Server Clustering

Oracle Application Servers form the core foundation of the Web and application layers for many large data-center environments. In this day and age of e-commerce and intranet site operations, Oracle Application Servers are the key components in a data-center environment. Furthermore, many large firms use Oracle EBS environments to manage business operations for large financial transactions and reporting. Oracle Application Servers are thus the middle-tier or application-broker component of Oracle EBS environments.

In order to implement true disaster recovery for high availability and protection against costly downtime and loss of application data, Oracle provides clustering and failover technology as part of the Oracle Application Server environments.

In our coverage of Oracle MAA, we introduced Data Guard, Streams, and Application Server clustering and failover.

The application tier can implement MAA architecture by deploying multiple redundant servers, as listed here, for highly available load-balanced components:

- Web servers
- BI Publisher (Forms) servers
- Parallel Concurrent Processing servers (on either the application tier or the database tier)

Redundant TCP/IP concentrators and hardware load balancers, such as BIG-IP, further enhance the EBS MAA for the application tier. Load balancers distribute client requests across multiple application-tier nodes, providing additional scalability and fault tolerance. Implementation requires addition and configuration of application-tier nodes and configuration of the load balancer. My Oracle Support Note 380489.1 describes the application-configuration options in detail. Configuration of load balancers is specific to the vendor.

Oracle Real Application Clusters

Oracle RAC provides a combination of options that could be considered a high-availability solution. It provides server-level redundancy and database-instance availability by clustering hardware and database resources. However, RAC is not a true disaster-recovery solution, because it does not protect against site failure or database failure.

The reason for this is that with an Oracle RAC configuration, the database is shared by nodes in the cluster and staged on shared storage—which makes it a **single point of failure**. If the RAC database is lost, the entire cluster will fail. Many people incorrectly assume that RAC is a true disaster-recovery solution, when in fact it is not. For a true disaster-recovery solution with Oracle, you would need to implement Data Guard to protect against site and data failure events.

Among the numerous enhancements to the Oracle 11*g* RAC technology, the following new features of Oracle 11*g* R2 RAC improve on high availability for Oracle database technology:

- **Oracle Automatic Storage Management Cluster File System (Oracle ACFS)**   A new scalable file system that extends Oracle Automatic Storage Management (ASM) configurations and provides robust performance and availability functionality for Oracle ASM files.

- **Snapshot copy for Oracle ACFS**   A utility that provides point-in-time copying of the Oracle ACFS file system to protect against data loss.

- **Oracle ASM Dynamic Volume Manager**   A tool that provides volume-management services and a disk-driver interface to clients.

- **Oracle ASM Cluster Filesystem Snapshots**   A functionality that provides point-in-time copying of up to 63 snapshot images with Oracle single-instance and RAC environments with 11*g* R2.

My Oracle Support Note 761564.1 provides information for the EBS R12 EBS installation requirements.

We are not going to cover how to install and configure operating systems and networking for RAC with EBS, since this is out of the scope this book and other references exist on these topics. Be sure to apply the latest required patches for RAC, Oracle, and EBS prior to configuring RAC with EBS. The EBS R12 documentation can be found at http://download.oracle.com/docs/cd/B53825_03/current/html/docset.html. The *Installation Guide: Using Rapid Install Release 12.1 (12.1.1), E12842-03* available in that documentation library provides detailed installation and upgrade instructions.

Oracle RAC Terminology Overview

For functional and technical Oracle-application administrators who are new to clustering technology and RAC, it is useful to briefly review the key terminology used in a cluster environment.

- **Automatic Storage Management (ASM)**   An Oracle database component that acts as an integrated file system and volume manager, providing the performance of raw devices with the ease of management of a file system. In an ASM environment, you specify a disk group, rather than the traditional data file, when creating or modifying a database structure such as a tablespace. ASM then automatically creates and manages the underlying files.

- **Cluster Ready Services (CRS)**   The primary program that manages high-availability operations in an Oracle RAC environment. The CRS process manages designated cluster resources such as databases, services, and listeners.

- **Parallel Concurrent Processing**   An extension of the concurrent-processing architecture. It allows concurrent-processing activities to be distributed across multiple nodes in an Oracle RAC environment, maximizing throughput and providing resilience to node failure.

- **Oracle Real Application Clusters (RAC)**   An Oracle database technology that allows multiple instances to work on the same data in parallel, reducing processing time significantly. An Oracle RAC environment also offers resilience if one or more instances become temporarily unavailable as a result of planned or unplanned downtime.

The Oracle Applications EBS naming conventions are as follows:

Convention	Meaning
Application tier	Machines (nodes) running Forms, Web, and other services (servers); sometimes also called the *middle tier*
Database tier	Machines (nodes) running the Oracle EBS database
Oracle	User account that owns the database file system (database ORACLE_HOME and files).
applmgr	User account that owns the application file system
CONTEXT_NAME	Variable that specifies the name of the application's context file used by AutoConfig; the default is *SID_hostname*
CONTEXT_FILE	Full path to the application's context file on the application tier or database tier. The default locations are as follows:

- application-tier context file:

    INST_TOP/appl/admin/*CONTEXT_NAME*.xml

- database-tier context file:

    RDBMS ORACLE_HOME/appsutil/*CONTEXT_NAME*. xml

APPS*pwd*	EBS database APPS user password

Configuration Prerequisites

In order to install RAC and enable EBS, we need to make sure that the prerequisites for installing EBS and configuring RAC are met. The basic prerequisites for using Oracle RAC with EBS Release 12.1.1 are as follows:

- If you do not already have an existing single-instance environment, perform an installation of EBS with rapid install; or apply the Oracle E-Business Suite Release 12.1.1 Maintenance Pack (patch 7303030, also delivered by Release 12.1.1 Rapid Install). The installation of EBS R12 12.1.1 has already been illustrated in the Installing EBS 12.1.1 section.

Set up the required cluster hardware and interconnect medium and install Oracle 11*g* R1 11.1.0.7 CRS, ASM, and relational database management system (RDBMS) as described in Chapters 3 and 9, along with the required interoperability patches described in the previous section under Upgrading an EBS 12 with the latest release of Oracle 11gR1 RDBMS bullet list or in My Oracle Support (formerly Metalink) note 802875.1. If you decide to implement Oracle 11gR2 RAC with Oracle EBS 12.1.1, the My Oracle Support (formerly Metalink) Note 823587.1 provides the details.

We will have the following Oracle Homes after the completion of these tasks:

ORACLE_HOME	Purpose
Rapid Install Database	Database ORACLE_HOME installed by Oracle EBS Release 12 rapidwiz. The ORACLE_HOME is created during the initial EBS installation. /u01/oracle/VIS/db/tech_st/11.1.0
Database 11g	Database ORACLE_HOME installed for Oracle 11g RAC Database. The ORACLE_HOME is created during the Oracle RDBMS RAC binaries installation. It will replace the binaries from the ORACLE_ HOME installed during the EBS installation. /u01/app/oracle/product/11.1.0/db_2
Database 11g CRS	ORACLE_HOME installed for 11g Clusterware (formerly Cluster Ready Services). The ORACLE_HOME is created during the Oracle Clusterware installation. /u01/crs/oracle/product/11.1.0/crs_1
Database 11g ASM	ORACLE_HOME used for creation of ASM instances. The ORACLE_ HOME is created during the Oracle ASM installation. /u01/app/oracle/product/11.1.0/db_1
OracleAS 10.1.2	ORACLE_HOME installed on application tier for forms and reports by rapidwiz. The ORACLE_HOME is created during the initial EBS installation. $INST_TOP/tech_st/10.1.2
OracleAS 10.1.3	ORACLE_HOME installed on application tier for HTTP Server by rapidwiz. The ORACLE_HOME is created during the initial EBS installation. $INST_TOP/tech_st/10.1.3

NOTE
The Oracle Homes for CRS, ASM, and RDBMS must be installed with Oracle 11g R1 and patched to Oracle 11.1.0.7. The patch number is 6890831.

For ASM and RDBMS Oracle home, install Oracle Database 11g Products from the 11g Examples CD after installing Oracle 11g R1 but prior to applying the patch for 11.1.0.7 (patch number 6890831).

After the successful installation of the Oracle 11g R1 CRS and ASM, the output of ./crs_stat-t -v should display the Clusterware services.

For the sample configuration for RAC and E-Business Suite, you need to verify that both CRS and ASM are installed and running on the ebsrac1 and ebsrac2 nodes of the cluster. As you can see, there are two instances belonging to ASM and two listeners for ASM on each node:

- ora.ebsrac1.+ASM1.asm on node ebsrac1,
- ora.ebsrac2.+ASM2.asm on node ebsrac2,
- ora.ebsrac1.LISTENER_EBSRAC1.lsnr on node ebsrac1, and
- ora.ebsrac2.LISTENER_EBSRAC2.lsnr on node ebsrac2.

Enabling RAC for Oracle R12 EBS—Rconfig

So far, we have a single-instance database that was created on a Unix-based file system for an Oracle R12 EBS environment. We will use rconfig to move this single-instance database to ASM and RAC and enable the sample Oracle R12 EBS database.

After logging on to the server using an Oracle OS user account, you will need to perform the following tasks:

1. Go to the $ORACLE_HOME/assistants/rconfig/sampleXMLs directory.

2. Make a copy of the template file ConvertToRAC.xml to convert.xml and convert1.xml.

3. Modify the content of convert.xml and convert1.xml identically with the exception of <n:Convert verify="ONLY">. (The possible values for Convert verify are ONLY, YES, and NO.)

4. Place <n:Convert verify="ONLY"> in the convert.xml file, and <n:Convert verify="YES"> in convert1.xml.

The utility is called rconfig, and it will be used along with the XML file to perform the following activities:

- migrating the database to ASM storage (if ASM is specified as a storage option in the configuration XML file),

- creating database instances on all nodes in the cluster,

- configuring listener and net-service entries,

- configuring and registering CRS resources, and

- starting the instances on all nodes in the clusters.

Please note that the Convert verify value ONLY performs a validation of the parameters and identifies any problems that need to be corrected prior to the actual conversion, but does not perform a conversion after completing the prerequisite checks. If you set Convert verify="YES", rconfig performs checks to ensure that the prerequisites for converting from a single instance to Oracle RAC have been met before it starts the conversion. On the other hand, if you set Convert verify="NO", rconfig starts the conversion without performing prerequisite checks. The content of the convert.xml file is displayed next.

In both the convert.xml and convert1.xml files, we will need specify the following information:

- the source of the preconversion E-Business Suite R12 RDBMS Oracle home of the non-RAC database—/u01/oracle/VIS/db/tech_st/11.1.0;

- the destination of the postconversion EBS RDBMS Oracle home of the RAC database—/u01/app/oracle/product/11.1.0/db_2;

- the SID for the non-RAC database and credentials—VIS;

- a list of nodes that should have RAC instances running—ebsrac1, ebsrac2;

- the instance prefix—VIS;

- the storage type (please note that storage type is ASM); and

- the ASM disk groups for the Oracle data file and FRA—DATA and FLASH.

The exact content of the convert.xml file is as follows:

```
<?xml version="1.0" encoding="UTF-8" ?>
- <n:RConfigxmlns:n="http://www.oracle.com/rconfig" xmlns:xsi="http://www
.w3.org/2001/XMLSchema-instance" xsi:schemaLocation="http://www.oracle.com/
rconfig">
- <n:ConvertToRAC>
- <!--
Verify does a precheck to ensure all pre-requisites are met, before the con-
version is attempted. Allowable values are: YES|NO|ONLY
-->
- <n:Convert verify="ONLY">
- <!--
Specify current OracleHome of non-rac database for SourceDBHome
-->
<n:SourceDBHome>/u01/oracle/VIS/db/tech_st/11.1.0</n:SourceDBHome>
- <!--
Specify OracleHome where the rac database should be configured. It can be same
as SourceDBHome
-->
<n:TargetDBHome>/u01/app/oracle/product/11.1.0/db_2</n:TargetDBHome>
- <!--
Specify SID of non-rac database and credential. User with sysdba role is
required to perform conversion
-->
- <n:SourceDBInfo SID="VIS">
- <n:Credentials>
<n:User>sys</n:User>
<n:Password>sys1</n:Password>
<n:Role>sysdba</n:Role>
</n:Credentials>
</n:SourceDBInfo>
- <!--
ASMInfo element is required only if the current non-rac database uses
ASM Storage
-->
- <n:ASMInfo SID="+ASM1">
- <n:Credentials>
<n:User>sys</n:User>
<n:Password>sys1</n:Password>
<n:Role>sysasm</n:Role>
</n:Credentials>
</n:ASMInfo>
- <!--
Specify the list of nodes that should have rac instances running. LocalNode
should be the first node in this nodelist.
-->
- <n:NodeList>
<n:Node name="raclinux1.gj.com" />
<n:Node name="raclinux2.gj.com" />
</n:NodeList>
- <!--
```

```
Specify prefix for rac instances. It can be same as the instance name for
non-rac database or different. The instance number will be attached to this
prefix.
-->
<n:InstancePrefix>VIS</n:InstancePrefix>
- <!--
Specify port for the listener to be configured for rac database. If port="",
alistener existing on localhost will be used for rac database.The listener
will be extended to all nodes in the nodelist
-->
<n:Listener port="" />
- <!--
Specify the type of storage to be used by rac database. Allowable values are
CFS|ASM. The non-rac database should have same storage type.
-->
- <n:SharedStorage type="ASM">
- <!--
Specify Database Area Location to be configured for rac database. If this
field is left empty, current storage will be used for rac database. For CFS,
this field will have directory path.
-->
<n:TargetDatabaseArea>+DATA</n:TargetDatabaseArea>
- <!--
Specify Flash Recovery Area to be configured for rac database. If this field
is left empty, current recovery area of non-rac database will be configured
for rac database. If current database is not using recovery Area, the
resulting rac database will not have a recovery area.
-->
<n:TargetFlashRecoveryArea>+FLASH</n:TargetFlashRecoveryArea>
</n:SharedStorage>
</n:Convert>
</n:ConvertToRAC>
</n:RConfig>
```

We can use the rconfig utility to verify the conversion process using the convert.xml file.

If you wish to specify a NEW_ORACLE_HOME, as is the case for the Oracle home of the freshly installed Oracle 11g Release 11.1.0.7, start the database from the new Oracle Home using the following command:

```
SQL>startup pfile=<OLD_ORACLE_HOME>/dbs/init<ORACLE_SID>.ora;.
```

Shut down the database. Create an spfile from the pfile using the following command:

```
SQL>create spfile from pfile
```

Move the $ORACLE_HOME/dbs/spfile*ORACLE_SID*.ora for this instance to the shared location. Take a backup of the existing $ORACLE_HOME/dbs/init<ORACLE_SID>.ora and create a new $ORACLE_HOME/dbs/init<ORACLE_SID>.ora with the parameter spfile=<Path of spfile on shared disk>/spfile<ORACLE_SID>.ora.

Start up the instance. Using netca, create local- and remote-listener tnsnames.ora aliases for database instances. Use listener_VIS1 and listener_VIS2 as the alias names for the local listener, and listeners_VIS for the remote-listener alias. Execute netca from $ORACLE_HOME/bin.

You will then need to do the following:

1. Choose the Cluster Configuration option in the netca assistant.

2. Choose the current node name from the list of nodes.

3. Choose the Local Net Service Name Configuration option and click Next.

4. Select Add and in the next screen enter the service name and click Next.

5. Enter the current node as the server name and the port 1521 defined during the ASM listener creation.

6. Select Do not perform Test and click Next.

7. Enter the listener TNS alias name for the local listener (LISTENER_VIS1).

8. Repeat the previous steps for the remote listener, with the server name as the secondary node and the listener name as LISTENERS_VIS.

Ensure that local and remote aliases are created on all nodes in the cluster.

After making sure that the parameters are valid and that no errors were identified that could cause a problem, we can start the real conversion using rconfig and the convert1.xml file.

After the completion of the Oracle R12 EBS database conversion from a single-instance database residing on a file system to an RAC database on the two-cluster RAC nodes, validate the conversion by viewing services produced by ./crs_stat-v command output.

After we install new Oracle 11g homes for ASM and RDBMS, we need to run AutoConfig (adautocfg.sh) on the database tier to make EBS aware of the changes.

Now we are going to enable AutoConfig on the new Oracle 11g 11.1.0.7 home database tier, so you will need to complete certain steps (in the order listed) to migrate to AutoConfig on the database tier:

1. Copy AutoConfig to the new RDBMS ORACLE_HOME for Oracle 11g R1.

2. Generate your database context file.

3. Prepare AutoConfig by completing the following AutoConfig steps.

4. Generate and apply AutoConfig configuration files.

5. Execute AutoConfig on all database nodes in the cluster.

6. Perform the following activities related to the Init file, tnsnames, and listener files.

Let's now see an explanation of each of these steps.

Copying AutoConfig to the New RDBMS ORACLE_HOME for Oracle 11g R1 11.1.0.7

Ensure that you have applied any patches listed in the prerequisites section previously. Update the RDBMS ORACLE_HOME file system with the AutoConfig files by performing the following steps:

1. On the application tier (as the applmgr user), log in to the APPL_TOP environment (source the environment file), and create an appsutil.zip file:

```
perl <AD_TOP>/bin/admkappsutil.pl
```

This will create appsutil.zip in $INST_TOP/admin/out.

2. On the database tier (as the Oracle user), copy the appsutil.zip file to the RDBMS ORACLE_HOME. You can also upload it using FTP. The following screenshot shows how to copy the file and how to make the file owned by the Oracle user.

3. Unzip the appsutil.zip file to create the appsutil directory in the 11*g* RDBMS NEW ORACLE_HOME after the copy:

```
cd <RDBMS ORACLE_HOME>
unzip -o appsutil.zip
```

4. Copy the jre directory from <OLD_ORACLE_HOME>/appsutil to 11*g* NEW_ORACLE_HOME/appsutil.

5. Create a <CONTEXT_NAME> directory under $ORACLE_HOME/network/admin. Use the new instance name while creating the context directory. Append the instance number to the instance prefix that you put in the rconfig XML file. For example, if your database name is VIS and you want to use "VIS" as the instance prefix, create the context_name directory as VIS1_<hostname> or VIS2_<hostname>, where the hostname can be either raclinux1 or raclinux2.

6. Set the following environment variables in the .bash_profile for Oracle RAC and EBS.

7. Deregister the current configuration using the APPS schema, FND_ CONC_CLONE .SETUP_CLEAN, executing the command SQL>exec fnd_conc_ clone.setup_clean; while logged into the database as apps user.

8. Copy the tnsnames.ora file from $ORACLE_HOME/network/admin to $TNS_ADMIN/ tnsnames.ora file and edit it to change the aliases for SID=<new Oracle RAC instance name>.

9. To preserve TNS aliases (LISTENERS_<service> and LISTENER_<asminstance>) of ASM, create a file named <context_name>_ifile.ora under $TNS_ADMIN, and copy those entries to that file.

10. Create listener.ora as per the sample file in the appendix. Change the instance name and Oracle home to match this environment.

11. Start the listener.

Generating Your Database Context File

From the 11*g* ORACLE_HOME/appsutil/bin directory, create an instance-specific XML context file by executing the following command in Linux:

```
cd <RDBMS ORACLE_HOME>
. <CONTEXT_NAME>.env
cd <RDBMS 11g ORACLE_HOME>/appsutil/bin
perl adbldxml.pl tier=db appsuser=<APPSuser>
```

Note that adbldxml.pl uses your current environment settings to generate the context file. Therefore, you must ensure that your environment is correctly sourced.

Also note if you build the context file for an EBS instance that runs on RAC, all your RAC instances have to be up and running while the adbldxml utility executes. This utility connects to all RAC instances to gather information about the configuration.

Preparing AutoConfig for Oracle R12 EBS with RAC

The context file acting as a centralized repository for the configuration needs to be updated so that after AutoConfig is run, all of the configuration-parameter files of the various components of EBS are aware of the implemented changes.

1. Set the value of s_virtual host_name to point to the virtual host name (VIP alias) for the database host by editing the database context file $ORACLE_HOME/appsutil/<SID>_hostname.xml.

2. Rename $ORACLE_HOME/dbs/init<Oracle RAC instance>.ora to a new name—init<racinstance>.ora.old—in order to allow AutoConfig to regenerate the file using the Oracle RAC–specific parameters.

3. Ensure that the following context variable parameters are correctly specified:
   - s_jdktop=<11g ORACLE_HOME_PATH>/appsutil/jre
   - s_jretop=<11g ORACLE_HOME_PATH>/appsutil/jre
   - s_adjvaprg=<11g ORACLE_HOME_PATH>/appsutil/jre/bin/java

4. Review prior manual configuration changes. The database context file may not include manual configuration changes made after the completion of Rapid Install. Before running the AutoConfig portion of this patch, review any modifications to specific configuration files and reconcile them with the database context file.

Generating AutoConfig Configuration Files

Now it is time to generate the AutoConfig configuration files so that all the changes get propagated to the configuration files of the EBS components. This step performs the conversion to the new context files by using the AutoConfig utility. Once it is completed, the previous configuration will not be available.

The database server and the database listener must remain available during the AutoConfig run. All the other database-tier services should be shut down.

Execute the following commands in Linux or Unix:

```
cd <RDBMS ORACLE_HOME>
/appsutil/bin/perl adconfig.pl
```

Running AutoConfig on the database node will update the RDBMS network-listener file. Be sure to review the configuration changes from the previous section. The new AutoConfig network-listener file supports the use of IFILE to allow values to be customized or added as needed.

Running AutoConfig on the database tier will not overwrite any existing init.ora file in the <ORACLE_HOME>/dbs directory. If no init.ora file exists for your instance, AutoConfig will generate one in the <ORACLE_HOME>/dbs directory for you.

Running AutoConfig might change your existing environment files. After running AutoConfig, you should always set the environment before you run any EBS utilities, in order to apply the changed environment variables.

Check the AutoConfig log file located in 11g at ORACLE_HOME/appsutil/log/<CONTEXT_NAME>/<MMDDhhmm>.

If ASM/OCFS is being used, make note of the new location of the control file:

```
sqlplus / as sysdba;
SQL> show parameters control_files
```

Perform all of these steps on all other database nodes in the cluster.

Execute AutoConfig on all database nodes in the cluster by running the $ORACLE_HOME/appsutil/scripts/adautocfg.sh command. Then shut down the instances and listeners. The following additional tasks must be completed to finalize the RAC setup for Oracle R12 EBS:

1. Edit the $ORACLE_HOME/dbs/<SID>_APPS_BASE.ora file on all nodes. If ASM is being used, change the control_files = <new location parameter from the *Generating and applying AutoConfig configuration files* section. Use the location of the control file in the previous step:

   ```
   sqlplus / as sysdba;
   SQL> show parameters control_files
   ```

2. Create an spfile from the pfile and then create a pfile in a temporary location from the new spfile, with the help of the following command:

   ```
   SQL>create spfile=<temp location> from pfile.
   SQL>create pfile=/tmp/init<ins1>.ora from spfile=<temp location>.
   ```

   Repeat this step on all nodes.

3. Combine the initialization parameter files for all instances into one init<SID>.ora file by copying all existing shared contents. All shared parameters defined in your init<SID>.ora file must be global, with the format *.parameter=value.

4. Modify all instance-specific parameter definitions in init<SID>.ora files using the syntax <SID>.parameter=value, where the <SID> variable is the system identifier of the instance.

Steps 3 and 4 refer to the init parameters from the old init EBS file to be modified in the parameter file or the RAC-enabled EBS. This states the necessity of modifying the old EBS init parameters into a new parameter file for the RAC-enabled EBS.

5. Ensure that the parameters LOCAL_LISTENER, diagnostic_dest, undo_tablespace, thread, instance_number, and instance_name are in the format <SID>.parameter—for example, <SID>.LOCAL_LISTENER=<local_listener_name>. These parameters must have one entry for an instance.

6. Create the spfile in the shared location where rconfig created the spfile from the init<SID>.ora pfile:

   ```
   SQL>create spfile=<shared location> from pfile;
   ```

7. Since AutoConfig creates the listener.ora and tnsnames.ora files in a context directory and not in the $ORACLE_HOME/network/admin directory, the TNS_ADMIN path must be updated in CRS. Run the following command as the root user:

   ```
   # srvctl setenv nodeapps -n <node> \
   -t TNS_ADMIN=<Full Path of ORACLE HOME>/network/admin/<context_
   directory>
   ```

8. Start up the database instances and listeners on all nodes. Run AutoConfig on all nodes to ensure that each instance registers with all remote listeners. Shut down and restart the database instances and listeners on all nodes. Deregister any old listeners and register the new listeners with CRS using the following commands:

```
# srvctl remove listener -n <nodename> -l <listener_name>
# srvctl add listener -n <nodename> -o <oracle_home> -l
<listener_name>
```

Conclusion

In this chapter we presented a comprehensive array of tools and methodologies to protect the availability and data integrity of the Oracle E-Business Suite environment. Using a framework as the reference point based on international standards, we discussed how to implement a disaster-recovery plan for Oracle EBS. Lastly, we discussed how to roll out a business-continuity plan with Oracle Data Guard and Oracle RAC for the Oracle E-Business Suite.

CHAPTER
27

Business Intelligence with OBIEE and ODI

usiness intelligence has risen to the cornerstone of importance for corporate enterprise resource planning environments. Executives and business leaders, as well as financial analysts, require a powerful and effective way to calculate, report, and analyze vast quantities of data generated from the core financial systems in the production Oracle EBS environments. Fortunately, Oracle comes to the rescue with a potent suite of products for business analysis and reporting in the Oracle Business Intelligence Suite.

In this chapter, we discuss the following topics:

■ Business intelligence,

■ Oracle Business Intelligence Enterprise Edition configuration for Oracle R12 EBS, and

■ Oracle Data Integrator (ODI) with Oracle R12 EBS.

Business Intelligence

What is business intelligence, you might ask. Business intelligence covers a wide gamut of technologies and business practices; it consists of a hodgepodge of reporting and analysis for interpreting the data from information systems to provide an intelligent and easy method for business analysts and executives to slice and dice facts to manage the business functions. In a nutshell, you need a quick and simple way to extract and report on the various sectors of the business by using the tools of corporate enterprise resource planning systems. For example, in the context of Oracle Financials, a corporate CFO may need to find out the total revenues for the past five years to provide a summary to the board of directors for the annual shareholder meeting. Business intelligence would rely upon tools such as Oracle Business Intelligence Enterprise Edition (OBIEE) to collect the data gathered from drill-down analysis instruments, such as Oracle Data Integrator (ODI), that extract the financial data from the E-Business Suite to create nice dashboard reports.

Dashboards for OBIEE with Oracle R12 EBS

Oracle Business Intelligence comes in standard and enterprise editions. The enterprise edition, OBIEE, permits an unlimited number of users, while standard edition is limited to 50. The Oracle Business Intelligence (BI) suite is rich in features, consisting of the following modules:

■ **Oracle BI Server**   A common enterprise business model and abstraction layer.

■ **Oracle BI Answers**   Ad hoc querying and reporting.

■ **Oracle BI Interactive Dashboards**   Useful interactive dashboards for accessing business intelligence and applications content.

■ **Oracle BI Disconnected Analytics**   A suite of tools for mobile applications to perform data analytics.

■ **Oracle BI Publisher (formerly known as XML Publisher)**   Tool for enterprise reporting and distribution of graphical, feature-rich reports.

■ **Oracle BI Briefing Books**   Snapshots of your dashboard pages to view and share in off-line mode.

■ **Hyperion Interactive Reporting**   Interactive ad hoc reporting tools for use with Oracle EBS.

- **Hyperion SQR Production Reporting**   Tools to generate professional reports with analytical features.
- **Hyperion Financial Reporting**   Center for creating nicely formatted reports in textbook-quality format for financial and management reporting.
- **Hyperion Web Analysis**   Tool for Web-based online analytical processing analysis, presentation, and reporting.

Since discussion of the Oracle Business Intelligence suite would require a book in itself, we will cover only how to create dashboards and reports for analysis of the Oracle Financials data with Oracle R12 EBS. Additional resources for using OBIEE are available online at www.oracle.com/technetwork/middleware/bi-enterprise-edition/documentation/index.html.

The first step is to install and configure a stand-alone Oracle Business Intelligence environment. Once you have tested the installation for OBIEE, you will need to register the environment with the Oracle R12 EBS landscape. You should see the main entry screen for OBIEE.

Configuring OBIEE with Oracle R12 E-Business Suite

Before you can create nifty dashboards for reporting against Oracle EBS with OBIEE, there are some key steps required to configure the Oracle R12 environment with OBIEE. Let's walk through the setup tasks to detail the process.

Fortunately, according to the support notes from Oracle, there are no prerequisite patches for configuring OBIEE with R12 EBS; all of the core functions required from Oracle EBS are contained already in the base EBS packages.

Embedding a URL to Open Oracle BI Interactive Dashboards

Follow these steps to create a form function and to assign it to the right menus and Responsibilities:

1. Log in to your Oracle EBS environment as a user with systems-administrator privileges. Choose the System Administrator Responsibility from the navigator pane within Oracle Application Manager. After you select the Responsibility from the left pane, the available menus are shown in the right pane.

2. Using these menus, create the function, menu, Responsibility, user, and profile, in that sequence. The following sections describe in brief how to do so. They assume some knowledge of how to navigate the Oracle E-Business Suite.

Creating the Function
From the Application menu, choose Function. This will take you to the Oracle EBS Function form. Enter the function name, user function name, and description, then save your changes.

In the Web HTML tab, enter **OracleOasis.jsp?mode=OBIEE&function=Answers**

Creating the Menu
Menus are generated as soon as they are updated. Start by selecting Menu under Application. If you are already in Forms, you can select Menu from the Top Ten List (see Figure 27-1).

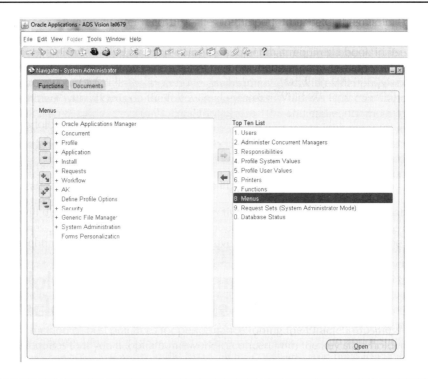

FIGURE 27-1.   *Configuring OBIEE with Oracle R12 EBS*

Create a new Standard menu and give it a name and user name. In the Function field, enter the name of the function created in the previous step.

NOTE
If a menu has only one function, then that is selected by default for the user; intermediate steps like displaying the function may be skipped altogether.

Assigning the Menu to a Responsibility

The menu that was created in the previous step needs to be associated with a Responsibility. You can either create a new Responsibility or reuse an existing one. To create a new responsibility, perform the following tasks (Figure 27-2):

■ Choose the application that you are creating the menu for; for the Responsibility Key, define any unique value. This key is used at the Oracle BI end because of its uniqueness.

■ Choose Oracle Self-Service Web Applications under the Application From, and under Data Group choose Standard and re-enter the application name.

■ For Menu, enter the value you created in the previous step.

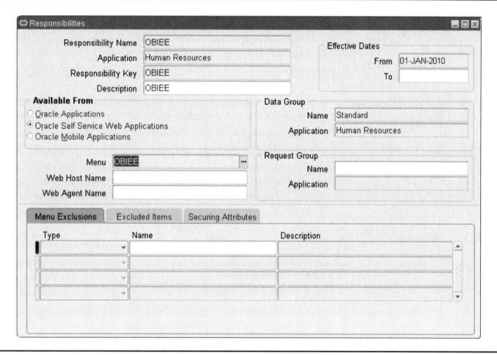

FIGURE 27-2. *Application setups for OBIEE with Oracle R12 EBS*

Assigning the Responsibility to a User

You can either create a new user or assign the Responsibility you just created to an existing user.

Assigning a Profile

The Profile form can be reached from the Top Ten List or from Application | Profile. A profile can be set for a Responsibility, a user, or a site. In our example we will set profile options for a Responsibility.

Check the Responsibility option and in the Profile field type **%oracle business%**. Click Find (see Figure 27-3). This will bring you to a new Form screen.

In the Profile Option Name field you should be able to find FND: Oracle Business Intelligence Suite EE base URL. Under Responsibility, enter the URL of your Oracle BI environment. The URL should be in the format http://BI.mysite.com:port.

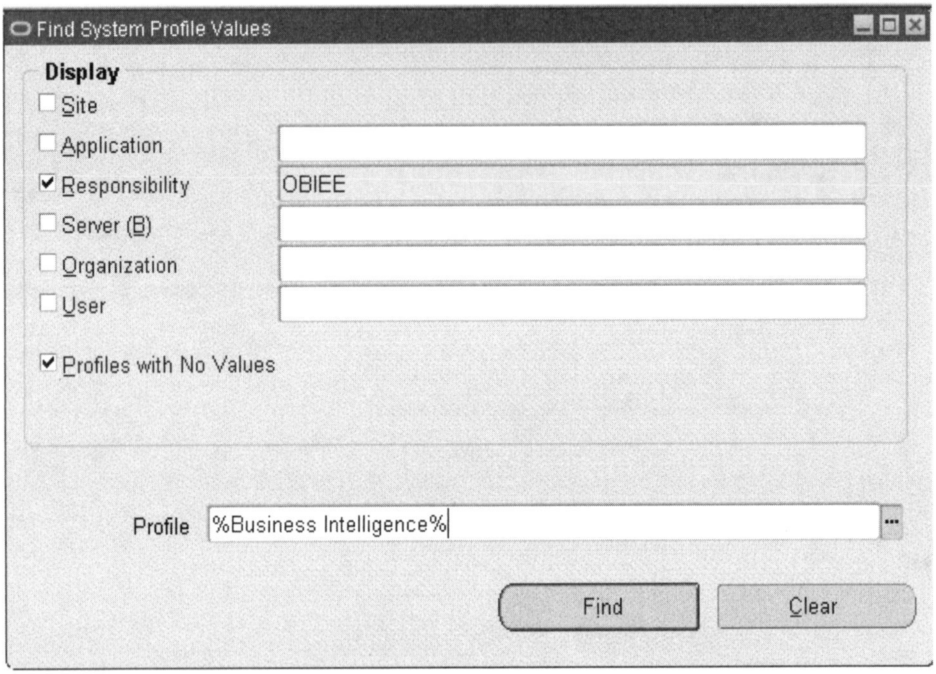

FIGURE 27-3. *Configure responsibilities for OBIEE users and Oracle R12 EBS*

Configuring Instanceconfig.xml for External Authentication

Modify the instanceconfig.xml file for the Oracle BI Presentation Services as shown here:

```xml
<?xml version="1.0"?>
<WebConfig>
<ServerInstance>
<CatalogPath>c:\temp\default</CatalogPath>
<DSN>AnalyticsWeb</DSN>
<Auth>
<ExternalLogon enabled="true">
<ParamList>
<Param name="NQ_SESSION.ICX_SESSION_COOKIE"
source="cookie"
nameInSource="EBSAppsDatabaseSID"/>
<Param name="NQ_SESSION.ACF"
source="url"
nameInSource="ACF"/>
```

```
</ParamList>
</ExternalLogon>
</Auth>
<!-- Other settings here. -->
</ServerInstance>
</WebConfig>
```

The nameInSource value for the cookie should be the same as the Oracle EBS application-database SID name. To verify the name of the cookie using Firefox, check the name of the cookie created under the domain where your Oracle EBS application middle-tier server is running. Please note that the cookie name is case sensitive. If you are using Internet Explorer, the cookie values can be obtained by connecting to EBS environment and entering **javascript:document.write (document.cookie)** in the browser address bar.

The steps described here in the subsections "Setting Up the Oracle E-Business Suite Connection-Pool Properties" and "Creating an Initialization Block Oracle EBS Context" are required for single-sign-on authentication. The steps described in the subsequent subsections are required to set up action links from Oracle BI to the Oracle R12 EBS environment.

Setting Up the Oracle E-Business Suite Connection-Pool Properties

Set up the Oracle EBS OLTP Connection Pool to connect to the Oracle E-Business Suite application database using the super user ID and password for the APPS user account.

The value of the Execute on Connect property should be call /* valueof(NQ_SESSION.ACF) */ APP_SESSION.validate_icx_session('valueof(NQ_SESSION.ICX_SESSION_COOKIE)'). See Figure 27-4.

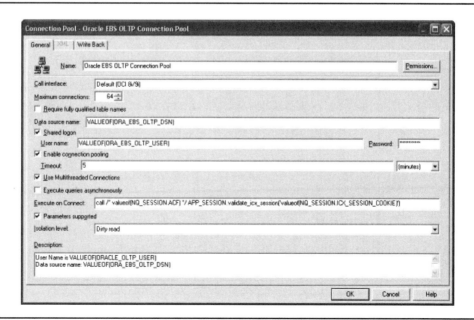

FIGURE 27-4. *Managing connection pools for OBIEE and Oracle R12 EBS*

If you receive an Oracle database error about not recognizing the APP_SESSION.VALIDATE_ICX_SESSION function call, then the second required ATG patch mentioned in Section 0 has not been applied.

Creating an Initialization Block for Oracle EBS Context

You will next have to create a new initialization block and set it to be the first one to run. This initialization block will need to be run using a connection pool defined from the earlier step. The target variables in the initialization block are shown in Figure 27-5. The connection pool should be the same as in the previous step: Oracle EBS OLTP Connection Pool.

The SQL for the initialization block should be the following:

```
select FND_GLOBAL.RESP_ID, FND_GLOBAL.RESP_APPL_ID, FND_GLOBAL.SECURITY_GROUP_
ID, FND_GLOBAL.RESP_NAME, FND_GLOBAL.USER_ID, FND_GLOBAL.EMPLOYEE_ID, FND_
GLOBAL.USER_NAME from dual
```

Creating an Opaque View for the Action-Link URL

In order to set up the action link, you will need to perform the following tasks:

- Determine the Oracle EBS Application page or function that you wish to link to. This includes finding the function ID of the page and the query-string parameters required by the page.

- Identify the Oracle EBS table that will support the parameters needed for the Oracle EBS function or page that you want to build action links to and create this physical table in the Oracle EBS OLTP schema as an opaque view.

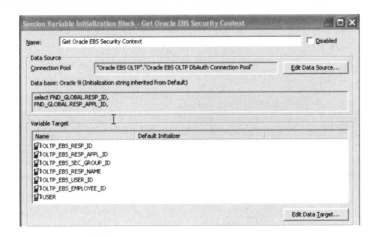

FIGURE 27-5.   *Connection pool management with OBIEE and Oracle R12 EBS*

An example is shown in Figure 27-6 using the OE_ORDER_HEADERS_ALL table for illustration; this table is at the core of the order header and supplies the header ID that we can use to join to the warehouse tables that contain the order-header information.

The action-link URL is generated by calling the FND_RUN_FUNCTION.GET_RUN_FUNCTION_URL() function in the Oracle EBS database schema. For example:

```
SELECT HEADER_ID, fnd_run_function.get_run_function_url(CAST(fnd_function.get_
function_id('ISC_ORDINF_DETAILS_PMV') AS NUMBER), CAST( VALUEOF(NQ_SESSION.
OLTP_EBS_RESP_APPL_ID) AS NUMBER), CAST( VALUEOF(NQ_SESSION.OLTP_EBS_RESP_
ID) AS NUMBER), CAST( VALUEOF(NQ_SESSION.OLTP_EBS_SEC_GROUP_ID) AS NUMBER),
'HeaderId='||HEADER_ID||'&pFunctionName=ISC_ORDINF_DETAILS_PMV&pMode=NO&pageFu
nctionName=ISC_ORDINF_DETAILS_PMV', NULL) as ORDER_HEADER_ACTION_LINK_URL FROM
OE_ORDER_HEADERS_ALL
```

The parameters to the function are the following:

```
p_function_id in number, p_resp_appl_id in number, p_resp_id in number, p_se-
curity_group_id in number, p_parameters in varchar2 default null, p_override_
agent in varchar2 default null
```

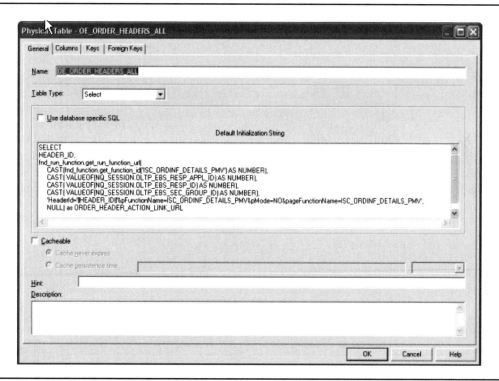

FIGURE 27-6. *OBIEE table management with Oracle R12 EBS Financials*

Here p_function_id is the function ID of the page that you want to navigate to; the next three parameters pass the security context to Oracle EBS. The fifth parameter is optional and is used if the page you are navigating to accepts parameters. In many cases if you want to navigate to a particular record on the page you are navigating to, you will need to supply the query-string parameters here. The function call returns a URL to the desired function with encrypted query-string parameters.

NOTE
The URL format returned by the function should look similar to http://host.mysite.com:8000/OA_HTML/RF. The "/RF" ending is hard-coded in the function.

The next step is joining this opaque view to the base fact table in the Data Warehouse schema. This join represents a join of tables in different database schemas and will, therefore, happen in the Oracle BI Server (Figure 27-7).

TIP
Ensure that sufficient filters are applied when requesting any columns from this opaque view, so that a small data set is returned to the Oracle BI Server to join with the results from the Data Warehouse schema. For demo environments, where the EBS table contains only thousands of rows, filters can be ignored. However, customer implementations will typically contain millions of rows, so appropriate filters are required.

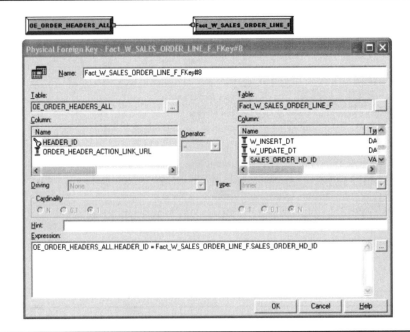

FIGURE 27-7. *OBIEE Configuration with Oracle R12 EBS filters*

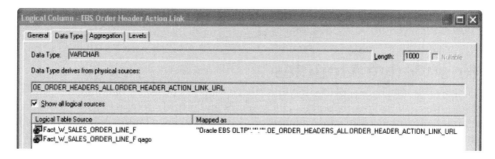

FIGURE 27-8. *Logical and Physical mapping of OBIEE data to Oracle R12 EBS*

Mapping the Logical and Presentation Layers
Map the URL column from the opaque view into the logical star where you want to create the action link. Then expose this logical column in the appropriate presentation catalog (Figure 27-8). Also ensure that the user who will be logging in to Oracle EBS is assigned access to the appropriate presentation catalogs.

Oracle BI Answers Configuration
When including the action-link column in a report, edit the column properties to indicate that the column is of type Hyperlink. That will automatically make it a clickable link in a BI Answers report. Further customization can be done to embed an image instead of the text.

Oracle BI Presentation Catalog Configuration
Ensure that the user who will be logging into Oracle EBS is set up in the presentation catalog with the appropriate permissions. You can make the dashboard that you want to embed into Oracle EBS the default dashboard for that user. This will take the user directly to that dashboard when he or she clicks on the hyperlink in Oracle EBS.

Oracle Data Integrator with Oracle R12 EBS
Most large corporate and public-sector data centers have volumes of legacy data from mainframe and Unix servers that need to be migrated to newer Oracle R12 EBS environments. In the past, this migration would have required armies of technical staff to create custom software programs to perform the painful extraction, transformation, cleansing, and loading processing from these legacy environments to Oracle Financials systems. Fortunately, Oracle Data Integrator (ODI) saves the day in terms of simplicity and ease of use compared to the alternatives of the past. You can quickly connect to third-party legacy systems and extract the source data to export to Oracle EBS systems. This allows you to migrate legacy data to new Oracle EBS environments. The migrated data can then be used within the Oracle EBS environment with OBIEE to create reports and dashboards after the modernization process is completed. The challenge in using ODI with Oracle R12 EBS is the configuration tasks required before you can extract data from source environments for import to Oracle R12 EBS. As they say, the devil is in the details. Let's walk through the steps to configure ODI with Oracle R12 EBS.

Oracle Data Integrator Knowledge Modules for Oracle EBS interact with the database tier to extract metadata and load data. While loading data, they also interact with the concurrent-processing server of the application tier.

Knowledge Modules

Oracle Data Integrator provides the Knowledge Modules (KMs) for handling E-Business Suite data. These specific EBS KMs support all EBS modules and provide comprehensive, bidirectional connectivity (through EBS objects tables or view and interface tables) between Oracle Data Integrator and the E-Business Suite, which enables you to extract and load data.

Before performing any installation, you should read the system requirements and certification documentation to ensure that your environment meets the minimum installation requirements for the products you are installing. The list of supported platforms and versions is available on the Oracle Technology Network at www.oracle.com/technology/products/oracle-data-integrator/index.html.

Creating an Oracle Physical Schema for Oracle Data Integrator

An Oracle physical schema must be created in the Oracle Data Integrator (ODI) repository database. The new schema will be used by ODI to process metadata operations against Oracle EBS environment. This schema must point to the Oracle schema that contains the synonyms pointing to the EBS tables. Additional guidelines and considerations are provided in the Oracle 11*g* Fusion Middleware Developer's Guide for Oracle Data Integrator.

Setting up the Integration Project

Set up a new Oracle Data Integrator project using EBS features as shown in the Oracle Fusion Middleware Developer's Guide for Oracle Data Integrator. Import the following KMs into your Oracle Data Integrator project:

- IKM E-Business Suite (Open Interface) and
- RKM E-Business Suite.

In addition to these specific EBS KMs, import the standard Oracle LKMs and CKMs to perform data extraction and data-quality checks with an Oracle database. For a list of available KMs, see the "Oracle Database" section in the Oracle Fusion Middleware Connectivity and Knowledge Modules Guide for Oracle Data Integrator.

Creating an Oracle Model for Oracle EBS

Create a new Oracle model using the logical schema you created earlier when configuring the Oracle EBS Connection using the standard procedure provided in the Oracle Fusion Middleware Developer's Guide for Oracle Data Integrator.

Reverse Engineer the Oracle R12 EBS Tables

The RKM E-Business Suite is able to reverse engineer the installed EBS tables, enriching them with information retrieved from the E-Business Suite integration repository. To perform a customized reverse engineering of EBS tables with the RKM E-Business Suite, use the usual procedure, as described in the "Reverse-Engineering a Model" section of the Oracle Fusion Middleware Developer's Guide for Oracle Data Integrator. This section details only the fields specific to EBS tables:

- In the Reverse tab of the Oracle model, select the RKM E-Business Suite.

- Set the RKM options as follows:

    Applications List   Enter the list of the applications' short names (such as INV and FA).

    Only Installed Applications   Set this option to "YES" to reverse engineer only installed and shared applications. If this option is set to "NO," all applications are reverse engineered.

    Min Rows   Leave the default value of 0 if you want to reverse engineer all the tables. If you want to reverse engineer only tables with a minimum number of rows, specify in this option that minimum number of rows.

    Description Mask   Specify the description mask for filtering the reverse-engineered objects based on their description in E-Business Suite.

    Flexfields   Set this option to "YES" to reverse engineer applications' flexfields.

    Interface Tables   Set this option to "YES" to reverse engineer applications' interface tables.

Specify the reverse mask in the Mask field in order to select the tables to reverse. The Mask field in the Reverse tab filters reverse-engineered objects based on their name. The reverse-engineering process returns the applications and tables as submodels and data stores. You can use Oracle EBS application as a source or a target of your integration interfaces.

Features of Oracle R12 EBS Reverse Engineering

Reverse engineering E-Business Suite tables involves the following features:

- The E-Business Suite modules are reversed as submodels. The submodel names correspond to the application names. Each application submodel is divided into submodels for tables, views, flexfields and interface tables.

- The tables or views and columns, as well as the primary and foreign keys, are reversed in the data stores.

- A submodel called Flexfield on <AppName> is created for each application. Data stores in the Flexfield submodel correspond to concatenated segment views of registered Key Flexfields for the application. These objects are a subset of views. The data stores in the Flexfields subfolder are named after the flexfields.

- Data stores in an interface-table submodel correspond to tables whose names contain the pattern "INTERFACE." These objects are a subset of tables.

Limitations of the Oracle R12 EBS Reverse-Engineering Process with Oracle Data Integrator

There are a few limitations of the functionality provided by Oracle Data Integrator to reverse engineer tables of application data for Oracle R12 EBS:

- Selective reverse engineering cannot be used with this Knowledge Module (KM). KM is used by Oracle EBS for training content modules with Oracle UPK and Oracle Tutor.

- The Min Rows option requires that Oracle statistics be computed on all tables.

- If the Oracle user defined in the Oracle Data Integrator data server is not the owner of the tables to reverse engineer, you must define synonyms for this user on these tables.

- Only Key Flexfields are supported; Descriptive Flexfields are not.

Designing an Interface

You can use E-Business Suite as a source and a target of an integration interface. The KM choice for an interface determines the interface's abilities and performance. The recommendations in this section help in the selection of the KM for different situations concerning loading and integrating EBS data.

Loading Data from E-Business Suite

When using E-Business Suite as a source, you extract data from the applications to integrate into another system (data warehouse, another database, etc.). Extracting data from E-Business Suite is performed with regular integration interfaces sourcing from an Oracle database. The Knowledge Modules working with Oracle database technology can be used for this purpose. For more information, see "Loading Data from Oracle" in the Oracle Fusion Middleware Connectivity and Knowledge Modules Guide for Oracle Data Integrator.

Integrating Data in E-Business Suite Through the Open Interface

Oracle Data Integrator provides the IKM E-Business Suite (Open Interface) to integrate data in E-Business Suite. The integration process into E-Business Suite is as follows:

- A set of open interface tables is loaded in a batch in a given transaction. This transaction is identified by a group ID. Note the following concerning the Group ID:
  - For the first table in the batch, create a group ID if it does not exist.
  - For the subsequent tables in the batch, use this group ID for loading tables.
  - When loading the last table in the batch, delete this group ID.
- If at any point in a batch it is required to call an E-Business Suite interface program, then you must validate and process data for the interface tables by executing an open interface program. The batch is finalized by the open interface program call that loads the base tables from the open interface tables.

These operations are supported by the IKM E-Business Suite (Open Interface). This IKM is used like the IKM Oracle Incremental Update and supports similar options to load the open interface tables. IKM manages the coupling between Oracle R12 EBS and third party applications. In addition, it can provide the options specific to open interfaces. For more information about the IKM Oracle Incremental Update, see "Oracle Database" in the Oracle Fusion Middleware Connectivity and Knowledge Modules Guide for Oracle Data Integrator.

Managing Group IDs

A transaction that integrates data into E-Business Suite is a batch identified by its group ID. For example, if you load several interface tables to create a product in E-Business Suite, all of these loading operations, as well as the calls to the validation and processing programs, will use this batch's group ID.

Creating a Group ID

You must force the creation of a group ID in the first integration interface that loads a group of interface tables in one single batch. To create a group ID in an integration interface, follow these steps:

Set the following in the KM options:

- Set OA_CREATE_NEW_GROUP_ID to "YES."

- Provide a group ID name in the OA_GROUP_ID_NAME option.

- Give a valid SQL expression for the Group ID value in the OA_GROUP_ID_EXPRESSION option. Use an Oracle database sequence value, for example <SEQUENCE_NAME> .NEXTVAL

In the integration-interface mapping, select the flag "UD1" for all the columns of the interface table you wish to load with the group ID value and set the mapping value to 0.

In the following integration interfaces belonging to a batch, you must use an existing group ID.

Using an Existing Group ID

To use an existing Group ID in an integration interface, follow these steps:

- Set OA_USE_EXISTING_GROUP_ID to "YES."

- Provide the group ID name in the OA_GROUP_ID_NAME option.

- In the integration-interface mapping, select the flag "UD1" for all the columns you wish to load with the group ID value and set the mapping value to 0.

- In the last integration interface that loads a batch of interface tables, you may delete a group ID that is no longer necessary.

Deleting an Existing Group ID

To delete an existing Group ID, follow these steps:

- Select the OA_REMOVE_GROUP_ID option.

- Provide the group ID name in the OA_GROUP_ID_NAME option.

In the integration-interface mapping, select the flag "UD1" for all the columns of the interface table you wish to load with the group ID value and set the mapping value to 0.

Executing an Open Interface Program

In Oracle Data Integrator integration interfaces, when a set of interface tables is loaded, it is necessary to call an open interface program in order to validate and process the data in the E-Business Suite interface tables. You can use an existing group ID in this call or create it in the same integration interface, if the Open Interface only contains a single table. The execution of the Open Interface program is started in the last integration interface of a package. This integration interface populates a set of Open Interface tables and usually deletes the group ID, if it is no longer needed.

To execute an Open Interface program, follow these steps:

- Set the SUBMIT_PROGRAM option to "YES."

- Provide the name of the program to call in the OA_PROGRAM option.

Specify the program parameters in the OA_ARGUMENTS option. The parameters are specified in the following format: argument_name => 'argument value', argument_name => 'argument value' etc. If one argument must take the value of the group ID, you must then specify argument Name => v_group_id.

You must also specify the context parameters for the session that will execute the program by setting the values of the following options:

- **OA_USER_NAME**   E-Business Suite user name
- **OA_REPONSIBILITY**   E-Business Suite Responsibility name
- **OA_LANGUAGE**   Language used for the Responsibility
- **OA_APPLICATION**   Application to which the Responsibility belongs

Conclusion

In this chapter we presented how to perform analysis and management with the Oracle Business Intelligence suite of tools for the Oracle E-Business Suite environment. We examined how to configure OBIEE with Oracle R12 EBS and concluded with a summary of how to set up Oracle Data Integrator with the Oracle E-Business Suite.

CHAPTER
28

Overview of CRM, HR, and Manufacturing

he focus of this book is the Financial applications, which are the more mature products at the core of the E-Business Suite product line. Because two of the major attractions of Oracle are its integration and common architecture, the other applications in the suite merit a brief discussion. The EBS applications share data internally and present a common look and feel to the user. The incremental cost of ownership of an additional module is low; all the applications use the same Oracle development tools, and EBS upgrades can be applied to the entire integrated system, which reduces costs for support and maintenance. Even those advantages are adding a significant value to the organizations, it is very important to understand the business processes and how these new modules will support them, and balance the out-of-the-box functionality with customizations in order to minimize the total cost of ownership of the E-Business Suite implementation.

The E-Business Suite product families are depicted in Figure 28-1. Goods and services flow right to left from their suppliers, procured through Purchasing, assembled into saleable products in Manufacturing, accounted for in Finance, and sold by sales staff using the Marketing and Sales modules. Money from customers flows left to right, paying suppliers for their input and employees (through the Payroll module of Human Resources) for their labor. The residue is the organization's profit.

Customer Relationship Management (CRM)

Oracle Receivables and Order Management are the cornerstones of the customer-oriented products within the Financials family. They process the back-office functions—maintaining shared customer master data and handling customer transactions from the point of order entry through billing and collection. The front-office customer-related corporate processes are handled by four product

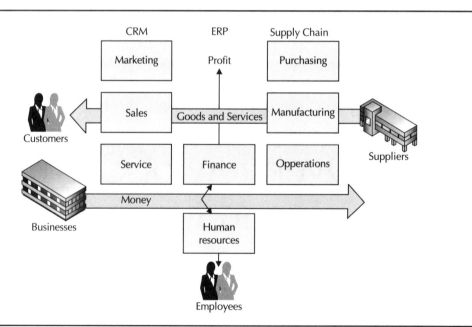

FIGURE 28-1. *E-Business Suite product families*

families: Marketing, Sales, Service and Channel Revenue Management. Often referred to as *Customer Relationship Management* (CRM), these four product families mirror the chronological evolution of a prospect from different angles.

Marketing creates demand for a product, Sales satisfies the demand, and Service follows up with postsale customer care. The new Channel Revenue Management product family allows the organization to manage all aspects of both direct and indirect channels, including partner life-cycle management, discount and rebates, sales collaboration, claims settlement, marketing, and performance measurement. Effective marketing and sales are elusive and occasionally counterintuitive. The reasons prospects do not buy are often more revealing than the reasons customers do. A swift and efficient response to repair faulty equipment or mail a spare part leaves customers with a strong positive buzz. They will buy again or tell their friends and colleagues. Good service can be a lower-cost way to increase sales than an expensive advertising campaign. Marketing professionals reckon it is 10 times harder to sell to a previous customer who has been dissatisfied than it is to sell to a new customer.

Marketing

Oracle Marketing is a set of analytical and campaign-management tools to publicize your company and its products and to generate the correct mix of demand for the company's products within target markets. Sales managers, salespeople, advertising managers, market researchers, and product managers carry out marketing functions.

Oracle Marketing

Oracle Marketing manages the marketing process. Marketing programs are analyzed, planned, and implemented to produce the desired product recognition. Marketing handles presales activity, generating leads, identifying prospects, and managing and tracking contacts. It supports telemarketing, team selling, and customer-base management. The system is designed for disconnected client operations; your representatives can enter their call notes and plans on a laptop, then upload them later.

Oracle Marketing lets you target qualified prospects, manage demand creation, fulfill literature requests, and track campaign effectiveness. Qualified leads are automatically transferred to your salespeople for immediate action. Overlapping campaigns can be run in parallel without duplicate information being sent to a single prospect. Additionally, customer responses from one campaign can be used to trigger other promotional efforts to a directly targeted group of prospects.

The relationships among prospects are varied and complex. You deal with different people and departments within the same organization and with organizations that are related to each other in any number of ways. Sales territories are defined along these imprecise boundaries. Sales and Marketing's schema for managing prospects not only handles prospect relationships, it also offers constructive help in sorting them out.

Contacts are the lifeblood of a sales organization. You need to know who they are, how they are related to each other, who has called on them, what the results were, what you have promised them, and what your next steps are. It is essential for all members of a sales team to share what they know, so that they present a common face to the prospect. There is an automated link with Order Management's shipping module to ship materials such as literature, kits, and trial packages.

Sales drive the rest of your business, whether you provide products or services. The company makes its plans for future periods on the best estimates from the sales force. From data on opportunities—how much, when, what, and how probable—Marketing creates forecasts that can be used by Oracle Inventory and Manufacturing.

Oracle Marketing Intelligence

Oracle Marketing Intelligence is a component of the Business Intelligence System. By monitoring marketing activities and measuring campaign success rates, it enables businesses to react early to market changes. Marketing Intelligence is integrated with Oracle Marketing and other CRM products such as Sales Intelligence, Customer Intelligence, and Call Center Intelligence.

Oracle Web Marketing

Oracle Web Marketing provides online marketing capabilities so that you can create real-time dynamic promotions and product recommendations for individuals as they surf your e-commerce site.

Along with other traditional marketing channels, such as e-mail, fax, direct mail, and advertisements, marketers today want to leverage Internet capabilities for marketing activities. The business benefits of Web marketing include direct, quick, and personalized interaction with customers, real-time message transfer, targeting of highly specific market segments, and direct and immediate selling. Using the Web Marketing functionality, you can create Web activities to cross sell, up sell, or make "buy this also" recommendations. When a Web activity executes, the resulting content is rendered on placements (physical locations) on applications such as Oracle iStore, iSupport, or Partner Portal, or other custom Web sites.

Marketing Encyclopedia System

The Marketing Encyclopedia System can be used to gather marketing insight and make it available to appropriate individuals. The information is published in a controllable manner to the appropriate people by classifying content into channels and assigning users to groups. Groups are given access to particular channels. If you do not know the correct channel to use when publishing a document, Marketing Encyclopedia System assigns the document to the correct channel by matching the document attributes to the channel attributes. The Marketing Encyclopedia encourages communication and effective exchange of information inside and outside an organization.

Sales

Oracle Sales is a suite of applications aimed at selling. Selling satisfies demand generated by marketing activities. Each application within Sales supports a different sales modality: online, via telesales, field sales force, inside sales, or distributors and value-added resellers. Oracle Sales ensures two things—common order processing and fulfillment, and common performance measurement—regardless of the sales modality.

A shopper who places an order on the Internet wants to be able to obtain delivery status from the telesales team later that same day. A customer who places an order with a field sales representative wants to be able to check the product configuration and specification of the order over the Internet. The challenge for the company is to have a single, unified back-office sales-fulfillment engine with any number of channels available to capture sales and respond to customer queries.

NOTE
The Oracle Sales Suite uses the Marketing Encyclopedia module as a data backbone, establishing and sharing sales-related information with Marketing.

Oracle Sales Online

Oracle Sales Online is a Web-based solution that provides salespeople, distributors, resellers, and sales managers with customer, opportunity, and product information. At its core is a sophisticated contact-management database. Before contacting a customer, a sales representative can review a list of products the customer has bought in the past and see the customer's outstanding service requests, payment history, and key contacts. Every individual dialogue—and topics arising, including sales opportunities—can be tracked, so that the customer is treated as an individual.

Oracle Sales Online also enables salespeople to create quotes using the latest inventory, price list, and discount information, through integration with Oracle Order Management and Oracle Configurator.

Oracle TeleSales

Oracle TeleSales is designed to meet the high-volume needs of inside salespeople in a call-center environment. Tight integration with the Oracle Telephony Manager provides representatives with a variety of tools to manage the sales process more effectively.

Call scripting is a requirement unique to telesales. Traditional scripts exist on paper; however, a database is a much better tool to follow the various paths a call may take. The direction of a conversation is determined by the prospect's previous responses. Oracle TeleSales can guide representatives through incoming and outgoing calls, collect information along the way, and fulfill requests for literature and follow-up.

The Oracle TeleSales Suite features a telephony application, Oracle Advanced Inbound and Outbound Telephony, that provides telephone access to all information contained in the E-Business Suite for inbound or outbound calling functions. Users can manage high-volume centralized or distributed call-center environments and operate blended-function service and sales call centers.

Oracle Field Sales for Mobile Devices

Oracle Field Sales for Mobile Devices enables organizations to deliver customer, opportunity, product, price, and quote information to a mobile sales force using the smartphone or tablet of their choice through its native Web browser.

Oracle iStore

Oracle iStore's powerful and scalable e-commerce site generator lets you easily create, track, and update business-to-business and business-to-consumer e-commerce sites for different customers, locations, languages, and more, while reducing order-to-fulfillment costs. Cross-sell and up-sell capabilities use unified, enterprise-wide customer data to personalize the customer experience and maximize per-customer purchases. Online credit-card payment can be integrated through Oracle iPayment; confirmed orders flow through Order Capture into Oracle Order Management (for sourcing, picking, packing, and dispatch) and from there into Oracle Receivables improving customer satisfaction while driving down customer-service costs.

Oracle Sales Compensation

Oracle Sales Compensation manages commissions and incentives to the sales force. A carefully optimized compensation plan drives your sales force. You structure the plan to put differing emphasis on different classes of business; the salespeople respond by working to bring in the business that is most lucrative for them. Compensation plans are engineered to reflect business logic; the application determines which sales events are eligible for incentive payments, which salesperson should receive credit, and how the credits should be calculated and paid.

Sales Compensation tags each sales-order line with a revenue-class category. You can define these categories on the basis of any combination of customer, product, service, industry, and market. For example, many companies give greater credit for sales to new accounts, for sales of strategic new products, or for sales in a strategically important industry. Such plans give salespeople the incentive to develop their knowledge of new products and new sets of customers. At its simplest, the credit for a sale equals the monetary amount of the sale times the compensation factor associated with the revenue class.

You can use a variety of sales agents—including a direct sales force, distributors, and external agents—each with their own plan. Representatives from more than one channel may participate in a given sale. The credit can be shared. For example, a matrixed sales organization may team an industry representative, a product specialist, and a territorial representative to land one sale. The three could share credit by splitting the revenue among themselves, each of the three could get full credit for it, or the sales plan could specify some other formula for assigning quota credit.

A company can recognize revenue at different points in the sales cycle, usually when an order is booked, when it is shipped and invoiced, and when the invoice is paid. Salespeople can likewise be credited with commission at these points, or the commission can be made payable in fractions at all three stages. The decision depends on the level of follow-through required from the salespeople.

Sales plans give money—but they can also take it back. The plan can pay salespeople a base salary or may pay a draw against future commissions. It can deduct commissions for sales that are canceled, returned, or not collected.

Most organizations set sales quotas for their representatives and pay commissions on the basis of quota attainment. A sales representative might have several quotas, such as new accounts, product lines, and services. A sale might apply to more than one quota. Compensation under each quota depends on the size of the sale and the plan for rewarding quota achievement. There might be sliding scales: a plan might state that each percentage of quota attainment up to 100 percent is worth $100; each point between 100 and 125 percent is worth $150; and all points over 125 percent of quota attainment are worth $200.

Oracle Receivables transactions drive sales compensation. Order Management collects the applicable data, such as the price list, salesperson, and revenue class, by the time an order is booked. It passes the data through to Receivables for invoicing and collection, and Receivables passes them to Sales Compensation. Inasmuch as Oracle Receivables is the system that feeds the General Ledger, making it the gatekeeper ensures that sales compensation ties out to actual revenue flows.

Tuning a sales-compensation plan is a tricky business, and often the problems are legion. Salespeople are notorious for exploiting ill-conceived compensation schedules. Representatives who are paid on business volume can "give away the store" with large amounts of unprofitable business. Ross Perot supposedly left IBM one January after attaining his maximum possible compensation for the year in the first month (he went on to build EDS and to found Perot Systems). Oracle Sales Compensation has a powerful graphical modeling facility that allows you to visualize the results of different sales scenarios. You want to be sure your salespeople are paid well enough—but not more than necessary—and that they are motivated to carry the company towards its strategic product goals.

Sales Compensation turns the complex rules you give for computing sales commissions into PL/SQL code that you can access. It gives you the opportunity to review and modify the programmed logic to be sure you get exactly what you want.

Oracle Sales Intelligence

Oracle Sales Intelligence is a further component of the Business Intelligence System. It provides an up-to-the-minute summary of sales, covering key focus areas such as the sales force, performance, sales effectiveness, revenue management, customer analysis, product analysis, channel analysis, and pipeline analysis.

Integration with Financials

Oracle Sales and Financials are tightly coupled. Order Capture executes order capture requests from other Oracle CRM applications, such as Oracle TeleSales, Oracle Sales Online, and Oracle iStore. Order Capture extends ordering capabilities beyond traditional products to include services, events and seminars, service-support agreements and renewals, and collateral requests. Oracle Configurator provides Oracle Sales Online, Oracle TeleSales, and Oracle iStore with guided selling, requirements-based product selection, and configuration validation for complex and custom-configured products and services.

Service

Oracle Service manages the installed base you create as you ship products. It maintains a database of customer products, or items you have shipped. Service on these shipped products can then be delivered over the telephone or on-site, or by having the customer return the product for "depot" maintenance at your site. The service can be covered by warranty, invoiced as delivered, or handled under a number of types of service contract. All employees who interact with customers have access to a wealth of historical and current information about each customer they are serving.

Service characteristics are one of the eight major attribute groups that Oracle Inventory carries on an Inventory Master item. Serviceable products have flags to indicate how service applies (it is serviceable, service is billable, and so forth), and the services themselves have product numbers. Oracle Inventory and Oracle Service manage the links between services and the products to which they apply, forming a two-way relationship.

Order Management populates the installed-base interface as it ships orders. It picks up the item number, service characteristics, serial number (if applicable), customer, and location. At that point, the customer's product and the inventory item take on lives of their own. The inventory item can continue to evolve and improve through engineering changes and new item-revision levels. The customer's product may or may not be improved through field upgrades, and its configuration might change through field maintenance. Oracle Bills of Material can recreate the "as built" configuration to support the service engineers.

Service can record changes that take place in the field. If five identical, nonconsecutively numbered items are shipped, the installed base will group them together. You need to update the record if the customer sells one and keeps the other four on maintenance. If there is a warranty replacement, it will record the new serial number. It can change most meaningful data at the level of the customer product item and can provide the necessary information when you need to track components within the product. It maintains the concept of a "system," a group of customer products (like a computer) that work together as a unit.

Order Management also manages customers and orders for service. Its return material authorization process handles customer returns for replacement, warranty service, and billable depot maintenance. Order Management sends billing data to Oracle Receivables over its standard interface. This tight integration means that customers, serviceable items, and services are defined only once within the EBS universe, and there is no duplication of the shipping, receiving, billing, and collection functions. An integrated view of sales and service is essential to measuring customer relationships.

Warranty service and service agreements provide vehicles for product maintenance. There are usually terms and conditions covering the length of the service, days of the week, and hours in the day for service; inclusion or not of repair parts; and shipping costs and similar considerations that affect the cost of delivering service. Oracle Service matches service requests against the terms of the agreement so it can deliver what the customer is authorized to receive.

Delivering service is a workflow process. The steps differ according to the product, but the procedure might, for example, move through several levels of telephone support, then to on-site service, and finally to depot service or replacement. Workflow enables you to apply business rules in routing service requests and to raise warnings when a problem remains unresolved for too long. Workflow can also help you keep up-to-date by confirming customer data as you log a call. This is often the way you learn who the ultimate customer of one of your dealers is, that customer names and locations have changed, or that a customer resold one of your products. You need this information to deliver service, but knowing who your customers are is also useful to marketing.

Depot maintenance, the heavy-duty repair you do in your own facilities, is a kind of manufacturing job. The following are the common steps for depot-level repair of a single customer return:

1. Estimate the cost of repair and decide whether the item is economical to repair.

2. Get a decision from the customer whether to repair, replace, or do nothing.

3. Create a nonstandard work order, routing the job through the necessary workstations to remedy the diagnosed problems.

4. Collect parts and resource-usage data at each station.

5. Put the repaired item back into inventory and let Order Management ship it back to the customer.

The depot-repair model, using Work in Process functionality, can collect very detailed data on the costs of maintenance. Engineering can use the database to assess mortality rates at a component level to improve quality, and you can use experience as the basis for your repair estimates and charges. The US Army develops bills of materials to use for depot-level maintenance. In planning to fix 100 tanks, it might order 20 new barrels, 50 new treads, and 30 fuel injectors based on past experience with the parts it expects to be consumed.

Oracle Customer Care

Customer-care representatives want to resolve customer problems efficiently and accurately. To do this, they need to be able to respond consistently, whether the customer calls, requests a callback on the Internet, or contacts the company by e-mail. The contact center is the core of the Oracle Customer Care application. With it, customer-care agents can record new or changed customer-contact information, raise service requests, record inquiries, and wrap up completed calls by recording the outcome.

Oracle Support

Oracle Support is an application for managing service requests, issuing notices of product defects, and logging requests for product enhancements. It is tightly coupled with Oracle Customer Care, with which it shares the contact center; service requests raised by Customer Care are resolved in Oracle Support.

Oracle Contracts

Oracle Contracts is a centralized repository for contract information that is made up of articles and rules. Articles are the terms and conditions of a contract in text form, whereas the rules provide the Contracts module with sufficient information to automate the terms and conditions. An article might state that a customer will be billed quarterly in arrears based on approved time sheets. The rule will trigger a process to bill the customer at the predefined intervals.

Oracle Field Service

Oracle Field Service automates the process used by support organizations to fix customer problems. The process starts with a call to the service center, followed by the dispatch of a field-support agent, through to the debriefing when the service request is closed. Billing information can be submitted, depending on the nature of the customer's service agreement.

Oracle Mobile Field Service

Oracle Mobile Field Service is a stand-alone wireless solution that provides field-service personnel with precise, up-to-date information about service duties assigned to them by office dispatchers.

Oracle Scheduler

Oracle Scheduler enables businesses to effectively manage the planning, scheduling, and routing of field-service personnel to optimize the scheduling of service calls.

Oracle Spares Management

Oracle Spares Management is an inventory system specifically designed with easy-to-use planning and parts-replenishment capabilities to control spare-parts inventories in geographically dispersed locations, even including service vehicles.

Oracle Customer Intelligence

Oracle Customer Intelligence is another component of the Business Intelligence System. It provides up-to-the-minute analyses of customer information, covering key focus areas such as customer acquisition, retention, profitability, satisfaction, loyalty, and life cycle, to understand the impact of different factors on customer retention.

Oracle iSupport

Oracle iSupport is a Web-based customer-care system that enables customer to obtain service and support in a self-help environment by offering immediate online order-status and inventory-check capabilities, order history, invoices, payment history, and online forums.

Channel Revenue Management

In today's economy, more global companies need to change their sales strategy in order to optimize the cost of their sales efforts. Apple, for example, now primarily sells its own products via its Web site and Apple stores, although it has allowed some other companies, such as Best Buy, to stock their computers as they have become more popular. Of course, in order to increase the number of items sold worldwide, Apple has allowed resellers to sell its products, too, like the iPhone and iPad. This is known as channel sales. Two thirds of all computing sales in the world are not direct sales like Apple's; instead, they are "channel sales," or "indirect sales." Channel sales is like outsourcing the costs of having your own far-reaching sales operations while still retaining an excellent portion of the sales profits. These days the relationship between the seller and the reseller is much closer, allowing for better cooperation and coordinated strategies. Channel sales does not just mean shipping your products off to a third party and hoping for the best; it means keeping your outsourced sales teams up to date with your products, ensuring that they are adequately informed, and regularly updating them on changes and issues in order for them to function at their best.

This new Channel Revenue Management product integrated into the E-Business Suite enables information-driven channel-revenue management by using consistent, accurate enterprise information and advanced tools for managing all aspects of both direct and indirect channels. From partner life-cycle management, discount- and rebate-program management, and channel-sales collaboration to claims settlement, marketing, and performance measurement, Oracle Channel Revenue Management increases channel effectiveness by using consistent enterprise information in every phase of the process. It provides a single, global basis of information to drive channel effectiveness across your sales, marketing, and finance divisions. Oracle Channel Revenue Management is seamlessly integrated with other E-Business Suite applications, including Oracle Sales, Oracle iStore, Oracle Marketing, Oracle Supply Chain Management, and Oracle Financials.

Oracle Accounts Receivable Deductions Settlement

Oracle Accounts Receivable Deductions Settlement is a solution that provides research, administration, analysis, and settlement functionalities to not only resolve but also pre-empt deductions. It features a centralized repository that tracks claims for any reason, promotional or operational, and enables all groups within the company to effectively communicate and collaborate with their customers.

Oracle Partner Management

Oracle's Partner Management solution enables companies to extend their business processes to work collaboratively with distribution-channel partners. From recruiting and managing partners through marketing, channel sales, and performance measurement, it manages the entire partner life cycle. Oracle Partner Management integrates seamlessly with Oracle Sales, Oracle Trade Management, Oracle Marketing, and Oracle iStore, as well as other EBS applications.

Oracle Channel Rebates and Point-of-Sale Management

Oracle Channel Rebates and Point of Sale Management administers trade spending programs for maximum return for both direct and indirect sales data. Closed-loop tool and solutions for planning, execution, and analysis enable companies to optimize the execution and impact of programs and promotions across the entire demand chain.

Oracle Price Protection

Oracle Price Protection enables manufacturers and distributors to automate and control the multiple business processes necessary to create and execute a price-protection transaction, with updates to Oracle Inventory, Oracle Purchasing, Oracle Cost Management, and Oracle Financials to ensure an accurate, automated, and seamless execution.

Oracle Supplier Ship and Debit

Oracle Supplier Ship and Debit enables distributors to more efficiently respond to changing market conditions by automating special price requests to suppliers. Distributors can close more sales, thus increasing profitability, through this closed-loop solution. Oracle Supplier Ship and Debit also reduces the cost of managing special pricing agreements and automates the execution and claims processes.

Human Resources (HR)

Oracle's Human Resources turns a prosaic record-keeping function into an area of strategic advantage. People represent the most significant element of cost for most companies, and their performance is essential to success. Oracle applications manage all aspects of hiring, training, managing, and compensating your staff. Because organization and personnel information is used by almost all Oracle applications, elements of Oracle Human Resources are present in every installation.

Payroll is the transaction-oriented system that handles the financial side of personnel—paying them. It also handles the financial side of deductions. Oracle Payables, the other payments system in the EBS family, also does payments to people. It commonly handles expense reimbursements, and sometimes commission checks and benefits payments, such as tuition payments to educational institutions. Payroll might need to account for the tax liabilities due on payments through Oracle Payables, and it can be used as a vehicle for expense reimbursements.

Oracle Human Resources

HR sees people in the context of the jobs and positions they fill within organizations. It maintains the Multi-Org hierarchy used throughout Oracle EBS. HR does a thorough job of tracking the time dimension; it can reconstruct the organizational structure and the way it was staffed at any point in history.

The way people are mapped to the organization becomes increasingly bureaucratic as an organization grows. Jobs in a large company are usually described generically—"payables supervisor" or "warehouse manager," for example. Job classifications are necessary for relating similar functions in different parts of the organization and for standardizing job requirements and pay grades. Positions are instances of jobs within a given organization. They figure into head-count and salary budgets. Your organization might have positions for three payables clerks. Finally, people fill positions, and not always exactly: the HR system has to accommodate situations in which the job title of an incumbent differs from the description for the position.

Not all organizations make careful distinctions among jobs, positions, and people, and it is not required to do so in Oracle EBS. You can, for instance, define an approval workflow by either people or positions. The term *"role"* is used in this broader context. As one example, you need to tell Oracle Web Customers who it is that fills the role of removing credit holds from orders. You determine in advance whether you will assign the role using a person's name or a position name.

Self-Service Human Resources extends the power of Oracle Human Resources to managers in the field and their employees. It provides workflow control over major HR activities such as hiring and performance appraisals. It also offers self-service support so employees can take control by updating their own records and arranging their own training.

You define qualifications, grade, and pay structures for jobs and positions. This standardization, to the degree you implement it, offers objective criteria for hiring and rewarding employees with raises and promotions. Records of individual employees show their past, present, and projected salaries, benefits, and monetary awards.

Salary administration is the immensely sensitive matter of determining each employee's worth to the company and compensating the employee appropriately. Oracle Human Resources provides the tools you need to compare and plan employee compensation based on job descriptions, performance, geography, seniority, and a host of other variables.

Regardless of the merits of individual employees, proposed salaries are constrained by budget considerations. Oracle Human Resources provides the base figures needed to feed the General

Ledger budgeting process and the tools to apply whatever adjustments are dictated by the budget. You can do detail-level salary planning in a spreadsheet.

Competency Management is the process of matching skills to requirements. Oracle Human Resources can match people's skills, training, and experience against job requirements. Storing definitions of the organization's goals and core competencies, Human Resources supports hiring, assessments and appraisals, and individual development to enable the company to grow the talent needed to support its strategic directions.

The first impression a candidate has of your company is through your recruiting. You have to evaluate a candidate, assess the fit between that person and the company, and sell him or her on joining. Oracle Human Resources manages candidates' applications, résumés, referrals, and other data. It keeps a record of contacts you have had with the candidate and the data you need to statistically evaluate your recruiting efforts.

Each organization within a company might be slightly different in its personnel policy. Certainly each country has different laws and customs. Acquired organizations might retain some of their own character, but might in other ways be made to conform to the parent. Different divisions and departments have their own characteristics.

Oracle Human Resources has the subtlety and flexibility to manage your company as it is. Virtually all Oracle EBS applications use organization data from HR, even if HR is not installed and used by your company; many use information about specific people. Purchasing identifies buyers; Order Management, Sales Compensation, Sales, and Marketing have salespeople; Bills of Material uses the hourly rate for people in defined positions to set standard costs; Work in Process captures the actual costs of human resources used in manufacturing. Projects computes revenue and billable amounts based on job title. Payroll pays people. All workflow processes have to identify people or positions in the approval process. Human Resources has more integration points than any system besides General Ledger.

Government takes a major interest in issues of employment. Human Resources produces a wide range of statutory reports; in the United States these include COBRA, OSHA, ADA, EEO, AAP, and VETS-100.

Oracle Payroll

Payroll applies Human Resources data to salaries and benefits to compute how much to pay and how to get the payment to the employee. Payroll management is an extremely demanding business function: highly complex, highly visible, and time critical. The tax rules encoded in a payroll system are country specific. Oracle Payroll supports national tax codes and regulations throughout the world.

Gross pay can be determined by salary, time cards, and payments such as commissions and awards. There can be any number of deductions to arrive at net pay. Many different types of rules govern deductions. To name a few obvious ones, income tax is proportional to income; medical insurance is usually a fixed amount; Social Security tax has an annual cap; loan repayments end when the obligation is fulfilled; garnished wages may be governed by rules specific to a jurisdiction. Deducted money has to be accounted for, consolidated for all employees, and sent to the agency on behalf of which it was deducted.

Income-tax rates are set by different levels of jurisdiction: federal, state, and local. The rules can get complex, with factors such as reciprocity between the workplace jurisdiction and the employee's residence. Oracle Payroll is integrated with Vertex Payroll Tax to keep the rates and rules up to date.

Vacation, paid time off, and sick leave are quasimonetary benefits with their own rules. They can be paid for in cash upon termination, but most of the time they are accounted as hours. Accumulated vacation appears on the books as an accrued liability, a benefit employees have earned but not yet drawn.

Mistakes can be corrected through restatements of pay and recomputations of payroll deductions for one or more past pay periods. The system has to make an appropriate accounting to the employee and the taxing bodies or benefit providers. It prepares quarterly and annual tax returns, including US forms W-2, W-3, W-4, 940, and 941.

Employees can be paid by check or direct deposit, from any number of bank accounts, and payment can be split. You can also use the payroll process to liquidate other obligations to employees, such as expense reimbursements. Labor-distribution rules let you split the payroll expense among ledger accounts, organizations, and other Accounting Flexfield segments to any level of detail you need. You can combine payroll accounting with Self-Service Time in the Oracle Projects family to reconcile the way you compensate labor with the projects and tasks that use it.

Oracle Training Administration

Oracle Training Administration supports the entire training function and can be implemented for both internal and commercial training purposes. With Oracle Training Administration, you can schedule and track training events and manage course enrollments. Updated employee-skills information is immediately available in the career-management functions within Human Resources. Oracle Training Administration is integrated with the Oracle Financials applications to administer the financial aspects of the training business.

Oracle Time Management

Oracle Time Management is a collection point for time and attendance data. It accepts, consolidates, and processes employee time against employer-specific parameters and legal requirements, such as base pay, overtime, shifts, vacation, work schedules, rotation plans, sick time, benefit codes, and mandates of union contracts. Validated time is processed to generate accurate payroll and paycheck information.

Manufacturing

This book has already covered many of the Manufacturing applications in detail, including Purchasing, Inventory, and Order Management. The basic manufacturing cycle is as follows: Customers enter demand for items through an order-entry application. Material Requirements Planning (MRP) translates that demand into requirements for parts at all levels—purchased parts, assemblies, and end items. MRP uses the bill of materials to determine what parts are needed and how long it will take to manufacture the products.

MRP takes into account current inventory quantities when determining what needs to be manufactured or purchased to meet the customer demand. MRP recommends work orders to manufacture the needed assemblies, and creates purchase requisitions to buy parts from suppliers. Work in Process manages work orders on the shop floor, routing them through the manufacturing process, issuing parts as they are needed, and tracking the resources and parts consumed until an assembly is finished and received into Inventory.

Other manufacturing applications are outside the flow of the shop floor. Oracle Engineering manages changes to bills of materials, such as the approval and timing of item-revision levels.

These represent changes in how the item is built. Capacity Planning uses resource constraints, such as machine capacity, work cells, and people, to determine how much can be built and what the best use is of plant capacity in terms of increasing profit and satisfying customers. Cost Management collects labor and material costs, which become available in the General Ledger for making more informed decisions about whether to make or buy products.

Oracle Bills of Material

Oracle's Bills of Material (BOM) manages the master files that describe how to make products. The item might be something that is made or something that is never actually made, such as a pick-to-order item, a model, an option, or a phantom assembly. Phantoms are an engineering convenience. A phantom represents a part that is consumed in a higher-level assembly as soon as it is manufactured. The items are called phantoms because they are never stored in inventory.

Each BOM includes the following:

- The item number and revision level of the product being made.

- A BOM name. When there is more than one way to make the same product, the BOM name serves to identify the particular recipe for assembly. For example, a loudspeaker is constructed by wiring the electronics to the speaker, bolting the assembly within a wooden cabinet, and covering with cloth (BOM1 = electronics + speaker + cabinet + cloth). Alternatively, the speaker subassembly could be bought in finished form and installed into the cabinet (BOM2 = speaker subassembly + cabinet + cloth).

- Routing records to show the work cells involved in making the item.

- A row for each component on the BOM. Components are parts, although it is convenient to include drawings, which are not consumed on bills. Options, option groups, and phantoms also appear as components. The row indicates the routing step where it is used.

- The resources used in manufacturing and the standard usage of those resources.

A BOM describes how to make something—for example, tricycle = 3 wheels + frame. The item being made can be a product for sale (tricycle) or an assembly that will go into something else (wheels to put on the tricycle). The raw materials for the assembly step (wheels and frame) and the product (tricycle) are all described as Inventory items.

The process can get more complex. The makeup of a bill can change over time (after July we use stamped plastic wheels instead of metal ones with rubber tires). It can have options (tricycle = frame + wheels + [optionally] decals). It might use other manufactured items. The frame could be made in-house (frame = body + fork + seat); in this case, the bill of materials has to be "exploded" through multiple levels to determine the raw materials that go into the final product.

It takes more than just materials to make a product. Assembling the tricycle takes labor, tools, and a place to work. Building the wheels takes a plastic-stamping machine and labor. Bills of Material works together with a routing to specify the kinds and quantities of resources needed to make an item. The item's routing also specifies the time needed to set up, produce, and clean up after making an item. The Order Management application can add up these times to compute an available-to-promise date, which can be quoted to a customer. The Master Scheduling/Manufacturing Request Program (MRP) application will use routing information to figure out when raw materials need to arrive for the manufacturing process. For example, if it takes two days to make the wheels, the plastic is needed on day 1, but the frame components can arrive on day 3.

The Order Management process uses bills of materials in two ways. When the customer orders a pick-to-order item (a phantom with a sale price), Order Management explodes it into the components on the bill of materials, which can go more than one level deep. Order Management then demands the piece parts from inventory and does the picking and shipping by piece part, printing a reference to the ordered BOM item on the packing slip so the customer doesn't get confused.

Configure-to-order items present options to the customer, enabling the customer to choose the ones he or she prefers. Pick-to-order items can also be configure-to-order. An example would be a great-books set: Order the basic product and you get Locke, Hume, and Adam Smith. Order the French option and you get Voltaire and Rousseau thrown in; the German option adds Goethe and Kant. This set would be structured as a three-level bill. Great Books, the top level, would be a model bill for ordering only. The next level would include a standard bill for the British authors and an option group specifying that the product can include either, neither, or both the French and German groups. The third level would be two standard bills: one for the French group and one for the German.

Assemble-to-order items are not made until the customer orders them. They can be standard or configure-to-order. Their distinguishing characteristic is that a final-assembly work order is created to make precisely what the customer orders.

Oracle Engineering

Oracle Engineering and Bills of Material both work with the BOM tables, but the emphasis in Engineering is on product development, while that of BOM is production. Engineering manages engineering-change orders. Whenever there is a change to the constituent items of an assembly or the way the assembly is made, the change needs to be planned and approved. Will the new bill of materials go into effect immediately? On some specified date? When the factory runs out of a particular component item? Purchasing needs to know what kinds of items to buy and customers might need to know what they bought.

Both engineering-change orders and item revisions are put into effect by date. The BOM exploder uses the composition of the bill as of the effective date of the explosion. It uses the same effective date to find the applicable item-revision level. Oracle Engineering manages engineering-change orders so that the item revision and the bill changes to make it have the same effective dates.

Oracle Inventory can track items down to the revision level. This enables you to move old products out of your inventory and to record in Oracle Service exactly what you have shipped to each customer.

Oracle Master Production Schedule

Oracle Master Production Schedule (MPS) supports the high-level decision of what products to make, feeding Material Requirements Planning so it can support the low-level decisions: which assemblies to make, what parts to buy, when, and in what quantities. Both processes are driven by demand, represented by forecasts and orders. MPS determines what high-level assemblies can be made and when they can be made, by matching the resources available with those required to satisfy demand. Some constraints are absolute; some can be bent. You might not be able to expand the factory overnight, but you can schedule a second shift or rent additional equipment. You execute the MPS process iteratively, trying different demand and resource assumptions to optimize profits while still meeting commitments.

MPS drives Material Requirements Planning, which plans the lower-level bill-of-material components. MRP, like MPS, checks resources and capacity to ensure that customer demand can be met with the existing resources.

Oracle Material Requirements Planning

MRP looks at requirements over time, out to a planning horizon. It projects material needs by time buckets and considers the cumulative time taken to manufacture each item. That computation includes the time to get materials from suppliers, the time to set up for manufacturing, the time to make however many layers of subassemblies are needed, and the time to assemble the final product. MRP recommends what to make and when to start making it, by backing off how long it will take to make an assembly from when it is needed. It generates requisitions to ensure that there will be enough parts to supply the manufacturing process at the time each job is scheduled. It will recommend expeditious action on parts whenever it projects a shortage.

The bill of materials is critical to both MPS and MRP. MPS balances the resource requirements associated with high-level items against total capacity. MRP explodes these high-level items' BOMs to find which components go into each item, then compares the date they are needed with the lead time to determine when it will have to place an order with the supplier. This is an area in which close relationships with suppliers are useful. When suppliers are allowed to see the plans MRP has generated for you to drive your organization, they can do a better job of anticipating your needs.

Oracle Work in Process

In discrete manufacturing, Oracle Work in Process (WIP) creates work orders to initiate and track the manufacture of a given number of a given item. Work orders describe how many of what assembly to make, when the assembly is supposed to be complete, and where to put it upon completion. Work orders use items issued from inventory for the parts and assemblies needed as input at each step.

The BOM and routing serve as a budget in creating a work order. Together they provide standard values for the material and resources to be consumed in the manufacturing process. WIP collects the actual data. There can be a budget for attrition due to parts getting lost, breaking, or not meeting the appropriate standards. Although a standard amount of labor is budgeted in the routing, WIP can capture the actual amount of labor used. The difference will be charged to variance accounts. Cost Management collects the actual figures, making it possible to update the standard costs as things change. The objective is to keep variances to a minimum and, of course, to continually improve the efficiency of the manufacturing process.

Oracle Manufacturing Execution Systems

Oracle Manufacturing Execution Systems (MES) is a new addition to the Oracle Discrete Manufacturing family in Release 12. MES enhances the basic WIP functionality with additional supervisor-workbench and workstation features.

The application allows process manufacturers to deploy Oracle Process Manufacturing directly on their shop floors as the manufacturing execution system. For most process manufacturers, this removes the requirement to invest in a third-party or homegrown MES, and helps reduce costs while eliminating integration and support headaches. Process Manufacturing eliminates many unnecessary and non-value-added activities by providing a structured and standards-based shop-floor execution tool set.

The MES Supervisor workbench includes a dashboard with the current operation's status where the department supervisor can monitor the operation progress, identify bottleneck operations, and assign alternate resources.

The MES Workstation workbench features clock-in and clock-out functionality to capture time spent on a work order, the ability to review the dispatch list and a single interface for multiple job operations.

Oracle Flow Manufacturing

The work-order concept does not adequately support all methods of manufacturing, especially assembly-line-style repetitive or flow methods. A major issue in all manufacturing methods is setup. The objective is to find the optimal trade-off between the carrying costs of the inventory that results from long production runs and the setup costs involved in short runs. Part consumption has to be recorded without waiting for the job to end. This is usually handled by back flushing; when 100 televisions roll off the assembly line, you know to decrease inventory by 100 tubes and 300 knobs.

Repetitive manufacturing is used to make long production runs of the same item, without incurring the long cycle times associated with items snaking their way through the factory from operation to operation and waiting in queues before each one of those operations. Repetitive manufacturing greatly reduces cycle time, but limits the flexibility and responsiveness of the factory.

Flow manufacturing is used for mixed-model manufacturing in which any number of items can be produced in any sequence. Flow manufacturing is very flexible and combines the efficiency of repetitive manufacturing with the flexibility of a work-order-based job shop.

Oracle Process Manufacturing (OPM)

Process manufacturing (or *continuous manufacturing*), such as petroleum refining, is very different from the discrete manufacturing we have been discussing. Raw materials and finished product are constantly flowing with varying potencies. Measurement and minimization of downtime become major issues, because the production process must be continually adjusted. As the ingredients change potency, the ratio of one ingredient to another must change to ensure consistency. Oracle Process Manufacturing (OPM) supports continuous manufacturing. Specific process-manufacturing techniques, such as formula and recipe management, are supported for food, drink, pharmaceutical, and chemical companies.

OPM and Financials Integration

The functional integration with Financials enables OPM purchasing receipts to be transferred into Oracle Purchasing and OPM fulfilled orders to be interfaced to Oracle Receivables, as well as allowing data feeds into Oracle General Ledger to generate journal entries whenever transactions are recorded in OPM that have an accounting significance.

OPM transactions are interfaced to and from Financials through standard interfaces—a model that all Oracle EBS applications conform to. The transaction flow is shown in Figure 28-2.

As Oracle has continued to mature its E-Business Suite applications, there has been a push to streamline and consolidate functions, taking the best practices in one area and combining efficiencies in another to bring most powerful application possible to bear. The integration between OPM and Oracle Financials has been improved to the extent that, starting with Release 12, they sharing the same model, no longer needing data replication.

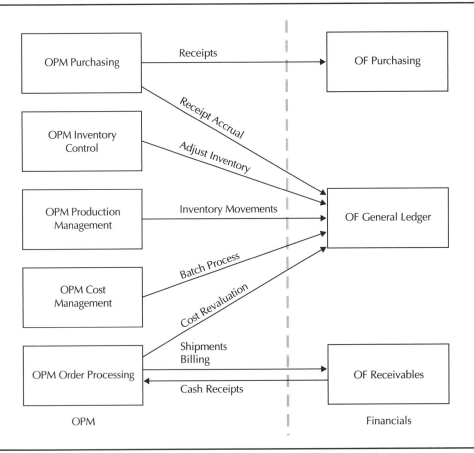

FIGURE 28-2. *Transaction integration between OPM and Oracle Financials*

OPM and Subledger Accounting

In prior releases, the Manufacturing Accounting Controller application was the tool that OPM used to determine how transactions were transferred to Oracle General Ledger and which account codes were used.

There are two challenges that will face companies that were comfortable with the Manufacturing Accounting Controller and are now faced with the new Subledger Accounting (SLA). While SLA works on a similar principle in the sense that it extracts and analyzes records from the material transactions table very much like the Manufacturing Accounting Controller, and accounting can be generated over and over to evaluate scenarios and review results before finally committing to a set of journals, that is where the similarities end. The first challenge is that the way rules are defined has been turned on its head. Oracle has introduced the concept of defining journal-entry templates and then applying those templates to transactions based on matching criteria. The accounting for each line within the template is derived from applying one or more rules, which generate each journal line. The rules consider criteria provided and then draw accounting from the identified sources. The sources can be predefined accounting parameters or custom PL/SQL functions that generate the accounting.

The second challenge is that analyzing the journal-entry results is no longer as simple as knowing one or two views or tables and utilizing simple tools to summarize the journal output. In order for SLA to function across multiple modules, it was necessary to build a series of tables and views that support a new HTML interface for researching and analyzing transaction journal entries.

The SLA engine lets the accounting department maintain sophisticated control over accounting and charts of accounts. Accounting rules can be defined against most attributes. For example, you can use an attribute of an item to redirect accounting to the proper category of cost of goods sold within the chart of accounts. You can also control and prevent the entry of user errors into the application. Incorrect entries can be redirected to proper accounts. For more information, see Chapter 4.

Oracle Quality

Oracle Quality unifies your company's quality specifications, processes, measurement results, and analysis at a corporate level. It is a valuable aid in developing complete and consistent procedures across the business, as required for ISO 9000 certification.

Quality applies to several elements of other Oracle applications. It manages the results of physical testing of items in the receiving and manufacturing processes. The results can be associated, among other things, with suppliers, receipts, WIP jobs, item-revision levels, subinventories, and finished goods that incorporate tested items.

Quality can also apply to business processes. You can assess how many overshipments your suppliers make, how many time sheets fail because they have improper accounting distributions, or how many newsletters are returned for invalid addresses. It only takes the following to measure quality:

- A way to identify the item being measured, such as item and serial number, or department and month.

- The property being measured, called the *collection element*. For items it might be weight; for a department, the number of unplanned absences.

- A collection procedure. Procedures might involve test equipment, be applied to every item or on a statistical basis, or be derived from other automated systems. Oracle lets you implement database triggers to collect quality records throughout the E-Business Suite.

There is no point in collecting quality data without a plan to use them. Employing what you collect involves

- specifications to establish acceptable values for the collection element and severity levels for departures from the standard, and

- prescribed actions to take in response to deviations from the standard, adjusted according to their severity. Oracle Quality makes extensive use of alerts to launch actions that range from sending a message to executing a concurrent job. You can force the system to take immediate action, such as returning a shipment or putting a hold on a payment.

Quality data are sometimes more useful for analysis than for immediate action. You might want to develop reports comparing your suppliers' success in meeting quality standards, or business departments' success in submitting time sheets by the deadline. Comparisons do not imply an absolute standard, and there could be reasons for the observed differences. There might be no need to take remedial action at a transaction level, such as bringing an issue up with your supplier.

However, you might use your knowledge of the quality problems to change your procedures. You might reassess your product engineering or provide your suppliers with more frequent feedback.

Cost is a constant consideration in measuring quality. Some costs of quality deficiencies can be measured. You can put a price on rework and returns to vendor. Opportunity costs such as customer dissatisfaction can only be estimated. However inexactly, you can estimate the value of improved quality to be some fraction of the costs associated with defective quality.

The costs of implementing quality procedures can be measured more easily. The major elements are the effort to put collection procedures in place, the costs of capturing quality transactions, the costs of acting on quality problems, and the costs of analysis. Oracle is a very efficient mechanism for determining the cost elements. Using Oracle Quality will tip the cost–benefit equation in favor of increased quality control in your enterprise. Using Oracle to take an enterprise-level view of quality provides you a number of benefits:

- You can use the E-Business Suite's built-in tools, such as alerts, triggers, and workflows, to create and act on quality transactions very economically.

- You have automatic access to Oracle's powerful analysis tools, such as the data warehouse and graphical presentation tools.

- You can propagate quality information throughout your process. The quality measurements for a batch of parts, for instance, can be associated with the finished item shipped to a customer.

- You can use an enterprise view to compare the quality of comparable processes throughout your organization.

- You can relate quality measurements to standards and procedures kept in documentary form, such as ISO 9000 processes.

Oracle Quality is a large concept. Unlike most other applications, you can implement it gradually by bringing more and more processes under its control as your business matures. Just as surely as quality is central to ISO 9000 and to the goal of reducing non-value-added work, Oracle will continue to extend Quality until it becomes a cornerstone of the EBS architecture.

Conclusion

Oracle E-Business Suite has thousands of customers attracted by the immense richness of the suite, covering business processes from CRM through Manufacturing and Human Resources. All of these integrate with the core Financials and Projects applications described in detail in this book.

All the EBS modules are built with a common Internet approach and standardized three-tier application architecture. For users, this means intuitive, easy-to-use screens and reports, underpinned by workflow processes that assist in getting the job done and reinforce company policies. For the technical team, it means simplified installation and support and built-in integration. E-Business Suite software is built using Oracle's own development tools, running on Oracle databases. Functional integration takes advantage of common processes and procedures wherever it makes sense from a business perspective.

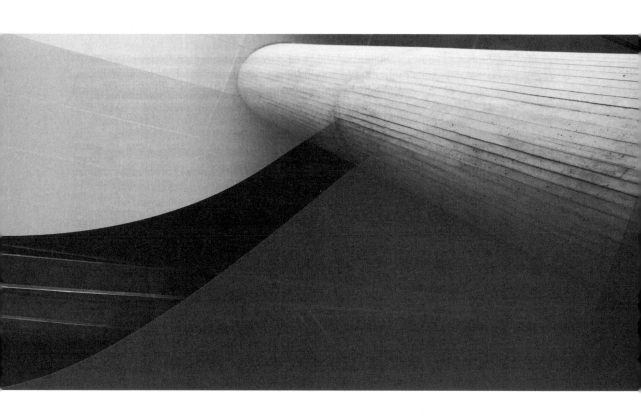

CHAPTER
29

Oracle Fusion
Applications—A Preview

racle Fusion Applications is the name of a new business software application that became generally available in October 2011. It may not sound like a new product—the market started talking about Fusion Applications several years ago. Oracle also adopted the name "Fusion" for the middleware architecture that became the standard for most of the Oracle applications many years ago.

Oracle's decision to build a new product from scratch was not well received by the community and the use of the name "Fusion" "brought confusion" to the organizations that were using Oracle products. One of the business challenges that Oracle faced after it acquired so many of the big software producers (such as PeopleSoft and Siebel) was the decline of organizations selecting or upgrading their systems, because of the lack of a defined path for the giant of Redwood Shores. Until Oracle started to mention a new product and unlimited support, many of them had stopped their plans to upgrade their applications and even to purchase Oracle applications.

As a result, Oracle stopped talking about Fusion Applications for quite some time, until in October 2010 one of the executives in charge of Fusion Applications performed a demo of the product live on stage in front of thousands of people at Oracle Open World.

There are several key factors that have challenged Oracle to invest in this brand-new product, besides the clear definition to the business software market on the roadmap of all the ERPs that Oracle acquired over the years. One of them is that today, many organizations are moving into service-oriented applications and want industry-standard applications platforms; the enterprise resource planning systems needed a change to adapt to this.

Also, since the "social-media revolution," businesses are changing. Companies see their employees connected through chat, social-networking sites, online communities, and all sorts of capabilities that are used for their personal lives and need to be part of their workspace as well.

All these changes have had an impact on the nature of how to make rapid decisions by switching from performing routine tasks to managing exceptions and requesting more automated activities. This shift in the way people work needed a corresponding move in enterprise software.

Another big transformation started to happen with the adoption of cloud computing for business. Now companies want to be able to deploy new technology in a fast and selective approach, on the premises or in the cloud. The new software has to respond to this desire and be flexible in a modular way, so that customers can deploy what they need where they want it to be deployed.

Given these market trends, Oracle has moved forward with this new product on the principles of a modern platform, best-practice business processes, new users' experience, cloud readiness, and collaboration with many clients and partners.

Fusion Applications—The New Standard for Business

After the arrival of Web 2.0, the new Internet revolution was the social-media revolution. Business software, which had enterprise resource planning systems built on old technology, needed to adapt to this new era.

Specifically for Fusion Applications, three main goals were set for the new product to become: the new standard for innovation, the new standard for work, and the new standard for adoption.

Building a product on open standards allows organizations to lower costs by having commonly available skills in the market place, lowering the risk of integration failure with other applications, making configuration easier, and maintaining and protecting configurations during upgrades. Companies have to adapt to the challenges of the market, and current systems have configurations that are difficult to change in a fast environment requiring rapid decisions. That is the niche Oracle envisions occupying with Fusion Applications: a business software that can be manipulated with simple changes in the configurations that can be applied to all other objects reflecting the new business model in a timely manner. All these changes are based on a new platform that has a role-based user experience, intelligent business processes and services, and a unified information repository. Every component is based on open standards, including Java, BPEL, XML, HTML, AJAX, RSS, mobile, and others.

Fusion Applications has a new standard for work founded on a role-based user experience. It is very frequent in global organizations that everyone wears multiple hats; to do work effectively, what they need is functionality that not only addresses those various roles but also bring together the right information for making decisions, connects the people who are needed for the work, and lets key resources get the job done. Figure 29-1 shows how business intelligence is integrated to Fusion Applications.

The Oracle Fusion Applications user experience is based on four questions: What do I need to know? What do I need to do? Who can help? How do we get it done?

These four questions are driving how organizations are trying to bring solutions to the business. Current problems such as having the information stored in multiple locations or changes that are not reflecting on-line, are forcing executives to wrong decisions. Figure 29-2 shows Fusion Tap, an iPad application for Fusion Applications.

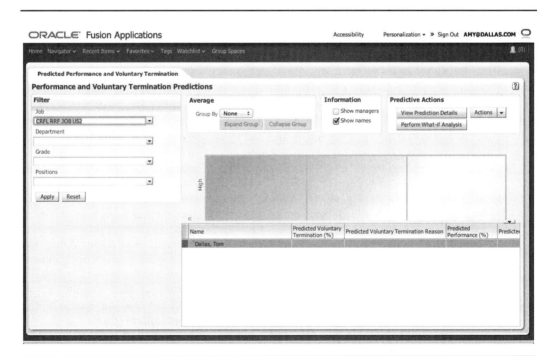

FIGURE 29-1. *Oracle Fusion Applications embedded analytics*

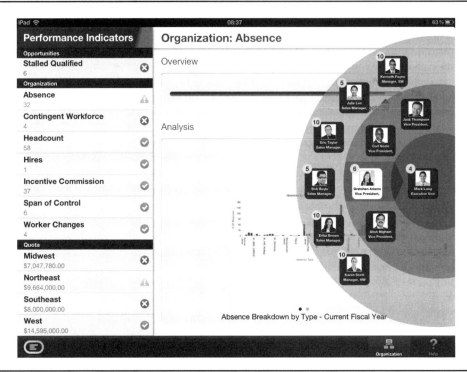

FIGURE 29-2. *Oracle Fusion Applications, iPad application showing HCM information*

Another key concept introduced in Fusion Applications is the user experience. By learning from past experiences, building extension or tailoring the user interface was time consuming. The hidden cost of those extensions was related to activities, such as patch application and upgrades where reviewing and testing was needed, and had to be added to the project plan.

The new concept of how Oracle Fusion Applications can be extended is a huge advantage. Composers are built on top of Fusion Middleware and supported by Fusion Middleware's Metadata Services. This is a vast advantage for the IT team, because it provides the ability to store changed metadata separate from the original metadata. So when patches or upgrades are applied, they affect the original metadata only. After a patch or upgrade, the changed metadata are reapplied, preserving the changes.

Another goal of the Fusion Applications strategy is to become the new standard for adoption. Oracle's pursuit of this goal gives Fusion Applications' users a complete choice of options—from suite to modules—and platform technology, from cloud to device.

Cloud computing is a style of computing in which dynamically scalable and often virtualized resources are provided as a service over the Internet. Users need not have knowledge of, expertise in, or control over the technology infrastructure in the cloud that supports them.

A private cloud runs within a firewall and is for the exclusive use of the enterprise. Certain applications may run on the premises, while others may run in public clouds. Even Oracle, which has one of the largest private clouds, also runs some applications in public clouds.

Public clouds are paid for as operational expenses, while private clouds are both capital and operational expenses. Enterprises need to examine trade-offs to determine what mix of private and public cloud computing is right for them. The new paradigm for hardware and software incorporates and integrates the concepts of infrastructure as a service, platform as a service, and software as a service. It also draws on other recent technology trends based on relying on the Internet to satisfy the computing needs of users.

Cloud computing is often characterized by

- virtualized computing resources,
- seemingly limitless capacity and scalability,
- dynamic provisioning,
- multitenancy,
- self-service, and
- pay-for-use pricing.

Oracle Fusion Applications gives the choice of deployment from a public to a private cloud. You can also take the most common option, of on-premises deployment, or a fourth choice: the hybrid approach, in which you can take the flexibility of using multiple platforms to decrease the total cost of ownership.

The other new concept is modularity. Oracle Fusion Applications has seven product families (see Figure 29-3): Financial Management, Human Capital Management, CRM Sales, Supply Chain Management, Procurement, Project Portfolio Management and Governance, Risk & Compliance. Within each of these families are many new modules.

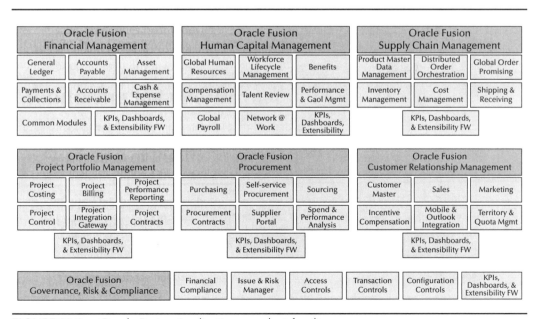

FIGURE 29-3. *Oracle Fusion Applications product families*

Conclusion

So what is the suggested strategy regarding Fusion Applications for companies that have E-Business Suite and are looking forward to upgrading to Release 12.1?

Continue on your current trajectory; follow the path of E-Business Suite. Given the Fusion Applications platform, many organizations will have the chance to adopt a coexistence strategy with their current environment and some Fusion Applications modules—such as Talent Management, Accounting Hub, Procure to Pay, or others—that are based on three co-exist pillars: Financials & Supply Chain Management, Human Capital Management and CRM Sales. Figure 29-4 shows a suite of products from Oracle Fusion Business Intelligence that can be integrated with multiple Enterprise Resource Planning systems.

In other words, the recommended course of action is to upgrade, adopt, and extend. Upgrade your E-Business Suite to the latest unlimited release. Take into consideration that Release 12.1 is the latest release and will be the base for the coexistence.

Adopt standards-based technology with Oracle Application Development Framework (ADF) for customizations or extensions, service-oriented architecture for integrations with legacy systems or extensions, Oracle Business Intelligence for reporting and dashboards, and the component of Oracle Business Intelligence Applications which brings a prebuilt solution for most of the business processes within Fusion Applications.

Technical components such as Oracle Identity Management (OIM)—part of Oracle Fusion Middleware—will allow your organization to manage the end-to-end life cycle of user identities across all enterprise resources, both within and beyond the firewall. You can now integrate Identity Management with your E-Business Suite instances and deploy applications faster, apply the most granular protection to enterprise resources, automatically eliminate latent access privileges, and

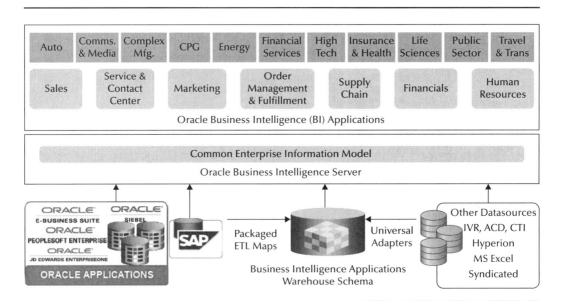

FIGURE 29-4. *Oracle Fusion Applications suite of products*

much more. Enterprise Manager is a key element for lowering the total cost of ownership and decreasing the maintenance costs of your IT team. Some metrics has shown that you can reduce your downtime by up to 90 percent, improve staff productivity by up to 75 percent, and reduce capital expenditures on servers by 20 percent or more.

In terms of hardware, a huge advantage in performance for E-Business Suite can be found in the Exadata and Exalogic solutions—also named Exastack. Some of the metrics performed by organizations running the E-Business Suite order-to-cash cycle show that the Exastack has one third the response time and twice the scalability of standard hardware.

Finally the proposal from Oracle is to extend the business value with Fusion Applications, implementing modules until you embrace the complete Fusion Applications solution.

Every organization running E-Business Suite should have a close look into Fusion Applications, but without leaving your enterprise resource planning system unattended with patches and upgrades. Oracle is providing an inflection point with Fusion Applications, but we do not necessarily have to move into it right away.

Oracle is committed to continue to invest in and provide unlimited support to the existing applications, but they are willing to have their customers adopt the new technology and extend their software solutions with Fusion Applications.

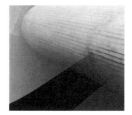

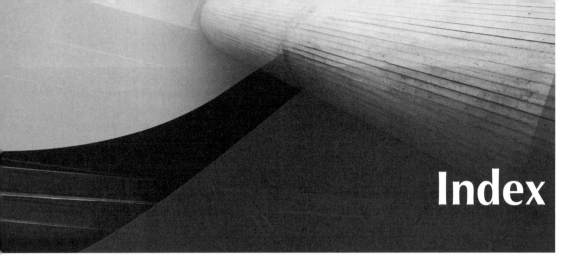

Index

B

H

J

N

O

Reach More than 700,000 Oracle Customers with Oracle Publishing Group

Connect with the Audience that Matters Most to Your Business

Oracle Magazine
The Largest IT Publication in the World
Circulation: 550,000
Audience: IT Managers, DBAs, Programmers, and Developers

Profit
Business Insight for Enterprise-Class Business Leaders to Help Them Build a Better Business Using Oracle Technology
Circulation: 100,000
Audience: Top Executives and Line of Business Managers

Java Magazine
The Essential Source on Java Technology, the Java Programming Language, and Java-Based Applications
Circulation: 125,000 and Growing Steady
Audience: Corporate and Independent Java Developers, Programmers, and Architects

For more information or to sign up for a FREE subscription:
Scan the QR code to visit Oracle Publishing online.